Linux® Bible

Candace Leiden and Terry Collings

Hungry Minds™

Hungry Minds, Inc.

New York, NY ✦ Cleveland, OH ✦ Indianapolis, IN

Linux® Bible

Published by
Hungry Minds, Inc.
909 Third Avenue
New York, NY 10022
www.hungryminds.com

Library of Congress Control Number: 2001016722

ISBN: 0-7645-4662-7

Printed in the United States of America

10 9 8 7 6 5 4 3 2 1

1B/RX/QU/QR/IN

Distributed in the United States by Hungry Minds, Inc.

Distributed by CDG Books Canada Inc. for Canada; by Transworld Publishers Limited in the United Kingdom; by IDG Norge Books for Norway; by IDG Sweden Books for Sweden; by IDG Books Australia Publishing Corporation Pty. Ltd. for Australia and New Zealand; by TransQuest Publishers Pte Ltd. for Singapore, Malaysia, Thailand, Indonesia, and Hong Kong; by Gotop Information Inc. for Taiwan; by ICG Muse, Inc. for Japan; by Intersoft for South Africa; by Eyrolles for France; by International Thomson Publishing for Germany, Austria, and Switzerland; by Distribuidora Cuspide for Argentina; by LR International for Brazil; by Galileo Libros for Chile; by Ediciones ZETA S.C.R. Ltda. for Peru; by WS Computer Publishing Corporation, Inc., for the Philippines; by Contemporanea de Ediciones for Venezuela; by Express Computer Distributors for the Caribbean and West Indies; by Micronesia Media Distributor, Inc. for Micronesia; by Chips Computadoras S.A. de C.V. for Mexico; by Editorial Norma de Panama S.A. for Panama; by American Bookshops for Finland.For general information on Hungry Minds' products and services please contact our Customer Care department within the U.S. at 800-762-2974, outside the U.S. at 317-572-3993 or fax 317-572-4002.

For sales inquiries and reseller information, including discounts, premium and bulk quantity sales, and foreign-language translations, please contact our Customer Care department at 800-434-3422, fax 317-572-4002 or write to Hungry Minds, Inc., Attn: Customer Care Department, 10475 Crosspoint Boulevard, Indianapolis, IN 46256.

For information on licensing foreign or domestic rights, please contact our Sub-Rights Customer Care department at 212-884-5000.

For information on using Hungry Minds' products and services in the classroom or for ordering examination copies, please contact our Educational Sales department at 800-434-2086 or fax 317-572-4005.

For press review copies, author interviews, or other publicity information, please contact our Public Relations department at 650-653-7000 or fax 650-653-7500.

For authorization to photocopy items for corporate, personal, or educational use, please contact Copyright Clearance Center, 222 Rosewood Drive, Danvers, MA 01923, or fax 978-750-4470.

 is a trademark of
Hungry Minds, Inc.

About the Authors

Candace Leiden is the Chief Technologist at the Cardinal Software Group, a training and consulting corporation. Forced to learn about computers because she was afraid of slide rules, Candace has worked as a software developer, a system and network administrator, and a database administrator and architect. She currently specializes in performance management and tuning for large production databases on a variety of Linux, UNIX, and Windows 2000 systems. Candace is also the author of *TCP/IP For Dummies*, published by Hungry Minds, Inc., and of more than 20 technical courseware manuals for large international corporations, the United Nations, and the U.S. Department of Defense on Linux, UNIX, and Oracle. She also speaks at technical conferences worldwide.

Terry Collings has been working in the computer field since 1981 and has experience in MS-DOS, Windows, Netware, and UNIX, as well as the hardware on which these systems run. He is an Instructional Technologist at Muhlenberg College in Allentown, Pennsylvania. He also teaches a wide range of computer and technology related courses in the evenings at Allentown Business School.

Credits

Acquisitions Editors
Terri Varveris
Sherri Morningstar

Project Editors
Barbra Guerra
Neil Romanosky

Technical Editors
Kurt Wall
Rick Orford
Kenneth Duncan

Copy Editor
S. B. Kleinman

Project Coordinator
Regina Snyder

Graphics and Production Specialists
Indianapolis Production Services

Quality Control Technician
Indianapolis Production Services

Media Development Manager
Laura Carpenter

Media Development Supervisor
Rich Graves

Permissions Editor
Laura Moss

Media Development Specialist
Travis Silvers

Media Development Coordinator
Marisa Pearman

Proofreading and Indexing
York Production Services, Inc.

Preface

Welcome to the world of Linux, a powerful operating system that started out as one of the best-kept secrets of the 1990s and has emerged as a power-house for the twenty-first century. Both the scientific and the commercial world have realized that, in the case of operating systems, you can get way more than you pay for. Both the Linux kernel and most tools, utilities, and applications that surround it are free! In fact, it's this "free"dom that first attracts many of us to Linux. You might have asked yourself, "Why are people so excited about this giveaway? Don't they real-ize you get what you pay for?" After snooping around Linux for a while, you'll realize (or perhaps already have) that the best things in life can be free — thanks to system developers who volunteer their time to program and test Linux.

Power and functionality aren't the only standards for operating systems. Many of us have been disappointed with powerful commercial operating systems because of reliability problems. Because of all the volunteers who work on Linux, it is probably the most widely tested operating system in use. The dedication of this international group of developers means that you and I can use an operating system developed not by a small group of programmers who work for one company in the United States but by many talented software developers worldwide. And did we mention that it's free?

Linux Bible is your guide to ferreting out the mysteries of the Linux operating sys-tem. Linux is one of the most tested and reliable operating systems available. And it's free. Wait! There's more! Linux is as loaded with features as one of those special knives you see on infomercials late at night when you can't sleep. You're not alone at that hour. Many Linux developers do their best work when the rest of us are sleeping (or watching those infomercials). Because of these hardworking developers — many of them volunteers — Linux runs on many different kinds of computers. You can run Linux on personal computers, workstation clients, giant mainframe servers, and everything in between. Also, there is a wealth of software available to run on Linux, from e-mail to word processing software to relational databases to programming languages and tools.

By the way, Linux is pronounced "Linnucks" with a short "i" and the first syllable accented. If your computer is equipped with audio, you can hear Linus Torvalds himself pronounce "Linux" at the following Web site:

```
http://uranus.it.swin.edu.au/~jn/linux/saylinux.htm
```

Why You Need This Book

This book holds the clues to using Linux, for beginners to advanced system and network administrators. We start with the basics and build your knowledge as far as you want to go — all the way to configuring, managing, and tuning Linux servers on the Internet. *Linux Bible* is intended to serve you throughout your Linux career. You can read the chapters in any order, depending on what you need to know. If you have already dabbled in Linux (or UNIX), feel free to skip around the topics or use this book as a reference to help you on specific topics.

Linux and UNIX beginners

You don't need any prior UNIX knowledge to learn Linux. If you've never used Linux or a UNIX operating system, I recommend that you start with Chapters 1, 2, and 3 and then skip to Part III, "Using Linux." Part III helps you navigate Linux and your files and directories. After Part III, you can move on to system administration and networking chapters.

UNIX veterans and system administrators

You want to find out the differences between Linux and commercial versions of UNIX. Chapter 1 describes why Linux is special and how the Linux philosophy differs from the UNIX approach. Chapter 3 helps you install different flavors of Linux. Part II provides concepts and the technical specifics of Linux system administration tasks. Don't forget to browse through Part III. Although the chapters are primarily end user–oriented, you may find some nifty hints and tips. Part IV describes how to get your Linux system connected to an intranet, the Internet, or both. Part V helps you monitor and tune your Linux system and network as well as customize your Linux kernel and secure your Linux system. Part V also shows you how to establish connectivity between Linux and Microsoft Windows. Some of the tools described in Part IV are standard UNIX tools. Others are Linux-specific tools that you want to know about. Keep this book close at hand to use as a reference throughout your system administration career.

TCP/IP network administrators

Sure, TCP/IP is TCP/IP on systems from UNIX to Windows 2000 to Macintosh to Linux. Even so, you need to read up on how to configure TCP/IP services on Linux in Part III. Part IV deals with the advanced Linux issues you run into when you add Linux to a mixed network that includes Microsoft Windows (95, 98, NT, and 2000) operating systems and mainframe systems. Make sure this book is easy to reach so that you can use it as a reference while you do your job.

Wannabe Linux programmers

Get the basics by reading through Parts I and II. Part II introduces you to writing shell scripts, filters, and awk/gawk programs. Part V builds on that introduction with chapters on shell scripting and Perl programming for system administrators.

What's Inside

Besides covering Linux from the basics to advanced mastery, this book is crammed full of hints for detecting Linux problems and solving various Linux riddles. All the examples in this book come from Linux operating systems running on both servers and client workstations, including some portable computers. There are lots of tips to help you understand how to get the most from the Linux operating system.

Part I: Getting Started with Linux

Chapter 1 gives you the background on Linux, GNU, licensing, various Linux distributions, and where people are using Linux (that would be everywhere). If you don't have a Linux system to practice on, Chapter 2 gives you some tips on what system information to collect and how to gather it before you start your Linux installation. Chapter 3 steps you through a sample Linux installation. Chapter 4 gives you a preview of some of the internal technical workings of Linux, such as process concepts, memory management, filesystems, device drivers, network protocols, and daemons.

Part II: Getting Started with Linux System Administration

Part II is about basic Linux system administration. Chapter 5 starts you off by explaining your responsibilities if you are (or are going to be) a system administrator. Chapter 6 illustrates various ways to start up (boot) and shut down your system and helps you decide which way is right for you. Chapter 7 is about installing software, such as databases and tools, on a Linux system. Chapters 8 and 9 are about managing devices, including disks, tapes, modems, serial and parallel ports, audio/video, and terminals. You need to read Chapters 10 and 11 if you are responsible for managing files, including backing them up and restoring them. Chapter 12 helps you set up accounts for users, or just for yourself if you are managing your own single-user workstation or PC. Chapter 13 tells you how to set up local and remote printers and how to manage and troubleshoot printing.

Part III: Using Linux

Chapters 14–16 provide a quick tour of using Linux, including how to log in, work with files and directories, use an editor, and run the most important commands and programs. Chapters 17–19 show you how to customize your environment, write simple shell scripts, and start to become a power user.

Part IV: Configuring and Managing TCP/IP Networking

The fourth part of this book explains basic network administration. If you plan on communicating with the outside world, such as the Internet, or even within your own private network, you need to understand how to configure TCP/IP and how to maintain it on a regular basis. Chapter 20 includes some basic network configuration information. Chapters 21–23 show you how to set up network services, such as DNS, NFS, and NIS, so that your computer can send messages to and share files with other computers on your network or on the Internet.

And while e-mail is instinctive and easy to use, it doesn't just magically appear on someone's computer. A system administrator needs to set up e-mail for users on Linux systems. Chapter 24 describes the basics of setting up e-mail and goes on to help you keep e-mail secure and to diagnose and solve e-mail problems on your system.

If your computer is on the Internet, is it going to be Web server or an FTP server? To see how to configure a Linux computer to serve up World Wide Web (WWW) or pages or FTP archives, read chapters 25 and 26.

Part V: Advanced System Administration and Network Administration

Chapter 27 explains how to set up repetitive system administration tasks to run automatically so you can go home and get some sleep. Chapter 28 helps you customize the Linux operating system by rebuilding its kernel — with up-to-date information available just prior to press time for this book. Chapter 29 shows you how to look for evidence of unfriendly intrusions and protect Linux from break-ins, viruses, and other nasty things.

If you'd like to write your own tools to manage your system, but the finer points of bash scripts and Perl programs seem like mysterious codes, read chapters 30 and 31. There you'll see examples of how to build simple tools and utilities to make a Linux system administrator's life easier. Chapters 32 and 33 explain how to snoop around your system and network to see how they are performing and how to troubleshoot problems and improve performance problems. If your Linux system lives on a net-work with Microsoft Windows, Macintosh, and other computers, read Chapter 34 to see how to integrate different systems into one network.

Part VI: Appendixes

The appendixes contain valuable information about the Linux directory structure, advanced commands, and where to find additional Linux resources on the Web — as well as information about the contents of the accompanying CD-ROM

How to Use This Book

You can read this book cover to cover if you want to start from scratch and become a Linux wizard. Personally, I find this approach rather daunting, and I don't think I have the discipline it would take to do this before the year 3000. Another way is to read what you need to get started and use the book as a reference when you need to learn something new or remember something you forget. Keep the book at your side if you are a system or network administrator.

Conventions used in this book

This book uses the following conventions when it explains how to do something on your computer:

- ✦ *Italic type* introduces new technical terms.

- ✦ **Bold type** indicates a command you would type on your computer keyboard.

- ✦ Output that you see on your computer looks like this: `make file`

- ✦ Commands that require no special privileges or security level are preceded by this prompt: $

- ✦ Commands that require a special level of privilege or security are preceded by this prompt: #

- ✦ Keys to press in combination are separated by a plus sign (+). For example, Ctrl+Alt+Del means press the Ctrl, Alt, and Delete keys together.

- ✦ When using the mouse, assuming you're right-handed, the term *click* means click the left mouse button once. The term *double-click* means click the left mouse button twice. *Right-click* means click the right mouse button once. The term *drag* means hold down the left mouse button and pull the mouse to where you want it. If you are left-handed, adjust these instructions to match your mouse setup.

Icons used in this book

The following icons appear throughout the book:

 Highlights a hint that can save you time or grief.

 Accents an interesting fact or related idea about the topic.

 Warns you of problems you might experience if you're not careful.

 Points to further explanations in other sections of the book.

 Points to files on the CD included with this book.

Acknowledgments

It takes a lot of people to put together a book — more people than I realized when I started this one. I'm grateful to the editorial and production staff at Hungry Minds for their support. Thanks also go to the team who assembled the software on the CD-ROM.

I would especially like to thank Terri Varveris, an extraordinary professional who kept everything and everyone going and held all the pieces together with unflagging good will. This book would not have happened without her. Thanks also to editors Barb Guerra, Neil Romanosky, and S. B. Kleinman.

Thanks also go to several contributors who worked long and hard. Ken Duncan not only wrote the chapters about Linux installation and installing software packages (chapters 3 and 7) but also provided high quality technical edits for certain chapters, including extra comments about readability that really helped. Terry Collings wrote about networking in chapters 20, 21, 22, 23, 25, 26, and 34. Kurt Wall spearheaded most of the author review, and I'm indebted to him for providing relief so that I could work on other projects. Rick Orford provided technical editing services. I also want to thank Michael Bellomo for contributing material to the e-mail and security chapters.

Thanks also go to Reza Malekzadeh of VMware, Inc., who provided the VMware software so that I could prove that you can get to Microsoft Windows from Linux without having to reboot (see Chapter 2). For those of us who are constantly going between, VMware saves the day.

And finally, a special acknowledgement and thanks to my resident technical genius (and co-author on *TCP/IP For Dummies*), Marshall Wilensky. Marshall can help you with just about any technical question you might have. Besides working with me on "normal" Linux installations, he helped me install and massage Linux on all sorts of unusual and old hardware to show where I could (and couldn't) get Linux up and running. Marshall also provided some of the screen captures in various chapters. He also acted as the network administrator, setting up and troubleshooting the heterogeneous network I created just for the examples in this book. Every time I went on a business trip, Marshall would take the network apart, pack it up for travel, and help set it up in remote hotel rooms for me — a tremendous job I would not have had the stamina or patience for on my own.

— *Candace Leiden*

Contents at a Glance

Contents

• •

Part II: Getting Started with Linux System Administration   55

Chapter 5: Linux System Management Responsibilities 57

Chapter 6: Managing Startup and Shutdown 65

Chapter 7: Installing Software Packages 73

Part III: Using Linux   215

Part IV: Configuring and Managing TCP/IP Networking   341

Getting Started
with Linux

What Is Linux?

Linux is simply a computer program: a special kind of program called an *operating system*. In fact, Linux looks a lot like a commercial UNIX operating system, but Linux is much more than UNIX. You can use it for the same purposes as any major operating system, including networking, software development, Web servers and browsers, e-mail, document processing, and financial applications. You might wonder, "Does the world really need another operating system?" But Linux is special. This chapter poses a series of questions about Linux. The answers show you what makes Linux so special.

Some Basic Linux Factoids

Here are a few brief Linux tidbits to get you excited about Linux. You can find other factoids sprinkled throughout the book.

+ The Linux operating system allows many users to share one computer.

+ Linux runs on all kinds of computers, from personal computers to giant supercomputers.

+ Users can run Linux in either text only mode or Windows mode, or in a combination of both.

+ Linux is free. The word "free" has different meanings, depending on who's using it. Be sure you understand what "free" means when you think about software. Keep reading to discover what "free" means with regard to Linux.

+ Linux does not require a lot of memory or expensive hardware. On a PC, you don't even need a Pentium strength processor. I have seen IBM/Lotus Development Corporation's Domino server software running on Linux on an old Intel 486 computer to serve dozens of Lotus Notes users.

+ Some flavors of Linux, such as DLX Linux and hal91 Floppy Linux, are so small that they fit on a 1.44 MB floppy disk.

Why is Linux Important?

Several factors make Linux an important and popular operating system:

✦ *Power and functionality.* The Linux operating system provides enough features and functionality that you can use it for almost any purpose on almost any type of hardware. For example, if you're a number cruncher, Linux runs on powerful computers used for scientific and technical purposes. On the other hand, if you just want to read your e-mail and write a few memos, you can use Linux on your PC or Mac. Between these two extremes, Linux functions well for just about any use you can think of. Chapter 2 describes some of the architectural features that enable Linux to provide such a high level of functionality.

✦ *Reliability.* Power and functionality aren't everything. Linux proves its reliability every day.

✦ *Availability.* You can get Linux easily from many different sources all over the world. Linux is not just an English-only operating system. Read the section about Linux distributions in this chapter to find a few of the places around the world where you can get Linux.

✦ *Price (free).* You need to understand exactly what "free" means with regard to Linux. Unlike most operating systems, you do not need to pay for Linux, although you must abide by the provisions of the GNU General Public License (GPL). You can read the basics about GNU and the GPL later in this chapter. To read the complete GPL, browse the Web site, `http://www.gnu.org/copyleft/glp.html`.

Is Linux UNIX?

Linux looks like UNIX and performs as well, but there is a big difference in how Linux was created and is being improved, and in how Linux is distributed and charged for. Linux is a UNIX-like operating system that contains no UNIX code. All the code in the Linux operating system is original and based on POSIX standards. Linux uses a lot of the GNU (GNU's Not Unix) software from the Free Software Foundation in Cambridge, Massachusetts.

Is Linux Free?

Yes. Unless you want to pay for it. Linux is free because of the work of Linus Torvalds, Richard Stallman, the Free Software Foundation (FSF), and a host of dedicated volunteers who believe that excellence does not have to be expensive. Linus developed the Linux kernel and gave it away. Richard mobilized developers to create the programs and utilities that surround the kernel to make a fully functional operating system.

A Software Free-for-All

The following fable is based on the birth of Linux. The names have not been changed to protect the innocent. The moral of this story is: "It's not necessarily a crime to pass software around."

It was a dark and stormy night. Richard Stallman put down his mystery novel. He was reading about an innocent soul who was being hunted for software piracy. "Why should it be a crime to copy software for friends or change the code to make it better?" he asked himself. Richard pondered this, and behold! The Free Software Foundation (FSF) was born. Richard created the GNU (GNU's Not UNIX) project to prove that software can be free.

And GNU software is free: anyone can copy it, distribute it, and change it. Linus Torvalds developed the Linux kernel and continues the open source policy — meaning that anyone can freely modify Linux kernel. Much of the software, aside from the kernel, that makes up the Linux operating system is from GNU.

When you install software for Linux, you may notice references to the GNU General Public License (GPL). The GPL states that "Linux is written and distributed under the GNU General Public License which means that its source code is freely-distributed and available to the general public."

What does Linux "free"dom really mean?

When most people hear the word "free," they think of price, but to Richard Stallman and Linus Torvalds, free means much more. Free is just the first part of the word "freedom," and you have the freedom to do the following with Linux:

1. Run Linux.

2. Hand out copies of Linux for free. For example, you can copy Linux from the Internet and give copies of your copy to all your friends and relatives.

3. Modify Linux, because you can get the original programming source code, change it to fit your needs, and rebuild the program.

4. Redistribute copies of your modified and enhanced version of the software. This way everyone can benefit from your changes.

5. Charge for any copies of Linux, modified or unmodified, that you provide to other people. You can charge to cover the cost of the software media (such as floppy disks or CD-ROMs), shipping and handling costs, and to offer a warranty on the software, as well as to make a profit.

Note

Copyleft is GNU's revolutionary twist on the copyright concept. Copyleft gives you the Linux freedoms listed above. It prohibits you from adding restrictions to Linux, such as denying others the ability to add to or change your new version. You have to make your source code available to the world.

Linus and the Kernel

Have you ever wondered why this operating system is called "Linux"? It's because Linus Torvalds is the father of Linux kernel, and the Linux kernel is the heart of Linux. He developed Linux when he was a student at the University of Helsinki. Today, programmers around the world work with Linus to add functionality to the Linux kernel and to keep it functioning on diverse hardware configurations. On a personal note, Linus must love penguins, since he chose the penguin as the official Linux mascot.

Note   If you want to know more about Linus Torvalds, check out *The Rampantly Unofficial Linus Torvalds FAQ* at `http://earthspace.net/~esr/faqs/linus/index.html`.

If Linux is free, why do some people charge for it?

You can download the Linux kernel and the software you need for a complete operating system from the Internet free of charge. Or, if you don't have access to the Internet, you can copy Linux from a friend, also free. If you have multiple computers, you can install your copy of Linux on each one without paying a license fee. And yet, if you browse software stores, catalogs, and Web sites, you find Linux being sold. Why buy something you can get for free? The answer is "time and convenience." Copying the pieces of Linux from the Internet can be time-consuming, and if you don't have a reliable high-speed connection, such as an ISDN line, your connection may break before you get everything you need. Reconnecting and starting over is no fun. So, to avoid tying up a telephone line and the pain of lost connections and corrupted copies, many people simply purchase a Linux distribution that includes the kernel, utility programs, and documentation on floppy disks or CDs. Or you can buy a book, like this one, that includes a Linux distribution and other handy bits and pieces on a CD.

You Need More Than the Kernel to Have a Linux Meal

Imagine a plate with a piece of fried chicken on it. If you're hungry, that piece of chicken is a start, but it's not a full meal. Now, use your hungry imagination to visualize a delicious fried chicken dinner, the chicken surrounded by potatoes, gravy, vegetables, a roll or bread, maybe even a piece of pie and some coffee or tea to finish the meal.

The kernel is the heart of any operating system, just as the chicken is the heart of a meal. But just as a meal is more than one piece of chicken, an operating system is more than a kernel. For an operating system to be useful, the kernel must be supplemented with all the trimmings: applications, a help system, system administration tools and utilities, Web server software, a Web browser, an installation procedure, and a user interface, often a graphical user interface (GUI). When all these components, including the kernel, are bundled together, you have a distribution. Linux distributions include Caldera, Red Hat, SuSE, and Mandrake. Chapter 2 lists even more Linux distributions.

Where Can I Get a Linux Distribution?

Lots of places. The easiest way is to buy a computer that has Linux pre-installed. The most common way is to copy Linux from the Internet.

 Chapter 2 explains how and where to find a Linux distribution.

Since the Linux kernel is under the GPL, you can copy it as many times as you want. You can get a copy from anyone who has Linux. If your Internet connection is slow, you can get a distribution on CD (if you're willing to pay for the convenience) from most companies that have created distributions.

Who Uses Linux? And for What?

You may be using Linux without even realizing it. If you browse the Web, you have probably accessed a Web server powered by Linux. If you've been to a hospital recently, your patient record may well have been stored on a Linux system. You can find people using Linux at research stations in Antarctica and on the high seas on research ships. Anyone who uses a computer can find a reason to use Linux. End users use Linux for e-mail, word processing, spreadsheets, browsing the Web — the same things users do on any operating system. Software developers build new software products using Linux compilers and tools. Scientific applications, such as signal processing and weather analysis, run on Linux. Linux is an excellent server platform for relational databases such as IBM's DB2, Informix, and Oracle. Linux is also great for networking and internetworking, such as providing a platform for Web servers. Of course, system and network administrators also use Linux to keep the operating system up and running for all the other users.

What Computers does Linux Run on?

Linux runs on little computers, even hand-held computers, big computers, old computers, and new computers. You can run Linux with as little as 4 MB of memory and 15 MB of hard-disk space, although I wouldn't recommend it if you want to use Linux as a server. Hardware platforms for Linux include:

✦ Palmtops, such as Palm Pilot and the IBM PC 110

✦ IBM PCs and PC compatibles, even those that are based on architectures as old as the Intel 386 CPU

✦ Macintosh PowerPC

✦ Amiga

✦ IBM mainframes (370/390, AS400)

✦ Hewlett-Packard PA-RISC

✦ Sun SparcStation

✦ Compaq Alpha (formerly Digital Equipment)

✦ Silicon Graphics workstations

Sizing and Scalability — How large can Linux go?

As of this writing, the largest Linux installation is IBM's Los Lobos supercomputer, consisting of a 512 CPU cluster. While IBM had to write a lot of code to support that level of scalability, the Linux kernel (2.4 and higher) supports multiprocessor scalability up to eight CPUs.

This choice of Linux hardware is one of the reasons for the rapidly growing popularity of Linux.

What Software Runs on Linux? Is it Free Too?

A wide variety of software is available for Linux — hundreds of programs. Some of it is free. Some of it is commercial software that you must pay for. TCP/IP internetworking software is built into Linux. Popular software for Linux includes:

- ✦ Domino R5 application server from Lotus
- ✦ Oracle, Informix, and DB2 (some of the most popular relational databases)
- ✦ Websphere Web application servers from IBM
- ✦ Netscape Communicator
- ✦ Netware
- ✦ WordPerfect
- ✦ ViaVoice speech recognition software
- ✦ Star Office suite
- ✦ Lots of games
- ✦ Microsoft MS-DOS and Windows emulators

Tip   A good place to see new Linux products demonstrated is the annual Linux World Conference and Expo, which is the world's largest Linux-only event and is held in major cities around the world. To see a schedule, browse `http://www.linuxworldexpo.com`. You can also check out the highlights from previous conferences at the linuxworldexpo site.

Summary

This chapter introduces you to Linux by listing a few quick factoids and answering some frequently asked questions about Linux in general.

✦   ✦   ✦

Getting Ready to Install Linux

If you're one of the lucky people who has a computer with Linux already installed, you can skip this chapter and the next one. All you have to do is turn your computer on and you can get to work — at least until you get another computer that doesn't have Linux installed on it. On the other hand, if you're like most people who use Linux, you already have a computer with some other operating system installed, probably a windowing-type operating system.

This chapter helps you prepare your computer for either a Linux-only installation or for a Linux installation that co-exists with your other operating system(s).

Caution   A computer with two operating systems installed is called a *dual-boot* computer. A computer with more than two operating systems installed is called a *multi-boot* computer.

Decisions, Decisions, Decisions

Before you start installing Linux, you need to make some choices.

1. Where are you going to get Linux?

2. What other operating systems do you want your computer to have besides Linux?

3. What kind of installation do you need - server, workstation, upgrade?

Where can you get Linux?

You can obtain Linux a number of ways. If you have a fast connection to the Internet, you can download it. You can borrow a friend's CD-ROM. Naturally, you can buy a complete distribution from a number of popular software stores or, best of all, you can buy this book and get it for free! This section discusses your options for obtaining Linux.

The easiest choice

Buy a computer with Linux installed and tested. Use Linux as the only operating system on your computer. For example, the IBM ThinkPad 600E comes preconfigured with Linux. Just turn it on and go!

Note   This chapter and the next assume that you are not taking the easy way—that you have a computer with another operating system that you want to preserve.

Other choices

If none of these choices work, here are the rest of the ways to obtain Linux:

✦ You can copy a Linux distribution from a friend's or a co-worker's CD-ROM.

✦ You can copy Linux from an FTP server on the Internet. On the Internet, you can browse the Web for locations, and use FTP (File Transfer Program) to copy Linux. Table 2-1 lists FTP sites for some major Linux distributions.

Note   Many of the sites listed in Table 2-1 are mirrored at other Internet locations.

✦ Buy this book! Many books on Linux include a CD with a Linux distribution.

Caution   If you buy a book just to get Linux on a CD, chances are good that it will not be the latest version available because Linux distributions are updated frequently.

✦ You can buy a Linux CD. With the source code for the Linux kernel being distributed free of charge, several companies have created distributions. Most distributions are available via FTP at no charge or, for convenience, on CD, usually for about $50.00 to cover development and packaging costs. Purchasing a product from a Linux distributor also entitles you to technical support, something you will not get from a free or downloaded version.

Table 2-1
Some Popular Linux Distributions

FTP server or URL	Distribution
ftp://ftp.caldera.com/pub	Caldera OpenLinux
ftp://ftp.sdn.ac.za/linux/distributions/linux-mandrake	Linux Mandrake
ftp://ftp.redhat.com	Red Hat Linux
ftp://ftp.debian.org	Debian GNU/Linux
ftp://ftp.cdrom.com	Slackware Linux

FTP server or URL	Distribution
`ftp://ftp.suse.com`	SuSE Linux
`ftp://ftp.turbolinux.com`	TurboLinux
`ftp://metalab.unc.edu/pub/` `Linux/distributions`	Mandrake, Debian, small-linux, slackware, SuSE, and more
`ftp://ftp.linux.org`	Most of the above and more

If you only want the Linux kernel, and not a full distribution, you can get the most recent version at `ftp://ftp.kernel.org/pub/linux/kernel`.

If you do not have FTP access, but you do have e-mail, you can get Linux by FTP-mail from `ftpmail@ftp.uni-stuttgart.de` or `ftpmail@garbo.uwase.fi`.

What kind of installation do you need?

The most common type of Linux installation is the server installation. You choose an installation type based on how you plan to use your computer. Most installation procedures ask you to choose from the installation options listed in Table 2-2.

Table 2-2	
Linux Installation Options	
Installation Option	*Purpose*
Workstation	For a single-user computer used either standalone or on a network.
Server	For a server on a network.
Custom	For a computer that used as both a server and a workstation.

Some distributions also include an upgrade installation for when you already have Linux installed and want to move to a new version.

What other operating systems need to co-exist with Linux

If you installed Linux on a computer with another operating system, you will need a boot manager. A *boot manager* is a small program that enables you to choose which operating system to boot when you start your computer. Boot managers are usually purchased separately from the operating system because most operating systems (Linux is an exception) assume you will not use another operating system. Many people installing Linux also run a Microsoft operating system, such as MS-DOS, Windows 95, 98, ME, NT, or 2000.

Caution

Regardless of how many operating systems you install, a computer can only run a single operating system at a time. For example, if you have booted Linux and decide that you need to work under Microsoft Windows 98, you must shut down Linux and restart your computer for the boot manager to load Windows 98.

Getting to Know your Hardware

Be absolutely sure that your hardware will work with Linux.

The key word is *absolutely*. The first time I tried to install Linux, I was *pretty* sure my hardware was OK, but not *absolutely* sure. After several hours and lots of grief, I learned that while Linux loved my hard disk, it hated my controller, and there was going to be no installation on that machine unless I changed some of the hardware.

Regardless of what distribution you plan to install, there are disk space and memory requirements. The installation also asks you about your system devices, including things that may seem unimportant, such as the mouse and the sound card. Table 2-3 lists the hardware information your Linux installation wants you to provide.

Tip

Be sure to determine how much memory and free disk space you have before you start the installation.

Linux is quite efficient, memory-wise. You can limp along on a Linux system with only 4 MB of memory if you do not use a GUI (graphical user interface). With a GUI, you need at least 8 MB, although 16 MB is more realistic.

Table 2-3 What you Need to Know about your Hardware	
Hardware Device	**Information Needed**
CPU (Central Processing Unit, AKA the chip)	Intel 386 and higher, Intel-type chips (e.g. AMD), Alpha, SPARC, MIPS, Macintosh PowerPC, PA-RISC.
Memory (RAM)	How much?
Hard drive(s)	Number, size, which drive connects to which controller? How much free space?
Disk controller(s)	SCSI, IDE, EIDE? Make and model?
CD-ROM	Make and model, type (IDE, SCSI)?
Monitor	Make and model, refresh rates?
Video controller	Make and model, video RAM size?

Hardware Device	Information Needed
Mouse	What kind (e.g. PS/2, serial)? Number of buttons, what driver (e.g. Logitech, Microsoft)? What COM port if serial?
Network Interface Card (NIC, network controller)	Make and model, TCP/IP information.

The next sections of this chapter describe the general hardware requirements for any Linux installation. You always need to check on the specific hardware that your particular distribution supports. The CD at the back of this book includes the latest version of Red Hat Linux and its hardware compatibility list available when this book went to press.

Tip   Most distributions publish a "hardware compatibility list" at their Web sites (see Table 2-1). A hardware compatibility list indicates what hardware the distribution is known to support. They are usually organized by device, such as CPU, mice, video cards, network cards, and so forth.

Now that you understand what you need to know about your hardware, how do you find the information? Don't start by opening up your computer and looking at each component. The make and model is usually somewhere on them, but that would mean pulling out circuit boards and chips. Who wants to do that? Besides, you have to get everything back into its original place. I tried this approach once, but while I could see where the model of my network card was imprinted, it was too small for me to read. Even after I got reading glasses, I couldn't make out that model number. You might be able to get the information you need from the manuals that came with your computer, if you can find them. A better way is to let your system tell you what you've got inside, starting with your Control Panel (see Figure 2-1 through Figure 2-4). The following sections illustrate how to find system and device information for a Microsoft Windows operating system.

Figure 2-1: Use the Control Panel to check your hardware settings

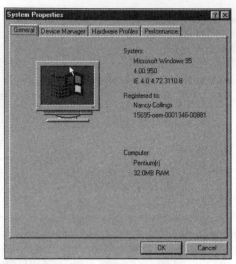

Figure 2-2: The System icon leads to the System Properties box

Figure 2-3: The Device Manager lists your hardware devices

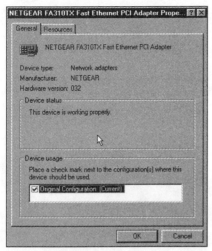

Figure 2-4: The Properties button directs
you to information about the selected device

A sample completed worksheet is shown next. The worksheet you fill out for your
own system will probably vary, so use the sample worksheet as a guide.

A sample completed pre-installation worksheet

Linux Installation Planning Worksheet

General System Information

Manufacturer: IBM ThinkPad

Processor: Intel Pentium

Speed: (266 MHz)

Motherboard   Make: Unknown   **Chip Set:** Triton II

Mouse: Logitech Trackpoint - PS/2 (If it's a serial mouse, list the COM port)

Keyboard: Standard 101/102-Key or Microsoft Natural Keyboard

Hard disk drive(s): Generic IDE   **Type:** <7   **Size:** (Each drive)

Boot: DOS/Windows 95

Disk Partition: C 1.99G, 1.24G used, 769 MB free, FAT, uncompressed, Size: 4GB

Disk Partition: D 1.81G, 0 used, 1.81 free, FAT, uncompressed   Size:

CD-ROM: E:/HITACHI CDR-S100 IDE/ATAPI

Continued

Continued

Video:

Video Card & Bus: IBM ThinkPad (Cyber9397) PCI

Video RAM: Don't know

Monitor: Laptop Display Panel (1024 X 768)

Max scan rate: Don't know

Ports: COM1 & LPT1, built-in infrared

Sound, video, & game controllers:

Crystal PnP Audio System CODEC

Crystal PnP Audio System Control Registers

Crystal PnP Audio System Joystick

Crystal PnP Audio System MPU-401 Compatible

US Robotics Wave Device for Voice Modem

PCMCIA (PC Card) Slot(s):

2 Texas Instruments PCI-1250 CardBus Controllers

Networking:

Modem: US Robotics Megahertz Telephony XJ-CC5560

On Serial port: COM1, Max speed: 115200

Computer hostname:

NIC (Network Interface Card) Type(s):

Dialup Adapter: None

AOL Adapter

Ethernet   token ring   FDDI   other

NIC Mfg: **Model:**

Network domain name: mountains.net

IP Address: 192.168.1.2

Network address: 192.168.1.0

Netmask: 255.255.255.0

Broadcast address: 192.168.1.255

Gateway(s): 192.168.1.1

DNS(s): 192.168.1.2

Summary

Planning is the most important phase of your Linux installation. Decide whether you need to run Linux along with another operating system. Know the hardware settings for your computer. Filling out a system worksheet saves valuable time in performing the actual installation. Chapter 3 guides you through the next steps — planning your filesystems and installing Linux.

✦   ✦   ✦

Installing Linux

This chapter focuses on the basic steps you need to perform to install Linux on a workstation as well as a server. We'll be looking primarily at Red Hat Linux with references to Caldera, Mandrake, and SuSE. I strongly recommend that you use the manuals that came with your distribution of Linux. As Linux is constantly undergoing development, I also recommend that you check the distribution's Web site for any product updates and/or bug fixes. The Web site for Red Hat is http://www.redhat.com.

You don't have to be a hardware technician or understand how hardware components work with each other. You do have to know on what kind of hardware you will be installing Linux. If you do not have all your hardware ducks in a row when you start the installation, it can be very difficult to go back during the installation process to effect changes on the fly. Similarly, editing a particular file after the install dialog is completed is not the ideal approach, though it is sometimes unavoidable.

The installation process is quite similar for the three distributions discussed in this chapter — Red Hat, SuSE, and Caldera. Each distribution takes you through a series of screens beginning with the language you wish to do the installation in and the language you will want to have your Linux system run in. The process continues with hardware decisions that you will have to make concerning your keyboard, mouse, video card, and so forth. With each new version and update for all three distributions, the installation process is becoming more stable and sophisticated, thereby making the installation process easier and more accurate for you, the user. Please keep in mind that the screens illustrated in this chapter and throughout this book are only examples and, considering the constantly and rapidly changing world of Linux, may not depict exactly what you see during your installation. The exact order of the installation path and the screens displayed will vary depending upon the distribution you choose and the actual version you install.

✦ ✦ ✦ ✦

In This Chapter

Understanding installation requirements

Partitioning your hard disk

Beginning the installation

Creating a boot disk

Configuring a loader

✦ ✦ ✦ ✦

Understanding Installation Requirements

Knowing your hardware is critical for a successful Linux installation. During the installation dialog, Linux will correctly detect your hardware; however, it is much better to be safe than sorry. Some components to pay particular attention to include hard drives, SCSI (Small Computer System Interface) or IDE (Integrated Drive Electronics), size, CD-ROM interface, mouse type, RAM, make, and model. Though the make and model of the monitor is not necessarily critical, the monitor must be able to support the screen resolutions of your video card. These are expressed in pixels (number of picture elements). For Windows 1024x768, horizontally and vertically is a typical setting. Table 3-1 provides a complete list of hardware elements that you should have on hand before you begin your Linux installation.

During the installation dialog you are given many opportunities to go back and change your decisions. However, I found that in many cases any new decisions were simply ignored by the dialog. This was especially true during the Mandrake installation where I specifically entered the pixels, and yet, the Linux "probe" determined a different value, which was incorrect.

Table 3-1	
Linux Installation Hardware Components	
Hardware Component	*Information Required*
Hard drives	Interface and size
Network card	IP address, host name, domain name
RAM	Amount of RAM
SCSI adapter	Make/model number
Monitor	Make/model, and refresh rates
Mouse	Type, number of buttons
CD-ROM	Interface adapter
Display adapter	Make/model number
Keyboard	Model/number of keys (101 standard)

Be prepared for the monitor and video card definitions during the installation dialog. With all four distributions installed—Red Hat (prior to version 7.0), Mandrake, Caldera, and SuSE—SuSE defining the correct refresh rates and resolutions was unclear. Although the installation dialogs for all distributions appeared to let me go back and change my definitions, more often than not this simply did not work out.

Refer to the X Window section later in this chapter for more detailed information on hardware components.

We have spent a lot of time going over the basic hardware you need to install your Linux system. You'll also need the following for a successful Linux installation:

✦ 16 MB of RAM

✦ 4 GB hard drive (300 MB to 1000 MB available)

✦ Pentium-class CPU

✦ IDE or SCSI disk controllers

✦ Color monitor

✦ CD-ROM drive

✦ Floppy drive

 Many other books and all the distributors will tell you that you don't need this much hardware to install Linux, and this is true, but with less you won't be able to do much after the installation is complete. Nor will you be able to use a GUI such as GNOME or KDE.

Partitioning your Hard Disk

Your Red Hat Linux system will require a minimum of two partitions: one large (size depending on the applications you choose to run) partition and a swap partition (for virtual memory), which will usually be twice the size of the RAM on your machine. You may want to create as many as eight to ten Linux native partitions for greater efficiency and easier disk management.

There are three ways to partition your hard disk: Disk Druid, which comes with the Red Hat CD-ROM, fdisk (yes, just like that old DOS program), or Partition Magic. Regardless of which method you choose, *be certain to back up your hard disk*. If you use fdisk or Disk Druid and you have existing data, you are almost certain to lose some of them. Partition Magic can work around your data but it is an additional expense — in time, quality, and money.

As long as I was going to incur an additional expense, I chose to invest in a new hard drive. By doing this I not only gave myself plenty of space to install Linux and select the packages and GUI of my choice, but I was also able to keep my Windows 95 system separate and thus eliminated all chance of losing any data. The choice is yours, but I recommend that you go with a new hard disk and use Disk Druid during the installation dialog to partition your hard disk. You can always use extra space, and disk drives are inexpensive.

Beginning the Installation

There are several ways to get Linux on your machine. The easiest and most reliable is to purchase a new machine with Linux already pre-installed. While this can be quick and save you a lot of work, it is usually not practical and also deprives you of the knowledge you will gain from performing the installation yourself. If you are one of the chosen ones about to purchase a new PC, you may want to consult a periodical such as *The Linux Journal,* one of the few magazines that covers Linux exclusively. You can find it on the Web at `fttp://www.linuxjournal.com/`.

More than likely you already have a PC running MS-DOS or some flavor of Windows. In this case, you will probably do your installation from a floppy disk or a CD-ROM. You can also install using FTP (File Transfer Program) or NFS (Network File System), but floppy and CD-ROM installations are the most common.

Creating a Boot Disk

To boot Red Hat Linux for the first time and start the Red Hat Linux installation program, you need a Red Hat boot disk. For this step, you should turn on your PC without any disk in the A: drive and then run Windows as usual.

Tip   You do not need a boot disk if you can start your PC under MS-DOS — not an MS-DOS window in Windows 95 — and access the CD-ROM from the DOS command prompt. If you run Windows 95/98, restart the PC in MS-DOS mode. However, you may not be able to access the CD-ROM in MS-DOS mode because the startup files — `AUTOEXEC.BAT` and `CONFIG.SYS` — may not be configured correctly. To access the CD-ROM from DOS, you typically must add a CD-ROM driver in `CONFIG.SYS` and add a line in `AUTOEXEC.BAT` that runs the MSCDEX program. Try restarting your PC in MS-DOS mode to see if the CD-ROM can be accessed. You also may not need a boot disk if your PC is capable of booting from the CD-ROM drive. To check if this is possible, go to your system BIOS and look in the section where you can choose the boot drives. If you can choose CD-ROM, select this and you can boot directly from the installation CD-ROM. If you succeed, skip the section describing making the Red Hat boot disk and continue with the text immediately following Figure 3-1.

Like the MS-DOS boot disk, the Red Hat boot disk starts your PC and the Red Hat Linux installation program. Once you install Red Hat Linux, you no longer need the Red Hat boot disk (except when you want to reinstall Red Hat Linux from the CD-ROMs).

The Red Hat boot disk contains an initial version of Red Hat Linux that you use to start Red Hat Linux, prepare the hard disk, and load the rest of Red Hat Linux. Creating the Red Hat boot disk involves using a utility program called `RAWRITE.EXE` to copy a special file called the Red Hat Linux *boot image* to a disk.

To create the Red Hat boot disk under Windows, follow these steps:

1. Open an MS-DOS window (select Start ➪ Programs ➪ MS-DOS Pro

2. In the MS-DOS window, enter the following commands at the MS-DOS prompt. (My comments are in parentheses, and your input is in boldface):

```
d:    (use the drive letter for the CD-ROM drive)
cd \dosutils
rawrite
Enter disk image source file name: \images\boot.img
Enter target diskette drive: a
Please insert a formatted diskette into drive A: and press -
ENTER- :
```

3. As instructed, you should put a formatted disk into the A: drive of your PC and then press Enter. The RAWRITE.EXE program copies the boot-image file to the disk.

After you see the DOS prompt again, you can take the Red Hat boot disk out of the A: drive and (if you haven't done so already) label it appropriately.

At this point you have all your hardware information handy and are ready to go. Place the bootable floppy or CD-ROM if available, in the appropriate drive and power up your system. The Linux banner screen will automatically appear, as shown in Figure 3-1.

Figure 3-1: The Red Hat Linux banner screen

At this point, the Red Hat Linux installation program is in control. The default graphical user interface (GUI) installation will automatically begin. The next screen to appear is the Language Selection screen, as shown in Figure 3-2.

Note   If you are familiar with the Red Hat Linux 6.0 installation, you will notice the addition of online help from the man pages on the left of the screen. This feature becomes especially helpful further along in the installation process.

For this particular installation I have highlighted English by using the down-arrow key. Clicking Next will take you to the next screen in the installation dialog — Keyboard Configuration. Figure 3-3 shows the Keyboard Configuration screen.

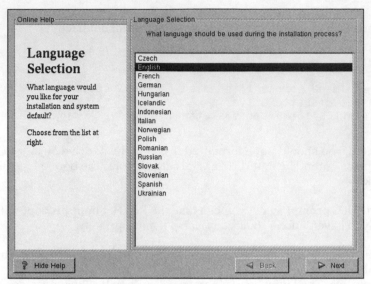

Figure 3-2: The Language Selection screen

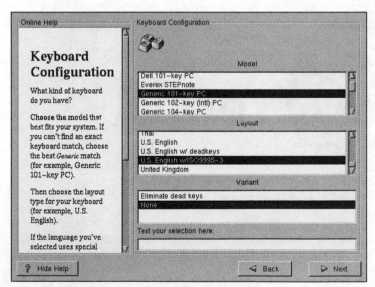

Figure 3-3: The Keyboard Configuration screen

Use the arrow keys to select the keyboard model that best matches your keyboard.

Note   For all four distributions—Red Hat, Caldera, Mandrake, and SuSE—I selected the Generic 101-key PC with layout and dead key defaults (for U.S. installations), and it worked nicely for all installations.

In the Layout subwindow select U.S. English (default). For the Variant subwindow, select None. Click Next to proceed to the Mouse Configuration screen, as shown in Figure 3-4.

 Note   The variant subwindow is for versions prior to 7.0.

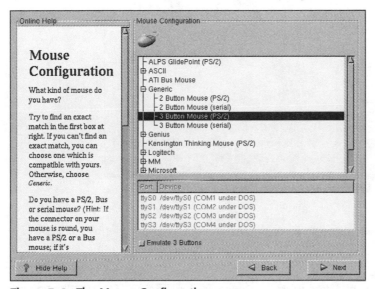

Figure 3-4: The Mouse Configuration screen

For version 6.1 and earlier and the other three distributions of Linux, select 2 Button Mouse. If you choose to emulate a three-button mouse, click on the checkbox in the bottom left-hand corner of the screen. This feature can be useful if you are going to be using X Window. To emulate the third mouse button in X Window, hold the left and right mouse buttons down simultaneously.

 New Feature   In version 7.1, your mouse properties are determined at the initial boot and load of the CD-ROM. Chances are you have a serial mouse, but if you are not sure, the help on the left side of the Mouse Configuration Screen, as shown in Figure 3-4, is very good. You should not have to override what Linux decides your mouse properties are, but if you feel the need, follow the preceding instructions at your own risk!

 Note   To alter your mouse configuration at a later date you will need to run the `/usr/bin/mouseconfig` command.

Click on the Next button to go the Welcome screen, as shown in Figure 3-5. Take a minute to read the text on the left portion of the screen.

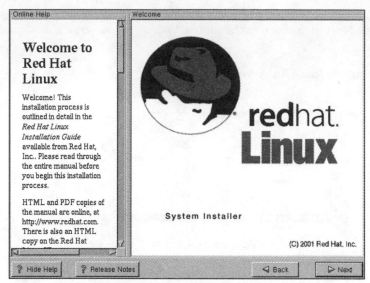

Figure 3-5: The Welcome to Red Hat Linux 7.1 screen

Click on the Next button to go to the Install Path screen to define the type of installation you will be performing.

Caution If you have not already backed up your hard drives/partitions on your system, this would be a good time to do so. Depending on the type of installation you select, data during this section *will* be destroyed.

In the section "Partitioning your Hard Drive" earlier in this chapter, I strongly recommended installing Linux on a clean or new hard drive. This is because of the potential for destroying data in this next part of the installation. On the Install Path screen you determine the type of Linux installation or upgrade you will be performing. Your options are Custom, GNOME Workstation, KDE Workstation, Server, and Upgrade. I recommend selecting the Custom installation, as this will enable you to select only the services and packages required for your system. Selecting a Server or Workstation installation will cause the Package Manager to select all available packages in the Linux distribution and will destroy all data in any existing Linux partitions. Figure 3-6 shows the Install Path screen.

Highlight the Custom icon and click Next to move to the Partitions screen of the installation dialog. Red Hat Linux uses a tool called Disk Druid to create partitions and file systems within these partitions. If you have not already created your partitions using fdisk or Partition Magic, as I recommended in the section "Partitioning your Hard Disk," you must do it now.

Note The Automatic Partitioning screen shown in Figure 3-7 gives you the choice of allowing the install program to automatically partition your hard disk or using Disk Druid or fdisk to partition your system. If you have pre-partitioned your system, select Disk Druid.

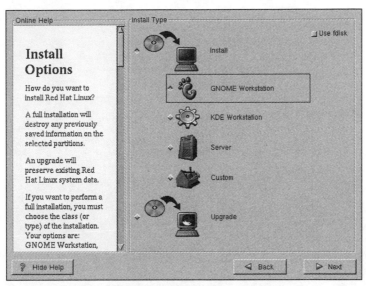

Figure 3-6: The Install path screen

Approximately 12 key directories define the Linux file system. Although you only need two partitions to install your Linux distribution—one for the entire file system and one for the swap space—disk space management is much easier if you create multiple native Linux partitions for some of these key directories. Table 3-2 provides an overview of the Linux filesystem hierarchy, including a brief description and the recommended size in megabytes (MB) for each file system.

Table 3-2
Linux Filesystem Hierarchy

Filesystem	Recommended Size	Description
/bin	16	Binary files for user commands.
/boot	16	Linux startup (boot) files
/usr	1300	X Window
/opt	512	Application packages
/var	256	Log and spool files
/home	1024-2048	User directories and files
/tmp	128	Temporary files
/	128	

The / partition typically contains the following key directories: /root, /bin, /dev, /etc, /lib, /boot, and /sbin.

Cross-Reference   See Chapter 10 for a detailed look at these key directories.

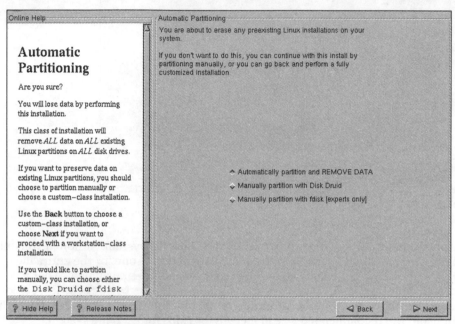

Figure 3-7: The Manual Partitioning screen

To add a partition using Disk Druid, click Manually Partition with Disk Druid. Click Next to display the Linux native partition you want to select for installation, where you will define the mount point, size, and device type. Figure 3-8 shows the Partitions Table screen.

New Feature   For version 7.1 to create the /root partition, highlight a mount point with a value of `<not set>` and a type of Linux native and click the edit pushbutton. You do not need a lot of space for the root partition; 128k will do. Click the use remaining space checkbox to allow for growth and click OK to add your /root partition. The swap partition is already defined for you on the Partitions Table screen.

To create the /rootpartition for versions prior to 7.0, enter **/root** in the Mount Point edit box, and **16** in the Size edit box. Do *not* click the checkbox for Grow to Fill Disk. Select Linux Native as the Partition Type and select HD*x* (*x* being the disk drive) for Allowable Drives. If you have multiple drives, spread your partitions across these drives for efficiency purposes. If you only have one drive, HDA will be your selection. Click OK to add the new partition to your system.

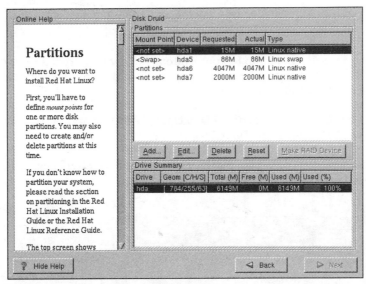

Figure 3-8: The Partitions Table screen

To create a swap partition, follow the same steps but leave the Mount Point edit box blank, and enter twice the value of the RAM on your system in the Size edit box. For example, if you have a 32-MB machine, enter **64** for size; on a 64-MB machine, enter **128** for size. Select Linux Swap as the Partition Type. Click OK to add the new partition to your system.

Table 3-3 describes the features of the additional pushbuttons for Disk Druid on the Partitions screen.

Table 3-3
Disk Druid Pushbuttons

Pushbutton	Function
Add	Adds a new partition. When you select it, a popup window appears.
Edit	Enables you to modify a highlighted partition on the Partitions screen. When you select it, a popup window appears displaying that partition's characteristics.
Delete	Deletes the highlighted partition. When you select it, a confirmation popup window appears.
Reset	Resets Partition table to original content.
Back	Terminates Disk Druid without making any changes.

Caution   If you select DOS as your partition type, your system will not run.

Click Add to add your swap partition to your system. Follow this procedure for all the partitions you wish to create. When all your partitions are created, click Next to go to the Choose Partitions to Format screen.

Note   All partitions will be created as Partition Type Linux Native except your swap partition, which will be Partition Type Linux Swap.

All the newly created partitions on your system should be formatted. Figure 3-9 shows the Choose Partitions to Format screen.

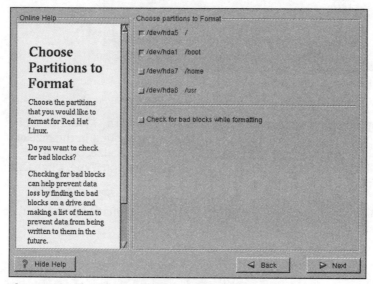

Figure 3-9: The Choose Partitions to Format screen

To format a newly created partition, highlight the requested partition and click the checkbox labeled "Check for bad blocks while formatting." By doing this, you prevent Linux from writing to any bad blocks on your disk in the future, and thus prevent data loss and ensure data integrity. When all of your partitions have been formatted, click on Next to go to the LILO Configuration screen.

Configuring a Loader

When you boot Linux, the kernel is loaded into your computer by one of several available *loader* programs. If you are running an Intel PC, you will be using LILO (Linux Loader). For a DEC Alpha, MILO is the loader program, and for SPARC compatible workstations, the loader program is SILO. Since we are running this installation dialog on an Intel PC, we will focus on installing LILO.

If for some reason you choose not to install LILO, you may start Linux from DOS by running loadlin.exe from the Dosutils directory on your CD-ROM. You can also load Linux via a network or a commercial boot loader such as System Commander.

Figure 3-10 shows the LILO Configuration screen.

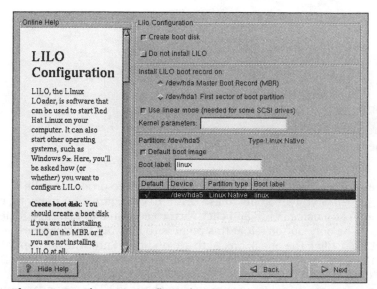

Figure 3-10: The LILO Configuration screen

Since this is a custom installation, you need to tell the computer how to boot your Linux system. Whether you will be running Linux as a standalone system or along with another operating system, you should choose to install LILO on the Master Boot Record (MBR). The only time you should choose the second option, First Sector of Boot Partition, is if you are using another boot loader. Also, click the Create boot disk checkbox. This boot diskette is always handy to have, and it's required if you're not installing LILO. Supply a name in the Boot Label edit box and click Next.

The actual installation of LILO will take place near the end of the installation dialog. In other words, although we are currently telling Linux we want to create a boot diskette, it will not happen right now but rather at the end of the installation process. Be prepared and have your floppy disk ready when prompted to create the boot disk. In versions prior to 7.1 the next screen in the installation dialog is the Network Configuration screen, as shown in Figure 3-11. In version 7.1, if your computer does not have a network card, you will go to the Time Zone Selection screen when you click on next. The Time Zone Selection screen is shown in Figure 3-12.

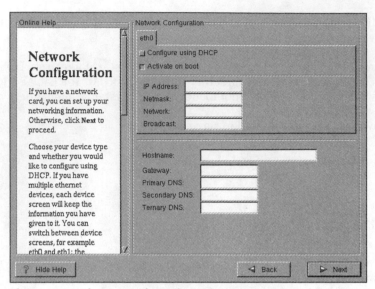

Figure 3-11: The Network Configuration screen

If your computer does not have a network card, click Next to proceed to the Time Zone Selection screen. If you are going to use DHCP to configure your network, click the checkbox Configure using DHCP and click Next to continue to the Time Zone Selection screen. The only option left at this point is to activate your network adapter at boot time. Click the check box Activate on boot. Enter the appropriate information in the edit boxes for IP Address, Hostname, Gateway, and Primary DNS. The Netmask, Network, and Broadcast edit boxes will be filled in automatically. (If this information is incorrect, make the appropriate changes.) The secondary and tertiary DNS edit boxes are optional. Verify that all the information is correct and click Next to go to the Firewall Configuration screen. This screen lets you choose the security level for your firewall. Click on Next to accept the default choice and go to the Time Zone Selection screen.

The Time Zone Selection screen, shown in Figure 3-12, offers two choices for setting your system clock. The first and most common is the Location option (Eastern Standard Time, Eastern Daylight Time, Central Standard Time, and so forth). The second option is the UTC offset or Universal Coordinated Time. During this installation dialog we are going to be using Eastern Standard Time.

New Feature In version 7.0 you can point the mouse anywhere on the displayed world map and select the desired time zone with a single click.

Highlight America/New_York and click Next to proceed to the Account Configuration screen.

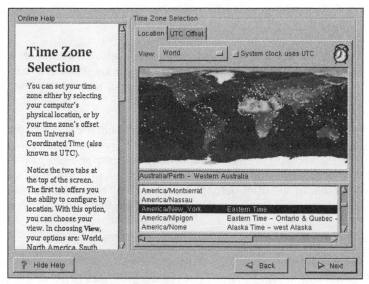

Figure 3-12: The Time Zone Selection screen

In this section we are going to create a minimum of two accounts: one root account and one user account. The Account Configuration screen has three parts. The top part of the screen is for defining the root password, the middle part of the screen is for defining a user account and password, and the bottom part of the screen is for displaying account names. Figure 3-13 shows the different components of the Account Configuration screen.

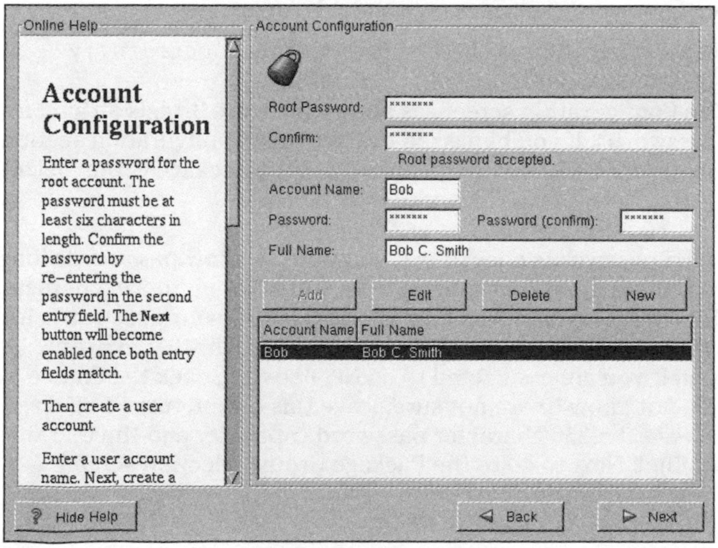

Figure 3-13: The Account Configuration screen

Enter the password for root in the Root Password edit box. Re-enter the password for root in the Confirm edit box.

Caution Remember that the root account is the all-powerful administrative account. With this account all things are possible. Don't choose an obvious password, like the name of your dog or cat. Passwords with both upper- and lowercase letters, as well as numbers or special characters, are harder to crack.

When you enter the password, only asterisks will be displayed, for security purposes. Once you have entered the root password you may create a user account by entering the name of the account in the Account Name edit box and the password in the Password edit box, and re-entering the password in the Confirm edit box. Enter the name of person the account belongs to in the Full Name edit box and click Next to go to the Authentication Configuration screen of the installation dialog.

At startup time, if you have forgotten the root password, you can recover it by following these steps:

1. At the LILO boot prompt enter `linux` `single` where `linux` is the name of your Linux boot partition (linux in this installation dialog).

2. Linux will then display the following prompt:

    Bash#

3. Use the `passwd` command at this prompt to receive this message:

    New UNIX password:

4. Type the new password and press Enter to receive this message:

    Retype new UNIX password:

5. Type the new password. This message should display:

    passwd: all authentication tokens updated successfully

The Authentication Configuration screen, as shown in Figure 3-14, is strictly for setting up network passwords. If you bypassed the Network Configuration section during the installation dialog, click Next to go directly to the Package Group Selection screen.

Click the Enable MD5 passwords checkbox if you want to allow passwords longer than the standard eight-character maximum. This will allow up to 256 characters. Clicking the Enable shadow passwords checkbox will store your passwords in a file called /etc/shadow rather than the usual /etc/passwd file. This file may only be read by the root account. If you are connected to an NIS network, click the Enable NIS checkbox. If you do not know or are not sure, leave this option turned off. I recommend that you activate the 256-character password capability and the Use shadow passwords option. Click Next to go to the Package Group Selection screen.

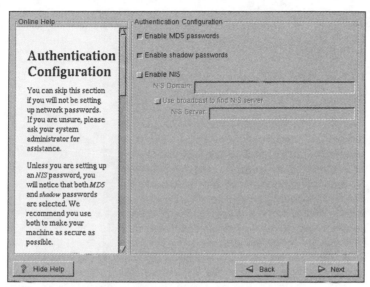

Figure 3-14: The Authentication Configuration screen

Since we are doing a custom installation, we can choose any or all of the packages on the Package Group Selection screen. Had we chosen the workstation installation option earlier in the installation dialog, all packages would be selected by default. If when you created your partitions you realized you had plenty of disk space, it might not be a bad idea to select all packages. This way you will not have to go back at a later date to install a package you may have missed. If you do need to install packages at a later date, you will use The Red Hat Package Manager (RPM). You can run RPM using the control panel in X Window. Each of the available packages is represented by an icon and a brief text description, as shown in Figure 3-15. To select a package, click the checkbox next to its icon. Use the scrollbar on the right to browse through the list of available packages.

Select your package groups carefully. For example, Printer Support and the X Window System are not automatically installed. You must select them manually. If you're using version 7.0, after selecting your packages click the Next button to go to the About to Install Screen, shown in Figure 3-16.

Caution

Version 7.0 users: At this point you'll see a small window that says "checking dependencies for packages selected?" If you pass this test, you will be presented with a screen depicting a monitor with a hand holding a wrench with a few bolts flying about (see Figure 3-16). If you fail this dependency test, your monitor will go black and your system will automatically re-boot off the CD-ROM. After this, the installation process will start from square one. This usually happens because of packages that were selected manually. Use caution!

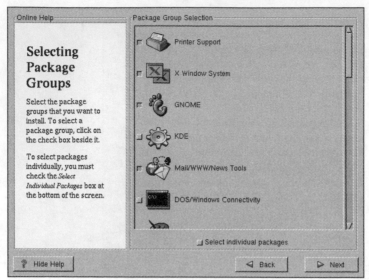

Figure 3-15: The Package Group Selection screen

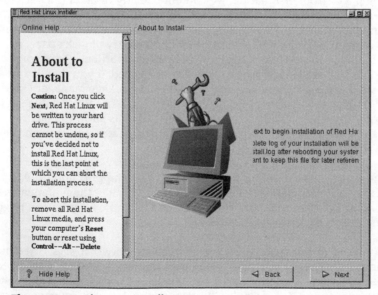

Figure 3-16: About to Install

If you are using a version prior to 7.0, click Next to proceed to the X Configuration screen of the installation dialog.

X Configuration will try and determine the type of video card and monitor you are using in order to find your computer's best display settings. Initially, the installation program will probe your system to determine the make and model of your video adapter. If the installation program probes successfully, it will list your hardware. Be sure to verify this information based on the research you did before beginning the installation. If the probe is unsuccessful, a list of video adapters and monitors will be displayed (as shown in Figures 3-17 and 3-18, respectively) and you will have to pick and choose. This list is quite extensive, so have your pre-installation notes ready just in case.

When you believe you have selected the correct hardware, click Next.

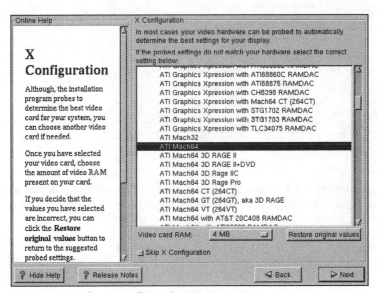

Figure 3-17: The X Configuration screen

Note Though this process is critical to the successful use of the GUI, do not agonize too much over getting the perfect display and resolution for your machine. If you do not select the correct hardware, the installation will still succeed and you will be able to correct this setting later by editing the XF86Config file (which we discuss in detail later in this chapter).

Confirm your selections by clicking Next to go to the About to Install screen or No
to go back and reconfigure X. If you see squiggly lines or a whiteout effect on your
monitor, click on No. Repeat this process until you have a reasonable video presen-
tation on your monitor.

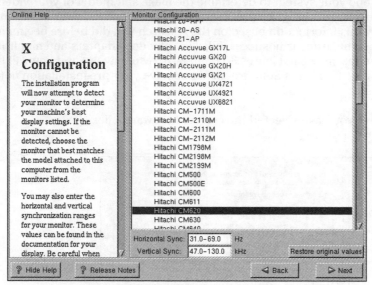

Figure 3-18: The Select Monitor Screen

Now that you have told the installation program everything there is to know about
your system and what features and hardware you would like to have, the actual
installation process is ready to begin. Click Next to begin the installation.

Figure 3-19 shows you a real-time list of how many packages you have selected and
how many have actually been installed. You can find the log of the installation process, including all errors and messages, in /tmp/install.log. The installation process
may take up to a couple of hours, depending on the speed of your machine.

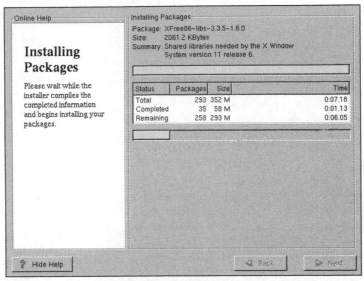

Figure 3-19: The Installing Packages screen

Once the package installation is complete, click Next to create the floppy boot disk the installation dialog requested earlier. Figure 3-20 shows the installation dialog screen for creating the floppy boot disk.

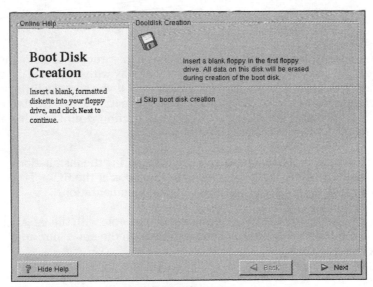

Figure 3-20: The Boot Disk Creation screen

Click Next to complete the installation and go to the Congratulations screen, shown in Figure 3-21.

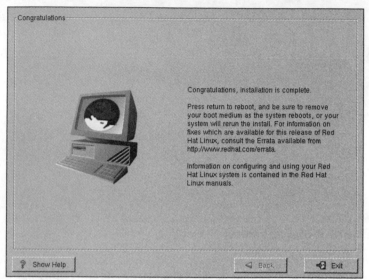

Figure 3-21: The Congratulations screen

Summary

Red Hat version 7.1 really does a good job of simplifying the process of installing Linux. There are still a couple of glitchy areas but if you stay with the Linux defaults and add your packages on at a later date, you will do well. If you spend a little time up front researching your hardware, and if you follow the detailed step-by-step instructions in this book and your distributor's documentation, your Linux installation should go smoothly and successfully.

If you have any questions or if some problems do arise during the installation process, you can consult the CD-ROM that comes with this book at the HOW_TOs. You can also go to your distributor's Web site and view its documentation.

Be sure to keep your system updated as frequently as possible with the latest and greatest available utilities in order to keep compatible with the new Linux applications being developed all the time.

✦   ✦   ✦

Inside Linux

This chapter gives you a peek inside the Linux kernel and
the Linux operating system. The kernel is like a car's
engine. You can't start the car without an engine. On the other
hand, if all you have is an engine, you can't go anywhere. You
need wheels and steering and a seat and more. The same concept applies to a kernel and an operating system. You can't
run an operating system without the kernel. On the other
hand, with only a kernel, you can't go anywhere or do anything on your computer and network.

A Linux user is like a car driver. To drive around, you don't
need to know anything about how or why a car works, nor do
you need to know how Linux does things behind the scenes to
be a Linux user. However, it helps to have a little background
when you see a command that seems bizarre or a mechanism
that appears cumbersome. Knowing a few nuts and bolts may
help you to understand why that command seems so strange
and how to use it more effectively. Just as an automobile
mechanic needs to know what's under the hood of a car, Linux
system and network administrators can get a head start on
their jobs by being familiar with the terminology and features
that sit "under the hood" of the Linux operating system.

Inside the Linux Kernel

The kernel, containing over seven million lines of code, is the
core of the Linux operating system. This small (yes — small, in
operating-system terms) and efficient kernel consists of different subsystems that provide the following services for the
Linux operating system:

- ✦ Support for and communication with hardware
- ✦ Process scheduling, providing multitasking
- ✦ Physical and virtual-memory management
- ✦ IPC (interprocess communication)

Cross-Reference Chapter 28 explains kernel options and how to customize and rebuild the Linux kernel.

Figure 4-1 shows the relationship of the Linux kernel to the operating system. One major benefit of the Linux kernel is that it allows you to load and unload components of the operating system as you need them. This capability is called *dynamic kernel module loading*. Many UNIX and other kernels do not provide dynamic kernel modules. You need to rebuild the kernel, shut down the system, and reboot to add functionality to the kernel. Linux kernel modules consist of code that you can dynamically link into the kernel at any time, even when users are working. When modules are no longer needed, you can remove them from the kernel, thereby keeping the kernel small and efficient.

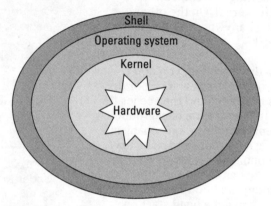

Figure 4-1: The kernel is the heart of the Linux operating system

Cross-Reference Without the kernel you could not run programs, but remember that the kernel is not the whole operating system. Most of the basic tools that comprise the operating system come from the GNU project (http://www.gnu.org) described in Chapter 1.

Understanding multitasking — A new concept for MS-DOS and Microsoft Windows users

Linux is a multiuser, multitasking operating system. The term *multiuser* means what it says — that many users can work on the same computer at the same time. Linux provides some security mechanisms to support multiuser computing. These security features include:

✦ User login and logout

✦ Password protection

✦ File and directory access control

Although computers can have multiple CPUs (Central Processing Units, such as the Intel Pentium or Compaq Alpha), let's use the typical example of a computer with one CPU. When you work on that single processor computer along with other users, the CPU can only do work for one user at a time. Yet, it seems like everyone is getting work done at the same time. The kernel has a little trick that makes it seem as if you are all doing processing work simultaneously. This trick is called multitasking, and the magic is that it fools you and all the other users into thinking that you are the only one working. *Multitasking* means that all users' tasks appear to run at the same time, though behind the scenes the operating system is really scheduling those tasks to take turns using the CPU. Linux and similar systems (for example, Compaq's OpenVMS, all flavors of UNIX, IBM's mainframe systems) are also called *timesharing*, meaning that all processes share the CPU in slices of time.

Caution If your computer contains multiple CPUs, everything works the same way, but there is more processing power available to share. However, don't assume that if you have two CPUs in your system, you have exactly twice the processing power to share. Because of various kinds of operating system overhead, you will have slightly less than twice the power. This ability to retain high-performance levels as the number of processors increases is called *scalability*. Distributions of Linux based on the 2.4 kernel scale work well with up to eight CPUs. Some vendors (notably IBM) have added code to increase the scalability to as many as 512 processors.

Understanding device drivers

One purpose of an operating system is to hide the intricacies of interfacing with hardware. If you want to send e-mail, you don't want to worry about whether your hard drive is a SCSI disk or an IDE drive. Device drivers are software loaded into the kernel that take care of the interface between hardware and the operating system.

A device driver is a program that controls a device—most often hardware—that is attached to your computer. There are device drivers for sound devices, printers, displays, CD players, floppy disk drives, touch screens, hard disks, clocks, Zip drives—and the list goes on. On Linux, device drivers also control non-hardware devices, called *pseudo-devices*, such as connections to network terminals. When you install Linux, most, and maybe all, of the device drivers you need are built into the kernel. Actually, more device drivers than you need are built into the kernel to satisfy different kinds of users with different hardware. If you buy a new type of device for which the kernel does not yet include a driver, you need to install the new device driver yourself.

Cross-Reference Chapter 28 explains how to edit and rebuild the kernel to add new device drivers and other options.

Understanding Linux process concepts

Every time you log in, Linux starts a process for you. Processes perform tasks within the operating system. Think of a process as a running program. While a program may look to you like a file consisting of lines of a programming language, such as C or COBOL, the computer sees a program as a set of data and instructions to the machine. The program is stored as an executable image on disk.

> **Note**   On Linux and UNIX, the term "exe" (pronounced "exee" with the first syllable accented) is a common nickname for an executable image.

The Linux kernel keeps track of your process context, which contains information about who you are, what you're doing, and where you are (in Linux). A process consumes system resources, such as the CPU and memory. Your process uses the CPU's to run its instructions and memory to hold those instructions and its data. Your process also opens files within filesystems. Linux keeps track of everyone's process and the system resources the processes use in order to manage system resources equitably for everyone. It would not be fair to the other users on the computer for one process to monopolize memory or CPU power. The kernel keeps track of you by building a data structure for each of your processes and links it with other data structures that represent the other processes on the computer. These data structures usually exist in physical memory, and only for the kernel to use.

As you use commands and run programs, Linux creates other processes for you. If you use a graphical user interface (GUI), Linux creates processes just to control your graphical environment. Figure 4-2 shows a list of processes displayed by the `top` command. The list is sorted by the amount of CPU time the processes are using. (`top` refers to *top CPU users*.) Don't worry about the extra system information you see in Figure 4-2. Chapter 32 explains each item.

```
─ Konsole <2>                                                            ? □ ×
  File   Sessions   Options   Help

 12:57pm  up  7:13,  1 user,  load average: 0.97, 0.36, 0.16
 68 processes: 65 sleeping, 3 running, 0 zombie, 0 stopped
 CPU states:  6.9% user,  19.5% system,   0.0% nice,  73.4% idle
 Mem:    47024K av,  45980K used,   1044K free,  30452K shrd,    8652K buff
 Swap:   64508K av,  22836K used,  41672K free                  12352K cached

   PID USER     PRI  NI  SIZE  RSS SHARE STAT  LIB %CPU %MEM   TIME COMMAND
  7353 root      18   0   592  592   404 R       0 17.6  1.2   0:07 slocate
   585 root       4   0  7024 6784  1152 R       0  4.8 14.4  20:58 X
  7334 root       6   0  1052 1052   840 R       0  2.5  2.2   0:02 top
   596 root       1   0  2636 1516  1100 S       0  0.9  3.2   0:31 kwm
  7328 root       0   0  4492 4492  2932 S       0  0.3  9.5   0:01 konsole
  7354 root       1   0  5412 5412  2876 S       0  0.1 11.5   0:01 ksnapshot
     1 root       0   0   124   68    56 S       0  0.0  0.1   0:02 init
     2 root       0   0     0    0     0 SW      0  0.0  0.0   0:00 kflushd
     3 root       0   0     0    0     0 SW      0  0.0  0.0   0:00 kupdate
     4 root       0   0     0    0     0 SW      0  0.0  0.0   0:00 kpiod
     5 root       0   0     0    0     0 SW      0  0.0  0.0   0:01 kswapd
   129 root       0   0   424  416   372 S       0  0.0  0.8   0:03 apmd
   218 bin        0   0    80   36     0 S       0  0.0  0.0   0:00 portmap
   270 root       0   0   288  224   176 S       0  0.0  0.4   0:00 syslogd
   280 root       0   0   452  164   132 S       0  0.0  0.3   0:00 klogd
```

Figure 4-2: The top command lists processes and system usage information

Jobs and processes — parents and children

A job includes a parent process and all child processes created (forked) by the parent. Linux tags processes with the following two identifiers:

✦ A pid (process id)

✦ A ppid (parent process id)

Note

All processes are ultimately descended from a system process called init. init's pid is always 1 on every Linux computer.

You don't need to know how many processes Linux creates on your behalf, but if you are monitoring your system's performance you need to understand that process creation is a fact of life, and that since processes consume system resources, a system administrator may need to control the number of processes allowed on the system at any given time. As you examine processes on the system, you can see which processes belong to the same job by matching pids with their ppids.

Cross-Reference

Chapter 32 shows a process status display and how to interpret it.

Understanding process states in relation to multitasking

As a process runs, it passes through various states. Linux processes may be in one of the following states:

Runnable   The process is either running (it is the current process) or ready to run (that is, it is waiting its turn to be scheduled to run on a CPU). Remember the multitasking concept. Even though only one process is current and running on any CPU at any one time, each user perceives that all processes are running simultaneously.

Waiting   The process is waiting for something to happen — for example, for a resource (other than the CPU) to become available. (If the process is waiting for the CPU, it is in a runnable state.) A common resource to wait for is the hard disk. Disks go very slowly compared to the CPU. Therefore, on a system with a fast processor and only one or two hard disks, you are likely to see users who have had their turn at the CPU and are now waiting their turn to read from or write to disk. The wait for disk is usually slower than the wait for CPU.

Stopped   The process has been signaled to stop. For example, a process that is being debugged might be stopped.

Zombie   The process is halted. On Linux, *halted* is different from *stopped*. Stopped can be restarted. Halted is not good. It usually means that parts are still hanging around, taking up space and system resources, but doing nothing — dead, but not buried.

Cross-Reference

Chapter 32 shows you how to monitor process statistics, including the process state.

Understanding how virtual memory relates to physical memory

Besides sharing memory with other processes, each Linux process has its own sep-arate virtual address space consisting of pages of memory that store the process context and anything else the process may need. The address space is called *virtual* because your page numbers are not the actual physical locations in memory. For example, virtual page number 4 might actually be the 10,000[th] physical memory page. Linux keeps special translation tables that map your virtual page numbers to the actual physical locations in memory. Figure 4-3 shows two separate virtual address spaces mapped through one of these special page translation tables into physical memory locations. Notice that besides showing separate virtual address spaces, the figure also shows the two processes sharing a page of physical memory (physical page 4).

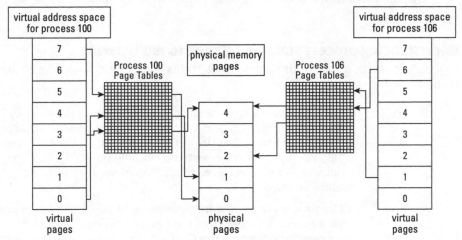

Figure 4-3: Virtual to physical memory mapping for process address spaces

One major advantage of maintaining a separate virtual address space for each pro-cess is that no process can adversely affect another.

Understanding virtual-memory management

Linux uses a demand-paged virtual-memory model. Memory is *virtual* because it looks to users as if there is an unlimited supply regardless of how much physical memory (RAM) sits in chips inside the computer. Linux uses a swap space on your hard disk as an extension of your computer's physical memory. Your computer pre-tends that the swap space is memory, thereby creating the illusion of much more memory than you actually have.

Memory is demand-paged because only those segments of a program or file that are actually in use (that is, in *demand*), are read from disk into pages of memory. If you need more pieces of program or data, more program or data segments are paged (read) into memory from your hard disk. To make room in memory for those new pages, the Linux kernel might have to page out (that is, discard from memory) to disk some in-memory segments that you no longer need. Also, if several instances of a program are running at once, those instances share physical memory in pages. This memory-page sharing reduces overall physical memory usage.

For example, suppose several people are using the same *shell* (a command-line interpreter) to execute commands. A shell is a program. It's much more efficient to keep a single copy of that shell in memory and let all processes needing a shell share that one in-memory copy. Dynamic libraries are another common way to share code among processes. Shared memory has a beneficial side effect — it reduces the amount of I/O (input/output) to and from disk, since shared code is only loaded into memory once, regardless of how many processes need to share it.

Note   Shared memory is also an interprocess communication (IPC) mechanism. IPC uses shared memory as a way for two processes to exchange data.

Understanding a little bit (a very little bit) about paging

Linux divides memory into manageably sized pieces called *pages*. The page size for Linux depends on the underlying hardware. On Compaq's Alpha AXP systems, a memory page is 8 KB (8192 bytes). On Intel-compatible processors (including other Compaq computers), the page size is 4 KB (4096 bytes). Regardless of page size, each Linux page has a unique number called the *page frame number* (PFN). When you run a program, one of the first things Linux must do is load the correct pages of code and data from disk into your memory address space. This process is called *paging in*.

When the amount of available physical memory becomes scarce, Linux's memory management system tries to free up more pages so they will be available when a process needs them. There is a special Linux program, called the *kernel swap daemon* (kswapd for short) that ensures that there are enough free memory pages to keep memory management working efficiently. At regular intervals, the kswapd looks to see if the number of free pages in the system is OK. If free pages are low, kswapd looks at two kernel variables. Kernel variables are values stored in the kernel. There are default values for the variables or the system administrator can adjust the values. kswapd checks that the free_pages_high variable is less than the number of free memory pages available; if it is, the kswapd decides that everything is okay and goes to sleep until its next scheduled wakeup call. If the free_pages_high variable exceeds the number of free memory pages, the kswapd goes into action to reclaim some pages by means of a technique called *paging out*. If the number of free memory pages goes below free_pages_high, the kswapd tries a variety of methods to reduce the number of physical memory pages that Linux is using. Even worse, if the number of free memory pages goes below free_pages_low, the kswapd must take extreme measures to reclaim some pages of memory.

Cross-Reference   Chapter 28 tells you how to adjust kernel variables such as free_pages_high and free_pages_low. Chapter 34 tells you why you might need to adjust them.

Understanding the buffer cache

Linux maintains several kinds of caches (memory areas). In each case, the purpose of the cache is to keep data in memory for faster access. Remember, hard disk access is still very slow compared to memory access. So, by maintaining caches, Linux is trying to make things go faster for you. One very important cache is the buffer cache.

The buffer cache contains buffers of data that are used by certain block-device drivers, usually hard-disk drivers.

Note   A block device is one that Linux accesses in fixed sized blocks of data, often 512 bytes. Even if you only need to read 20 bytes, your disk access is one block. If you need to read more than 512 bytes, say 1500 bytes, for example, your disk access consists of multiple blocks. It's a lot more efficient to do three disk reads, one per block, than 1500 disk reads, one per byte.

These buffers contain blocks of data that have either been read from a device or are being written to it. When you request a disk read, Linux checks the buffer cache first. If your data are already in the buffer cache, Linux does not need to read from the physical block device; that is, the hard disk. Remember, access to the buffer cache (memory) is much faster than access to disk.

Understanding filesystems

A filesystem consists of a set of directories and files in the Linux directory tree. One advantage of filesystems is that you can use files and directories without understanding any disk geometry, such as how many tracks or cylinders are on your disk, or which bits and bytes hold your files. You even access hardware through the filesystem via device special files located in a directory called /dev.

Tip   Remember this (it comes up often in the system-administration section): In Linux, devices look like files to users.

In Sync

Storing programs and data in memory provides much faster access than reading everything from a disk file. However, memory is temporary storage. When your system shuts down or crashes or there's a power failure, the data in memory are lost. This is why memory is called *volatile storage*. So Linux needs a mechanism to ensure that shutting down the system doesn't lose data. Linux writes the in-memory data to disk automatically and on a regular basis. This writing of volatile data to permanent storage is called *syncing*.

Another advantage of using Linux is filesystem flexibility. Linux supports more than a dozen filesystems with various formats for local and remote network filesystems, including the formats in the following list. (The ext2 filesystem was developed specifically for Linux.)

✦ ext2

✦ Microsoft MS-DOS FAT16

✦ Microsoft Windows 95 VFAT

✦ NFS (Network Filesystem)

✦ UNIX System V

✦ Xenix

✦ UFS (UNIX Filesystem)

✦ ISO 9660 CD-ROM filesystem

✦ OS/2 HPFS

✦ Minix (a bare-bones UNIX that drove Linus Torvalds to create the Linux kernel)

Note You do not need to recognize what kind of filesystem your files are stored in. To a user, files are files. Just go ahead and use them. For example, neither you nor the programs you need to run need to know that your home directory is in ext2 format on the first IDE drive connected to your system.

You can use very different filesystem formats on your computer all at the same time. Regardless of how many different filesystems you use on a single computer, Linux combines all your filesystems into one tree structure. As you create additional filesystems, Linux adds each new filesystem into this one file-system tree.

Cross-Reference As you will see in Chapter 10, filesystems live in Linux disk partitions, which live on devices.

Understanding Networking Features

Communication of any kind requires a set of rules that each side understands. In networking terminology, those rules are *protocols*. Linux supports many networking protocols (that is, rules for communication) including:

✦ TCP/IP

✦ UUCP

✦ IPX (from Novell)

✦ AppleTalk (from Apple Computer)

Connecting with TCP/IP

TCP/IP (Transmission Control Protocol/Internet Protocol) is a set of networking protocols that allows computers to communicate over a local or wide-area network. TCP and IP are only two of the protocols in the TCP/IP suite. The Internet runs on TCP/IP, and that is the protocol that Part IV of this book describes.

Most TCP/IP networks use Ethernet or token ring as the physical network-cabling scheme. Linux supports both Ethernet network interface cards (NICs) and token-ring adapters, including those for portable computers, such as pocket and PC Card Ethernet interfaces.

If you don't have a NIC in your computer, don't worry. If you have a telephone line and a modem, Linux can connect you to the Internet (or any dialup network) with two protocols from the TCP/IP set:

 ✦ SLIP (Serial Line Internet Protocol)

 ✦ PPP (Point-to-Point Protocol)

Connecting with other network protocols

Besides TCP/IP, Linux users can also communicate with Microsoft operating systems (Windows for Workgroups, Windows 95/98/Me/NT/2000) via Samba, a program based on SMB, the Server Message Block protocol. Samba lets you share files, printers, and serial ports. You can also run Samba over the Internet on top of TCP/IP.

Note   The SMB protocol originated at Microsoft.

Cross-Reference   See Chapter 34 for more information on SMB, including how to configure Samba.

Linux also supports Apple's AppleTalk protocol for Macintosh connectivity.

UUCP (UNIX-to-UNIX Copy) is an older protocol for transferring files, electronic mail, and electronic news between UNIX (and Linux) machines over telephone lines by modem. UUCP was quite popular a few years ago when TCP/IP was not the *de facto* network standard.

Delving into Daemons

Daemons are programs that run in the background and provide services for you. These daemons usually start automatically when your system starts up. Daemons provide many functions, including:

✦ Networking and remote access

✦ Internet services, such as telnet and FTP

✦ E-mail

✦ Newsgroups

✦ Scheduling commands and programs to run automatically and unattended

✦ World Wide Web servers

✦ Printing

✦ Remote filesystems

✦ Logging system errors and events

Cross-Reference

You can read about specific daemons throughout this book, in the chapters that deal with the functions the daemons control. For example, you can read about the line printer daemon (lpd), in Chapter 13, "Managing Printers and Printing."

The common convention is to end the names of daemons with the letter "d." Look at the right-most column in Figure 4-2. That column displays the name of the program that the process is running. Find the commands that end with d. Those processes are daemons. As a user, you don't need to worry about them. As a system administrator, you need to make sure the ones on your system keep running.

Note

Although daemons usually start automatically when the computer boots up, as a system administrator you may need to start some daemons manually, depending on how your system is configured.

Understanding Shells

The shell is the outermost layer of the Linux operating system, the way the car chassis is the outer layer of an automobile. A shell is the program that lets you talk to Linux. Your shell executes your commands. Logging in places you in a shell so that you can type commands and run programs. Although the system administrator usually assigns you a default shell, you can choose which shell you want to use after you log in. You can even change between shells during your session. If you use a GUI, your graphical interface functions as a graphical shell. This section concentrates on command-line shells.

Most shells look pretty much the same at first glance. They all display a prompt at the beginning of the command line. Default prompts include $ and %, but you can assign any kind of prompt you want, from the name of your computer to a reminder to pick up milk on the way home from work. The common commands are mostly the same in any shell. For example, the ls command always displays a directory listing. However, shells differ in the finer points of how they interpret commands. Some of these differences include:

✦ The way you define variables.

✦ The way you can recall the commands that you have typed, and the way you edit those commands.

✦ The way shells read your mind about file names. Some shells enable you to type a partial file name, conveniently completing the name for you.

✦ The way shells read your mind about commands. Some shells enable you to type a partial command, conveniently completing the command for you.

Tip Think of the shell as your Linux home, in the way that a shell is home to a hermit crab. If you need more room or other capabilities, you can move to a new shell. You can even move back to the old shell if you get homesick.

What is a shell script?

A shell script is a set of shell commands and statements that you put together in a file. You run the script interactively or you can schedule the script to run automatically and unattended at a later time.

Note A shell script is similar to a MS-DOS batch file, but can be much more powerful.

The variations in the different shells' commands and statements usually become apparent when you start to write complex shell scripts.

What shells are out there?

The major UNIX shells (to which the Linux shells are similar) are:

✦ The Bourne shell (also simply called *the shell* because it was the first shell), named after its creator, Philip Bourne.

✦ The restricted Bourne shell (rsh), which provides a limited set of Bourne shell features, for sites with security concerns

✦ The C shell, developed by William Joy, named because its command language resembles the C programming language.

✦ The Korn shell (combines features of Bourne and C and adds a few of its own), named after its creator, David Korn.

✦ The Bourne Again Shell (bash) written by William Fox, of the Free Software Foundations

Lots of different shells are available for Linux. GNU's Bourne Again shell (bash) is the shell you see in this book's examples. The Bourne Again shell is included with most Linux distributions. It is a variation of a powerfully enhanced Bourne shell and provides mind-reading (automatic command and file name completion), command history and recall, command editing, and job control.

 Chapters 17, 18, and 30 provide a detailed look at bash and at shell scripting.

tcsh, modeled after the C Shell (csh) with enhancements is an example of the many other shells, most of which are free and available for downloading from the Internet. The Z shell (zsh) is one of the newest shells available.

Researching RPC (Remote Procedure Call) for IPC (Interprocess Communication)

IPC (interprocess communication) is the heart of client/server communication. RPC (Remote Procedure Call) is a communications protocol that processes and programs use to communicate with each other. One program — the client — asks for a service from a different program (the server) running somewhere on the network. The server program may be on the same computer as the client program. The advantage to using RPC is that programmers can implement client/server computing without having to understand any technical network details. Linux programmers use RPC to implement IPC. As a system administrator, you may need to install RPC software.

Summary

One major benefit of the Linux kernel is that it allows you to load only the software components you need, thereby conserving system resources, such as memory. It also provides demand page virtual memory and true multitasking, which contribute to the power of Linux as a multiuser operating system.

Linux processes, daemons, and shells deliver a wide range of functionality.

Linux supports a wide range of filesystems and network protocols so that computers running Linux can easily co-exist and interoperate with other different operating systems.

✦   ✦   ✦

Getting Started with Linux System Administration

Linux System Management Responsibilities

This chapter is for the beginning system administrator. If you are an experienced Linux system administrator, you know what you have to do and are probably too busy to read this chapter. Get to work!

System administration is everything that you do to keep a computer up and running and meeting users' needs. Keeping a computer up and running usually means daily maintenance, such as backing up files and directories and restoring them if necessary, checking filesystems for corruption and repairing them if needed, making sure that all startup and shutdown procedures work as planned, setting the system clock, and monitoring disk space. "Meeting users' needs" means different things depending on the computer and the users. It may be as simple as creating accounts for users, installing new software, and protecting the security of your computer, or it may be as involved as managing not just one computer, but multiple computers on a network, and also managing the network itself—including file servers, print servers, Web servers, fire-wall software, and network security.

The chapters in Part II start with the basics, such as ensuring that you understand the hardware on your system, and move on to advanced techniques, such as tuning the computer(s) for best performance, configuring an intranet, and being responsible for your computer's connection to the Internet. You may not need to perform all the tasks described in Part II today. However, as a system administrator in today's networked environment, one of your challenges is to be able to handle new responsibilities that grow along with your network. The good news is that as your role grows, you have the chapters in Part II to help you perform your new duties.

Oh, the Responsibility!

System-administration duties are numerous, diverse, and frequent. Even if your system is running well and making all your users happy, you can find lots of things to do, such as update application and operating system software, monitor performance and plan for future users and system growth. You may not need to do every job listed in this chapter. Not every activity on this chapter's list is required for every computer. Some sites do require that every job in this chapter be done, and many companies and organizations spread system-management tasks across a team of system and network administrators. If you have no teammates, and you need to do everything listed in this chapter, don't despair. You're not alone. You have this book. The following chapters in Part II describe the how-tos for each activity listed below.

It's Super to be Root

Yes, you know your own name, but if you are a Linux system administrator, you are known to the computing community as ... the *superuser*, root for short. The superuser has all privileges on the system, and a lot of the responsibility. When you install Linux, the installation procedure creates an account for the superuser with the username root and a user ID of 0. The installation procedure also asks you to select a password for root. The following sections of this chapter describe your responsibilities as root, the superuser. A non-privileged user (that is, a user with a regular account) cannot perform system administration tasks.

Getting Started with System Management

If you're a Linux system administrator setting up a new Linux environment, you need to perform some basic tasks to get the system ready for users. First of all, you need to be familiar with your hardware. You don't have to know how to fix hardware, but you need to know what you've got and how to configure software for it.

Once you've inventoried your hardware, you should configure the devices, such as terminals, disks, printers, and such optional goodies as PC cards, CD players, game controllers, and whatever else you and your users decide is important. Your next step is to configure a help system and software applications for users, back up your virgin system, and create accounts so that users can log in. After you get done with these basic chores, you can go ahead to configuring the network and performing advanced system-management work.

Configuring the help system and man pages

Even if you are the only user on your computer, one of the first things to do is get the Help system running. Whether you want graphical help or the more traditional man pages, you need to make sure that all the necessary files are available. For the man pages, you need to decide how you plan to store them—for example, in compressed format or not. This may be a networking decision if you decide to use another computer's help system.

Booting (starting up) and shutting down the computer

Even if your computer is supposed to run 24-7, you may need to shut down and reboot in case of an emergency or a strange system hang or crash. You may also need to customize the startup and system-initialization procedures.

Chapter 6 helps you understand what goes on behind the scenes when your system boots and explains shutdown and startup options and run levels. Chapter 6 also warns you of the dangers of not following proper shutdown and startup procedures.

Working with hardware devices

Hardware isn't plug-and-play on Linux. The system administrator needs to configure new hardware and make sure it is available to users. Configuring hardware may be as simple as adding a hardwired terminal or as complex as adding a new disk drive for which you need to change partition sizes and create filesystems. When working with hardware, you may also need to edit and rebuild the kernel to make the new device known.

Chapters 9 and 10 tell you how to configure devices. Chapter 10 discusses the steps to follow to configure filesystems. In Part V, "Advanced System Administration and Networking," Chapter 28 explains how to edit and rebuild the kernel.

Installing (and uninstalling) software

You read how to install the operating system software in Chapter 3. The system administrator needs to install new software and upgrade existing software—both operating system and application software—to new versions. After you install or upgrade the software, don't forget to test it to see if it works. Then you can inform users that they have something new to play with (or work with) and tell them where to find the new or upgraded programs. Most Linux software comes in "packages" that contain executables, configuration files, man and info pages, copyright information, documentation, and sometimes source code.

Usually you install and uninstall software with a package manager program, such as RPM, the Red Hat Package Manager; spm, the Slackware package manager; or dpkg, the Debian Linux package manager. All package managers, regardless of your distribution, do the same thing: they unpack the software components in the package, ensure that any pre-requisite software is installed, and install the software components into the proper directories.

Tip   Kpackage is a GUI interface to the RPM, Debian, and Slackware package managers. Kpackage is part of the K Desktop Environment.

Sometimes, depending on the software, you may use `tar`, the tape archive program.

Cross-Reference   Chapter 8 explains how to install programs using RPM and tar.

Backing up and restoring directories and files

The job of backups and restores usually falls under daily maintenance. You create a backup strategy and schedule, automate the procedures, and schedule those procedures to run. Unfortunately, backups and restores may also turn out to be part of disaster recovery. Disaster recovery can be anything from saving a user who has accidentally deleted a crucial file to saving a computer that has lost or corrupted its operating system. You need to know the best and fastest way possible to restore a single file or filesystem or even the whole operating system.

Cross-Reference   Chapter 12 gets you ready for various backup and restore tasks, from daily scheduled backups to a critical operating-system restore.

Configuring and managing user accounts

After you have installed your operating system and application software, configured hardware devices, customized startup and shutdown procedures, and backed up your system, you're ready to let users start working. Actually, you're almost ready. You need to get ready for your users by creating accounts with usernames and passwords for all users. You also need to create home directories for them. You may want to assign the users to groups as well. As time goes by, you may also need to modify or update some users' accounts, perhaps disabling or deleting them.

Cross-Reference   Chapter 12 explains how to create and manage user accounts.

Managing printers and printing

Do you need to install and configure a printer on your system? Or will you use a printer that is attached to another computer on your network? Or will you use a printer that is attached directly to the network? You also need to be able to manage print queues and spooling directories. If you have a printing problem, you need to be able to troubleshoot it.

Cross-Reference   Chapter 13 tells you how to make printing available to your users, and how to configure queues and troubleshoot printing problems.

Configuring and Managing Your Linux System in a Network

Linux and networking go together like Holmes and Watson, or maybe it's Watson and Holmes. In any case, it's hard to separate networking from Linux. Linux is the platform of choice for more than half the Web servers in the wide world. Some Linux administrators function as THE network administrator for their organizations. Most Linux system administrators perform at least some of the network administration tasks I mention in this section.

Configuring network hardware

Does your network connect with an Ethernet or token-ring wiring scheme? Or do you need to maintain an intranet (an internal network of networks) that includes both kinds of wiring? You need to be able to identify your computers' network devices — for example, network-interface cards — and configure them. Then you need to be able to configure the TCP/IP protocols that your networking environment uses.

 Cross-Reference Chapter 20 shows you how to configure NICs (network-interface cards) and routers.

Setting up your computer to connect to a TCP/IP network

The TCP/IP suite, the protocols of the Internet, consists of dozens of protocols besides the two for which it is named. One of your first TCP/IP tasks is to assign IP addresses and possibly subnet (divide) your network. You probably want to connect to the Internet as well. If you want to provide dialup networking with modems you need to configure PPP, the Point-to-Point protocol, as well. You may also need to connect your computer or your network to a "foreign" set of network protocols, such as AppleTalk or SNA, IBM's System Network Architecture, so that you can communicate with Macintoshes and IBM mainframes. If you are connecting your computer or LAN to the outside world (someone else's network, including the Internet), you also need to deal with security mechanisms such as firewall and encryption software.

Configuring other TCP/IP services

After you have connected your computer to the network, you probably still have some work to do with more advanced TCP/IP services. Some of your remaining network tasks will probably include some or all of the following configurations:

✦ The Domain Name Service (DNS), so that your computer can find other computers.

✦ The Network File Service (NFS), so that users can share files transparently.

✦ Network Information Services (NIS), if you want to share system files in a LAN (local area network).

✦ E-mail protocols, daemons, and services, such as POP3, SMTP, IMAP4, and sendmail.

✦ FTP (File Transfer Protocol) services, so that users (either on a LAN or a WAN, including the Internet) can copy (and possibly write) files from a central archive that you set up.

✦ World Wide Web services, so that you can configure your Linux computer as a Web server.

Cross-Reference

The chapters in Part IV give you explanations and examples of setting up a TCP/IP network as mentioned in this subsection, including connecting to the Internet.

Advancing your System Administration Skills

After you get your system set up for users, including networking, it's time to look into some advanced system-administration utilities and tools. The techniques listed in this section help you secure your computer and manage it more efficiently.

Automating tasks

You can use the `at` and `cron` tools to schedule repetitive jobs such as backup to run unattended while you do other work or maybe even take a night off to party. You need to configure `cron` by setting up a file to hold entries that specify what to do and when to do it. If you grant end users access to `cron`, they can schedule their own tasks to run automatically when the computer is less busy.

Cross-Reference

Chapter 28 tells you how to configure and use cron to automate tasks.

Rebuilding the kernel

As time goes by, you may need to add device drivers into the kernel or change some kernel variables to tune your computer. You should understand what the system configuration file does and where to find it. Finally, you need to know when you can make dynamic changes to the kernel and when you need to edit the system configuration file, rebuild, and reboot your new kernel.

Cross-Reference

Chapter 28 gives you the details you need to understand how to rebuild your operating system kernel.

Protecting a Linux system

Many Linux computing environments are friendly and open, where passwords and file-access permissions are the only security mechanisms needed. This type of easy-going atmosphere is typical in scientific and academic settings. Most commercial sites need more security, and Linux provides options for using encrypted passwords, secure dialup access, secure terminals, and security auditing. In addition to understanding how and when to use optional security mechanisms, a system administrator also needs to know how to check for break-in attempts and viruses.

Chapter 29 reviews basic Linux security methods and introduces optional techniques that system administrators can use to provide enhanced security.

Monitoring and tuning Linux system performance

No matter how carefully you configure a system, there will be a day when someone complains, "The computer seems slow." There are lots of reasons that performance can slow down. Perhaps you've added lots of new users and applications. Perhaps you have a hardware problem. You need to be able to monitor daily system performance. If you can use monitoring tools effectively, you may be able to anticipate performance problems and prevent them from happening. If performance does slow down, you need to be able to figure out what is causing the slowdown and how to fix it. Consider this: Maybe performance isn't slow at all, but some cranky user's perception is distorted. In this case, you need to be able to produce facts and figures that support your position.

Chapter 32 explains how to set up regular performance monitoring, how to anticipate and forestall performance problems, and how to optimize and tune a Linux system when necessary.

Summary

This chapter divides system administration into three categories:

✦ Basic system configuration

✦ Network configuration

✦ Advanced system administration and tuning

Depending on your current system administration skills and your computer's (network's) needs, you may need to understand all the concepts and tools in all the system and network-administration chapters, or only those advanced capabilities that you have not yet experienced.

The following chapters get you started with the technical details of basic system administration.

✦   ✦   ✦

Managing Startup and Shutdown

The terms *booting* and *starting up* are synonymous in computer jargon. Both terms refer to starting the computer and loading an operating system. The process is called booting because the computer pulls itself up by its own bootstraps.

Understanding the Boot Process

When a computer starts up, the first thing it does is load a tiny program called the *bootstrap loader* — LILO, for example. Different types of computers find the bootstrap loader differently. On a PC, assuming no floppy disk is loaded, the BIOS reads the master boot record (MBR) from the boot sector (at the beginning of the first hard disk) to find the bootstrap loader program. The bootstrap loader knows where to find Linux, so off it goes and loads the compressed Linux kernel. The kernel takes over and uncompresses itself. The kernel then follows these steps, displaying extensive boot messages along the way:

1. Load device drivers.

2. Mount the root filesystem (/).

3. Run the init process (named /sbin/init).

At this point, the init process takes over and does the following:

4. Decides which system initialization files to run depending on the run level you select when you start booting.

5. Starts daemons for your run level.

6. Assuming you are booting to run level 3 (full timesharing and networking) `init`:

- Creates `getty` processes. `getty` processes post a login prompt on terminals so users can log in.

- Continues executing system initialization files until the computer is running at the selected run level.

7. Performs general housekeeping tasks, such as cleaning the /tmp directory.

Understanding run levels

A run level is the software mode, such as multi-user or single-user mode, to which the Linux kernel (and all versions of UNIX) boots or shuts down. The `init` process decides which system processes to create based on the run level you specify when you boot or shut down. For example, if you are booting to single-user mode, `init` doesn't need to spawn any `getty` processes because no users can log in. When you boot to full multi-user mode (run levels 3, 4, or 5), `init` needs to spawn the `getty` processes so that users can login to the system. Different versions of Linux (and UNIX) supply different numbers of run levels. Table 6-1 lists the run levels that most versions of Linux have in common.

Table 6-1 Typical Linux Run Levels	
Run Level	**System State**
0	Halted
1, S, s	Single user
2	Multiuser without networking
3	Multiuser; boots to text mode login without X Window
4	Unused but equivalent to run level 3
5	Multiuser; boots to X Window login prompt
6	Reboot

 Note   Some Linux versions boot to the X Window login prompt in run level 4.

Investigating init

The first thing init does when it takes over the boot sequence from the kernel is read the file /etc/inittab to see what the default run level should be. This file contains an entry for each process that should be started for the various run levels. Figure 6-1 shows an /etc/inittab file from a Red Hat Linux system. Each entry consists of four fields separated by colons:

✦ *Label*, the unique identifier (1–4 characters) of the entry.

✦ *Run level(s)*, the run levels where the entry's action should occur — for example, the value 1,2,3 means perform the action for run levels 1, 2, and 3.

✦ *Action*, the action to perform for this entry. Although actions can vary slightly among different flavors of Linux, the most common actions are:

- initdefault — Enter the specified run level as soon as booting completes. If there is no initdefault, wait for the system administration to type a run level at the console. Ignore the process field.

- sysinit — Execute the process during booting and before any boot or bootwait actions. Ignore the run level field.

- boot — Execute the process while the system is booting. Ignore any run levels.

- bootwait — The same as boot, but wait for the process to finish before going on to the next step.

- ctrlaltdel — Execute the process when someone presses Ctrl+Alt+Del.

- wait — At the specified run level, start the process and wait for it to finish before going on to the next step.

- respawn — Restart the process if it terminates. This usually applies to getty processes.

- powerfail — Execute the process listed if there is an automatic signal (SIGPWR) from your UPS (Uninteruptible Power Supply) if power is interrupted. You must have the powerd (power daemon) running for this to work.

- powerwait — Same as powerfail, except wait for the process to complete before going on to the next step.

- powerokwait — Read the file /etc/powerstatus. If the file contains the value OK, the power has come back

✦ *Process*, the process (program) to start.

On the CD-ROM The actions above are the most common ones. Check the man pages on the CD for a complete list of inittab actions.

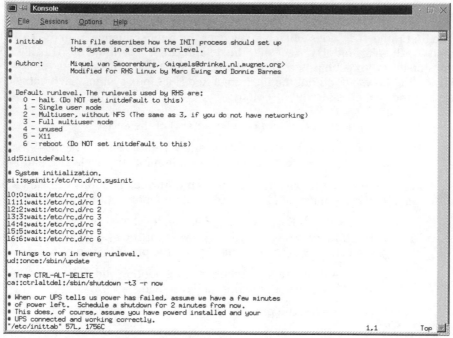

```
 🔲🔲 Konsole                                                                          ⤬ □ ✕
   File   Sessions   Options   Help
🔲
# inittab        This file describes how the INIT process should set up
#                the system in a certain run-level.
#
# Author:        Miquel van Smoorenburg, <miquels@drinkel.nl.mugnet.org>
#                Modified for RHS Linux by Marc Ewing and Donnie Barnes
#
# Default runlevel. The runlevels used by RHS are:
#   0 - halt (Do NOT set initdefault to this)
#   1 - Single user mode
#   2 - Multiuser, without NFS (The same as 3, if you do not have networking)
#   3 - Full multiuser mode
#   4 - unused
#   5 - X11
#   6 - reboot (Do NOT set initdefault to this)
#
id:5:initdefault:

# System initialization.
si::sysinit:/etc/rc.d/rc.sysinit

l0:0:wait:/etc/rc.d/rc 0
l1:1:wait:/etc/rc.d/rc 1
l2:2:wait:/etc/rc.d/rc 2
l3:3:wait:/etc/rc.d/rc 3
l4:4:wait:/etc/rc.d/rc 4
l5:5:wait:/etc/rc.d/rc 5
l6:6:wait:/etc/rc.d/rc 6

# Things to run in every runlevel.
ud::once:/sbin/update

# Trap CTRL-ALT-DELETE
ca::ctrlaltdel:/sbin/shutdown -t3 -r now

# When our UPS tells us power has failed, assume we have a few minutes
# of power left.  Schedule a shutdown for 2 minutes from now.
# This does, of course, assume you have powerd installed and your
# UPS connected and working correctly.
"/etc/inittab" 57L, 1756C                                              1,1          Top
```

Figure 6-1: The /etc/inittab file lists process to start automatically at various run levels

The Linux Bootdisk HOWTO describes the technical details of creating a customized root-maintenance floppy.

Always remember to update your emergency boot and customized root floppies if you change your kernel or software significantly.

Booting from an Emergency Boot Floppy

If your system becomes unbootable, you can try booting from the emergency boot floppy you created when you installed Linux. The emergency boot disk contains a generic kernel that should be enough to boot your system into single-user mode. Then you can use the programs on the emergency repair disk to fix the problem that made your computer unbootable.

The most common reason for an unbootable system is a corrupted root filesystem. Unfortunately, sometimes the emergency floppy does not have everything you need to fix your system. For example, if you backed up your root filesystem using a specialized backup program, that specialized backup program won't be on the standard emergency-repair floppy. The solution is to build a customized root floppy in addition to the emergency-repair floppy. Put whatever extra programs and files you need to fix boot problems that depend on more software than is on the emergency repair disk.

Understanding Shutdown Options

In addition to booting, run levels apply to shutting down your computer. For example, if your computer is halted, it's at run level 0. If you're not already a UNIX user, you might be surprised to find that you can start up part way and that shutting down does not necessarily mean that "It is safe to turn off your computer." Linux shutdown options include:

✦ Shutting down to single-user mode so that only the system administrator can work.

✦ Shutting down to a halted state, which requires power cycling the system to restart it.

✦ Shutting down and automatically rebooting.

Shutting down Linux does not mean turning the computer off. The term, *powering off* means turning your computer off. You should never power off your computer without shutting it down first unless you have absolutely no choice — for example, if your computer is so confused that it is totally frozen and will not let you shut it down. You have several choices as to how you shut down your system, but turning off the power is not one of them.

Caution   If you power off your computer without following a proper shutdown procedure, you could be in trouble. Multitasking systems usually have work going on in the background that should be cleanly shut down. At the least, your filesystems won't be cleanly umounted. Yes, umounted — `umount` is Linux/UNIX for `dismount`. If files are not cleanly umounted, the system takes extra time at the next startup. At worst, the buffer cache won't be written back to disk. Data can be lost, and even worse, the filesystem(s) might become so corrupted that they cannot be repaired.

Cross-Reference   You can review the purpose of the buffer cache in Chapter 5.

A complete Linux shutdown procedure to a halted state follows these steps:

1. Disable new logins.

2. Close all files.

3. Cleanly terminate all processes.

4. Sync the disks (*syncing* the disks writes all cached data to disk).

5. Log the shutdown in a file.

6. Turn off accounting and disk quotas (if you enabled them).

7. Unmount filesystems.

8. Display a message that the computer is halted and that you can turn off the power.

Although you type the shutdown command, it's actually the init process that does most of the work of shutting down. The shutdown command signals the init process (remember init is process 1) to change the run level.

Tip   Think of shutting down as a way to change to a lower run level, not necessarily as a method of turning off your computer.

Shutting down and halting (going to run level 0)

Use the shutdown command with the -h option to shut down your system and halt it. You need to tell the shutdown command when to shut down, and it's a good idea to add a message to your users as to why you're shutting down and when the system will be available again. The first command below shuts down and halts the system immediately (now). There's no time to send a message to the users. The second command shuts down and halts the system in 15 minutes and sends a user-friendly message. The third command does the same thing as the second command, but replaces the absolute time (23:18) with a relative time (+15 minutes).

```
# shutdown -h now

# shutdown -h 23:18 'The system is shutting down in 15 minutes.
Please log out. The system will be available in 1 hour. Happy
New Year!'

# shutdown -h +15 'The system is shutting down in 15 minutes.
Please log out. The system will be available in 1 hour. Happy
New Year!'
```

Note   Notice the # prompt that precedes the shutdown command in the figure above. # is traditionally the root prompt. Only the superuser or someone with superuser equivalence can execute the shutdown command.

Each user logged in sees the shutdown message. The message looks like this on users' screens:

```
Broadcast message from root (ttyp0) Thu Dec 31 11:03:25 1999...

The system is shutting down in 15 minutes. Please log out. The
system will be available in 1 hour. Happy New Year!
```

Shutting down and immediately rebooting (going to run level 6)

If you want to shut down and reboot immediately, use the shutdown command with a -r option. There are two examples below. When you can, it's always more user-friendly to give users time to finish what they are doing and a reason why the system is going down.

Note Don't type the # character in the examples below. Remember that Linux displays the # character for the root prompt.

```
# shutdown -r +5 "Quick shutdown and reboot in 5 minutes to fix
a hardware problem"
```

```
# shutdown -r now
```

You usually shut down with an immediate, automatic reboot if you have been performing some kind of system configuration task that requires a reboot for the task to take effect — for example, if you have edited and rebuilt the kernel.

Tip If you give the three-fingered salute (Ctrl+Alt+Del) on a PC running Linux, most systems run the `shutdown -r now` command automatically. However, you can configure the default action for the Ctrl+Alt+Del sequence. If you don't want users randomly rebooting their computers, configure Ctrl+Alt+Del to do nothing. To do so, change the line in /etc/inittab that reads

```
ca::ctrlaltdel:/sbin/shutdown -t3 -r now
```

so that it reads

```
ca::ctrlaltdel:/bin/false
```

This change disables Ctrl+Alt+Del as a means to reboot the computer.

Shutting down to single-user mode (going to run level 1)

Many people, especially PC users, think that shutting down means that no one can work on the computer. Linux has a shutdown option that makes the system appear shut down to regular users, but enables the system administrator to keep working on the console. To bring a system down to single-user mode, simply type the `shutdown` command without an option. Even though you don't use a command option, you can still give your users a time and a warning message:

```
# shutdown +10 "Maintenance shutdown will occur in 10 minutes.
Please finish your work and log out."
```

Shutting down to single user mode is useful for system administration tasks that you prefer to do without users logged in, such as a complete backup or a critical restore of a database. When you are finished with system maintenance, you can either halt the system or reboot to timesharing mode. Pressing Ctrl+D automatically takes the system to full timesharing with networking.

Note Run levels S and s are aliases for run level 1, single-user mode.

init is Also a Command

Now that you understand what the init process does, it's time to learn that init is also a command to use for changing run levels. The difference between init and shutdown is that shutdown only moves to lower run levels. You can use init to move up or down the run-level scale. Red Hat Linux uses run level 6 to mean full timesharing and networking mode. So if you are in single-user mode, you can type

```
# init 6
```

instead of pressing Ctrl+D to go to full timesharing, multiuser mode.

Note   init is one of the few commands that does not require a dash (-) in front of the option.

Tip   A special purpose of the init command is simply to reread the /etc/inittab file without performing a run-level change. You need to do this if you add new terminal lines, so that init creates getty processes to enable users to log in on the new terminals. If you forget to run the init command, your new terminals remain useless until you reboot. You reread the inittab file with the command below. The q option means *query* the inittab file.

```
init q
```

Troubleshooting

init tries not to gobble up system resources if you have introduced some sort of error in the /etc/inittab file. If init continuously respawns the same entry more than 10 times in two minutes, it displays an error message on the system console and stops respawning. After five minutes or an init q command, whichever comes first, init begins respawning again.

Summary

This chapter described how booting and shutting down work, as well as how run levels in the inittab file affect startup and shutdown. This chapter also showed you how to boot and shut down your system, and how to move between various run levels. The next chapter presents options and techniques for configuring your computer's help system(s).

✦   ✦   ✦

Installing Software Packages

This chapter discusses installing different pieces of software to keep your Linux system up and running, as well as adding enhancements and applying patches (also known as fixes). In Chapter 3 we talked about installing packages during system installation. During the installation, the packages were installed by the installer program. In this chapter, we will learn how to install packages using other methods.

This chapter also discusses the Tape Archiver, or tar — how to make tape backups, how to make archives for specific files, and more.

Using Red Hat Package Manager (RPM)

RPM (Red Hat Package Manager) is used during the installation of Red Hat Linux and to apply patches or fixes supplied by Red Hat.

Tip   **See the Red Hat FTP site at** ftp://ftp.redhat.com/
pub/redhat/updates/.

Since Linux is an open source system, many folks around the world develop features or support for new devices such as video cards. These types of upgrades keep Linux a state-of-the-art operating system and provide a rewarding experience to the developers. In all probability you will use RPM to add these enhancements to your Linux system as well.

The Red Hat Package Manager section of this chapter also discusses the following topics in both command mode and graphical mode using GnoRPM. (Additionally, we will briefly discuss using RPM for other open Linux systems such as Caldera and SuSE.)

✦ Installing new packages or installing a package not included in the initial installation.

✦ Removing a package from the original installation. As some packages may be rather large, doing this can recover significant disk space.

✦ Applying kernel patches.

✦ Verifying that a package has all the required pieces in the right places and is actually working.

✦ Querying packages to verify version numbers, files owned by a specific package, what type of files these are, and much more!

Using tar

The Linux GNU version of tar is far more powerful and flexible than the standard UNIX version. One of its most widely used features is the capability to not only archive files but to compress them at the same time. While software companies often use it to create and compress their distributions (also known as *tarballs*), tar is still used by individual developers to back up to various storage media such as tape drives or CD-ROMs.

Like many Linux commands, tar has a vast amount of switches that you can turn on to execute many different options. To review all the various tar options, refer to the man pages in your Linux system (man tar). The first argument supplied to tar must be A, c, d, r, t, u, or x, followed by any of the optional functions. The last argument supplied to tar is always the names of any directories and files to be archived. When you are supplying only a parent directory to tar, all child or subdirectories will be archived by default as well. Use the following syntax to archive files with tar:

```
tar a|c|d|r|t|u|x [z][v] f filenames
```

Table 7-1 describes the arguments Acdrtux:

Table 7-1	
Arguments to be Supplied to tar	
Argument	**Description**
-A, --catenate, --concatenate	Append tar files to an archive.
-c, --create	Create a new archive find differences between archive and filesystem.

Argument	Description
-d, --delete	Delete from the archive (does not support magnetic tapes).
-r, --append	Append files to the end of an archive.
-t, --list	List the contents of an archive.
-u, --update	Only append files that are newer than copy in archive.
-x, --extract, --get	Extract files from an archive.

The z option will tell tar whether you are creating or extracting your files from a compressed or zipped format. -compress or -uncompress must be used along with the z option for compressed/uncompressed files. -gzip or -ungzip must be used along with the z option if you are working with zipped or unzipped files.

Note   If you are extracting from a compressed or zipped file, the -z option is required.

The v option will force tar to operate in what is called *verbose mode*. Simply put, a list of files being created or extracted will be printed.

Table 7-2 provides a complete (at the time of this writing) list of all the available options for tar.

Table 7-2
Available tar Options

Option	Description
--atime-preserve	Don't change access times on dumped files.
-b, --block-size N	Block size of Nx512 bytes (default N=20).
-B, --read-full-blocks	Reblock as read (for reading 4.2BSD pipes).
-C, --directory DIR	Change to directory DIR.
--checkpoint	Print directory names while reading the archive.
-f, --file [HOSTNAME:]F	Use archive file or device F (default /dev/rmt0).
--force-local	Archive file is local.
-F, --info-script F -new-volume-script F	Run script at end of each tape (implies -M).
-G, --incremental	Create/list/extract old GNU-format incremental backup.

Continued

Table 7-2 *(continued)*

Option	Description
-g, --listed-incremental F	Create/list/extract new GNU-format incremental backup.
-h, --dereference	Ignore blocks of zeros in archive (normally means EOF).
--ignore-failed-read	Don't exit with non-zero status on unreadable files.
-k, --keep-old-files	Keep existing files; don't overwrite them from archive.
-K, --starting-file F	Begin at file F in the archive.
-l, --one-file-system	Stay in local filesystem when creating an archive.
-L, --tape-length N	Change tapes after writing N*1024 bytes.
-m, --modification-time	Don't extract file modified time.
-M, --multi-volume	Create/list/extract multi-volume archive.
-N, --after-date DATE, --newer DATE	Only store files newer than DATE.
-o, --old-archive, --portability	Write a V7 format archive, rather than ANSI format.
-O, --to-stdout	Extract files to standard output.
-p, --same-permissions, --preserve-permissions	Extract all protection information.
-P, --absolute-paths	Don't strip leading slashes (/) from file names.
--preserve	Like -p -s.
-R, --record-number	Show record number within archive with each message.
--remove-files	Remove files after adding them to the archive.
-s, --same-order, --preserve-order	List of names to extract is sorted to match archive, create extracted files with the same ownership.
-S, --sparse	Handle sparse files efficiently.
-T, --files-from F	Get names to extract or create from file F.
--null	-T reads null-terminated names, disable -C.
--totals	Print total bytes written with --create.
-v, --verbose	Verbosely list files processed.
-V, --label NAME	Create archive with volume name NAME.
--version	Print tar program version number.
-w, --interactive, --confirmation	Ask for confirmation for every action.
-W, --verify	Attempt to verify the archive after writing it.

Option	Description
`--exclude FILE`	Exclude file *FILE*.
`-X, --exclude-from FILE`	Exclude files listed in *FILE*.
`-Z, --compress, --uncompress`	Filter the archive through `compress`.
`-z, --gzip, --ungzip`	Filter the archive through `gzip`.
`--use-compress-program PROG`	Filter the archive through `PROG` (which must accept-d).
`--block-compress`	Block the output of compression program for tapes.
`-[0-7][lmh]`	Specify drive and density.

The following examples illustrate a few uses of the `tar` command. If you wanted to create an archive of your printer spool file, you could type the following command:

```
# tar czvf /backup/spool.tar.gz /var/spool
```

In the preceding command, the c indicates that you are creating an archive. The z tells tar to filter the output through gzip to compress the file into gzipped format. The v indicates verbosity (remember, this is a list of the files being archived). The f tells `tar` to create a file called spool.tar.gz in the /backup directory (it must already exist).

To get a list of the files archived on a tape the command would be

```
# tar tvf /dev/st0
```

The t tells `tar` to "get the files from." The v once again provides a listing of the files (verbosity). Notice that even though f is specified, there is no corresponding file name. This is because tape drives are considered character devices and not files. In this type of situation, specify the name of the device, in this case /dev/st0.

Note Many of the `tar` options for tape may not be supported if your tape drive is connected via a parallel port. Consult your distribution user guide to determine which options are only supported for a SCSI tape drive.

As you can see, `tar` can provide you with a vast variety of capabilities and options. There are other utilities besides `tar` that provide archival capabilities. Some of these include `cpio` (copy in-out), `dump`, which is only available to system administrators (it uses the ext2 filesystem), `afio`, which is just like `cpio` except that it compresses individual files during the backup, and `BRU`, which is a commercial backup and restore product.

One more system that should be mentioned and is worth looking into is Amanda. Amanda actually uses `tar` to organize and run backups for you. It will provide any required automation (with limited effort on your part) for you and is capable of running quick remote backups from multiple clients to the tape drive attached to your server. The RPM for Amanda is available on the Red Hat FTP site and detailed information may be found at www.cs.umd.edu. At the UMD home page, type **Amanda** in the search box.

What is a package?

Very simply, a package is the way Red Hat (and other distributions like Caldera and SuSE) combines into one file all the necessary components (such as files and programs) that comprise a software product. These are commonly called RPM files or more often than not just plain RPM.

When you went through the installation process in Chapter 3, "Installing Linux," the installation program actually used the rpm command to unload, unpack, and copy files to their respective directories.

What is RPM?

RPM is the primary tool used for installing, upgrading, and removing software on your Linux system. RPM is an extremely easy way to manage and maintain the packages on your Linux system. It manages what is on your Linux system, keeps track of required dependencies, and provides notification if certain dependencies for a specific package are not met. RPM can be run in command or graphical mode. The basic format for RPM in command mode is:

```
rpm function packagename.rpm
```

The most common functions used with the rpm command are -i to install and -e to remove or uninstall a package.

The *function* symbolic is case-sensitive.

In addition to installing and removing packages, some other common functions that you will use RPM for include:

✦ Getting information (like build number and version) about a specific package.

✦ Listing the files included in a package.

✦ Identifying which package a file belongs to.

✦ Updating an existing package.

Using RPM in command mode — basic operations

RPM in command mode can be used in an X terminal window or on the console. Table 7-3 illustrates the more common RPM commands that you can use.

Table 7-3
RPM in Command Mode

Function	Description	Full Command
-q	Check version and build number.	rpm -q *packagename*.rpm
-qi	Get info about a specific package.	rpm -qi *packagename*.rpm
-ql	List the files contained in a package	rpm -ql *packagename*.rpm
-qpl	List the files contained in an uninstalled package.	rpm -qpl *packagename*.rpm
-qf	Find out which package(s) a file belongs to.	rpm -qf *filename*
-U	Update an existing package.	rpm -U *packagename*.rpm
-Uhv	Update an existing package and display a progress bar.	rpm -Uhv *packagename*.rpm
-F -v ./*.rpm	Update all packages contained in the current directory.	rpm -F -v ./*.rpm
-I ftp	Install packages from an FTP site.	rpm -i ftp://ftp. redhat.com/pub/redhat/ rh-2.0-beta/RPMS/ foobar-1.0-1i386.rpm

RPM has many more functions and options than those listed in this table. Check the man pages (man rpm) or use the rpm command rpm -help to list these options. Also, you can visit the Web site www.rpm.org.

Using RPM in graphical mode — basic operations

GnoRPM is the graphical interface tool that is used to interact with RPM from the Gnome desktop display. The only requirement is that you have X Windows (2x) installed on your Linux system. Using menus, toolbars, trees, and a display window of the packages in your system, you can easily run RPM by pointing and clicking.

 GnoRPM is the graphical tool for RPM that runs under X Windows (2x) for Red Hat versions 6.0 and later. Prior to version 6.0, GLINT was the graphical tool used to interact with RPM.

GnoRPM may be started in two ways. If you wish to start GnoRPM from an X terminal window simply type **gnorpm** at the shell prompt. GnoRPM may also be started within the GNOME desktop panel under system. Figure 7-1 illustrates the GNOME desktop panel with the system option shown.

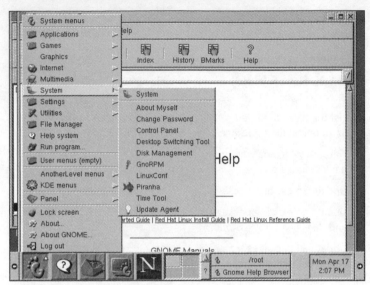

Figure 7-1: GNOME desktop panel

Once GnoRPM is started the primary GnoRPM window appears, as shown in Figure 7-2.

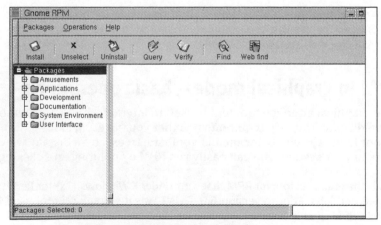

Figure 7-2: Primary GnoRPM graphical window

The GnoRPM interface window has five basic parts, which are:

Package Panel   This panel, on the left of the window, enables you to browse the packages in your Linux system.

Display Window   This window, adjacent to the package panel, enables you to see the different packages in the various folders in your system.

Toolbar   The toolbar, across the top of the package panel and the display window, contains the pushbuttons for installing, unselecting, uninstalling, querying, and verifying all the packages in your system. It also contains a find pushbutton and a Web find pushbutton.

Menu   This menu, located above the toolbar, contains text-based commands.

Status Bar   This bar, located below the package panel and display window, shows the number of packages selected.

Note   You must be logged in as root to install, uninstall, or upgrade packages.

Selecting packages using GnoRPM

Once the primary GnoRPM graphical window is displayed you can expand the package list in the display window by clicking on one of the trees in the package panel. Each tree contains a group of packages and each group can contain subgroups. The Amusements tree contains the groups Games and Graphics. If you double-click the Games group, you will see the contents represented by icons in the display window, as shown in Figure 7-3.

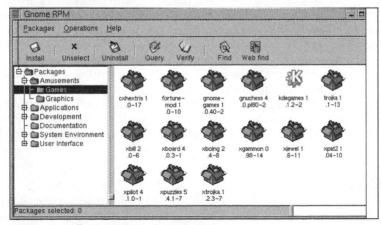

Figure 7-3: Expanded display window

To select an individual package simply left-click the icon. This highlights the icon and enables you to perform the toolbar functions on it. If you change your mind about the package that you selected, use the unselect pushbutton on the toolbar or simply click in any white space.

Querying packages

The query pushbutton on the toolbar of GnoRPM is the easiest and simplest way to find out all the pertinent information about a package. Figure 7-4, the Package Info window, illustrates the information you see when you click the query pushbutton on the toolbar.

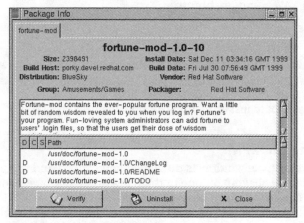

Figure 7-4: Package Info Window

The Package Info window is divided into three parts. The top part shows the size of the package, the user who installed the package, the installation and build dates of the package, and the name of the distributor of the package. The bottom half of the Package Info window contains the display area, which is further divided into two parts. The top part of the display area provides a text description of the package. The bottom right-hand part of the display area provides you with the path showing where the package resides on your Linux system. The bottom left-hand side of the display area indicates if the package is a Documentation file [D] or a Configuration file [C]. The [S] column indicates the *state* of the package. If the package were missing any files (which would probably make it unusable) that information would show up here.

Verifying packages

You can verify a package in two ways. The first way is to click the Verify pushbutton on the Package Info window at the bottom left-hand side of the window (as shown in Figure 7-4). The second way is to select the package and use the Verify pushbutton on the GnoRPM toolbar, the result of which is shown in Figure 7-5.

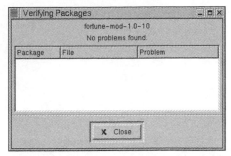

Figure 7-5: Verifying Packages window

The Verifying packages window shows the name of the package in the top half of the window. If any problems are detected with the package being verified, the messages will be displayed in the bottom half of the window or display area. If there are no problems, the message *No Problems Found* will be displayed under the package name in the list area of the window.

Uninstalling packages

When you uninstall a package from your Linux system, the selected application and any associated files will be removed from your machine. To uninstall a package, select it and then click the Uninstall pushbutton on the GnoRPM toolbar. After you click the Uninstall pushbutton the removal window, shown in Figure 7-6, will appear. If you really want to uninstall the package, click the Yes pushbutton.

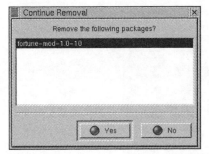

Figure 7-6: Continue Removal window

Caution

If there are no file-dependency problems, the package will be instantly uninstalled. There will be no confirmation windows.

If there are dependency issues with any files, these will be displayed in the Dependency Problems window, shown in Figure 7-7.

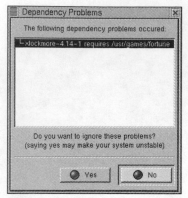

Figure 7-7: Dependency Problems window

Caution If you get the Dependency Problems window, be sure to investigate the messages displayed. Remember you are working in root and ignoring any of these messages can severely harm your Linux system.

Installing packages using GnoRPM

To install a package, select the package on the Primary Window by highlighting its icon as shown in Figure 7-3, and then click the Install pushbutton on the GnoRPM toolbar. This will display the Install window with a file manager display on the left side of the window, as shown in Figure 7-8. Select the package that you want to install by left-clicking and then click the Add pushbutton on the right side of the Install window.

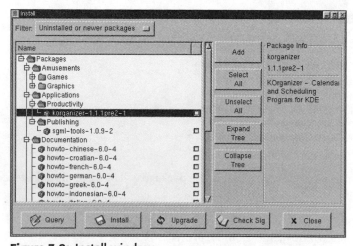

Figure 7-8: Install window

GnoRPM will now search the default path `/mnt/cdrom/RedHat/RPMS` for the package that you selected. If the package you are installing is not in this path, you will be presented with the Preferences or Add Packages window.

In Figure 7-9, the Preferences window, you can browse the default selection path by clicking the Browse pushbutton, or you can pick a different path in the RPM Directories section of the window to find the path where your package resides.

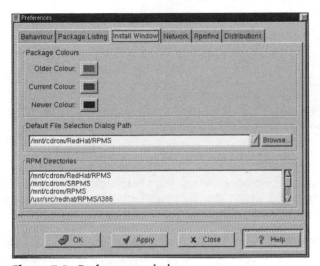

Figure 7-9: Preferences window

To change the path for your package, highlight the appropriate path and then click the Apply and OK pushbuttons at the bottom of the Preferences window.

Note If the package you are installing on your Linux system already exists, use the Upgrade pushbutton on the bottom of the Install window to move to a newer release of your package.

You can also install packages from the Package Info window (refer to Figure 7-4). When you query a package that has not been installed, an Install pushbutton will be displayed at the bottom of the Package Info window. Click this pushbutton and follow the steps as described in the "Installing packages using GnoRPM" section found earlier in this chapter.

Using the Rpmfind pushbutton on the GnoRPM toolbar

Packages may also be downloaded from the Web for installation. If you click the Rpmfind pushbutton on the toolbar, you will get the Rpmfind window as shown in Figure 7-10.

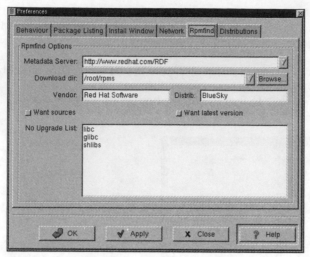

Figure 7-10: Rpmfind

To download a package using the Rpmfind option, supply the appropriate URL in the Metadata Server edit box, and supply the path on which you want the package to reside in the Download dir edit box. Click Apply and OK.

Caution   You will find many versions of the package you want to install at numerous Web locations. Since there is no verification process with the Rpmfind option, you should query the package you want to download and install to be certain it is the right package for you.

Note   If you choose to download your package from the Primary GnoRPM graphical window as shown in Figure 7-2, use the Web find tab and follow the same procedures as described for Rpmfind above.

Using RPM on Non-Red Hat Linux Distributions

Other open Linux distributions provide RPM and a graphical interface tool even though RPM was developed by Red Hat. I describe two examples next — Caldera and SuSE.

RPM on Caldera OpenLinux

For Caldera OpenLinux you can use the command line as I described earlier in the "Using RPM in command mode — basic operations" section, or you can use GnoRPM by following the graphical COAS menu to kpackage. kpackage is the KDE graphical equivalent to GnoRPM. To use the `kpackage` utility from the KDE desktop, select `kpackage` from Utilities on the pull down menu. If you are not already signed in as `root`, you will be prompted for the root password in the standard COAS dialog box. After you enter the password, you can browse the package database of your Linux system: you will see the main window of `kpackage`, as shown in Figure 7-11.

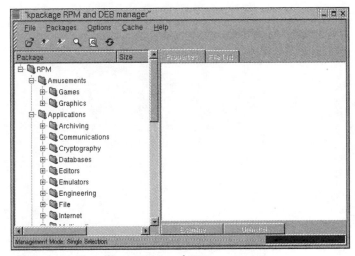

Figure 7-11: kpackage RPM and DEB manager

Using RPM on SuSE OpenLinux

To use GnoRPM on SuSE OpenLinux, follow the steps in the "Using RPM on non-Red Hat Linux distributions" sections above. To access SuSE's graphical installation and configuration tool, YaST (Yet another Software TOOL).

Summary

As you can see, `tar`, Command-based RPM, and the GnoRPM graphical RPM tool are very powerful features of your OpenLinux system. As you will most likely be logged on as root, you should always exercise extreme caution when using these tools. With these tools you can take care of all your package maintenance in a clean efficient manner and you will be able to keep your OpenLinux system current and running smoothly. For more detailed and up-to-date information on packages, be sure to check the Web site `www.rpm.org` regularly.

✦   ✦   ✦

Managing Devices

Devices are hardware. A computer's operating system, which is software, uses special programs called *device drivers* to communicate with its attached hardware, the devices. Linux and all modern operating systems use device drivers to talk to hardware. The device driver is a program that translates instructions between the kernel and hardware devices.

Drivers are part of the kernel. The kernel works with the device drivers and a set of device special files in the /dev directory to provide user access to the various devices connected to your computer.

Understanding Device Special Files

The /dev directory contains files known as device special files, which Linux uses to represent all the different types of hardware devices on your system. For example, Linux uses the /dev/mouse file for reading input from the mouse. By organizing access to hardware devices in this way, Linux effectively makes the interface to a hardware device look like any other piece of software. This means that you, in many cases, can use the same syntax that you use with software to perform operations on computer hardware devices. For instance, you can use the cat command to send a file to the screen display, the null device (/dev/null), or to a filesystem.

All Linux systems support the usual devices you need to work with, such as disks, tape drives, printers, game controllers, and modems. Each Linux device has at least one device special file in the /dev directory to represent it. You use device special file specifications to refer to your Linux devices. For example, most Linux distributions refer to the mouse as the file, /dev/mouse, and the system console as /dev/console. Linux uses device special files for reading input and writing output from and to hardware.

Note   This file-oriented approach to devices is very effective from an operating-system point of view. By representing hardware with files, Linux programmers can use the same approach to accessing hardware and software. This makes certain kinds of system programming easier.

Linux devices for Windows, DOS, and OS/2 users

To access devices on a Windows, DOS, or OS/2 operating system, you explicitly specify a device name. For example, if you are accessing a floppy disk drive, you call it A:. On Linux, you don't use explicit device names. You use file specifications. The typical floppy device file specification on Linux is /dev/fd0 (floppy disk 0). If you have an extra floppy drive, Linux calls it /dev/fd1. An IDE hard drive (known as C: on DOS, Windows, and OS/2) is /dev/hda (hard drive a).

Now, let's complicate things. On the laptop computer, flyingpenguin, there are over 100 /dev/fd* files. From what you've read so far, it's reasonable to think that flying-penguin has 100 floppy drives. Think again! I only have two physical floppy drives. Floppy disks come in different flavors: double- or single-sided, high or low density. Linux uses a different device special file to represent each possible floppy disk con-figuration. For example, if I am using a 1.44 MB floppy (1,440 KB), there is a file called /dev/fd01440 for my first floppy drive, and another file, /dev/fd11440, for my second floppy device. If I need to write to some sort of old, low-density floppy, Linux enables me to do that by providing several choices of files in the /dev direc-tory. You can examine your floppy device special files in either command or graphi-cal mode. To look at the device special files in command mode, use the `ls` command or the `file` command at the console, at a terminal, or in a GNOME or KDE terminal window. The examples below show the files in /dev that point to two different floppy drives. Notice that to represent two floppy drives, the Linux instal-lation procedure created many more than two files to be sure that it supports what-ever unusual and/or ancient floppy drives you may have.

Tip   You don't need to be logged in as root to examine device special files. Whenever you can, log in with your non-privileged username to avoid accidents that may damage your system.

```
miss_scarlet@flyingpenguin$ ls /dev/fd0*
/dev/fd0            /dev/fd0h1200   /dev/fd0h720    /dev/fd0u1743
/dev/fd0u3840
/dev/fd0CompaQ     /dev/fd0h1440   /dev/fd0h880    /dev/fd0u1760
/dev/fd0u720
/dev/fd0D360       /dev/fd0h1476   /dev/fd0u1040   /dev/fd0u1840
/dev/fd0u800
/dev/fd0D720       /dev/fd0h1494   /dev/fd0u1120   /dev/fd0u1920
/dev/fd0u820
```

```
/dev/fd0H1440    /dev/fd0h1660    /dev/fd0u1440    /dev/fd0u2880
/dev/fd0u830
/dev/fd0H360     /dev/fd0h360     /dev/fd0u1660    /dev/fd0u3200
/dev/fd0H720     /dev/fd0h410     /dev/fd0u1680    /dev/fd0u3520
/dev/fd0d360     /dev/fd0h420     /dev/fd0u1722    /dev/fd0u360
---------------  Output edited to save space  -----------
miss_scarlet@flyingpenguin$ ls /dev/fd1*
/dev/fd1         /dev/fd1h1200    /dev/fd1h720     /dev/fd1u1743
/dev/fd1u3840
/dev/fd1CompaQ   /dev/fd1h1440    /dev/fd1h880     /dev/fd1u1760
/dev/fd1u720
/dev/fd1D360     /dev/fd1h1476    /dev/fd1u1040    /dev/fd1u1840
/dev/fd1u800
/dev/fd1D720     /dev/fd1h1494    /dev/fd1u1120    /dev/fd1u1920
/dev/fd1u820
/dev/fd1H1440    /dev/fd1h1660    /dev/fd1u1440    /dev/fd1u2880
/dev/fd1u830
/dev/fd1H360     /dev/fd1h360     /dev/fd1u1660    /dev/fd1u3200
/dev/fd1H720     /dev/fd1h410     /dev/fd1u1680    /dev/fd1u3520
/dev/fd1d360     /dev/fd1h420     /dev/fd1u1722    /dev/fd1u360
---------------  Output edited to save space  -----------
```

Here are the results of the `file` command. Notice that each file is labeled as a "block special" file. The "Categorizing special files" section in this chapter describes block special files.

```
miss_scarlet@flyingpenguin$ file /dev/fd0* |more
/dev/fd0:       block special (2/0)
/dev/fd0CompaQ: block special (2/4)
/dev/fd0D360:   block special (2/12)
/dev/fd0D720:   block special (2/16)
/dev/fd0H1440:  block special (2/28)
/dev/fd0H360:   block special (2/12)
/dev/fd0H720:   block special (2/16)
/dev/fd0d360:   block special (2/4)
---------------  Output edited to save space  -----------

miss_scarlet@flyingpenguin$ file /dev/fd1* |more
/dev/fd1:       block special (2/1)
/dev/fd1CompaQ: block special (2/5)
/dev/fd1D360:   block special (2/13)
/dev/fd1D720:   block special (2/17)
/dev/fd1H1440:  block special (2/29)
/dev/fd1H360:   block special (2/13)
/dev/fd1H720:   block special (2/17)
/dev/fd1d360:   block special (2/5)
---------------  Output edited to save space  -----------
```

How do you create a device special file?

First of all, you rarely have to create device special files. The Linux installation procedure loads hundreds of them on your system to support the most commonly used devices (and lots of uncommonly used ones too). However, if you buy some new type of device or a non-standard device that doesn't have a device special file, you can run the MAKEDEV script to create a device special file in the /dev directory. If you needed a serial device named ttyS17, you would type the following lines in a terminal window or on a text mode terminal:

```
cd /dev; MAKEDEV ttyS17
```

Caution   Be sure to be root when you use the MAKEDEV command. Don't forget that MAKEDEV is one of those rare Linux words that are completely uppercase.

Categorizing Device Special Files

Linux divides the device special files into the following three categories, based on how the device performs I/O:

✦ Character special files for serial access devices (such as such as tapes, serial lines, and USB ports).

✦ Block special files for random-access block devices, such as disks.

✦ Named pipes for certain kinds of interprocess communication.

Table 8-1 lists some Linux devices with their device special file names.

Note   While you refer to devices by their device special file names, you cannot open and read the files in the /dev directory. Device special files are in machine-readable format only.

Character special files

Character special files represent devices that perform I/O on a character-by-character basis. Terminals and printers are common character special devices. Character devices are often called *raw devices* because the I/O is done in a stream of characters. Hard disks, on the other hand, store data in blocks addressed by cylinder and sector.

Cross-Reference   Chapter 9 discusses hard disk geometry.

Block special files

Block special files represent devices — such as disks — that perform I/O in complete blocks of data. Let's say that you only want to read one word in a disk file. Linux retrieves an entire block (512 bytes) of data on the disk and puts the block into a buffer in memory. Then Linux and the filesystem work together to extract and return just the word you want.

Tip
Block I/O devices also need to act like character I/O devices. Behind the scenes, a block of data is made up of characters. Therefore, every block device and special file has a corresponding character device and special file. Linux automatically reads data character by character and assembles it into blocks for block devices, such as disks.

Named pipes

A named pipe is actually a FIFO (first in first out) buffer—that is, an area in memory that processes information on a first come, first served basis. Linux system processes use named pipes as an interprocess communication (IPC) mechanism. For example, one daemon schedules printing for all users on a system. The print command (1p) communicates with the daemon via a named pipe.

Note
There are other IPC mechanisms, such as Remote Procedure Calls (RPC) that do not use device special files.

Inspecting the /dev directory

Many of the devices in the /dev directory are in logical groups. Table 8-1 lists some of the most commonly used devices in the /dev directory.

<table>
<tr><td colspan="2" align="center">Table 8-1
Commonly Used Device Special Files</td></tr>
<tr><td>*Device Special File*</td><td>*Description*</td></tr>
<tr><td>/dev/console</td><td>The system console—that is, the device combination (e.g. monitor and keyboard) that is physically connected to your Linux system; also called /dev/tty0.</td></tr>
<tr><td>/dev/hd*</td><td>IDE or EIDE hard drives. Each IDE disk has a separate file for every partition on that disk. The /dev/hda1 device refers to the first partition on hard drive hda. The device /dev/hda refers to the entire hard disk hda.</td></tr>
<tr><td>/dev/sd*</td><td>SCSI hard drives. Each SCSI disk has a separate file for every partition on the disk. The /dev/sda1 device refers to the first partition on hard drive sda. The device /dev/sda refers to the entire hard disk sda.</td></tr>
<tr><td>/dev/fd*</td><td>Floppy disk drives. /dev/fd0 is the first floppy drive. If you have another floppy drive, /dev/fd1 is the second floppy drive.</td></tr>
<tr><td>/dev/st*</td><td>SCSI tape drives. /dev/st0 is the first SCSI tape drive.</td></tr>
</table>

Continued

Table 8-1 (continued)	
Device Special File	Description
/dev/vc*	Linux considers terminals to be consoles. These files support virtual consoles that you can access by pressing the Alt key with the F keys (Alt+F1 through Alt+F6). Virtual consoles provide separate simultaneous local login sessions.
/dev/pty*	Pseudo-terminals, used for remote logins.
/dev/ttyS*	The serial interface ports on your computer. /dev/ttyS0 corresponds to COM1 under MS-DOS. If you have a serial mouse, /dev/mouse is a symbolic link to the appropriate ttyS device to which your mouse is wired.
/dev/tty*	Serial terminals, such as those hardwired to your computer.
/dev/cua	Another name for serial ports, usually used with dial-out modems.
/dev/null	The null device—the bit bucket—a black hole. Linux throws away anything you write to /dev/null.

Managing Serial Devices

A serial port is an I/O (Input/Output) device that moves data into and out of your computer serially—that is, one bit of data at a time. Computers use serial ports to connect to other devices, including terminals, modems, other computers, and printers. Serial devices, such as "dumb" terminals and modems, are connected to your serial ports. Most PC compatibles have at least two serial ports.

Note   There are many types of I/O devices besides serial ports, such as parallel ports, disk controllers, network interface cards (NIC), universal serial buses (USB), and more.

One common type of device attached to serial ports is the tty (teletype) device (/dev/tty*). Linux has three classes of terminals: virtual consoles (vc); pseudo-terminals (ptys), used by network and X Window terminals; and serial devices, such as hardwired terminals and modems. Modems are ttys, because they permit interactive sessions over a serial connection from a remote computer over a telephone line.

Tip   If you are a Microsoft operating system user, you know /dev/ttyS0 as COM1 and /dev/ttyS1 as COM2.

When you use the `file` command on the serial port device files, you see that they are character I/O devices. You can also see the device type if you use `ls -l` to list your serial devices. The first column contains a "c," which stands for *character device*. The following example shows both ways to list your serial port device special files. Notice that the computer named flyingpenguin has device special files to support four serial ports.

```
[root@flyingpenguin}# file /dev/ttyS*
/dev/ttyS0:    character special
/dev/ttyS1:    character special
/dev/ttyS2:    character special
/dev/ttyS3:    character special

[root@flyingpenguin}# ls -l /dev/ttyS*
crw-------    1    root    tty    4,  64    May 5   1998   /dev/ttyS0
crw-------    1    root    tty    4,  64    May 5   1998   /dev/ttyS1
crw-------    1    root    tty    4,  64    May 5   1998   /dev/ttyS2
crw-------    1    root    tty    4,  64    May 5   1998   /dev/ttyS3
```

Note When you examine your device special files, your output may differ from that in this book. The output depends on your hardware, your Linux distribution, and the version of the distribution you are running. For example, the output above comes from flyingpenguin running Red Hat Linux 6.1. The Red Hat Linux 7.1 upgrade procedure on flyingpenguin created many more /dev/ttyS files even though the physical number of serial ports remained the same.

Tip You can also install a special multiport serial board that allows your PC to have up to 256 ports so that the PC functions as a login server for multiple users on "dumb" character-based terminals. If you use one of these serial boards, remember that its device special files may not be named according to the ttyS convention, to avoid confusion with the two built-in serial ports.

On the CD-ROM "The Linux Serial HOWTO," a detailed paper about configuring and troubleshooting serial ports, includes multiport serial devices that connect terminals and banks of modems to your Linux system. You can find a link to this HOWTO on the CD-ROM.

On a portable computer, such as a notebook or a laptop, you may have one of the following:

✦ A 9-pin male serial port.

✦ An RJ-11 telephone jack if you have an internal modem.

✦ A PC Card modem card with an RJ-11 telephone jack.

Tip If you insert your portable computer into a docking station to use the docking station's serial ports, those serial ports usually have 25-pin connectors.

On the CD-ROM Read the PCMCIA HOWTO for detailed information on PC Card connections. To read the most recently updated information about PC Card configuration, read the Linux PCMCIA Information Page. Links to the HOWTO and the Information Page are on the CD-ROM.

Terminals — Serially

The first serial device you read about below is the terminal. However, not all terminals are serial devices. Some are network devices. The "dumb" terminal and all of Linux's consoles are serial. Before you get into details about configuring serial terminals, you need to understand the types of terminals that you can use with Linux.

There are lots of different types of terminals, including "dumb" character-based terminals, "smart" graphical X-based terminals, and terminal emulation windows. Dumb terminals are so named because they simply transmit characters between the screen and the computer. Dumb terminals have no brain (processor) inside, so while they have only the most basic logic, they're easy to configure and use. The VT100 type terminal from Digital Equipment Corporation (now part of Compaq Computer) is the most common "dumb" terminal, but there are many others including the Digital's VT200 series, and terminals from IBM, Hewlett Packard, Bull, and Wyse. Most dumb terminals display 24 lines of 80 or 132 characters. "Dumb" terminals are serial devices.

X terminals are "smart" graphical terminals that allow you to use the X-based GUI of your choice, such as KDE, GNOME, or Motif. X terminals are more complicated to configure than dumb terminals because they have a brain (processor) and memory inside them. The software for X terminals is usually loaded into their memory from across the network. Since X terminals connect to Linux over a network, they are pseudo-terminals (ptys). The X protocol lets you display bitmapped graphics, such as a Paint program or a graphical Web browser. Terminal emulation windows also let X users run the same text-based applications they would run on a dumb terminal.

Terminal emulation windows are graphical applications that run on smart X terminals to emulate dumb terminals. Many Linux tasks are so simple that it's often easier to type a command than to point and click and navigate through windows and menus. For example, I prefer to use the `ls` command to list my files in a terminal emulation window rather than launch the File Manager or Caldera's Disk Navigator. You can mix terminal emulation windows with graphical windows on the same computer. The following figure shows one character-based terminal emulation window sharing the KDE desktop with Caldera's graphical disk navigator application. Both windows show the same directory listing, /home. Terminal emulation windows usually emulate the VT100 terminal.

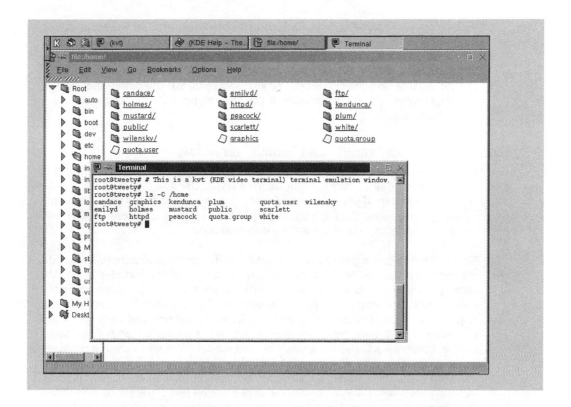

The Linux device special files for serial ports are /dev/ttyS0, /dev/ttyS1, and so on. You can use the `setserial -a` command on the console or in a terminal emulation window to see all attributes for a specified serial port, as below.

```
root@tweety# setserial /dev/ttyS0 -a
/dev/ttyS0, Line 0, UART: 16550A, Port: 0x03f8, IRQ: 4
        Baud_base: 115200, close_delay: 50, divisor: 0
        closing_wait: 3000
        Flags: spd_normal skip_test
```

Getting started with "dumb" terminals

If you use Linux (except for X Window use) with a computer monitor and keyboard, you are using a terminal. It looks like a PC to you, but Linux recognizes your monitor and keyboard as a terminal.

Note   A console is a terminal you use to monitor and control your computer or network.

Tip

Virtual consoles enable non-graphical users to have different text workspaces, just as a GUI enables graphical users to have different windows. Linux provides virtual consoles (VCs) when you're the superuser (root) and not running X. When you work in console mode, which is text-only, you can switch between consoles using special console keys (Alt+F1, Alt+F2, Alt+F3, and so forth). The device special files, /dev/vcs* represent virtual consoles. If you're working in a VC, /dev/vc0 is your first virtual console.

Some notes about "smart" and "dumb" terminals

"Dumb" terminals on serial lines are called tty devices. If you're working on a standard terminal, your device name might be /dev/tty01. Use the `tty` command below to determine the name of your terminal device. Linux responds with the name of the terminal you're using. Figure 8-1 shows that Linux uses a different file to identify each terminal emulation window on the same desktop.

Note

Terminal emulation applications are plentiful. Different Linux distributions provide different applications. Any distribution that includes GNOME includes a GNOME terminal. Any distribution that includes KDE includes a kvt (KDE video terminal). Most recent distributions also include konsole for KDE. Figure 8-1 shows that three different terminal emulation programs, kvt, konsole, and terminal each generated a window. The three terminal application you use is mostly a matter of personal choice. konsole is a fairly new application that is built on more modern technology and a more comprehensive usage of X Windows features than terminal and kvt. If you plan simply to work in your shell, any terminal emulation application is going to satisfy your needs. If you need to run sophisticated text applications in your terminal emulation window, especially those that contain a pseudo-graphical interface, konsole offers more functionality.

Note

The first terminals were teletypes hardwired to a computer.

Managing "dumb" terminal devices

Managing dumb terminals is easy. Usually, all you need to do is connect the terminal to a serial port in your computer, plug the terminal into the wall and let Linux do the rest. Linux automatically identifies the type of terminal you're using when you log in. How does Linux know how your terminal should work? It consults terminfo, the terminal information database in /usr/share/terminfo/*/*. Terminfo, a large set of subdirectories and binary files, describes all the character cell terminals known to your Linux distribution. Usually you don't need to touch the terminfo database. However, if a vendor developed a new terminal and you purchased it, the vendor would also supply a terminfo entry for this new device. Your job would be to insert the information for the new terminal entry into the terminfo database. The subdirectories under /usr/share/terminfo use the first letter of the terminal type as a naming convention. The binary files are named for the terminals. For example, type the following `ls` command to see all the entries for VT100 terminals.

```
miss_scarlet@flyingpenguin$ ls /usr/share/terminfo/v
v200-nam     vi200-rv       visa50       vt100-nav-w   vt200-js      vt320-w-nam
v320n        vi300          visual603    vt100-s       vt200-old     vt320nam
v3220        vi300-old      vitty        vt100-s-bot   vt200-w       vt330
v5410        vi50           vk100        vt100-s-top   vt220        vt340
vanilla      vi500          vp3a+        vt100-top-s   vt220-8      vt400
vapple       vi50adm        vp60         vt100-vb      vt220-8bit   vt400-24
vc103        vi55           vp90         vt100-w       vt220-js     vt420
vc203        vi550          vremote      vt100-w-am    vt220-nam    vt420f
vc303        vi603          vs100        vt100-w-nam   vt220-old    vt420pc
vc303a       viewpoint      vs100-x10    vt100-w-nav   vt220-w      vt420pcdos
vc403a       viewpoint3a+   vsc          vt100nam      vt220d       vt50
vc404        viewpoint60    vt-61        vt102         vt300        vt50h
vc404-s      viewpoint90    vt100        vt102-nsgr    vt300-nam    vt510
vc414        vip            vt100-am     vt102-w       vt300-w      vt510pc
vc414h       vip-H          vt100-bm     vt125         vt300-w-nam  vt510pcdos
vc415        vip-Hw         vt100-bm-o   vt131         vt320        vt52
venix        vip-w          vt100-bot-s  vt132         vt320-k3     vt520
versaterm    vip7800-H      vt100-nam    vt200         vt320-k311   vt525
vi200        vip7800-Hw     vt100-nam-w  vt200-8       vt320-nam    vt61
vi200-f      vip7800-w      vt100-nav    vt200-8bit    vt320-w      vt61.5
```

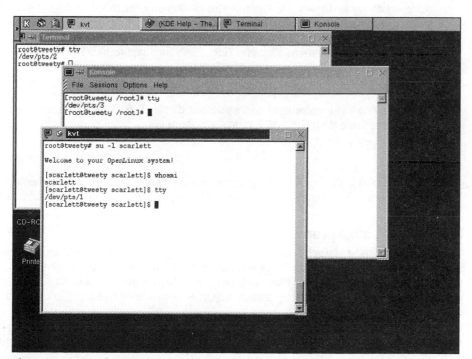

Figure 8-1: Use the tty command to determine the file that represents your terminal (or terminal window)

The file-naming convention for the binary files in the terminfo database follows two rules:

1. The subdirectory name is the first letter of the terminal model name. For example, the VT100 binary files reside in the path /usr/share/terminfo/v and binary files that support IBM terminals in the path /usr/share/terminfo/i.

2. The file names include the terminal's model name. In the directory listing of above, notice that the terminfo database supports most of Compaq's VT series terminals, including the popular VT100 and the ancient VT52.

Note   The Red Hat Linux terminfo database is about 2 MB for both versions 6.x and 7.x.

termcap is an older, declining way for Linux to describe your terminal. It is a very large file, /etc/termcap (*terminal capabilities* file) that holds definitions for all the keystrokes on all the character cell terminals Linux knows about. Linux maintains termcap in addition to terminfo in order to retain compatibility with older programs that were written before terminfo became the preferred terminal capability database. The Linux installation procedure creates the termcap file.

Caution   Linux can occasionally become confused as to your terminal type, especially if you accidentally try to display a binary file. This confusion may cause problems in how your terminal reacts to keystrokes, especially control characters, arrow keys, and the backspace key. To be absolutely sure that Linux knows what your terminal type is, export the environment variable, TERM, in your .bashrc file. The export command below sets my terminal type to VT100.

```
export TERM=vt100
```

The following echo command and its output display the value of the TERM environment variable for a GNOME terminal emulator window.

```
echo $TERM
xterm
```

Note   The examples in this book use bash. If you use a different shell than bash, the name of the environment variable and the syntax for exporting it may be slightly different.

Changing terminal properties

The stty command reports on and sets terminal options, such as control characters, parity, and whether to echo typed characters. To see all the stty options, read the man page. It's more than most people want to know about stty. The example below illustrates these three commonly used formats of the stty command:

stty -a	Show all your terminal settings.
stty *control-charac key*	Set a key to generate a character. For example, the command "stty erase <CTRL-m>" tells the terminal to erase the last character you typed whenever you press <CTRL+M>.
stty sane	When your terminal is completely messed up, reset it to sanity.

```
miss_scarlet$ stty -a
speed 9600 baud; rows 23; columns 80; line = 0;
intr = ^C; quit = ^\; erase = ^?; kill = ^U; eof = ^D; eol = <undef>;
eol2 = <undef>; start = ^Q; stop = ^S; susp = ^Z; rprnt = ^R; werase = ^W;
lnext = ^V; flush = ^O; min = 1; time = 0;
-parenb -parodd cs8 -hupcl -cstopb cread -clocal -crtscts
-ignbrk -brkint -ignpar -parmrk -inpck -istrip -inlcr -igncr icrnl ixon -ixoff
-iuclc -ixany -imaxbel
opost -olcuc -ocrnl onlcr -onocr -onlret -ofill -ofdel nl0 cr0 tab0 bs0 vt0 ff0
isig icanon iexten echo echoe echok -echonl -noflsh -xcase -tostop -echoprt
echoctl echoke
```

The following command sets the job control suspend function to be control D:

```
miss_scarlet$ stty susp ^D
```

Terminals, getty, and login

Three programs, init, getty, and login, work together so that you can log into a
Linux system from a serial terminal connection. The getty program controls logins
from terminals (via serial lines) and the console (not running X). The init program
(job 1) starts a separate getty program for each terminal that allows logins. Each
getty program displays a login prompt and waits for a user to type a username.

The getty performs three tasks:

1. Reads the username.
2. Checks terminal characteristics, such as the speed, especially for dial-in
   connections.
3. Runs the login program, which reads the password.

If the username/password combination is valid, the login program starts the shell. If
the username/password combination is not valid, init starts a new getty program
without letting the user log in. When the user logs out from the terminal, the shell
finishes. The init program sees that the shell has terminated and starts a new
getty. In this way, init sees to it that the login prompt is always ready and waiting
for a user.

How does getty know about your terminal?

When getty realizes that you want to log in, it checks your terminal characteristics
by reading the file /etc/gettydefs. The gettydefs (getty definitions) file stores the
first terminal speed to try as well as the next speed to try if the first speed causes
the terminal display to look like garbage. gettydefs also supplies other settings for
each serial terminal line, such as what the login prompt should look like. Each entry
in /etc/gettydefs includes five fields separated by the hash character (#): label#
initial-flags # final-flags # login-prompt #next-label.

The label is a name that usually includes the preferred terminal speed. The initial flags field includes the starting settings for the terminal. The final flags usually specify the value SANE. The login-prompt field is the prompt that should appear on the terminal display. The final field, next-label, usually specifies a series of speeds to try if the terminal is not responding properly. The lines below are three entries from the gettydefs file on the flyingpenguin computer. (The lines that start with ""a hash are comment lines.) The first two entries are for modem lines. The third entry is for a terminal.

```
# 9600 fixed-baud modem entry
F9600# B9600 CS8 CRTSCTS # B9600 SANE -ISTRIP HUPCL CRTSCTS #@S login: #F9600
# 230400 autobauding Modem entry with hard flow control
230400# B230400 CS8 CRTSCTS # B230400 SANE -ISTRIP HUPCL CRTSCTS #login:#115200
# 19200 fixed baud Dumb Terminal entry
DT19200# B19200 CS8 CLOCAL # B19200 SANE -ISTRIP CLOCAL #@S login: #DT19200
```

Logging in from the network

While a local terminal login uses a separate physical serial line for each terminal user, a network terminal login uses a separate virtual network connection for each user. Since there is no way to predict how many virtual network connections might be active at any one time, there is no way to know how many getty programs to run. Also, users have different choices as to how to log in across a network, such as telnet and rlogin.

Caution — Don't Step in a Terminal Security Hole

Allowing the all-powerful root user to log in from any terminal on the network may be a security hole. Our office has a public "Welcome" terminal in reception. Visitors can try out certain applications there. We don't want them trying to guess the root password to invade our systems, so the public terminal is not a secure terminal. Linux defines a secure terminal as one that allows root logins. The file /etc/securetty lists the names of the ttys where root is allowed to log in. The file format requires one tty device (minus the /dev/ prefix) per line. If the securetty file does not exist, root is allowed to log in on any serial terminal (including dialup terminals). The following display shows that only eight serial terminals permit root logins to flyingpenguin.

```
root@flyingpenguin# cat /etc/securetty
tty1
tty2
tty3
tty4
tty5
tty6
tty7
tty8
```

Instead of creating a swarm of getty programs, Linux uses daemons (detached programs) to handle network logins. For example, there is a daemon for telnet named telnetd to listen for and handle incoming telnet login requests, and a daemon for rlogin, rlogind, to listen for and handle rlogin requests. These daemons automatically start when you boot Linux to full timesharing and networking mode (run levels 3 or 5). When a daemon receives a remote login request, it starts a copy of itself to handle that request; the original daemon continues to listen for other login requests. The new daemon (the one that is the copy) validates the user name much as getty does. The following excerpt from the ps -elf command shows the individual copies of telnetd for each telnet user. The rightmost field in the ps output shows the program that each process is running. Both miss_scarlet and professor_plum have telnetted into the computer and have two processes each: login and bash.

```
root@tweety# ps -elf
F S UID        PID  PPID  TTY  TIME       CMD
100 S root       1     0  0  Mar23 ?      00:00:04 init [5]
             ****** This ps output is edited **********

140 S root     402     1  0  Mar23 ?      00:00:00 inetd
000 S root    1428     1  0  Mar24 ?      00:00:00 ksnapshot
100 S root    1429  1422  0  Mar24 ?      00:00:00 GNOME-pty-helper

000 S root    2986   402  0  19:03 ?      00:00:00 in.telnetd:
bigbird.cardinalconsulting.com
100 S root    2987  2986  0  1903  pts/2  00:00:00 login -- miss_scarlet
100 S miss_sca 2988  2987  0  19:03 pts/2 00:00:00 -bash

000 S root    3028   402  0  19:09 ?      00:00:00 in.telnetd:
bigbird.cardinalconsulting.com
100 S root    3029  3028  0  0  19:09 pts/3 00:00:00 login -- professor_plum
100 S professo 3032  3029  0  0  19:10 pts/3 00:00:00 -bash
```

Getting started with modems

Since modems are serial devices, the serial port device special files, /dev/ttyS* represent them, for example, /dev/ttyS1. For convenience, Linux usually also lets you refer to a modem as /dev/modem. The file /dev/modem is a symbolic link to /dev/ttyS1. You use the ln -s command to create symbolic links, which conveniently function as file-name aliases. If your Linux installation procedure recognizes your modem, it creates the symbolic link for you. If you do not have a file /dev/modem, and you want to refer to your modem that way for convenience, type the command below, using the serial port to which your modem is connected (my modem is on /dev/ttyS1).

```
[root@flyingpenguin]# ln -s /dev/ttyS1 /dev/modem
```

Tip   When you display a long listing (ls -l) for the modem, you can see the link pointing to the original serial port device special file at the end of the listing, as below. The listing also shows that /dev/modem is a symbolic link because the first character in the listing is an l, indicating a symbolic link file type.

```
[root@flyingpenguin]# ls -l /dev/modem
lrwxrwxrwx 1 root 10 Dec 6 15:32 /dev/modem -> /dev/ttyS1
```

Getting familiar with modem terminology

If you have configured modems for other operating systems, the terminology should be familiar. If this is your first time configuring a modem, take a minute to understand the following terms:

✦ winmodem — Many PCs come with "semi-modems," part hardware and part software, called *winmodems*. These winmodems work fine with Microsoft Windows, but not usually with Linux. The Lucent LT WinModems are an exception. Winmodems lack certain hardware found in regular modems. Your computer's CPU emulates the "missing" parts.

Note   A winmodem that works with Linux, such as the Lucent LT WinModem, is called a "linmodem."

✦ Baud rate — Baud was the unit for data transmission speed until it was replaced by bps (bits per second), a more accurate term. *Baud* and *bps* are often used interchangeably.

Note   The term *baud* — named after J.M.E. Baudot, the inventor of the Baudot telegraph code — means the number of signaling elements (such as bits) that occur each second. At slow data transmission speeds, since only one bit of information (signaling element) fits in each electrical change, the baud rate is the same as the number of bits per second (bps). For example, 300 baud means a transmission rate of 300 bps. However, at high transmission rates, you can squeeze more than one bit into an electrical signal. Therefore, baud rate and bits per second are different. When you deal with higher transmission rates (4800 and above), refer to the speed as bps. For example, a 9600 bps modem may have a baud rate of 2400. Most of the time, when people other than electrical engineers refer to baud, they are using a technically inaccurate term. They should be saying "bps."

✦ Parity — A way of verifying that no data are lost or corrupted during transmission.

Tip   If you aren't sure whether your modem works with Linux, go to the Linux Modem Compatibility Database, http://www.o2.net/~gromitkc/20000326a.html.

Managing modems

Modems are easy to set up. Follow these steps:

1. Connect the modem hardware to your computer. Be sure to read the documentation that comes with the modem.

2. Use the `ls -l` command to check for the symbolic link /dev/modem. If the link is not there, and you want to refer to the modem as /dev/modem, use the following `ln -s` command.

```
[root@flyingpenguin]# ln -s /dev/modem /dev/ttyS1
```

3. Use the `chmod` command to grant permissions on the device special file so that people can dial out.

4. Provide users with a dialer program, such as minicom, or set up a PPP (Point to Point Protocol) link so that users can connect to an Internet Service Provider (ISP).

Tip

How do you know which port your modem is on? You can use the command `wvdial` to scan your serial ports for a modem. If the scan finds a modem, it lists the modem's device special file and attributes.

```
miss_scarlet@tweety$ wvdial
--> WvDial: Internet dialer version 1.41
--> Initializing modem.
--> Sending: ATZ
    ------------ wvdial output truncated --------------
```

Modem software

There are several communication packages available for using a terminal to dial out on a modem. They enable you to dial into another computer. Minicom is a modem program that DOS users might recognize. Seyon is a popular X-based communications package. When you run one of these programs, it seems as if your terminal is directly connected to the remote computer. The following example shows what the minicom interface looks like.

```
miss_scarlet@flyingpenguin minicom

minicom: WARNING: please don't run minicom as root when not
maintaining it (with the -s switch) since all changes to the
                  configuration will be GLOBAL !.

Welcome to minicom 1.83.1

OPTIONS:History Buffer,F-key Macros,Search History Buffer,
Compiled on Aug 24 2000, 10:09:47.

                    Minicom Command Summary

           Commands can be called by CTRL+A <key>

               Main Functions                 Other Functions

Dialing directory..D  run script (Go)..G | Clear screen.......C
Send files........S   Receive files....R | cOnfigure Minicom..O
comm Parameters....P  Add linefeed.....A | Suspend minicom....J
```

```
Capture on/off.....L  Hangup...........H │ eXit and reset.....X
send break.........F  initialize Modem.M │ Quit with no reset.Q
Terminal settings..T  run Kermit.......K │ Cursor key mode....I
lineWrap on/off....W  local Echo on/offE │ Help screen........Z

        Select function or press Enter for none.

            Written by Miquel van Smoorenburg 1991-1995
            Some additions by Jukka Lahtinen 1997-1999
              i18n by Arnaldo Carvalho de Melo 1998
Press CTRL+A Z for help on special keys

AT S7=45 S0=0 L1 V1 X4 &c1 E1 Q0
OK
CTRL-A Z for help │ 38400 8N1 │ NOR │ Minicom 1.83.1 │ VT102 │
X
AT S7=45 S0=0 L1 V1 X4 &c1 E1  Leave Minicom?
OK                             Yes        No
```

Cross-Reference   Chapter 21 details how to set up a PPP connection. You use a PPP connection for communicating across telephone lines between two computers. Your Internet service provider (ISP) may provide you with a PPP connection so that the server at the ISP can pass your requests to the Internet and send Internet data and Web pages back to you.

Fax modem

efax (/usr/bin/efax) is a program that lets you send and receive faxes on Class 1, 2, and 2.0 modems. Some of the many modems that the efax program supports are AT&T Dataport, Cardinal Digital Fax Modem, Digicom Scout+, and USR Sportster (V.32 and V.34).

Tip   efax automatically answers all incoming calls if you add the following entry to /etc/inittab:

    s1:45:respawn:/bin/sh /usr/bin/fax answer

An efax README file, by the programmer, Ed Casas, is at http://casas.ee.ubc.ca/efax. The efax Web page also links to patches, new releases, and known bugs.

Caution   Older versions of Red Hat Linux support Class 2.0 modems, but Red Hat states that the support is "untested."

Input devices

Keyboards and pointing devices, such as the mouse, glidepad, trackpad, and the little red device in the middle of my ThinkPad keyboard (called a TrackPoint), are input devices. You need a keyboard, but you don't need a mouse to run Linux as long as you don't plan to use a GUI (XFree86, the open-source implementation of the X Window System). Even if you don't configure X, you can still use a mouse on a text-based Linux system. Certain text-based tools and utilities enable you to move the cursor through their menus with either the arrow keys or a mouse.

Configuring your keyboard

Keyboards are easy to configure. Linux supports just about any keyboard—certainly all the keyboards that work in DOS. The Linux installation procedure asks what kind of keyboard you have—including the national language to use for language specific key mappings, such as slovene, uk english, us english, thai, and so on. If you don't know the make and model of your keyboard, that's okay. Linux offers you the generic 101-key keyboard. After you complete the Linux installation, you probably won't need to do any post-installation keyboard configuration. If you want to, you can configure the repeat rate and the delay time. You can also remap the default actions of key values, such as Delete, and map keys to national language characters.

The repeat rate is how fast the keyboard repeats a keystroke when you hold down a key. The delay is how long the keyboard waits to repeat a keystroke after you start holding down a key.

Modifying the keyboard repeat characteristics

Most people are satisfied with the defaults for keyboard rate and keyboard delay, but if you press heavily on the keys, you may find that characters repeat when you only mean to type a single character. To change the repeat rate and/or the keyboard delay time, use the kbdrate program. Running kbdrate without command-line options sets the repeat rate and delay time to the default that your Linux distribution establishes for your particular hardware.

The default keyboard repeat rate depends on the underlying hardware architecture. The default keyboard repeat rate for my IBM ThinkPad laptop (or any Intel-based system) is 10.9 characters per second (cps), and the delay time is 250 milliseconds (ms). This rate also holds for computers based on the Motorola 68000 architecture (Apple Macintosh computers). On Sun workstations (or any computer based on the SPARC-chip architecture), the default kbdrate values are 5 cps and 200 ms.

The kbdrate command-line option to set your repeat rate is -r. The range for -r is from 2 to 30. The option to set your delay time is -d. The time for -d can be one of four values: 250, 500, 750, or 1000. If you select a rate or time that kbdrate does not support, pick the closest valid value. In the following example, the kbdrate -d command attempts to set the delay time to 5 on a SONY VAIO (Intel architecture) notebook. However, the output shows that the keyboard repeat rate defaults to 250 ms since Linux does not support 5 on any hardware.

```
miss_scarlet@tweety$ kbdrate -d 5
Typematic Rate set to 10.9 cps (delay = 250 ms)
```

If you have configured X on your computer, you can run xset to change keyboard, mouse, and screen characteristics. You can run xset from any terminal emulation window. To find out what your xset characteristics currently are, type xset -q, as in the example below. (See Table 8-2.)

```
root@flyingpenguin$ xset -q
auto repeat:  on     key click percent:  0     LED mask:
00000000
   auto repeat delay:  500      repeat rate:  30
   auto repeating keys:  00ffffffdffffbbf
                         fa9fffffffdffdff
                         ffffffffffffffff
                         ffffffffffffffff
   bell percent:  50      bell pitch:  400      bell duration:  100
Pointer Control:
   acceleration:  2/1      threshold:  4
Screen Saver:
   prefer blanking:  yes      allow exposures:  yes
   timeout:  600      cycle:  600
Colors:
   default colormap:  0x21      BlackPixel:  0      WhitePixel:  1
Font Path:
   unix/:7100
Bug Mode: compatibility mode is disabled
DPMS (Energy Star):
   Standby: 1200      Suspend: 1800      Off: 2400
   DPMS is Disabled
Font cache:
   hi-mark (KB): 1024   low-mark (KB): 768  balance (%): 70
```

Table 8-2
Keyboard Characteristics you Can Change by Running xset

Characteristics	Command Options
bell on/off, volume, pitch, and length	xset -b
key click on/off, volume	xset -c
LED lights on/off	xset -led
autorepeat on/off	xset -r*

* xset can toggle autorepeat on and off, but it cannot set a specific rate.

Modifying key mapping

If some form of English is your native language, you have probably not had problems getting keyboard keys to type the letters of your alphabet. However, if your alphabet has special characters, such as umlauts or accent graves, you understand that sometimes you have to modify the mapping of keys to letters so that when you press a key, you get the letter you need. There are two parts to key mapping:

✦ Getting Linux to interpret your keypress as a special character, such as a *u* with an umlaut

✦ Having a font available that displays the special character

Why Linux Needs Separate X and Text Programs for Configuring Keyboards

As you've probably read more than once, Linux usually provides more than one way to get a job done. In most cases, choosing from the different approaches is a matter of your personal preference. This is not the case for keyboard configuration programs, however. You need to use a separate set of programs for configuring keyboards in text mode — such as a Linux console versus keyboards attached to an X display running KDE or GNOME. Here's the reason why: The keyboard driver program controls keypresses when you are in text mode. Each key you press generates a code, which Linux looks up in a keymap to translate the code into an action to perform. When you are in X mode, X itself controls the keyboard (the mouse, too). Therefore, you have two categories of keyboard programs: those that talk to the keyboard driver and those that talk directly to X.

Linux has separate keymap directories for various supported hardware architecture. The location of these directories varies with your distribution and architecture. For example, TurboLinux for the PPC (PowerPC) stores keymaps in /usr/lib/kbd/keytables/ defkeymap.map.

The following `file` commands show the hardware subdirectories that contain keymaps under Caldera Linux eserver and under Red Hat Linux. Under each hardware subdirectory are gzip-compressed keyboard maps for national languages or, in the case of the i386 subdirectory, more subdirectories based on the type of keyboard you have.

```
Prof_plum@tweety$ file /usr/share/kbd/keymaps
/usr/share/kbd/keymaps/amiga:    directory
/usr/share/kbd/keymaps/atari:    directory
/usr/share/kbd/keymaps/i386:     directory
/usr/share/kbd/keymaps/include:  directory
/usr/share/kbd/keymaps/mac:      directory
/usr/share/kbd/keymaps/sun:      directory

miss_scarlet@flyingpenguin$ file /usr/lib/kbd/keymaps/*
/usr/lib/kbd/keymaps/amiga:     directory
/usr/lib/kbd/keymaps/atari:     directory
/usr/lib/kbd/keymaps/i386:      directory
/usr/lib/kbd/keymaps/include:   directory
/usr/lib/kbd/keymaps/mac:       directory
/usr/lib/kbd/keymaps/sun:       directory
```

Note A *qwerty* keyboard is a keyboard where the first six letters are *q, w, e, r, t,* and *y.* Other keyboard attributes, such as shape, ergonomic features, number of keys, and special function keys have nothing to do with a keyboard's "qwerty-ness." Qwerty is the most common (not necessarily the most efficient or ergonomic) English-language keyboard, modeled after the standard English-language type-writer. The network of computers used to generate the examples in this book serves as an example of how widespread the qwerty model is. In fact, all the computers came factory-equipped with "qwerty" keyboards. These computers are built on either Intel compatible or Alpha architectures, and the makers include IBM, Gateway, Dell, and Sony.

Figure 8-2 shows a few of the national-language keymap files supported by the Linux "qwerty" keyboard. To use the `loadkeys` command to load any of these national language files, type the command followed by the name of the keyboard map file (without the suffix ".gz").

Tip If you have a non-U.S. default keyboard, you need a keyboard map. The `kbdconfig` command loads a selected keymap before exiting and configures your machine to use that keymap automatically after rebooting.

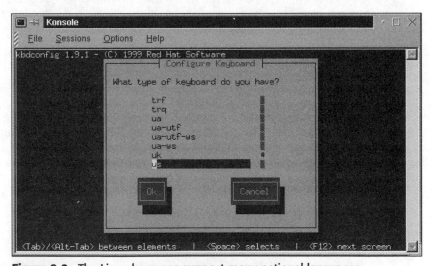

Figure 8-2: The Linux keymaps support many national languages

Caution Anyone who has read permission on the device special file /dev/console can run `loadkeys` and thereby change the keyboard mapping for all virtual consoles.

Configuring pointing devices and mice

There are two characteristics you should find out about your pointing device or mouse before you start to configure it:

✦ The mouse interface.

✦ The mouse protocol.

The interface concerns the hardware characteristics of the mouse, such as the I/O ports it uses. The kernel uses the mouse interface to determine how to read data. The protocol concerns the mouse's software characteristics. The kernel sends mouse data to applications. The applications need to understand the mouse protocol to interpret this data. A pointing device looks like a mouse to Linux. For example, Caldera OpenLinux eServer considers the glidepad on tweety, a SONY notebook, to be a PS/2 mouse.

The Linux kernel currently supports the following bus mouse interfaces:

✦ Inport (Microsoft)

✦ Logitech

✦ PS/2

✦ ATI-XL

✦ Two- or three-button

✦ Pointing device, such as a TrackPoint

✦ Touchpad, glidepad

✦ USB devices

Caution

The Linux 2.4 kernel, released just as this book was going to press, includes much better USB support, especially for hotplugging, or inserting USB devices, such as mice or keyboards. Unfortunately, at the current time, not enough USB drivers are available to make the new USB features widely useful. Perhaps by the time you read this, the general availability of USB drivers will have improved.

You configure a pointing device during the Linux installation procedure. If you add a different pointing device from the one you used during installation, you may need to reconfigure it. You can change basic mouse attributes, such as mouse motion and whether the mouse is left- or right-handed from either the GNOME Control Center or from the KDE main menu. From the KDE menu, for example, select Settings, followed by Input Devices, and select the mouse attributes from the Input Devices Properties window. To completely reconfigure the mouse, you have several choices of mouse configuration tools, depending on your distribution.

Note

The menus for the mouse configuration tools described in this section are not X-based GUIs. They are text-based menus that work with either a mouse or other pointing device or with a keyboard.

Your mouse configuration tool choices include:

✦ The Red Hat mouse configuration tool, usually `/usr/sbin/mouseconfig`, runs on many distributions in addition to Red Hat and is a menu-driven configuration tool.

✦ Xmseconfig is another menu-driven mouse configuration tool. Xmseconfig lets you select the mouse protocol, the mouse device, the baud rate, as well as three-button mouse emulation attributes. An example of the first xmseconfig screen (running on Caldera OpenLinux eserver) follows.

```
root@tweety# xmseconfig
Note: the `Logitech' protocol is only used by older Logitech
mice. Most current models use the `Microsoft' or `MouseMan'
protocol.

     Key   Function
     ----------------------------------------------------
      a  -  Apply changes
      b  -  Change to next baud rate
      c  -  Toggle the ChordMiddle button
      d  -  Toggle the ClearDTR button
      e  -  Toggle the Emulate3button button
      l  -  Select the next resolution
      n  -  Set the name of the device
      p  -  Select the next protocol
      r  -  Toggle the ClearRTS button
      s  -  Increase the sample rate
      t  -  Increase the 3-button emulation timeout
      3  -  Set buttons to 3
      4  -  Set buttons to 4
      5  -  Set buttons to 5
     ----------------------------------------------------
You can also use Tab, and Shift-Tab to move around and then
use Enter to activate the selected button.
                    Dismiss
```

Caldera's COAS configuration tool also has a section for reconfiguring a pointing device. Select Peripherals from the COAS menu, followed by Mouse, to configure your mouse.

Tip You need to be running as root to use most mouse configuration tools.

Configuring Parallel Port Devices

When it comes to parallel port devices, most people think of printers.

Cross-Reference Chapter 13 describes how to configure printers.

However, Linux supports a profusion of external devices that connect to a personal computer's parallel printer port. Some of these devices, such as the Iomega Zip drive can connect to different interfaces, such as a parallel port and a SCSI bus.

Besides parallel port printers, Linux supports parallel devices including parallel port scanners, Iomega Zip and Ditto drives, Web cams, the Colorado Trakker 250 external tape device, ATAPI CD-R and CD-RW, even a clock radio. The Parallel Port Information Page at `http://www.torque.net/linux-pp.html` includes a list of links to parallel port driver projects.

There are several HOWTOs for configuring commonly used parallel port devices, such as the Iomega Zip drive. If you have a parallel port device currently unsupported by Linux, read the Linux I/O Port Programming mini HOWTOs to see how to get started writing your own driver.

Leaving the Memory Device Special File Alone

Believe it or not, Linux has a device special file to represent your computer's physical memory as a device special file — /dev/kmem. The `file` command tells you that /dev/kmem is a character special file. The device special file, /dev/mem, contains an image of your computer's physical memory. If you are a Linux wizard and brave, you can use /dev/mem to examine your physical memory and even patch the system.

If you are not a Linux wizard, and you work with /dev/kmem, you may destroy your system. One wrong keystroke is all it takes.

The device special file /dev/port is similar to /dev/mem with the I/O ports included.

Working with Tape Devices

Linux supports several types of tape drives, including streaming QIC (quarter inch cartridge) tape drives. A single tape drive may have several device special files, one for each different tape characteristic. For example, one physical tape drive may have two device special files that govern when a tape rewinds: one file for the logical rewind tape device (rewindon close — that is when your application finishes writing to a tape), another file for the logical norewind tape device (You do not want the tape to rewind when the application closes) That same physical tape drive may have other separate device special files for high density and low density. For a quarter inch streaming tape drive, for example, you may see the following files:

| /dev/rft0 | QIC 117, rewind on close |
| /dev/nrft0 | QIC 117, no rewind on close |

Tip

Most Linux installation procedures create the file /dev/tape as a symbolic link to the drive that is the system's default tape device.

Cross-Reference

Chapter 11 shows you how to use tape as a backup medium.

On the CD-ROM

The ftape HOWTO contains hints and tips for using the ftape floppy tape driver under Linux. There is a link to this HOWTO on the CD-ROM.

Adding New Hardware

When you add new devices to a Linux system you may need to configure them. If a device is fairly common, Linux probably has a device driver for it. If not, you must load the device-driver program first before you can use the hardware.

New Feature

In the next version of the kernel (2.4*x*) there is a big change in how to discover hardware. The 2.4*x* kernels will support a feature called "devfs" (a "device filesystem"). It's virtual in that it dynamically represents the state of a system as the kernel "sees" it.

Tapes and More Tapes

Linux supports several types of tape drives. The following table lists just a few commonly used device special file names for some Linux tape drives.

Device Special File	Tape Device
/dev/tpqic11	QIC-11 streaming, rewind
/dev/tnpqic11	QIC-11 streaming, norewind
/dev/rft0	QIC-117, streaming rewind
/dev/nrft0	QIC-117, streaming norewind
/dev/qft0	Floppy tape, streaming, rewind
/dev/nqft0	Floppy tape, streaming, rewind
/dev/st0	SCSI tape, rewind
/dev/nst0	SCSI tape, norewind

New Feature

kudzu, a program that detects and configures new hardware, is a new utility developed by Red Hat. It runs on Red Hat Linux 6.1 and higher. You can also download kudzu packages that run on a wide variety of other distributions, including Mandrake, Kondara Jirai, RawHide, Connectiva, ASPLinux. When you start kudzu it refers to the database, /etc/sysconfig/hwconf, to check your computer's hardware configuration. If you have added or removed hardware, kudzu enables you to configure/unconfigure and updates its hwconf database. kudzu builds its database from data in the files:

```
/etc/conf.modules (the module configuration file)
/etc/sysconfig/network-scripts/ifcfg-* (the NIC
configuration files)
/etc/X11/XF86Config (the X Window System
configuration file)
```

Visit http://rpmfind.net/linux/RPM/ to search for kudzu RPM packages.

Exploring New Device Features in the 2.4 Kernel

Just as this book was going to the printer, Linux released the 2.4 kernel. This section briefly discusses the 2.4 kernel's additions and enhancements that affect device management.

PCMCIA support has been moved into the kernel. In the 2.2 kernel, PCMCIA support required a set of user utilities available separately. By moving PCMCIA into the kernel, the performance of PCMCIA devices, especially important on laptop computers, will improve significantly.

The new kernel also supports more IDE devices, such as parallel port tape drives, large disks that run off floppy drives, and so forth. Especially useful for users with older systems is that ISA Plug and Play devices are now supported in the kernel and do not require editing obscure configuration files. Moreover, you can boot your system from such devices, say, from ISA Plug and Play IDE controller.

For Linux users coming from a UNIX environment, support for logical volume management now exists. A *logical volume* is a way to combine multiple disks for sections of multiple disks into a single, logical disk, or volume. For example, suppose you have a 1 GB disc and you create a /home partition on it using 600 MB. Then you run out of space and decide that you need 1 GB in /home. Before the 2.4 kernel, you would have to add a new disc, create a new /home, and copy the existing /home onto the new disk.

Logical volumes, and logical volume management (often abbreviated *LVM*), on the other hand, lets you add a 400MB section of an existing (or new) disk to the current /home partition. Another LVM tool allows you to resize existing filesystems LVM has long been an important feature of the major UNIX operating systems and Linux system administrators and DBAs have waited for it to appear on Linux.

Summary

Linux uses device special files to represent hardware. You initially configure hardware devices during the Linux installation procedure. The installation creates the device special files that represent the hardware that your Linux distribution supports. After installing Linux, if you need additional device special files to represent new hardware, you can use the MAKEDEV command to create device special files. Using MAKEDEV is not usually necessary; the Linux installation makes such a large set of device special files that the files you need for new devices are almost always present.

Linux categorizes device special files as *block I/O oriented* or *character I/O oriented*. Terminals are an example of character I/O oriented devices, and disk drives are an example of block I/O oriented devices. Consoles and hardwired terminals and modems are Linux serial devices — character devices that plug in to your computer's serial port. X terminals terminals are pseudo-terminals (ptys) — character devices that connect to the network. Both terminal types have sets of associated device special files.

Hard disks are both block and character I/O oriented, and therefore have a double set of device special files. Chapter 9 details hard-disk geometry and how to reconfigure disk partitions.

The new Linux 2.4 kernel further increases the breadth and depth of Linux device support.

✦   ✦   ✦

Managing Disk Devices

Disks of any kind — floppy disks, CD-ROMs, Zip disks, and even RAM disks, (which are not physical disks but areas of memory that act like disks) — perform one function: storing data. The physical and logical storage concepts that provide the foundation for this very simple function are a little more complicated. Before you can store data on a disk, you need to set the disk up so that the operating system and applications recognize where and how to place data. Getting the disks ready for data usually means partitioning them and building a filesystem in the partitions. Then you can store and retrieve data from the disks. This chapter and the next, Chapter 10, "Managing Filesystems and Swap Space," describe how to prepare disks to store data on Linux. Most of this chapter explains how to create various Linux partitioning schemes for hard disks. This chapter also tells you how to manage floppy disks, CD-ROM disks, Zip disks, and RAM disks under Linux.

Introducing Hard Disk Concepts

Your goal as a system administrator is to make it possible for users to access data. To do that, you need to create filesystems to hold the data. Before you can create filesystems, you must create partitions to hold the filesystems. Filesystems live in partitions. Partitions live on disks. These concepts lead to the idea of physical disks versus logical disks.

Understanding physical versus logical disks

As an end user, you need have no idea of how hard disks and partitions work. All you need to know is the path to your data, such as /home/miss_scarlet/files. You don't need to know on which device your data reside or what kind of device holds your data.

As a system manager, you need to know all of the above so that your users can access data without even knowing what a disk is! The first concept you need to understand is that of a physical disk versus a logical disk. The *physical disk* is the piece of hardware you hold in your hand and cable into your computer cabinet. You think of it in hardware terms — size and controller type — as something like "The 20-gigabyte IDE disk in slot number 1" or "the 10-gigabyte SCSI disk." A *logical disk* is part or all of a physical disk. Applications request data access from logical disks, such as "Get the first 100 records from the file /home/miss_scarlet/weapons." Operating system programs translate this logical I/O request into a physical I/O request that figures out where (on what block, track, sector, and cylinder) the data reside. Linux calls logical disks *partitions*. If you have four partitions on one hard disk, Linux sees that single physical disk as four separate logical disk drives.

Looking inside a hard disk

A hard disk consists of *platters* — slender magnetized disks that hold data. On each platter's surface there is a read-write head that accesses data. The platters rotate and the heads move in and out from the edge to the center of the platters. Platter rotation plus head movement allows access to all parts of all surfaces.

Examining hard-disk geometry

Many disk utilities, such as fdisk, cfdisk, and Red Hat's Disk Druid manipulate a disk's geometry. *Disk geometry* refers to disks in terms of cylinders, heads, sectors, and tracks. Figure 9-1 shows that disk surfaces are made up of concentric rings called *tracks*. Each track is subdivided into sectors. A sector is the smallest unit a disk can handle. So if you only need one byte of data, the disk controller retrieves at least one block from a sector (usually 512 bytes). Dividing the disk into tracks and sectors helps the controller find files on disk and allocate disk space for files.

If you were to take a single sector on the top platter and follow it all the way down through each platter in the drive, you have what is called a *cylinder*. Cylinders are the building blocks of hard-disk geometry. When Linux is able to place a file in the same cylinder, the heads (the instruments perform the actual reads and writes) don't have to do much in-and-out movement across tracks. The less head movement that takes place, the faster disk I/O will be.

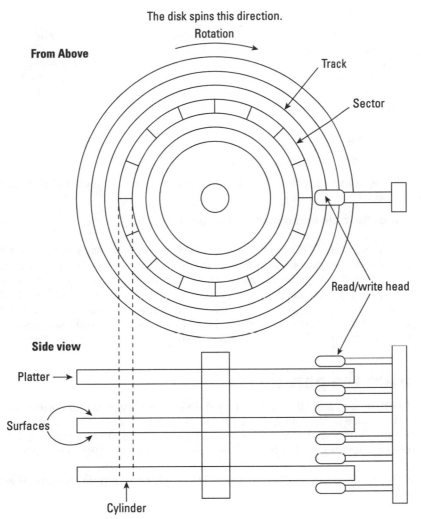

Figure 9-1: Hard-disk geometry

Adding in the controller

Each hard disk communicates with the CPU through a SCSI or IDE disk controller. The controller tells the read/write heads where to move, when to move, and how much data to read from or write to the disk. Today's smart controllers also cache data to improve I/O performance and have the ability to identify bad blocks and sectors.

Booting BIOS

When you turn on your Intel-compatible computer, the BIOS (Basic Input/Output System) program executes a quick check called the Power On Self Test (POST) to make sure that important subsystems, such as RAM, floppy and hard disks, keyboards, mice, video cards, and the CPU, are functioning properly. Next, the BIOS reads the master boot record (MBR) from the first sector of the first hard disk. The MBR includes a small program, called a *boot loader*, that

✦ Reads the partition table.

✦ Finds the active, bootable, partition.

✦ Reads the active partition's boot sector, that is, the first sector of the bootable partition.

✦ Executes the code found in the active partition's boot sector.

Why tell you about the BIOS? Even though it is completely transparent and internal to the workings of the computer, you need to know a little about the BIOS because it has a restriction that influences Linux systems. In particular, older versions of the LILO (LInux LOader) boot loader, the standard Linux boot loader, could not boot an operating system installed on cylinder 1024 or higher, which meant one had to be careful to place Linux's kernel below that limit, or the system would not boot. However, the version of LILO on this book's CD-ROM does have this limitation.

Where are the partitions?

Now that you understand the basics of hard disk geometry, you can understand the output from Linux's partitioning programs, such as fdisk and cfdisk. You need to be able to understand these geometry terms before you can even start to think about changing partitions. You have a choice of tools for repartitioning disks.

Note This choice of tools is another example of Linux giving you more than one way to perform a task.

The fdisk program has been around since time (or at least UNIX) began. There are variations on fdisk — the cfdisk and sfdisk programs — that have nicer interfaces. Red Hat Linux provides the Disk Druid to help you partition. Commercially available programs, such as PartitionMagic, make partitioning easier. All these programs let you examine partitions and change, move, and delete them. With cfdisk, you use the arrow keys to highlight the menu options you want, and press Enter to execute the command. You do not need X to run the menu-driven cfdisk. Figure 9-2 shows the basic cfdisk output for a SCSI disk (/dev/sda) with one primary and five logical partitions. You arrow or tab through the menu at the bottom to highlight the function you wish to perform. For example, to delete partition sda9, first arrow to sda9 to highlight its data line. Then you would move through the menu and highlight Delete choice, and press Enter to delete the partition.

Tip   At this point, you have not really deleted the partition; you have marked it for dele-tion. You must select the Write choice from the menu to delete the partition and return its sectors to free space. After you press Enter, you get another chance to change your mind and roll back your changes. The partitioning program prompts you to confirm the Write.

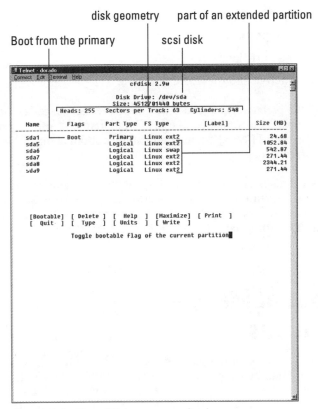

Figure 9-2: The cfdisk program displays a menu interface for managing partitions

Creating Many out of One — The Partition Story

Every Linux disk contains a partition table at the beginning of the disk, at sector 0, track 0, before any system files or user files. The Linux installation writes the parti-tion table. Programs that restructure partitions, such as Red Hat's Disk Druid, cfdisk, sfdisk, fdisk, and the commercial PartitionMagic product, write to the partition table. The partition table consists of one to four entries, one per partition (logical disk). Each entry describes the attributes of the partitions:

✦ The type of partition, a two-digit hexadecimal number that indicates the operating system and filesystem that use the partition. For example:

- Windows 95 FAT 32 = 0b
- Linux (files) = 83 or 85
- Linux (swap) = 82
- BSDI UNIX = b7 (files) or b8 (swap)

✦ The starting location of the partition.

✦ The ending location of the partition.

✦ Whether the partition is active and therefore bootable.

Tip   You can get a list of all the partition types and associated hexadecimal codes that your Linux distribution supports by running the `cfdisk` program and arrowing or tabbing over to select the choice [Type] on the menu at the bottom of the display. The list is at least two screens long.

Figure 9-3 shows two physical disks containing four logical disks. The figure pictures the hard disks with their partition tables and partitions. One hard disk has only one partition that extends across the entire disk. In this case, the logical and physical disk are the same. The other hard disk contains three partitions and some free space.

Creating Many out of Many — Partitioning Partitions

Figure 9-4 shows four possible entries in the partition table. The architecture of IBM-compatible PCs limits the number of primary partitions on hard disk to four. A *primary partition* is one that can be booted at Linux startup. However, the large disk drives now available make four partitions inefficient for normal use. A workaround exists, however. It is called an extended partition. An *extended partition* is a partition that holds other partitions called logical partitions. A *logical partition* is the actual disk space on which data will be stored. When you create an extended partition, Linux builds a special extended-partition table. Figure 9-5 shows one physical disk with an extended-partition table and logical partitions.

Tip   There is no limit to the number of logical partitions you can create on one physical hard disk. However, for performance reasons involving the management of the partitions, it is best to create no more than 12 logical partitions per physical disk.

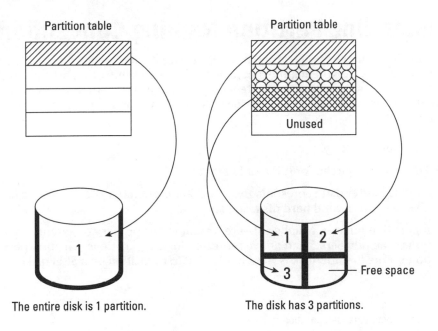

Partition table

Partition table

Unused

1 2

3 ── Free space

The entire disk is 1 partition.

The disk has 3 partitions.

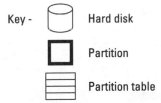

Key - Hard disk

Partition

Partition table

Figure 9-3: The partition table points to logical disks (partitions) residing on physical hard disks

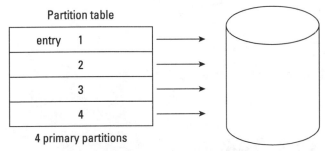

Partition table

entry	1
	2
	3
	4

4 primary partitions

Figure 9-4: Partition table with four partitions

Understanding Partition Naming Conventions

In the previous chapter, you learned how Linux uses device special files to identify hardware devices. As you might expect, Linux also represents disk partitions in the /dev directory. Each partition and extended partition has its own device special file. Figure 9-5 shows an IDE disk with four partitions, where each partition name consists of:

✦ The /dev directory.

✦ The device type (hd for IDE or sd for SCSI).

✦ A device letter that represents the physical disk number — a is the first hard disk, b is the second hard disk, and so forth.

✦ A partition number. Numbers 1–4 represent either primary or extended partitions. The numbers 5 and above represent logical partitions. The first partition on the first IDE disk is /dev/hda1. The first partition on a SCSI disk is /dev/sda1.

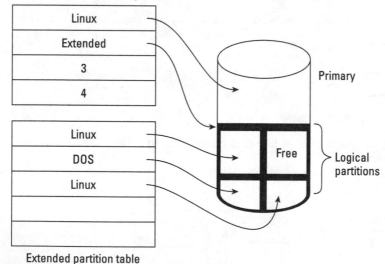

Figure 9-5: Extended and logical partitions on a disk

Repartitioning for Linux

Multiuser production systems usually need more than the single Linux and swap partitions that the most basic installation procedure creates. After you install Linux and live with it for a while, you may decide that you need more partitions.

Why repartition?

There are three reasons to repartition your disk(s) after installing Linux:

1. You need more room. Either you've run out of room on a partition and no one can add any new files to it, or you don't have enough swap space to support optimal performance for your applications.

2. You've gotten a new physical disk that you need to partition before users can create files and directories.

3. You need to improve disk I/O performance by redistributing the system and user files and directories and adding additional swap space.

During the Linux installation procedure, you created disk partitions. If you're a Linux or UNIX novice, you probably created two partitions — one for the Linux operating system and user files and one for swap space — on one hard disk. This partitioning scheme is fine for testing and learning Linux. When it comes to production systems that support many users and applications, however, this very basic partitioning scheme may be a problem because of the disadvantages described in Table 9-1.

Table 9-1
Disadvantages of Improperly Designed Disk Partitions

Disadvantage	Impact
Low availability in case of disk problems.	If your Linux partition is unavailable for any reason, your entire Linux system is unavailable.
Long backup time.	When you back up your entire disk, you can't break the backup into separate concurrent operations.
Swap disk performance.	Linux systems often perform better with more than one swap partition. Swapping to the disk with the operating system can cause a bottleneck.
Disk I/O performance.	You can't spread applications, users, and files across multiple disk drives. The Linux disk speed becomes a bottleneck.

For a small to medium production system, the following partitioning guidelines give you room for future growth:

✦ On your first physical hard disk (the system disk):

- /boot — 16 to 24 MB. This partition only contains enough data and configuration information to boot the system.

- / — 1 GB. The root partition stores all of the files necessary to have a basic, functioning Linux system after it boots.

- /usr — 2 to 3 GB. This partition contains almost all of the applications, such as editors, Web browsers, mail clients, and so forth, installed on the system.

- /var — 1 GB (depending on how many products you install). If you have a third hard drive, move /var to there.

✦ On your second physical hard disk (a user disk):

- /home

- Other user filesystems

✦ On your third hard disk (if you have one):

- /var

✦ Spread swap space (twice the size of physical memory (RAM)) across two physical disks. If you are running a large relational database system such as Oracle or Informix, make swap space three to four times the size of the physical memory. For optimum performance, put one of your swap partitions on a separate hard drive from the operating system and from very active users.

✦ If you have more than two physical hard drives, create large partitions for users — for example, user1, user2, user3.

Alternative partitioning schemes are discussed in the remaining sections of this chapter. The appendixes in the Multi-Disk-HOWTO show various partitioning examples. The HOWTO also has worksheets for you to fill out if you need to locate your partitions to get the absolute fastest disk I/O performance. This kind of fine-tuning can be helpful for benchmarking and in high-response data-entry applications. In real life, many system administrators don't have the time or the need to wring the last drop of performance out of their disks.

How to repartition

If you need to repartition disks after you install Linux, you have two main choices:

✦ Partitioning non-destructively (no risk of destroying existing data).

✦ Partitioning destructively (destroying existing data and later recovering them).

The sections below explain various non-destructive and destructive repartitioning strategies. Regardless of the software you use, the steps to repartitioning are the same:

1. Plan ahead, deciding which program you are going to use to do the repartitioning. This chapter illustrates using the cfdisk program. Whether you use fdisk, cfdisk, or sfdisk is strictly a matter of personal preference.

2. Examine your existing partitions. Find out their size, where they start and end. Figure 9-6 shows you how to use the `cfdisk` program in a terminal window to inspect your partitions. If you want to use a graphical program, you can show information from the KDE Control Panel or look at GNOME's Detailed System Information display. See Figure 9-7 for KDE's System Information display and Figure 9-8 for GNOME's Detailed System Information/Disk Information display.

3. Decide what strategy (described in the next few subsections) you are going to use to make more room and add Linux and/or swap partitions.

4. Obtain any new hardware you need.

5. Back up the data in any partition you plan to destroy and recreate.

6. Run your choice of program.

7. Repartition.

Figure 9-6: You can get detailed information by highlighting and selecting a partition from `cfdisk`'s initial partition display

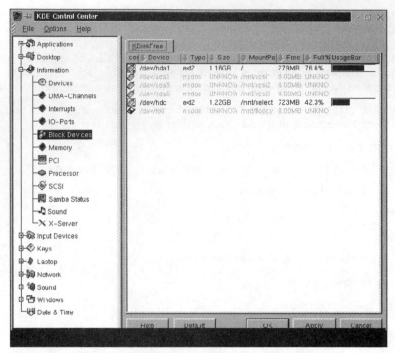

Figure 9-7: KDE System Information shows an overview of all your partitions

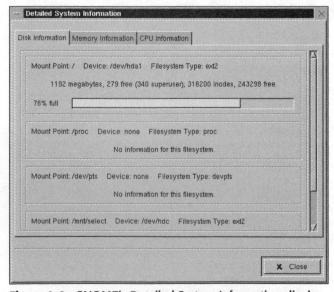

Figure 9-8: GNOME's Detailed System Information display
shows detailed information about your partitions

Tip

Call us paranoid! Even if we are non-destructively repartitioning, we back up the data. There could be some unexpected problem, such as a power failure or hardware crash, that might wreck your data.

Non-destructive repartitioning — The preferred strategy

Non-destructive enables you to make more space for Linux without destroying any existing on-disk data. When you need to add disk space for Linux, always try to do it non-destructively. To add new Linux partitions without destroying existing data you need one of the following:

✦ A new hard disk with no files or directories on it yet.

✦ Some unallocated free space.

✦ A partition you no longer need or use.

Creating Linux partitions on a new physical disk

This is the easiest way to get more space for Linux. New hard drives are affordable for most people and there is no risk of destroying data. Use your favorite partitioning software to create as many partitions as you need.

Tip

To create a new partition with `cfdisk`, select an area of free space from the display and select the menu choice New. `cfdisk` prompts you for the size of the partition and displays the maximum amount of space you have available. `cfdisk` automatically calculates the starting and ending positions of the partition for your disk's geometry. Remember to select the Write option from the menu to make your new partition permanent.

Using unallocated free space for Linux partitions

This solution is as easy and risk-free as using a new physical disk. Figure 9-9 shows one physical hard disk with free space and how it looks after using the free space for a Linux partition.

Restructuring an unused partition

In real life, it's rare to have unused partitions. Perhaps you have a partition you are using for testing another operating system. When testing finishes, you can reuse the partition for Linux. You need to follow three steps:

1. Back up the data on the partition in case you need them later (optional, but recommended).

2. Delete the partition, using `cfdisk`'s Delete menu option. `cfdisk` moves the space from the deleted partition to free space.

3. Create a Linux partition to replace the partition you just deleted, using the cfdisk New menu option.

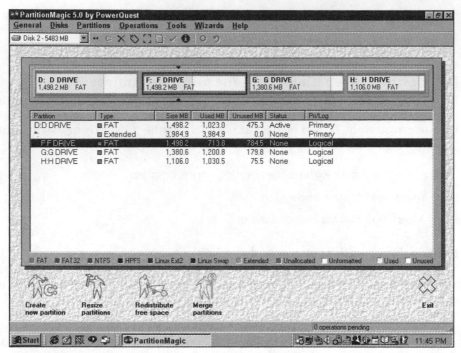

Figure 9-9: Using Partition Magic to create a Linux partition in free space keeps existing data safe

Figure 9-10 shows the hard disk before and after restructuring of an old unused Windows NT partition.

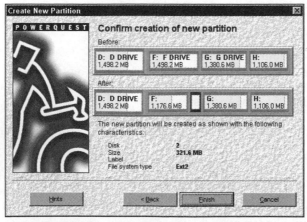

Figure 9-10: Restructuring an unused partition into Linux keeps existing data safe

Destructive repartitioning — The last resort

If you have no unallocated free space, can't buy a new disk drive, and have no unused partitions that you can reclaim, the only way to make more Linux partitions is to take space from an existing partition. This is the riskier method because you must be very careful not to destroy the existing data. Basically, you delete the large partition and build smaller partitions into its space. Follow these steps:

1. *Absolutely* back up all data in the original partition. Here's a handy form of the cp command that enables you to make a quick copy of an entire directory in a backup directory.

   ```
   cp -av original_source_directry bakup_destination_directry
   ```

2. Optionally, and admittedly paranoidly, restore the data to be sure the backup is completely functional. Backups have been known to be corrupted. Candace's rule: The more likely you are to need your backup, the more likely it is to be corrupted.

3. To resize the partition, delete it and create new partitions (cfdisk new menu option) from the resulting free space. Divide the free space into multiple new partitions according to your needs.

4. Restore the data you backed up from the original partition into one of the new partitions.

Caution   Measure twice, cut once. No matter what partitioning software you use, before you write the partition table, always double-check that your partitions do not overlap.

Cross-Reference   Chapter 32, "Monitoring and Optimizing Linux Performance," gives guidelines for spreading users and applications across multiple hard disks to reduce I/O contention and bottlenecks.

Floppy Disks

Unlike hard disks, floppy disks only have one platter. Like hard disks, though, floppy disks contain tracks and sectors. The two corresponding tracks on both sides of a floppy make up a cylinder. Most floppy disks come preformatted, and all you need to do is mount the floppy filesystem. If you need to format a floppy disk, use the fdformat command shown in the following example.

```
# fdformat /dev/fd0H1440
Double-sided, 80 tracks, 18 sec/track. Total capacity 1440 kB.
Formatting ... done
Verifying ... done
#
```

Tip

When using the `fdformat` command, you usually need to specify the exact device special file for the capacity of your floppy disk. In other words, you can't use the handy symbolic links /dev/fd0 or /dev/fd1. However, if you really want to use a symbolic, first run the `setfdprm` command to set the floppy device's parameters. The following example has the same effect as the preceding example above:

```
$ setfdprm /dev/fd0 1440/1440
$ fdformat /dev/fd0
Double-sided, 80 tracks, 18 sec/track. Total capacity
1440 kB.
Formatting ... done
Verifying ... done
$
```

If the `fdformat` command returns an error, the floppy disk probably has unreadable spots, called *bad blocks*. Usually Linux automatically locates bad blocks and works around them. If you get a read error, however, you may need to run the `badblocks` command manually to find the bad blocks and fix them, if possible, or mark them as bad so they will not be used in the future. The following `badblocks` example finds two bad blocks, numbered 718 and 719.

```
# fdformat /dev/fd0H1440
Double-sided, 80 tracks, 18 sec/track. Total capacity 1440 kB.
Formatting ... done
Verifying ... read: Unknown error
#
# badblocks /dev/fd0H1440 1440
718
719
#
```

Tip

The `badblocks` command has a verbose option, `-v`, if you want to see more detailed information. If a disk is badly damaged, you won't be able to fix the bad blocks, and you should discard the disk. You can also use the `badblocks` command on hard disks. However, modern hard disks automatically take care of bad blocks so that you never see them. If you need to run the `badblocks` command on a hard disk, your disk is probably damaged beyond repair.

CD-ROMs

You don't partition CD-ROMs because they are read-only devices. You simply mount them into the Linux directory tree. Chapter 10 shows you how to mount CD-ROMs. The device special file names for CD-ROMs vary with the manufacturer, but you can refer to the symbolic link /dev/cdrom, which points to your actual CD-ROM. The example below shows that the `ls -l` command on the CD-ROM symbolic link displays the actual CD-ROM in the far right-hand column.

```
# ls -l /dev/cdrom
lrwxrwxrwx 1  root      22 Feb 11:54 /dev/cdrom -> sonycd535
```

There are various audio CD players available for Linux. The GNOME CD Player (represented by both a window on the desktop and an icon on the panel) is an example. The CD Player lets you play audio CDs through your computer's sound card. Before you can use the CD Player, you must have read access to your CD-ROM's device file (/dev/cdrom is the link). If the CD Player fails to play your CDs, log in as root and use the following command to give all users read access to the CD-ROM device:

```
root@tweety# chmod a+r /dev/hdc
```

Caution

The preceding chmod example uses the device special file, not the symbolic link (/dev/cdrom), because symbolic links are always readable and writable by all users. The permissions on the linked file, in this case, /dev/hdc, are the permissions that have to change.

Figure 9-11 shows the GNOME CD Player interface. The buttons resemble those found on other CD Players, such as the one provided with Windows 9x or MacOS.

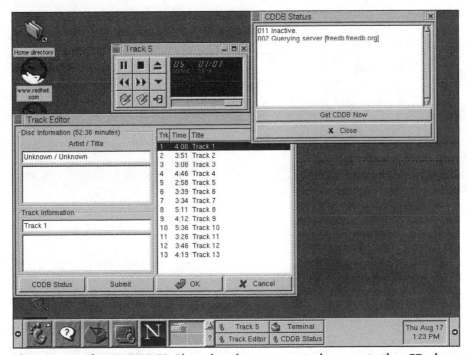

Figure 9-11: The GNOME CD Player has the same controls as most other CD players

Summary

Disk devices range from removable disks such as Zip and Jaz disks, floppies, and CD-ROMs and CD-RWss to hard disk drives on EIDE, IDE, or SCSI controllers. Linux supports all of these disk types and many more.

A partition is where the operating system writes files on a hard disk. The hard disk itself is a physical device. The partitions on the hard disk are logical devices. Therefore, partitioning lets one physical disk contain multiple logical disks. Linux partitions can be primary or extended with logical partitions. A filesystem tells the operating system what format to write the files in. Now that you understand advanced partitioning concepts and commands, go ahead to the next chapter, which explains how to create filesystems in partitions.

✦   ✦   ✦

Managing Filesystems and Swap Space

Filesystems hold directories and files. Swap space works with physical memory (RAM) to implement virtual memory (VM). When you create filesystems, you need to decide where (in what partition) to put the filesystem, what type of filesystem your environment requires, when and how the filesystem will be available, and who will be permitted to store files and directories in the new filesystem. You also need to decide which tool you want to use to build your filesystem. Your choices include the text-based programs, such as mkfs, and graphical tools such as linuxconf or COAS, depending on your Linux distribution. This chapter walks you through a case study where you add more disk space to your system. You start with four disks, *n* partitions, and *n* filesystems. The case study takes you step by step through all the work you need to do in order to make the new disk ready for users. At the end of this chapter, you have five disks, *n* partitions, and *n* filesystems. This chapter also shows you how to add additional swap space to your system in one of the new partitions you create.

Creating Filesystems

Disk partitions contain either filesystems or swap space. In addition to its native ext2fs filesystem, Linux also supports many other filesystems, including FAT, FAT32, VFAT, NT, HPFS, and more. Like all modern operating systems, Linux also utilizes swap space, using either a swap file (like Windows) or, more often, a disk partition specifically designed as swap space.

Cross-Reference   Chapter 9 explains how to build raw, uninitialized disk sectors into partitions that function as logical disks.

One or more filesystems hold the Linux directory hierarchy. No matter how many files, directories, and disks are on your Linux system, they all make up a single directory hierarchy. The Linux directory hierarchy is an upside down tree: / is the root, other directories make up the branches and twigs, and the files are the leaves. A filesystem is a group of directories and files on the Linux directory tree. Figure 10-1 shows one filesystem on the Linux directory tree.

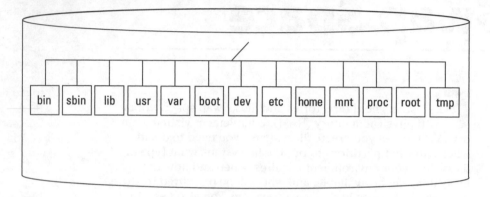

Generic Linux Directory Tree
1 Filesystem, 1 Hard Disk

Figure 10-1: This Linux directory tree only has one filesystem

Getting started

You need to follow these steps to create a new filesystem:

1. Plan ahead.

    a. Decide on a filesystem type.

    b. Determine how much space you need for your new filesystem.

    c. Choose or create an empty directory to function as the new filesystem's mount point.

    d. Decide on what attributes your new filesystem needs.

2. Find or create a partition for your filesystem.

3. Make the new filesystem with the `mke2fs` command.

4. Mount the new filesystem into the Linux directory tree with the `mount` command.

5. Create any needed subdirectories and files in your new filesystem with the `mkdir` command.

6. Set file and directory ownerships and permissions in your new filesystem with the `chown`, `chmod`, and `chgrp` commands.

Planning your filesystems

By default, the Linux installation procedure automatically creates one filesystem for you—the root filesystem in the / directory. All other directories and files reside under / in the root filesystem. Unless you set up your Linux system as a single user workstation or a very small server with only a few users, you should add additional filesystems to improve performance and make system maintenance easier. Adding other filesystems doesn't necessarily mean changing the structure of the directory tree. By adding other filesystems, you are allowing the tree to consist of several grafts instead of being one monolithic tree. You may also need to access data on floppy disk or CD-ROM filesystems. Figure 10-2 shows the same Linux directory tree as Figure 10-1. The difference between the two figures is that Figure 10-2 uses four filesystems to create the same tree.

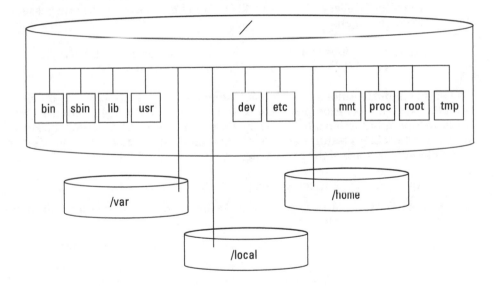

Generic Linux Directory Tree
4 Filesystems (/home, /local, /var, /) on their own disks

Figure 10-2: Four filesystems build this Linux directory tree

If a tree loses a limb, the other limbs and root can still live and grow. The same is true of the Linux directory tree. If you lose a single filesystem, some files and directories become inaccessible. However, users can still function and do at least some of their work with the files and directories that remain.

Caution

All filesystems depend on the directories and files in /, the root filesystem. No tree, whether a Linux directory tree or a living tree, can survive without roots. If the Linux root becomes inaccessible, all of Linux becomes inaccessible. Mirroring the root filesystem (maintaining an exact copy) helps to ensure that the root will always be available. You can read more about mirroring in Chapter 32, "Monitoring and Optimizing Linux Performance."

Choosing a filesystem type

Before you build a filesystem in a partition, you need to decide what type of filesystem to create. Linux supports several filesystem types. The filesystem type determines how Linux structures and formats data in the partitions. By default, the Linux installation procedure creates one filesystem, /, of the native type ext2fs (second extended filesystem). The ext2fs is the only filesystem that provides native Linux security using traditional UNIX file ownership and file permissions. ext2fs is the most commonly used and feature-rich Linux filesystem. Other filesystem types may "fake" some of these security features, but they do so poorly. For example, in an MS/DOS filesystem root owns all files, regardless of who creates them. This is because the MS/DOS filesystem has no file ownership, so the Linux kernel assumes that root owns the files.

Tip

You can find bug fixes and enhancements to ext2fs programs at the MIT Web site, `http://web.mit.edu/tytso/www/linux/e2fsprogs.html`.

Linux also supports various "foreign" filesystem for file compatibility with other operating systems. For example, in Linux, you can read and write files from Microsoft Windows operating systems because Linux supports the MS/DOS filesystem. Foreign filesystems lack Linux features and have limitations when compared to Linux's own ext2fs filesystem. Some of the foreign filesystems that Linux supports are:

MS/DOS	For compatibility with FAT filesystems.
umsMS/DOS	An extended MS/DOS filesystem that allows long filenames, file ownership, and permissions.
vfat	An MS/DOS filesystem that allows long filenames.
iso9660	The international standard CD-ROM filesystem with the Rock Ridge extensions that allow long filenames and permissions.
hpfs	The OS/2 high-performance filesystem.
nfs	A networked filesystem that enables many computers (possibly running different operating systems) on a network to share one file system.

Cross-Reference

This chapter describes local filesystems. Chapter 22, "Configuring the Network Filesystem," describes NFS filesystems and how to create and maintain them.

What Filesystems are Available on your Computer?

Different Linux systems may support different filesystems, depending on how you installed Linux and whether or not you edited your kernel or loaded any dynamic modules. Filesystems are either built into your kernel or are dynamically loadable modules.

Loadable modules are device drivers, including filesystems that you can add to memory at runtime instead of building permanently into the kernel. Chapter 28 shows you how to load filesystem support dynamically.

Display the contents of the file /proc/filesystems to find out which filesystems are built in to your kernel. The following example shows how to use the cat command (in a terminal window or at a non-graphical console) to display built-in filesystems. Your output may differ depending on whether you've added or removed filesystems from your kernel.

```
# cat /proc/filesystems
        ext2
nodev   proc
        iso9660
nodev   devpts
```

To find out which loadable filesystems are active on your computer, list the contents of the subdirectory under /lib/modules for the version of your kernel.

The nodev option above means to treat device special files regular filenames as opposed to special files associated with a device.

The following example shows how to list your loadable modules directory by inserting the regular expression `uname -r` into the ls command. The backticks surround the uname -r command, which expands to the version of your kernel.

```
# ls -l /lib/modules/`uname -r`/fs
total 842
-rw-r--r-- 1 root   root   14824 Sep 27 1999 autofs.o
-rw-r--r-- 1 root   root    6516 Sep 27 1999 infmt_aout.o
-rw-r--r-- 1 root   root    3136 Sep 27 1999 binfmt_java.o
-rw-r--r-- 1 root   root    6080 Sep 27 1999 binfmt_misc.o
-rw-r--r-- 1 root   root   77665 Sep 27 1999 coda.o
-rw-r--r-- 1 root   root   44662 Sep 27 1999 fat.o
-rw-r--r-- 1 root   root   84788 Sep 27 1999 hfs.o
-rw-r--r-- 1 root   root   13604 Sep 27 1999 hpfs.o
-rw-r--r-- 1 root   root   50412 Sep 27 1999 lockd.o
-rw-r--r-- 1 root   root   33526 Sep 27 1999 minix.o
-rw-r--r-- 1 root   root   10413 Sep 27 1999 MS/DOS.o
-rw-r--r-- 1 root   root   43449 Sep 27 1999 ncpfs.o
-rw-r--r-- 1 root   root   44107 Sep 27 1999 nfs.o
```

Tip   The filesystem that you choose to make inside a partition depends on the situation. The best filesystem to choose for general Linux operations and performance is ext2fs. However, if you need to manage data to share across operating systems, choose the foreign filesystem that is compatible with the data.

Deciding how much space you need for your new filesystem

The amount of space you need for your filesystem depends on what kind of files and data users plan to store. If you are creating a filesystem wherein programmers will store multiple listings, binary files, and test data, be sure to build in lots of extra space. Programmers usually need lots of disk space. You can allocate less space to casual users, such as those who use the Internet mostly to surf the Web and read and write e-mail. If the filesystem is going to store application data files, be sure to check with the developers to see what kind of space requirements the applications have. For example, a relational database system usually needs enough filesystem space to support large files.

Tip   Relational database systems usually reside in filesystems. However, it is possible to build certain relational databases in raw partitions. Work with the DBA (Database Administrator) to see what the database storage plan is.

Deciding on what attributes your new filesystem needs

When you create a filesystem, you can set the attributes, such as read and write privileges, whether regular users can mount the filesystem, and so on. You can also accept the Linux default options, which include read-write and mountable only by root.

Attaching your disk drive — the hardware side

When you buy a new disk drive, be sure Linux supports it.

On the CD-ROM   The CD-ROM included with this book contains the Linux Hardware Compatibility HOWTO. If you don't find your drive on the list, browse the Web site for your distribution to see the most current hardware compatibility list.

After you install your new drive in your computer, boot Linux and look for a message saying that Linux recognizes your new disk. The format of the message will vary depending on whether you've attached an IDE or a SCSI drive. If the messages zoom by too quickly on the screen, use the dmesg command to review them or check the boot messages in the system log. If you've used a Linux-supported hard drive and controller, the kernel sees your drive.

Cross-Reference   Chapter 28, "Rebuilding the Kernel," describes how to rebuild a Linux kernel.

Attaching your disk drive — the Linux software side

After the kernel recognizes your new disk hardware, you need to make sure that a device special file exists for the new device. Suppose this new disk is the sixth SCSI disk you've attached. The device special files in /dev for SCSI disks 1–5 already exist (/dev/sda through /dev/sde). You need to check the directory listing for /dev/sdf.

Finding a Partition to Hold a New Filesystem

When you installed Linux, you defined at least one disk partition. If you created extra partitions for future growth, you can build a filesystem in one of those unused partitions. If you have neither a new disk nor an unused partition, you need to appropriate some space away from other partitions or unallocated free space, create a partition from the space you just grabbed, and build a filesystem in the new partition.

 Cross-Reference Chapter 9, "Managing Disk Devices," describes how to create partitions.

Once you have added a disk and created the filesystems, the next thing to do is to tell Linux about them. Although the kernel knows the disk is there, it does not know what to do with it. Use the following steps to incorporate the new disk into your system.

1. Check the integrity of the newly created filesystems. The -f option tells e2fsck to check the filesystem even though it appears to be intact.

```
# e2fsck -f /dev/hdd5
# e2fsck -f /dev/hdd6
# e2fsck -f /dev/hdd7
# e2fsck -f /dev/hdd8
# e2fsck -f /dev/hdd9
```

2. Create the mount points.

```
# mkdir /home/detectives
# mkdir /home/hackers
# mkdir /home/programmers
# mkdir /home/suspects
# mkdir /home/victims
```

3. Edit /etc/fstab and add these lines:

```
/dev/hdd5   /home/detectives    ext2   defaults   2 1
/dev/hdd6   /home/hackers       ext2   defaults   2 1
/dev/hdd7   /home/programmers   ext2   defaults   2 1
/dev/hdd8   /home/suspects      ext2   defaults   2 1
/dev/hdd9   /home/victims       ext2   defaults   2 1
```

4. Mount the partitions.

```
# mount /dev/hdd5
# mount /dev/hdd6
# mount /dev/hdd7
# mount /dev/hdd8
# mount /dev/hdd9
```

5. Create any needed subdirectories and files in your new filesystem with the mkdir command.

6. Set file and directory ownerships and permissions in your new filesystem with the chown, chmod, and chgrp commands.

Formatting (creating) the new filesystem with the mke2fs command

Building a filesystem into a partition is similar to formatting a disk under MS-DOS. You can use either the `mkfs` (make filesystem) or the `mke2fs` (make ext2fs) command to format filesystems into your partitions.

Caution   Be very sure that you are formatting your new filesystem into an empty partition. If you format a new filesystem over an existing filesystem, the existing filesystem and all its data will be destroyed.

The `mke2fs` command formats ext2fs filesystems only. The `mke2fs` syntax is

    mke2fs [options] device [block-count]

where *device* is the device special file for the partition that you are formatting, and *block-count* is the number of blocks on that device. Specifying the block-count is optional because `mke2fs` automatically calculates the correct filesystem size. Other `mke2fs` options include:

-b	The number of bytes in each block of the filesystem.
-f	The number of bytes in each fragment (ignored by `mke2fs`).
-c	Check the device for bad blocks before creating the filesystem.
-i	The number of bytes each inode should manage.
-n	The number of inodes that Linux should reserve for the filesystem.
-m	The percentage of blocks reserved for the root user (overhead).
-s	The sparse-super-flag, either 1 (on) or 0 (off). Do not use "on" (1) with kernels version 2.0 or less. Only some 2.1 kernels support the "on" value. All 2.2 kernels support "on."
-v	Display verbose messages.
-L	Set the specified volume label for the filesystem.
-S	Reinitialize superblock and group descriptors.

The following examples create filesystems on IDE (hd) disk 4 (d). The partitions are numbered 5–7.

    # mke2fs -c /dev/hdd5
    # mke2fs -c /dev/hdd6
    # mke2fs -c /dev/hdd7

The `mkfs` command originated with UNIX and works with Linux as well. You use the `-t` option to tell `mkfs` what type of filesystem to make. For example, if you use `mkfs` to format an ext2 filesystem, you need to type:

    # mkfs -t ext2 /dev/hdf7

For our case study, we need a partition of type MS/DOS to hold files that we can read on both Linux and MS-DOS. The example below creates an MS/DOS filesystem on the new hard drive's partition 8:

```
# mkfs -t msdos /dev/hdd8
```

1. **Choose or create an empty directory to function as the new filesystem's mount point.** Now that you have filesystems, you need to make them available to users. Do this by mounting them into the existing directory tree. The Linux directory tree is a collection of connected filesystems. The filesystems can be of various types. To *mount* is to connect a filesystem to the Linux directory tree. To *umount* is to disconnect a file from the Linux directory tree.

Umounting is not a word you can find in an English dictionary. It comes from the Linux command umount, which means unmount or dismount. This book uses the term umounting to remind you not to type "un" when using the umount command.

When you connect a filesystem to the Linux directory tree, you mount that filesystem into a directory called a *mount point*. The Linux boot procedure always mounts the root filesystem into the / directory.

Create an empty directory to serve as a filesystem mount point. Linux allows the mount point directory to contain files. However, if you mount a filesystem into a mount point that contains files, you must hide the files until you umount the filesystem. Mounting a filesystem on top of files does not destroy the files.

2. Mount the new filesystem into the Linux directory tree with the mount command. The mount command will also report the filesystem types and any options (readonly, synchronous, and so on) in effect on these. You might have to use the fdisk -l command to find any unmounted filesystems (that might not be listed in your /etc/fstab file) under Linux. Solaris has a similar command called prvtoc (print volume table of contents).

3. Create any necessary subdirectories and files in your new filesystem with the mkdir command.

4. Set file and directory ownerships and permissions in your new filesystem with the chown, chmod, and chgrp commands.

Mounting Filesystems Automatically

When Linux starts, it automatically mounts all filesystems listed in the file system table (fstab) in the file /etc/fstab. You can control which local and remote filesystems should be mounted automatically at boot time by editing the fstab.

Mounting local filesystems automatically

When you install Linux, the installation program creates the fstab (/etc/fstab) to specify what filesystems should be automatically mounted when the system boots. The following is a typical /etc/fstab file:

```
# /etc/fstab: File system Table for mounting at boot time.
#
# filesystem   mount point       fs type       options dump pass
/dev/hda2      /                 ext2          defaults 0      1
/dev/hda3      none              swap          sw       0      0
/dev/cdrom     /cdrom            iso9660 ro
proc           /proc             proc          defaults 0      0
```

Tip   The first three lines (starting with hash characters) are comments. I like to insert the column headings to remind me of what I'm looking at.

Each of the next three lines specifies a filesystem to be mounted at system startup. Each entry in the fstab consists of six columns:

✦ *Filesystem* — The partition that holds the filesystem.

✦ *Mount point* — The directory that holds the filesystem.

✦ *Fs type* — The type of the filesystem, such as swap, ext2fs, and so forth.

✦ *Options* — Special mounting options, separated by commas if there are multiple options. Options include:

  • defaults — Default options that work for most filesystems. For details, see the man page for mount.

  • errors=remount-ro — Mount the filesystem for read-only access if fs2k finds errors.

  • sw — Swap partition.

  • ro — Read only. Always mount a CD-ROM as ro.

  • noauto — Do not automatically mount the filesystem at startup. This option has the same effect as not including the filesystem in /etc/fstab.

  • user — Enables any user to mount the filesystem. Without this option, only root can mount the filesystem.

✦ *Dump flag* — Whether the dump command creates a backup of the filesystem or not. Either 0 or no value says not to dump (back up) the filesystem.

✦ *Pass flag* — The order in which fsck checks filesystems at boot time. Either 0 or no value says not to fsck the file.

Tip   Use a pass value of 1 for the root filesystem (/) so that fsck checks it first. Use 2 for other filesystems.

Tip

While the system administrator should mount most filesystems, you might want to allow users to mount the floppy disk with the following fstab entry:

```
/dev/fd0        /mnt/floppy   vfat    noauto,user
```

Using /mnt for temporary mounts

Each time you change CD-ROMs you need to umount and mount the device (/dev/cdrom). The example below mounts the CD as an iso9660 format with the read-only (`ro`) option onto the /mnt directory.

```
root@flyingpenguin# mount -t iso9660 -o ro /dev/cdrom /mnt
```

Figure 10-3 shows the mounted filesystems before and after the root user mounts the CD-ROM.

BEFORE

root@flyingpenguin# mount
/dev/hda1 on / type ext2 (rw)
/proc on /proc type proc (rw)
/dev/hda5 on /local type ext2 (rw)

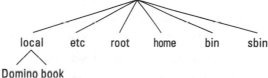

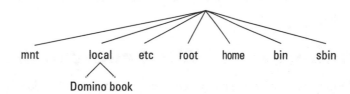

AFTER

root@flyingpenguin# mount –t iso9660 –o ro /dev/cdrom /mnt
root@flyingpenguin# mount
/dev/hda1 on / type ext2 (rw)
/proc on /proc type proc (rw)
/dev/hda5 on /local type ext2 (rw)
devpts on /dev/pts type devpts (rw,gid=5,mode=620)
/dev/hdc on /mnt type iso9660 (ro)

Figure 10-3: Before and after mounting the CD-ROM

Linux only displays messages if the CD fails to mount correctly. The Linux installation creates the /mnt directory specifically for temporary mounts. You do not have to use /mnt. It is just a Linux convenience. You can mount the CD into any directory you want.

Repairing Corrupted Filesystems after Power Failures or Hardware Problems

Linux is one of the most stable operating systems. However, even stable operating systems may crash unexpectedly — perhaps because of a power outage or a bad application. If your system crashes, your file systems are not properly umounted. When your system reboots, the fsck (filesystem check) program runs automatically to check each of your filesystems for errors. Most of the time, the file system check can detect and repair filesystem problems automatically.

Occasionally (very rarely), a serious hardware problem, such as a bad hard drive or corrupted memory chip, may damage a filesystem. If fsck can not repair the damaged filesystem (unless it is the root filesystem), it displays a message about the damage, and the boot procedure leaves you in single-user mode or in a recovery shell so that you can try to repair the damage manually. If the root filesystem is ruined, you must reboot into your distribution's recovery shell, such as the standalone shell (sash), and try to fix the problem without mounting the root filesystem.

Tip   Be prepared for emergencies such as a non-recoverable filesystem. Be sure to have the following recovery resources available:

The boot/root emergency disk set, and/or

The LILO emergency boot disk, and

A recent backup copy of your important files — just in case!

Mounting Non-Native Filesystems

Mounting non-native filesystems on a Linux system is comparable to mounting a native one with these differences: Non-native filesystems do not support the same options as the ext2 filesystem or, in some cases, what an option means with respect to the ext2 filesystem is not the same as what it means when applied to, for example, an OS/2 HPFS filesystem.

Caution   Be sure your kernel has support (either built-in or loaded) for the filesystem you want to mount. For example, Linux boot messages show that the fd0 device is recognized, but if you try to mount /dev/fd0 without kernel support, you get a message telling you that the filesystem is not supported.

Working in the Standalone Shell (sash)

sash is a shell that contains built-in commands that you can execute even if all filesystems, including the root, are umounted. Working in sash is useful when you need to recover from certain system failures, including filesystem failures. For example, if your fstab file becomes corrupted and booting fails, you can use the built-in `-ed` command to edit the fstab file and fix the problem. Generally a built-in command begins with a hyphen (or minus) (-) to distinguish it from the regular Linux program of the same name. For example, if you type `ls`, you are trying to invoke the /bin/ls program. Typing `-ls` means you want to run the built-in sash form of the command. Table 10-1 lists the built-in commands that sash supports.

<table>
<tr><td colspan="2" align="center">Table 10-1
Built-in sash Commands</td></tr>
<tr><td>*Command*</td><td>*Function*</td></tr>
<tr><td>`help`</td><td>Displays the list of built-in commands and their usage.</td></tr>
<tr><td>`alias`</td><td>Displays or defines an alias for a command.</td></tr>
<tr><td>`aliasall`</td><td>Defines aliases for all of the built-in commands that begin with a dash (-).</td></tr>
<tr><td>`unalias`</td><td>Turns off the specified alias.</td></tr>
<tr><td>`cd`</td><td>Changes the working directory.</td></tr>
<tr><td>`exec`</td><td>Executes a specified program, replacing sash.</td></tr>
<tr><td>`exit`</td><td>Exits from sash.</td></tr>
<tr><td>`prompt`</td><td>Displays a prompt and reads the input.</td></tr>
<tr><td>`setenv`</td><td>Defines environment variables.</td></tr>
<tr><td>`source`</td><td>Execute commands in the specified script.</td></tr>
<tr><td>`umask`</td><td>Sets the mask for setting default permissions.</td></tr>
<tr><td>`-chattr`</td><td>Changes ext2fs attributes on the files specified.</td></tr>
<tr><td>`-chgrp`</td><td>Changes the group ID for files.</td></tr>
<tr><td>`-chmod`</td><td>Changes the permissions for files (accepts octal permissions only).</td></tr>
<tr><td>`-chown`</td><td>Changes the ownership uid for files.</td></tr>
<tr><td>`-cmp`</td><td>If two files are different, compares file attributes such as size and byte counts.</td></tr>
<tr><td>`-cp`</td><td>Copies files.</td></tr>
<tr><td>`-dd`</td><td>Copies files (more options and complexity than `-cp`).</td></tr>
<tr><td>`-echo`</td><td>Echoes the arguments supplied, expanding wild cards.</td></tr>
<tr><td>`-ed`</td><td>Runs the editor in line mode, not full screen mode.</td></tr>
<tr><td>`-file`</td><td>Displays file types and attributes.</td></tr>
<tr><td>`-find`</td><td>Finds files that meet the conditions specified in the command options.</td></tr>
<tr><td>`-grep`</td><td>Searches for patterns in files.</td></tr>
</table>

Continued

	Table 10-1 *(continued)*
Command	***Function***
-gzip	Compresses files into archives using the gzip algorithm.
-gunzip	Unzips (decompresses) gzipped archives.
-kill	Sends a signal to a process or list of processes.
-ln	Creates hard and symbolic links.
-ls	Displays directory listings.
-lsattr	Displays file attributes for ext2fs files (dashes mean attributes are not set).
-mkdir	Creates directories.
-mknod	Creates a device special file.
-more	Displays file contents one page at a time.
-mount	Mounts a filesystem.
-mv	Moves files from source to destination. Performs renaming.
-printenv	Displays the values of all the environment variables.
-pwd	Displays the current working directory.
-rm	Removes files.
-rmdir	Removes directories.
-sum	Calculates checksum for a file.
-sync	Performs a sync system service to write dirty blocks to disk.
-tar	Creates, lists, and extracts files from a tar archive.
-touch	Creates a file.
-umount	Umounts a filesystem.
-where	Displays the path of a program that lies on the PATH environment variable.

Each physical disk drive has a name that indicates how it's connected to the computer. The device names are as follows:

/dev/hda	IDE disk—primary master
/dev/hdb	IDE disk—primary slave
/dev/hdc	IDE disk—secondary master
/dev/hdd	IDE disk—secondary slave
/dev/sda	SCSI disk 1

/dev/sdb	SCSI disk 2
/dev/sdc	SCSI disk 3
... ...	
/dev/sdg	SCSI disk 7
... ...	

When a disk is divided into partitions, the Linux device name is extended by the addition of the partition number. The partition device names are as follows:

/dev/hda1	First partition on IDE disk 1
/dev/hda5	Fifth partition on IDE disk 1
/dev/hdb2	Second partition on IDE disk 2
/dev/hdc6	Sixth partition on IDE disk 3

Configuring and Assigning Disk Quotas

After you create a filesystem, you may decide to restrict how much of that filesystem any user or group can use. You do this by assigning disk quotas.

Tip   Even though Linux calls them *disk quotas,* the quotas are really on filesystem usage.

Checking the kernel for quota support

You need quota support in the kernel before you can assign disk quotas. Nearly every Linux distribution includes kernel support for disk quotas, but you should do a sanity check to be absolutely sure quota support is there. If you are compiling your kernel from source code, answer to the CONFIG_QUOTA option when you run the kernel configuration tool that comes with your distribution.

Disk Rule #1

No matter how much disk space you have, users will fill it up faster than you expect.

Disk quotas limit the amount of disk space each person can use. You can limit disk space on a per-user or per-group basis. For example, if you know that programmers keep lots of old (unneeded) copies of files, you can restrict each individual programmer to a certain amount of space. Or you can add all the programmers to a group, restrict the amount of space available to the entire group, and let the programmers work out space usage within their group.

Checking that you have the quota packages

Most distributions include the quota packages. As with kernel support, it's worth-
while to do a sanity check to be sure the packages are there. You can use your distribution's package manager to check. The following example uses rpm (the -qa
options query all installed packages) to check through all packages and pipes the
output through grep to search for the string quota.

```
root@flyingpenguin# rpm -qa | grep quota
quota-1.66-11
```

Configuring the filesystem for quotas

Even though they are called "disk quotas," you enforce quotas on a per-filesystem
basis. You do this by editing the filesystem's entry in /etc/fstab. You must also create quota files for either group or user or both in the /home directory. The touch
commands shown in the following listing create the file and the chmod command
sets rw file access permissions on both group and user quota files.

Package Managers

Remember that Linux provides you with multiple ways to do your work. Some distributions
provide both rpm and their own package manager. For example, the rpm command in the
preceding example came from tweety, a Caldera OpenLinux eServer. The following example
comes from the same computer's graphical kpackage that runs under COAS.

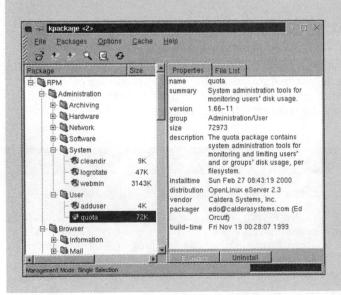

```
root@tweety# touch /home/quota.group
root@tweety# touch /home/quota.user
root@tweety# chmod 600 /quota.group /quota.user
```

Managing disk quotas

Managing disk quotas involves enabling and disabling quotas on filesystems, monitoring how much space users are using, enabling users to check how much of their quotas they've used and how much of their quotas remain, and setting and changing users' quotas.

Enabling and disabling disk quotas

You use the quotaon and quotaoff commands to turn disk quotas on and off. The syntax is as follows:

```
/usr/etc/quotaon [-vug] filesystem . . . filesystem
/usr/etc/quotaoff [-vuga] filesystem . . . filesystem
```

The quotaon command enables disk quotas on one or more filesystems that you specify. The quota files listed in the section, "Configuring the filesystem for quotas," must exist before can you run the quotaon command.

The quotaoff command disables disk quotas on the filesytems you specify. Table 10-2 lists the options you can use with the quotaon and quotaoff commands.

Table 10-2
quotaon and quotaoff Options

Command	Option	Function
quotaon	-a	Verify that all the read-write filesystems in the fstab that are marked with the quota flag should have quotas enabled.
	-v	Display a message as quotas for each filesystem are enabled.
	-u	*User quotas*: Enable per-user quotas (this is the default option).
	-g	Enable group quotas.
quotaoff	-a	Disable quotas on all filesystems in the fstab.
	-v	Display messages for each filesystem when quotas are disabled.
	-u	Disable user quotas.
	-g	Disable group quotas.

Only root can turn quotas on and off. The following commands enable and disable quotas for all filesystems with quotas flagged in the fstab:

```
root@tweety# quotaon -a
root@tweety# quotaoff -a
```

Tip   Although -u (user quotas) is the default, I included it in the command anyway. When writing scripts, always specify all options, even the defaults. This makes it easier to edit and maintain the scripts later.

Assigning quotas to users and groups

Use the edquota command to set quotas for users and groups. Only root can assign quotas. The edquota command reads the quota definitions from the quota file and runs either vi or your default editor (EDITOR variable) so that you can edit quota values. Since the quota files are in machine-readable format, you must use the edquota command to edit those files. The only options on the edquota command are -u (user) and -g (group). Running edquota for new user kendunca, who has not yet created any files, generates the following vi output:

```
root@tweety# edquota /user.quota

Quotas for user kendunca
/dev/hda2: blocks in use: 0, limits(soft = 0, hard = 0)
        inodes in use: 0, limits (soft = 0, hard = 0)
~
~
~
"/tmp/EdP.aTQjGBh" 3 lines, 130 characters
```

Running edquota performs the following operations:

✦ Extracts the quota definition for the user or group that you specify into a temporary file.

✦ Invokes an editor so that you can edit the temporary file.

✦ Stores the edited entry in the quota file.

Tip   Only edit the hard and soft limits and the grace period. The soft limit is the lower space limit at which the quota system warns the user. The hard limit is the space limit beyond which the user can have no more space. Any user who tries to create a file after hitting the hard limit gets an error message. This can occur at inconvenient and sometimes surprising times. For example, a user can get a *quota exceeded* message when sending e-mail. The user may wonder what this has to do with e-mail since he or she is not creating any files. Wrong! The e-mail program tries to create a temporary file in the user's directory. When the temporary file creation fails, the user receives the *quota exceeded* message.

The grace period is the time to wait before warning the user that he or she has exceeded the soft limit. If you use a grace period of one day, the user learns quickly about the overage and has time to clean up files before hitting the hard limit.

Caution   Editing any field beside the hard and soft limits can corrupt your quota files.

If you want to limit the number of files a user can store instead of the amount of space a user can take up, set a quota for inodes. Inodes are filesystem structures that point to files. If a user's quota is 100 inodes (file pointers), a user can have no more than 100 files in a quota-enabled filesystem, regardless of space usage. The system administrator can edit the kendunca entry to look like this:

```
Quotas for user kendunca
/dev/hda2: blocks in use: 0,limits(soft = 1000,hard =512
    inodes in use: 0, limits (soft = 10 , hard = 5)
~
~
~
-- INSERT --
```

After the system administrator saves the quota file and runs the quotacheck command, the user, kendunca, can use between 512 and 1000 disk blocks to create between five and 10 files.

Note   Usual practice places quotas on disk blocks and leaves inode quotas at 0 (unlimited).

Checking on quota usage

Any user can check how much quota he or she has used with the quota command. The root user can check any user's quota by using the -u option on the quota command. The quota command displays the user's hard and soft limits and how many 1024-byte disk blocks the user is currently using. See the following example.

```
kendunca@tweety$ quota
Disk quotas for user kendunca (uid 502):
Filesystem blocks quota limit grace files quota limitgrace
/dev/hda2      172  1000  1500  none  6    0    0
```

The repquota program generates a quota-usage report like the following:

```
root@tweety# repquota -vau
```

The quotacheck program scans filesystems for files and directories owned by users and groups subject to quotas, and updates the quota files. As root, you should run quotacheck automatically as part of the Linux boot procedure to keep your quota file(s) up to date. You can also run quotacheck manually, as in the following example:

```
root@tweety# quotacheck
Scanning /dev/hda2 [/] done
Checked 1680 directories and 24020 files
Using quotafile /quota.user
Updating in-core user quotas
Using quotafile /quota.group
```

Note   The options for the `quotacheck` program include the same options as for other quota programs: `-a`, `-v`, `-u`, `-g`. `quotacheck` also uses the `-R` option together with `-a`, which checks all filesystems except /, and the `-d` option, to display debug information, such as inode and hard-link information.

Setting up automatic quota checking at boot time

You should customize your Linux initialization procedure so that each time the system boots it automatically enables quotas and checks for users who exceed their quotas. Some distributions automatically check quotas and turn quotas on at boot time. For example, both Caldera OpenLinux and Red Hat Linux do this. Look in the /etc/rc.d/rc*.d/*quota files to see the complete scripts that run at boot time and as you change run levels.

Caution   Large downloads can fail because they use more space than a user's disk quota allows. If users have this problem regularly, you need to increase their quotas or disable disk quotas. Another workaround is to have users download to the /tmp directory. Then you can move the files to another directory. Remember that the Linux boot procedure cleans out /tmp, so downloaded files may disappear. On the other hand, if your system is a server that is usually up and running, too many large downloaded files in /tmp may eventually fill your filesystem.

When is a filesystem not a filesystem?

/proc is called a *virtual filesystem* because it exists only in memory. It uses no disk space, yet it behaves like any other filesystem. The following example shows a listing of the /proc filesystem.

```
[/proc]$ ls
1      420    4812   5146   cmdline        interrupts   mdstat       pci         sys
2      433    4813   525    cpuinfo        ioports      meminfo      rtc         tty
3      440    4814   526    devices        kcore        misc         scsi        uptime
399    447    4853   527    dma            kmsg         modules      self        version
4      466    5      528    fb             ksyms        mounts       slabinfo
402    474    5130   529    filesystems    loadavg      mtrr         sound
412    4810   5132   530    fs             locks        net          stat
416    4811   5135   bus    ide            mca          partitions   swaps
[/proc]$
```

The numbered filenames are different on every computer. The numbers are directory names that represent processes running on the computer at the time that you execute the listing. The file self in the example above is a link to the process that is executing the `ls` command. The next listing shows a directory listing for process 5132. Each file stores information that the operating system uses to keep track of the process. The cmdline file, for example, records the command line that started the process. The cwd file contains links to the current working directory for process 5132. The status file tracks the process ID, the parent's process ID, the shell the process is using, the process state, the user OD (UID) and group ID (GID) for the process, and the process' virtual memory usage (Vm). The next listing shows the contents of the status file for process 5132. Table 10-3 describes what some of the /proc process files represent.

```
[/proc]$ ls 5132
cmdline  cpu  cwd  environ  exe  fd  maps  mem  root  stat
statm  status
[/proc]$
 [/proc/5132]$ cat status
Name:    mutt
State:   S (sleeping)
Pid:     5132
PPid:    5130
Uid:     501       501      501       501
Gid:     100       100      100       100
Groups:  100
VmSize:      1980 kB
VmLck:          0 kB
VmRSS:       1220 kB
VmData:       156 kB
VmStk:         16 kB
VmExe:        376 kB
VmLib:       1340 kB
SigPnd: 0000000000000000
SigBlk: 0000000000010000
SigIgn: 0000000000001006
SigCgt: 0000000008014001
CapInh: 0000000000000000
CapPrm: 0000000000000000
CapEff: 0000000000000000
```

Table 10-3
/proc Process information Files

File	Information
cmdline	The current command line.
cwd	A link to the current working directory.
environ	A list of all the current environment variables.
exe	The program that is currently executing.
fd	A subdirectory that contains information about all files the process has open. 0=stdin, 1=stdout, 2=stderr.
maps	Memory maps.
root	A link to the root directory (/).
stat	Process statistics.
statm	Memory-utilization statistics.

Configuring Swap Partitions

You use the `swapon` and `swapoff` commands to mount swap partitions.

Note   Swap partitions are "raw" — they are not formatted with filesystems. They do not have mount points.

If you list a swap partition in the fstab, swapping is automatically on when your system boots. Use the `swapon` command to enable swapping manually, as follows:

```
# swapon -a
```

This command turns on swapping for all swap devices listed in /etc/fstab. If you want to enable swapping on a specific swap partition, type the `swapon` command and the swap partition device special filename, as follows:

```
# swapon /dev/hda3
```

If you need to fix a swapping problem or change the swapping partition(s), you must first disable swapping. Use the `swapoff` command to disable all swapping, as follows:

```
# swapoff -a
```

If you need to disable swapping on a particular partition, perhaps to increase its size, use the `swapoff` command followed by the partition name, as follows:

```
# swapoff /dev/hda3
```

Note   Linux does not require that you use a dedicated swap partition. However, unless you have very little RAM (less than 16 MB), a swap partition is usually going to help performance.

Sizing swap space

How much swap space you need depends on the kinds of applications that run on your system. A common guideline is to make swap space the same size as physical memory. Certain applications, such as relational database applications, often need more swap space — from two to three times the size of physical memory. The `free` command displays the amount of free and used memory, including swap space. The example below uses the `-m` option to display the sizes in megabytes rather than the default kilobytes. The example below shows that the flyingpenguin computer has 124 MB of RAM and three times that amount of swap space.

```
root@flyingpenguin# free -m
          total      used       free     shared    buffers     cached
Mem:        124       112         12         61         20         56
-/+ buffers/cache:                34         90
Swap:       580         0        580
```

Tip The previous example shows that no swap space is currently being used. When you monitor any kind of system-resource use, be sure to monitor regularly over time. Based on the results of the free command, you might deduce that flying-penguin does not need its large swap space, and decide to reuse the space for data. However, this one snapshot of memory use does not reflect that at peak times, an active database application uses much more swap space than it does at slower times.

The maximum size of a swap partition depends on the hardware architecture. For the Intel family of x86 and PowerPC computers, the maximum size of a swap partition is approximately 2 GB. It is 128 GB on Compaq's Alpha hardware architecture, 1 GB on Sun's SPARC architecture, and 3 TB (terabytes) on Sun's SPARC64 architecture. In Linux, RAM and swap space aggregate to form virtual memory. For example, if you have 16 MB of RAM and 32 MB of swap space, you have about 48 MB of virtual memory.

Caution For older Linux kernels (2.1 and earlier), the swap-partition limit is 128 MB. You can create a swap partition larger than 128 MB, but Linux does not use the space over 128 MB. If you want more than 128 MB of swap for these earlier kernels, you must create multiple swap partitions.

Swapping

Linux performs two types of swapping:

✦ Moving some of a process's in-memory pages of data and code between physical memory (RAM) and a swap partition.

✦ Moving the entire process context and all its pages between physical memory (RAM) and a swap partition.

Swapping pages of data and code for a process may not degrade performance significantly if Linux does it occasionally for a few processes at a time. Here's how it works conceptually. Every process has a working set of in-memory pages that the CPU can access. Linux assumes that you may try to re-access recently used pages and keeps these pages in physical memory (RAM) whenever there is enough memory to hold them. Holding a working set of recently used pages in main memory only works if your system has enough RAM to support the working-set concept. If RAM cannot support the in-memory page requirements of the processes running on a computer, the kernel moves the processes' in-memory pages of data and code to a swap partition on disk. Swapping the pages out causes an action called a *page-out*. If a user accesses one of these swapped pages again, a *page-in* (from the saved page in the swap partition to the in-memory working set of pages) occurs. You can monitor page-outs (po) and page-ins (pi) with the ps command. If you see heavy paging activity accompanied by a substantial system slowdown, your computer is *thrashing*. That is, the computer is using most of its CPU power to move data back and forth between memory (the working set of recently used pages) and disk (the swap partition).

Where should you put swap space?

Ideally, it shouldn't matter too much where you put your swap partition(s) because ideally your system doesn't swap. For most system administrators in the real world, where you put swap space affects system performance, especially disk I/O performance. For best performance, distribute swap space over multiple disk partitions on different hard drives with different controllers. If you cannot put multiple swap partitions on separate hard drives, the next best solution is to put your swap partition on a fast disk with many heads that is not busy.

New Filesystem Features in the 2.4 Kernel

The new 2.4 kernel has several new features that enhance its filesystem support. The following list highlights the key changes.

✦ Devices, discussed in Chapter 8, have traditionally required hundreds of entries in the /dev filesystem and had bizarre looking names, such as /dev/fd0H1440 and /dev/midi0. A new, optional, filesystem, called devfs, dramatically reduces the size of this directory, organizes the device names into easily understood directories, such as /dev/ide for IDE devices, and makes the names of individual devices more understandable. For example, /dev/hda1, the first partition on the first IDE disk under the old way of organizing the /dev directory, becomes /dev/ide/host0/bus0/target0/lun0/part1 in devfs.

✦ HPFS, the OS/2 filesystem, is now writeable.

✦ The kernel now supports *raw devices* — disks, or disk partitions, that are not formatted. Reading and writing a raw device does not require the kernels buffering layer, but occurs on the device itself. This feature is typically used by high-powered database management systems, such as Informix and Oracle, to provide very fast I/O. In addition to better performance, raw devices improve data reliability because they permit data to be written to disk immediately without waiting for a buffer cache to be flushed.

Summary

This chapter discussed how to create and manage filesystems using the `mke2fs`, `e2fsck`, and `mount` commands. It also explained the key role of the /etc/fstab file and the options available for controlling when, how, and if users can access a given filesystem. Using the quota system, you learned how to limit the amount of disk space users can use on a filesystem. Finally, you learned about the /proc filesystem, which stores vital information about a running Linux system.

✦   ✦   ✦

CHAPTER

11

◆ ◆ ◆ ◆

Devising a backup
strategy

Using cpio

Using tar

Using dump and
restore

Using a commercial
backup solution

◆ ◆ ◆ ◆

Backing Up and Restoring Filesystems

Performing regular backups is one of the most important jobs anyone that owns a computer can do. Even though Linux is an extremely reliable operating system, stuff happens. You may lose files because of hardware failures, power outages, unexpected problems, and, most often, user error. If you have reliable backups stored away, you can recover from just about anything, even if a natural disaster destroys your computer. Linux provides three utilities for performing backups that meet different needs. For system backups, dump is the preferred utility. For personal backups, non-privileged users can run tar or cpio.

Backup Terminology

There are a few terms you should understand before going further into this chapter:

> ◆ *Full backup* — An archive of an entire filesystem, usually created with the dump command.
>
> ◆ *Incremental backup* — An archive of only those files and directories that have changed since the last full backup, also created with the dump command.
>
> ◆ *Personal backup* — A user-created archive of files and/or directories owned by that user, usually created with tar.
>
> ◆ *Image backup* — A bit-by-bit physical backup of the image on a hard disk, usually created with cpio.
>
> ◆ *Archive* — A file that contains copies of other files. Archive files also store control information about the owner, date-timestamp, and permissions of each file in the archive.

Devising a Backup Strategy

Since backing up filesystems is so important, most sites need a documented backup strategy. That way, when you go on holiday, you know that your substitute can continue to keep your site's filesystems available and recoverable. When you design your site's backup strategy, you need to answer the following questions:

✦ How often will you perform full backups?

✦ Will you use dump to perform ext2fs backups? dump, which functions very similarly to tar, is the traditional utility for making backups in Linux and UNIX environments.

✦ Will you supplement full backups with incremental backups?

✦ What backup media will you use? What is the device special file name for the backup device?

  • Hard disks

  • Tape drives

  • SCSI

  • IDE

  • CD-ROM

  • Iomega Zip and Jaz drives

✦ How will you automate the backup procedures?

✦ What backup utilities will you use?

✦ How much storage do you need for the backup archives?

✦ Will you store a fireproof copy of the backup archives at an outside site? Doing so is a good idea in many situations. In some industries, in fact, such as banking and insurance, maintaining a fireproof, offsite backup is required by law.

✦ If you are backing up filesystems that are not ext2fs, what program will you use?

Check the hardware compatibility list (Hardware-HOWTO) to be sure your backup medium is listed. The most recent hardware howto is available at many Web sites. The primary site is the Linux Documentation Project home page at http://www.linux.org/help/ldp/howto/Hardware-HOWTO.html.

For the most recent compatibility list, go to the Linux Hardware Database (LhD) on the Web at http://lhd.datapower.com/. The LhD is a repository of compatibility and performance ratings for hardware that runs under Linux. The LhD also includes information about device drivers and hints for getting devices to work with Linux.

Using cpio (Copy-In/Out)

cpio—copy-in/out—is a UNIX/Linux archiving and copy program. The examples in this section use GNU cpio. You can run cpio in any of three modes:

✦ *Copy-out*—Creates and archives files in a cpiotar archive.

✦ *Copy-in*—Extracts files from an archive.

✦ *Pass-through*—Combines copy-out and copy-in to copy files from one directory to another or one file system to another. Does not use an archive file.

Creating a cpio archive (copy-out mode)

When you use cpio to create an archive, you pass it a list of files and the name of the archive file to hold them. Since cpio takes its input from standard input (the keyboard, by default), one way to pass the files to the archive is to use the ls command and pipe | its output of the directory listing to the cpio command. By default, cpio sends the archive to stdout (the screen), so you must redirect (>) the archive to a disk file, as in the following example, which lists the bitmapped graphic files and pipes the list to the cpio -ov (copy-out, verify) command to archive all the graphics files in the /root directory. It also redirects the cpio archive to the file bitmaps.cpio.

```
root@flyingpenguin# ls *.bmp | cpio -ov > bitmaps.cpio
70881 blocks
```

To create the archive on a floppy disk, simply substitute the device special file name for the output. If the archive is too large to fit on a single floppy, cpio will prompt you to insert the next floppy.

```
root@flyingpenguin# ls *.bmp | cpio -ov > /dev/fd0
70881 blocks
```

Use the file command on the new archive to assure yourself that it is, in fact, a cpio archive:

```
root@flyingpenguin# file bitmaps.cpio
bitmaps.cpio: cpio archive
```

Extracting files from a cpio archive (copy-in mode)

When you use cpio in copy-in mode to extract files from an archive, cpio tries to put the files in your current working directory if you do not specify another location. The following example changes the default destination directory to the /root/restored_bmp directory and uses the -i and -v options (copy-in, verbose messages) to extract all the files in the archive bitmaps.cpio.

```
root@flyingpenguin# cd /root/restored_bmp
root@flyingpenguin# ls
root@flyingpenguin# cpio -iv < /root/bitmaps.cpio
27atallow.bmp
fg1501.bmp
fg1502.bmp
fg1504.bmp
fg1505.bmp
fg1506.bmp
fg1507.bmp
fg1509.bmp
fg1510a.bmp
fg1510b.bmp
fg1510c.bmp
fg1510d.bmp
fg1511.bmp
```

Tip

cpio does not overwrite existing files unless you include the – option on the command line. Note the messages in the following example:

```
root@flyingpenguin# cpio -iv < bitmaps.cpio
cpio: 27atallow.bmp not created: newer or same age
version exists
cpio: fg1501.bmp not created: newer or same age version
exists
cpio: fg1502.bmp not created: newer or same age version
exists
```

You pass the command a list of files and name the archive file to hold them. Since cpio takes its input from stdin (the keyboard, by default), one way to pass the files to the archive is to list them and pipe (|) the output of the directory listing to the cpio command.

```
root@flyingpenguin# cpio -iv < bitmaps.cpio
cpio: 27atallow.bmp not created: newer or same age version
exists
cpio: fg1501.bmp not created: newer or same age version exists
cpio: fg1502.bmp not created: newer or same age version exists
cpio: fg1504.bmp not created: newer or same age version exists
```

Copying directory trees (passthrough mode)

Passthrough mode lets you copy entire directory trees, including subdirectories and files, from one location to another. Passthrough mode also keeps the original file ownerships and permissions. Passthrough mode is especially useful when you need to move all or a large part of a filesystem to another partition. For example, on flyingpenguin, I kept all files for this book in the root filesystem in directory /root/book. Figure 11-1 shows a filesystem that is about to fill its partition and the solution to the problem.

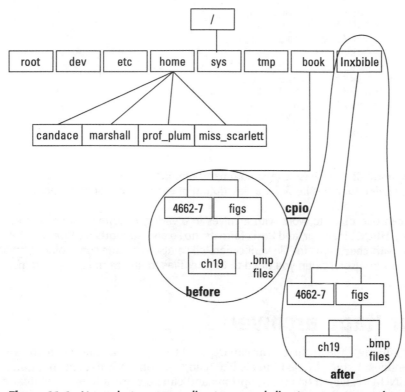

Figure 11-1: Use cpio to move a directory or subdirectory tree to another filesystem

The following commands move the book directory tree into the /docs/lnxbible directory tree. The first command is `find` with the `-print` option to list each full file name on the book directory path on its own line. The `cpio` command after the pipe uses three options:

-v   To list `cpio`'s progress in verbose mode.

-d   To create subdirectories (such as /lnxbible/book/figs) as needed to match the original subdirectory structure.

-p   To run in passthrough mode.

```
root@flyingpenguin# pwd
/root
root@flyingpenguin# find book/* -print  |cpio -vpd /lnxbible
lnxbible/book/4662-7
lnxbible/book/4662-7.fig.makeconfig.txt
lnxbible/book/figs
lnxbible/book/figs/7645-4662-7-fig27-1.bmp
lnxbible/book/figs/7645-4662-7-fig27-2.bmp
lnxbible/book/figs/7645-4662-7-fig27-3.bmp
lnxbible/book/figs/mountfloppy.bmp
```

```
lnxbible/book/figs/gimp1.bmp
lnxbible/book/figs/gimp2.bmp
lnxbible/book/figs/gimp3.bmp
lnxbible/book/figs/ch19
lnxbible/book/figs/ch19/ch19firstscript.bmp
lnxbible/book/figs/ch19/4662-7-ch19.txt
lnxbible/book/figs/ch20/4662-7-ch20.doc
lnxbible/book/figs/ch20/4662-7-ch20.txt
lnxbible/book/figs/ch22/4662-7-ch22.doc
lnxbible/book/figs/ch22/4662-7-ch22.xls
        ---- output edited  ----
```

Each mode of cpio has its own command options. See the man pages on the CD included with this book for a description of each option for each mode.

You can use cpio to work with archives in a variety of formats, including ASCII, binary, HPUX binary, tar, and Posix formats. cpio also supports crc format—that is, ASCII with checksums for file verification. cpio also supports some older formats. This can be useful when you need to transfer files to and from legacy systems.

Using tar (tape archiver)

Despite the name, tape archiver, tar can be used to create backups on many sorts of storage devices. Using tar on Linux is like using tar on UNIX except that Linux supplies GNU tar, which has more options and can compress files dynamically. The first tar option must be either A, c, d, r, t, u, or x. Then you list any other options, followed by the tar file or device for the archive and the files or directories to archive.

Table 11-1 describes only a few of the command options for tar—those that are useful for personal backups.

Chapter 7 describes how to install software from tarballs, tar archives created by software vendors. For a more complete list of tar options, see Chapter 7.

Table 11-1
Useful tar Options for Personal Backups

Option	Description
v	Display verbose messages.
c	Create the archive.
f	Specify the name of the archive (or the device special file) to read or write.
t	List the contents of the archive.

Option	Description
z	Tell tar that the archive is compressed.
x	Extract files from the archive.
u	Update the archive with files that are newer than the tar copy.
r	Append more files to an existing archive.
A	Append tar files to an archive.
d	List the differences between the contents of the archive and the filesystem.

The following example uses the c, v, and f options to create an archive in /tmp named bitmaps. The archive contains compressed versions of all files in the /root directory that end with .bmp.

```
miss_scarlet@flyingpenguin$ tar czvf /tmp/bitmaps /root/*.bmp
tar: Removing leading `/' from archive names
root/27atallow.bmp
root/fg1501.bmp
root/fg1502.bmp
root/fg1504.bmp
root/fg1505.bmp
root/fg1506.bmp
root/fg1507.bmp
root/fg1509.bmp
root/fg1510a.bmp
root/fg1510b.bmp
root/fg1510c.bmp
root/fg1510d.bmp
root/fg1511.bmp
root/fg1512.bmp
root/fg1513.bmp
root/fg1514.bmp
root/fgsb1502.bmp
root/at01.bmp
root/at02.bmp
root/bashrc01.bmp
```

The following example reviews the archive to see which files are in it. The t option tells tar to list a table of contents. The z option reminds tar that the archive is compressed. The f option lists the file that is the archive. The v option, as usual, displays verbose messages.

```
miss_scarlet@flyingpenguin$ tar -tvzf /tmp/bitmaps
-rwxr-xr-x root/root    215650 2000-01-09 20:21:20
root/27atallow.bmp
-rw-r--r-- root/root   1440054 2000-03-24 10:31:26 root/4622-7
fg1501.bmp
-rw-r--r-- root/root   1440054 2000-03-24 10:31:29 root/4622-7
fg1502.bmp
```

```
-rw-r--r-- root/root    1440054 2000-03-24 10:31:31 root/4622-7
fg1504.bmp
-rw-r--r-- root/root    1440054 2000-03-24 10:31:34 root/4622-7
fg1505.bmp
```

Tip   When you use options with `tar`, you can omit the dash (-) or not as you wish. GNU `tar` accepts both.

The following example extracts all files in the archive to the working directory, newpics.

```
miss_scarlet@flyingpenguin$ cd newpics
miss_scarlet@flyingpenguin$ ls
        (no files listed)
miss_scarlet@flyingpenguin$ tar -zvxf /tmp/bitmaps
/root/27atallow.bmp
/root/fg1501.bmp
/root/fg1502.bmp
/root/fg1504.bmp
        (output truncated)
```

Note   If `tar` tells you a compressed archive does not appear to be a tar archive, check to see if you omitted the `z` option on `tar`it. Despite what the `tar` messages say in the following example, there is no problem with the archive. The command simply needs the `z` option to read the archive.

```
miss_scarlet@flyingpenguin$ tar -tvf /tmp/bitmaps
tar -tvf /tmp/bitmaps
tar: Hmm, this doesn't look like a tar archive
tar: Skipping to next file header
tar: Only read 1885 bytes from archive /tmp/bitmaps
tar: Error is not recoverable: exiting now
```

Using dump and restore

If you are a system administrator, `dump` is the backup utility you probably use the most. `dump` is the system backup utility for archiving complete filesystems. You must be the superuser (root) to run `dump`. `restore` is the companion utility for restoring complete filesystems or individual files from `dump` archives.

Using dump

You use the `dump` command to create full and incremental backups of ext2 filesystems. A full backup is a backup of an entire filesystem. An incremental backup contains files that are newer or more recently modified than the date of the last full backup.

dump Factoids

dump **only dumps ext2 filesystems.**

If a dump **archive is larger than the backup medium, the** dump **command automatically breaks the archive into as many volumes as needed.**

You use level numbers to control incremental backups. The file /etc/dumpdates stores the filesystem name, incremental level, and creation time for each dump **archive.**

dump **estimates the number of tapes your backup needs (even if it's a disk-to-disk backup).**

dump **displays its progress at periodic intervals, including estimates of the number of blocks to write, the estimated number of tapes** dump **needs, the time to completion, and the time to change the tape.** dump **bases its estimates on your behavior. For example, if you go out to lunch, and** dump **waits one hour for you to mount a new tape,** dump **revises its estimate based on the assumption that it will take you one hour to mount every tape. This revision process is constant during each backup session.** dump **(with the** -W **option) tells you the current backup status of your filesystems: if** dump -w **doesn't list a filesystem, that filesystem's backup has not been listed in /etc/dumpdates or that filesystem has never been backed up. See the following example:**

```
root@flyingpenguin# dump -W
Last dump(s) done (Dump '>' filesystems):
  /dev/hda5  (/local) Last dump: level 0, Date Sat Jul 29 07:41
```

The syntax for the dump command is

```
dump [-0123456789acnu] [-B records] [-b blocksize] [-d density]
      [-f file][-h level] [-s feet] [-T date] filesystem

   dump [-0123456789acnu] [-B records] [-b blocksize] [-d
density] [-f file]
      [-h level] [-s feet] [-T date] directory
   dump [-W | -w]
```

Table 11-2 describes the options for the dump command.

Table 11-2
dump Options

Option	Description
0	Full backup level, dumps the entire filesystem.
1-9	Incremental levels, default = 9.

Continued

Table 11-2 *(continued)*	
Option	**Description**
u	uupdate Update /etc/dumpdates.
b *n*	Blocksize *n*; the number of Kbytes kilobytes per dump record.
B *n*	Number of dump records— *n*— per volume; overrides dump's automatic calculation of tape size based on length and density.
c	Use cartridge tape defaults, 8000 bpi, 1700 feet of tape.
d *int*	Set the density to the specified integer; defaults to 1600BPI.
f *file*	The backup device, either a device special file, or a disk file to hold the dump archive; can also be a remote device or file.
T *date*	Instead of looking in /etc/dumpdates, use the specified date as the starting time.
W	Reads /etc/dumpdates and /etc/fstab to see which files should be dumped. Displays those files.

Dumping to a tape device

Remember when you dump to a single tape device that that device might have multiple device special files. It's up to you to specify the device special file that meets your needs. For example, if you plan to use two dump commands to back up two filesystems to the same tape, you need to use the no-rewind tape device on the first dump command. If you forget the n in the device special filename, the tape automatically rewinds, and your second dump archive overwrites the first. The following example shows that there are six device special files that represent one streaming tape device. The file /dev/nqft0 represents the no-rewind floppy-tape device.

```
root@flyingpenguin# file /dev/*qft0*
/dev/nqft0:    character special (27/4)
/dev/nrawqft0: character special (27/36)
/dev/nzqft0:   character special (27/20)
/dev/qft0:     character special (27/0)
/dev/rawqft0:  character special (27/32)
/dev/zqft0:    character special (27/16)
```

The following command dumps the /local filesystem on flyingpenguin to the streaming tape device with no rewind:

```
root@flyingpenguin# dump -0uf /dev/nqft0 /local
```

Cross-Reference   See Chapter 8, "Managing Devices," for more information on tape special files and characteristics.

The following command dumps the /local filesystem to the first SCSI tape drive and has the tape drive rewind when the dump completes:

```
root@flyingpenguin# dump -0uf /dev/st0 /local
```

Dumping to a disk file

The following `dump` command creates a level 0 dump (`-0`), updates the /etc/dump-dates file (`u`), sets the length of the "tape" to 50000 feet (`-s 50000`), dumps to a file (`-f /root/localfsdump`), and dumps out the /local filesystem.

```
root@flyingpenguin# dump -0u -s 50000 -f /root/localfsdump /local
  DUMP: Date of this level 0 dump: Sat Jul 29 07:41:20 2000
  DUMP: Date of last level 0 dump: the epoch
  DUMP: Dumping /dev/hda5 (/local) to /root/localfsdump
  DUMP: mapping (Pass I) [regular files]
  DUMP: mapping (Pass II) [directories]
  DUMP: estimated 654134 tape blocks on 0.77 tape(s).
  DUMP: Volume 1 started at: Sat Jul 29 07:41:43 2000
  DUMP: dumping (Pass III) [directories]
  DUMP: dumping (Pass IV) [regular files]
  DUMP: 53.19% done, finished in 0:04
  DUMP: DUMP: 655359 tape blocks on 1 volumes(s)
  DUMP: finished in 563 seconds, throughput 1164 KB/s
  DUMP: Volume 1 completed at: Sat Jul 29 07:51:06 2000
  DUMP: Volume 1 took 0:09:23
  DUMP: Volume 1 transfer rate: 1164 KB/s
  DUMP: level 0 dump on Sat Jul 29 07:41:20 2000
  DUMP: DUMP: Date of this level 0 dump: Sat Jul 29 07:41:20 2000
  DUMP: DUMP: Date this dump completed: Sat Jul 29 07:51:06 2000
  DUMP: DUMP: Average transfer rate: 1164 KB/s
  DUMP: Closing /root/localfsdump
  DUMP: DUMP IS DONE
```

Tip   Why specify the tape length when this `dump` archive is being written to a disk file? `dump`'s default options are tape-oriented. With no tape options, `dump` assumes that you are backing up to an ancient 1600 bpi (bits per inch) tape and makes all its volume estimates based on that default tape drive. When I tried to dump the /local filesystem to a disk file, `dump` originally estimated that I would need about 17 of these ancient tapes, and stopped after dumping (to disk) the amount that would fill one tape and prompting:

```
DUMP: Change Volumes:
DUMP: Is the new volume mounted and ready?: ("yes" or
"no")
```

Since I didn't want to respond 17 times to that prompt, I aborted the `dump` (Ctrl+C), and tricked `dump` into believing that the disk file was a very long tape (50000 feet).

Dumping to a remote device or file

If you use the - option, you can specify a device or file on the network. For example, to dump to the remote system tweety you would use the following format:

```
# dump -f tweety:fp_dumpfile
or
# dump -f tweety:/dev/nrmt0h
```

Caution   You need to refer to the remote tape drive as it is named on the remote computer. The fact that the remote machine must enable you to rsh to it without a password is a security risk.

Checking on the dump output

After the dump completes, you can sanity-check the output in various ways. The following example uses the file command on an on-disk dump archive. The file command, in addition to verifying that the output is in fact a dump, displays the following information:

✦ The date the archive was created.

✦ The level.

✦ The date of the previous backup.

✦ The filesystem that was backed up, by name and device.

✦ The hostname of the computer.

✦ The dump flag listed in fstab.

```
root@flyingpenguin# file local*
localfsdump: new-fs dump file (little endian), This dump Sat Jul 29 07:41:20 200
0, Previous dump Wed Dec 31 19:00:00 1969, Volume 1, Level zero, type: tape head
er, Label none, Filesystem /local, Device /dev/hda5, Host flyingpenguin.cardinal
consultin, Flags 1
```

The simple ls -l command lists the file name, size, and date of the dump archive:

```
root@flyingpenguin# ls -l local*
-rw-r--r--   1 root     tty       671078400 Jul 29 07:51 localfsdump
```

Since dump creates a table of contents within the archive, you can use the restore command to list information about the dump. Using the restore command puts you into a mini-shell where you can examine the dump, add files to it, or extract files. The example below uses the options -i to invoke the interactive mini-shell to and --f to specify that the dump archive is a disk file.

```
root@flyingpenguin# restore -if localfsdump
restore > ?
Available commands are:
  ls [arg] - list directory
```

```
     cd arg - change directory
     pwd - print current directory
     add [arg] - add `arg' to list of files to be extracted
     delete [arg] - delete `arg' from list to be extracted
     extract - extract requested files
     setmodes - set modes of requested directories
     quit - immediately exit program
     what - list dump header information
     verbose - toggle verbose flag (useful with ``ls'')
     help or `?' - print this list
If no `arg' is supplied, the current directory is used
restore > what
Dump   date: Sat Jul 29 07:41:20 2000
Dumped from: the epoch
Level 0 dump of /local on flyingpenguin.cardinalconsulting.com:/dev/hda5
Label: none
restore > verbose
verbose mode on
restore > ls
.:
     2 ./
     2 ../
 67321 DominoKits/
    13 communicator-v461-export.x86-unknown-linux2.0.tar
    11 lost+found/
136681 notesdata/
  2041 save/

restore >quit
```

Cross-Reference

The "Restoring filesystems, directories, and files" section later in this chapter tells you how to use the `restore` command to restore files and filesystems.

Performing incremental backups

When you use `dump` to perform incremental backups, the `dump` messages tell you when the last backup was done. In the following examples you can see the complete set of messages from the first incremental performed on the /local filesystem, followed by an excerpt from the next incremental.

```
root@flyingpenguin# dump -2uf /root/incremental_localfs2 /local
  DUMP: Date of this level 2 dump: Sat Jul 29 13:19:23 2000
  DUMP: Date of last level 0 dump: Sat Jul 29 07:41:20 2000
  DUMP: Dumping /dev/hda5(/local) to /root/incremental_localfs2
  DUMP: mapping (Pass I) [regular files]
  DUMP: mapping (Pass II) [directories]
  DUMP: estimated 166 tape blocks on 0.00 tape(s).
  DUMP: Volume 1 started at: Sat Jul 29 13:19:31 2000
  DUMP: dumping (Pass III) [directories]
  DUMP: dumping (Pass IV) [regular files]
  DUMP: DUMP: 117 tape blocks on 1 volumes(s)
  DUMP: finished in less than a second
  DUMP: Volume 1 completed at: Sat Jul 29 13:19:31 2000
```

```
DUMP: level 2 dump on Sat Jul 29 13:19:23 2000
DUMP: DUMP: Date of this level 2 dump: Sat Jul 29 13:19:23 2000
DUMP: DUMP: Date this dump completed: Sat Jul 29 13:19:31 2000
DUMP: DUMP: Average transfer rate: 0 KB/s
DUMP: Closing /root/incremental_localfs2
DUMP: DUMP IS DONE

root@flyingpenguin# dump -3uf /root/incremental_localfs3 /local
  DUMP: Date of this level 3 dump: Sat Jul 29 13:21:10 2000
  DUMP: Date of last level 2 dump: Sat Jul 29 13:19:23 2000
  DUMP: Dumping /dev/hda5(/local) to /root/incremental_localfs3
```

Restoring filesystems, directories, and files

restore is the companion to dump with one difference. dump only backs up complete filesystems; restore restores complete filesystems, directories, or any number of files from a dump archive. You can use the restore command with no options except for -f, the device from which to restore. restore's interactive mode (-I) enables you to use commands such as ls, cd, and pwd to move through the archive. When you want to select a file to restore, type add at the prompt. After you've selected the files you want to restore, type extract to start restoring files. The following example uses the interactive option to find, add, and extract a file from the backed-up filesystem.

Restoring files interactively

The following example uses the interactive option to list, add, and restore (extract) one file to the current working directory.

```
root@flyingpenguin# # restore -ivf /root/incremental_localfs3
Verify tape and initialize maps
Tape block size is 32
Dump    date: Sat Jul 29 13:21:10 2000
Dumped from: Sat Jul 29 13:19:23 2000
Level 3 dump of /local on flyingpenguin.cardinalconsulting.com:/dev/hda5
Label: none
Extract directories from tape
Extract directories from tape
Initialize symbol table.
restore > ls
.:
 2 ./      2 ../     12 passwd

restore > add passwd
restore > extract
Extract requested files
You have not read any tapes yet.
Unless you know which volume your file(s) are on you should start
with the last volume and work towards the first.
Specify next volume #: 1
extract file ./passwd
Add links
```

```
Set directory mode, owner, and times.
set owner/mode for '.'? [yn] n
restore > quit
```

Note Again, restore assumes your dump archive is on a tape, even though you specify a file. This is why it asks you to specify a volume.

Restoring a complete filesystem

The following example restores the full backup of the /local filesystem we performed in the section "Dumping to a disk file." The restore command uses the -C option to read the dump archive and compare its contents with files already on disk. restore --C changes its working directory to the root of the filesystem that was dumped (/local) before comparing the tape with the files.

```
# restore -Cvf /root/localfsdump
Begin compare restore
Verify tape and initialize maps
Tape block size is 32
Dump   date: Sat Jul 29 07:41:20 2000
Dumped from: the epoch
Level 0 dump of /local on flyingpenguin.cardinalconsulting.com:/dev/hda5
Label: none
filesys = /local
Initialize symbol table.
Extract directories from tape
Extract directories from tape
comparing ./communicator-v461-export.x86_unknown-linux2.0.tar (size: 14305280,
mode: 0100644)
restore: ./save/domino-19990607/old-installation: does not exist (-1): No such
file or directory
comparing ./DominoKits/linux_na.tar (size: 132939776, mode: 0100644)
comparing ./notesdata/mail/jkirk.nsf (size: 6029312, mode: 0100600)
Check the symbol table.
```

Caution The restore command writes to the current directory when extracting files. Be careful to cd to the correct directory before running restore. If you are running restore interactively, you can use the cd command within the interactive mini-shell.

Restoring an archive from multiple volumes

Since you can write successive dump archives to a single tape, you may need to use the mt command to position the tape. For example, when you need to restore the second archive on the tape, using mt as in the following code positions the tape (/dev/nrst0) to the beginning of the second dump archive. The -f option tells mt the device special file name. To move the tape, use the fsf option followed by the number of files to move forward.

```
root@flyingpenguin# mt -f /dev/nrst0 fsf 1
```

Controlling a Tape Drive with mt

The `mt` command is the tape-control program. The `mt` command takes a wide variety of options. The options listed below are the ones most useful for performing dumps and restores. The syntax for `mt` is as follows:

```
mt [-h] [-f device] operation [n] [arguments...]
```

The following table lists a few mt options.

Option/Operation	Description
h	List the operations (very minimal help).
fsf n	Go forward n files.
bsf n	Go forward n files.
asf n	Rewind and position tape at the nth file.
offline	Rewind and unload the tape.
erase	Erase tape.
status	Display tape status.
load	Load SCSI tape into the drive.
lock	Lock SCSI tape-drive door.
unlock	Unlock SCSI tape-drive door.
setdensity n	Set SCSI tape density to n.

Tip   If you define the TAPE environment variable, the `mt` command uses that device as the default device. If you do not define the TAPE variable, `mt` uses /dev/tape as the default device.

Note   You cannot use the mt command to position the tape on a remote device.

Scheduling dump levels

This section explains how to use `dump` to create finer-grained backups and suggests a backup strategy that uses `dump`.

Saving backup time by using all the levels

The `dump` command supports up to 10 different levels of backups. Level 0 is the full backup. Levels 1–9 are the incremental backups. Many sites schedule full backups once a week, supplemented by daily incremental backups. A major consideration in formulating your backup strategy should be how often to perform full and incremental backups on each filesystem and at what level. To use an example, a production system for a real-world company that develops compilers and tools might include eight filesystems spread over five hard disks. Table 11-3 describes the kind of activity that occurs on each disk and the corresponding backup schedule.

Table 11-3
Filesystem Activity

FS	ActivityFile Update Frequency	Full	Incremental
/	Rarely updated.	Monthly	Daily
/local updated	Rarely updated.	Monthly	Only if
/tmp	Throw-away temp files.	Never	Never
/usr	Read- only files.	Only if upgraded	Never
/var	Depends on sys admin.	Weekly	Daily
/user1	Home directories for programmers working on the cc project, shared cc project files.	Weekly	Daily
/user2	Home directories for programmers working on the editor project, shared editor project files.	Weekly	Daily
/user3	Home directories for programmers working on the FORTRAN project, shared FORTAN project files, home directories for office staff, including management (mostly e-mail).	Weekly	Daily

Table 11-3 shows that four filesystems require weekly full backups and daily incrementals. That's four weekly invocations of dump at level 0 and five daily invocations of dump at a level higher than 0. Since these are large filesystems and take a few hours to back up, the system administrator decides to stagger the full schedule, doing a full backup of /user1 on Monday, of /user2 on Tuesday, of /user3 on Wednesday, and so on. Your decisions as to when to perform full backups may differ from this strategy. For example, if you have multiple backup media, you might go ahead and perform all full backups in parallel to different devices on the same day. If your filesystems are small, and only take an hour or two to back up, you may also choose to perform all full backups on the same day to keep the backup strategy simpler. Whatever you choose is a function of the environment in which you work.

Tip

Some sites, with small to medium filesystems and fast backup devices, perform full backups every day, eliminating the need to perform and organize incremental backups.

If you do an incremental backup on Monday evening to pick up new and modified changes since Sunday, you might make that a level-2 backup. If, on Tuesday, you do another incremental backup on new and modified files since Monday, you might choose level 4. You might choose to label Wednesday's incremental backup level 6. The actual numbers are not important. The important fact is that each succeeding incremental is numbered higher than the previous one. If you don't like using 2, 4, and 6, you could use 1, 2, and 3, or 1, 7, and 8. Anything works as long as the level numbers increase.

Let's examine what happens with the multi-level scheme described above when you need to perform a restore. You perform a level-0 (full) dump on Sunday, a level-1 dump on Monday, a level-2 dump on Tuesday, a level-3 dump on Wednesday, and a level-4 dump on Thursday. The advantage of using all the level numbers is that each daily incremental dump will most likely be quite small and take very little time and tape. On Friday, Professor Plum mistakenly removes his entire home directory. As the system administrator, it's your job to restore the home directory to the state it was in after the last backup (level-4 on Thursday). You must follow these steps:

1. Restore Professor Plum's home directory from Sunday's level-0 (full) dump.

2. Restore his home directory from Monday's level-1 dump.

3. Restore his home directory from Tuesday's level-2 dump.

4. Restore his home directory from Wednesday's level-3 dump.

5. Restore his home directory from Thursday's level-4 dump.

Note

If Professor Plum created or modified any files in his home directory on Friday before the restore, he must recreate them himself. They are not available on any dump.

Therefore, to restore Professor Plum's home directory to its state as of the last dump requires five restore operations, done in the correct sequence. This type of restore — one that relies on multi-level dumps — is time-consuming. Also, the more steps in the restore process, the more chance for human (your) error.

Using only a few levels to manage restores more safely and efficiently

If you use only a couple of levels (for example, level 0 and one other level) in your dump strategy, the time to perform the daily incremental dumps increases each day on an actively updated filesystem, as does the amount of tape it takes to hold the daily dumps. However, you save time and effort when you have to restore. For example, instead of incrementing the level number on each daily dump, you could choose to use the same level each weekday. So Sunday's full dump would still be level 0, but the daily dumps would be the same level — any level number greater than 0 works. Suppose you use level 7 for Monday's through Thursday's dailies. You are now performing a *differential* backup. This means that Monday's daily dump records changes since Sunday's full dump. Tuesday's level-7 daily records all changes (including Monday's) since Sunday's full dump. After Tuesday, Monday's level-7 dump is irrelevant. Wednesday's level-7 daily records all changes (including Monday's and Tuesday's) since Sunday's full dump. After Wednesday's daily, Monday's and Tuesday's dumps are irrelevant. You perform Thursday's daily at level 7 as well. Each day, the differential between Sunday and that day is larger than on the previous day. When you need to restore Professor Plum's home directory on Friday, you only need to restore from Sunday's full backup (level 0) and Thursday's daily differential (level 7). The restore goes faster because there are only two operations, and there is less risk of human error affecting the restore process.

Using Commercial Backup Solutions

If you need a large-scale backup solution, especially for mission-critical systems, you should look into commercial and/or freeware packages, some of which act as a frontend for dump and restore, and some of which use proprietary formats. These products help you perform all sorts of sophisticated operations, such as automating managing tape changers and robots to perform gigantic backups. One example of a commercial solution is BRU for Linux from Enhanced Software Technologies, Inc (http://www.estinc.com). BRU is a high performance backup and restore utility designed for reliability, speed, flexibility, and ease of use. Besides backup and restoration, you can use BRU to perform tar and cpio functions.

There are other products available besides BRU. When you research which commercial backup solution is right for your environment, look for features that include:

Reliability | You want to be sure that your backup is uncorrupted. There is nothing so horrifying to a system administrator as having to restore a critical filesystem and finding out that a dump archive was somehow corrupted when it was created. Look for a backup product that provides multiple levels of data verification and that notifies you if the backup has validity problems.

Hardware compatibility | Be sure to get a product that supports a wide range of hardware — including hardware you might have in the future. Supported hardware to consider includes disk drives, removable disks like the Iomega Zip and Jaz drives, floppy disks, and a wide range of tape drives, such as 1/4-inch QIC drives, DLT, 4mm, 8mm, MLR, TRAVAN, streaming SCSI tapes, and old reel-to-reel magtapes.

Performance	Find a product that can detect and recover from errors so that you don't need to stop and restart the backup procedure. Look for products that provide high-performance buffering features and that know how to set media characteristics, such as block size and tape size, to optimal values.
Ease of use	Whether it's a graphical interface or a command-line interface, look for a product that doesn't take a long time to learn how to use. Also, be sure that the product can automate everything you need.
Multi-filesystem compatibility	If you use other filesystems beside ext2fs, you might find that a backup product that can back up most or all of the filesystems you use to be a convenient time-saver.

Summary

For filesystem backups, dump (along with its complement, restore) is the preferred tool. dump only backs up complete filesystems. Flexibility in performing incremental backups comes from the levels that are stored in the file /etc/dumpdates. tar is a useful tool for short or personal backups. cpio copies files and directories in many formats, including some old formats (for compatibility with legacy systems).

✦　　✦　　✦

Configuring and Managing User Accounts

When you installed Linux, the installation procedure created an account for you with the username root and the password you selected. However, if you want to use Linux as a multiuser timesharing system, users need accounts before they can log in.

Note   You need to be the superuser (have a user ID of 0) to create and manage user accounts.

As the system administrator, you create individual accounts consisting of a username, password, and home directory for each user. You may also seed each user's home directory with a few shell scripts that set up the user environment. In a graphical environment, each individual user takes charge of customizing his or her desktop and windows.

Managing Accounts

After you've created user accounts, you need to manage those accounts. Managing user accounts includes:

✦ Adding accounts for new users

✦ Modifying user accounts

✦ Disabling user accounts

✦ Removing user accounts

Adding new user accounts

You can create and manage accounts at the command line or in your graphical interface. If you work in the command-line interface, you can choose to create an account either by manually editing the system account file (/etc/passwd) or by running a shell script that prompts you for user information and edits the /etc/passwd file for you. This chapter shows examples of a graphical method and both command-line methods. You choose how you want to create user accounts. No matter what method you choose, these are the steps you follow to create a new user account:

1. Create the new user's account entry in the /etc/passwd file.

2. Set the user's password (`passwd` command).

3. Create the user's home directory (`mkdir` command).

4. Copy startup and initialization files into the user's home directory (`cp` command).

5. Set the file ownership of the user's directory and files. If you forget to do this, you own the user's home directory and files, and the user will have problems working in the directory (`chown` command).

Tip   Before editing the /etc/passwd file, make a copy of it just in case you make a mistake.

Creating an account by editing the passwd file

No, I didn't forget to spell check. The system file that holds account information is /etc/passwd. Each account has an entry in the /etc/passwd file. It's a plain text file, so it is easy to read and edit. You can display /etc/passwd on your screen. You can print it. And you can use your favorite editor to edit it. A very basic way to add or modify an account is to edit the /etc/passwd file.

What Editor Should You Use on the /etc/passwd File?

You can use any editor you want, but vi has two special versions:

  ✦ vipw (for /etc/passwd)

  ✦ vigr (for /etc/group)

Each of these editors is vi with a special twist: it sets a lock flag on the passwd or group file so that only one vi user can edit those files at a time. If you use something besides vipw, it's possible that another superuser could be editing the passwd file at the same time and overwriting your new accounts.

Tips about /etc/passwd

Here is a list of tips about the fields in the /etc/passwd file:

✦ *user* is the username for the account.

✦ *password* is an encrypted password. You do not edit it in the /etc/passwd file. You use the passwd command to set a password. The passwd command does the encryption. When you look at a /etc/passwd file, the encryption is the reason the password looks like gibberish. If you see a password field that says "*" or "No Logins," no one can log into that account. Only the superuser can change another user's password.

✦ *uid* is the numerical user ID for this account. A uid of 0 means that the user has all the privileges of the superuser. It's good practice to keep uids unique, although it's not strictly necessary. If a user has accounts on multiple computers in your network, remote access and file transfers work better if the uid is the same on all systems, because it makes it easier to identify who is doing what on any given system, for example, who owns which files and who is running what processes.

✦ *gid* is the default group ID for this account. If a user belongs to multiple groups, you set the default gid in the /etc/passwd file, and the other group memberships in the /etc/group file.

✦ *comment* is usually the user's full name, but it can be any kind of documentation that identifies the user.

✦ *home* is the path to the user's home directory.

✦ *shell* is the user's default shell. If this field is blank, the shell defaults to /bin/sh.

To create a new user account, open the /etc/passwd file with an editor, open a new line, and add an account for the user. When you are finished, exit the editor, saving the changes. The entries in a passwd file contain the following fields separated by colons:

```
user:password:uid:gid:comment:home:shell
```

Caution   Using vipw and vigr only works if all superusers agree to use them for editing the passwd and grp files. vipw and vigr are the only editors that look for the locked file flag. If you use vipw and another superuser uses emacs, the emacs editor will not see the locked file flag, and the two superusers may bury each other's passwd edits.

After you create the entry in the /etc/passwd file, finish creating the account by following these steps:

1. Create the home directory.
2. Set the password.
3. Copy the files listed in Table 12-1 into the new directory.
4. Set the directory and file ownership for the new user.

The following short listing shows a sample /etc/passwd file with a new entry for the user gnuuser.

```
gnuuser:x:515:100:GNU User:/home/gnuuser:/bin/bash
```

The user's account name is gnuuser. The x where the password should be indicates that shadow passwords are used on this system. The user ID and group ID are 515 and 100, respectively. The user's full name is GNU User. gnuuser's home directory is /home/gnuuser and the shell gnuuser uses is /bin/bash.

Table 12-1 lists some of the files you might copy into a user's home directory. These files set up the user's environment by defining environment variables, setting the user's command search path, and establishing useful command aliases. Although you can store these "seed" files anywhere on disk, the most common location is the directory /etc/skel.

Table 12-1
Seed Files that Help Construct the User Environment

Filename	Purpose
.bash_logout	Contains commands executed when the user logs out.
.bashrc	Contains commands that configure interactive shell sessions.
.login	Contains commands that configure a login shell.
.inputrc	Contains configuration directives for the bash shell's key bindings.
.emacs	Contains configuration directives and Emacs commands executed when Emacs (or Xemacs) is first started.

Getting the scoop on groups

Linux acknowledges three types of users:

✦ You

✦ The members of your group

✦ The rest of the world (other)

Root is a Group

So far, you've seen root used to mean the top directory in Linux and the username of the superuser. root is also the name of a pre-defined group. The Linux installation procedure creates a system group with gid (group ID) 0 and automatically makes root a member of that group. On Red Hat Linux, that group is named root. In the long listing below of the root directory (/), you can see that most system directories are owned by user root and group root.

```
$ ls -l /
total 44
drwxr-xr-x    2 root    root     2048 Nov  3 07:33 bin
drwxr-xr-x    3 root    root     1024 Nov  3 07:30 boot
drwxr-xr-x    4 root    root    11264 Nov 19 10:55 dev
drwxr-xr-x   38 root    root     3072 Nov 19 09:55 etc
drwxr-xr-x   10 root    root     1024 Nov  2 20:15 home
drwxr-xr-x    2 root    root     1024 Nov  1 13:23 initrd
drwxr-xr-x   12 root    root     1024 Nov  1 13:19 install
drwxr-xr-x    6 root    root     2048 Nov  3 07:32 lib
drwxr-xr-x    2 root    root    12288 Nov  1 12:50 lost+found
drwxr-xr-x    8 root    root     1024 Nov  1 13:01 mnt
drwxr-xr-x   11 root    root     1024 Nov  3 07:27 opt
dr-xr-xr-x   42 root    root        0 Nov 19 10:55 proc
drwxr-xr-x    7 root    root     1024 Nov  2 21:12 root
drwxr-xr-x    2 root    root     3072 Nov  3 11:52 sbin
drwxr-xr-x    2 root    root     1024 Nov  3 11:52 shlib
drwxrwxrwt    8 root    root     1024 Nov 27 08:36 tmp
drwxr-xr-x   23 root    root     1024 Nov  1 13:18 usr
drwxr-xr-x   14 root    root     1024 Nov  3 11:52 var
```

Each user is responsible for protecting his or her directories and files. Linux supports groups to make security easier when users need to share files. Each user belongs to one group by default and can belong to several more groups, although only one group can be active at any given time. The system administrator creates these groups according to how users need to share files, usually by function, such as a programmers' group, a managers' group, a tech writers' group, and so on. Certain software packages automatically create groups and populate them with users when you install the software.

Creating groups by editing the /etc/group file

You use the /etc/group file to create groups and add any users who need to belong to more than one group. In the sample /etc/passwd entry shown earlier, gnuuser's group ID was 100. As the first line in the following excerpt from /etc/group shows, a group ID of 100 corresponds to the users group, which also shows that erik, marc, and kurt are members of the users group. In addition, the user erik is also a member of the groups programmer and backup.

```
user::100:erik,marc,kurt,gnuuser
backup::105:erik
programmer::106:erik
```

Tip   Before editing the /etc/group file, make a backup copy of it first!

Adding new users graphically

You can point and click your way to creating users and groups if you use a GUI such as GNOME or KDE. (You follow the same basic steps for both.) If you are working with the GNOME interface, follow the specific steps below to invoke the LinuxConf utility, which provides a User account manager:

1. Click the gnome's foot (the Main menu).
2. Point the cursor at the System entry.
3. Select the LinuxConf utility.
4. Scroll down to the User accounts and examine the Normal configuration options.
5. Under Normal, click User accounts to display a windowpane containing a list of all current user accounts.
6. Click the Add button at the bottom of the User accounts pane.

Now you are ready to create a new account.

1. Click the checkbox labeled *The account is enabled*.
2. Fill in the boxes for login name, full name, group, supplementary groups, home directory, command interpreter, and user ID. Optional fields are marked with the abbreviation *opt*.
3. When you have filled in the boxes, type Accept.
4. In the Change password dialog, type the user's password, and then click the Accept button.
5. Confirm the user's password by retyping it. Click the Accept button again. You can see the user account you just created in the User accounts pane.
6. Click Quit to make the changes permanent on your computer.

Even if you opt to use GUI tools to create user accounts, make sure you learn how to do it manually, also. Why? Because not all Linux systems have GUI tools for user account creation installed. The slower, manual method is the only method guaranteed to work on any Linux system.

Cross-Reference   Chapter 25, "Configuring an ftp Server," explains how to set up an ftp server.

Creating Accounts for Non-Login Use

Some software and services require accounts even though no users will log in. The documentation for such software tells you what to name the account. To provide anonymous FTP (the TCP/IP File Transfer Protocol) services, for example, you need to permit users to download files from your server without having to log in to a valid account. You need to create an account named ftp with the password /bin/false to prevent anyone from actually logging in using the account name ftp.

Modifying existing user accounts

If you need to change any user-account characteristics, you can re-edit the /etc/passwd file or rerun the graphical LinuxConf. When LinuxConf displays the pane of existing users, select the one you want to edit and follow the steps for creating a new user, changing only the information you want to edit.

Disabling and deleting user accounts

If a user no longer needs to log in to a Linux system, you can either disable that user's account or remove it entirely. If the user is going away temporarily, you can disable the account manually by changing the password to /bin/false, which prevents the user from logging in. When the user returns to work, all you need to do is change the password back and notify the user. Although a user is gone, other people may need to access the files. This is another situation where disabling the account is a better choice than removing the account altogether.

Tip   Another way to disable an account is to write a small program that prints a warning message. In the /etc/passwd file, make that program the default shell for the account being disabled. Chapter 30, "Shell Scripting for System Administrators," gives an example of a program that delivers an "account disabled" message.

When Can a User Change /etc/passwd?

Users don't have the necessary file permissions on /etc/passwd to edit the file directly or to run a graphical utility such as LinuxConf to change password settings. However, Linux provides the following commands so that the user can change certain fields in his or her own /etc/passwd entry:

   ✦ chfn — Change the value of the comment field.

   ✦ chsh — Change the value of the default shell.

   ✦ passwd — Change the value of the password.

If you decide to remove an account completely, delete the entries in the /etc/passwd and /etc/group files and delete the user's home directory and all files and subdirectories. Some Linux distributions include a special program for removing users and their files and directories. Usually, the program is named userdel or, in some cases, deluser. The reason for the name difference is that each distribution customizes these programs (which are usually scripts) according to their own needs and preferences. To determine how to use them, you should read the documentation that comes with your Linux distribution.

Caution   Be sure to back up the departed user's files and directories before removing them just in case someone else needs to access them.

Summary

Managing accounts for Linux users is a straightforward task if you follow the steps outlined in this chapter. Whether you edit the files manually or use a GUI is a matter of personal preference. The end result is the same either way. The next chapter helps you set up printing for the users whose accounts you create.

✦   ✦   ✦

Managing Printers and Printing

Linux offers a choice of printing systems. The most commonly used Linux printing system is the mature lpr command, which is a descendant of the Berkeley Software Distribution's (BSD) UNIX lp system. While we might like to think of lp as standing for Linux printing, it really stands for line printer. If you're a DOS/Windows user, printing on a time-sharing system such as Linux offers more capabilities and is much more flexible than what you are used to.

Note   There are other print systems besides lpr. LPRng is a more modern and enhanced descendant of lpr and easier to administer for large numbers of computers and printers. LPRng adds features such as dynamic redirection of print queues, more verbose diagnostic messages, multiple printers serving a single queue, more powerful security checks, and an improved permission strategy. You can read about and obtain LPRng at ASTArt Technologies by visiting http://www.astart.com/lprng/LPRng.html. The Debian distribution offers a choice between plain lpd and LPRng during installation.

What Printers Work with Linux?

Most major printer manufacturers have several models that work well with Linux.

Caution   Don't assume because a manufacturer has Linux-compatible printers that your model is also supported. For example, several Lexmark printers work well with Linux, but as of this writing, my Lexmark 7000 model does not work with Linux. Maybe someone is writing a driver for it right now. Maybe a later release of Linux will include a driver. Since this is Linux, I could write my own driver. My solution is to buy an inexpensive printer that I know supports Linux easily.

Linux Printing Factoids

Multiple users can print on the same printer at the same time. Printer sharing is automatic.

No user except root can control the printer.

Linux enables you to print to any printer on the network, including a printer attached to your own computer, a remote printer attached to someone else's computer or a print server, a printer directly attached to the network, even printers on different operating systems such as Windows 95/98/NT/2000 and Mac OS.

The daemon lpd waits for print requests from users and sends them to the printer.

If you're a UNIX user, especially a BSD UNIX user, printing on Linux should be familiar.

To avoid grief, you should use a printer known to have a driver program that works with Linux. You might also be able to convince a printer to work with Linux by pretending it is something else. For example, you might be able to get an unsupported Lexmark printer to work by getting it to use an Epson driver, but if you don't like irritation and don't have lots of free time, get a printer you know works with Linux.

On the CD-ROM The Printing HOWTO contains a link to the Linux Printing Support Database, which contains a list of software printer drivers and a nifty summary of printers known to work with each driver.

The Linux Printer Support Database, at `http://www.linuxprinting.org/printer_list.cgi`, enables you to look up a printer by type (such as inkjet, laser, and so on) or by vendor. The database also lists printers under the compatibility categories Perfectly, Mostly, Partially, and Paperweight. When buying a printer, try to go for the Perfectly category. Definitely avoid the Paperweights. They don't work at all with Linux.

Printing with Linux

When users print, it can be as simple as pressing a button or typing a simple command. However, behind the scenes, Linux printing involves special files, directories, and programs. If you're the system administrator, you need to know where these files and directories are and what they're for. You also need to know how to start and stop the daemon.

Understanding the terminology

Spool stands for simultaneous peripheral operations online. Spooling is the process whereby the lpd (line printer spooling daemon) stores a temporary copy of the file to be printed in a directory on the hard disk before sending the file to the printer. Using spooling means that when you type a print command, such as lpr, you don't need to wait for the printer to finish printing before you can execute another command. It also means that if the printer is busy with someone else's job, your file can queue up in the spooling directory and print automatically when the printer is ready.

The *spool directory* is the location the system administrator creates and lists in the /etc/printcap file that holds temporary copies of files before they print. The printing system automatically deletes the temporary files after they print. The default spool directory is /var/spool/lpd on most Linux and UNIX systems, but you can declare any directory to be the spool directory by setting the sd entry in the printcap file.

Queuing is using a print command or button to send your files to the spool directory where they wait in line for lpd to send them to the printer.

While most Linux distributions offer easy-to-use print-configuration utilities, you can also configure printing manually by editing the /etc/printcap file.

The section "Setting up the printcap file" describes the manual configuration process whereby you can set up Linux or UNIX printing for any distribution. This chapter also describes some Linux distribution-specific graphical print-configuration tools. You can configure printing either manually or with a handy graphical tool, depending on your personal preference and the tools available in your Linux distribution.

What happens when someone prints

Remember that Linux represents devices, including printers, as files. If you use the ls or file command to examine the files in the /dev directory, as in the example below, you should see one or more character device files, named lp followed by a number, that represent printers. These are the parallel port printers:

```
[root@flyingpenguin} $ file /dev/lp*
/dev/lp0: character special (6/0)
/dev/lp1: character special (6/1)
/dev/lp2: character special (6/2)
```

If you are used to Microsoft numbering conventions for printers (for example, LPT1, LPT2, and LPT3), you should know that Linux printer-numbering conventions start with 0. For example, the printer on your PC that you know in DOS as LPT1 is /dev/lp0 in Linux. If you have a serial port printer, the port you think of as COM1 in DOS is /dev/ttys0 in Linux.

The printer daemon, lpd (Line Printer Daemon) starts at boot time. It listens for requests to perform services such as spooling files, printing files waiting in the print queue, displaying the jobs in the print queue, or removing jobs from the print queue. For each service, lpd creates a child process to handle the request so that lpd can keep listening for requests. The lpd determines which printers it spools for by reading the file /etc/printcap. The printcap file contains the name of the spool directory for each printer and holds information about each printer that your computer can access. Each time a user runs the `lpr` command to print, `lpr` contacts lpd through /dev/printer. The `lpr` command passes information (the file to print, how to print it, and who is doing the printing) to the lpd. The lpd sends the file to the printer.

The lpd that starts at boot time is the master lpd. When you send files to different printers, the master lpd starts an lpd for the printer you are using. Therefore, at any time the number of lpds running may be equal to the number of printers connected to your system plus the master lpd. Each child lpd remains active as long as files are queued for its printer. When the spool directory for a printer is empty, the child lpd terminates. The master lpd is always active.

The GUI printing utilities update the printcap file automatically when you add a printer. You can also configure printing by editing the printcap file yourself with any text editor.

Configuring the Linux Print System

To set up printing on a Linux computer, you must follow these steps:

1. Check that the kernel includes printer support.

2. Make sure you have the necessary driver- and printer-control software for your printer.

3. Physically connect the printer to a computer or a network.

4. Test the hardware connection.

5. Start the line printer daemon (lpd).

6. Add a printer entry to the /etc/printcap file or run a Linux graphical tool that edits the printcap file automatically.

7. Enable spooling and printing.

8. Test printing.

I'll describe each of these steps in detail in the following subsections.

Confirming that the kernel supports printing

Before you start to configure a printer, be sure that your kernel supports the lp device. Usually your kernel will have printer support built in, but there are a couple of different ways to be sure.

One way is to display the devices file from the proc filesystem, /etc/proc, and check for the lp device. In the example below, the lp device shows up as IO device 6.

```
root@flyingpenguin# more /proc/devices
Character devices:
  1 mem
  2 pty
  3 ttyp
  4 ttyS
  5 cua
  6 lp
  7 vcs
 10 misc
 29 fb
 36 netlink
128 ptm
136 pts
162 raw
254 pcmcia

Block devices:
  1 ramdisk
  2 fd
  3 ide0
  9 md
 22 ide1
```

You can also check the boot messages and look for lp support.

Getting the printer driver

The Linux installation process builds a kernel with numerous printer drivers. However, if you have a very new (or sometimes very old) printer, the driver may exist but not in your kernel. If a new stable kernel is about to be released, check to see what new devices are supported. For example, the new kernel, v2.4, contains support for many new printers and also for an old DECWriter III (also known as the DEC LA120) printer that you need ribbons for. If no new stable kernel is imminent, you may be able to download the driver you need from the Web. You can find the Web site for downloading printer drivers at the Linux Printing Support Database, http://www.linuxprinting.org/printer_list.cgi or at individual printer vendors' sites.

On the CD-ROM The Linux Hardware HOWTO document lists most hardware supported by Linux and helps you find the necessary drivers. Section 21 points you to printer information. Check the HOWTO to see if your printer is supported. If the HOWTO on the CD-ROM does not include your printer, don't give up. There is a link to this HOWTO on the CD-ROM. Developers are constantly writing drivers to add new printer support. Check the Web site `http://www.linhardware.com/LDP/HOWTO/Hardware-HOWTO.html`. This site contains the most recently updated Hardware HOWTO, and your printer may have been added since this book was printed.

Connecting and testing the printer hardware

Read the documentation to see how to connect the printer to your computer or network.

Tip If you don't have documentation for your printer, check the vendor's Web site. Most printer manufacturers keep the technical specifications for their products online.

After you connect the printer, test the hardware to be sure that the printer and cable are working. Most printers have a self-test function that prints a test page. Read your printer documentation to see how to run the self-test. When you're sure the hardware is working, test its connection to your computer. There are a few different ways to do this.

If your computer can boot another operating system, boot the alternate operating system and print from it. If you can print from another operating system, you know that your printer cabling is working.

Caution Beware of Winprinters. Winprinters are incompatible printers because the internal printer control language and the details of the printing mechanism are not public. The vendor provides a Windows driver only. If you have a Winprinter, it will pass the hardware tests, but you will not be able to connect to Linux — or it will take you much research and grumbling to hack a workaround.

With Linux booted, log in as root and make sure that your device special files are linked to the physical printing device. You can do this by running the `lptest` program, `etc/lptest`, which sends a set of test output to the printer you specify. The test output is 79 characters wide and prints over more than one page. The following example shows a few lines of a successful `lptest` output.

```
[root@flyingpenguin} $ /etc/lptest > /dev/lp0
!"#$%&'()*+,-./0123456789:;<=>?@ABCDEFGHIJKLMNOPQRSTUVWXYZ[\]^_`abcdefghijklmno
"#$%&'()*+,-./0123456789:;<=>?@ABCDEFGHIJKLMNOPQRSTUVWXYZ[\]^_`abcdefghijklmnop
#$%&'()*+,-./0123456789:;<=>?@ABCDEFGHIJKLMNOPQRSTUVWXYZ[\]^_`abcdefghijklmnopq
$%&'()*+,-./0123456789:;<=>?@ABCDEFGHIJKLMNOPQRSTUVWXYZ[\]^_`abcdefghijklmnopqr
%&'()*+,-./0123456789:;<=>?@ABCDEFGHIJKLMNOPQRSTUVWXYZ[\]^_`abcdefghijklmnopqrs
&'()*+,-./0123456789:;<=>?@ABCDEFGHIJKLMNOPQRSTUVWXYZ[\]^_`abcdefghijklmnopqrst
'()*+,-./0123456789:;<=>?@ABCDEFGHIJKLMNOPQRSTUVWXYZ[\]^_`abcdefghijklmnopqrstu
()*+,-./0123456789:;<=>?@ABCDEFGHIJKLMNOPQRSTUVWXYZ[\]^_`abcdefghijklmnopqrstuv
```

Tip If you want to run a mini-test, you can tell lptest the width (in characters) and length (in lines) of the output, e.g. /etc/lptest 50 10, which prints test output 50 characters wide and 10 lines long.

If you have a serial printer, another way to use lptest is to send its output directly to the serial port, as follows:

```
[root@flyingpenguin} $ /etc/lptest > /dev/ttys0
```

As root, you can also test printing by using the cat command to redirect a file to the printer you want to test. In the example that follows, replace mytest.txt with the name of your test file, and replace the device special file with the file for your printer.

```
[root@flyingpenguin} $ cat mytest.txt > /dev/lp1
```

Setting up printer-control software

It's likely that your installation procedure installed the packages you need to support printing. You can check that the packages are installed by running rpm to query the package database. The most commonly used print system is lpr, which contains the print spooling daemon, lpd. This package provides basic print services. Use rpm as in the following example to find it. If you're not sure of the name, rpm -qa lists all the packages installed.

```
root@tweety} rpm -q lpr
lpr-0.41-2
```

Besides the lpr package, you need supplemental packages to support the more powerful and flexible features of Linux printers. Those packages include the groff text formatter (to display man pages and other documents created by the troff program). The Linux installation procedure usually adds these filters and text formatters automatically. The example below uses the rpm -q command to query the package database for the groff text formatter.

```
root@tweety} rpm -q groff
groff-1.11a-9
```

The example below shows how to pipe the rpm output through grep. This is useful if you don't know the exact name of the package you're looking for. In the following example, I was searching for the ImageMagick and ghostscript filters, but I wasn't sure about the spelling and case so I piped the output through grep, searching for partial names. The rpm command tells me that both packages are already installed.

```
root@tweety} rpm -qa | grep agick
ImageMagick-4.2.9-1
root@tweety} rpm -qa | grep script
ghostscript-fonts-5.10-3
ghostscript-5.10-10
```

Table 13-1 lists some popular printing packages. These packages run on a variety of architectures, including Alpha, SPARC, PowerPC, Intel x86 and compatibles. Check the Web site, `www.rpmfind.net/linux`, for specific architecture support. The package column displays the name only. For the most recent version number for each package, browse the Web site, `www.rpm.org`.

Table 13-1 **Printer Configuration and Text/Image** **Formatting and Filtering Packages**	
Package	**Function**
lpr	Traditional print spooler and configuration package.
LPRng	LPRng (next generation) Print Spooler (works with UNIX and NT as well as Linux).
LPRng-lpd	Enhanced replacement for the usual Linux print-spooler daemon.
APS-Filter	The ultimate magic print filter.
magicfilter	Another customizable, extensible magic printer filter.
ImageMagick	Image format conversion and display under the X Window System.
ghostscript	PostScript interpreter that enables you to print PostScript on a non-PostScript printer.
ghostview	PostScript viewer and print previewer (depends on ghostscript).
groff	A document-formatting tool.
mpage	Prints multiple pages of text on one paper page.
printtool	GUI printer-configuration tool.
rhs-printfilters	Red Hat print filters to use with printtool or printerdrake.
tunelp	Configuration tool for lp device parameters.
enscript	Text converter, ASCII and GNU text to PostScript, displays PDF (Acrobat) files.
enscript-fonts-koi8	Enscript fonts.
HP-printcap	Printcap configuration tool and utilities for HP Laserjet printers.
lpstyl	Apple StyleWriter family print spooler.
mpdist	GUI based (Motif) PostScript pretty printers tool.
lout	Another document-formatting language and tool.
pcps	Tool for printing text files on a PostScript printer.
psutils	Assorted PostScript utilities.
t1utils	Tools for using PostScript Type 1 fonts.

Tip It makes a difference whether you get your printing packages from a European or American Web site. The European version of most printing packages defaults to A4 size paper. Most American versions default to 8.5 x 11 inch paper. You can override both defaults with an option on the lpr command.

Starting the printer daemon (lpd)

The lpd must be running before you can configure a printer. The lpd usually starts when you boot Linux because the rc startup files (in the directories, /etc/rc.d/rc*.d) start and stop the lpd automatically. If you need to start and stop the lpd manually, you can start it from a graphical print utility, as in Figure 13-1, or you can type the following command in a terminal window or a non-graphical console:

```
root@tweety> /usr/sbin/lpd
```

Setting up the printcap file

The following sections guide you through setting up the printcap file.

Inside the /etc/printcap file

The following printcap file shows a Canon BJC300 printer locally attached to the Red Hat computer flyingpenguin. Since there is only one entry in this file, flyingpenguin can only see that one printer. The line that begins with ##PRINTTOOL3## describes the printer.

Note The hash symbol, #, is a comment character.

```
[root@flyingpenguin] cat /etc/printcap
# /etc/printcap
#
# Please don't edit this file directly unless you know what you are doing!
# Be warned that the control-panel printtool requires a very strict format!
# Look at the printcap(5) man page for more info.
#
# This file can be edited with the printtool in the control-panel.

##PRINTTOOL3## LOCAL bjc600 360x360 letter {} BJC600 8 {}
lp0:old_printer_in_the_loft_office\
        :sd=/var/spool/lpd/lp0:\
        :mx#0:\
        :sh:\
 :pl#61:pw#80:\
        :lp=/dev/lp0:\
:if=/var/spool/lpd/lp0/filter:
```

The Red Hat graphical printer configuration utility, `printtool`, inserted the comments lines. Different graphical printer tools insert different comments. You can also edit in any comments you want. The next line contains the name of the printer (and any alternate names) that you can use in print commands. Notice that you can refer to this printer as lp0 or as old_printer_in_the_loft_office. The ability to give the same printer different descriptive names is a nice feature of the Linux print system. If the employee who sits in the loft office would like to refer to this printer as Kens_printer, you can edit the line and add another name. The system administrator would probably print to lp0; most users would print to old_printer_in_the_loft_office, and Ken would print to Kens_printer. The lpd understands that these three names are the same physical printer.

Each line that follows the printer's name(s) is a symbol that describes a printer capability, such as the number of lines on a page or the location of the spool directory. Table 13-2 lists most of the possible symbols. You do not need every symbol in your printcap file. It depends on the printer and whether you can accept default values for capabilities you don't define. The preceding printcap file defines only six symbols.

Tip

Name your print queues something meaningful to non-technical users, such as color_printer_in_the_loft_office. Do not name the printer for the vendor's make or model. The old printer in the loft office is a Canon BJC-600. Naming a print queue CanonBJC600 means a lot of extra phone calls for the system administrator from users asking, "What's the printer in the loft office called?" Additionally, if I put another printer in there, I can name it black_white_laser_printer_in_loft_office, and most users will get it. Three months from now, when color_printer_in_the_loft_office breaks, and you replace it with a Lexmark color inkjet, you won't need to change the print queue name. Users can continue to print to color_printer_in_the_loft_office without ever knowing that the hardware has changed.

Table 13-2
printcap Symbols

Symbol	Meaning	Default Value
af	The location of the printer accounting file, if you are using printer accounting.	
br	The baud rate, if the printer is connected to a serial port.	none
if	The location of the text file input filter.	none
ff	The formfeed character.	
fo	Automatically sends a formfeed before printing.	true
lf	The location of the error log file.	/dev/console

Symbol	Meaning	Default Value
lo	The location of the lock file.[1]	none
lp	The default local printer.	/dev/lp
mx	The maximum file size the printer will accept.	0 (unlimited)[2]
of	The name of the output file filter.	
pl	The number of lines for the page length.	66
pw	The number of characters in a line (printer width).	132
rm	The name of the remote computer, if you are setting up a remote printer.	/dev/null
rs	Restricts printing to users who have accounts on the printer's local computer.	false
sb	Prints a single line banner before printing the file.	
sc	Suppresses multiple copies, i.e. enables users to print only one copy at a time.	false
sd	The location of the spool directory.	/usr/spool/lpd
sh	Suppresses headers on burst pages.	

1. The lock file is a two-line file that keeps multiple daemons from being active simultaneously. The first line in the lock file is the process ID of the daemon. The second line is the control file name of the current job being printed.

2. On some Linux distributions, the mx default is 1000 blocks.

Note

Each printer that your computer can access needs an entry in the printcap file. If you are accessing a remote printer that is physically connected to another computer on the network, the entry is brief, naming the remote computer that hosts the printer, the local spool directory, and the name of the printer. The printer name on the local computer and the remote computer can be different. The following is the entry for a network-attached printer. This printer, a Hewlett Packard LaserJet 4000, is not connected to any computer. The lp symbol equates local printing with the null device because this printer is directly attached to a network. The rm symbol points to the IP address for the printer.

```
lp1|HP4000|net_printer:\
:lp=/dev/null:\
:sh:\
:rm=192.168.0.71:\
:lf=/var/log/hp4k_errs:\
:af=/var/log/hp4k_acct:\
:sd=/var/spool/lpd/hp4k:
```

Finishing touches

To finish setting up printing, you need to create the spool directory, set the spool directory ownership and access privileges, and create the status and lock files in the spool directory. The following commands show these final steps:

```
root@tweety# mkdir /var/spool/tweety_print
root@tweety# chown root.lp tweety_print
root@tweety# chmod 775 tweety_print
root@tweety# touch tweety_print/lock
root@tweety# chown root.root tweety_print /lock
root@tweety# chmod 004 tweety_print /lock
root@tweety# touch tweety_print /status
root@tweety# chown root.root tweety_print/status
root@tweety# chmod 664 tweety_print/status
```

Tip   Consider creating a man page or a Web page that provides information about each printer at your site, including location, capabilities, and what computers can print to it. If you don't use a magic filter, include some sample commands for printing various file types, including images, PostScript, and PDF.

Using Printing Commands

After you have connected a printer and configured a print system, you and your users can print files. This section describes basic user commands for printing (spooling), checking the status of your print jobs, and removing jobs before they print.

Printing files

The lpr command prints a text document by sending the document to the spooling directory, and the lpd sends it to your printer. The following examples show the lpr command in action.

```
root@tweety> # print a text file on the default printer
root@tweety> lpr 4622-7fg13-7.txt
root@tweety> # Use the -P option to print on a specific printer
root@tweety> lpr -PLab_Printer 4622-7fg13-7.txt
```

Note   If you want to print to a device other than the default lp, you can export the PRINTER variable in your .bashrc file. The PRINTER variable overrides the value of the system default printer. For example, if you wanted to print to the Lab_Printer regularly, you would export the variable as follows:

```
# Put a line like this in the .bashrc file
#    in your home directory
export PRINTER=Lab_Printer
```

Once you define the PRINTER variable, your output automatically goes there. If you want to print to another printer, the -P option on the lpr command overrides your PRINTER variable.

The lpr command has various options for formatting output. See the man page for the lpr command that comes with the CD-ROM in the back of this book for a complete listing of options.

Table 13-3 lists some of the more common options for the lpr command.

Table 13-3 lpr Command Options	
Option	**Purpose**
-b	Do not print a banner or header.
-i*n*	Indent *n* columns. (Not all printers support this option.)
-K*n*	Print *n* copies.
-m*address*	On successful completion, mail a message to *address*.
-P*printer*	Print on *printer*. If -P*printer* is omitted, print to the PRINTER variable or default printer.
-w*n*	Set the page width to *n* characters
-F*filter*	If there is no magic filter installed, specify the filter flags manually.

When Does print Not Mean Print?

The Linux pr command is a formatter. It does not actually spool files. You can use the pr command to pretty up text files and pipe the output to the lpr command, which actually spools your file with its extra formatting. For example, to add a page number and page header to each page of output, you would type the pr command, followed by any command options and the file name, and pipe the entire command line through lpr, as below:

```
miss_scarlet@tweety$ pr -h "My Special Clue Report" -l52 cr.txt |lpr
```

The preceding command uses the -h option to generate a custom header and the l option to specify that each printed page should be 52 lines long. The pr command formats a default page header that contains two blank lines, a line containing the formatting date, the file name, and the page count, followed by two more blank lines. The pr command options enable you to change the header format, specify columnar output, double-space the output, set the page width and length, set margins, number the lines in the output, and show non-printable characters.

If you have a GUI such as GNOME or KDE, you can print from the File menu. Figure 13-1 shows a text file selected in the KDE Disk Navigator (which is similar to Windows Explorer); Print is selected from the File menu. Clicking on Print sends the file to the spool directory, just as typing lpr in a terminal window does. If you use the lpr command, you can add options to control the formatting, such as page orientation and size. A GUI enables you to set those options by pressing buttons.

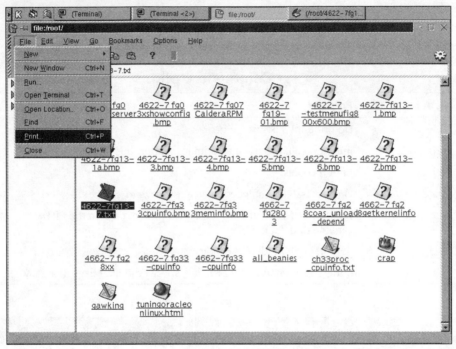

Figure 13-1: Hate command mode? Point and click to print

Checking the status of your print jobs

The lpq (line printer queue) command reports on your print job as in the following example. The lpq command lists print jobs by their job number and owner. With no options, the lpq command lists all jobs in the print queue.

```
root@flyingpenguin# lpq
Remote_Printer_Tweety is ready and printing
Rank     Owner          Job   Files            Total      Size
active   prof_plum      031   SillyReport.ps   5233782    bytes
1st      miss_scarlet   034   weapons.txt          240    bytes
1st      miss_scarlet   042   victims.jpeg        5472    bytes
```

Using the lpc command to manage print services

If you're the system administrator, you are responsible for controlling and managing printer operations. You use the lpc (line printer control) program to manage queuing and printing and to report on printer status. The lpc program controls printing in the following ways:

✦ Reports the status of the line printer daemon, printers, and spooling

✦ Enables and disables printers

✦ Enables and disables spooling (queuing)

✦ Reorders jobs in a print queue

✦ Redirects print jobs to different printers

✦ Holds print jobs in the queue so that they do not print when their turn comes

✦ Releases print jobs so that they go from the queue to the printer

✦ Stops printing (to solve a printer problem)

✦ Restarts printing, as well as restarting print jobs that were interrupted when printing was stopped

You can invoke lpc commands in two ways. If you are only going to run a single lpc command, you can add it to the lpc invocation, as in the following example:

```
candace@tweety$ lpc status
Printer          Printing       Spooling      Jobs    Server     Slave
lp@tweety        enabled        enabled       0       none       none
lp5@tweety       enabled        enabled       0       none       none
```

Note   The preceding lpc status output comes from tweety, which runs the LPRng printing software.

Another way to run lpc is to invoke it with no arguments and enter lpc commands at the lpc prompt, as in the following example:

Note   The lpc status below comes from flyingpenguin, which runs the older and more commonly used lpd software. Compare the following output to the output in the preceding example. Although the underlying print systems are different, both lpc status commands show the same basic information.

```
miss_scarlet@flyingpenguin> lpc
lpc> status
lp:
          queuing is enabled
          printing is enabled
          no entries
          no daemon present
```

```
        lp0:
                queuing is enabled
                printing is enabled
                1 entry in spool area
                lp0 is ready and printing
        lpc> exit
```

The following printcap file is for the printers on flyingpenguin, which were listed in
the previous example by the lpc status command. The first printer, lp0, is a Samba
(Server Message Block protocol) printer attached to a Microsoft Windows 98 computer. The second printer, lp0, is locally attached to flyingpenguin.

```
miss_scarlet@flyingpenguin>$ cat /etc/printcap
# /etc/printcap
#
# Please don't edit this file directly unless you know
#    what you are doing!
# Be warned that the control-panel printtool requires a
#    very strict format!
# Look at the printcap(5) man page for more info.
#
# This file can be edited with the printtool in the
#    control-panel.

##PRINTTOOL3## SMB bjc600 360x360 letter {} BJC600 8 {}
lp:\
        :sd=/var/spool/lpd/lp:\
        :mx#0:\
        :sh:\
        :if=/var/spool/lpd/lp/filter:\
        :af=/var/spool/lpd/lp/acct:\
        :lp=/dev/null:
##PRINTTOOL3## LOCAL bjc600 360x360 letter {} BJC600 8{}
lp0:\
        :sd=/var/spool/lpd/lp0:\
        :mx#0:\
        :sh:\
        :lp=/dev/lp0:\
        :if=/var/spool/lpd/lp0/filter:
```

Table 13-4 lists common lpc commands. All the commands in Table 13-3 (except
topq) take either all or the name of a printer (or printers) as an argument. If you
omit the argument to the lpc commands, all is the default.

Table 13-4
lpc Commands

Command	Function
Help	List the lpc commands.
help *command*	Describe a specific lpc command.
Abort	Kill the active print job and the lpd, and disable printing.
disable	Disable spooling only, and finish printing jobs that are already queued. Do not queue new print requests.
enable	Enable spooling only.
Down	Disable spooling, stop printing, and put out a message.
Up	Enable spooling and restart printing.
Stop	Disable spooling after the current print job finishes, and disable printing.
Start	Enable printing and restart the daemon(s) for listed printers.
hold	Suspend a spooled job. Allow a held job to print.
topq	Move the specified job numbers or specified users' jobs to the head of the queue.
status	Display the status of the lpds and queues.
exit	Exit from the lpc program.

The disable command kills the lpd associated with the specified printer(s). The enable command starts the lpd associated with the specified printer(s). hold is a toggle and is not available on all systems. Its meaning depends on the status of the job. The topq command takes either job numbers or usernames as arguments.

Removing jobs from the print queue

Use the lprm command to remove a job from the print queue. lprm removes the spooled file and any temporary files associated with it from the spooldirectory. For example, the following command removes miss_scarlet's weapons.txt job.

```
root@flyingpenguin# lprm 34
034 dequeued
```

If you type lprm with no options, it removes all print jobs you have queued. For example, if Miss Scarlet types the following command, she removes all of her print jobs.

```
root@flyingpenguin# lprm
034 dequeued
042 dequeued
```

Note   You can only remove jobs that you own unless you are root. Root can remove any job from any print queue. For example, to remove all jobs from the Lab_Printer root can simply type:

```
root@flyingpenguin# lprm Lab_Printer
```

Root can also remove jobs owned by a specific user. For example, to remove the SillyReport file you can see spooled in the preceding lpq example, root types

```
root@flyingpenguin# lprm prof_plum
```

Using a GUI Tool to Set up Printing

Different Linux distributors offer their own GUI printing-administration and -configuration tools that automatically create entries in the printcap file based on your choices. Caldera OpenLinux's GUI tool is the printer configuration tool that is part of COAS (Caldera Open Administration System). Red Hat's GUI tool is called printtool. You can use printtool to add both local printers and remote printers. With all GUI tools, you configure your printer and print queue by selecting items from menus and clicking on buttons.

Using Caldera Open Linux's COAS printer configuration

You start COAS by clicking on the COAS icon on the main taskbar or by selecting COAS from the KDE main menu, as shown in Figure 13-2. When you start the printer configuration tool, a window similar to the one in Figure 13-3 appears. The exact appearance of the window depends on what (if any) printers are already configured. The printer configuration window in Figure 13-3 has two tabs: Printer and Daemon.

Starting and stopping the lpd (line printer daemon)

You can only print if the daemon is running. You start and stop the lpd (line printer daemon) from the Daemon menu in the printer configuration tool's main window.

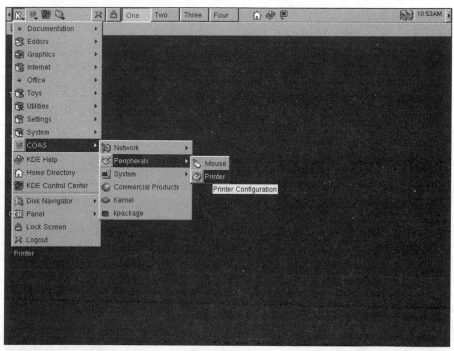

Figure 13-2: The COAS Printer Tool Window

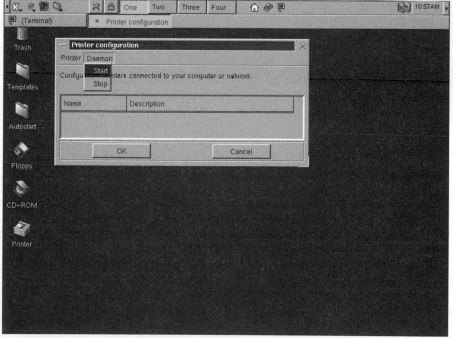

Figure 13-3: The Printer and Daemon tabs

Adding a printer to your system configuration

To add a printer to your system, follow these steps:

1. Select Add from the Printer menu in the printer configuration tool's main window. The Select printer model window appears. It will look like the window in Figure 13-4.

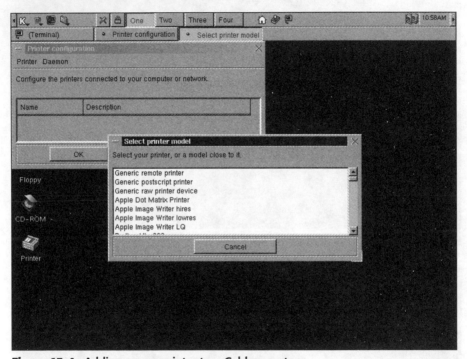

Figure 13-4: Adding a new printer to a Caldera system

2. After you select your physical printer device from the list, you'll see the Printer name window. Give the printer a logical name, such as lp, lp1, or the like. See Figure 13-5.

3. After you click OK to continue, you'll get the Printer attributes screen shown in Figure 13-6. Printer attributes include paper size, the device special file that represents the printer, and the data speed (get the speed from the printer documentation or manufacturer's Web site). Click OK after you set all the attributes.

4. Click Save in the next window to save your printer configuration. After you save the configuration, click OK to save the attributes and create the printer queue. COAS will stop and restart the lpd so that the daemon recognizes the new printer. Figure 13-7 shows that the daemon recognizes the new printer.

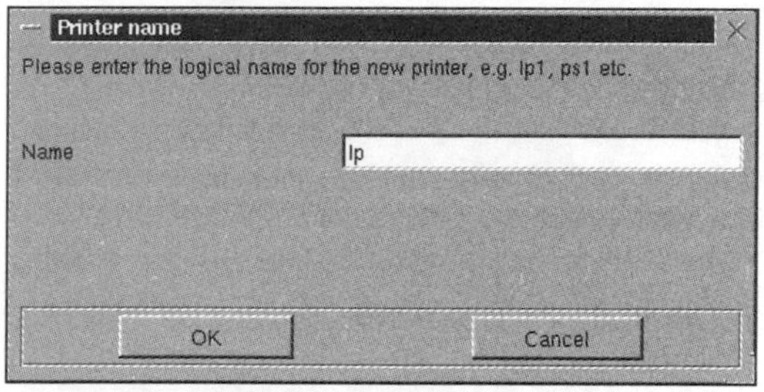

Figure 13-5: Naming the printer

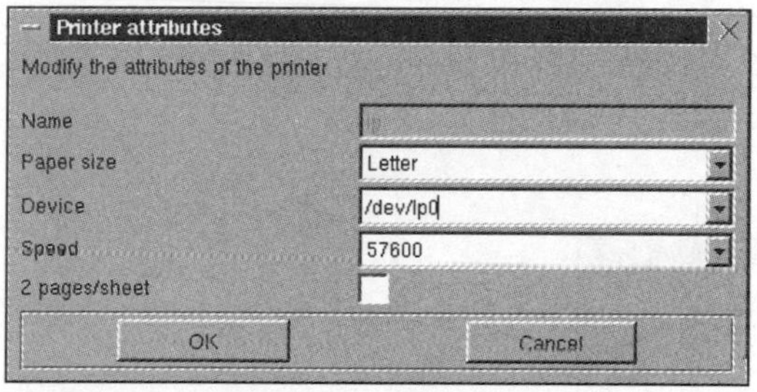

Figure 13-6: Setting the printer attributes

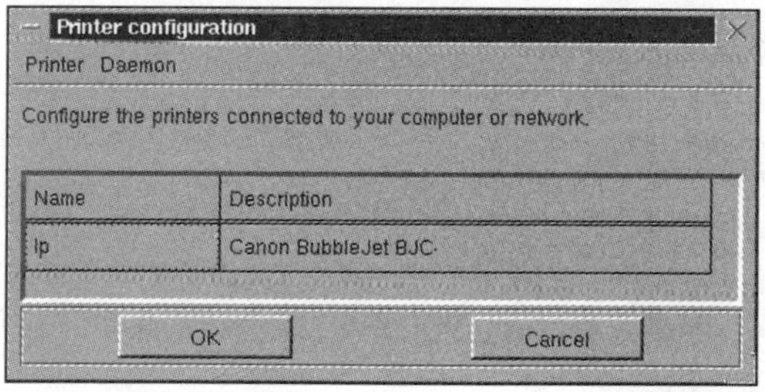

Figure 13-7: The lpd recognizes the new printer

Editing printer attributes

To change a printer's attributes, select the printer from the Printer configuration window (Figure 13-3) and click the Printer tab to display the menu. Choose Edit from the menu. This will bring up the Printer attribute window, where you can add and change attributes. (Typical changes include adding alternate printer names and changing the spool directory.) Click OK when you're finished with the changes, and click Save to save the edited configuration. If you are setting up a queue to a remote printer, be sure to fill in the Remote host and Remote queue boxes at the bottom of the screen. In Figure 13-8, the system administrator edits the printer attributes on the computer, tweety, to add alternate names for 1p. The following example shows the printcap file generated by the COAS printer configuration tool after root edited the 1p printer.

```
#     /etc/printcap on tweety (Caldera OpenLinux)
#
# Please don't edit this file directly unless you know what you are doing!
# Be warned that COAS requires a very strict format
# Other applications (like WordPerfect) cannot cope with LPRng-extensions
# to the syntax (those are best hidden in a 'lpd-printcap')
#
# The preferred method to modify this file is COAS.
lp|2ndFloorColor|Emily's printer:\
    :lp=/dev/lp0:\
    :br=#57600
    :rm=:\
    :rp=:\
    :sd=/var/spool/lpd/lp:\
    :mx#0:\
    :sh:\
    :if=/var/spool/lpd/lp/printfilter:
```

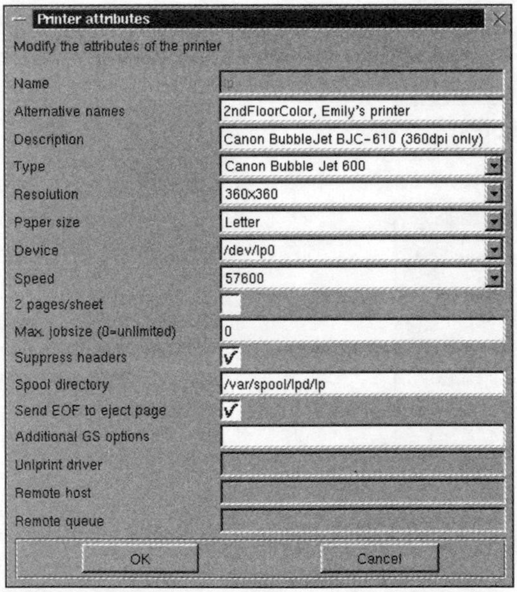

Figure 13-8: The Printer attributes window

Removing a printer

When you permanently disconnect printer hardware, don't forget to remove it from your Linux software configuration. Select the printer from the Printer configuration window and click Remove to remove all software traces of the printer, including its entry in the printcap file.

Using Red Hat Linux's printtool

Red Hat's printtool program is another easy-to-use graphical interface for configuring printers. You need to log in or su to the root user. To run printtool, go to the Control Panel and press the printtool button or run printtool from a terminal window. If you use a terminal window, typing /usr/bin/printtool creates the printtool main window. If you have already added some printers, the main window will show all the printers in the printcap file. You can add a new printer or select existing printers to remove or edit. All saved changes edit the printcap file automatically. To add a new printer, click the Add button and select options such as local, remote, or LAN manager printer. The printtool program will show you which parallel printer device special files it has detected.

Note If printtool does not show at least one of the device special files /dev/lp0, /dev/lp1, or /dev/lp2, either your printer is not on or physically connected, or your kernel does not yet support printing.

Remote Printing to Another Linux (or UNIX) Computer

Remote printing is easy to set up. If you want to print to a remote printer attached to another computer, you need to create a simple entry in the printcap file that identifies the print queue as remote and gives the location of the remote computer.

To allow remote computers to print to your printer, you must list the machines in the file /etc/hosts.lpd. If you specify the rs flag in the printcap entry for a printer, lpd only allows remote users (users logged in on other computers) who have accounts on the remote computer (the machine with the printer attached).

```
#   printcap file on flyingpenguin (Red Hat)
#   REMOTE djet500 lp3|candys_office|HPdeskjet:\
:sd=/var/spool/lpd/HPdj1:\
#   Print jobs from flyingpenguin will automatically come out on
#        tweety's printer
:rm=tweety.cardinalconsulting.com:\
:rp=candys_office:\
:lp=/dev/null:\
:sh:
```

Note Even though the printer is on a remote computer (tweety), you still need a local spool directory. If the remote computer is busy or offline or the network connection is down, print jobs from the local computer wait in the spool area until the remote printer is accessible.

The TCP/IP networking protocols take care of the behind-the-scenes communications that make remote printing so easy on Linux.

Remote Printing to Non-Linux Printers

Linux packages NetWare networks.

Printing to printers attached to computers running Microsoft operating systems

You can print to Windows 95/98, Windows NT, LanManager, and Samba printers by sending a print queue through the smbclient to a TCP/IP based SMB print service. You run the script smbprint to set up this interface to Windows printing.

Cross-Reference   Read Chapter 34, "Integrating Linux into Heterogeneous Networks" for detailed information on using Samba.

You put the configuration file (/etc/smb.conf) for the printer into the spool directory and list the pathname for the smbprint script as the :if line in the printcap file, as in the following example:

```
lp|remote-smbprinter:\
    :lp=/dev/null:sh:\
    :sd=/var/spool/lpd/lp:\
    :if=/usr/local/sbin/smbprint:
```

Tip   You should read the documentation inside the smbprint script for more information on how to configure printing to remote Windows printers. You can also use smbclient to submit a file directly to an SMB printing service without involving lpd. See the man page for smbclient.

What to Do if Something Goes Wrong

If you can't print, always check the hardware. Things that seem obvious can be easy to overlook. For example, did the printer come unplugged from the wall or uncabled from the computer or network? Is there paper in the printer? If you can't print, try these hardware sanity checks to see whether you have a hardware problem:

✦ If your computer has another operating system loaded, such as DOS or Windows, boot the alternate operating system and see if you can print. If you can print from the other operating system, you know that your printer hardware, printer, cable, connector are okay, then you must have a Linux configuration issue.

✦ If, as root, you can redirect a file to the printer device, /dev/lp, then the print hardware is working and you have a Linux configuration issue.

Here are a couple of other printing problems that you might encounter:

Problem:	When you try to print, your file doesn't spool.
Solution:	Use ps or lpc to check whether the lpd is running. If it is not, restart the daemon.
Problem:	Your spool directory fills up its partition. Users can't create or edit new files, or spool to the associated printer.
Solution:	Preventive maintenance. Don't let this happen in the first place. Create a text file called minfree in each spool directory. The minfree file should list the minimum number of disk blocks to leave free, even if it means not spooling a request. You might be thinking, "My users will never have that many print requests." Don't be fooled. A runaway job might spool for hours or days without anyone noticing until it fills the disk. I filled my own disk with e-mail messages from cron when I was testing a job that ran every minute of every day of every week.
Problem:	Everyone's print job seems to run except yours.
Solution 1:	Try to print from a different application. Your printing problem may be application-related.
Solution 2:	If you're printing to a remote printer, make sure that you haven't been excluded from the rg (remote group) line in the printcap file.
Problem:	Printing starts to work, but stops after printing a few pages.
Solution:	Check the mx parameter in your /etc/printcap file. If it's set lower than some of the file sizes you need to print, edit the printcap file and increase mx.

Tip   There are various ways to print a man page. The simplest way is to pipe the man page to the lpr command. The example below prints the pr man page.

```
miss_scarlet@tweety$ man xterm | lp
```

A filter is a program that manipulates input in some way before sending the input to an output device, such as stdout or a printer. Linux's *magic filters* manipulate files based on their type. A magic filter saves the system administrator time and trouble in configuring a printer for multiple output formats. A magic filter understands most input file types, such as PDF, PostScript, and text, and produces the right output format for each file type. For example, if you print a PostScript file, the magic filter "magically" figures out that the file is PostScript and activates a program that can get the printer to output the PostScript format. If you've ever tried to print a PostScript file without a filter, you've printed the control information, which is huge, as well as the data. Try to separate the data from the control information and you'll see why you need a filter. The filter performs the actions contained in the control information, such as formatting text and setting up headings, and outputs the data neatly. A magic filter works with specialized printing programs that you install on your system. When you print a file, the magic filter finds the appropriate filter for your output so that you don't need to worry about formatting the output as part of the printing process. The most popular magic filters are magicfilter and APSfilter.

 Note   The term *magic filter* refers to programs that format your output. The name magicfilter refers to one of the magic filter programs.

 On the CD-ROM   There is a link on the CD-ROM to the NHF (Newbieized Help File) entitled "What is an APSfilter?" This NHF also includes a printcap file with five different entries for one printer. This printcap file illustrates how to enable a printer to output differently formatted files, based on APSfilters.

 Tip   GhostView is a PostScript viewer, i.e. a front end to GhostScript that enables you to preview a PostScript file on your screen before printing it. If your Linux distribution does not come with GhostScript and GhostView, you can get them at the GNU project's FTP site, `ftp://prep.ai.mit.edu/pub/gnu/`.

 Tip   One way to print TeX files is to convert them to PostScript and print them using GhostScript. First you need to convert them from TeX to DVI (device-independent) format with the `tex` command. Then you need to convert the resulting DVI file to PostScript with the `dvips` (dvi to PostScript) command.

```
$ tex yourfile.tex
$ dvips yourfile.dvi
```

Replace `yourfile` with the name of the file you want to print. After you convert the file to PostScript, you can use the `lpr` command to print it.

Summary

In this chapter you saw:

✦ How the Linux lpd printing system works.

✦ How to configure both local and remote printers and the /etc/printcap file either with commands or with graphical tools.

✦ How to use commands or graphical tools to start and stop the printer daemon (lpd).

✦ How to use the `lpc` program to manage spooling and printing.

You also got a review of standard Linux printing commands and the basic idea behind using print filters. You saw examples from both the `lpr` and LPRng printing systems. As you look at printcap files from each, you can't tell the difference. LPRng is an enhanced `lpr` system that uses the same commands and files (with additional options and capabilities).

This is the last chapter in Part II, "Getting Started with Linux System Administration," where you've learned to set up basic services for users. Part III deals with user commands. For more system administration topics go to Part IV, "Configuring and Managing TCP/IP Networking," and Part V, "Advanced System Administration and Networking."

✦　　✦　　✦

Using Linux

Logging in and Starting to Use Linux

This chapter helps get you started using Linux by introducing the GNOME graphical user interface (GUI) and showing you how to customize it to your liking. Unlike Windows, Linux allows you to choose from several popular GUIs and, if you do not like GUIs at all, you are always free to use a basic command line, text-mode interface.

Deciding on a UI (User Interface)

Before you log in to Linux, you need to decide what kind of user interface you plan to use. Linux offers you a choice of interfaces — character cell or graphical. A *character cell* (sometimes called *text mode*) interface, such as MS-DOS, is text-based. Linux calls this character cell interface the *command-line interface* (CLI). A *graphical-user interface* (GUI) is mouse- or pointer-based — point and click, drag and drop, such as Mac OS or Microsoft Windows.

Do you do windows?

Linux's graphical desktop environments (and there are several) are based on the X Window System. In addition to the command line, this book shows you two different graphical environments: GNOME, the newest environment with a GUI, and KDE, another popular desktop environment for Linux. Both interfaces will seem familiar to Windows users (with some differences). GNOME and KDE fill the need for an easy-to-use desktop for UNIX workstations, similar to the Mac OS and Microsoft desktop environments. GNOME is the newest graphical desktop environment.

A Word about X

MIT's (Massachusetts Institute of Technology) Project Athena developed the X Window System (X) to be a vendor- and operating-system-independent windowing system that specifies the internal workings of windows. X understands the graphical capabilities of your computer and provides enough flexibility on top of the graphical mechanics for developers to build different graphical interfaces, such as GNOME and KDE on Linux. These interfaces may look different, but underneath the hood they work the same. This may seem like a fine distinction, but X's focus on internal workings instead of appearance leads to the different-looking interfaces, such as GNOME and KDE, that are used in this book, and to the older, commercial Motif. If you install Linux on your computer, you must install the X Window System if you want a GUI. Then individual users will be able to decide whether they want to look at GNOME- or KDE-style windows.

What Goes on Top of X?

X by itself does not provide a GUI. X is called a display engine with *hooks* for windowing programs to attach to. These "hooks" enable windowing programs, called window managers, to define the GUI's appearance. You need to layer a Window Manager on top of X to achieve the distinctive look and feel of a GUI.

Caution   Installing the X Window System is usually the most complicated part of an operating-system installation.

GNOME and external window managers

As of this writing, there is only one window manager that is 100% compliant with GNOME. That is the Enlightenment window manager. Most of the GNOME screenshots in this book use the Enlightenment window manager.

Note   Unlike KDE, which comes with its own built-in window manager, GNOME uses an external window manager. You can use just about any window manager with GNOME, but the more GNOME-compliant a window manager is, the more functionality it offers.

Caution   Don't rule out GNOME because you don't have the Enlightenment Window Manager software. For the most part, GNOME can work with window managers that are partially compliant. You may not be able to use a fancy feature, such as multiple-desktop management, but the GNOME basics are there. Table 14-1 lists Window Managers that are partially compliant with GNOME or are currently being made compliant.

A Few Words about Window Managers

The *window manager* is software that controls the placement, borders, and appearance of your windows. GUIs such as KDE and GNOME work with window managers to provide your screen environment. For example, GNOME doesn't decide where your windows should go; it communicates with the window manager to learn the locations of your windows.

Table 14-1
Where to Find Window Manager Software

Window Manager	URL
Enlightenment	http://www.enlightenment.org
FWVM	http://www.fvwm.org/
Icewm	http://www.kiss.uni-lj.si/~k4fr0235/icewm/ http://icewm.sourceforge.net
Window Maker	http://www.windowmaker.org
AfterStep	http://www.afterstep.org/
GnoWM	http://www.pce.net/wdomburg/gnoWM
WmG	http://ductape.net/~reeve/

Note The GNOME Software Map lists window managers that work with GNOME (http://www.gnome.org/applist/list-martin.phtml?catno=12) and any restrictions they may have.

Why would you do anything *but* windows?

To Microsoft Windows and Apple Macintosh users, a GUI seems the logical choice of an interface to Linux. You point, click, and go. Why mess with commands and syntax? The answer has three parts:

✦ X is greedy. It requires memory, lots of memory. If you run Linux in a small amount of RAM, 4 to 8 MB for example, you may find that using a GUI leaves barely enough memory for your computer to crawl rather than run.

✦ Some GUI functions call the command line in a terminal window. If you're going to wind up working in a terminal window, why not just go there directly?

✦ If you decide to write shell scripts to automate system administration tasks (and you will), you need to understand how to use commands.

✦ The GUIs available for Linux still do not eliminate the necessity for the CLI because, at this point in time, the CLI is still required for configuring certain Linux behavior.

Getting Started

Linux is a multiuser, multitasking operating system. The term, *multiuser*, means what it says — that many users can work on the same computer at the same time. Linux provides some security mechanisms to support multiuser computing. These security features include:

✦ User login and logout

✦ Password protection

✦ File and directory access control

Logging in

Since Linux is a multiuser operating system, before you can work you must identify yourself to Linux by entering your username and password. The system administrator creates an account with a username, initial password, and home directory. Whether you see a login prompt or window when your computer starts up depends on whether you are using the graphical X Window System (X for short) or a character-based terminal or terminal window.

Linux offers you a choice of several possible interfaces, including a plain text-based shell, the X-based GNOME (GNU Network Object Model Environment), and KDE (K Desktop Environment).

Figure 14-1 shows user Marshall logging in to a GNOME window. Figure 14-2 shows the same user logging in to a terminal window. When you log in successfully, Linux puts you into a command interpreter called a *shell*. In a terminal window, you know you are in a shell because you see the shell prompt. The most common shell prompts are $, %, and #. You can customize your shell prompt to be almost any set of characters you want.

Multitasking — A New Concept for MS-DOS and Microsoft Windows Users

Multitasking means that while all users' tasks appear to run at the same time, behind the scenes the operating system is scheduling those tasks to take turns using the CPU (Central Processing Unit). Linux and systems are also called *timesharing systems*, meaning that all processes share the CPU in slices of time.

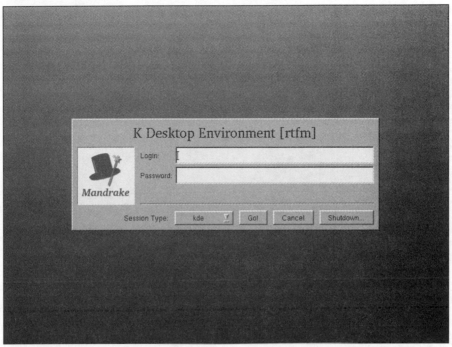

Figure 14-1: A user logs in through a GUI

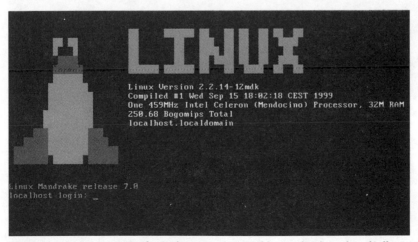

Figure 14-2: In a terminal window, a successful login displays the shell prompt

Linux is case-sensitive. CANDACE is not the same username as Candace or candace or CaNdAce. Figure 14-3 shows what happens if you type your username or password wrong.

Figure 14-3: This user forgot that her username is Candace, not candace

Changing your password

After you log in for the first time, you should use the `passwd` command to change the password that the system administrator assigned to you. All the normal warnings about passwords apply. Notice in Figure 14-4 that you can't see the password being typed. That's because Linux doesn't let anyone, even you, see your password on the screen.

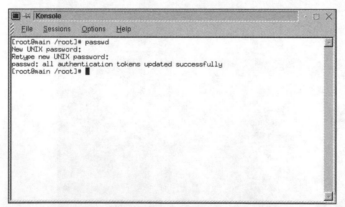

Figure 14-4: I use the `passwd` command to change my original password in a terminal window

The previous warning about case sensitivity also applies to passwords. If you forget your password, you must ask the system administrator to set a new password for you. Since your password is encrypted, the system administrator cannot look up your forgotten password.

For security reasons, most system administrators set up Linux so that you need to change your password on a regular basis—often every 30 or 60 days. When you get the message that your password will expire, you need to change your password as in Figure 14-4.

Logging out

When you are done with your Linux session, you should log out by using the logout command. Logging out ensures that no other user can work within your session or access your files and e-mail without permission. Logging out also tidies up your environment, closing files, releasing file and record locks, and reminding you to cancel any jobs that may be running in the background. Figure 14-5 shows a terminal window user logging out with the logout command.

Some other ways to log out are:

✦ Pressing Ctrl+D.

✦ Typing exit at the command-line prompt.

✦ Selecting Log Out from the graphical main menu.

When you log out, windowing environments such as GNOME and KDE remember where your windows are and which applications you were using, so that they can re-open them for you the next time you log in. This is called *session management*. The command-line interpreter does not provide this convenience.

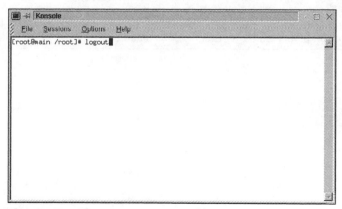

Figure 14-5: The logout command logs you out of Linux

Getting Online Help

Once you've logged in, what next? Linux, like most systems, supplies an online help system called the man (manual) or reference pages. The *man pages* hold the complete system documentation for commands and system configuration files. GNOME and KDE provide help facilities in addition to the man pages.

Using the man pages to get online help

The man pages range from spotty to comprehensive to almost incomprehensible. Some man pages provide examples. Many do not. Man-page help for a topic may be one sentence or six pages. Because of the inconsistency of the man pages, you may prefer to use the help facilities provided by your GUI.

Table 14-2 lists the commands you use to access the man pages. Figure 14-6 shows how to use the man command to display the man pages for the passwd command.

| Table 14-2 | |
Commands for Accessing the man Pages	
Command	*Purpose*
man	Displays complete help on the topic, including a description of the topic, cross-references, related files, and known problems.
apropos	
(man -k)	Lists all the commands that contain the keyword you are looking for as well as brief help for each command listed. You can also use apropos to search on partial words, for example, *fil* instead of *file*.

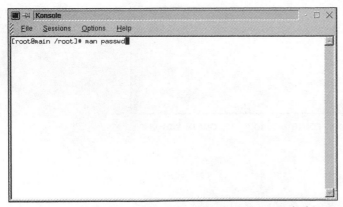

Figure 14-6: Using the man pages is one way to get help

Using your GUI's help facility

You may find your GUI help facility an easier place to start than the man pages.

To get quick tips about the functions of the icons and buttons you see on your screen, hold the mouse or pointer over the icon or button. Figure 14-7 shows how the help magically appears when you hover over a graphical element.

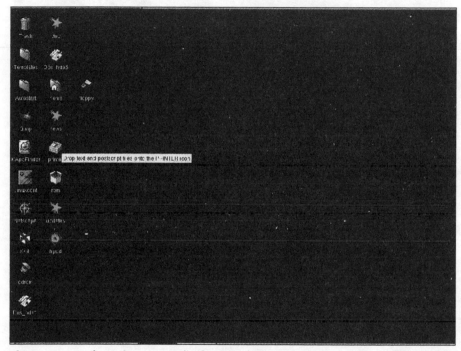

Figure 14-7: A hovering cursor displays quick tips on screen elements such as icons and buttons

You can also click the Help icon as shown in Figure 14-8. We are using the GNOME interface in this example. Pressing the F1 key also displays help functions. Figure 14-9 shows an example of the GNOME help browser.

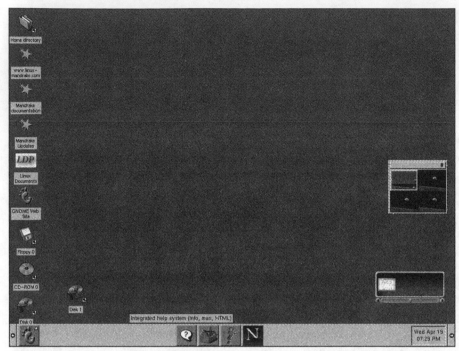

Figure 14-8: Click on the Help icon to bring up the help contents and index

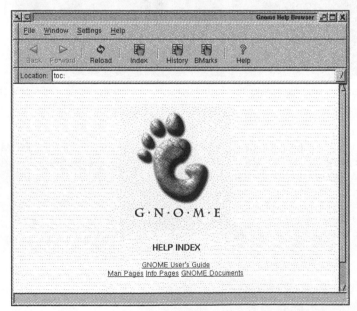

Figure 14-9: Use the GNOME help browser to see both Linux and GNOME help

Tip The GNOME help browser does not have a search function. You must page through the topics.

Getting to Know GNOME

Figure 14-10 shows GNOME running immediately after installation but before configuration to suit my environment. I see the desktop and the main GNOME panel.

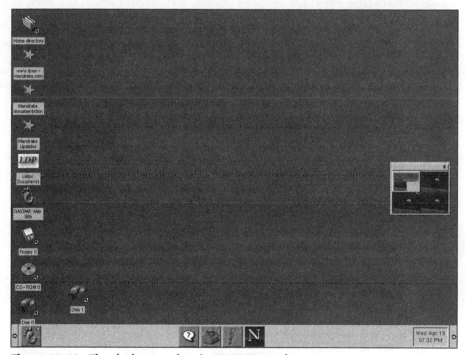

Figure 14-10: The desktop and main GNOME panel

Caution Depending on how you configure your environment, your GNOME display might look very different from Figure 14-10. This is because of GNOME's high degree of configuration flexibility.

The GNOME main panel (the bar with the foot on it at the bottom of Figure 14-10) is the heart of GNOME. The main panel contains a set of applets and menus.

The arrows on each side of the panel hide and unhide the panel. The foot on the left side of the main panel is the Main Menu button. Click on the Main Menu button to see a menu containing applications, such as Netscape Navigator, and commands, such as logout.

Most of the screen is your desktop, just as it is in any Windows-based GUI. You can put the items you use most on your desktop and double-click an item to activate it.

Understanding GNOME Basics

Using the GNOME panel is mostly intuitive for anyone who has used another GUI. The following sections describe the basics of working with panels, including using the main menu, adding new panels, and adding applications to panels. Panels contain applets and launchers. An *applet* is an X application, such as the clock. A *launcher* starts (launches) applications the way a shortcut does in the Microsoft Windows GUI. There are three kinds of launchers:

✦ Menus, such as the main menu (the footstep in the lower left-hand corner of Figure 14-10)

✦ Buttons, such as the Close Session button (just to the right of the main menu footstep)

✦ Drawers, which contain a panel that holds other launchers and applets

Using the main menu

The main menu is your starting point for running Linux applications. Installing GNOME builds the main menu.

Cross-Reference   You can read about how to customize the menu in a later section of this chapter.

The main menu works the same with GNOME as it would in any other GUI. Figure 14-11 shows the screen after a user presses the foot to display the main menu.

Running applications

GNOME provides different ways for you to run applications:

✦ From the main menu.

✦ From Application Launcher icons.

✦ From the File Manager (gmc). You can double-click any executable file to run it.

✦ From the Run Program item on the main menu. For example, if you want to run the Emacs editor, select Run Program and type emacs in the dialog box. See Figure 14-12.

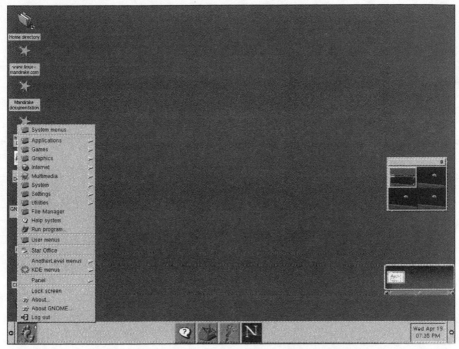

Figure 14-11: The main menu includes applications and other menus

Customizing Your Environment

GNOME is very adaptable. For instance, you can change how your desktop looks by changing colors, fonts, and borders, moving and adding panels and drawers and more. In fact, you can have four different desktops going at once! Look at the main panel in Figure 14-10 to see four desktop buttons. Besides the main panel, you can create multiple customized panels and determine what applets and commands to include. You can also add launchers to your desktop.

Using Control Center capplets

The GNOME Control Center enables you to customize your GNOME environment using tools called *capplets*. The Control Center consists of two parts, the main workspace and the capplet menu. To launch the Control Center, go to the Main Menu ⇨ Settings ⇨ Control Center. To configure your environment, double-click a capplet from the menu. Figure 14-13 shows how to change your desktop theme.

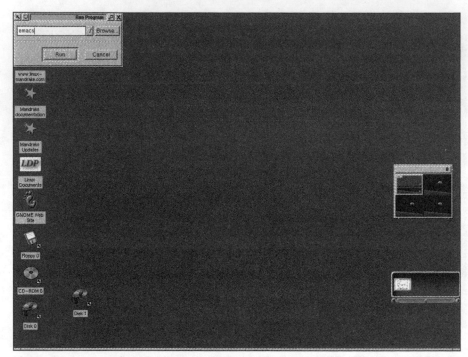

Figure 14-12: Use the Run Program item to run a program that you can't find on a menu or a panel

Table 14-3 lists some popular capplets and their functions.

Table 14-3
GNOME Capplets

Capplet	Customizes
Background properties	Background color and wallpaper.
Screen saver	Screen saver properties, e.g. speed, password, power management.
Theme selector	Desktop theme.
Window manager	Which Window Manager to use.
Default editor	Which editor, for example, vi, Emacs, to use with GNOME.
MIME types*	Which image to associate with a file type.
Keyboard bell	Sound and volume of the bell signal.
Sound events	Sounds associated with various GNOME events.

Capplet	Customizes
Keyboard properties	Auto-repeat and audible key clicks.
Mouse properties	Left- or right-handed operation and mouse speed.
Session manager	Prompt to confirm (or not) on logout and automatically save session changes when you log out.

* Multipurpose Internet Mail Extensions, originally developed for handling different types of e-mail and attachments. GNOME lets you extend the concept to defining how certain MIME types should be automatically handled.

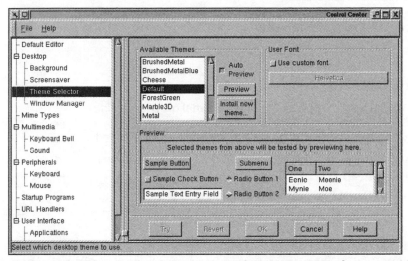

Figure 14-13: Use capplets from the Control Center to customize your environment

Creating launchers on the desktop

You can add a launcher to your desktop by positioning your mouse on the desktop and right-clicking. When you select New ➪ Launcher from the pop-up menu, a dialog box for the launcher appears as in Figure 14-14. Fill in the dialog box. The name of the launcher is the file name of the program to run (with no extension). The comment appears in the balloon that a hovering mouse displays. The command is the command you would type on a terminal to run the program. After you create the launcher, if you need to edit its properties, simply right-click the launcher to move it along the panel, to move it to a different panel, or to remove it.

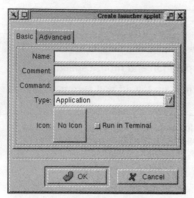

Figure 14-14: Add a launcher to run applications with a click of the mouse

Moving panels

You have a choice of three ways to move a panel on your desktop:

+ Dragging the panel with the middle mouse button pressed.

+ Dragging the panel with the left and right mouse buttons pressed simultaneously.

+ Using the Panel Configuration dialog box.

Adding a new panel to your desktop

Select Add New Panel from the Main Menu ➪ Panel menu. Choose Edge or Corner Panel as in Figure 14-15. Figure 14-15 shows both edge and corner panels.

Tip   You can toggle between panel types by moving your mouse to a panel and right-clicking. When the pop-up menu appears, select either Convert to edge panel or Convert to corner panel.

Adding applications and applets to panels

If you would like to add applications and applets to your panels, you must create icons, called *application launchers,* to start those applications. Right-click the panel and select Add New Launcher from the pop-up menu. To add an applet, such as the clock, to a panel, right-click the panel and select Add new applet. Figure 14-16 shows the dialog box that you fill in to set the properties for your new application launcher.

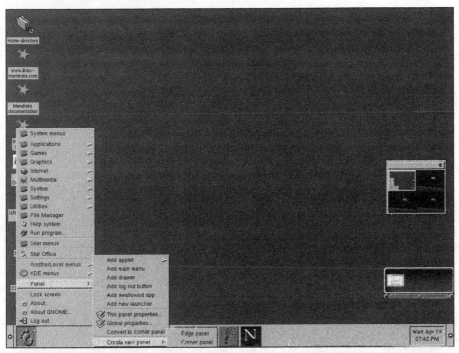

Figure 14-15: Use the Main Menu to add corner or edge panels

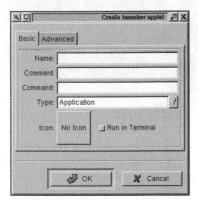

Figure 14-16: Set the properties for your new application launcher in the Create Launcher dialog box

Adding menus to panels

Follow these steps to add a menu to your panel:

1. Right-click the title bar of a menu.

2. Select Add this as menu to panel from the pop-up menu.

You can add system directories to a panel as menus by dragging them from the File Manager and dropping them on the panel.

Grouping applications into drawers

Drawers enable you to group applications together. Figure 14-17 shows a drawer button sitting on a panel. That drawer button groups together a set of application launchers. Click the drawer button to display the menu of applications. Click again to hide the menu.

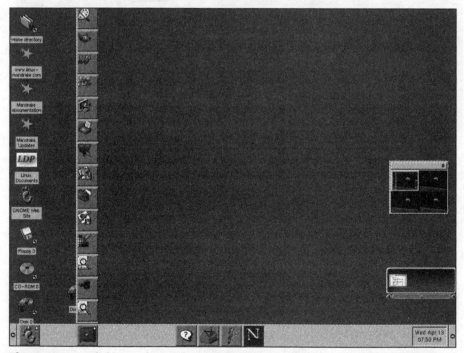

Figure 14-17: Clicking a drawer button displays a menu of applications for quick launching

There are two ways to put a drawer on your panel:

✦ Right-click the panel and select "Add drawer" from the pop-up menu.

✦ If you want your drawer to hold a set of menus from the main menu, right-click the title bar of that menu and select Add this as drawer to panel from the pop-up menu. See Figure 14-18.

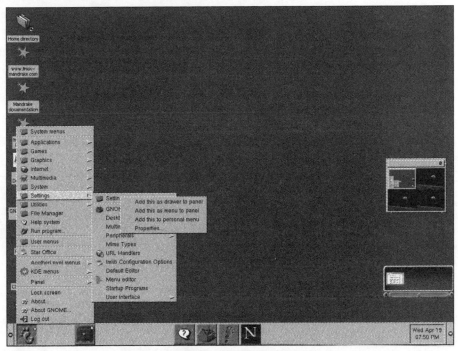

Figure 14-18: You can put a set of menus into a drawer

Summary

This chapter showed you how to get started by logging in, changing your password, and logging out. It also showed you examples of graphical interfaces. Besides the Command Line Interface, you have a choice of graphical interfaces based on the X Window System. While GNOME is the newest and most flexible GUI, KDE is more mature and has more applications at the time of this writing. Either GUI includes:

✦ A help browser

✦ Panels

✦ Launchers

✦ Applets

✦ Customizing capabilities

✦   ✦   ✦

Working with Files and Directories

If you're new to Linux or UNIX, this chapter introduces you to using common Linux commands for working with files and directories. If you're an MS-DOS user, some of the Linux commands may look familiar. That's because many of the commands available in MS-DOS were copied from UNIX. Table 15-1 lists the commands you discussed in this chapter.

Getting Started with Linux Directory Concepts

All modern operating systems include the concept of a file saved in a directory on disk. The directory is a collection of files, like a folder in the Microsoft Windows operating systems. As promised at the beginning of this chapter, Table 15-1 lists the most commonly used commands for working with files and directories.

Table 15-1
Common Linux Commands for Working with Files and Directories

Command	Function
ls	List files in a directory listing.
pwd	Display your working directory.
cd	Change to another directory.
mkdir	Create a new directory.

Continued

	Table 15-1 *(continued)*
Command	*Function*
rm	Delete (remove) a file.
rmdir	Delete (remove) a directory.
chmod	Control who can access your files.
cat, more, head, tail	Display the contents of your files.
man	Get help.
find	Find the location of files.
file	Learn about the file type.

Linux File and Directory Factoids

✦ All file names and directory names are case-sensitive.

✦ Directories can hold other directories (subdirectories).

✦ Directories and subdirectories are organized into a tree structure (hierarchy).

✦ Files are at the bottom of the directory tree.

✦ The root directory is the top directory in the Linux directory tree. A single forward slash (/), called "slash," represents the root directory.

✦ Installing Linux automatically creates the root directory and system subdirectories.

✦ A path is the route to a file. A full pathname lists the subdirectories and file name separated by forward slashes, for example, /home/bookfiles/chapter1 (pronounce the slashes).

✦ Linux doesn't use drive letters. All you need to know is the directory path to the file.

✦ Linux, unlike MS-DOS and the earliest version of Windows, allows you to use up to 256 characters in file names, unlike the 8.3 format to which you may be accustomed. You can even use spaces in a file name if you enclose the file name in quotation marks.

✦ Linux can access lots of different filesystems, including filesystems for Windows 2000, 95, and 98, OS/2, and UNIX.

✦ The system administrator creates a home directory for you. This is where you start when you log in.

A Quick Tour of a Linux Directory Tree

Figure 15-1 is a diagram of the Linux directory tree for a computer I use named red-bird. Directly underneath / are important subdirectories, such as /bin, /etc, /dev, and /opt, that hold system files and programs. On redbird, /home contains each user's home directory. The system administrator creates the home directories. Each circled group makes up a filesystem.

Cross-Reference   See Chapter 12 if you are the system administrator and need to create users' home directories.

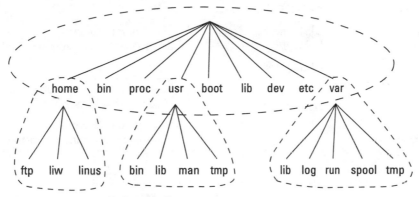

Figure 15-1: A typical Linux directory tree

Using full pathnames

The path to my home directory is /home/candace. I used the `mkdir` command to create several subdirectories under my home directory to organize my files. You can see that I have paths to old mail files (/home/candace/oldmail), and book files (/home/candace/lnxbible/chapters and home/candace/lnxbible/graphics).

Moving around in the directory tree

You use the `cd` (change directory) command to move around in the directory tree. You tell the `cd` command where to go by specifying a full pathname, a relative pathname, or a shortcut for a relative pathname. Table 15-2 shows a variety of ways to use the `cd` command.

Tip   **.** is a shortcut that represents your current directory, that is, where you are in the directory tree.

.. is a shortcut that represents the parent of your current directory (.), i.e. one directory above you in the directory tree).

Both **.** and **..** are relative paths.

Table 15-2
Using Pathnames with the cd Command

Pathname	Example	Effect
Full path	cd /home/candace/ lnxbible/chapters	Changes your current directory to the directory specified.
Relative path	cd chapters	
	c	Moves to the chapters subdirectory of your current directory.
Shortcut (..) to the directory above you	cd ..	Moves to the parent directory of your current directory.

Finding out where you are in the directory tree

You should always be aware of two directories: your home directory and your working directory. You read about your home directory earlier in this chapter.

Your *working directory* is the directory where you are currently located. For example, when you first log in, your working directory is automatically set to your home directory. It's easy to forget where you are after you use the cd command a few times to move to different directories. If you are confused, use the pwd (print working directory) command to find out where you are.

Tip   Whenever you need to get to your home directory, type the cd command without any arguments.

Note   A command argument is a parameter that you pass to a command. For instance, when you cd to a directory, the name of the directory is an argument to the cd command.

Using a Graphical Interface to Tour your Files and Directories

The GNOME and KDE file managers give you a graphical interface to your files and directories. This interface is similar to Microsoft Windows Explorer. The graphical file manager displays two windows:

✦ The tree window (on the left) displays all the directories in your computer's directory tree.

✦ The directory window (on the right) displays the files in the directory you select from the tree view.

Listing Files and Directories

The ls command displays a list of files and directories. If you type ls without any arguments, it displays the files and subdirectories in your current working directory. Here are some ls hints:

✦ If you use a directory as an argument to ls, Linux displays a list of files in that directory.

✦ If you use a file name as an argument to ls, Linux simply lists that file.

✦ You can use either full or relative pathnames as arguments to the ls command to list files and directories.

Tip You can use the tilde (~) character as a quick substitute for the name of your home directory in any command. For example, I can replace /home/candace with just one character, the tilde. If I need to list files in user scarlet's home directory, I can also use the tilde as a shortcut to her home, for example, ~scarlet. The variable HOME is another shortcut to your home directory. When using a variable, be sure to precede it with a $ to signal your shell to translate the variable's meaning.

Using wildcards in file and directory names

Most commands for working with files and directories understand two common wildcards, * and ?.You can refer to a file by its full pathname or, if it's in your working directory, simply by its file name. In either case, wildcards can let you type less. For example, for all files that start with the letter s, you can either type all their names or type s followed by the * wildcard. For all files that have the letter s anywhere in their names, type *s*, meaning zero or more characters, followed by s, followed by zero or more characters.

Note   The process of changing the *' into a file name is called *wild-card expansion* and is done by your shell. The ? wildcard represents exactly one character. The * wildcard represents zero or more characters.

Another wildcard is ?. The ? wildcard expands to one character only. Therefore, the command `ls ~/lnxbible/chapters/chap?.doc` lists files for chap1 through chap9, but not chap10.

Caution   You cannot use the * wildcard to match file names that start with a period (.). These files are called *hidden files*. Although they're not really hidden, they don't show up on normal `ls` listings. Read on to find out how to use `ls` to display hidden files.

Tip   To see hidden files using the GNOME File Manager, select Preferences from the Settings menu and click the File Display tab.

Tip   Linux has a useful pattern-matching feature for wild-carding that works on groups of files. For example, if you have a set of files named chapter1.doc through chapter99.doc, and you want to display a long listing of only the first six files, you can put the wild pattern to match inside a charset, as shown in the following example. A charset is a group of characters enclosed in brackets ([ ]). The shell understands that a charset range such as [1-6] means 1, 2, 3, 4, 5, and 6.

```
ls -l chapter[1-6].doc
```

Caution   Here's yet another case-sensitive gotcha: The charset range [A-Z] represents only the uppercase letters. [a-z] represents the lowercase letters.

Getting more information from ls

The `ls` command, when executed without any other arguments, is not terribly informative. It only lists the names of the files and directories in the current directory, which is not always terribly useful. For example, how can you tell which names are directories and which are folders? You can use options to expand the functionality of the command. For example, typing `ls -F` identifies files and directories and more.

Note   In addition to arguments, such as filenames, most Linux commands take options. These options usually begin with a -.

Table 15-3 lists some useful options for the `ls` command. Check the man pages on the CD to see a complete listing of `ls` command options.

Table 15-3	
Useful Options for the ls Command	
Command + Option	*Description*
ls -l	Display a long listing.
ls -a	List all files, including hidden files.
ls -c	Sort the listing by file-creation time.
ls -r	Sort the listing in reverse alphabetical order.
ls -s	Show the size (in kilobytes).
ls -R	List subdirectory contents recursively.

Caution Be careful of case sensitivity. Most, though not all, Linux command options are lowercase.

Getting clues from ls -l listings

The long listing gives you detailed information about a file or directory, including what kind of file you are listing, when it was created, who the owner is, when the file was last modified, and the size of the file.

Note Don't worry about understanding all the codes listed in the sidebar table. For now, - and d are important. You can read about the rest of the codes as you go through other chapters.

Deciphering file types in ls -l

The first column of a long listing tells you what kind of file you are looking at — if you know how to break the code. If the first column is -, it's easy: you are listing a regular file. The other codes are a little more mysterious. The following table lists the codes and their meanings.

First column	*Meaning*
-	Regular file
d	Directory
c	Character I/O file
b	Block I/O file
l	Symbolic link

Finding files

You can use the `find` command to list files. `find` lets you specify more file attributes than `ls`. For example, you can find and list files by various dates, by file access permissions, or by type. Table 15-4 lists some useful options for the `find` command. Check the man pages on the CD to see a complete listing of `find` command options.

 Note   Don't worry if you don't understand all the options below. You'll read about them throughout the book.

Table 15-4
Useful Options for the find Command

Option	Description
-print	Display the names of the files found.
-ctime x	Find files created x days ago.
-atime x	Find files accessed x days ago.
-perm x	Find files with access permissions x.
-size xk	Find files bigger than x kilobytes.
-type f	Find files only.
-type d	Find directories only.
-type l	Find symbolic links only.
-name file name	Find files with the specified name (you can use wildcards).
-user username	Find files owned by username.

Figuring Out What's in a File

You cannot type or edit binary files (those that are not text). The `file` command is a super-useful command that you can use to find out what kind of file you have. For example, if you're not sure how to refer to your CD drive, use the `file` command on the files in /dev/*. The `file` command tells you the device type of all your device files.

Displaying the Contents of Files

Linux provides several ways for you to see the contents of your files. How do you decide? It's a matter of personal preference. Table 15-5 lists some of the available options.

Note The `less` command is a typical Linux play on words because `less` does more than `more`.

<table>
<tr><td colspan="2">Table 15-5
Commands that Display File Contents</td></tr>
<tr><td>*Command*</td><td>*Display Function*</td></tr>
<tr><td>more</td><td>Go forward one screen at a time. Press Enter to go ahead one line at a time and the space bar to go ahead one screen at a time.</td></tr>
<tr><td>less</td><td>Page forward or backward one screen at a time.</td></tr>
<tr><td>head</td><td>Display the first few lines of a file. You can specify how many lines to display (ten is the default).</td></tr>
<tr><td>tail</td><td>Display the last few lines of a file. You can specify how many lines to display (ten is the default).</td></tr>
<tr><td>cat</td><td>Display the entire file on your screen.*</td></tr>
</table>

* `cat` is short for "concatenate the file to the screen."

Managing your Personal Files and Directories

Most people need to do more than just move around the Linux directory tree and list files. If you're like most Linux users, you need to manipulate files in the following ways:

✦ By creating and removing directories

✦ By copying, renaming, moving, and removing files

✦ By setting file-access permissions to grant or deny other users' access to your files

Miss Scarlet needs to store information about suspicious characters in a new subdirectory. To do this she plans to:

1. Create a new subdirectory, suspects, under her home directory (using the `mkdir` command).

2. Copy files from Professor Plum's subdirectory, /prof_plum/people/* to her new subdirectory (using the `cp` command).

3. Delete her own suspects file from her new subdirectory (using the `rm` command).

4. Give her suspects directory the new name friends.

Sharing and protecting your files and directories

The following listing shows part of a recursive, long listing (`ls -lR`) of the user col's home directory. You can see the file-access permissions beginning at the second character. These access permissions determine who can do what with col's files. Since col created these files and subdirectories, he owns them and can do anything with them, including use the `chmod` command to change the access permissions. Table 15-6 lists the three types of file and directory access permissions and what they allow.

```
$ ls -lR /home/col
/home/col:
total 3
drwxr-xr-x   2 col      users        1024 Nov  1 13:21 Desktop
drwxr-xr-x   2 col      users        1024 Jan 10 20:42 mail
drwxr-xr-x   5 col      users        1024 Jan 10 20:44 src

/home/col/Desktop:
total 2
-rw-r-r-    1 col      users         631 Feb 18  2000 OpenStore.kdelnk
-rw-r-r-    1 col      users         642 Feb 18  2000 Register Now!.kdelnk

/home/col/mail:
total 40
-r-r-r-    1 col      users       39755 Jan 10 20:42 george

/home/col/src:
total 3
drwxr-xr-x   4 col      users        1024 Jan 10 20:44 etc
drwxr-xr-x   3 col      users        1024 Jan 10 20:44 home
drwxr-xr-x   5 col      users        1024 Jan 10 20:44 usr

/home/col/src/etc:
total 2
drwxr-x--   2 col      users        1024 Jan 10 20:44 ircd
drwxr-xr-x   3 col      users        1024 Jan  6 20:03 rc.d

/home/col/src/etc/ircd:
total 0

/home/col/src/etc/rc.d:
total 1
drwxr-xr-x   2 col      users        1024 Jan  8 05:05 init.d
```

```
/home/col/src/etc/rc.d/init.d:
total 0

/home/col/src/home:
total 1
drwxr-xr-x   7 col       users       1024 Jan 10 20:44 ircd

/home/col/src/home/ircd:
total 5
drwxr-xr-x   3 col       users       1024 Jan 10 20:44 etc
drwxr-x--   2 col       users       1024 Jan 10 20:44 lib
drwxr-x--   2 col       users       1024 Jan 10 20:44 log
drwxr-x--   2 col       users       1024 Jan 10 20:44 run
drwxr-x--   2 col       users       1024 Jan 10 20:44 usr

/home/col/src/home/ircd/etc:
total 1
drwxr-x--   2 col       users       1024 Jan 10 20:44 ircd

/home/col/src/home/ircd/etc/ircd:
total 0

/home/col/src/home/ircd/lib:
total 0

/home/col/src/home/ircd/log:
total 0

/home/col/src/home/ircd/run:
total 0

/home/col/src/home/ircd/usr:
total 0

/home/col/src/usr:
total 3
drwxr-xr-x   3 col       users       1024 Jan  6 20:03 doc
drwxr-xr-x   4 col       users       1024 Jan  6 20:03 man
drwxr-x--   2 col       users       1024 Jan 10 20:44 sbin

/home/col/src/usr/doc:
total 1
drwxr-xr-x   3 col       users       1024 Jan  6 20:03 ircd-2.10.3

/home/col/src/usr/doc/ircd-2.10.3:
total 1
drwxr-xr-x   4 col       users       1024 Jan  8 05:05 doc

/home/col/src/usr/doc/ircd-2.10.3/doc:
total 2
drwxr-xr-x   3 col       users       1024 Jan  8 05:05 Juped
drwxr-xr-x   3 col       users       1024 Jan  8 05:05 Nets
```

```
/home/col/src/usr/doc/ircd-2.10.3/doc/Juped:
total 1
drwxr-xr-x   2 col       users       1024 Jan  8 05:05 US-Admin

/home/col/src/usr/doc/ircd-2.10.3/doc/Juped/US-Admin:
total 0

/home/col/src/usr/doc/ircd-2.10.3/doc/Nets:
total 1
drwxr-xr-x   2 col       users       1024 Jan  8 05:05 Europe

/home/col/src/usr/doc/ircd-2.10.3/doc/Nets/Europe:
total 0

/home/col/src/usr/man:
total 2
drwxr-xr-x   2 col       users       1024 Jan  8 05:05 man5
drwxr-xr-x   2 col       users       1024 Jan  8 05:05 man8

/home/col/src/usr/man/man5:
total 0

/home/col/src/usr/man/man8:
total 0

/home/col/src/usr/sbin:
total 0
```

Table 15-6
File and Directory Access Permissions

Permission	Meaning	Action(s) Allowed on a File	Action(s) Allowed on a Directory
r	Read	Read	List the contents.
w	Write	Write, edit, delete	Create and delete files in that directory.
x	Execute	Run a program or shell script	cd into the directory.

Use the chmod command to assign the permissions in Table 15-6 to three classes of users: the owner of the file, the group to which the file belongs, and the world (all other users).

Deciphering permission lists

The long listing (ls -l) displays a file or directory's permissions in nine characters. Look at the permissions on one of the files (not a directory!) shown in the recursive listing of the user col's home directory. Ignore the first hyphen. It means that this is a regular file, not a directory or any kind of special system file.

Tip A hyphen in a listing means that the field is empty. If the hyphen is in a permission field, it means that there is no access.

The text string, rwxr–r– is really three groups of permissions for the owner, the group, and the world. The first three characters (rwx) represent the permissions granted to the file's owner. Miss Scarlet has all (rwx) permissions. The next three characters (r–), represent the group's permissions on the file. The group that owns this file is bad-guys. Any user who belongs to the group can read this file, but cannot alter or execute it. The last three characters (r–) mean that other users (the world) can read this file, but cannot write or execute it.

Using the chmod command to set file and directory permissions

Only the file/directory owner or system administrator may use the chmod command to change permissions. To change permissions, give the chmod command the following three arguments:

✦ For whom you are setting the permission. This will be one or more of the following: a (all), u (user), g (group), or o (other). Note that a is equivalent to ugo.

✦ Whether you are granting or revoking permissions. + grants permissions; - revokes permissions.

✦ The combination of permissions that you are granting or revoking (rwx).

Table 15-7 lists some frequently used chmod commands.

Tip You can set permissions on groups of files by using wildcards with the chmod command.

Table 15-7
Frequently Used chmod Commands

Command	Effect
chmod a+r *file**	Allow all users to read any file in the current directory that starts with *file*.
chmod ogu +r *file?*	Another way to allow all users to read all files that start with *file* and end with a single alphanumeric character.
chmod +r *file*	Another way to allow all users to read the file named *file*. If you do not specify a user or group, Linux assumes a (all).
chmod o -rwx *file*	Remove permission to access the file in any way from others except the owner and owner's group.

Cluing in to groups

Besides being owned by a specific user, files are also owned by a particular group. The system administrator defines groups and adds users to those groups. A user always belongs to at least one group. For convenience, the system administrator may also add a user to additional groups. Groups are convenient when you want to allow access for several people to a file. For example, if Miss Scarlet wants to allow Professor Plum, Mrs. White, and Colonel Mustard to be able to cd into her weapons subdirectory, she can use the chmod a+x command to make the directory accessible to everyone. If the system administrator creates a group (let's call it bad-guys), Miss S. only needs to make her weapons subdirectory accessible to that group. You can choose which way works for you. If you are security-conscious, wise use of groups gives you more options and flexibility.

The system administrator defines groups by the type of users who share files on the computer. For example, at a publishing house, Linux users may be in the groups named writers, editors, managers, and guests. The group names on my niece Emily's computer are friends, parents, and relatives.

Caution   The permissions granted to a file depend on the permissions of the directory in which the file is located. In the previous example, you've seen that Miss Scarlet gives permission for her group to have full access to the knife file. However, unless the group bad-guys has r and x access to the file's directory, group members cannot access the file.

Tip   You don't need to worry about setting individual permissions on your files if you set the permissions on your home directory to rwx——. When no one (besides you) has permission to access your home, no one can access anything in or below your home.

The last three characters (r—) represent the permissions granted to every other user on the system. For example, a directory with rwx on it for every other user on the system gives read and write access to that directory.

Getting octal with umask — why bother?

The chmod command accepts octal numbers as arguments as well as the symbolic characters r, w, and x. In octal numbers, the number 7 represents rwx. If you use octal numbers with the chmod command, you use three numbers, one each to represent the owner, group, and world. For example, to grant all permissions on all files to all users, you type:

```
chmod 777
```

All files you create after typing the chmod command inherit the 777 permission. If you're not a diehard techie, you might be wondering why bother with octal numbers when you can use meaningful symbols instead? The answer is that there is a

Using the GNOME File Manager with Your Files

You can do everything using a GUI that you can do with the commands described in this chapter. Right-click any file to choose the following properties and actions from a popup menu:

Open	Delete
Open with	Move
View	Statistics
Edit	Permissions
Copy	

GNOME File Manager—File and Command Menu Guide

Menu	Option	Function	Shell Command
File	Create New Window	Open a new File Manager Window.	
	New ⇨ Terminal	Open a GNOME terminal window and automatically go to the directory you selected in the main window.	cd
	New ⇨ Directory	Create a new directory.	mkdir
	New ⇨ [application name]	Open a new application.	
	Open	Open the selected file.	
	Copy	Launch the Copy dialog box.	cp
	Delete	Remove the selected file.	rm
	Move	Launch the Move/Rename dialog box.	mv
	Show Directory Sizes	Display the size of directories in the Detail or Custom view.	ls -l
Commands	Find File	Search for files.	Find
	Edit Mime Types	Associate applications with file types.	
	Run Command	Run one command.	
	Run Command	Run preloaded commands. in panel	
	Exit	Exit all GNOME functions.	

very useful command, umask. The bad news is that umask isn't very user friendly. Unlike chmod, umask only accepts octal numbers. umask makes your life easier by letting you set a default access privilege for all files. If you use umask in your login environment file, you don't need to use chmod to set every file's permissions explicitly.

Cross-Reference The system administrator should also use the umask command in a system initialization file to set system-wide default protections for those users who don't protect their own files. Chapter 30 tells you how to do this.

Here's the most commonly used umask command. Use it for friendly open systems. It grants rwx permissions to all users:

```
umask 022
```

If you don't want to share everything you own with everyone on your computer, try this umask command. It grants rwx to you, the owner, r-x to your teammates in your group, and -- (no permission) to the rest of the world.

```
umask 027
```

Are you a disk hog?

Some Linux system administrators impose disk usage quotas so that they can control how much disk space each user is allowed to take up. However, many Linux systems operate in a friendly, trusting way. If you work on one of those friendly systems, be nice! Regulate your own disk-space usage. Linux, since it doesn't keep multiple versions of files, helps keep disks tidy. It's up to you, however, not to clog the disk by keeping old files that no one needs. Use the du command to find out how much disk space you are using. You can use du to show the disk usage for a single file or for an entire tree of subdirectories. The example below shows the disk space used by a subdirectory and its files. The du output displays file sizes in blocks (usually of 512 bytes) by default. You can change the display by using either the -b option (display in bytes), the -k option (display in kilobytes), or the -m option (display in megabytes).

Tip After you download compressed files (for example, .zip or .gzip) from the Internet, the compressed archive remains. To save disk space, either move the original compressed archive to a backup medium, such as a tape or CD, or delete (rm) them.

Summary

This chapter got you started as a Linux user. You learned commands for moving around the Linux directory tree and manipulating files, including commands that tell you how much disk space you're using. You also learned how to protect your files and how to look at a listing of someone else's files and decipher the file permissions on those files. Finally, you got a look at some basic print commands.

You also learned some commonly used command options, but remember that most of the commands covered in this chapter can take more options than the ones described here. The best place to see all the options and what they do is in the man pages (provided on your CD).

The next chapter shows you how to use vi, a Linux text editor. If you want to use more advanced commands, Chapter 30 gets you started and also shows you some handy techniques for binding commands together.

This chapter shows that you can use either the command-line interface or a graphical interface. While the graphical interface may seem easier for Linux novices, try to learn the commands. As you move from one Linux computer to another, you can't be sure that the optional GUI will be installed or that you will have access to a graphical display. (Lots of Linux users find themselves on dumb terminals from time to time). However, you can always count on the commands to be there.

✦   ✦   ✦

Using an Editor

Sooner or later, you're going to need to edit a text file.
Linux gives you a wide choice of text editors, including:
vi, ex, ed, emacs (GNU, lucid, and other variants), pico, jove,
and joe.

Choosing an Editor

Your choice of an editor depends on your personal preference
and what you have available. vi (visual editor) is not the
newest or most powerful editor you can use. So why does this
chapter concentrate on it? Because vi is the most common
editor in the Linux (and UNIX) world. The only editor that you
are guaranteed to find on any Linux system is vi.

Understanding vi Modes

vi operates in three modes — each one guaranteed to beep
you into submission if you don't get the concept. The modes
are:

- ◆ Command
- ◆ Insert
- ◆ ex

By default, vi starts in command mode. Command mode is the
mode that enables you to type editing commands, such as dd
for delete line, wq to save the file and exit vi, and other standard file editing commands. From command mode, you can
also change to either insert or ex mode. To change modes, do
one of the following:

- ◆ To enter command mode, press the Esc key.
- ◆ To enter insert mode, press i.
- ◆ To enter ex mode, first enter command mode, then
  type :.

Insert mode is the mode that permits you to perform basic editing, such as editing existing text and adding new text to a file. To change from command mode to insert mode, you can press i to insert text at the cursor's current location or you can press a to append characters at the space immediately following the cursor's current location. When you are done typing text, return to command mode by pressing Esc (the Escape key).

When using vi, listen for beeps from the computer's internal speaker. If you try to enter or edit text when you are not in insert mode, vi beeps at you. If you ignore this warning, you may have one or two typos in your file, or you may wind up utterly corrupting the file you are editing. The beep is vi's way to tell you that you need to change modes. Another common mistake new vi users make is to accidentally press the Caps Lock key. Be aware that vi, like most Linux applications, is case-sensitive, so, for example, R pressed in command mode replaces all text until you press the Esc key, but r in command mode only replaces the current character.

Tip   To see your current mode displayed at the bottom of your screen, enter command mode and type :showmode. The default is not to show you the mode — just to beep if you get into the wrong mode.

Understanding ex-mode concepts

Use ex mode to invoke vi's extended command set. These extended commands are based on the older UNIX editor, ex. ex commands appear on the bottom line of the screen, regardless of where your cursor is. For example, when you type : in command mode, you move into ex mode. Quitting (:q!), saving (:w), and saving changes and exiting (:wq) are ex operations. After typing an ex command, press Enter to execute it.

Note   Because ex-mode commands appear on the last line of your vi window, you may also hear ex referred to as *last-line mode*.

A Quick Tour of vi

This section presents an introduction to vi. You won't find an encyclopedia of vi features here — only the ones you need to know to get started.

On the CD-ROM   You can refer to the man page for vi if you're interested in learning the really fancy features.

Making vi the Default Editor for GNOME

A capplet is GNOME's term for a configuration tool in the GNOME Control Center. Capplets come from the GNOME developers; you can also write your own capplet tools and associate them with GNOME applications.

Use the Default Editor Capplet to select your default editor when using GNOME. After you select vi, the GNOME File Manager automatically launches vi when you try to open files associated with editing. If you think vi is *vile*, you can choose another editor from the Default Editor Capplet's selection list. The figure below shows how to make vi your editor for GNOME windows.

 Cross-Reference   You can read about the GNOME Control Center in Chapter 14.

Starting vi and creating a new text file

To start up vi in the command-line interface, type v i followed by the file name you want to edit. vi starts in command mode. If you are starting to edit a new file, vi shows you a screen with a column of tildes (~), as shown in Figures 16-1 and 16-2. Figure 16-1 shows how to start vi in the GNOME GUI. Since vi is in command mode, you can not enter text yet. vi assumes that whatever you type is a command. Here's your first vi command: i, to insert text at the cursor. Type i for insert, followed by the text you want to enter. Figure 16-2 shows an example.

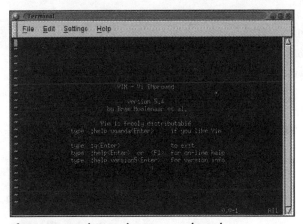

Figure 16-1: vi starts in command mode

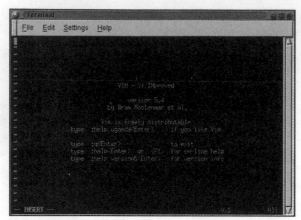

Figure 16-2: Don't forget to type i command to insert text

Exiting vi

After you've typed in your file, you will want to save it and exit vi. Table 16-1 lists the options you have in command mode. You can either exit, write, or quit. Figure 16-3 shows how the screen looks after you use :wq to save your file.

	Table 16-1	
Commands for Exiting vi		
Command	**Effect**	
ZZ	Save your edits and leave vi.	
:wq	Save your edits and leave vi (*write* & *quit*).	
:w	Save the file and continue editing (a good tip if your system is not reliable, e.g. subject to mysterious power outages).	
:q!	Leave vi without saving edits (quit-bang).	
:x	For a file you did not change, leave vi and do not update the file's date and time.	

Depending on your terminal-emulation software, your escape key may not actually send an Esc sequence to vi. If this happens, you need to find out what key you can substitute for Esc. A common Esc substitution key is the function key F11.

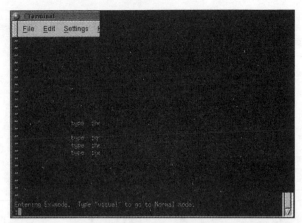

Figure 16-3: The : indicates an ex-mode instruction

Modifying an existing file

To change an existing file, enter vi by typing vi and the file name you want to change. Maybe you can use the arrow keys to move around in the file, and maybe not. It depends on your terminal emulator. The commands in Table 16-2 always work to move the cursor. Perform the following steps:

1. Enter vi, naming the file I want to change vi family.txt.

2. Move the cursor to the duplicate line (see Table 16-2) and type j as many times as it takes to get to the line, or arrow down or use a number to tell vi how many lines to jump down — for example, 5j to go five lines down.

3. Delete the entire line and type dd. Table 16-4 lists some delete keystrokes.

4. Move the cursor to "Emma Lee" using the keys described in Table 16-2.

5. Delete "ma Lee" and use the x keystroke listed in Table 16-4.

6. Insert/append "ily" and try the i or a keystrokes listed in Table 16-3.

7. Move to the end of the file, just after the last character. (See Table 16-3 for a list of keystrokes for inserting and appending text.) Type a for append and press Enter followed by the new line.

8. Be sure to be in command mode and save the changes by typing :wq.

Table 16-2
Cursor Movement Keys that are Always Available

Keys	Function
h	Move the cursor left one character.
9h	Move the cursor left 9 characters.
J	Move the cursor down one line.
20j	Move the cursor down 20 lines.
k	Move the cursor up one line.
22k	Move the cursor up 22 lines.
l	Move the cursor right one character.
7l	Move the cursor right 7 characters.
CTRL+F	Move forward one screen of text.
CTRL+B	Move back one screen of text.
CTRL+D	Move down one half screen of text.
CTRL+U	Move up one half screen of text.
G	Go to the bottom of the file.
1G	Go to the top of the file.

Tip   If you lose track of where you are in the file (this sometimes happens as you switch among modes), hit Ctrl+G.

Table 16-3
Keystrokes for Inserting and Appending Text

Keystroke	Function
I	Insert text at the cursor.
o	Open (start) a new line directly below the current line and insert text.
O	Open (start) a new line directly above the current line and insert text.
a	Append text immediately following the cursor.
A	Append text at the end of the current line.
R	From the cursor, keep replacing text until you press Esc.
r	Replace one character at the cursor.

Table 16-4
Keystrokes for Deleting Text

Keystroke	Function
dd	Delete the current line.
D	Delete from the cursor to the end of the current line.
x	Delete the character under the cursor.
dw	Delete from the cursor to the end of the current word.

You can manipulate the delete commands by adding a modifier (a number, G, or $, or some combination thereof) to the command. The examples listed here use the number 4. You can use any number that makes sense in the file.

4x	Delete four characters at the cursor.
4dd	Delete four lines starting with the current line.
d4w (or 4dw)	Delete four words starting with the current word.
d4$	Delete from the current line to the end of the fourth line.
d1G	Delete from the cursor to the top of the file.
dG	Delete from the cursor to the end of the file.

Cross-Reference For those catastrophes when vi can't recover your file, read Chapter 6 to see how to restore a file from a backup.

Recovering from Mistakes Tiny or Disastrous

If you have made a small mistake, you can undo it with the u or U keystrokes. U undoes the changes on the current line. u undoes the last command. If you have made a huge mistake, you can quit (:q!) or you can discard your changes, return to the state of your previous edit, and start editing over again in one step (:e!).

If your system crashes, (it doesn't happen often with Linux, but it does happen, especially if you have a hardware problem), you can tell vi to recover by using the -r option the next time you type vi. For example, if the system crashes while I'm editing clues.txt, after the system starts up, I type

```
vi -r clues.txt
```

This vi option almost always recovers what you think you lost.

Searching for text

You need to be in command mode to search for text. Figure 16-4 shows what it looks like to search through the family file. To search forward, use the / key followed by the text string for which you are searching. Then press Enter. For example, to search forward for the string excelle, type:

```
/excelle
```

To search backward, use the ? key.

```
?excelle
```

Tip   To repeat your last search in the same direction, type n. To repeat the search in the opposite direction, type N.

Figure 16-4: You can search for text forward and backward

Substituting text

You should use the s (substitute) command in ex mode to replace one text string with another. You start the s command with a range of lines wherein the substitution should occur. The s command below changes all suspects to victims from the beginning of the file to the end of the file (1, $) and asks you to confirm the edits (c). If you don't want to be asked about the edits, you can use g for the global option.

```
1,$s/suspects/victims/c
```

More Ways to Change Text

If the substitute command isn't enough for you, you can use the change (c) command to change the text under the cursor or to the left or right of the cursor. Table 16-5 shows some common change commands.

Table 16-5
Change Commands

Command	Function
cwx	Changes the current word to x, where x is the new text.
ncwx	Changes the next n (where n is a number) words to x, where x is the new text.
c$x	Changes text from the cursor to the end of the line to x, where x is the new text.
ccx	Changes the current line to new text, where x is the new text.

Summary

The concept of vi modes was the trickiest part of this chapter. I've been using vi for 17 years, since I was just a wee baby, and I still beep. Just remember, beeping is not a bad thing. It keeps you in the mode. This chapter also covered how to use vi to create new files and edit existing files, including:

✦ Moving around the file.

✦ Inserting text.

✦ Appending text.

✦ Searching and replacing text.

✦ Deleting text.

✦ Saving your changes (or not) and exiting vi.

With the text editing skills you learned in this chapter, you can edit any file. If you want to go further with vi, look at the man pages. vi has a rich set of commands, including moving (*yanking*) text to buffers and creating macros to perform repetitive editing tasks. If you love vi so much that you want more, browse the vi lovers' Web site, http://www.cs.vu.nl.

✦　　✦　　✦

Getting to Know bash

Ashell is a program that talks with the operating system on your behalf. You talk to the shell, the shell talks to Linux. The shell's main purpose is to run other programs. When you type a command that is a program, such as `ls`, your shell asks Linux to display a directory listing for you. GUIs also function as shells, communicating with the operating system for you. Microsoft Windows, GNOME, and KDE are graphical shells.

Chapter 4 lists some popular command-line shells available on Linux.

The most commonly used Linux shell is *bash*—which stands for *Bourne again shell*. The name Bourne Again Shell is a pun on the traditional UNIX Bourne shell that was written by Steven Bourne. Its pathname is /bin/bash.

If you are interested in international standards conformance, bash is intended to comply with the IEEE Posix Shell and Tools Specification 1003.2.

bash tries to be the best of all possible shell worlds, maintaining compatibility with the original Bourne shell (/bin/sh) as well as including handy features from other shells.

This chapter shows you how to use bash, the default Linux shell, to manage your jobs and processes, and how to combine shell commands into scripts to make repetitive tasks easier and quicker.

Chapter 16 introduces you to using command options.

Comparing a Linux Shell to the MS-DOS Shell

If you're a MS-DOS user, every time you've typed a command at the C: prompt you've used the DOS shell, C:\WINDOWS\COMMAND.COM. Just like any UNIX or Linux shell, the DOS shell executes the commands you type at the prompt. However, Linux shells are much more powerful than the DOS shell because Linux shells offer features such as rich scripting languages and the capacity to run multiple processes simultaneously from the command line or in one terminal window.

Using Nifty bash Features

bash (and other shells) provides useful features that make your life easier when you are working with commands. Some of the features that you might want to take advantage of include:

✦ Getting bash help

✦ Using shortcuts to make typing easier

✦ Automatically completing command names and file names

✦ Recalling and editing previous commands

✦ Using aliases to substitute for long command names

✦ Combining commands on one line

✦ Automatically sending the output from one command into another command (piping)

✦ Sending screen I/O from the display to files (I/O redirection)

Getting bash help

You can get help from the bash man page:

```
man bash
```

When is a Command Not a Command?

Some of the commands you use are really commands built into bash (or any other shell). Built-in commands include `cd` and `pwd`. Other "commands" are actually programs that your shell executes for you, such as `cp` and `ls`. Should you care whether you are executing a built-in command or a program? Not really. You never need to know whether you are executing a command or a program. Your shell always knows what to do. This book uses the term *command* to refer to both built-in shell commands and programs.

The bash man page is quite long and involved. bash itself has a built-in help system. You type the `help` command at your bash prompt to see a list of all help topics. You type the `help` command followed by a specific topic name to see information about a particular command (see Figure 17-1).

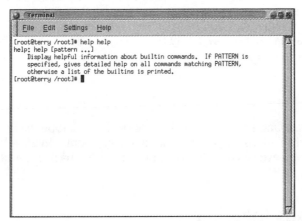

Figure 17-1: Use the bash help system

You can also use `info`, a command to read documentation from various sources. If you type the `info` command followed by the `info` argument, as in Figure 17-2, you see a menu for learning how to use the info program. After you have typed the command shown in the Figure 17-2, read the instructions and type the h command, to take `info` lessons.

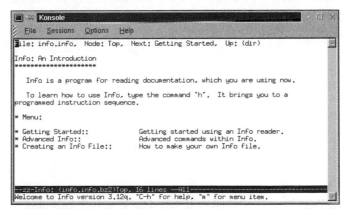

Figure 17-2: Info is a text-based hyperlink document browser

Letting bash complete file names and command names

Suppose you forget the exact name of a program? You can search through directories looking for it, but that search takes time and is tedious. Or you can let bash help you. One of bash's niftiest features is command-line completion. You type as much of the command as you remember and then hit the Tab key, and bash fills in the command for you. In the example below, I only type linux and hit the Tab key. bash fills in the rest of the command for me. I save three keystrokes.

```
linux<TAB>
linuxconf
```

If there is more than one command that starts with the letter(s) you type, bash lists all the commands that match. You can, if you're so inclined, type only the first letter of the command, but the more letters you type, the smaller the list bash returns to you. See Figure 17-2.

Stringing commands together

So far, the examples you've seen in this chapter put each command on a separate line, like so:

```
cd
pwd
ls
```

Since most Linux commands are short, the preceding example doesn't require much typing. For convenience, however, Linux offers you the ability to type those commands together on a single line:

```
cd;pwd;ls
```

Notice that you need to separate the commands with a semicolon (;). You aren't really saving much typing because you're substituting a semicolon for pressing Enter. Nonetheless, grouping commands together usually feels easier. It's up to you to decide on Enter versus the semicolon.

Note   A separator character, such as the semicolon, is called a *delimiter*.

Taking advantage of command history and recall

Command-line history and editing should be on everyone's top-ten list of handy shell features. If you want to recall a command you typed a few minutes ago, you don't need to retype it. Command-line history and recall let you simply press the up-arrow key to get the previous command back. In fact, you can bring back any command in your history by pressing the up-arrow key until you see the command displayed. To re-execute the command, press Enter. If you arrow back too many commands, press the down arrow to go forward toward your most recent commands. You can also edit the command you recall from the history list. If you mistype a long and complex name, such as a file name or environment variable name, you can recall it and simply correct the mistake rather than retyping the whole command.

Command-history tips

The following list provides some tips and hints to help you get the most out of bash's command-line history and editing features. Rather than try to use all of them at once, practice using one or two of them until they become habits, then add one or two more. In this way, you will gradually become proficient at the command-line.

+ bash keeps a history of your previous commands in, ~/.bash_history (the .bash_history file in your home directory).

+ bash keeps your history list across login sessions so that you can execute a command, log out, log back in, and re-execute the command from the history list.

+ The `history` command recalls a list of past commands. By default the `history` command lists your last 500 commands starting with the most recent.

+ Use a number as an option to the history command to limit the display.

+ You can re-execute commands without retyping them. Use the bang (!) character to recall a command. For example, typing `!4092` and hitting Enter will recall the 4,092nd command you typed earlier and also executes it. (The `history` command shows you the command numbers.)

+ You can also recall commands by name rather than by number. For example, typing `!history` will recall and automatically re-execute the last `history` command you typed

+ When you recall a command, you can change it before you re-execute it. Use the carat (^) character to substitute words on the command line. To display the last five commands, I would type `history 5`. If I wanted to display the last eight commands, I could type `^5^8<ENTER>` to change the 5 to an 8 and automatically execute the new command.

+ You can change the number of commands kept in your history list by defining the `HISTSIZE` environment variable. The section titled "Using environment variables" later in this chapter explains environment variables in more detail.

+ If you have more than one terminal window open in a graphical environment, each window has a separate history list.

Command-recall tips

Use these keystrokes to edit recalled commands.

✦ After you recall a line with either an arrow key or !, your cursor will be at the end of the line. Press Ctrl+A to move to the beginning of the command line.

✦ Ctrl+E (for *end*) moves the cursor to the end of the command line.

✦ Ctrl+K *kills* (deletes) all characters from the cursor to the end of the command line.

✦ Ctrl+A, Ctrl+K combination deletes an entire command line.

✦ Ctrl+Y (for *yank it back*) pastes at your current cursor location what you killed.

Redirecting input and output

When you type a command at the shell, bash reads in the command and sends output from the command back to your screen—or an error message if you did not type the command correctly. bash sees your physical screen as three logical displays—one for supplying input and two for displaying output—and gives each logical display a symbolic name:

1. An input device, called stdin (standard input).

2. An output device, called stdout (standard output).

3. An error device, called stderr (standard error).

bash has a feature called I/O (input/output) redirection that uses the symbolic names in the previous list. You can tell bash to:

1. Take command input from a file instead of from the keyboards.

2. Send command output to a file instead of displaying it on the screen.

3. Send error messages to a file instead of displaying them on the screen.

Use the special symbols in Table 17-1 to redirect input, output, and error messages to files.

Table 17-1
I/O Redirection Symbols

Symbol	Meaning
>	Redirect output to a file or device.
>>	Redirect output, appending to an existing file or device.
2>	Redirect error messages to a file or device.

Symbol	Meaning
2>>	Redirect error messages, appending them to an existing file or device.
<	Receive input from a file instead of the keyboard.

Figure 17-3 shows how to redirect output and errors to a file.

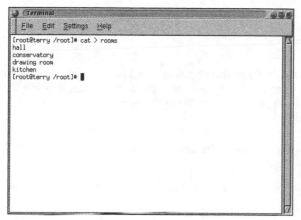

```
Terminal
File  Edit  Settings  Help
[root@terry /root]# cat > rooms
hall
conservatory
drawing room
kitchen
[root@terry /root]# █
```

Figure 17-3: Use symbols to redirect screen output to files

Tip   You know from Chapter 16 that the cat command displays a file — conCATenates the file to the screen. Here is another way you can use cat: to create a new file by redirecting the cat output to a file. Type the cat command followed by the data the way you want them to appear in the file. When you are done, press Ctrl+D, the end-of-file (EOF) character. The following example creates a file named rooms and loads it with data.

```
cat > rooms
hall
conservatory
drawing room
kitchen
<CTRL+D>
```

Piping one command into the next

A pipe (short for *pipeline*) takes the standard output of one command and uses it as the standard input to another command. The pipe operator is the vertical bar (|). Pipes are another bash feature that save you time and make life with Linux easier. Suppose you try to get a long listing of all files in all subdirectories recursively (ls -lR) starting with the root filesystem (/). The listing scrolls by so fast you can't read it. You have a couple of possible options:

Build Powerful Commands with Pipes

If you need to search a long list for an environment variable, piping the output through a search command, grep, saves you from having to look through screens of output. For example, my printenv command returns a couple of dozen environment variables. Why should I look at all the variable definitions if I only need to see the history variables? By piping the output of printenv to the grep (search) command followed by the text string I want to search for, I can reduce the output to exactly the variables I want to see. Notice that I only need to type a partial variable name (HIST).

```
[root@flyingpenguin /root]# printenv | grep HIST
HISTSIZE=1000
HISTFILESIZE=1000
```

A pipe lets you send screen output directly to the printer without first creating a file. In the following examples, I send a long directory listing directly to the printer. I can skip the steps of redirecting the output to a file and submitting the file to the printer.

```
[root@flyingpenguin /root]# ls | lpr
```

The following example prints my entire list of environment variables.

```
[root@flyingpenguin /root]# printenv | lpr
```

1. Redirect the output of the ls command to a file, and then use more or less to browse the file, as below:

```
ls -lR / > allfiles.lis
more allfiles.lis
```

2. Pipe the output of the ls command directly to the more command, as below:

```
ls -lR / | more
```

Both of these solutions give you exactly the same result. However, if you use a pipe (solution 2), you can skip a step.

Note   The command to print is lpr.

You can pipeline any number of commands. The example below pipes three commands, ls (list files), sort (sort the listing in reverse order), and head (only print the first 10 lines of the listing).

```
[root@flyingpenguin /root]# ls | sort -r | head
```

Understanding Variables

The shell uses variables to represent internal Linux values such as pathnames, terminal types, user IDs, process IDs. Variables furnish information to programs running on your Linux system. For example, Linux provides an environment variable called HOME that contains the pathname of your home directory. Any program that needs to know where your home directory is can find out by checking the value of the HOME variable. You can use these variables too. A variable is an item, such as a pathname, that contains a value. The shell substitutes the value for the variable name. Variables provide a quick and easy way to create a shortcut with a meaningful name. Linux automatically defines some variables, and you can also define your own variables. For example, bash automatically provides a variable called UID that contains the value of your user id. If you need to know your user id, you can use the echo command to display the value of the UID built-in variable. When you use the echo command to display a variable, be sure to precede the variable name with a $ character to make the command expand the variable to its value. Figure 17-4 shows how to use the echo command to display the value of some built-in shell variables.

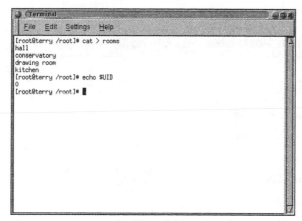

Figure 17-4: Precede the variable name with a $ when using the echo command

Using built-in shell variables

bash defines and sets the values for the special built-in variables listed in Table 17-2. Linux uses these variables internally, and you can use them too, as in Figure 17-5.

Caution

Only Linux should set the values for the built-in shell variables listed in Table 17-2. If you change the value of any of these variables, you may affect the way Linux works.

If, for some reason, you need to manipulate one of these built-in variables, you can define your own variable, assign it the value from the built-in variable, and use in any way you need as the following script demonstrates.

```
# Lines that start with "#" are comments
echo $UID
0
# Define a variable, myuid
# Make myuid's value the same as the built-in UID
myuid=$UID
#Display both variables
echo $UID, $myuid
0, 0
# Set the value of myuid to be 6, but don't touch #the built-in
UID
myuid=6
# Notice the new value for myuid
echo $UID, $myuid
0, 6
```

Table 17-2
Built-In Variables Set by bash

Variable Name	Used As
UID	User id
PPID	Parent pid (process id)
PWD	Current working directory
OLDPWD	Previous working directory
BASH	Pathname of bash
BASH_VERSION	Version number of bash
SHLVL	Count of number of times bash is started
OSTYPE	Operating system
HOSTTYPE	Type of computer*

* For any Intel-based computer, including 486 and Pentium (586), the value is always i386.

Defining your own local variables

Any Linux shell, including bash, lets you define variables to help you work quicker and more easily. A long pathname, such as /home/emily/collections/beanies/bears, is a lot to type, especially if you access files in the bears directory often. If you define a variable named bears, you can simply use $bears/maple in commands to get to the maple file. To assign a value to a variable, type the variable name followed by an equals sign followed by the value. The following command sets the value of a variable named bears to the full pathname of the bears directory. The bears variable is local—that is, it can only be seen by the instance of the shell where it is defined.

```
bears=/home/emily/collections/beanies/bears
```

To use a variable, insert the $ character in front of the variable name, as shown in Figure 17-5.

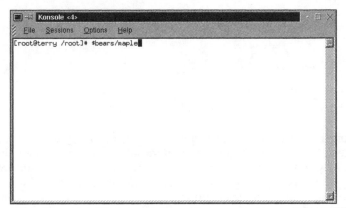

Figure 17-5: Variables make handy shortcuts

Caution When you define a variable locally (such as bears in Figure 17-5), the variable is only available to the shell in which you define the variable.

The set command, in Figure 17-6, shows a list of all variables for your shell.

Using environment variables

Your environment includes your shell, your home directory, and your terminal type. Environment variables are globally available variables that control your shell environment's configuration. The variables are called global because they are available to all bash shells, including those that you may not realize Linux spawns for you. Instead of defining variables locally, you can make them global by exporting them across your entire environment. bash gives you two syntax choices for defining environment variables:

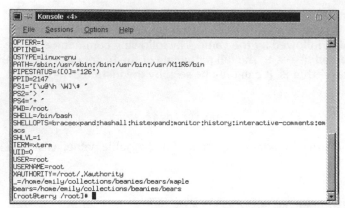

Figure 17-6: Use the set command to display all your shell variables

```
bears=/home/emily/collections/beanies/bears
export bears
```

```
export bears=/home/emily/collections/beanies/bears
```

I prefer the second one because I'm always trying to save time and typing. Both do exactly the same thing: they define the environment variable and export the value to all shells that you may run, basically making the variable global for you until you log out. Linux includes a set of standard environment variables listed in Table 17-3. Some examples of environment variables include:

✦ The PATH variable, which you can use to define your frequently used directory/subdirectory paths.

✦ The PS1 variable, which you can use to customize your prompt.

✦ The EDITOR variable, which sets up a default editor for you to use in various situations.

✦ The bears variable in the example above (because it is exported).

Various components of Linux automatically set default values for some of the environment variables in the table below. For example, bash sets a default value for MAILPATH, and the X Window System sets the default value for DISPLAY. If Linux doesn't set the value, you can set it yourself if you want to use it in a command or shell script.

Caution   Remember, Linux is case-sensitive. That includes variable names.

Table 17-3
Linux Environment Variables

Variable Name	Purpose	Default Automatically Set
PATH	The directory path to search to find commands.	Yes
HOME	Your home directory.	Yes
MAILCHECK	How often (in seconds) to check for new mail.	No (If you don't set MAILCHECK, bash doesn't check)
MAILPATH	A list of directories to check for mail.	Yes
PS1, PS2, PS3, PS4	Appearance of the primary and continuation prompts.	
MANPAGER	The program that displays man pages on screen.	Yes (/usr/bin/less)
MAIL	The file that holds your mail when it arrives. Your mail reader checks this file.	Yes
LOGNAME	Your login name.	Yes
HISTFILE	File name where bash keeps command history.	Yes
HISTSIZE	Number of commands bash remembers you typed.	Yes
PROMPT_COMMAND	Command to execute before displaying the PS1 prompt.	No
TERM	Declares your terminal type.	Yes
DISPLAY	Tells X which computer is the display server. If you are displaying graphical input and output from a remote computer, you must reset the default.	Yes (0.0)
ENV	The shell to execute a script under.	No
FCEDIT	The editor to use for the fc command.	No
Noclobber	Do not overwrite files.	No

Who Sets Environment Variables?

Besides the components that you already know about (bash and you) that set environment variables, there are other parts of Linux that set environment variables. For example, the X Window System sets the variable DISPLAY. init — the mother of all processes — (see Chapter 6) also sets environment variables, such as the default for PATH, the run level, and the console. Many applications have installation procedures that define environment variables for that application.

You can use the printenv command to display your environment variables. The set command shows environment variables, plus built-in shell variables and local shell variables.

Setting the PATH variable

When you use a command, how does the shell find the executable image for the command? For example, if you type ls, how does your shell know that the ls command is in the /bin directory? The shell uses the environment variable PATH to find the executable files for ls and for all the commands you type. The PATH variable lists the directories for the shell to search. When you define the PATH variable, separate the directories in the list with a colon (:) as in the following code.

```
echo $PATH     #the default PATH
/usr/local/sbin:/sbin:/usr/sbin:/usr/bin
echo $HOME
/home/miss_scarlet
echo $bears
/home/emily/collections/beanies/bears
# Build a PATH consisting of the existing PATH
# with the values of $HOME and bears added
export PATH=$PATH:$HOME:$bears
echo $PATH
/usr/local/sbin:/sbin:/usr/sbin:/usr/bin:
/home/miss_scarlet:/home/emily/collections/beanies/bears
```

When you type a command, your shell looks in the directories listed in PATH to find the executable image for the command. For example, if you type ls *, your shell first looks for /bin/ls, then /usr/bin/ls, and so on. Don't forget to include your current working directory in your PATH. This enables you to write a program or shell script and execute it from your current directory.

Note   The PATH variable doesn't work with files that are not executable, such as text files. For example, the shell will not use PATH to locate the files foo and bar if you type ls, those file names are assumed to be complete. The shell only uses PATH to locate the cp executable.

The shell won't look for commands in any directories that are not on your PATH, including your current directory. Look at what happens when a directory is not on your path:

```
# First, check out the value for PATH
echo $PATH
/usr/local/sbin:/sbin:/usr/sbin:/usr/bin:
# Test the ls command
ls *
admin    emily    ftp    miss_scarlet    notes    prof_plum
# Change the PATH variable
export PATH=$bears
# Verify that the value of PATH has changed
echo $PATH
/home/emily/collections/beanies/bears
# Try the ls command again
ls *
bash: ls: command not found
# bash can't find the executable image file for ls
# OK. Use the full path of the ls command
/bin/ls
admin    emily    ftp    miss_scarlet    notes    prof_plum
```

Setting the bash prompt

The environment variable that represents your primary bash prompt is PS1. The primary bash prompt is the prompt that precedes your commands. If a long command runs to the following line on the screen, bash displays a secondary continuation prompt. The environment variable that represents the secondary prompt is PS2. bash allows your commands to extend across four screen lines. The environment variables for the third and fourth lines are PS3 and PS4. Figure 17-7 shows a variable definition for the primary bash prompt followed by definitions for the continuation prompts.

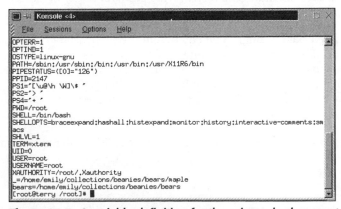

Figure 17-7: A variable definition for the primary bash prompt

The default prompt for bash users is the character string comprising the user name, the computer's fully qualified domain name, and the current working directory, enclosed by brackets. By defining the environment variable PS1 in a system initialization file, /etc/profile, the system administrator can create a prompt that all users inherit. The excerpt from /etc/profile in Figure 17-8 shows the system-wide prompt being set to the combination of user name, host name, current working directory. Table 17-4 describes what the strange characters mean.

```
/etc/profile
  File   Edit   Options   Help

# /etc/profile

# System wide environment and startup programs
# Functions and aliases go in /etc/bashrc

PATH="$PATH:/usr/X11R6/bin"
PS1="[\u@\h \W]\\$ "

# In bash2 we can't define a ulimit more than 0 for user :-(
[ "$UID" = "0" ] && {
ulimit -c 1000000
                } || {
ulimit -c 0
}

if [ `id -gn` = `id -un` -a `id -u` -gt 14 ]; then
        umask 002
else
        umask 022
fi

USER=`id -un`
LOGNAME=$USER
MAIL="/var/spool/mail/$USER"

HOSTNAME=`/bin/hostname`
HISTSIZE=1000
HISTFILESIZE=1000
export PATH PS1 HOSTNAME HISTSIZE HISTFILESIZE USER LOGNAME MAIL

for i in /etc/profile.d/*.sh ; do
        if [ -x $i ]; then
                . $i

                                         INS  Line: 1 Col: 1
```

Figure 17-8: The system administrator sets a system-wide prompt in /etc/profile

If you prefer a customized bash prompt, you can define the PS1 variable to change your prompt to include almost any information you want, such as date, time, your name, your computer's name and/or address, your birthday-gift wish list. You can even make your prompt display in color and in interesting fonts. For example, Figure 17-8 shows four KDE terminal windows, each with a different prompt so that I can tell the windows apart at a glance.

Tip   If you work on different computers in a network, setting PS1 to the host name reminds you where you are.

You can use special character sequences to customize your bash prompt even further. Each character sequence must begin with the backslash character (\). For example, the character sequence \t makes the current time (in 24-hour HH:MM:SS format) part of your bash prompt. Figure 17-9 shows the global bash configuration script that sets the PS1 variable. Table 17-4 lists some of the backslash-character sequences that you can use to configure your bash prompt environment variables.

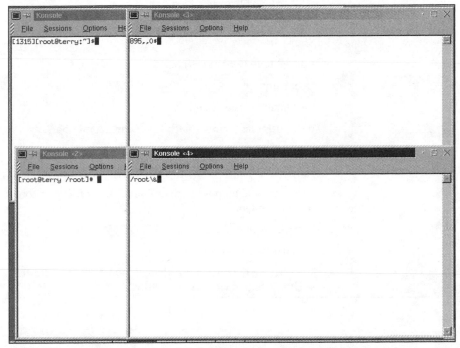

Figure 17-9: /etc/bashrc sets global values for key bash environment values

Cross-Reference You can find the complete list of special backslashed character sequences to use in your prompt variable in the man page for bash.

Table 17-4	
Backslashed Characters Controlling bash Command Prompts	
Character Sequence	*Function*
\a	Bell sound (ASCII character 7).
\d	Date ("Weekday Month Date").
\e	<ESC> (ASCII character 33).

Continued

Character Sequence	Function
\h	Host name.
\H	Fully-qualified domain name for the host.
\n	New line (linefeed).
\r	Carriage return.
\s	Shell name.
\t	Current time (24-hour HH:MM:SS).
\u	User name.
\v	bash major version number.
\V	bash major and minor (patch-level) version numbers.
\w	Full path of the current working directory.
\W	Current working directory name.
\#	The command number, such as 68 for the sixth-eighth command of your session.
\!1	The history number for the command.
\\	One backslash (\) character.
\[?\]	The ellipsis (?) represents a string of non-printing characters, such as a terminal control sequence.

Table 17-4 *(continued)*

Creating Shortcuts and New Commands with Aliases

Most Linux commands are short, but you can make them shorter by using the alias command to create command "nicknames." For example, when I list files, I almost always use the -la option so that I can see complete information for my files, including the hidden files. The following creates an alias for the ls command. Using aliases allows you to set the options you typically use with a given command so that you do not need to type them. Since I am aliasing ls to itself, I am redefining the command. I could also create a different alias and define a new command — lsl — to continue to use ls to display a short listing and my new lsl command to display the long listing.

```
alias ls='ls -la'
ls
total 3
-rw-r-r--  1   miss_sca   miss_sca   111   Nov 22   15:48   error.txt
-rw-r-r--  1   miss_sca   miss_sca   64    Nov 23   01:00   rooms
-rw-r-r--  1   miss_sca   miss_sca   33    Nov 22   14:36   weapons

# Remove the ls alias so that ls is back to normal.
unalias ls
# Test ls.
ls
error.txt    rooms      weapons
# Now let's try another alias for ls
alias lsl='ls-la'
# Test our new command, lsl
lsl
total 3
-rw-r-r--  1   miss_sca   miss_sca   111   Nov 22   15:48   error.txt
-rw-r-r--  1   miss_sca   miss_sca   64    Nov 23   01:00   rooms
-rw-r-r--  1   miss_sca   miss_sca   33    Nov 22   14:36   weapons
```

Tip If you frequently use the same command with the same options, create an alias to reduce typing.

If you want to create aliases that are available to all users, define them in the file, /etc/bashrc, the system-wide bash initialization file.

Tip Remember that aliases are shell-specific. If you want to use your aliases in other shells besides bash, you need to define them for those shells. To have all your aliases ready for you whenever you're in a shell, define them in the shell initialization files, .bashrc for the bash shell, .cshrc for the C shell, for example. Read the next section to find out how to use shell-initialization files.

Customizing Your Environment with Initialization Scripts

A shell script (script for short) is a text file that you create with a text editor. Scripts contain a group of commands the shell executes. You use scripts to automate many tasks in Linux. For example, if you want to keep your environment consistent from login to login, you can repetitively define your environment variables and aliases each time you log in and create new shells. Or you can write scripts that contain all your variable and alias definitions. You can set these scripts up to run automatically whenever you log in or start a new shell. The scripts you use to set up your environment are called *initialization* scripts.

Cross-Reference The following chapter shows other uses for shell scripts.

Initialization scripts contain commands that customize your environment, such as by defining your path, terminal setup, environment variables, and aliases to make your work easier. There are two types of initialization scripts: *system-wide* and *personal*. The system-wide script is /etc/profile. The system administrator creates and maintains /etc/profile, using it to produce a consistent environment for all users, such as default-file access permissions and system-wide aliases that everyone can use. Personal initialization scripts for bash users include:

- ✦ .bash_profile
- ✦ .profile
- ✦ .bashrc

Linux automatically executes the commands in your startup scripts each time you log in or create a new process. You don't need any startup files, but they perform the necessary repetitive housekeeping that you must otherwise do manually. For example, you could interactively set up your terminal and define your variables and aliases each time you log in and activate a shell, but if you define your environment inside your startup scripts, Linux saves you time and typing by doing the work automatically for you. System administrators usually create startup files for users and put them into each user's home directory. You are free to change these startup files to suit your own needs if the system administrator makes the files write-accessible for you.

When do initialization scripts execute?

Your login shell starts when you log in. Linux invokes additional instances of bash shells whenever you run a shell script or program. Therefore, you can have several shells invoked at the same time. Your login shell invokes the initialization script, $HOME/.bash_profile. Each successive shell invocation executes the $HOME/.bashrc script. Therefore, it makes a difference where you put commands and variable and alias definitions that should run automatically. If you define your PATH variable in the $HOME/.bashrc script, you will not be able to use that variable until Linux invokes another shell for you when you run a program or a shell script.

Tip   Put things that you need at login in your .bash_profile script. Put shell-specific configuration variables and commands in your .bashrc script. If you don't have a .bash_profile script in your home directory, Linux looks for a script called .profile to execute when you log in. If your login shell is the Korn shell, Linux also looks for the .profile script when you log in.

Tip   After you modify an initialization script — .bashrc, for example — how do you get the changes to take effect without logging in again or starting a new shell? The source command is your answer. After you execute the command in Figure 17-10, a new .bashrc takes effect.

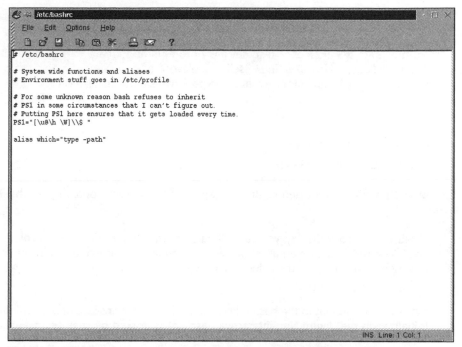

```
# /etc/bashrc

# System wide functions and aliases
# Environment stuff goes in /etc/profile

# For some unknown reason bash refuses to inherit
# PS1 in some circumstances that I can't figure out.
# Putting PS1 here ensures that it gets loaded every time.
PS1="[\u8\h \W]\\$ "

alias which="type -path"
```

Figure 17-10: Use the source command after modifying .bashrc.

What should go in initialization scripts?

What sort of commands should you put in an initialization script? Commands you always execute after you login are good candidates for initialization script, as are variables you often find yourself setting. If you have to often find yourself cding to the same directory buried deeply in the filesystem, assign that path to a short variable, and put the assignment in an initialization script. You can also create aliases in these scripts.

Knowing what to put in each initialization script is very important. For example, if you define an alias in your .bash profile script, that alias will only be available in your login shell. If a command or an application spawns another shell, the alias will not be available.

In your .bash_profile script, put configuration variables and commands that only need to be done once, at login. Some of the functions that a .bash_profile script typically performs include:

✦ Exporting variables to your entire environment.

✦ Setting the default file permissions with the umask command.

Fancy up your Shell

The bashPrompt package enables you to set bash prompts and create themes. You can download the package, which like Linux itself is the work of dedicated volunteers, from `http://bash.current.nu`. As of this writing, the package is a pre-release version.

✦ Setting the terminal type.

✦ Displaying a login message.

Put things that you cannot define globally, such as alias definitions, in your .bashrc script.

 Tip   If you have a color display, you can tell bash to list different file types in color. In your .bashrc file, define an alias for the `ls` command to use color, as in the following line of code. Yes, the color option requires two hyphens (`--`).

```
alias ls = 'ls --color=auto'
```

 Tip   Set your `PS1` prompt in the bash initialization file, .bashrc, instead of in your login initialization file, .login. Non-interactive bash shells, forked by shell scripts, unset `PS1`.

 Tip   Before modifying the `PS1`, `PS2`, `PS3`, and `PS4` variables permanently in your .bashrc file, define them interactively so that you can be sure you're satisfied with how your prompts look.

 Caution   Most of the themes require extended VGA fonts, which you can download from `http://home.earthlink.net/~us5zahns/enl/ansifont.html`.

 On the CD-ROM   You can read more details about the bashPrompt package and the bash prompt in general in the bashPrompt HOWTO. There is a link to this HOWTO on the CD-ROM.

Taking Advantage of Multitasking to Control Your Jobs

The Linux kernel manages multitasking by switching among multiple processes so quickly that all processes seem like they're executing at the same time. This section shows you the practical use for multitasking. How would you like to do three (or more) things at once? For example, let's say you need to browse the Web, run a shell script to see who's using the most disk space, and run a program to check to see if anyone has tried to crack your system today? You can save time by running a disk hog script and the security program as you're surfing the Web. Sure, if you have a GUI, you can open three windows at once to do all three tasks. However, just the act of opening those windows gobbles up lots of system resources, such as memory and CPU. And that's before you do any work in the windows. Also, what if you don't have a GUI installed? In that case, can you even consider doing three things at once? YES! Because Linux is a multitasking operating system, you don't need to use multiple windows to perform multiple tasks at the same time. All you have to do is run some jobs in the background, leaving your shell free for you to do something else in the foreground.

Note   Although you usually hear the terms *job, process,* and *program* used interchangeably, technically a job consists of a process and all the child processes it spawns (forks).

Understanding multitasking terminology

There are three terms you need to understand before investigating this section further:

✦ Background processing

✦ Foreground processing

✦ Job control

Background processing enables you to get more work done. When you put the command in the background, your shell launches a process to execute the command and gives the process an id, which you can see with the ps command. When the background process is launched, the shell comes back to you for another command to run (in either the background or foreground). While there is no limit to the number of background processes you can run, remember that each process uses memory and other system resources.

Caution   Be careful if you run interactive programs in the background. If a program running in the background prompts you for input, it sits and waits for you and no work gets done. You can deal with this minor inconvenience by bringing the interactive program to the foreground, entering your response, and moving the program back into the background.

Foreground processing is regular interactive processing. You run a command and wait for it to complete.

Job control means managing your jobs and their processes, such as changing the status of a job. bash provides the following job-control functions:

✦ Moving running programs into the background.

✦ Bringing background programs to the foreground.

✦ Suspending a program's execution.

✦ Resuming a suspended program.

✦ Listing jobs.

✦ Terminating the program.

Moving between the foreground and background

You use special characters and commands to control jobs and programs:

To put a running program into the background	type & after the command.
To suspend a running program	type **Ctrl+Z.**
To list all suspended programs	type jobs.
To return a running program to the foreground	type fg.
To terminate a program	type kill followed by % and the job number.

Figure 17-11 shows some of bash's powerful job-control handling.

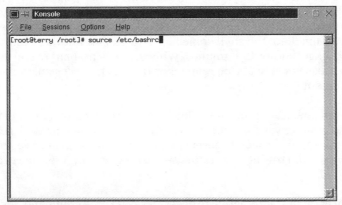

Figure 17-11: bash provides job control to help you do many things at once

Summary

This chapter showed you some of flexibility that bash provides. Although Linux commands are short and modular, bash enables you to build your own complex commands by grouping commands together and taking advantage of I/O redirection and pipes. This chapter also demonstrated how to use different variables, including how to use them to customize your environment, such as by changing your command prompt and defining a default path to follow to find commands. You can also use environment variables to create nicknames for directory paths. bash also supports aliases, which allow you to customize commands and to create command shortcuts. Job control, with foreground and background processing, gives you powerful capabilities for efficiently running and managing several programs at once.

Now that you understand some bash basics, the next chapter introduces you to some practical advanced commands and takes you to the next stage of working with bash — writing bash shell scripts.

✦　　✦　　✦

Shell Scripts

ow that you know a few user commands and how to
work with basic bash features, it's time to move to a
new level. This chapter helps you write shell scripts that use
those bash commands. Linux uses scripts of many different
types. Some scripts use a special interpreter just for running
scripts, such as perl or python. Your shell (command line
interpreter) executes another type of script — a shell script.
This chapter gets you started writing simple shell scripts.

Cross-Reference See Chapter 32 for an introduction to perl scripting.

Shell scripts are text files that contain commands. A bash
shell script consists of bash commands. Although you can
write scripts to run under any shell, this chapter concentrates
on bash scripts. There are only minor differences among most
scripts, regardless of the shells you intend them to run under.
After you create a shell script, you run your script instead of
the individual commands contained in the script. You can also
schedule your script to run automatically. This chapter
describes how to:

- ✦ Write a bash script.
- ✦ Make the name of your script an executable command.
- ✦ Run a script automatically.
- ✦ Pass user input to a script.
- ✦ Determine whether a script runs successfully or not.

Understanding the Advantages of Shell Scripts

Shell scripts save you time and typing. You can also pass
these savings on to other users on your computer and even
your network.

CHAPTER 18

In This Chapter

Understanding the
advantages of shell
scripting

Writing and
executing your first
script

bash syntax rules and
quirks, including
metacharacters

Adding functionality
to bash scripts

Comparing values
and basing actions
on conditions

Using flow control to
follow different logic
paths

Saving time and typing

When you repeatedly use the same group of commands, it makes sense to write a shell script. For example, suppose you back up your newly modified personal files each day using `tar`, a personal backup utility. Your backup procedure probably uses these five commands:

`cd`	Move to the directory that holds the files you need to back up.
`pwd`	Verify that you are located in the right directory.
`find * -mtime 0`	Find all the files modified in the past 24 hours.
`tar`	Back up the files into an archive (even though `tar` means *tape archive*, you can use it to write a backup archive to disk).
`cp`	Copy your backup archive to a safe place.

Instead of typing these commands every day, you can write them into a script. Then you can use one command every day to run the script. You can make a script executable so that all you need to do to run it is type its name.

Saving even more time and typing

If you are too busy to remember to run your script every day, you can save even more time by submitting your script to the cron system so that cron runs the script every day at the same time. Besides saving time, automating your `tar` backup with cron means that there is no chance for you to forget to run your backup script. Chapter 27 explains how to use cron. When the cron system finishes executing your backup script, it e-mails you a notification of the status of your backup.

Sharing your time savings with other users

You can set the permissions on your backup script so that everyone can use it. This saves time for the other users on your system—they don't need to figure out how to write a personal backup script. If you're working in a networked environment, users on other computers on the network can share your script as well. Not only have you saved your colleagues time, you have saved disk space by eliminating the need for each and every user to store some kind of backup script on disk.

See Chapter 27 to learn how to use the cron system to automate shell-script processing.

How is Scripting Different from Programming?

The difference between a script and a program is that a script is a text file. You write the commands in the file and execute the file with no intermediate steps — instant gratification. If you want to know what a script does, you simply print it or display it on your screen. Programs, on the other hand, require an extra step besides writing them and running them. A program must be compiled from its source code. A programmer writes the source code in a programming language and submits the source code to a compiler. The compiler generates executable machine code that only the computer can read. If you need to know what a program does, you cannot read the executable code. You must find the source code that matches the executable.

Although you do not compile scripts as you do programs, shells, including bash, support most programming language constructs, such as:

- ✦ Variable declarations and interpretation

- ✦ Parameter passing

- ✦ Logic and flow control constructs (`if...then...else` blocks, `and`, `or`, `not`)

- ✦ Case statements

- ✦ Looping constructs (`until`, `while`, `for`)

- ✦ Functions (built-in and user-defined)

- ✦ Comments to document what the script is doing

Writing and Executing Your First bash Script

The first line in any script should say which shell should execute the script. The first line — that is, the line that invokes the shell — has two parts:

- ✦ The hash-bang — The character combination #! Don't confuse the hash-bang with the comment character (#). Some people call the hash-bang the *shebang*.

- ✦ The path of the script, e.g. /bin/bash for bash, /bin/csh for the C shell, /bin/sh for the Bourne shell.

Caution If you forget this important first line, your script may not execute the way you expect. In fact, in some cases, if your script runs under the wrong shell, it may not execute at all.

Note   /etc/shells is a text file that stores the pathnames for all login shells on your computer.

Writing your first script

Your first script uses commands you already know:

cd   Change directory

pwd   Print working directory

echo   Display text

The script below also uses the built-in variable HOME.

Cross-Reference   Chapter 17 explains how to use variables in shell commands.

Here's the text file that includes the hash-bang and the commands. I created my file with the vi editor. You can use your favorite method of creating a new file.

```
#!/bin/bash
#This is a comment. Some more comments follow.
#The filename of this script is /root/myfirstscript.
#This script displays the name of your current working
#directory.(echo;pwd)
#Next it displays the name of your home #directory.(echo)
#Then it moves you to your home directory(cd)and shows #that
you are really there.(echo;pwd)
#
echo "Your current directory is "
pwd
echo $HOME
cd
echo -n "Your current directory is now   "
pwd
#That's all folks
```

Tip   If you want the prompt and the user's response to be on the same line, you can suppress the default behavior of the echo command by using the -n option. This option suppresses the new line (linefeed) that normally appears after the echoed text and the name of your current working directory. Note the difference between the first echo command (without -n) and the second echo command.

Running your first script

Linux provides you with three different ways to execute shell scripts:

✦ Name the shell on the command line.

✦ Make the script executable so that you can run it like a Linux command.

✦ Use the dot (.) character to run the script. This is called "sourcing."

Invoking the shell to run a script

The first way to run a script is to invoke the shell (/bin/bash) followed by the name of your script, as shown in the following listing. The first time the user tries to run myfirstscript, he or she gets the error No such file because the file for the script is not in the home directory. Therefore, the user needs to try again and type the full pathname of the script file, /root/myfirstscript.

Tip　　Use full pathnames to avoid errors.

```
$ /bin/bash myfirstscript
myfirstscript: myfirstscript: No such file or directory
$ /bin/bash /root/myfirstscript
Your current directory is
/home/kwall

Your current directory is now /home/kwall
$
```

The next listing shows the default permissions for myfirstscript. Everyone has read permission. Read permission enables you to run the shell script. When you type the script's pathname at the prompt, bash automatically invokes a subshell to run the script. No one, not even the file's owner, gets execute permission by default on a script file.

Note   A subshell is a shell that runs under its parent's control.

```
# ls -l myfirstscript
-rw-r--r--   1 root     root      451 Nov 27 09:06 myfirstscript
#
```

Running an executable script

Another way to run a shell script is to make a script executable. It would be more convenient to skip the shell invocation and just type the script pathname as a command. If you want to permission run the script like a command, simply by typing the file name, you need to grant execute permission on the script file. The next listing shows how to use the chmod command to change the script's permission to executable (x) for all (a).

```
# chmod a+x myfirstscript
# ls -l myfirstscript
total 2
-rwxr-xr-x   1 root     root      451 Nov 27 09:06 myfirstscript
#
```

Running a "sourced" script

You can also run a script using the source command. The dot (.) character is shorthand for source. You can use either form below to source a script.

```
$ source .bash_profile
$ . .bash_profile
```

The source command is especially useful when you edit one of your environment scripts (the scripts that begin with a dot), such as .bashrc. After you edit one of these files, you need to run the script so that the changes take effect. Use the source command to ensure that all changes, such as exported variables, descend to all shells and subshells in your environment. You learn more about the effects of sourcing a script later in this chapter.

bash Syntax Rules and Quirks

As you look at the examples in this book, you may notice that bash uses special characters as a kind of shorthand. Brevity is typical of all versions of Linux, UNIX, and the shells. For example, Chapter 15 describes wildcard shortcuts that you can use in file and directory names, and Chapter 17 tells you how to use job-control symbols such as the pipe (|) and ampersand (&).

Using metacharacters

Metacharacters are characters that have special meaning for the shell. Table 18-1 lists the metacharacters with special meaning for bash. You already understand how to use several metacharacters, such as a slash (/) to separate the parts of a pathname or a semicolon (;) to separate commands on one line. When you read or write bash scripts, you are likely to see or use some of the following metacharacters:

✦ Double quotation marks (")

✦ Single quotation marks (')

✦ Backticks (`)

✦ Backslashes (\)

Using double quotation marks to define values that include spaces

Enclose text strings with spaces in double quotation marks (") so that bash interprets the whole string, as in the following example:

```
$ export suspects="Miss Scarlet Professor Plum"
$ echo $suspects
Miss Scarlet Professor Plum
```

 Cross-Reference I am using the export command to define and export variables in one step. You can also set local variables without exporting them. See Chapter 17 for more information on defining and exporting variables.

Look at the same example below without the double quotation marks. bash does not see the entire value of the suspects variable.

```
$ export suspects=Miss Scarlet Professor Plum
$ echo $suspects
Miss
```

Using single quotation marks

Use single quotation marks (') when you do not want the shell to interpret and expand variable names or reserved characters such as the dollar sign ($) and backslash (\).

The following example compares using double quotation marks and single quotation marks with the same echo command:

```
$ echo "$USER is" $USER
root is root
# That's not what I want. Let's try single quotes.
```

```
$ echo '$USER is' $USER
$USER is root
# Now let's see what happens with a reserved character.
$ echo "$$"
1365
$ echo '$$'
$$
```

Using back quotes to store the results of a command in a variable

Use the back quote (`) — also called the *backtick* — character to enclose a command. The backtick key is usually on the tilde (~) key above the Tab key. The backticks store the output from the command into a variable. For example, if you need to find Emily's full name in a database of suspects, you can use the grep command to search for her. Enclose the grep command in backticks, and bash stores the result of your search in the following variable:

```
$ export prime_suspect='grep Emily suspectfile'
$ echo $prime_suspect
Miss Scarlet Emily
```

Cross-Reference

The grep **command is a search command. It searches for a text string within a file. The basic syntax for** grep **is:**

```
grep expression file
```

Using the backslash to escape "specialness"

Metacharacters may cause confusion at times. Suppose you need to search a document for the ampersand (&) character. How does bash decide whether you are trying to do background processing or simply looking for an ampersand? When you want a metacharacter to behave as a normal text character, you can precede it with a backslash (\) to prevent the shell from interpreting it as special. This is known as *escaping*, though it has nothing to do with the Esc key on your keyboard.

You know from Chapter 17 that when you use the echo command to display the value of a variable, you must precede the variable with a $. If you try to include a $ in a variable's name, bash generates an error:

```
$ export id_var=Miss$scarlet
$ echo $id_var
Miss
```

The preceding example shows that bash gets so confused by the $ that it does not recognize the correct value for the variable id_var. The following example shows how to escape the $ with a \.

```
$ export id_var=Miss\$scarlet
$ echo $id_var
Miss$scarlet
```

	Table 18-1	
	Some Shell Metacharacters	
Character	**Class**	**Meaning to bash**
$	General	Identify a variable to bash.
#	General	Start a comment.
#!	Shell scripts	Declare which command interpreter to use to run a script.
.	Shell scripts	Execute (via source) a script without forking a subshell.
*	Wild card	Match one or more characters.
?	Wild card	Match one character only.
&	Job control	Run a command in the background.
>	Job control	Redirect standard output.
<	Job control	Redirect standard input.
>>	Job control	Redirect and appends standard output.
2>	Job control	Redirect standard error.
|	Job control	Pipe the output from one command to another.
" "	Quoting	Include spaces in a text string.
' '	Quoting	Do not interpret variables or metacharacters in a string.
` `	Quoting	Use the result of a command as a value in a variable.

Using the backslash to dress up your script's output

You can refine your script's output by backslashing characters within the echo command. For example, \t inserts a tab, as in the following command:

```
$echo "\t$OSTYPE\t$PPID\t$USER"
        1320        Linux      Miss_Scarlet
```

Table 18-2 lists some commonly backslashed characters and their functions.

	Table 18-2	
	Commonly Used Backslash Characters	
Backslash Character	**Function**	
\a	Ring the bell (alert sound).	
\b	Display a backspace.	
\n	Insert a linefeed (newline).	
\c	Omit the trailing linefeed (newline).	
\r	Insert a carriage return.	
\t	Insert a tab.	

Getting the white space right

White space means space characters or tab characters. Usually you use white space to make your scripts and commands easier to read. However, there are times when white space or the lack of it can cause errors. For example, when you are defining and exporting variables, white space generates syntax errors that may be hard to understand, as in the following example.

This looks nice, but it doesn't work!

```
$ id_var = 1
bash: id_var: command not found
$ export id_var = 1
export: =: not a legal variable name
export: 1: not a legal variable name
```

This looks cramped, but it works!

```
$ id_var=1
$ export id_var=1
```

When you are comparing values in an if-test, you need to use white space before and after the operator — for example, " = ". You also need to surround the if-test with square brackets ([ ]). You must use white space between the left bracket and the variable being tested and between the value and the right bracket as in the following example.

```
if [ $id_var = "1000" ]
```

If you forget any white space in a comparison, bash generates syntax errors.

The Top Two Syntax Rules for White Space

1. Include white space in an if-test.

2. Don't include extra white space in a variable definition.

Cross-Reference A later section in this chapter, "Comparing Values and Basing Actions on Conditions," describes if-tests in more detail.

Adding Functionality to Your Scripts

bash provides you with a rich set of features and commands so that you can write scripts that vary from utter simplicity to the complexity of the file /etc.rc.d/rc4.d/ S25netfs, which checks that networking is up and mounts network file systems. Some common features that may help you write useful scripts are the ability to:

✦ Prompt users for input so that you can run scripts interactively.

✦ Pass positional parameters to the script from the command line so that you can run scripts non-interactively.

✦ Compare values.

✦ Follow conditional decision paths.

✦ Loop based on text and numeric values.

Prompting users for input

You can write scripts that prompt users for input. Use the read command to read a user's input from stdin (standard input, usually the keyboard). The script in the following listing, getname.sh, uses the echo command to display prompts for a user's ID and name. The read command accepts the user's input and stores it in the user-defined variables id_var and name_var.

Cross-Reference Chapter 17 tells you how to define and use variables.

```
#!/bin/sh
# getname.sh -
# Get user's ID and name and store these values in variables
```

```
echo -n "Enter your user ID: "
read id_var
echo -n "Enter your first name: "
read name_var

echo "User ID = $id_var"
echo "User Name = $name_var"
```

Reading input from a file

You can also use the read command with the input redirection character (<) to read a line from a file and store the line in a variable of your choice. The commands below read the first line from the suspects database ($HOME/suspectfile), store the results in my_var, and display (echo) the contents of my_var.

```
$ read my_var < $HOME/suspectfile
$ echo $my_var
Miss Scarlet Emily          ·
```

Using variables in scripts

Variables are containers for values. Variables hold user input, text and numerical values, and even the results of complex commands.

You don't need to predefine the variables, id_var and name_var, in getname.sh. The read command automatically creates the variables and stores the input in them. In other scripts you may need to define variables, as in the following floppy_setup script. This script creates and exports a variable, FLOOPY, that is a shortcut for a vfat (Microsoft Windows compatible) file system on a floppy disk. The script then creates an alias, mfl, that uses the FLOOPY variable to mount the file system.

```
#!/bin/sh
# floppy_setup - Setup and mount a floppy-based
# VFAT filesystem
export FLOOPY="/dev/fd0H1440"
alias mfl='mount -t vfat $FLOOPY /mnt/floppy'
mfl
```

Passing positional parameters on the command line to scripts

When you run the script in the following listing, you must run it interactively because the script expects you to input your ID and name. If you want that script to run unattended, by cron, for example, you need a way to pre-input the ID and name.

Shells provide a set of predefined command-line parameters called *positional parameters* to pre-accept input to a script. Each predefined parameter begins with a $. When you run a script, you type the values for the parameters on the command line following the name of the script. Inside the script you refer to the values by their positions on the command line. For example, a script refers to the first parameter passed in as $1. Table 18-3 lists the command-line parameters that you can use to pass values to a script.

Understanding the Scope of Variables

A variable's **scope** refers to the shells and subshells where the variable is visible. When you export a variable, as in floppy_setup, you make the variable global to the shell where you export it and to all the underlying subshells. If you run the floppy_setup script, everything seems to work. However, after you run the script you cannot see the value of the FLOOPY variable because it is no longer set. This is not a mistake. Here's what happens:

1. Before you run the script, you are in a bash shell, looking at your prompt. This is the parent shell.

2. When you run the floppy_setup script, the parent shell forks a subshell to run your script. This is the child shell. This child shell sets the FLOOPY variable.

3. The FLOOPY variable's scope is *global*, meaning it extends to all subshells that may be forked off from the floppy_setup script. These are the child's children, or the parent's grandchildren.

4. All child and grandchild shells can see the value of the FLOOPY variable.

5. After you exit the floppy_setup script you are back at the parent level.

6. The parent doesn't see the FLOOPY variable because a variable's scope only extends inward to subshells. Another way to say this is to say that descendants inherit a variable. Ancestors do not inherit outwards from their children or grandchildren.

There is a way to make the FLOOPY variable visible to the parent shell. Instead of running the script in the usual way, you need to source the script. Sourcing a script means that the parent script does all the work without forking any subshells. The parent shell is the shell that exports the FLOOPY variable. Therefore the FLOOPY variable is global from the outer level (the parent) all the way through to any children (subshells) the parent may later create. One way to source a script is to type a dot followed by a space and the pathname of the script. Another way to source a script is to use the source command. The following listing shows both ways to source the floppy_setup script.

```
$ . floppy_setup
$ source floppy_setup
```

Table 18-3	
Command Line (Positional) Parameters for Scripting	
Parameter	**Meaning**
$#	The number of parameters you are passing in to the script.
$0	The name of the script.
$1	The first parameter passed in to the script.
$2	The second parameter passed in to the script.
$3	The third parameter passed in to the script.
$n	The nth parameter passed in to the script. (It can't be larger than $9).
$*	A text string containing all the parameters.
$$	The pid (process ID) of the current shell.
$?	The exit status of the last command.

The next listing shows the getname.sh script modified to accept command-line parameters instead of interactive input for id_var and name_var.

```
#!/bin/sh
# getname.sh - Display user's ID and name and store passed
# as arguments to the script

id_var=$1
name_var=$2

echo "User ID = $id_var"
echo "User Name = $name_var"
```

Tip

If your script creates files for each user who runs the script, use the $$ character to create unique file names. Remember that $$ is the pid of the script, which is unique. For example, if your script wrote the home directory listing into a file, one file for each user running the script, you could use this command in your script:

```
ls $HOME > /tmp/homedir.$$
```

Using $$ to build a unique file name enables several people to run the same shell script at the same time

Testing for success (or failure)

Every command and every script returns an exit status — success or failure — into the reserved variable, ?. Normally the Linux and UNIX operating systems use the numeric value 0 to indicate success and any non-zero value to indicate failure. (The

Shuffling Through Positional Parameters

The shell only uses nine parameters ($1–$9). Suppose you need a tenth parameter? The shell does not provide $10, but it provides the `shift` command as a workaround. `shift` removes the first parameter from the parameter list and shuffles the other parameters left. $2 shifts left to become $1, $3 becomes $2, and so on. What was originally the tenth parameter becomes $9. When you shift parameters, $1 falls off the list. The original value of $1 is lost forever. The shift command also changes $* and $@. Here's a fragment of a shell script that shows how the `shift` command works.

```
$ cat paramscript
#!/bin/bash
# paramscript
echo $1 $2 $3 $4 $5 $6 $7 $8 $9 $10
# Prove that you have to shift to make param 10 work.
shift
echo $1 $2 $3 $4 $5 $6 $7 $8 $9
# Run the paramscript.
# Assume it has executable permission.
#
$ paramscript me you him her it them they us nous vous
me you him her it them they us nous me0
you him her it them they us nous vous
```

most common failure value is 1.) You can also define your own exit status. The following Linux statements come from the Red Hat 6.1 file /etc/rc.d/rc6.d/S01reboot, the script that reboots the system. They check to see if you invoked rebooting correctly. If not, the script exits with a failure (1) status.

```
echo "$0: call me as \"rc.halt\" or \"rc.reboot\" please!"
exit 1
```

 Cross-Reference Chapter 30 is about more advanced shell scripting techniques, including defining and using your own exit status.

 Cross-Reference See the section "Comparing Values and Basing Actions on Conditions" for more about testing a script's exit status.

You can test for many more conditions than success or failure. No matter what you test, from a simple value such as `true` to a complex condition such as "Who is the best detective—Holmes, Poirot, Clouseau, or Morse?" the result of any test is either true (0, success) or false (not 0, failure). Use the test command to:

✦ Compare text strings

✦ Compare numbers

✦ Find out the length of a text string

Quick and Easy Status Testing

Use the *control operators*, `&&` and `||`, at the end of a command to tell bash whether or not to execute the command that follows. `&&` tells bash, "If my current command succeeds, go ahead and execute the next command." `||` tells bash the opposite—"If my current command fails, do not execute the next command." The following code snippets show two examples that use these exit-status shortcuts. They also introduce the `exit` command, which exits the subshell with the exit status of the last executed command. In the first example, if the `ls` command fails, bash exits the script. The second line displays `/tmp is there` if the `ls` command succeeds. Note that both examples redirect output to /dev/null to avoid cluttering the screen.

```
Using the && and || control operators in status tests allows you
to execute one statement based on the success or failure of
another statement.$ ls getname.sh 2> /dev/null || exit
```

In this case, the `exit` statement is executed whether or not the `ls` command succeeds or not.

```
$ ls /tmp > /dev/null && echo "/tmp is there"
```

In this case, the `echo` statement only executes if the `ls` command succeeds.

✦ Combine conditions

✦ List file characteristics

There are two formats for the test syntax. The script in the following listing, beanie.sh, uses both flavors of test. Both syntax forms generate exactly the same results:

```
test [expression] (where expression is the condition to test)
if test -f /tmp/beanie tests to see if the beanie file exists
[ expression ] (The [ stands for "test".)
if [ -f /tmp/beanie ] also tests to see if the beanie file
exists
#/bin/sh
# beanie.sh - Test for existence of /tmp/beanie

echo "Using 'test'"
if test -f /tmp/beanie; then
    echo "/tmp/beanie exists"
else
    echo "/tmp/beanie does not exist"
fi

echo "Using '['"
```

```
if [ -f /tmp/beanie ]; then
    echo "/tmp/beanie exists"
else
    echo "/tmp/beanie does not exist"
fi
```

Note   Most of the other examples in this book use the second form of the `test` command—the one where you don't actually type the keyword `test`. I find the second format to be more intuitively understandable when I'm reading through the code for a script. Your preference may vary.

Testing for everything

The following tables describe everything you can test for. If you are a bash beginner, you may want to start with the most common tests—string and numeric. Most people don't need all the functionality listed in Tables 18-4 and 18-5 to get their work done.

Table 18-4
Comparison Tests for Numbers, Text, and Logical Operations

Comparison Type	Test Operator	Meaning (true if)
Text string	`-z`	String is 0 length
	`-n`	String is not 0 length
	`=`	Strings are the same
	`!=`	Strings are not the same
	`string`	String is not NULL
Numeric	`-eq`	Numbers are equal
	`-ne`	Numbers are not equal
	`-ge`	First number equal to or greater than second
	`-gt`	First number greater than second
	`-le`	First number equal to or less than second
	`-lt`	First number less than second
Logical	`!`	Negate
	`-a`	AND
	`-o`	OR

Table 18-5 **Tests for File Conditions**	
Test Operator	**True if File is**
-d	Directory
-s	Not empty (size is greater than 0)
-f	Regular file
-b	Block special file
-c	Character special file
-r	Readable file
-w	Writable file
-x	Executable file
-h	Symbolic link
-u	Setuid
-g	Setgid

Comparing Values and Basing Actions on Conditions

By itself, if doesn't compare values. To compare values you must use the test command within the if block. The if statement tests the status of your command(s). If the command is successful (also called true or 0) in Linux, bash executes the commands that follow the then statement. If the command is not successful (also called false in Linux), bash does not execute the commands that follow the then statement. bash goes on to the commands that follow fi.

Using the simplest if statement

The simplest if statement is a block of code that follows the following syntax pattern:

```
if [some condition]
then commands
fi
```

Note

The if statement tests the status of a command, not the value of a comparison. In other words, bash does the comparison, for example, 5 = 6. If the results are true, if returns an exit status of 0 (success).

Tip If you need bash to treat a numeric value as an integer, you must declare it as an integer. When working with monetary values, be sure to use integer variables.

Tip When you are comparing values that look like numbers and the comparison does not seem to work, try using the text-string operators.

Be Careful: A Number is not Always Numeric

The data values that you use in bash have a data type, usually integer (a whole number) or text (a character string). As with any programming language, bash data types come built into bash. bash understands how to process and store its data types. The default bash datatype is text.

Values that look like numbers may actually be text strings. When comparing numbers that are text, you may be surprised by the results. For example, the number 500 is more than 60. However, if you declare 500 and 60 as text variables, 500 is less than 60 because of ASCII character-sorting rules.

The following example shows what happens when a user tests the value 1000 as a number. It looks like a number to a human eye, but Linux sees it as the text string 1000.

```
[root@flyingpenguin] echo $id_var
1000
[root@flyingpenguin]cat number_script
if [ $id_var == 1000 ]
then
      echo "It works"
fi
[root@flyingpenguin]/bin/bash number_script
[: ==: binary operator expected
```

The preceding error message is not that clear, but it means that you tried to use a numeric operator on a text string. Look at the following example below to see what happens when you test 1000 as text.

```
[root@flyingpenguin] echo $id_var
1000
[root@flyingpenguin]cat text_script
if [ $id_var = "1000" ]
then
      echo "It works"
fi
[root@flyingpenguin]/bin/bash text_script
It works
```

Evaluating more complex if statements

The `if...then...else` statement lets your script follow a decision path if the condition you specify is true and an alternate path if the condition is false. The `if...then...else` syntax is a block of code that follows the following form:

```
if [condition]
then
    commands
else
    commands
fi
```

The `if...then...else` block works like this:

✦ If *condition* is true, the shell executes the *commands* that follow `then`.

✦ If *condition* is false, the shell executes the *commands* that follow `else`.

If you need to act based on multiple conditions, you can add complexity to your code by using an `if...then...elif...fi`

```
if [condition]
then
    commands
elif
    commands
    . . .
elif
    commands
else
    commands
fi
```

The ellipsis indicates that you can have multiple elif blocks. If *condition* is false and more conditions follow, the shell executes the command:

```
elif (else if)
```

`fi` ends the conditional block, and the shell processes the statement(s) following the block.

Tip   You don't need to use all sections of the `if...then...else` syntax to satisfy the syntax rules. All you need are `if`, `then`, and `fi`. The following excerpt shows a simple `if...fi` block:

```
#/bin/bash
if [ $HISTFILESIZE -gt "1000" ]
then echo "That's a big history file"
fi
```

If the history file size (the predefined variable HISTFILESIZE) is more than 1000 lines, tell the user that it's a big file. If the history file is less than or equal to 1000, the script takes no action.

Caution

bash is very picky about syntax for conditional expressions and variable definitions. Be sure to enclose comparisons in square brackets — [ ] — and use spacing as shown in the preceding script fragment. The white space within the brackets can be either spaces or tabs.

The script in the next listing uses the $# positional parameter to test how many arguments the user types on the command line. The script contains two decision paths:

+ If the user doesn't type both command-line parameters for ID and name, write a message to the file that the user must input both ID and name.

+ If the user types both parameters — for ID and for name — go ahead and follow the main code in the script.

```
#!/bin/sh
# Get user's ID and name and store these
# values in variables

if [ $# -ne 2 ]; then
    echo "USAGE: getname ID NAME"
else
    id_var=$1
    name_var=$2
    echo "User ID = $id_var"
    echo "User Name = $name_var"
fi
```

Caution

Don't forget to end the if...then...else block with fi. If you don't, the script will fail and bash will complain that the if statement is malformed.

Using "if" to test for success or failure

You can test the exit status of the commands in your script and write if...then...else blocks (or other decision constructs) based on whether the command succeeded or not. For example, the script in the next listing, backup.sh, makes a backup copy of a file using bash's ?? operator. This is a simple way to keep the previous version of the file in case you need to revert to the original.

```
#!/bin/sh
# backup.sh - Make backup copy of a file

cp $1 $1.$$
if [ $? -eq 0 ];then
```

```
        echo "Copy succeeded"
else
        echo "Copy failed"
fi
```

Using Flow Control to Follow Different Logic Paths

Flow-control statements are conditional statements that you use to execute one or more commands if a given condition is true. You can also use flow-control statements to run commands until or while a condition is true.

Using for loops to repeat actions

Use a for loop to repeat actions a certain number of times. The for syntax includes a do loop, as in the following example:

```
for variable in list
do
    statements
end
```

Using a list instructs bash to execute the statements following do once for each value in the list. The keyword in separates the variable for the list.

Note   The keyword in functions as an equal test. It tells Linux to make the variable equal to each value in the list.

Each time it goes through the loop, bash assigns the current item in the list to the variable you name. You can give the variable any name you want. By naming the variable, you are telling bash to reserve space in memory for the list items. bash handles it from there. The list is a set of values separated by spaces or a command that outputs a list of values, such as the file command. The next command makes backup copies of the files in a user's home directory. The script follows these steps:

1. Name the variable something meaningful; in this case we call it orig_files.

2. Pass in the list. In this case, the list contains the results of the ls command.

3. For each value in the list (i.e., each file found by the ls command), execute the following command:

   a. If the file is not a directory, copy it to the backup directory.

   b. Test for a successful copy.

   c. Notify the user if the copy fails.

More Examples of for Loops

The code fragments below show various ways of beginning for loops. Remember that the keyword in works like an equality (-eq, =).

```
for 1 2 3
for var in "$@"
loop_var="1 2 3"
for loop_var
```

```
#!/bin/sh
# backup.sh - Make backup copy of a file

for orig_file in $(ls)
do
        if [ ! -d $orig_file ]; then
                cp $orig_file /tmp/$orig_file.$$ || echo
"Failed to copy $orig_file"
        fi
done
```

Tip Instead of typing a list of values, you can define a variable to hold those values and pass just the variable to the for loop. bash automatically expands the variable into your list. Use this syntax:

```
for variable
do
    statements
done
```

Repeating actions while a specified condition exists

Use a while loop to execute commands while a condition is true (0). The loop ends as soon as the condition becomes false. The loop may not execute at all if the condition is false immediately.

The syntax for a while loop is:

```
while expression
do
    statements
done
```

Repeating actions until a specified condition exists

Use an until loop to execute commands until a condition is true (0). The loop ends as soon as the condition becomes true. The loop may not execute at all if the condition is true immediately.

Caution   Be careful when you code the `until` loop. The loop might never end if the condition never becomes true. This situation is called an endless loop.

The syntax for an `until` loop is almost identical to the syntax for a `while` loop:

```
until expression
do
     statements
done
```

The following script shows both a `while` and an `until` loop based on the same condition. Even though the code is almost identical, bash processes the loops a different number of times because of the subtle difference between *while a condition remains true* and *until a condition becomes true*.

Note   You can also structure `while` and `until` loops to process negatively—that is, until or while a condition is false (1). For example:

```
while [ x !== 1 ]
#!/bin/sh
# loop.sh - Using while and until loops

VAL=10
i=0

while [ $i -le $VAL ];
do
     i=$[$i+1]
done
echo "Using the while loop: i = $i"

i=0
until [ $i -eq $VAL ];
do
     i=$[$i+1]
done
echo "Using the until loop: i = $i"
```

Caution   Be careful when you code the `while` condition. The `while` loop might never end if the condition never becomes false. A loop like this is called an *endless loop*, and can devour CPU and memory resources. Depending on what the loop does, endless loops can actually use so many system resources that performance degrades noticeably or, in the worst case, the system hangs.

Using the case statement to evaluate multiple choices

Use the case statement to execute statements depending on several different conditions. The case statement is often used to replace a complex if...elif...fi block or in other situations where one option must be chosen from many. The syntax for the case statement is as follows:

```
case word in [ pattern1 | pattern2 ])
        commands;;
?)
    commands;;
esac
```

The last condition should be an asterisk (*), which represents the default case. The default case enables you to write code to execute even if none of the conditions is met. Each condition is associated with all the commands until bash reaches two semicolons (;;). The following listing shows case.sh, which illustrates how to use the case statement.

```
#!/bin/sh
# case.sh - Using the case selection structure

function usage
{
    echo 'Press a, b, c, or q. Type "q" and press ENTER to exit'
}

clear
usage
read OPT
while [ true ]
do
    case $OPT in
        a ) echo 'You pressed "a"' ;;
        b ) echo 'You pressed "b"' ;;
        c ) echo 'You pressed "c"' ;;
        q ) exit 0 ;;
        ? ) usage ;;
    esac
    read OPT
done
```

Summary

After reading this chapter, you should understand the benefits of using bash scripts to perform repetitive tasks. True to form, bash gives you different ways to run shell scripts. Take your pick, but don't forget to include the hash-bang (#!) on the first line. This chapter gets you started writing scripts by showing you how to

✦ Use variables in bash scripts.

✦ Use special metacharacters with quotes in bash scripts.

✦ Prompt and accept input from script users and files.

✦ Use positional parameters as an input source to scripts.

✦ Test the exit status of scripts.

✦ How to compare values in scripts with if-tests.

✦ How to control the logic flow of bash scripts with different types of loops.

✦   ✦   ✦

Discovering Filters

A *filter* is a program that reads input — either from stdin (standard input) or a file — processes that input, and outputs the results to stdout (standard output) or to a file. Linux filters range from simple tools, such as wc (word count) to complex programming tools such as gawk, a text processor. You've already read about some simple filters, cat, head, and tail, in Chapter 15. This chapter adds more sophisticated filters to your repertoire of Linux tools.

Using wc to Check More than the Number of Words

The wc (word count) filter lets you see how much you have written — in numbers of characters, words, or lines (terminated with a newline). In addition to counting the words in a file, wc counts lines and characters. You can let wc take its input from stdin (your keyboard) and deliver its output to stdout (your screen), as in the following example:

```
$ wc
4 lines made up of
ten words and
47
characters
<CTRL/D>
    4      10      47
```

The default output from wc lists the number of lines (4), the number of words (10), and the number of characters (47).

Tip   Did you count the characters in the example above? You can only see 43 characters. Linux sees the 43 and also four linefeeds — one at the end of each line of typed input.

Using input and output files with wc

The next example shows how you can tell wc to take its input from a file. Since there is no output file specified, wc delivers the result, including the name of the input file, to the screen.

```
$ wc /etc/passwd
      30      44     1320 /etc/passw
```

If you want wc to deliver the result to an output file, use the redirect character (>) to send the results to a file, as in the following example. Then display or print the file or send it to another program for additional processing.

```
$ wc /etc/passwd > passwdcnt
$ cat passwdcnt
      30      44     1320 /etc/passwd
$
```

Using wc options

The previous examples show the default output from wc: the count of lines, words, and characters. The options to wc let you determine which counts you want to see. As a programmer, you probably only want to count the lines of code you write. A typesetter, on the other hand, might be interested in how many characters need to be printed. The three wc options are:

-l   counts only lines

-w   counts only words

-c   counts only characters

A system administrator might count the lines in the passwd file to see how many accounts are on the system, as in the following example. The number of words and characters in the passwd file are irrelevant.

```
$ wc -l /etc/passwd
      30 /etc/passwd
$
```

Getting Acquainted with sort

sort alphabetizes your input (either from stdin or from a file) and displays the sorted list. The format for the sort command is:

```
sort [OPTIONs]... [FILEs]...
```

sort factoids

If you don't specify an input file, sort accepts values from the keyboard. In the following example the user types in a list of names, and sort alphabetizes the list and returns the sorted list to the screen.

```
$ sort
miss_scarlet
emily
Miss_Scarlet
Professor Plum
MISS_SCARLET
mr. green
sherlock holmes
Professor Moriarty
Morse
<CTRL/D>
          (sort displays this on the screen)
MISS_SCARLET
Miss_Scarlett
Morse
Professor Moriarty
Professor Plum
emily
miss_scarlet
mr. green
sherlock holmes
$
```

The sort command reorders lines in a file based on ASCII (American Standard Code for Information Interchange) rules. ASCII decrees that uppercase letters precede lowercase letters. You can see this happen in the example above. Professor Plum comes before miss_scarlet because his name appears in the file in upper case. The three values for miss scarlet do not sort together because of differences in case.

sort has three key advantages that make it especially helpful:

✦ You can sort more than one file.

✦ sort automatically merges the output if you sort multiple input files.

✦ You can choose to redirect the sorted output to a file.

sort tips

By default, sort retains all duplicate values. For example, both files below (miss_scarlet.doc and nancy_drew.doc) contain the value weapons. The sorted output shows weapons twice — once per input file.

```
$ cat miss_scarlet.doc
weapons
friends
confession.txt

$ cat nancy_drew.doc
suspects
weapons
solved_cases.txt
dead.letter

$ sort miss_scarlet.doc nancy_drew.doc
confession.txt
dead.letter
friends
solved_cases.txt
suspects
weapons
weapons
$
```

Use the sort command's -u option to reduce duplicates to one value, as below.
sort displays the sorted output on the screen. Notice that the two occurrences of
weapon become just one.

```
$ sort -u miss_scarlet.doc nancy_drew.doc
confession.txt
dead.letter
friends
solved_cases.txt
suspects
weapons
$
```

You can combine the sorted output from multiple files, as shown below, by using
the -o option:

```
$ sort -uo combined miss_scarlet.doc nancy_drew.doc
$ cat combined
confession.txt
dead.letter
friends
solved_cases.txt
suspects
weapons
```

If you need to sort in alphabetical order, ignoring case, you can use the -f option to
tell sort to "fold" uppercase and lowercase letters together. The example below
sorts the same names as in the "sort factoids" section above. The three values for
Miss Scarlet's name appear together because the -f option ignores ASCII case
rules.

```
$ sort -f
miss_scarlet
emily
Miss_Scarlet
Professor Plum
MISS_SCARLET
Mr. Green
sherlock holmes
Professor Moriarty
Morse
<CTRL/D>

emily
MISS_SCARLET
Miss_Scarlet
miss_scarlet
Morse
Mr. Green
Professor Moriarty
Professor Plum
sherlock holmes
$
```

Do you need to sort in reverse order? Use the -r option. The example below sorts
two files and displays the reversed output on the screen.

```
$ sort -ru miss_scarlet.doc nancy_drew.doc
weapons
weapons
suspects
solved_cases.txt
friends
dead.letter
confession.txt
$
```

Caution   Don't try to sort a file into itself using redirection, for example, sort myfile >
myfile. sort opens your file for output and zeroes it out to get ready for the
sorted output. The problem is that now there are no lines left to sort as input.
Always use a separate output file.

Sorting by columns

By default, sort uses the whole line as the sort key. If multiple lines start with the
same character, sort breaks the tie by checking the next character. If there's
another tie, sort goes on to the third character, and so on. The example below displays the clues file, and then sorts the clues file using the default line-by-line sort:

```
$ cat clues
emily    duncan    lead pipe      rope     revolver
helen    duncan    chair          cat      fingerprint
prof     plum      pipe           shoe     tobacco
colonel  mustard   glass          monocle  bumbershoot
kate     duncan    hoe            shovel   fertilizer
jacques  clouseau  kato           poisson  parapluie
$
$ sort clues
colonel  mustard   glass          monocle  bumbershoot
emily    duncan    lead pipe      rope     revolver
helen    duncan    chair          cat      fingerprint
jacques  clouseau  kato           poisson  parapluie
kate     duncan    hoe            shovel   fertilizer
prof     plum      pipe           shoe     tobacco
$
```

You can see that the clues file sorted in first-name order.

You can also sort by fields. Each field is a group of non-blank characters. The line below contains 51 characters and six fields. Linux numbers fields starting at 0. The first two fields (f0 and f1) are last and first name fields. The remaining four fields are clues.

```
emily      duncan    lead pipe      rope     revolver
 f0          f1       f2   f3        f4         f5
             +1       +2   +3        +4         +5
```

By default, sort would order the lines in this file by first name. If you want to order the data by a different field, such as last name, you need to tell sort which group of characters to use as the sort key. You tell sort where to find the sort key by indicating the key's starting position and ending position. To specify a key's starting position, use a + followed by a field number (*fields* are delimited by whitespace: one or more spaces or a tab). To specify a key's ending position, use a - followed by the field number of the field or fields you want to use as the sort key. For example, the command below uses the last name (field 1) plus the rest of the line as a sort key. The sort key includes all characters after the last name because the command includes no ending position. That is, it does not end with - *number*.

Note   A sort *key* is a contiguous group of characters that is used to compare and order lines in a file.

Caution   sort considers that blanks precede letters and numbers in the alphabet. Look at the example below where I try to sort by the last-name (+1) field.

```
$ sort +1 clues
kate     duncan    hoe            shovel   fertilizer
prof     plum      pipe           shoe     tobacco
helen    duncan    chair          cat      fingerprint
```

```
emily    duncan   lead pipe     rope     revolver
jacques  clouseau kato          poisson  parapluie
colonel  mustard  glass         monocle  bumbershoot
```

The sort below uses the last name field (+1) as the sort key and tells `sort` to ignore blanks. Now the lines are sorted into correct last-name order.

```
$ sort +1 -b clues
jacques  clouseau kato          poisson  parapluie
kate     duncan   hoe           shovel   fertilizer
helen    duncan   chair         cat      fingerprint
emily    duncan   lead pipe     rope     revolver
colonel  mustard  glass         monocle  bumbershoot
prof     plum     pipe          shoe     tobacco
```

Table 19-1 lists some helpful `sort` options.

Table 19-1
Handy sort Options

Option	Function
-b	Ignore leading blanks in a sort- key field.
-f	Fold lower- and uppercase letters together, e.g. make "B" = "b."
-i	Ignore unprintable characters.
-n	Sort numerically.
-r	Sort in reverse order.
-o FILE	Put the sort output into a file, where FILE is the file specification.
-t SEP	Use SEP as the field separator where SEP is a character that acts as a field separator, e.g. to sort spreadsheet data, sort -, file (the comma is the separator between spreadsheet fields).
--help	Display sort help, including a list of options.
--version	Display the version of sort.

Tip

When you sort large files, the sort command may create temporary files in the /tmp directory (by default) to hold intermediate results. The /tmp directory is in the root file system, which can be a busy file system from a disk I/O point of view. If the applications that run on your computer do lots of sorting, you can improve disk I/O performance by moving sort's temporary files to a less busy file system. To control sort's temporary directory, define the variable TMPDIR to point to the full path of a directory. sort then creates the temporary files in TMPDIR. When sort finishes, it automatically deletes the temporary files.

Why define a separate temporary directory in `TMPDIR` instead of using /tmp? The primary reason is security. First, /tmp is readable by all users, so if a `sort` command executed against, say, the file /etc/shadow, abruptly died instead of terminating normally, `sort` would not have a chance to delete its temporary file in /tmp/, leaving encrypted passwords in a file that anyone could look at and, potentially, decipher. There are other security risks associated with /tmp as well, so you might consider browsing the Web site http://www.bugtraq.org for all of the gory details.

Searching with the greps

The search commands, `grep`, `egrep`, and `fgrep` are some of the most popular filters. `grep` and the extended form, `egrep`, search for text strings and regular expressions in text files. `fgrep` searches for text strings only, rather than regular expressions. `zgrep` works like `grep` and `egrep`, but on compressed (gzipped) files. The examples in this chapter use `egrep` and `fgrep`, although `grep` is very similar.

Chapter 18 includes a table that lists and describes metacharacters that you can use in regular expressions.

The syntax for using members of the `grep` family is:

```
grep [-lots of options] string or reg_expression file(s)
```

or

```
grep -E expression file(s)
fgrep [-lots of options] string file(s)
zgrep [-lots of options] string or reg_espression compressed files
```

The example below uses the simplest form of `egrep` to find all the files in /home/emilyd that contain the text string `Erin`.

```
tweety$ egrep Erin /home/emilyd/*
/home/emilyd/all_beanies: Princess    Ewey Squealer Erin
/home/emilyd/favorite_beanies: Princess    Erin    Curly
```

The output shows the entire line of each file that contains the string `Erin`. The following example shows that using `fgrep` to search for the text string `Erin` returns the same output as using the `egrep` command.

```
tweety$ fgrep Erin /home/emilyd/*
/home/emilyd/all_beanies: Princess    Ewey Squealer Erin
/home/emilyd/favorite_beanies: Princess    Erin    Curly
```

When you start using regular expressions for searching, `fgrep` does not return output. `fgrep` only searches for text strings.

If you want to search for a text string that includes a space or characters such as parentheses, such as `Emily Duncan's Beanies` or `(string_in_parens)`, you must enclose the string in double quotes (`" "`). See the following example.

```
tweety$ egrep "Emily Duncan's Beanies" /home/emilyd/*
/home/emilyd/all_beanies:Emily Duncan's Beanies
tweety$ egrep "Emily Duncan's Beanies" home/emilyd/*
/home/emilyd/test:(string_in_parens)
```

Caution   If you forget to enclose the entire string in double quotes, bash returns an error.

Searching with regular expressions

A regular expression is a search pattern for text strings. Linux uses special characters that resemble arithmetic operators to represent text strings. For example, a commonly used regular expression in searching is:

```
[0123456789]
```

This regular expression means "match any single character in the list." It is useful for searching for numbers. You can use any list of characters as a regular expression by enclosing the list in square brackets (`[` and `]`).

Cross-Reference   You already know from Chapter 18 that the asterisk (*) is a special character, also called a wildcard or a metacharacter, that matches any one or more characters.

Tips for "egrep-ing" with regular expressions

You can create search ranges by enclosing the starting character of the range, a hyphen (-), and the last character of the range in square brackets. For example, the command:

```
egrep [1-5] beanies_ratings
```

searches for the top five beanies, (`1-5`).

Be careful with ranges versus search strings. While the preceding command returns the top five beanies, the following command returns any beanie with a 1 or a 5 in the rating:

```
tweety$ egrep [15] beanies_ratings
Brittania         5
Osito            25
Erin Princess     1
almond           15
valentino        35
```

Remember that Linux is case-sensitive. To override case-sensitivity, use the -i (ignore case) option:

```
tweety$ egrep -i emily *
all_beanies:Emily Duncan's Beanies
often_searched_words:Emily
ften_searched_words:emilyd
```

You can negate a list. If you type a carat (^) as the first character of the list, egrep matches any character not in the list.

To search for the ^ character as part of the list, type it anywhere in the list but first.

To search for the] character as part of the list, make it the first character of the list.

egrep's -n option is handy because it numbers the lines it finds, as follows:

```
egrep -n "v" beanies_ratings
12:valentino              35
13:valentina              9
```

If you search for the same patterns in different files, you should know about the -f option. This option enables you to create a file that lists the patterns. Then you can input the file path to egrep whenever you want to find those words. This -f option is quite useful for semi-automating egrep commands. The following example displays the contents of the file often_searched_words and searches for those words in all the files in the current working directory (*) and in the passwd (/etc/passwd) file.

```
tweety$ cat often_searched_words
Emily
Erin
Duncan
emilyd
tweety$ egrep -nf often_searched_words * /etc/passwd
all_beanies:1:Emily Duncan's Beanies
beanies_ratings:5:Erin      Princess    Lucy
favorite_beanies:2:Princess    Erin     Curly
often_searched_words:1:Emily
often_searched_words:2:Erinoften_searched_words:3:Duncanoften_s
earched_words:4:emilyd
/etc/passwd:21:emilyd:x:500:100:emily duncan :/home/em
```

Tip   Notice that a space separates the names of multiple files to be searched with egrep.

If you want to create a search window — that is, to display a certain number of lines before and after your search string or regular expression — use the -B and -A options. The command below tells egrep to display the 10 lines immediately preceding and the 12 lines immediately following the search string:

```
tweety$ egrep -B 10 -A 12 [15]*beanie_ratings
```

To find files that have no match with the search string, use the -L option.

To display non-matching lines, use the -v option.

Tips for formatting "egrep-ed" output — Using filters within a filter

Sometimes you don't need all the information that egrep provides. You can use egrep command options to filter certain egrep output. Here are a few formatting options for egrep:

-l   Filter all output except the file name. Use egrep -l to list only the file names that match your search string.

-s   Suppress error messages about directories and unreadable files, such as egrep: /root/Disktop: Is a directory.

-c   Suppress egrep's normal output and display only a count of the matching lines.

-cv   Display a count of the non-matching lines.

-h   Does not display the file names in the output.

If you want to find, for example, all uppercase characters of all the numbers between 0 and 9, you can save considerable typing by using one of the following predefined character classes.

[:alnum:]   Find 0–9 A–Za–z.

[:alpha:]   Find all alphanumeric characters.

[:lower:]   Find all lowercase characters.

[:upper:]   Find all uppercase characters.

Using awk

The awk language is like many Linux commands and programs: it's named after its creators, Alfred Aho, Peter Weinberger, and Brian Kernighan. gawk is an enhanced version of awk written and maintained by the GNU project (Paul Rubin and Jay Fenlason, in particular). Both gawk and awk include advanced search and character-string-handling capabilities. There are other versions of awk besides the original and gawk (GNU awk), including nawk and POSIX awk. POSIX awk conforms to the IEEE's Portable Operating System Interface industry standard. gawk, as typical of GNU software, is based on POSIX awk. This chapter shows you how to write and run standalone gawk programs (also called scripts). You do not compile awk/gawk programs.

gawk uses a pattern-matching/processing system. When gawk matches a pattern you submit, it processes an action against the pattern. A major benefit of gawk is that it can process actions against the same pattern in multiple files. The pattern-action format of a gawk program looks like this:

```
pattern1  { action1 }
pattern2  { action2 }
    and so on through as many pattern-action pairs as you need.
```

Tip   As with most of Linux, gawk offers you various ways to do the same thing. As you examine the examples in this section, you may find another way to do the same thing. Experiment.

Getting started with gawk

The easiest way to use gawk is to use it interactively — write a simple gawk script right on the command line. The gawk script below accepts input from the keyboard (stdin) and displays the results on the screen (stdout). The interactive syntax for gawk is

```
$ gawk pattern {action}
```

Depending on what you need to do, you can omit either the pattern or the action, but not both. If you omit the action, the default is to print all lines in the file matching the pattern. If you omit the pattern, the default action is to perform the action on all lines in the file.

Note   The combination of pattern and action is called a *gawk rule*. You can put one or more rules in a gawk program.

Invoking gawk

You can start gawk interactively either from a KDE, GNOME, or X terminal window, or from the command line in a virtual console or on a non-Windowing terminal. gawk can accept input from various sources, such as a file, from the keyboard (stdin), or from a pipe (|) from another program. gawk's output can go to the screen (stdout), can be piped into another program, or can be redirected into a file.

Note   The gawk examples that follow are extracted from GNOME and KDE terminal windows on a Caldera OpenLinux computer. You can use exactly the same syntax on any other Linux distribution.

Writing your first gawk program — Hello World

The traditional starting point for learning a programming language, whether it's C++ or FORTRAN or Visual Basic, is to learn the Hello World program. Following this tradition, the example below shows your first gawk program — Hello World. To run this gawk program yourself, the first thing you need to do is invoke gawk. All you have to do is type gawk. Then, type a gawk rule. A rule consists of a pattern or an action or both. In this first example there is no pattern and one action. Surround the rule in single quotes (' '). Always enclose the action in braces ({ }). The action executes a common gawk command, print. Be sure to enclose the string you are printing in double quotes (" "). When you're done typing, press Enter, and the program will run. When the following program runs, it appears to do nothing at first. You have to press a key to see the text string.

```
tweety$ gawk '{ print "To say Hello, world?press any key" }'

To say Hello, world?press any key

To say Hello, world?press any key
^D
tweety$
```

Remember, if there is no pattern, gawk performs the action based on input. Where does gawk get the input? In this case, gawk expects input from the keyboard (stdin). So you need to press a key (any key) to tell gawk to go ahead and process the action. That action executes the print statement for each line of input — that is, each time you press a key. In the example above, when you press a key (this example uses the Enter key), gawk prints the message on your screen. When you press the Enter key again, gawk prints the message again. If you press a key twice, gawk receives two lines of input. According to the laws of gawk, it processes the action every time it receives input. If you were to press a key 100 times, you would see 100 Hello World messages. I think you get the point. To exit from the gawk program, hit Ctrl+D when you're done pressing keys. As you can see from the example, after gawk receives Ctrl+D, it returns to the shell prompt.

Note   While the preceding example is simple, the syntax is not intuitive. The quotes and braces, and other features that you will see later, cause some users to say that however useful gawk may be, it's very "gawk"y. The same holds true for the original awk. It can seem quite "awk"ward.

It wouldn't be Linux if there weren't more than one way to do the same thing. Here's another way to write a Hello World gawk program. In contrast to the preceding example, this example uses both a pattern and an action. Because you include a pattern, gawk does not expect any input either from stdin or from any other input source, such as a file.

```
tweety$ gawk 'BEGIN { print "Hello, world" }'
Hello, world
```

Here are some syntax notes on the preceding Hello World program:

✦ First, type gawk to invoke gawk processing.

✦ The pattern comes next. In this case, the pattern is BEGIN.

✦ Follow the pattern with the action enclosed in braces ({ }). The action is simply to print `Hello World` on the screen (stdin). `print` is a gawk command.

✦ Don't forget to surround the whole rule (pattern + action) in single quotes.

Here's a third way to print the Hello World message. You can provide a file to gawk as the input source. In the example below, the message is inside the hello_file. The example uses the `cat` command to display the file. The following gawk command has no pattern and one action. The action, as always, is within braces, which are inside single quotes. Notice that after the action, you type the name of the input file. If this file is not in your current working directory, you should type its full pathname, for example, /home/miss_scarlet/hello_file.

```
tweety$ # Before we gawk, let's display the hello_file
tweety$ cat hello_file
Hello World
tweety$ gawk ' { print $0 }' hello_file
Hello World
tweety$
```

In the example above, you see the input file used to hold the data — in this case, a text string that is input for gawk. You can also use a file to hold the patterns and/or actions you want to submit to gawk. The next example displays the Hello World message using two files. The first file, gawk_action, holds the action(s). The `-f` option tells gawk to get its instructions from a file. You do not have to place the name of the file, hello_file in the previous example, inside single quotes, but the =braces are still required. The next file (hello_file) holds the data that the gawk_action file should process.

> **Note**   You can give the files any valid file name.

```
tweety$ cat gawk_action
{ print }
tweety$ gawk -f gawk_action hello_file
Hello World
tweety$
```

Using BEGIN and END

gawk programs have three parts:

1. What happens before gawk receives any input (pre-processing).

2. What happens during processing.

3. What happens after gawk processes the input (post-processing).

BEGIN and END Factoids

Here are some things to remember about how BEGIN and END behave with gawk:

1. They really are uppercase keywords.

2. gawk does not use the BEGIN and END keywords as a tests. They simply mark the beginning and end of a code block.

3. If there are multiple BEGIN patterns, gawk merges all the actions that go with the BEGINs. All the actions behave as if they had been written into one BEGIN.

4. gawk performs BEGIN actions before reading any input.

5. gawk merges multiple END statements and patterns into single END statements and patterns, and then executes the END after processing all of the input or when it runs into an existing exit statement.

6. Unlike other gawk patterns, BEGIN and END patterns must have actions.

For example, in the command gawk 'BEGIN { print "Hello World" }', the BEGIN statement says to print Hello World before accepting input. After printing Hello World, gawk accepts any input that might exist. In this case there is no input, so gawk simply prints the message and exits.

Note The spaces between the opening and closing braces and the words print and World are not required. They are there to improve readability.

Using expressions and variables with gawk

You can use predefined program expressions and both arithmetic and Boolean operators to write complex patterns and actions. Table 19-2 lists some commonly used gawk predefined expressions.

Table 19-2
gawk Predefined Expressions

Expression	Meaning
BEGIN { action }	Perform the action before processing any input and before performing any other actions that might be in the program.
END { action }	Process all input and all other actions before performing the action.
NF	The number of fields in the currently processed record.

Continued

Table 19-2 (continued)	
Expression	**Meaning**
NR	The number of records that have been processed.
FS	The field separator for multiple input fields.
OFS	The field separator for multiple output fields.

Using field separators in gawk input

Suppose you wanted to use gawk to filter and display only the personal names of the last six people who have accounts on your system. You can use gawk to read each line of the passwd file and extract the fifth field (the personal name field). Then you can pipe the output of gawk into the tail command to display only the last six names. By default, gawk expects the fields to be separated by white space, either spaces or tabs. You know from Chapter 12 that the /etc/passwd file separates fields with colons (:). Therefore, you need to use FS to notify gawk to expect a different field separator (:). In the following example, the first action sets the field separator to be a colon and the second action prints the fifth field.

Note Two of the lines in the passwd file have an empty personal-name field. Therefore, gawk displays blank lines for two of the users' accounts.

```
tweety$ gawk '{ FS = ":"} {print $5}' /etc/passwd | tail -6

col mustard
emmi peacock
inspector morse
sherlock holmes

tweety$
```

The next example also operates on the passwd file. This time, gawk displays the user name (account name) in the first field as well as the personal name in the fifth field, and uses the output field separator (OFS) to separate the two fields.

```
tweety$  gawk '{ FS = ":"} { OFS = " ... "} {print $5,$1}'  etc/passwd | tail -6
 ... squid
col mustard ... colonel_mustard
emmi peacock ... mrs_peacock
inspector morse ... morse
sherlock holmes ... sherlock
 ... testing
tweety$
```

Note In the preceding example, you can now see the user names for the lines that had a blank personal name.

Using comparison operators in gawk programs

You can evaluate and compare values and expressions in gawk programs. Table 19-3 lists gawk comparison operators.

	Table 19-3 Comparison Operators	
Operator	**Meaning**
==	Equals
!=	Does not equal
>=	Is greater than or equal to
>	Is greater than
<=	Is less than or equal to
<	Is less than
&&	Logical AND (both conditions must be true)
||	Logical OR (either condition must be true)

Note These operators are the same as those in the C programming language.

The following gawk example filters data from the passwd file and generates a simple report. The report lists accounts that have the same UID (user id) and GID (group id). It also lists all accounts that use the default shell—that is, who have no shell listed in the passwd file. Finally, the gawk example below reports on the number of records in the passwd file that were processed.

Tip The comment lines explain each line of gawk code that follows. The indented lines are just for appearance to make the code easier to read.

```
tweety$ gawk '
> # Give the BEGIN pattern two actions. Set the FS and OFS.
> BEGIN { FS = ":" }
> # The OFS is a TAB. It doesn't show up, but gawk accepts it.
>       { OFS = "" }
> # If there are only six fields in the record, there is no shell.
```

```
>  NF==6    { print $1, " uses the default shell" }
>  # If the first and fourth fields are equal, the UID = the GID
>  $3==$4    { print $1, " has the same user and group id" }
>  # When all records are processed, display the number of records.
>  END   { print NR, " records processed" }
>  # Don't forget the last single quote and name the data file.
>        ' /etc/passwd
default_user uses the default shell
root has the same user and group id
bin has the same user and group id
daemon has the same user and group id
nobody has the same user and group id
gdm has the same user and group id
squid has the same user and group id
testing has the same user and group id
31 records processed
tweety$
```

Caution   Be careful with operators. When initializing the formatting expressions, such as FS and OFS, you can use a standard = symbol. When working with values, you must use the == operator.

Generating simple reports with patterns only

In the example that follows, we use awk to find all the people whose offices are on the ground through third floor. The example includes the pattern ' /^[0−3]/ '. No action is necessary since the default action displays the information that matches the pattern. Breaking the pattern apart, the pieces are:

'   '   The single quotes tell the shell not to interpret anything between them as special shell characters.

/   /   Slashes surround the pattern meaning that the pattern is a regular expression.

^   Means match the pattern at the beginning of the line.

[0-3]   Means that the pattern to match is 0, 1, 2, or 3.

Cross-Reference   Chapter 18 lists expressions commonly used for shell scripting. You can also use these expressions in gawk programming.

First, display the entire offices file.

```
tweety$ cat offices
1A      Miss Scarlet
1B      Professor Plum
2C      Mr. Green
4A      Mrs. Peacock
```

```
2A        Colonel Mustard
4F        Sherlock Holmes
5F        Dr. Watson
3C        Mrs. White
```

Now use gawk interactively to find all lines in the office file that begin with 0, 1, 2, or 3. To use gawk interactively simply invoke gawk, followed by the gawk program (pattern and/or action lines), and include any input files to process.

```
tweety$ gawk '/^[0-3]/ ' offices
1A        Miss Scarlet
1B        Professor Plum
2C        Mr. Green
2A        Colonel Mustard
3C        Mrs. White
```

You usually run gawk interactively, as in the preceding code example, if the gawk patterns and actions are simple and you only need to run them once.

You have already seen that another way to run gawk is to store your gawk program in a file. If you save your gawk commands in a file, you can invoke gawk on the command line using the -f (for gawk file) option, and pass the name(s) of the gawk file and any input data files for processing to gawk. The following example uses the input file approach (gawk -f), generates the same report as the previous example, displays the gawk program, named office_search, and then runs the program against the offices data file.

```
tweety$ cat office_search
# gawk script
# finds tenants on the ground through third floors
/^[0-3]/
#
tweety$ gawk -f office_search offices
1A        Miss Scarlet
1B        Professor Plum
2C        Mr. Green
2A        Colonel Mustard
3C        Mrs. White
```

This method of running gawk is convenient if you have medium to complex patterns and actions and if you may need to run this gawk program again.

The next way to run gawk is to create a gawk script to run as a command. You must tell bash to process the file with gawk -f. You do this with the hash-bang (#!) just as you saw in Chapter 18, where the #! tells bash to process the script through the bash shell.

Defining a variable in a gawk program

How many people have offices in the building? To use gawk to find the answer, have it perform actions on the input file named offices. In this example, you do not need patterns. The actions are surrounded by braces. The first action tells gawk to print the text strings There are and occupied offices in the building. In between the two text strings is a variable named lcv, which the programmer makes up. Any name will do. I used lcv because to me it means "line count variable." The second action tells awk to keep a count of the lines in the file. You could say

```
lcv = lcv + 1
```

The expression ++lcv is a shortcut that means the same as lcv = lcv + 1. Either expression counts the lines in the file. The action to count the lines in the file automatically repeats until all the lines are processed. Here's what the gawk script named count_offices looks like:

```
tweety$ cat count_offices
#! /usr/bin/gawk -f
# gawk script to count the offices in the building (lines in
the file)
END     {
        print "There are ", lcv, "occupied offices in the
building."
        }
{ ++lcv }
# end of gawk script.
```

Next, use the chmod command to make the gawk program executable.

```
tweety$ chmod a+x count_offices
```

Use the ls command to be sure that the count_offices program has execute permissions set.

```
tweety$ ls -l count*
-rwxr-xr-x   1 root     root       192 May 13 14:00 count_offices
```

Run the gawk program as a command and pass it the offices data file for input.

```
tweety$ /home/miss_scarlet/count_offices offices
There are eight occupied offices in the building.
tweety$
```

When should you program with gawk?

Now that you have learned the basics of gawk, you might wonder when gawk is the right tool to use and, conversely, when you should *not* use it. Use gawk when you have to perform the same processing on one or many text files, when you need to extract specific text from a file, and when you need to generate some sort of report, but do not have a lot of time in which to create a program using a language such as C or C++. Another situation in which gawk excels is one-liners — short command lines that perform a needed task, such as reformatting the output of, say, the ps or ls commands.

Naturally, there are many situations for which gawk is the wrong tool. If you find yourself writing a gawk program longer than 100 lines, you are unloading a dump truck with a spoon. That is, you are using the wrong tool. Consider using Perl or even a traditional programming language. If speed is the paramount concern, a compiled program (written in C, C++, or another compiled language is a better solution than gawk because gawk is an interpreted language. Compiled programs are ready to run because they are already in a format that a CPU can understand. Interpreted programs, on the other hand, have to be translated from text to an intermediate format, and then passed to the interpreter. Consequently, the general rule (there are exceptions) is that interpreted languages execute much more slowly than compiled languages.

Finally, gawk is not the appropriate tool to use if the problem you need to solve involves a lot of mathematics. Even though gawk can perform basic arithmetic, it is inadequate to the task of higher math and heavy computation. FORTRAN is a better solution in this case.

Gawk summary

The following list summarizes the key points of the preceding discussion of gawk. Although gawk's syntax may seem "gawkward," the trade-off for its peculiar syntax is that gawk programs can be much smaller than programs in more traditional programming languages and still be just as powerful, particularly when manipulating text.

✦ Use gawk for matching text patterns and manipulating them record by record.

✦ gawk uses a pattern-action pair to do your work.

✦ You can omit either the pattern or the action, except for BEGIN and END.

✦ gawk numbers fields from $1 to $n (the last field in the record). $0 is the entire record.

✦ You can run gawk interactively or you can tell it to take its commands from a file.

✦ If you make a gawk program executable, you can run it as a command.

Streaming Through Files with sed

sed is a text filter called a **stream ed**itor, which is the origin of its odd name. The term *stream editor* means that a program performs some sort of processing on the flow of data coming from standard input and then sends the result to standard output. Unlike a global editor such as vi, sed does not change its input file. It changes the data, usually text, it receives from standard input. For example, suppose that everywhere in this book, we spelled Miss Scarlet's name wrong—we used two t's. We can use sed to edit all 34 chapters at once, changing every occurrence of Scarlett to Scarlet. You can use sed interactively or you can run it from a script.

How does sed work?

sed, although called a stream editor, does not work like other editors. You type the commands for processing input records, and the results of that processing go to your screen or an output file. You don't use a traditional editing interface, moving the cursor and changing text. Here's an example:

```
tweety$ sed -e '/Scarlett/d' *
```

It doesn't look anything like vi, does it? First you invoke sed by typing its name with the -e option. Next you type the action you want sed to perform. In the example above, you want sed to find every occurrence of the word Scarlett and delete it (d). You enclose the text to find in slashes (/ /) and follow the slash with the action to perform (d for delete). Enclose the whole thing, text plus action, in single quotes. Finally, you name the file(s) to operate on. In the example above, you're telling sed to perform the delete on every file (*) that it finds the word Scarlett in.

These are the behind-the-scenes steps sed performs:

1. Determine where in the input to apply your instructions. If you have not told sed where to start and stop, go to Step 2 below.

2. Apply the instructions you type—such as d to delete, s to substitute, w to write to a file, = to display the line number on stdout—to every line in the input.

3. If you have specified beginning and ending line numbers or beginning and ending matching patterns, sed only applies your instructions to the input between your beginning and ending markers.

Note   The lines that your instructions say to process are called *addresses*. Addresses can be patterns enclosed in slashes, as in the previous example, or line numbers.

Stepping through some simple sed examples

The example below tells sed to delete the third line in the suspects file. This basic sed command simply uses the d instruction preceded by the line number of the line you wish to delete. If you want to delete line 3 in more than the suspects file, submit a list of files to sed. sed displays the newly edited suspects file on the screen since the example does not tell sed to write the output to a separate file.

```
tweety$ cat suspects
Miss Scarlet
Mrs. Peacock
Sherlock Holmes
Professor Plum
Jack
Colonel Mustard
tweety$ sed -e '3d' suspects
Miss Scarlet
Mrs. Peacock
Professor Plum
Jack
Colonel Mustard
tweety$ # Line 3, Sherlock Holmes, has been deleted.
```

If you want to delete all suspects from line 3 to the end, change your sed stream to list line 3 followed by a comma (,) and use $d to say "go all the way to the last line," as in the example below. The output shows that only the first two lines of the input remain.

```
tweety$ sed -e '3,$d' suspects
Miss Scarlet
Mrs. Peacock
```

Caution

In the examples above, you saw sed perform the deletions and display the results on the screen (stdout). However, if you display the file again, you see that the deletions were not permanent. All the lines in the file remain. If you want sed to write the deletions to a permanent disk file, you need to redirect the output to a new file, as follows:

```
tweety$ sed -e '3,$d' suspects
Miss Scarlet
Mrs. Peacock
tweety$ cat suspects
Miss Scarlet
Mrs. Peacock
Sherlock Holmes
Professor Plum
Jack
Colonel Mustard
tweety$ # oops! the deletions weren't permanent
tweety$ sed -e '3,$d' suspects > new_suspects
tweety$ # Check for permanent deletions
tweety$ cat new_suspects
Miss Scarlet
Mrs. Peacock
tweety$ #Now we have a new file with only 2 lines
```

Always redirect the output into a new file. If you try to redirect output into the input file, you destroy the input file before sed can operate on it.

Besides using line numbers and simple patterns to tell sed where to process text and what to do to the text, you can also use regular expressions. Regular expressions are one of sed's most powerful features. The following example uses the regular expression /^/ to mean the beginning of the line. The example tells sed to find every line in the unsolved_crimes file with Scarlett in it, and substitute (s) the beginning of the line with the word misspelled.

```
tweety$ sed -e '/Scarlett/s/^/misspelled/' unsolved_crimes
misspelled101A  Miss Emily Scarlett
1044    Professor Hank Plum
misspelled1049  Miss Emily Scarlett and horse
1077    Mrs. Hannah Peacock
1078    Mrs. Hannah Peacock
1088    archcriminal Marshall Wilensky
tweety$
```

Summary

Linux provides several commands and programming languages for filtering data.

✦ wc enables you to get statistics on a file, not in terms of how many bytes long the file is, but in terms of how many lines or words you have written.

✦ sort enables you to order data records by different fields.

✦ The grep family enables you to search for plain text and complex regular expressions in files.

✦ gawk (and its parent, awk) enable you to write programs to manipulate data and generate reports that range from one-liners to pages of complete output.

✦ sed enables you to filter and edit data in multiple files at once.

You can combine any of these filters with pipes and redirection to make them even more powerful.

✦   ✦   ✦

Configuring and Managing TCP/IP Networking

IV

In This Part

Chapter 20
Configuring the
Network

Chapter 21
Configuring the
Domain Name
System (DNS)

Chapter 22
Configuring the
Network File System
(NFS)

Chapter 23
Configuring Network
Information Services
(NIS)

Chapter 24
Configuring E-mail
and Other
Communication
Services

Chapter 25
Configuring an FTP
Server

Chapter 26
Configuring a Web
Server

♦ ♦ ♦ ♦

Configuring the Network

This chapter will provide a simple overview of the TCP/IP protocols as they apply to networking with Linux. TCP/IP is complex and many books have been written on this topic alone. If you want to learn more about TCP/IP, look for *TCP/IP for Dummies*, a Hungry Minds book by Candace Leiden. After the description of TCP/IP, I'll explain how to configure such a network in a Linux environment.

Introducing TCP/IP

The letters TCP/IP are an acronym for Transport Control Protocol/Internet Protocol. They refer to a family of protocols used for computer communications. TCP and IP are just two of the separate protocols contained in the group of protocols developed by the Department of Defense into what is sometimes called the DoD Suite, but is more commonly known as TCP/IP.

In addition to Transport Control Protocol (TCP) and Internet Protocol (IP), this family also includes:

+ Address Resolution Protocol (ARP)
+ Domain Name System (DNS)
+ Internet Control Message Protocol (ICMP)
+ User Datagram Protocol (UDP)
+ Routing Information Protocol (RIP)
+ Simple Mail Transfer Protocol (SMTP)
+ Telnet

These protocols provide the necessary services for basic network functionality. In this chapter you'll take a closer look at them to gain a better understanding of how the network works.

To be able to send and receive information on the network, each device connected to it must have an address. The address of any device on the network must be unique and have a standard, defined format by which it is known to any other device on the network. This device address consists of two parts: the address of the network to which the device is connected, and the address of the device itself (its *node* or *host* address).

Devices that are physically connected to each other (not separated by routers) have the same network address but different node or host addresses. This would be typical of an internal network at a company or university. These types of networks are often referred to as *intranets*.

The two unique addresses we have been talking about are typically called the *network layer* addresses and the *Media Access Control* (MAC) addresses. Network layer addresses are IP addresses and must be assigned to the device. The MAC address is built into the card by the manufacturer and refers only to the lowest-level address by which all data are transferred between devices.

Transmitting data across the network

Now that you know a little about addressing you need to learn how the address, and also the data, are transmitted across the network. This information is transmitted in small pieces called *packets* or *datagrams*. Why is it necessary to use small pieces of data called packets instead of just sending the entire message as one long stream of data? The two reasons for this are:

✦ Sharing resources

✦ Error correction

Let's look at the first, sharing resources. If two computers are communicating with each other, the line would be busy. If these computers were sharing a large amount of data, other devices on the network would be unable to transfer their data. If the long stream of data is broken into small packets, each can be sent individually, and the other devices can send their packets between the packets of the long stream. Since each packet is uniquely addressed and contains instructions on how it should be reassembled, it does not matter that a stream of data is not transmitted all at once and arrives in small pieces.

The second reason for breaking the data into packets concerns error correction. Because the data are transmitted across media that is subject to interference, they can become corrupt. One way to deal with the corruption is to also send a checksum with the data. A checksum is a running count of the bytes sent in the message. The receiving device compares its total to the total transmitted. If these numbers are the same, the data are good, but if they are different, either the checksum or the data themselves are corrupt. The receiving device then asks the sender to resend the data. If the data are broken into small packets, each with its own checksum, it is easier to ensure that a good message arrives; if there is some corruption, only a small portion needs to be resent instead of the entire message.

In the description of packets I mentioned unique addressing and reassembly instructions. Packets also contain data. So each packet is made up of two parts: the header that contains the address and reassembly instructions, and the body that contains the data. Keeping all this information in order is the protocol. The protocol is a set of rules that specifies the format of the package and how it is used.

As I mentioned earlier, all addresses must have two parts: the network part and the node, or host, part. Addresses used in TCP/IP networks (IP addresses) are four bytes long and are written in standard dot notation (as a decimal number separated by dots — for example, 192.168.1.2). The decimal numbers must be between 0 and 255 to conform to the requirement that they be one byte each. IP addresses are divided into classes, the most significant being classes A, B, and C. Table 20-1 shows valid numbers for these classes.

Table 20-1	
IP Class Addresses	
Class	*First Byte*
Class A	0–127
Class B	128–191
Class C	192–233

The class division allows for efficient use of the address numbers. If the division were the first two bytes to the network portion and the last two bytes to the host portion, then no network could have more than 2^{16} hosts. This would be impractical for large networks and also wasteful for small networks.

IP Address Assignments

So far you've learned about packets and addresses for transmitting data across networks. How are the addresses assigned to the devices? There are a few ways to assign IP addresses to the devices, depending on the purpose of the network. If the network is internal, an intranet that will not be connected to an outside network, then any class A, B, or C network number can be used. The only requirement is choosing a class that allows for the number of hosts to be connected. While this is possible, in the real world this approach would not enable you to connect to the Internet.

A more realistic approach would be to register with one of the domain-registration services and request an officially assigned network number. An organization called the InterNIC maintains a database of all assigned network numbers to ensure that each assignment is unique. After obtaining a network number, you may assign the host numbers. Nearly all IP devices require manual configuration; you will look at assigning IP addresses later in this chapter when you actually set up your own network. For now, let's continue with our discussion of how TCP/IP works.

You have now seen that each device has a unique network and node address, called an IP address. Earlier this was described as the Network layer address. Also introduced in the section describing the Network layer address was the Media Access Control, or MAC, address. The MAC address was defined as the lowest level at which communication occurs. On an Ethernet network, this address is also called the Ethernet address. So in reality, this is the address that is ultimately necessary for transmitting data. For data to be transmitted, the IP address must be mapped to the Ethernet address of the device. The mechanism that makes this possible is the *Address Resolution Protocol*, or ARP.

To determine the Ethernet address of a node on the same network, the sending device sends an ARP request to the Ethernet broadcast address. The Ethernet broadcast address is a special address that all Ethernet cards are configured to listen to. The ARP request, containing the sender's IP and Ethernet addresses, as well as the IP address it is looking for, asks each device for the Ethernet address that corresponds to a particular IP address. The device whose address matches the request then sends a reply to the sender's Ethernet address. The sender is then able to send its data to the specific address it received in response to its ARP request. This works for sending data between devices on the same network, but what about devices on different networks? For this you need a router.

Routers allow networks not physically connected to each other to communicate. A router must be connected physically to each network that wants to communicate. The sending node must be able to send its request to a router on its own network and the receiving node must also be on a network connected to a router. The sending node sends its request to the router on its network. This router is typically called the *default gateway* and its address must be manually configured in the sending node's configuration files. You will perform this configuration later in this chapter.

The router receives the request from the sending node and determines the best route to use to transmit the data. The router has an internal program, called a *routing table*, which it uses to send the data — either to another router if the other network is not directly connected, or directly to the other network if it is. If the router cannot find the destination network in the routing table, it considers the packet undeliverable and drops it. Typically, if the packet is dropped, the router sends an ICMP Destination Unreachable message to the sender.

You can configure routing tables manually or acquire them dynamically. Manual configuration requires the person setting up the router to provide all the information about other networks and how to reach them. This method is often quite impractical because of the size of the file required and the constantly changing information.

Dynamic acquisition means that the router sends a message using *Routing Information Protocol* (RIP). RIP is a protocol that enables routers to share details with other routers concerning networks and their location. Ultimately, the purpose of everything you have looked at so far — packets, IP addresses, and routing — is to give users access to services such as printing, file sharing, and e-mail.

You are almost near the end of this brief look at the TCP/IP family of protocols and have arrived at TCP. Transmission Control Protocol (TCP) is encapsulated in IP packets and provides access to services on remote network devices. TCP is considered a *stream-oriented reliable protocol for the following reasons*. The transmission can be any size because it is broken down into small pieces (as you saw earlier). Lost data are retransmitted, and out-of-order data are reordered. The sender is notified about any data that cannot be delivered. Typical TCP services are File Transfer Protocol (FTP), Telnet, and Simple Mail Transfer Protocol (SMTP).

Networking in Linux

Every Linux distribution includes networking support and tools that you can use to configure your network. In this section you'll learn how to configure a computer for connection to an internal and external network.

Even if the computer is not connected to outside networks, an internal network address is required for some applications. This internal address is known as the *loopback* and its IP address is 127.0.0.1. You should first check that this network interface is working before you begin to configure your network cards. To do this, you can use the ifconfig utility to get some information. If you type ifconfig at a console prompt, you will be shown your current network-interface configuration. Figure 20-1 shows the output of the ifconfig command.

If your loopback is configured, the ifconfig will show a device called lo with the address 127.0.0.1. If this device is not shown, you can add it by using the ifconfig command as follows:

```
ifconfig lo 127.0.0.1
```

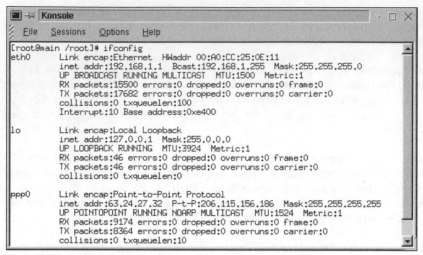

Figure 20-1: The ifconfig utility shows the current network-interface configuration

You then need to use the route command to give the system a little more information about this interface. For this you type:

```
route add -net 127.0.0.0
```

You now have your loopback set up and the ifconfig command will show the device lo in its listing.

Configuring the network card

To configure a network card, you follow the same procedure that you use to configure the loopback interface. You'll use the same command, ifconfig, but this time you will use the name eth0 for an Ethernet device. You will also need to know the IP address, the netmask, and the broadcast addresses. These numbers will vary depending on the type of network you're building. For an internal network that will never connect to the outside world you can use any IP numbers. There are IP numbers that are usually used for such networks, and they are shown in Table 20-2.

Table 20-2 Reserved Private Network Addresses		
Network Class	Netmask	Network Addresses
A	255.0.0.0	10.0.0.0–10.255.255.255
B	255.255.0.0	172.16.0.0–17.31.255.255
C	255.255.255.0	192.168.0.0–192.168.255.255

If you are connecting to an existing network, it is necessary to get the IP address, netmask, and broadcast address from the network administrator. You will also need to have the router and domain-name server addresses. We'll look at this in more detail in the "Connecting to the Internet" section later in this chapter.

In this example you will configure an Ethernet interface for an internal network. You need to issue the following command:

```
ifconfig eth0 192.168.1.1 netmask 255.255.255.0 broadcast 192.168.1.255
```

This results in the creation of device eth0 with a network address of 192.168.1.1, a netmask of 255.255.255.0, and a broadcast address of 192.168.1.255. A file called ifcfg-eth0 is created in /etc/sysconfig/network-scripts. Figure 20-2 shows a listing of this file showing the information that you just entered. The line onboot=yes tells the kernel to configure this device at system startup.

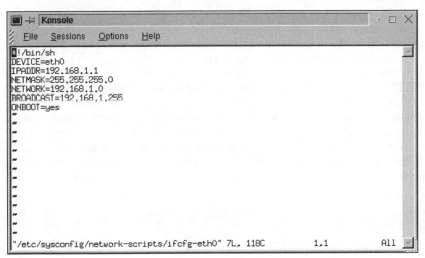

Figure 20-2: The configuration file for the network device eth0

Configuring an internal network

Now you have a network device configured for one computer. To add additional computers to your network, you just need to repeat what you've done so far on the other computers you want to add. The only change is that you need to assign a different IP address. For example, the second computer on your network could have the address 192.168.1.2, the third 192.168.1.3, and so on.

Note   This section does not cover the physical requirements for building a network, such as cabling, hubs, and so forth.

In addition to configuring the network cards on each of the computers in the network, you need to modify three files on each computer. These files are all located in the /etc directory and they are:

```
/etc/hosts.conf
/etc/hosts
/etc/resolv.conf
```

Let's begin with /etc/hosts.conf. This file contains configuration information for the name resolver and should contain the following items:

```
order hosts, bind
multi on
```

This configuration tells the name resolver to check the /etc/hosts file before attempting to query a nameserver and to return all valid addresses for a host found in the /etc/hosts file instead of just the first.

The next file, /etc/hosts, contains the names of all the computers on the local network. It's not difficult to maintain this file for a small network, but for a large network it is often impractical to keep the file up to date. Figure 20-3 shows a network containing three computers. The first two addresses — localhost and 192.168.1.1 — are the same computer, and the other two addresses are different computers on the same network. In most networks, the IP addresses are assigned dynamically, so usually this file would just show the loopback interface and the local host's name.

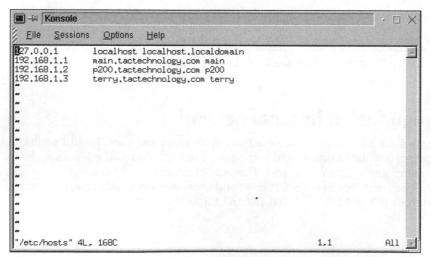

Figure 20-3: The /etc/hosts file contains a listing of the computers on your network

The last file you need to configure is /etc/resolv.conf. This file provides information about name servers used to resolve host names. You will look at Domain Name Servers (DNS) in the next chapter. Figure 20-4 shows a typical resolv.conf file listing.

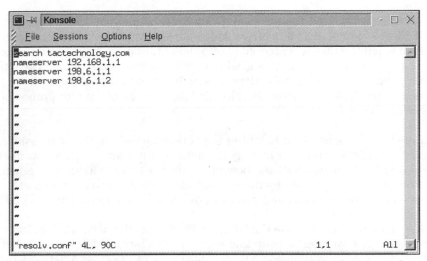

```
■ -₩ Konsole                                          - □ X
  File  Sessions  Options  Help
Search tactechnology.com
nameserver 192.168.1.1
nameserver 198.6.1.1
nameserver 198.6.1.2
~
~
~
~
~
~
~
~
~
~
~
~
~
~
~
"resolv.conf" 4L, 90C                    1,1           All
```

Figure 20-4: The /etc/resolv.conf file contains a listing of the domain and nameservers on the network

Connecting to the Internet

You have learned how easy it is to build an internal network, but now you need to learn how to connect to the outside world. You need to do a few more things before you can do this, including configuring a router, obtaining an IP address, and finally, making the connection to outside networks. We'll begin with obtaining an IP address.

Where do IP addresses come from?

Earlier in this chapter you saw that IP addresses used on the Internet are assigned by the InterNIC. Now let's take a closer look at the makeup of IP addresses and how you can extend them through subnetting.

To start, let me clear up a basic cause of misunderstanding. IP numbers are not assigned to hosts; they are assigned to network interfaces on hosts. Even though many computers on an IP network have a single network interface and a single IP number, it is possible for a single computer to have more than one network interface. In this case, each interface has its own IP number. Even though this is true, most people speak of *host addresses* when what they really mean are *IP numbers*.

Note   Just remember that the host address is simply shorthand for the IP number of this particular interface on this host. Many (if not the majority) of the devices on the Internet have only a single interface and thus a single IP number.

In the current (IPv4) implementation of IP numbers, IP numbers consist of four bytes (8 bits) — a total of 32 bits of available information. This results in large numbers, even when they are represented in decimal notation. To make them easier to read and organize, they are written in what is called *dotted quad* format. The numbers you have seen earlier in this chapter — such as your internal network IP address, 192.168.1.1 — were expressed in this format. Each of the four groups of numbers can range from 0 to 255.

Part of the IP number of a host identifies the network on which the host resides; the remaining bits of the IP number identify the network interface. Exactly how many bits are used by the network ID and how many are available to identify interfaces on that network is determined by the network class. Earlier you learned that there are three classes of networks, and you saw how they are composed in Table 20-1.

Class A IP network numbers use the left quad to identify the network, leaving three quads to identify host interfaces on that network. The farthest left bit of the left byte in a class A address is always a 0, so a maximum of 128 class A network numbers are available, each one containing up to 33,554,430 possible interfaces.

The network numbers 0.0.0.0, known as the *default route*, and 127.0.0.0, the *loopback network*, have special meanings and cannot be used to identify networks. You saw the loopback interface when you set up your internal network. We'll look at the default route when you set up your connection to the "Internet in the configuring a router" section of this chapter. If you take these two network numbers out, there are only 126 available A class network numbers.

Class B IP network numbers use the two left dotted quads to identify the network, leaving two dotted quads to identify host interfaces. The farthest left bits of the left byte of a class B address are always set to 10. This leaves 14 bits to specify the network address, or 32,767 available B class networks. The first dotted quad in a class B network can range from 128 to 191, with each network containing up to 32,766 possible interfaces.

Class C IP network numbers use the left three quads to identify the network, leaving right quad to identify host interfaces. The leftmost three bits of class C addresses are always set to 1, 1, and 0, or a range of 192 to 255 for the leftmost dotted quad. This means that there are 4,194,303 available class C network numbers, each containing 254 interfaces. There are also IP addresses set aside for internal networks, as you saw in Table 20-2. IP numbers can have three possible meanings.

The first of these is an address of a network, which is the number representing all the devices physically connected to each other. The second is the broadcast address of the network, which is the address that allows all devices on the network to be contacted. Finally, the last meaning is an actual interface address. Let's look at a class C network for an example.

✦ 192.168.3.0 is a class C network number.

✦ 192.168.3.42 is a host address on this network.

✦ 192.168.3.255 is the network broadcast address.

Network mask and subnetting

When you set up your Ethernet device, eth0, you used the ifconfig utility to pass some information that was written to the ifcg-eth0 file. One of these parameters was the network mask. What is a network mask and what is it used for?

The network mask is more properly called the *subnetwork mask*, but it is generally referred to as the network mask or just netmask. The determining factor in subnetting is the network mask and how it is understood on a local network segment. In setting up your network card you used a netmask of 255.255.255.0. In this case all the network bits were set to 1 and the host bits were set to 0. This is the standard format for all network masks. Table 20-2 showed the network masks for the three classes of networks.

There are two important things to remember about the network mask. First, the network mask affects only the interpretation of IP numbers on the same network segment. Second, the network mask is not an IP number; it modifies how IP numbers are interpreted by the network.

A subnet allows you to use one IP address and split it up so that it can be used on several physically connected local networks. This is a tremendous advantage as the number of available IP numbers is rapidly diminishing. You can have multiple subnetted networks connected to the outside world with just one IP address. By splitting the IP address, you can use it on sites that need multiple connectivity, and eliminate the problems of high traffic and difficulty of management.

There are other advantages to subnetting: it allows different network topologies to exist on different network segments within the same organization, as well as reducing overall network traffic. Subnetting also allows for increased security by separating traffic into local networks.

Before you can subnet your network, you need to make some choices and gather some information.

First you need to decide the size of each of your subnets so you can determine how mnay IP addresses you need. Earlier in this chapter you set up an Ethernet interface using the reserved internal class C network number 192.168.1.0. You will continue to use this number, which gives you up to 254 interfaces.

Every IP network has two addresses that you cannot use: these are the network IP number itself and the broadcast address. Whenever you subnetwork the IP network you are creating additional unusable addresses: each subnet, like the IP network itself, will have an unusable network IP address and broadcast address. The more you subnet the more IP addresses you lose, so don't subnet your network more than necessary.

Next, you need to determine the subnetwork mask and network numbers. The network mask for an un-subnetworked IP network number is simply a dotted quad of which all the network bits of the network number are set to 1 and all the host bits are set to 0.

Subnetworking takes one or more of the available host bits and makes them appear as network bits to the local interfaces. If you wanted to divide your class C network into two subnetworks, you would change the first host bit to 1 and get a netmask of 11111111.11111111.11111111.10000000 or 255.255.255.128. This would give you 126 possible IP numbers for each of your subnets. Remember that you lose two IP addresses for each subnet. If you wanted four subnetworks, you would need to change the first two host bits to ones, which would give you a netmask of 255.255.255.192. You would have 62 IP addresses available to you on each subnetwork. Table 20-3 shows an example of subnetting your class C network.

Table 20-3
Subnetting a Class C Network

Number of Subnets	Subnet Mask	Number of Hosts
2	255.255.255.128	128
4	255.255.255.192	62
8	255.255.255.224	30
16	255.255.255.240	14
32	255.255.255.248	6
64	255.255.255.252	2

Now all you need to do is assign the appropriate numbers for the network, the broadcast address, and the IP address for each of the interfaces, and you're nearly done. Table 20-4 shows these numbers for subnetting your class C network into two subnets.

	Table 20-4			
Subnetting Your Class C Network into Two Subnets				
Network	**Netmask**	**Broadcast**	**First IP**	**Last IP**
192.168.1.0	255.255.255.128	192.168.1.127	192.168.1.1	192.168.1.126
192.168.1.128	255.255.255.128	192.168.1.255	192.168.1.129	192.168.1.254

Configuring a router

You have successfully created two subnets from your class C network, but the individual network segments will not be able to communicate with each other yet. You still have to configure a path for them, and you will do this using a router. Earlier in this chapter you learned that a router is necessary for separate networks to communicate with each other. You also learned that each network must be connected to a router in order for this communication to take place. This router is called the *gateway*.

In Linux, you can use a computer with two network interfaces to route among two or more subnets. To be able to do this you need to make sure that you have IP Forwarding enabled. All current Linux distributions have IP Forwarding compiled as a module, so all you need to do is make sure the module is loaded. You can check this by entering the following query at a command prompt:

```
cat /proc/sys/net.ipv4/ip_forward.
```

If forwarding is enabled, the number 1 will be returned; otherwise the number 0 will be returned. Figure 20-5 shows the output of the previous query.

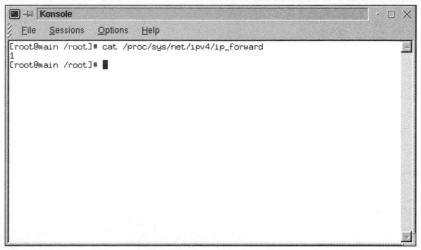

Figure 20-5: cat /proc/sys/net/ipv4/ip_forward shows that forwarding is enabled

To enable IP forwarding, type the following command:

```
echo "0" > /proc/sys/net/ipv4/ip_forward
```

Continue your setup using the two subnets you created earlier in the chapter with the information in Table 20-4.

Let's assume that a computer running Linux is acting as a router for your network. It will have two network interfaces to the local LANs using the lowest available IP address in each subnetwork on its interface to that network. The network interfaces would be configured as in Table 20-5.

Table 20-5
The Configuration of the Network Interfaces

Interface	IP Address	Netmask
eth0	192.168.1.1	255.255.255.128
eth1	192.168.1.129	255.255.255.128

The network routing the computer would use is shown in Table 20-6.

Table 20-6
The Network Routing

Destination	Gateway	Mask	Interface
192.168.1.0	0.0.0.0	255.255.255.128	eth0
192.168.1.128	0.0.0.0	255.255.255.128	eth1

You're nearly finished now: just one more step. Each computer on the subnet has to show the IP address for the interface that will be its gateway to the other network. For the computers on the first subnet, the 192.168.1.0 network, the gateway would be 192.168.1.1. Remember that you used the first IP address on this network for the gateway computer. The computers on the second subnet, 192.168.1.128, would use 192.168.1.129 as the gateway address. You can add this information using the route command as follows:

```
route add -net 192.168.1.0 and then
route add default gw 192.168.1.1
```

This sets up the route for local (internal) routing as well as setting up the external route for your first subnet. You need to repeat the preceding commands, substituting the appropriate numbers for the second subnet. You have now successfully set up two subnets and established communication between them. Next we'll look at connecting to the Internet.

There are several ways to connect to the Internet, the most common being a point-to-point (PPP) connection, using a cable modem, Digital Subscriber Loop (DSL) or dedicated lines such as T-1 or T-3. In this section you will learn about establishing a point-to-point connection

Configuring a point-to-point (PPP) connection

A PPP connection is a dialup connection that requires a modem and an analog phone line, and it is by far the most common way to connect to the Internet. It is relatively easy to set up PPP on a Linux system, especially using a graphical method called kppp. Kppp is part of the K Desktop Environment (KDE), which is included with most major distributions of Linux. In this section, we'll set up a PPP connection using KPPP.

Start the kppp program as follows:

1. From the K menu choose Internet ⇨ kppp. The screen shown in Figure 20-6 will appear.

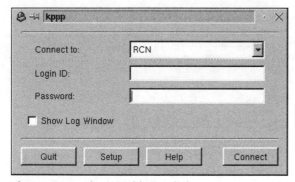

Figure 20-6: The initial kppp dialog screen

2. Click Setup to create a new connection. Figure 20-7 shows the dialog box used to create a new connection.

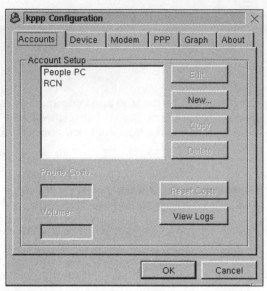

Figure 20-7: The KPPP Configuration screen

3. Click New to open the New Account setup box as shown in Figure 20-8.

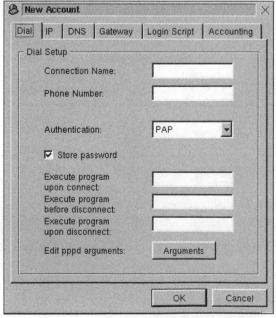

Figure 20-8: The New Account setup box enables you to enter information about your Internet Service Provider (ISP)

Note When you established your Internet account with your ISP, you should have received setup information. You will need to use this information to set up KPPP.

In most cases the default choices will work, but it is always a good idea to check them to be sure nothing is wrong.

Proceed as follows:

4. In the Connection Name box, enter a name for this connection.

5. In the Phone Number box, enter the number you dial to connect to your ISP. Usually PAP Authentication will work, so you will not need to change this.

6. After you have entered the necessary information, click OK. When the KPPP Configuration box appears, the Connection Name you chose will be shown in the Account Setup section.

7. Click the Device tab. Figure 20-9 shows the Device page.

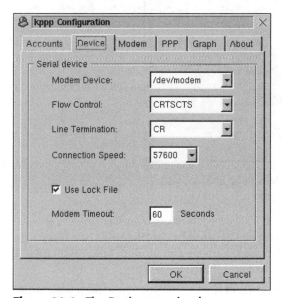

Figure 20-9: The Device page is where you enter details about your modem

Refer to Figure 20-9 while reading steps 8 through 10.

8. The Device dropdown box is where you tell KPPP the location of your modem. The default setting here is /dev/modem, which is a symbolic link to the actual modem device. It is usually best to specifically tell the system the location of

your modem (/dev/ttyS0 to /dev/ttyS3). `ttyS0` corresponds to `com1` in the DOS/Windows world, `ttyS1` to `com2`, and so on. So if your modem is installed on `com1` in Windows, it is /dev/ttyS0 in Linux.

9. The default settings for flow control and line termination usually work, so no change is necessary here.

10. The connection speed should be 115200 for a 56K modem and 57600 for any other modem.

11. Next, click the Modem tab. Figure 20-10 shows the Modem page.

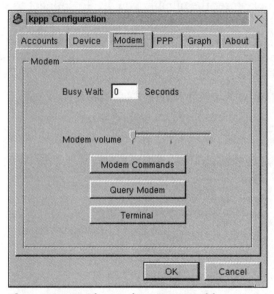

Figure 20-10: The Modem page enables you to set the modem volume and test your configuration

12. To set the delay between redial attempts in the event of a busy signal, enter a number in the Busy Wait box. Choose the modem volume by moving the slider bar right to increase and left to decrease.

13. To see if you chose the correct device for your modem, click on the Query Modem button. If your modem is correctly configured, you should see an output box like the one shown in Figure 20-11.

Note   If you have chosen the wrong port, you will see a message like the one shown in Figure 20-12. You will have to go back to the Device tab in step 7 and choose a different port.

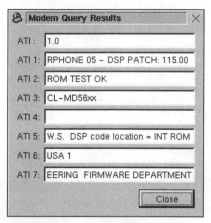

Figure 20-11: The result of the modem query shows that the modem is responding

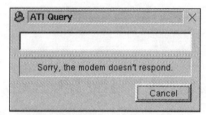

Figure 20-12: The result of the modem query shows that the port is not configured correctly

14. When the result of the modem query shows that the modem is working correctly, everything is properly configured. Click the OK button to save your profile.

15. When the initial kppp screen reappears, as shown in Figure 20-5, enter your User ID and password in the appropriate boxes and click Connect. If all is well, you will see a screen like the one in Figure 20-13.

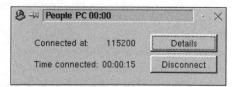

Figure 20-13: A successful connection has been made by KPPP

16. If you want to check the status of your connection, use the `ifconfig` command, the results of which are shown in Figure 20-14.

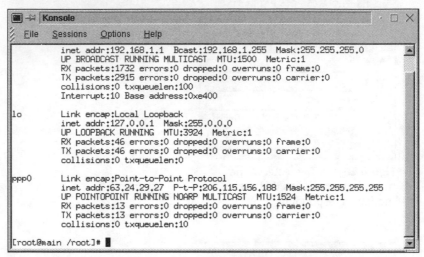

Figure 20-14: The ifconfig command shows the PPP connection

Connecting an internal network to the Internet (IP masquerading)

So far you have configured an internal network consisting of two subnets, configured a router for connectivity between the networks, and made a PPP connection. Assuming that you made the connection to the Internet through your router, you just need to make a few configuration changes, and every computer on your network will be able to connect to the Internet through your one PPP connection. IP masquerading enables you to connect a TCP/IP network to the outside world using a single server and a single IP address.

Current Linux distributions make IP masquerading available as a module, so you just need to load the module and enable the appropriate configuration. You already enabled IP forwarding when you configured your router, so now all you need to do is set up a simple packet filtering firewall using a utility called `ipchains`. You will look at Linux security in Chapter 29, so we don't need to go into it now. The `ipchains` utility will give you enough protection for the moment.

To set up masquerading, you need to type the following commands:

```
ipchains -P forward DENY
ipchains -A forward -s 192.168.0.0/24 -j MASQ -d 0.0.0.0/0
```

This is all you need to do to enable the firewall rules and start masquerading.

Of course, you want masquerading enabled whenever you boot the computer, so it would be a good idea to make a script file that enables IP forwarding as well as the `ipchains` utility. Be sure to include the command to start IP forwarding (shown earlier in this chapter) as well as the preceding `ipchains` commands.

Connecting to a "foreign" network

In addition to providing you with native TCP/IP networking support, Linux also enables you to connect to networks that use different protocols. You can connect to networks that use AppleTalk, the Apple networking protocol, Internetware Packet Exchange (IPX), used on Novell networks, and Microsoft Windows. Chapter 34 explains how to connect to these "foreign" networks.

Summary

In this chapter you learned about the TCP/IP protocol suite and how it works to enable communication across networks. Then you learned how to configure a network interface card. You used subnetting to create two internal subnetworks and configured a router so that they could communicate with each other. Finally, you set up a point-to-point connection to the Internet and enabled IP forwarding and masquerading so that every computer on your internal network could have Internet access.

✦ ✦ ✦

Configuring the Domain Name System (DNS)

In this chapter you will learn how to install and configure the Domain Name System that provides name address resolution. Name address resolution is, simply stated, the conversion of people-friendly names into computer-friendly numbers. Remember from the last chapter that each interface on the network has an IP address. This address is expressed as a dotted quad group. These groups of numbers present no problem to the computers in the network, but it is very difficult for humans to remember many groups of numbers. So you need a way to be able to enter names and then have these names converted into numbers. Each time you go to a Web site and type its address into your browser, the Domain Name System (DNS) goes to work. You enter names that are easy for you to understand and the names are resolved into numbers that the computers find easy to understand. This is the function of name address resolution.

What is Name Address Resolution?

Let's take a look at domain names and their organization using the domain name `tactechnology.com`. The first part of this domain name, `tactechnology`, is the name of the company, institution, or organization. The next part after the period (*dot* in today's vernacular) is called the *top-level* domain. In addition to the com top-level domain, there are a few more. Table 22-1 shows the top-level domains in the United States.

<table>
<tr><td colspan="2" align="center">Table 22-1
Top-Level Domain Names</td></tr>
<tr><td>*Top-Level Domain*</td><td>*Meaning*</td></tr>
</table>

Top-Level Domain	Meaning
com	Typically used for businesses www.tactechnology.com).
edu	An educational institution (www.muhlenberg.edu).
gov	A U.S. government agency (www.whitehouse.gov).
mil	A branch of the U.S. military (www.army.mil).
net	Typically used for network-affiliated organizations (www.tellurium.net).
org	A non-commercial organization (www.lvcg.org).
int	An international organization (www.wipo.int).
us	The U.S. domain with each state as a lower level (www.state.pa.us).

There are also top-level domains in other countries: each of these has a two-letter suffix, such as fr for France, or su for Switzerland. Not all of the top-level domains are the same as the top-level U.S. domains, but a company in France could be http://www.frenchcompany.com.fr.

Large domains may be further broken down into subdomains. For example, the U.S. Department of Justice site is www.usdoj.gov. The Justice Department includes many agencies, such as the Immigration and Naturalization Service. To find the INS, you would go to the subdomain www.ins.usdoj.gov. An individual computer in the INS would also have a hostname, for example Mexico. The complete name for this computer would then be mexico.ins.usdoj.gov: you could find its IP address by using the DNS to look it up.

Why Not Just Use the hosts File?

When you type in a host name, your system uses resources on your system to resolve that name into an IP address. One of these files is the /etc/nsswitch.conf (name service switch) file, which contains a line telling the system where to look for host information. Figure 21-1 shows the /etc/nsswitch file and the hosts line.

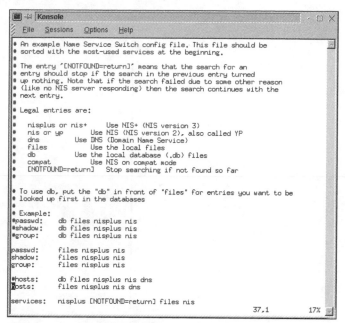

```
■ -☆ Konsole                                            · □ ×
  File   Sessions   Options   Help
# An example Name Service Switch config file. This file should be
# sorted with the most-used services at the beginning.
#
# The entry 'ENOTFOUND=return]' means that the search for an
# entry should stop if the search in the previous entry turned
# up nothing. Note that if the search failed due to some other reason
# (like no NIS server responding) then the search continues with the
# next entry.
#
# Legal entries are:
#
#   nisplus or nis+    Use NIS+ (NIS version 3)
#   nis or yp          Use NIS (NIS version 2), also called YP
#   dns           Use DNS (Domain Name Service)
#   files              Use the local files
#   db                 Use the local database (.db) files
#   compat             Use NIS on compat mode
#   ENOTFOUND=return]    Stop searching if not found so far


# To use db, put the "db" in front of "files" for entries you want to be
# looked up first in the databases
#
# Example:
#passwd:    db files nisplus nis
#shadow:    db files nisplus nis
#group:     db files nisplus nis

passwd:     files nisplus nis
shadow:     files nisplus nis
group:      files nisplus nis

#hosts:     db files nisplus nis dns
hosts:      files nisplus nis dns

services:   nisplus ENOTFOUND=return] files nis
                                            37,1         17%
```

Figure 21-1: The nsswitch.conf file tells the resolver routines
where to look for IP addresses

The information following the word `hosts` tells the system to first look at the local
files, then to look in the NIS database, and finally to use the Domain Name Service
(DNS) to resolve the names into IP numbers. One of the local files that will be
searched is the /etc/hosts file. Remember that in Chapter 20 we talked about the
hosts file. The hosts file contains IP addresses and host names that you used on
your sample network. So why not use this file for name resolution? Well, you could
on a small internal network that you controlled and that did not have very many IP
addresses — but not on a large network, as it would be impossible to keep it up to
date. There would be IP addresses over which you had no control.

After looking in the hosts file and failing to find the address, the next file the system
checks is /etc/resolv.conf. This file contains the IP addresses of computers known
as domain name servers, which are listed in /etc/resolv.conf as nameservers.
Figure 21-2 shows the /etc/resolv.conf file on one of the computers in the
tactechnology.com domain.

Two namerservers are listed in the file shown in Figure 21-2. You could list up to
three nameservers, but two is enough to allow a connection to one of the nameservers in case the other nameserver is down or not reachable. There is no point
listing more than three nameservers, as any over three are ignored.

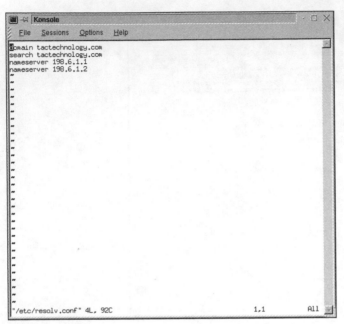

Figure 21-2: The /etc/resolv.conf file points to domain name servers used to resolve IP addresses

Installing the Software

So far you have learned about name address resolution and the structure of domains in the United States. Now you need to learn about the Domain Name System servers that resolve the name into IP numbers. The most common DNS server used in current Linux distributions is BIND, or the *Berkeley Internet Nameserver Daemon*. The latest release of BIND is version 9.0.0, and you can get it from the Internet Software Consortium at www.isc.org.

Depending on the distribution installed on your system, and how frequently you update, your version of BIND may differ.

A very convenient way to install the latest version of BIND is to look for the distribution-specific package. Check the Web site for your distribution to locate the rpm file for BIND. On my system, which is running Mandrake, I installed the rpm file using the Kpackage manager, as shown in Figure 21-3. You can also install the rpm file at the command line by using the rpm command.

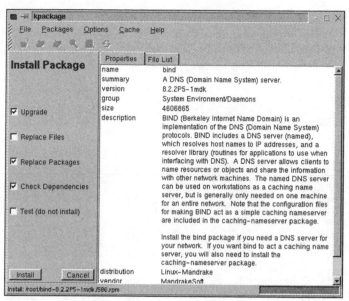

Figure 21-3: Installing the latest version of BIND using the Kpackage manager

Installing the package installs all the files you need to set up DNS. The installation creates a directory /var/named and places in it two files, /var/named/named.ca and /var/named/named.local. These files are used for localhost lookups. Two files are created in the /etc directory, /etc/named.conf and /etc/named.boot. Four files are created in /usr/sbin. These files are:

/usr/sbin/named	Nameserver daemon
named-boot	Perl script that converts named.boot files to named.conf files.
named-xfer	Transfer program for external zone files.
ndc	Nameserver daemon control program; a shell script that interacts with the named daemon to provide status information, and that can also be used to start, stop, or restart the named daemon.

Types of domain servers

There are two types of domain servers — primary masters and secondary masters. A top-level domain server, one that provides information about the domains shown in Table 22-1, is typically referred to as a root name server. A search for www.muhlenberg.edu would look to the root name server for .edu for information.

The root name server would then direct the search to a lower-level domain name server until the information was found. You can see an example of this by using the `nslookup` command to search for the root name servers for .edu, as shown in Figure 21-4.

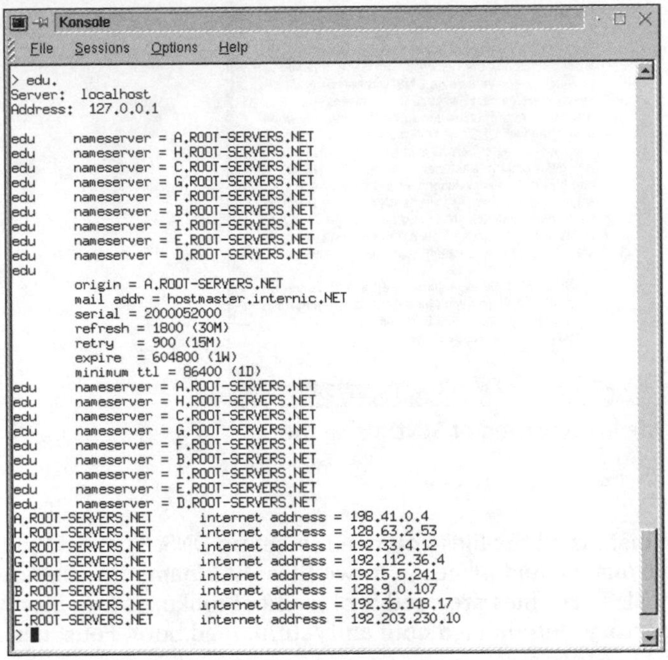

```
━ -ₓₓ Konsole                                        · □ ✕
  File   Sessions   Options   Help

> edu.
Server:  localhost
Address:  127.0.0.1

edu      nameserver = A.ROOT-SERVERS.NET
edu      nameserver = H.ROOT-SERVERS.NET
edu      nameserver = C.ROOT-SERVERS.NET
edu      nameserver = G.ROOT-SERVERS.NET
edu      nameserver = F.ROOT-SERVERS.NET
edu      nameserver = B.ROOT-SERVERS.NET
edu      nameserver = I.ROOT-SERVERS.NET
edu      nameserver = E.ROOT-SERVERS.NET
edu      nameserver = D.ROOT-SERVERS.NET
edu
         origin = A.ROOT-SERVERS.NET
         mail addr = hostmaster.internic.NET
         serial = 2000052000
         refresh = 1800 (30M)
         retry  = 900 (15M)
         expire = 604800 (1W)
         minimum ttl = 86400 (1D)
edu      nameserver = A.ROOT-SERVERS.NET
edu      nameserver = H.ROOT-SERVERS.NET
edu      nameserver = C.ROOT-SERVERS.NET
edu      nameserver = G.ROOT-SERVERS.NET
edu      nameserver = F.ROOT-SERVERS.NET
edu      nameserver = B.ROOT-SERVERS.NET
edu      nameserver = I.ROOT-SERVERS.NET
edu      nameserver = E.ROOT-SERVERS.NET
edu      nameserver = D.ROOT-SERVERS.NET
A.ROOT-SERVERS.NET      internet address = 198.41.0.4
H.ROOT-SERVERS.NET      internet address = 128.63.2.53
C.ROOT-SERVERS.NET      internet address = 192.33.4.12
G.ROOT-SERVERS.NET      internet address = 192.112.36.4
F.ROOT-SERVERS.NET      internet address = 192.5.5.241
B.ROOT-SERVERS.NET      internet address = 128.9.0.107
I.ROOT-SERVERS.NET      internet address = 192.36.148.17
E.ROOT-SERVERS.NET      internet address = 192.203.230.10
> █
```

Figure 21-4: A search for the top-level root name servers for .edu

The listing shows all of the root name servers for the .edu domain. You can continue the search for the second-level domain by adding the name of the domain you are looking for, as shown in Figure 21-5.

A server is listed as an authoritative server when it contains the information you want and can provide you with that information. In the previous figure, two servers are shown, one a primary master and the other a secondary master. The secondary master contains the same information as the primary master and is intended as a backup in case the primary goes down or is not available. Where does the information come from? The answer is that the servers contain configuration files with domain name information that they provide when asked. In the next section you will learn how to configure a server to provide domain-name information.

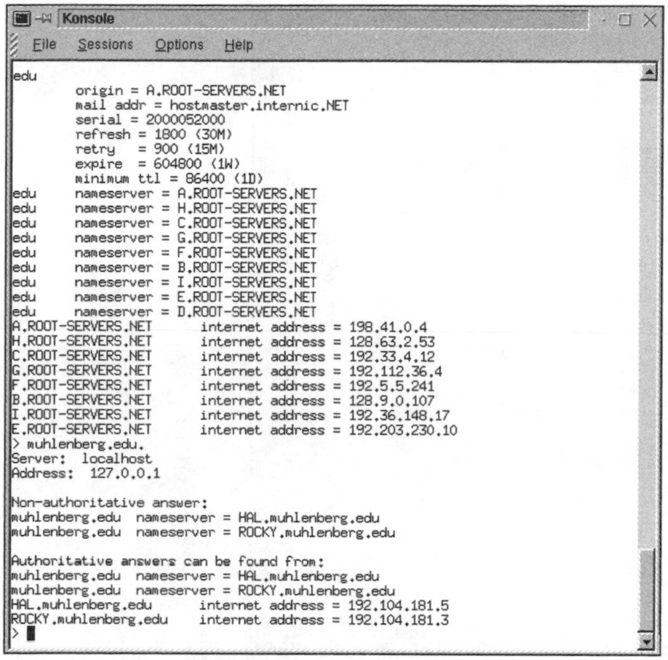

```
edu
        origin = A.ROOT-SERVERS.NET
        mail addr = hostmaster.internic.NET
        serial = 2000052000
        refresh = 1800 (30M)
        retry  = 900 (15M)
        expire = 604800 (1W)
        minimum ttl = 86400 (1D)
edu     nameserver = A.ROOT-SERVERS.NET
edu     nameserver = H.ROOT-SERVERS.NET
edu     nameserver = C.ROOT-SERVERS.NET
edu     nameserver = G.ROOT-SERVERS.NET
edu     nameserver = F.ROOT-SERVERS.NET
edu     nameserver = B.ROOT-SERVERS.NET
edu     nameserver = I.ROOT-SERVERS.NET
edu     nameserver = E.ROOT-SERVERS.NET
edu     nameserver = D.ROOT-SERVERS.NET
A.ROOT-SERVERS.NET      internet address = 198.41.0.4
H.ROOT-SERVERS.NET      internet address = 128.63.2.53
C.ROOT-SERVERS.NET      internet address = 192.33.4.12
G.ROOT-SERVERS.NET      internet address = 192.112.36.4
F.ROOT-SERVERS.NET      internet address = 192.5.5.241
B.ROOT-SERVERS.NET      internet address = 128.9.0.107
I.ROOT-SERVERS.NET      internet address = 192.36.148.17
E.ROOT-SERVERS.NET      internet address = 192.203.230.10
> muhlenberg.edu.
Server:  localhost
Address:  127.0.0.1

Non-authoritative answer:
muhlenberg.edu  nameserver = HAL.muhlenberg.edu
muhlenberg.edu  nameserver = ROCKY.muhlenberg.edu

Authoritative answers can be found from:
muhlenberg.edu  nameserver = HAL.muhlenberg.edu
muhlenberg.edu  nameserver = ROCKY.muhlenberg.edu
HAL.muhlenberg.edu      internet address = 192.104.181.5
ROCKY.muhlenberg.edu    internet address = 192.104.181.3
> ▌
```

Figure 21-5: A search for the second-level domain shows the authoritative nameservers

File Configuration

Before you begin to configure your server you need to take a closer look at the files you'll be configuring. We'll begin with the /etc/named.conf file, which is shown in Figure 21-6.

Let's look at this file in more detail beginning with the lines starting with //. These are comment lines and anything following them is ignored by the system.

The sections of the file start with a statement. Information about the statement is contained within curly braces and terminated by a semi-colon as follows:
{ *information about server* };

The first section is called options and contains information about the location of the files used by named. The directory is /var/named. Other sections of the /etc/named file refer to files contained in /var/named. If you specify the directory here, you won't need to list the entire path to the file, just the name of the file.

```
// generated by named-bootconf.pl

options {
        directory "/var/named";
        /*
         * If there is a firewall between you and nameservers you want
         * to talk to, you might need to uncomment the query-source
         * directive below.  Previous versions of BIND always asked
         * questions using port 53, but BIND 8.1 uses an unprivileged
         * port by default.
         */
        // query-source address * port 53;
};

//
// a caching only nameserver config
//
zone "." {
        type hint;
        file "named.root";
};

zone "0.0.127.in-addr.arpa" {
        type master;
        file "named.local";
};

zone "tactechnology.com" {
        notify no;
        type master;
        file "tactech.com";
};

zone "1.168.192.in-addr.arpa" {
        notify no;
        type master;
        file "tac.rev";
};
"/etc/named.conf" 38L, 705C                              1,1             All
```

Figure 21-6: The /etc/named.conf file from the
tactechnology.com domain

The remainder of the listings in /etc/named.conf are called zone. These zones refer
to files called *zone files*.

The first zone file is known as the *cache file*: it references a file called named.root
that contains information about all the root name servers in the world. This information changes and needs to be updated periodically. Figure 21-7 shows the contents of this file.

The next zone file contains information about the localhost. The file referenced
here is named.local and contains information about the local domain. Figure 21-8
shows the contents of this file.

The next zone file provides name lookup information about the domain
tactechnology.com, and the final zone provides reverse lookup. Reverse lookup
enables you to enter an IP number and obtain the corresponding name. Now you
will look at these files more closely.

Another item appearing in the named.conf file in the zone sections is the type of
server, shown following the word type. In this case, all the servers are shown as
master because each nameserver is master of its own domain.

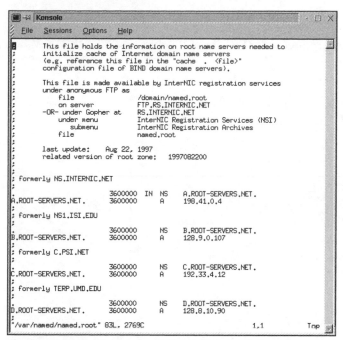

Figure 21-7: The named.root file contains a listing of root name servers worldwide

Figure 21-8: The named.local file contains information about the internal network 127.0.0.1

Zone files

Zone files contain resource records (RR) about IP addresses. Figure 21-9 shows a typical zone file.

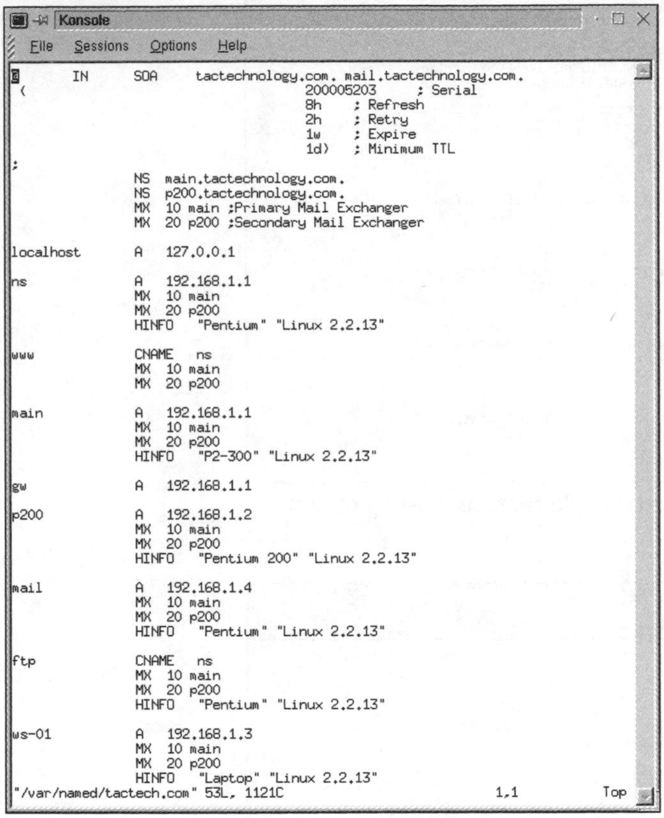
Konsole
File Sessions Options Help
@ IN SOA tactechnology.com. mail.tactechnology.com. (
200005203 ; Serial
8h ; Refresh
2h ; Retry
1w ; Expire
1d) ; Minimum TTL
;
NS main.tactechnology.com.
NS p200.tactechnology.com.
MX 10 main ;Primary Mail Exchanger
MX 20 p200 ;Secondary Mail Exchanger
localhost A 127.0.0.1
ns A 192.168.1.1
MX 10 main
MX 20 p200
HINFO "Pentium" "Linux 2.2.13"
www CNAME ns
MX 10 main
MX 20 p200
main A 192.168.1.1
MX 10 main
MX 20 p200
HINFO "P2-300" "Linux 2.2.13"
gw A 192.168.1.1
p200 A 192.168.1.2
MX 10 main
MX 20 p200
HINFO "Pentium 200" "Linux 2.2.13"
mail A 192.168.1.4
MX 10 main
MX 20 p200
HINFO "Pentium" "Linux 2.2.13"
ftp CNAME ns
MX 10 main
MX 20 p200
HINFO "Pentium" "Linux 2.2.13"
ws-01 A 192.168.1.3
MX 10 main
MX 20 p200
HINFO "Laptop" "Linux 2.2.13"
"/var/named/tactech.com" 53L, 1121C 1,1 Top

Figure 21-9: The zone file for the tactechnology.com domain

A zone file can contain many types of RRs, listed in the order in which they generally appear in the zone files. In the next section, I'll explain them.

Types of resource records

The *start of authority* (SOA) is the first line in the zone file. The SOA identifies the nameserver as the authoritative source for information about this domain. There is only one SOA in each zone file, and it contains the following data:

```
@  IN  SOA  main.tactechnology.com.
   mail.tactechnology.com. (
                          2000052101   ; Serial
                          8h           ; Refresh
                          2h           ; Retry
                          1w           ; Expire
                          1d)          ;Minimum TTL
```

Here is an explanation of each item in the SOA.

✦ The first character in the SOA line is a special symbol that tells the system to look at this domain.

✦ IN means Internet.

✦ main.tactechnology.com. is the authoritative server for this domain.

✦ mail.tactechnology.com. is the e-mail address of the administrator.

✦ Note the trailing period after the domain names. If this is not included, the domain name will be appended to the entry.

✦ The opening parenthesis enables you to extend the first line so that anything between the opening and closing parentheses will be considered one line.

✦ The information within the parentheses is passed to other nameservers, secondary masters, that use this information to update their records.

✦ The line containing 2000052101;Serial is the serial number of the file. Secondary servers compare this information with their stored information: if there has been no change, it is not necessary to download this file. If the information has changed — if the serial numbers are different — the file is downloaded by the secondary server to update the information. The serial number can be any number you want as long as it can be incremented to indicate a revision to the file.

✦ The semicolon indicates that what follows to the end of the line is a comment.

✦ Refresh is the amount of time the server should wait before refreshing its data.

✦ Retry is the amount of time the server should wait before attempting to contact the primary server if the previous attempt failed.

✦ Expire is the amount of time after which the data will expire and be purged if the secondary master is unable to contact a primary master.

✦ TTL specifies the time to live for the data. This parameter is intended for caching nameservers and tells them how long to hold the data in their cache.

All of the information contained by the SOA may be placed on one line, but it is usually written as shown in the preceding example. The order of the items is significant in the SOA header and should always follow the example shown previously. (The examples shown here are for my system, your entries should contain information relevant to your system.)

Continuing with the explanation of the zone file, the next items are:

NS	Name servers in this domain.
A	The IP address for the name.
PTR	Pointer for address name mapping.
CNAME	Canonical name.
MX record	Mail-exchange record.

The tactech.com zone file lists two MX addresses, one followed by the number 10 and the other by the number 20. Any mail sent to tactechnology.com would go to main.tactechnology.com because it has a lower number. Priority is determined by the number assigned to the server, with the lowest number receiving the highest priority. So main is the primary mail server and p200 is the secondary mail server. If main is unable to receive mail, the mail will go to p200. p200 will try to send it to main since it is its primary mail server also. When main is again able to receive mail, it will receive all the mail that p200 has received.

TXT	Text information. Enables entry of descriptive information.
WKS	Well-known service. Enables entry of descriptive information.
HINFO	Host information. Usually shows type of hardware and software.

The last zone file shown in the named.conf file in Figure 21-6 is called tac.rev. This file provides information for reverse lookups. In the previous example, you searched for tactechnology.com by using the domain name. This is called *forward address resolution* since it is more common than the alternative, using an IP address to find a name. This is called *reverse address resolution*. All you need to do is enter the IP address and the server will return the domain name. Figure 21-10 shows the reverse lookup zone file for tactechnology.com.

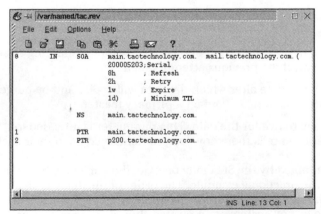

Figure 21-10: The reverse lookup zone file for tactechnology.com

Caching server

Now that you know which files you need to configure and the information you need to put in them, you are ready to set up your own domain name servers. You will set up a caching server for your domain. Begin by verifying the zone information in /etc/named.conf. When you installed the BIND package, the /etc/named.conf file was created, and it contained zone information for your localhost, but you need to check it to be sure. You are looking for the two zone lines, one indicated by a dot, referencing the file named.root, and the other by 0.0.127.in.addr.arpa., and referencing named.local. Figure 21-11 below shows the file listing for the generated file.

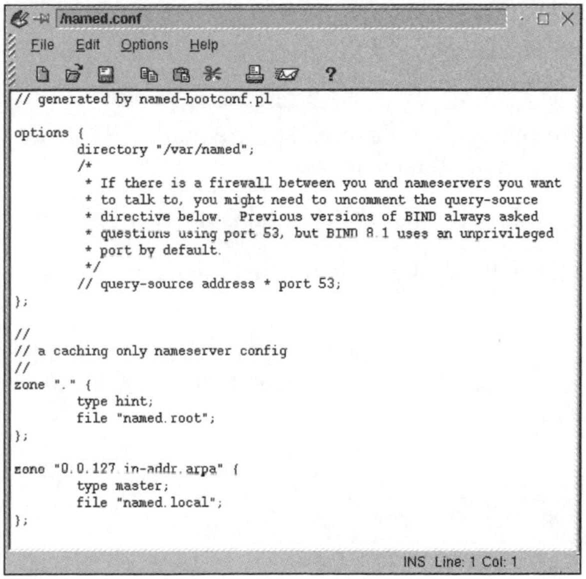

```
// generated by named-bootconf.pl

options {
        directory "/var/named";
        /*
         * If there is a firewall between you and nameservers you want
         * to talk to, you might need to uncomment the query-source
         * directive below.  Previous versions of BIND always asked
         * questions using port 53, but BIND 8.1 uses an unprivileged
         * port by default.
         */
        // query-source address * port 53;
};

//
// a caching only nameserver config
//
zone "." {
        type hint;
        file "named.root";
};

zone "0.0.127.in-addr.arpa" {
        type master;
        file "named.local";
};
```

Figure 21-11: The named.conf file generated during BIND installation

Next, you need to configure the /var/named/named.local file. This file will contain the domain name tactechnology.com, a sample domain you have used for many examples in the networking section of this book. Substitute whatever name you want to use for your domain. Figure 21-12 shows the named.local file for tactechnology.com.

Refer to the section "Why Not Just Use the hosts File?" for illustrations of the files mentioned in the remainder of this section. You need to check the /etc/nsswitch file to be sure it contains the following line:

```
hosts:    files    nis    dns
```

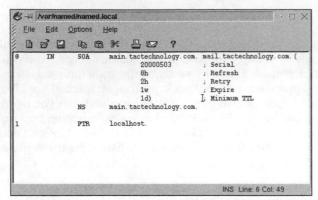

Figure 21-12: The named.local file for the domain tactechnology.com

You also need to check the /etc/resolv.conf file to make sure that the IP address (127.0.0.1) of your localhost is listed as a nameserver.

Finally, you need to check that your /etc/host.conf contains the word `bind`.

After you have completed all these tasks, it is time to start the named daemon and check your work.

Type `ndc start` at a command prompt, wait for the prompt to return, and then type `nslookup`. If you see a screen like the one in Figure 21-13, you have successfully configured a caching server.

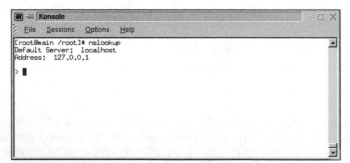

Figure 21-13: The nslookup command can be used to find name servers, in this case your localhost

Next, you will set up a name server for your domain. The procedure is similar to and not much more difficult than what you have already done.

Go back to the /etc/named.conf file and add two more zones, one for the forward lookup of your server and one for the reverse lookup. For the forward lookup you need to add the following:

```
zone "tactechnology.com" {
   notify no;
   type master;
   file "tactech.com";
};
```

For the reverse lookup, add this:

```
zone "1.168.192.in-addr.arpa" {
   notify no;
   type master;
   file "tac.rev";
};
```

After you modify the /etc/named.conf file it should look like Figure 21-14.

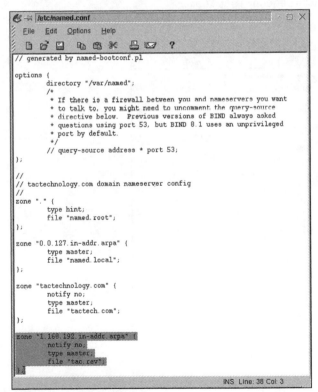

Figure 21-14: The /etc/named.conf file with the forward and reverse lookup zones added

Now you need to create the zone files referenced by the /etc/named.conf file. First you will create the file /var/named/tactech.com by beginning with the start of authority section (SOA). For an explanation of the information contained in zone files, refer to the section "Zone files" earlier in this chapter.

```
@   IN   SOA   tactechnology.com. mail.tactechnology.com. (
                        200005203    ; Serial
                        8h           ; Refresh
                        2h           ; Retry
                        1w           ; Expire
                        1d)          ; Minimum TTL
```

Next, add name server and mail-exchange information.

```
        NS      main.tactechnology.com.
        NS      p200.tactechnology.com.
        MX      10 main    ;Primary Mail Exchanger
        MX      20 p200    ;Secondary Mail Exchanger
```

Finally, add information about your localhost, mail, ftp, and Web server. You can also add information about every workstation on your network. Figure 21-15 shows the complete zone file for `tactechnology.com`.

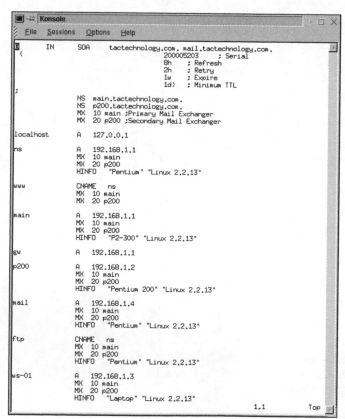

Figure 21-15: The zone file for the tactechnology.com domain

Next, you will set up the reverse lookup zone file, which is called tac.rev. Again, you need to start with the SOA header:

```
@   IN  SOA  main.tactechnology.com. mail.tactechnology.com.(
                200005203;Serial
                8h          ; Refresh
                2h          ; Retry
                1w          ; Expire
                1d)         ; Minimum TTL
```

Next, add the information about your nameservers and their IP addresses.

```
             NS        main.tactechnology.com.

1            PTR       main.tactechnology.com.
2            PTR       p200.tactechnology.com.
```

After you finish creating this file, it should look like Figure 21-16.

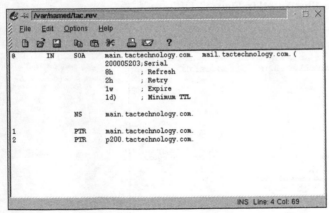

Figure 21-16: The completed reverse lookup zone file for tactechnology.com

If you have followed all these instructions, your name server should be working. You need to check your work again. But before you do, let's look at some of the tools available to you for checking name server information.

DNS Tools

Earlier in the chapter, when you set up a caching name server, you checked your work using a program called nslookup. nslookup is one of several programs you can use to obtain information about your name servers that will help you to fix problems.

nslookup, as its name implies, is a program that you can use either interactively or non-interactively to look up name servers. Entering nslookup at a command prompt will start the search for a name server by looking in the /etc/resolv.conf file. If you are running a name server on your system, nslookup will search your localhost (127.0.0.1) as it is the first listing for a name server in /etc/resolv.conf. You can also tell nslookup to search for a specific server by entering a hyphen and the name of the desired server after the command. After nslookup starts, it shows the DNS server that it will use for searches and a prompt for entering commands.

You can use many commands with nslookup, the most common being:

✦ ls —Lists information about the domain in question.

✦ set —Changes search information for lookups.

The set command also has many options, but the most common option is to set the query type. You can change the query type to any of the RR types you saw earlier in this chapter, plus a few other types. For example, if you wanted to see the mail servers on the tactechnology.com domain, you could change the query to look for mail servers as illustrated in Figure 21-17.

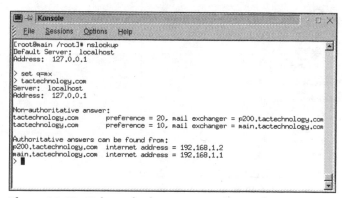

Figure 21-17: Using nslookup you can choose the type of information you wish to query

Another utility that is useful for obtaining information about a name server is dnsquery. dnsquery provides a lot of information by default and is easy to use. Figure 21-18 shows sample output from dnsquery.

The last utility to look at is dig. You can use dig for debugging and obtaining other useful information. You can use it to get the latest updates from the InterNIC about root servers, and then use this information to update the /var/named/named.root file. Figure 21-19 shows the output of a dig request to the InterNIC name server.

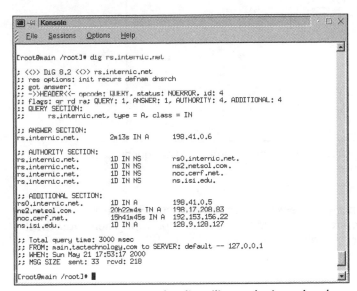

Figure 21-18: dnsquery is an easy-to-use utility that provides a lot of information

```
Konsole
File   Sessions   Options   Help
[root@main /root]# dig rs.internic.net

; <<>> DiG 8.2 <<>> rs.internic.net
;; res options: init recurs defnam dnsrch
;; got answer:
;; ->>HEADER<<- opcode: QUERY, status: NOERROR, id: 4
;; flags: qr rd ra; QUERY: 1, ANSWER: 1, AUTHORITY: 4, ADDITIONAL: 4
;; QUERY SECTION:
;;      rs.internic.net, type = A, class = IN

;; ANSWER SECTION:
rs.internic.net.        2m13s IN A      198.41.0.6

;; AUTHORITY SECTION:
rs.internic.net.        1D IN NS        rs0.internic.net.
rs.internic.net.        1D IN NS        ns2.netsol.com.
rs.internic.net.        1D IN NS        noc.cerf.net.
rs.internic.net.        1D IN NS        ns.isi.edu.

;; ADDITIONAL SECTION:
rs0.internic.net.       1D IN A         198.41.0.5
ns2.netsol.com.         20h22m4s IN A   198.17.208.83
noc.cerf.net.           15h41m45s IN A  192.153.156.22
ns.isi.edu.             1D IN A         128.9.128.127

;; Total query time: 3000 msec
;; FROM: main.tactechnology.com to SERVER: default -- 127.0.0.1
;; WHEN: Sun May 21 17:53:17 2000
;; MSG SIZE  sent: 33  rcvd: 218

[root@main /root]#
```

Figure 21-19: You can use the dig utility to obtain updated root server information

Let's get back to checking the results of your efforts to set up a domain name server for your sample network.

You made some changes to the /etc/named.conf file, so before you can check what you did, you need to restart the named daemon. (You must restart the named daemon whenever you make changes to /etc/named.conf.) To do this, just type `ndc restart`.

Now you can run nslookup to see if you can find your name server. After nslookup starts, it returns the name of your localhost. Now you need to look for your name server by using the set command to change the query type to look for name servers. Figure 21-20 shows the entire process of running nslookup and changing the query type, and the results of the query.

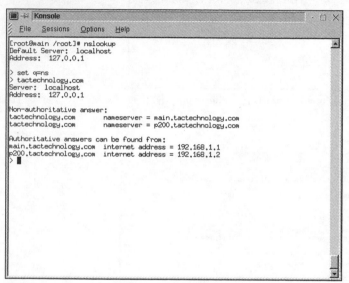

Figure 21-20: The results of the nslookup command with query type set to name server

The last thing you need to check is the reverse lookup. Start nslookup in the default mode by typing nslookup at the command prompt. Then enter the IP address of your server, which is 192.168.1.1. Figure 21-21 shows the result of this query.

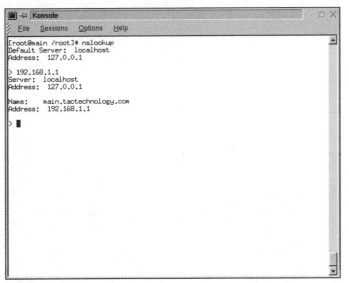

Figure 21-21: The reverse lookup of your IP address returns the name of your server

That's it! You have successfully set up a domain name server on your system.

Summary

In this chapter you learned about the Domain Name System (DNS). You looked at name address resolution and found out how names that are easy for people to remember are converted to numbers that are the basic language of computers. You obtained the BIND software package and installed it on your system, and located the files that you needed to configure for BIND to work. After configuring the files, you set up a caching name server and tested its operation. You then configured a primary master name server, looked at some of the diagnostic utilities available for the BIND package, and used them to test your name server.

✦   ✦   ✦

Configuring the Network File System (NFS)

The Network File System (NFS) was developed by Sun Microsystems in the 1980s to enable file and directory sharing across the network. Computers configured for NFS can share their directories and filesystems with other computers on the network, even those using different operating systems. By using NFS, a computer on the network can access files and programs on other computers as if they were on its own disk drives. This saves disk space, as it is not necessary to place the same files and programs on each computer to provide identical functionality. In this chapter you will learn how to configure NFS on a Linux system as a server as well as a client computer.

Installing the Software

Current Linux distributions have support for NFS compiled into the kernel as modules. Modules are a convenient way of loading options that you want to use and then unloading them when you don't want them. You can check which modules are loaded in your system by typing lsmod at a command prompt. Figure 22-1 shows the modules currently loaded.

Loading modules at boot time on a Linux system is dependent on the distribution you have installed. Refer to the distribution specific documentation that came with the distribution to determine which modules can be loaded automatically and which need to be manually loaded. For NFS, you need to have the modules sunrpc and nfsd loaded. If these modules are loaded, they will appear in the listing shown from the lsmod command. If they are not loaded, you can use the insmod command to load them. You can manually load modules on any Linux system by using the insmod command, as shown in Figure 22-2.

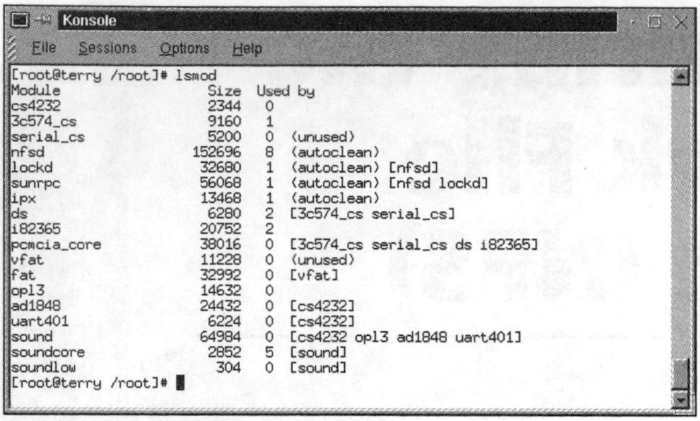

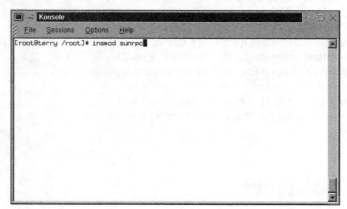

Figure 22-1: The output of the lsmod command shows the modules loaded on your system

Figure 22-2: You can use the insmod command to manually load modules

NFS Configuration Options

Using NFS you can configure a PC to be a server, a client, or both. Each of these options is explained in the following subsections.

Configuring a server

To configure a computer as a server, follow the sequence described in The NFS Daemons and also Exporting filesystems. If you followed the steps successfully, you will have an NFS server.

The NFS daemons

After you have ensured that the modules necessary for NFS functionality are loaded, you can move on to loading the daemons. The daemons you need for NFS are mountd and nfsd, but before you learn about them, you need to learn about the portmapper. The portmapper is a program that converts remote procedure calls (RPC) into DARPA port protocol numbers. (DARPA is an acronym for the Defense Advanced Research Projects Agency; you may remember from Chapter 21 that the TCP/IP protocol suite was developed by the Defense Department.) The portmapper needs to be running, so you should start it now by typing portmap at the command prompt. To check that the portmapper is running, use the ps aux command; you should see something like what's shown in Figure 22-3.

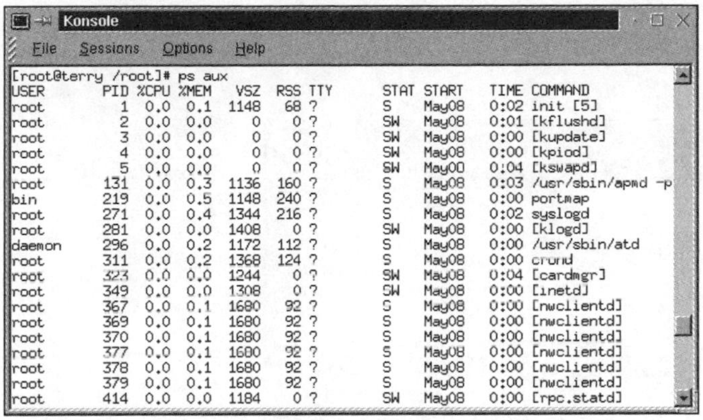

Figure 22-3: The ps aux command shows that the portmapper program is running

The portmapper program needs to be started every time the computer is booted, so it would be a good idea to place the script for this program with your system startup scripts in /etc/rc.d, /etc/init.d, or /etc/rc.d/init.d.

Exporting filesystems

Before you start the mountd and nfsd daemons, you need to decide to which directories and files you want to give access. You do this by placing this information in the /etc/exports file. Figure 22-4 shows a sample exports file.

In the example from Figure 22-4, the filesystem /linbib is available to the computer called main. The (rw) gives read and write access to main. Many other options are available: these are listed in the exports man page as shown in Figure 22-5.

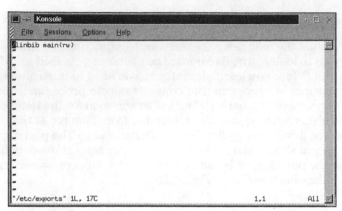

Figure 22-4: The exports file contains information about the directories available to client computers

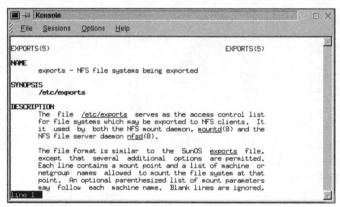

Figure 22-5: The exports man page contains information about using the exports file

Now you can start the NFS daemons by typing `mountd` and `nfsd` at a command prompt. Depending on the distribution, these programs may be called rpc.mountd and rpc.nfsd.

Since you are setting up your server for the first time, you saved a step by editing the /etc/exports file before you started the daemons. Anytime the /etc/exports file is changed, you must make those changes known to the NFS daemons. In this case, you made the changes before you started mountd and nfsd. To notify the daemons of changes in /etc/exports after they are already running, you can use a program called `exportfs`. To check that the daemons are running, you can use the command `rpcinfo -p`. Figure 22-6 shows the result from the `rpcinfo -p` command.

Error Messages

If you receive the following message, the portmapper is not running:

```
pcinfo: can't contact portmapper:
RPC: Remote system error - Connection refused
```

If you receive the following message, one or both of the daemons are not running:

```
no remote programs registered
```

You should stop and restart the portmapper and the daemons by following the instructions in the previous NFS Daemons section.

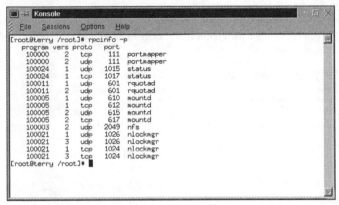

Figure 22-6: The output from the rpcinfo -p command shows that the portmapper, mountd, and nfsd are running

You can stop the daemons from running by using the `kill` command as follows:

```
killall -HUP /usr/portmap
killall -HUP usr/sbin/rpc.mountd
killall -HUP usr/sbin/nfsd
```

If you receive output like what's shown in Figure 22-6, then the portmapper, mountd, and nfsd are all working properly. The NFS server is now configured.

Configuring the NFS Client

Configuring a NFS client is even easier than setting up a NFS server. As with the server, NFS must be compiled in the kernel or available as a module. Current distributions already have NFS enabled as modules, as you saw earlier in this chapter.

Some distributions automatically enable the NFS filesystem. Check to see if the modules are already loaded by using the `lsmod` command. Remember that you can manually load modules by using the `insmod` command followed by the name of the module.

Mounting NFS filesystems

After the modules are loaded on the client, you have to mount the filesystem that was previously exported by the server. You do this by using the `mount` command. To mount the file-system example you used earlier, you need to enter the following:

```
mount terry:/linbib /mnt/laptop
```

Note   This is what I type on my system. On your system you will need to type the name and paths of your directories.

You can now change to this directory and look at its contents as shown in Figure 22-7.

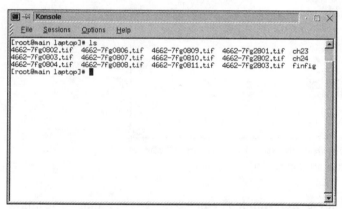

Figure 22-7: After mounting the exported filesystem, you can view its contents

Error Messages

Sometimes, instead of mounting the filesystem, `mount` will return an error message. The following message indicates that the information in the exports file is incorrect, or it was changed and the daemons were not notified.

```
Mount:/linbib failed, reason given by server: Permission denied
```

This message shown below means that one or both of the daemons are not running on the server.

```
Mount clntupd_create: RPC Program not registered
```

Mount command options

There are some options you can use with the mount command to improve performance (speed) of file transfers and also to handle server crashes. We will look at rsize and wsize. These represent the size of the blocks used for reading and writing data. The default size is 1024 bytes and the maximum size is 8192 bytes. Using the largest size can increase performance, but sometimes causes problems during file transfers. You can experiment with these numbers to obtain the best performance.

If the server crashes while it is being accessed, the program accessing it will hang on the remote computer. When the server comes back on line, the program will continue from where it was hanging. From the user's perspective, there is no intervention necessary to resume using the NFS files. The user does not need to do anything to resume using the NFS files.

As an alternative to typing the mount command to access the NFS server, you can make this an automatic process at boot time on the client PC. All you need to do is add the mount information to the /etc/fstab file. Using the computer from previous examples, your entry in the fstab file would be:

```
terry:/linbib /mnt/laptop nfs rsize=8192,wsize=8192 0 0
```

Note This is what I type on my system. On your system you will need to type the name and paths of your directories.

Unmounting the filesystem

Unmounting the filesystem is quite easy and requires just one command. Using our previous example, the command is:

```
umount /mnt/laptop
```

NFS Security

NFS is inherently insecure: after all, it is designed to allow file sharing over the network. Any time you open up your filesystem, you are inviting trouble, but with some care you can increase your overall security. Let's begin by looking at the NFS server and some areas where you can increase security.

Server security

By default, the NFS client and server trust each other. If you take no steps to change this, you are asking for trouble. If a malicious cracker breaks into the client's root account, it is not too difficult to then break into the server's root account. In many cases, the goal of someone breaking into a system is to gain root access. With root access, the transgressor can do anything to your system. So what can you do?

You can tell the server not to trust the client's root account by using an option in the exports file. You previously exported the /mnt/scsi3 filesystem with the following command:

```
/mnt/scsi3 main(rw)
```

By adding the following `root squash` option, you restrict the client root access to root level files on the server.

```
/mnt/scsi2 main(rw,root_squash)
```

Note   The `root_squash` option is actually the default on current Linux distributions (kernel 2.2 and above).

The portmapper

To secure the portmapper, you can use two files that you saw in Chapter 21. These two files are /etc/hosts.allow and /etc/hosts.deny. The /etc/hosts.deny file tells the system who is denied the use of services. The /ect/hosts.allow tells the system who is allowed to use services.

Figure 22-8 shows the /etc/hosts.deny file used by the NFS server in our example in this chapter.

```
Konsole
File   Sessions   Options   Help
[root@terry /root]# rpcinfo -p
  program vers proto   port
   100000    2   tcp    111  portmapper
   100000    2   udp    111  portmapper
   100024    1   udp   1015  status
   100024    1   tcp   1017  status
   100011    1   udp    601  rquotad
   100011    2   udp    601  rquotad
   100005    1   udp    610  mountd
   100005    1   tcp    612  mountd
   100005    2   udp    615  mountd
   100005    2   tcp    617  mountd
   100003    2   udp   2049  nfs
   100021    1   udp   1026  nlockmgr
   100021    3   udp   1026  nlockmgr
   100021    1   tcp   1024  nlockmgr
   100021    3   tcp   1024  nlockmgr
[root@terry /root]#
```

Figure 22-8: The /etc/hosts.deny file denies services

In Figure 22-8 you can see that the portmap shown in the /etc/hosts.deny file is denying service to all. This means that no one can access the portmap on this server. So no one could use your NFS filesystem without your permission. You can grant permission by listing those you trust in the /etc/hosts.allow file.

Figure 22-9 shows the listing from the /etc/hosts.allow file from the NFS server. You can see that any PC on network 192.168.1.0 is allowed access.

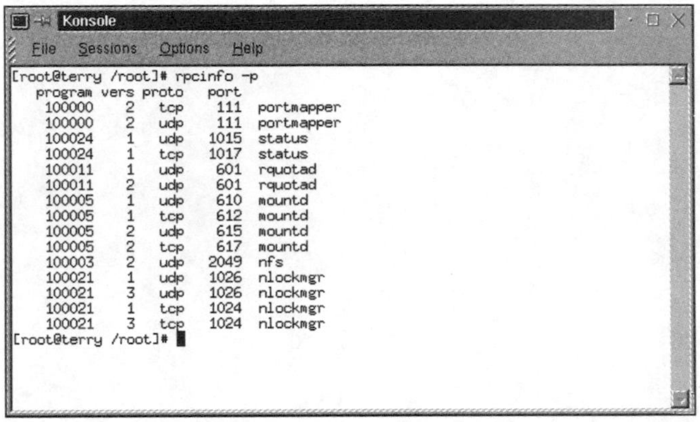

Figure 22-9: The /etc/hosts.allow file tells the system whom you trust and will allow to use your services

The number shown in the file is the IP address number and network mask of the network. In this case 192.168.1.0 is the network and 255.255.255.0 is the subnet mask.

Client security

Earlier I said that the server and client trust each other and that this was not a good thing. You can limit the access of the server to the client with some mount options. By using the nosuid option you can forbid suid programs to work on the NFS filesystem. This prevents the server's root account from obtaining root on the client PC. To implement this, place the nosuid option in the client's /etc/fstab file in the option's column.

Summary

In this chapter you learned about the Network File System (NFS). You looked at the modules required by the kernel, the portmap program, and the mountd and nfsd daemons. Then you configured a NFS server and exported a filesystem. You then configured a client PC and mounted and unmounted the exported filesystem. Finally, you looked at NFS security and implemented a few simple procedures to make your system more secure.

✦   ✦   ✦

Configuring Network Information Services (NIS)

NIS is an acronym for *Network Information Services,* a program that was released by Sun Microsystems in 1985.

Note At the time of its release NIS was called Yellow Pages, or just YP, but was subsequently changed to NIS because of trademark conflicts. Since it was called YP when first introduced, many of the commands used in NIS begin with the letters yp.

NIS is designed to enable the sharing of files across the network to make the administrator's job easier. With NIS, a user can log into the network from any host and have access to his/her files as if the login were from his/her own host. NIS enables this by maintaining a list of files that are available to the hosts through NIS servers in a NIS domain. The files shared contain configuration information with the most commonly shared files being the following:

`/etc/passwd`	Contains user account information.
`/etc/group`	Contains group definitions.
`/etc/hosts`	Contains hostnames and IP addresses.
`/etc/services`	A listing of port numbers for network services.
`/etc/protocols`	Lists text-name-to-protocol-number conversions.

`/etc/aliases`	Contains alias listings for mail.
`/etc/netgroup`	Contains a listing of networks, users and hosts.

The Difference between NIS and NFS

In Chapter 22 you learned about the NFS — what it does for the network and how it is configured. From the description of NIS in the previous section, it would seem that NIS and NFS serve the same purpose, so why do you need both? Although they are similar, there are significant differences between the two.

NFS was designed to enable users to share a common filesystem across the network by linking a group of filesystems into one. In order to be so linked, there must be consistent UID and GID numbers on each separate filesystem. In the past, this meant that system administrators had to manually copy files between systems. In a large network with many different filesystems this created problems, such as determining where to store the master information and how to ensure that it was accurate and up to date. So in an attempt to solve these problems, Sun released NIS (YP) not too long after the release of NFS.

As you saw previously, NIS files shared across the network contain configuration information about users, groups, passwords, protocols, and more. These files are stored on NIS servers and exported as maps to other NIS servers and clients. NFS, on the other hand, actually enables sharing of entire filesystems. Basically, you can say that NIS contains the information necessary for the system to provide the services furnished by the NFS, and exports this information to the other servers and clients on the network.

Configuring NIS Domains

Any system that will be using NIS must be part of an NIS domain, and the domain must have an NIS domain name. Your NIS domain name must be different from your IP network domain name: there is no connection between the two.

Each NIS domain needs to have at least one *master server*. The master server contains all the NIS databases. Additional NIS servers in the same domain are known as *slave servers*: they contain copies of the NIS databases from the master server. Computers on the NIS domain that are not master or slave servers are *clients*. Changes made to the master server databases are sent to the slave servers. The slave servers provide fault tolerance in case the master server goes down, and they speed up database searches by providing information to clients closer to a slave than to the master server. Database information is stored in DBM files using information obtained from ASCII databases. The configuration files listed earlier in this chapter can be converted to DBM using a program called `makedbm`.

To name the domain, use the following command:

```
domainname  name of domain
```

name of domain is the actual name you want to use for the NIS domain. Since you want this domain to be available every time you boot the PC, this command should be placed in one of the rc startup scripts on each PC in the network.

You can also configure the domain using a GUI that will vary depending on the distribution you are using. It is always best to refer to the system-specific documentation supplied with your distribution.

Checking for NIS Programs

Before you begin to set up your NIS domain, you need to be sure you have the necessary software installed on your computers. Current distributions supply the necessary programs as RPMs, which are usually on the installation CDs. If you have downloaded the distribution, make sure that you also downloaded the NIS programs. On a Mandrake system, for example, the programs are:

```
yp-tools-2.3-1mdk.i586.rpm
ypbind-3.3-2_1mdk.i586.rpm
ypserv-1.3.7-1. mdk.i586.rpm
```

You can install these programs by using the rpm command at a command prompt, or by using a GUI such as kpackage, as shown in Figure 23-1. yptool and ypbind are used by NIS clients and ypserv is used by the NIS servers.

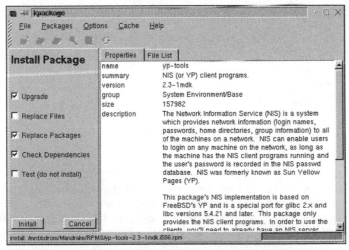

Figure 23-1: Using kpackage to install the rpm needed for NIS

After you have performed the necessary installations, you can proceed to configuring your servers and clients. We will begin by configuring the master NIS server.

Configuring the NIS Master Server

As you learned earlier, there are two types of NIS servers, master server and slave server. Each domain can have only one master server, but can contain any number of slave servers. Now you will configure the NIS master server.

First, you need to check that you have the files that NIS needs on the master server. These files are located in the /etc directory and were listed earlier in this chapter. Be sure to remove any expired accounts and make sure that all the information is correct. Next, you will run a program that will convert these files into NIS map files.

The program you need to run is called ypinit, and if you use the -m option, it will automatically generate the map files. Figure 23-2 shows the ypinit -m command.

Figure 23-2: The ypinit command shows the host that will be the master server and the files created in /var/yp/mainnis

The ypinit command looks in the /var/yp directory to get the information it needs to make the NIS maps. A new directory is created in /var/yp named for the domain name. In our example, the domain name is called mainnis, so the directory created is /var/yp/mainnis. All the maps created by the ypinit program are placed in this directory.

`ypinit` enables you to enter the names of other servers if you desire. When you have entered all the servers you want, press Ctrl-D to continue. A list of all NIS servers is then displayed and you need to hit Y to continue. When the command prompt returns, the program has finished running and you can move on to the next step.

You need to place the domain name and server name in the /etc/yp.conf file. Figure 23-3 shows this file. The server name can be the name or IP address of the server. The server name and IP address should be listed in the /etc/hosts file. (You set this up when you configured your Ethernet card in Chapter 20.)

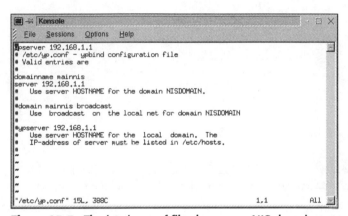

Figure 23-3: The/etc/yp.conf file shows one NIS domain name and the master server

Another file you need to configure, or at least check, is /etc/nsswitch.conf. This file is the name service switch file and it tells the system where to look for information about system services. You need to check that NIS is listed for passwd, group, and shadow. Figure 23-4 shows that NIS will be queried for these three items.

Now you need to start the NIS server by issuing the `ypserv` command. You should place this command in one of the rc startup scripts so the daemon will start every time the system boots.

Finally, you need to start the `ypbind` daemon so the server can find the maps. You should also start this daemon by placing the command in one of the system rc scripts.

Configuring the NIS Slave Server

Now that the master is running, you can configure NIS slave servers if you want. Configuring a slave requires the following steps (be sure to use the correct path for your filesystem):

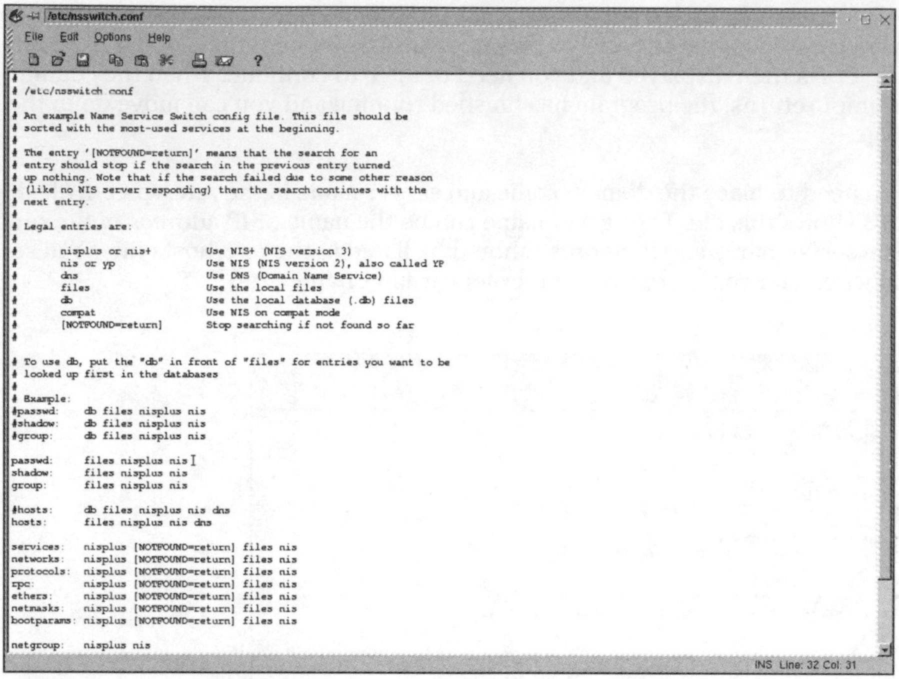


```
#
# /etc/nsswitch.conf
#
# An example Name Service Switch config file. This file should be
# sorted with the most-used services at the beginning.
#
# The entry '[NOTFOUND=return]' means that the search for an
# entry should stop if the search in the previous entry turned
# up nothing. Note that if the search failed due to some other reason
# (like no NIS server responding) then the search continues with the
# next entry.
#
# Legal entries are:
#
#       nisplus or nis+         Use NIS+ (NIS version 3)
#       nis or yp               Use NIS (NIS version 2), also called YP
#       dns                     Use DNS (Domain Name Service)
#       files                   Use the local files
#       db                      Use the local database (.db) files
#       compat                  Use NIS on compat mode
#       [NOTFOUND=return]       Stop searching if not found so far
#

# To use db, put the "db" in front of "files" for entries you want to be
# looked up first in the databases
#
# Example:
#passwd:    db files nisplus nis
#shadow:    db files nisplus nis
#group:     db files nisplus nis

passwd:     files nisplus nis
shadow:     files nisplus nis
group:      files nisplus nis

#hosts:     db files nisplus nis dns
hosts:      files nisplus nis dns

services:   nisplus [NOTFOUND=return] files nis
networks:   nisplus [NOTFOUND=return] files nis
protocols:  nisplus [NOTFOUND=return] files nis
rpc:        nisplus [NOTFOUND=return] files nis
ethers:     nisplus [NOTFOUND=return] files nis
netmasks:   nisplus [NOTFOUND=return] files nis
bootparams: nisplus [NOTFOUND=return] files nis

netgroup:   nisplus nis
```

Figure 23-4: The /etc/nsswitch file shows where the system will look for service configuration information

1. Log into the server as root.
2. Enter the domain name of the server using the `domainname` command as described in the section "Configuring NIS Domains."
3. Enter the `ypbind` command.
4. Enter the `ypinit` command as follows: `ypinit -s` *`name of your main server`* (in our example it would be `main.tactechnology.com`).
5. To test the configuration type: `ypmatch` *`username`* `passwd`. This will show the password for the user you name.

Configuring the NIS Client

To configure the NIS client you need to do the following:

1. Set up the domain name by using the `domainname` command as described in the section "Configuring NIS Domains."
2. Start the `ypbind` daemon.

Note Remember to place the `domainname` command in the rc startup scripts so it is active at each boot.

Modify the passwd and group Files for Use with NIS

You also need to place an entry in the /etc/passwd and /etc/group files to direct the search for name matches to the NIS server if no match is found in the local file. So to the end of these files you need to add the following line:

```
+:*:0:0:::
```

The plus sign tells `ypbind` to query the NIS master.

That's all there is to it.

Summary

In this chapter you learned about the Network Information System (NIS). This system provides password and login information to the entire network. By using NIS, you enable your users to access their own files from any network-connected PC. You looked at the modules required by the kernel and the programs you need to run NIS. Then you configured a NIS master and slave server. And finally, you configured a NIS client PC.

✦ ✦ ✦

Configuring E-mail and Other Communication Services

Electronic mail is a way you can communicate with other computer users without making more work for your local postal worker. Electronic mail, more familiarly known as *e-mail*, is in many ways very similar to postal mail, or, as system administrators like to call it, *snail mail.* Like regular mail, e-mail must be sent to a specific person at a specific location or the message won't get through. Of course, the specific location is not the recipient's physical location, but the electronic address of the recipient's e-mail server.

It is difficult to overestimate the power and importance of e-mail. Recently, a computer journal performed a time-analysis study of how the typical office worker used a computer. Amazingly, the amount of time spent writing, reading, or responding to e-mail was over 30%! Clearly, e-mail is important to computer users. Indeed, many people used the Internet solely for e-mail until the development of the World Wide Web. For that reason alone, it is important to understand as much as possible about how e-mail works, how to set it up, and which programs to use or make available to Linux users.

E-mail from Start to Finish

An e-mail message starts with a user — the sender — and ends with a user — the recipient. Along the way, a variety of programs may process the message, and the message may travel through several intermediate way stations before it reaches the recipient's destination. Message transport relies on network protocols. This chapter describes configuring e-mail to run across TCP/IP protocols.

Chapter 20, "Configuring the Network," introduced the TCP/IP protocol suite.

Before you configure an e-mail client or server, you should understand as much as possible about how e-mail works and which programs to use or make available to Linux users. As a system administrator, you may have to configure three elements to provide e-mail services for users:

1. Programs:

   • A Mail User Agent (MUA) so that users can read and write e-mail.

   • A Mail Transfer Agent (MTA) to deliver users' e-mail messages from one computer to another across a network.

   • A Local Delivery Agent (LDA) to append messages to users' mailbox files.

   • An optional mail notifier program so that users know when new mail comes in.

2. The TCP/IP protocols that store e-mail messages and transfer e-mail between MTAs.

3. Miscellaneous communication and mail storage components:

   • Ports

   • Mail queues

   • Mailbox files

The following sections of this chapter follow an e-mail message from creation to receipt to describe how the programs, protocols, and miscellaneous components cooperate. Later you see how to configure these software components to build a complete e-mail system for either a single-client machine or for an e-mail server that provides mail services for many networked users.

Users work with MUAs. They never see the MTA at work. System administrators work with MUAs to read and write mail. They may also work with MTAs, the protocols, and the mailbox storage components and ports, which are invisible to e-mail users.

Following the Mail Trail across the Internet

In the next example, Miss Scarlet on flyingpenguin.cardinalconsulting.com (running Red Hat Linux) decides to send mail to Professor Plum at opus.redbird.net (running Caldera OpenLinux eServer). Both flyingpenguin and opus are up and running and connected to the Internet. The following sections trace Miss Scarlet's message from her keyboard, out of her computer, across the Internet, and ultimately, on to Professor Plum's screen.

Starting at the beginning — Composing the message with an MUA

Miss Scarlet needs a program to compose her message. This program is a Mail User Agent (MUA). You use an MUA to write and read mail messages. MUAs are also called mail clients. MUAs come in two varieties: GUI (Graphic User Interface) and non-GUI (command line interface). Netscape Messenger is a popular MUA. Lotus Notes also has MUA functionality built into it, so that you can send and receive e-mail using the Notes GUI.

If you prefer the command line interface, or if you are running Linux without a graphical desktop, you can run one of the many text-based mail clients, such as mail, mailx, elm, pine, or mutt.

Miss Scarlet's message looks like this:

```
To: professorplum@opus.redbird.net
Date: Thu, 18 Jan 2001 17:14:16 -0500
Subject: Anacron job 'cron.daily'
Security Alert:
/etc/cron.daily/tripwire-check:
****    Error: Tripwire database for
flyingpenguin.cardinalconsulting.com not found. ****
```

After typing her message, Miss Scarlet presses the send key. At this point, it seems like the MUA is done, but it has one more job to do. Miss Scarlet's MUA passes her message to another program, a Mail Transport Agent (MTA), for further processing. MUAs and MTAs work together to get messages from senders to recipients. The MUA is the program that most users see and work with. You use an MUA to read and write mail. The MTA is a program that handles your e-mail behind the scenes, delivering it to or receiving it from your MUA.

Tip   If you use the Emacs editor, try RMAIL, an MUA that runs inside Emacs.

Crossing the Internet with MTAs

Contrary to popular belief, electronic mail does not magically leave the sender's machine and pop up on the recipient's screen. When Miss Scarlet finishes typing an e-mail message and sends it to Professor Plum, her MUA goes behind the scenes to establish a connection with her default MTA, most often a program called *sendmail*. The MTA takes over from there. The MTA on flyingpenguin passes Miss Scarlet's message to the MTA on opus, Professor Plum's computer. Miss Scarlet's MTA reads the "To" information in the message and translates Professor Plum's opus.redbird.com address into a numeric IP address. The MTA on flyingpenguin opens a connection across the Internet so that it can communicate with another MTA that lives on opus. The MTA to MTA communications go through a logical structure called a port. Port 25 is the commonly used port where MTAs communicate when handling mail messages.

At this stage of the message trail, we have two MTAs—one from flyingpenguin, representing Miss Scarlet, and the other from opus, representing Professor Plum, communicating through port 25. The two MTAs communicate using the SMTP (Simple Message Transfer Protocol).

Note

TCP/IP protocols are described in technical detail in a series of numbered public documents called RFCs (Request for Comments), maintained by the RFC Editor under the IETF (Internet Engineering Task Force). The document that defines the SMTP standard is RFC821. All RFCs are available at www.rfc-editor.org.

At this point, Professor Plum's MTA has received Miss Scarlet's message. The next step is for the receiving MTA (Professor Plum's) to add a header to Miss Scarlet's message. The header includes tracking information. If a message goes through multiple MTAs, each MTA adds header information.

LDAs and mailboxes

After adding the header, Professor Plum's MTA hands the message over to another program called a Local Delivery Agent (LDA). The LDA adds the message to Professor Plum's mailbox file.

Note

A commonly used LDA on Linux systems is the procmail program.

Most Linux mailboxes reside in files identified by username in the directory with spool/mail somewhere in its name. For example, Professor Plum's mailbox is /var/spool/mail/prof_plum because he uses Caldera OpenLinux. Miss Scarlet, on the other hand, uses Red Hat Linux, and her mailbox file is named /usr/spool/mail/ miss_scarlet.

Tip

Different Linux distributions store mailbox files in different locations. See your distribution's documentation for the location. You can override Linux's choice of a mailbox file by setting the MAIL environment variable to point to the specific location where you want your mail to be stored. You can set the MAILPATH environment variable to point to a list of directories to check for mailbox files. Another handy environment variable is MAILCHECK. By defining MAILCHECK, you set the frequency (in seconds) at which bash checks for new mail.

Cross-Reference

Chapter 17 describes how to use environment variables.

Back to the beginning—Using an MUA

When Professor Plum reads his mail, his MUA accesses his mailbox file and— *voila!*—Miss Scarlet's message appears on his screen.

Notifiers on the side

Another program on the message trail is a mail notifier — a utility that watches your mailbox file and tells you that new mail has arrived. A mail notifier is nice to have, but it's not essential in the whole e-mail story.

All of the Linux shells have a built-in mail notifier that typically looks at your mailbox file once a minute. If new mail has arrived, the shell displays a message just before it displays the next system prompt. It won't interrupt a program you're running. You can adjust how frequently the mail notifier checks and even which mailbox files to watch.

If you use a GUI, you can use fancier mail notifiers. Some of these programs play sounds or display pictures to show you that there's new mail.

Tip

One of my favorite mail notifiers is the graphical xbiff. When you run xbiff, a small picture of a traditional U. S. postal mailbox appears. If you have no mail, the flag on the mailbox is down. When mail arrives, the flag goes up and the mailbox beeps.

Besides being useful and cute, xbiff has an interesting legend attached to its name. The story is that in the olden days of UNIX, the author of the first mail notifier had a dog named Biff. Whenever the postman arrived, biff barked. Therefore, biff became the name of the UNIX mail notifier. It's just a short leap from biff to graphical xbiff.

More about MTAs

A Mail Transport Agent or MTA is a daemon, such as sendmail or smail, that handles the delivery of e-mail. Because MTAs work behind the scenes, users do not normally encounter them. System administrators configure MTA characteristics, such as what directories sendmail should look in to find system files, whether sendmail will recognize your host by alternate host names, which MUAs sendmail will run with.

Comparing E-mail Cases

Now that you've tracked the sending, delivery, and receipt of a message in the section, "Following the Mail Trail", let's look at some other examples of both local and networked mail delivery and which protocols and programs you need to run to satisfy each case.

One user

Your computer must have a network connection (either modem for dial-up networking or NIC for LAN/WAN networking).

Incoming mail is delivered directly to you. Your computer must run an MTA (both to receive incoming mail and to send outgoing mail).

You don't need the POP3 or IMAP4 protocols. Your MUA does all the work.

Note POP3 and IMAP4 are irrelevant here because your client MUA can directly read your mail out of your local mailbox file on your computer.

SOHO (Small Office, Home Office)

Instead of running an MTA, you can connect to a mail server on your intranet or on the Internet. You need a client to match the server that holds your mail, for example, a POP3 client (such as Netscape Messenger) for a POP3 server, an IMAP4 client (such as Eudora) for an IMAP4 server, a Web browser (such as Netscape Navigator) for Web mail on a Web server.

Tip For both of these examples, you can connect to the mail server via dial-up networking (see the PPP chapter) or via a permanent connection such as cable modem, DSL, LAN, or WAN.

Medium organization without a dedicated mail server

Your organization has an intranet collection of computers networked together on a LAN with no dedicated mail server. All computers run an MTA and function as described in the one-user case. For example, Miss Scarlet's mail is stored on Miss Scarlet's computer, Professor Plum's mail is stored on his computer, and so forth for each member of your organization.

Medium organization with a dedicated mail server

Just as the SOHO example had POP3 / IMAP4 / browsers, this example has the same. The difference is that the mail server to which you connect is a single computer shared by everyone on your intranet. That machine is your mail server.

Deciding on How to Serve E-mail

As a system administrator, you decide which computer should function as the mail server and whether it should be dedicated to mail or also used for other things. The advantages of a shared mail server are:

✦ When you run a mail server, you can backup everyone's mail from one computer, rather than having to perform a separate backup on each user's computer.

✦ You only need to configure the MTA once. (Well, twice. Once for the mail server computer to send/receive Internet mail and once for all the other computers on the intranet to work only with the mail server.)

✦ You really only have to worry about doing performance management and capacity planning for the mail server.

✦ Only the mail server needs to have access to the Internet to implement e-mail for all the users.

 Note A dedicated mail server is really a type of file server. It simply serves files of one type—e-mail files.

Understanding How the Protocols Fit into the Mail Trail

As your message moves from MUA to MTA to MTA to MUA, it flows across various TCP/IP protocols. This section provides a few more details about SMTP, POP3, and IMAP4.

Understanding SMTP

SMTP, which stands for *Simple Mail Transfer Protocol,* is the TCP/IP protocol that transfers e-mail messages among computers on an intranet or on the Internet. MTAs use SMTP to communicate. SMTP defines how messages move from one computer's MTA to another's MTA, but not what path the message follows. A message may go directly from the MTA on your computer to the MTA on your recipient's computer. Or, a message may proceed through multiple MTAs on intermediary computers on the network via a process called *store and forward.* Store and forward technology dictates that as each message travels through the network on the way to its destination, it may pass through any number of other computers on that network, where the MTA briefly stores the message before forwarding it on to the next computer on the route.

If a destination address is not local to the MTA, in other words, if you are writing to someone out on a network, the MTA decides whether to:

✦ Forward the message to the destination MTA (if your MTA knows the address of the receiving MTA).

✦ Send the message to an network gateway for further deciphering of the recipient's address.

✦ Forward the message to an intermediate MTA on the way to the final destination. When the mail message finally arrives at the destination MTA, the message is again stored in the recipient's mail spool until a MUA at the destination host retrieves it.

Note If you're interested in the behind-the-scenes technical details of how SMTP works, read the documents that define SMTP's function and workings. These documents are called RFCs (Request for Comments) and are available from the RFC Editor site of the IETF (Internet Engineering Task Force) at www.rfc-editor.org. The RFCs for SMTP are RFC 821 and 1869.

The SMTP protocol is strictly about moving messages from one computer to another. Although SMTP doesn't care about the content of an e-mail message, it does limit the formatting attributes of the message. SMTP can transfer only ASCII text. It can't handle fonts, colors, graphics, attachments, or any other of those fancy e-mail features that you may already know and love.

Tip If you like to send multimedia e-mail, such as Miss Scarlet's scream, movies of your suspects, or a picture of Colonel Mustard, you need to read the next section about MIME coming up.

Adding MIME to SMTP

Since SMTP by itself transports only text, MIME — *Multipurpose Internet Mail Extensions* — enables senders to enhance the body of an e-mail message. MIME enables the body of e-mail messages to have all those cool enhancements such as colors, sounds, and animation, while still allowing them to be delivered by SMTP.

Tip For the original Internet documentation of MIME, see RFCs 2046 through 2049.

Are you asking, "How do they do that?" It depends on your MUA. You must use a *MIME-compliant* mail user agent; that is, your MUA must know how to generate MIME message bodies. When you compose your sophisticated e-mail message, your MIME-compliant MUA encodes the deluxe features into a text-only representation that SMTP can transfer. The message can then pass through the necessary intermediary computers as usual, and none of them needs anything special to process your enhanced message.

When the message arrives at its final destination, your correspondent also needs a MIME-compliant MUA in order to decode the fancy features. Without a MIME-compliant MUA, the recipient of your message may not be able to do much with it.

Tip S/MIME secures communications between an e-mail sender and the recipient. For example, Candace and niece Emily need secrecy for sharing important Beanie news.

Understanding POP3 — the Post Office Protocol version 3

E-mail can only arrive at a computer that is connected to a network, such as the Internet. If you work on a computer that is not continuously connected, you may miss e-mail deliveries from the Internet. POP3 is a protocol that solves the problem of potential e-mail loss by allowing a computer that is continuously connected to the Internet — such as a POP3 mail server — to receive and store your e-mail for you. When you're ready to read mail, connect to the POP3 mail server and download your e-mail to your own computer where you can read it with your MUA. POP3 was originally designed to allow home computer users to download their e-mail from their ISP (Internet Service Provider).

Note   You need an e-mail client (MUA) that understands POP3 to communicate with a POP3 mail server. POP3-aware MUAs for Linux include pine, emacs, Netscape, and mutt.

Caution   Using POP3 can present problems for traveling users. For example, if Professor Plum "pops" his e-mail from the server to flyingpenguin on Monday and is using his opus notebook on a business trip on Tuesday, all the mail he "popped" to flyingpenguin is unavailable on opus.

Understanding IMAP4 — The Internet Message Access Protocol, version 4

IMAP4 provides sophisticated client/server functionality for handling e-mail. IMAP4 has more features than POP3. IMAP4 permits you to store your e-mail on a networked mail server, just as POP3 does. The difference is this: POP3 requires you to download your e-mail before your MUA reads it; IMAP4 allows your e-mail to reside permanently on a remote server from which you can access the mail from your office, your home, or anywhere else you happen to be.

Note   You need an e-mail client (MUA) that understands IMAP4 to communicate with an IMAP4 mail server.

Caution   POP3 and IMAP4 do not interoperate. While there are e-mail clients and servers that speak both protocols, you can't use a POP3 client to communicate with an IMAP4 server or an IMAP4 client to communicate with a POP3 server. When you configure an e-mail server, you must decide whether your users need POP3 or IMAP4 functionality (or both) IMAP4 servers usually require much more disk space than POP3 servers because the e-mail remains on the mail server unless the users or system administrator deletes it.

When E-mail Problems Happen

E-mail is very rarely lost in transport. This is quite an accomplishment when you consider the volume of e-mail sent each day. On occasion, e-mail messages get garbled or misrouted, just as a Post Office sometimes does with snail mail. E-mail can become garbled or lost due to lightning storms and other causes that disrupt power supplies. Most e-mail problems are the result of user or system administrator error. Probably the most common e-mail "problem" is using an incorrect e-mail address.

Misconfiguring an e-mail server causes e-mail problems. Make sure that mailboxes sit in the right directory for your distribution. If you add filesystem quotas to mailboxes, be aware that at some point, users may not be able to receive new messages until they (or you) clean up the mail files.

How routing facilitates travel on the mail trail

Routing is the process of moving network packets between networks. A router is a combination of hardware and software that extends a LAN (Local Area Network) by connecting different network segments. The router permits each connected network to maintain its independent identity and address. For example, the Cardinal network used in the examples in this book is actually three different LANs linked together.

Tip   A router is usually a dedicated computer running specialized software, but you can also run routing software on any general-purpose computer. The computer must have two NICs (Network Interface Cards) and be connected to two or more network segments. Configuring routing software on Linux is beyond the scope of this book.

If you're a network beginner, check out *TCP/IP for Dummies*, published by Hungry Minds, Inc., for more details on how routing works and which routing protocols to choose.

While routing works with all networking applications, this section describes how routing works with e-mail message transmissions. When Miss Scarlet in Singapore sends e-mail to Professor Plum in Johannesburg, her message (broken into parts called packets) travels from her local network to the Internet and across the planet via multiple routers set up by ISPs (Internet Service Providers) with connections and transport agreements. Routers are aware of the various network paths e-mail can take across the network to its final destination. Each router knows about other routers and can choose the most efficient path for e-mail to follow. This efficient path may change as network devices change and as network traffic increases and decreases.

For example, on Monday, the most efficient path for Miss Scarlet's e-mail may be from her home network to a network in Malaysia to the final destination network. On Tuesday, however, the most efficient path may be from her home network to a network in Australia to a network in Nairobi to the final destination. Why would the path change from day to day (or even minute to minute)? Perhaps the network in Singapore is not available because of hardware problems. Maybe the Singapore network hardware is fine, but the network is very congested because of increased traffic, and the routers have decided that a longer path is actually more efficient.

Routers figure out the most efficient path by using routing protocols such as RIP, the Routing Information Protocol; OSPF, the Open Shortest Path First; BGP, the Border Gateway Protocol (used by the Internet's routers); and CIDR (Classless Inter-Domain Routing), which cooperates with BGP and/or OSPF.

Configuring the Server Side

The previous sections of this chapter provide technical concepts and how-it-works information. The following sections describe how-to and when-to: when you need to and how to configure protocols and the sendmail MTA.

Configuring sendmail

There are a number of mail transport agents available for Linux, including Qmail, smail, and sendmail. The most widely used MTA is sendmail, which is the default MTA for most Linux distributions.

Note   You may be wondering why one of the oldest MTAs is the most commonly used. Some of the newer MTAs — particularly smail — are easier to configure and manage. But, if you are configuring a computer to handle lots of e-mail connections and messages, you still need the power of sendmail.

Checking that sendmail is installed and running

Before you start to configure sendmail, be sure that it's installed on your computer. It probably is. Almost all Linux installation procedures install sendmail. But just to be sure, check it out. The example below shows how to check using the rpm -q command. The output not only shows that sendmail is installed, but which version of sendmail is installed.

```
root@flyingpenguin# rpm -q sendmail
sendmail-8.11.0-8
```

Next, make sure that sendmail starts when your computers boot. There are several ways to check whether sendmail is running. Pick your favorite. The example below uses my favorite version of ps to look for sendmail. Notice that the terminal field is a "?" and that sendmail is listening on port 25.

```
root@flyingpenguin# ps -auwwx | grep sendmail
root  8977  0.0  0.3  1388  472  ?  S  12:16   0:00 sendmail:
accepting connections on port 25
```

Tip

If you have it on your system, you can also use the `chkconfig --list` command to query the system's runlevel information to see if sendmail is running.

You can also use telnet to check whether sendmail is running. You telnet to yourself (localhost) and tell telnet specifically to use port 25. The example below shows that telnet is not running on the emperor system:

```
root@emperor# telnet localhost 25
Trying 127.0.0.1...
telnet: Unable to connect to remote host: Connection refused
```

Working with the sendmail configuration file

The ancient UNIX mythology declares sendmail to be complex to configure. If you look at its configuration file, /etc/sendmail.cf, you can understand how this legend started. In the days of UNIX past, system administrators had to build this file themselves. But that's no longer the case. Linux provides you with a default sendmail configuration file that works for most sites. Your default sendmail configuration file accepts mail deliveries to your computer, sends mail deliveries from your computer, and allows your computer to be used as a relay host.

Note

Sometimes a message has to be relayed through more than one machine. When your computer relays a message, you are allowing it to be used as a relay host.

If you need to edit the configuration file at all, you may only need to make a couple of minor changes. Here are the key lines a Red Hat Linux Sys Admin might want to edit in /etc/sendmail.cf. These are NOT in the order you'll find them in the file. In the example below, the cardinalconsulting.com domain is set up to be a relay host.

```
# Copyright (c) 1998-2000 Sendmail, Inc. and its suppliers.
#        All rights reserved.
# Copyright (c) 1983, 1995 Eric P. Allman.All rights reserved.
# Copyright (c) 1988, 1993
#The Regents of the University of California. All rights
#reserved.
#
# By using this file, you agree to the terms and conditions
# set forth in the LICENSE file which can be found at the top
# level of the sendmail distribution.
##############################################################
#######
#####            SENDMAIL CONFIGURATION FILE
#####
##############################################################
#######
        | File edited here |
```

```
==========
# "Smart" relay host (may be null)
DS

CHANGE THE LINE TO DEFINE THE NAME OF THE MAIL RELAY HOST
(GATEWAY COMPUTER THAT HAS THE RESPONSIBILITY FOR
SENDING/RECEIVING INTERNET MAIL). NOTE -- NO SPACES!

DSmailrelay.cardinalconsulting.com
==========
# my official domain name
# ... define this only if sendmail cannot automatically
#        determine your domain
#Dj$w.Foo.COM
```

Fortunately, you do not have to be a sendmail expert in order to perform most configuration chores. In most cases, all you need is one of the predefined configuration files in /usr/lib/sendmail.cf. The basic process is to modify one of the predefined configuration files for your own needs, regenerate /etc/sendmail.cf using the m4 macro processor, as explained in a moment, and then test your configuration. This method enables you to make incremental changes, minimizing the risk of major problems. Most Linux distributions come with a generic sendmail configuration file (/etc/sendmail.cf).

Understanding and managing the mail queue

There may be a reason why e-mail messages can't go out immediately. Perhaps your network is down. Maybe your intranet's connection to the Internet is sporadic. Maybe the recipient's computer is unavailable. Whatever the reason, users can continue to compose e-mail with their MUAs. When they send the mail, sendmail puts the message into the mail queue and keeps trying to send at intervals defined for the sendmail daemon. You can find out what these intervals are by checking the initialization script that starts sendmail.

The brief excerpt below is from the file /etc/rc.d/rc2.d/S80sendmail. The first line defines the interval to retry as one hour (1h). You can specify the interval in h (hours), m (minutes), or s (seconds). Depending on your distribution and version of Linux, you may see different programming styles setting the queue. This Red Hat version defines the variable QUEUE and sets it to 1h. Some distributions hardcode the interval right into the sendmail command (sendmail -q1h). The last two lines of the excerpt show the sendmail startup command. The -q$QUEUE in the last line sets the retry time to 1 hour. The -bd option in the next to last line of the excerpt starts sendmail as a daemon.

```
QUEUE=1h
fi

# Check that networking is up.
[ ${NETWORKING} = "no" ] && exit 0
```

Behind the sendmail Scenes with the m4 Macro Processor

What is a macro? A *macro* is a symbolic name for a long string of characters, much like a keyboard macro is a shorthand way to type a long series of keystrokes. Sendmail gets its rules from the entries in a sendmail macro file. The location of the generic sendmail macro file varies depending on your distribution. For example, Red Hat's file is /usr/lib/sendmail-cf/cf/generic-linux.mc. On Caldera it's /usr/share/sendmail/cf/cf/generic-col2.2.mc.

The rules in sendmail macro file generate the default sendmail configuration file, sendmail.cf. The m4 is a macro processor that reads the macro file and generates the configuration file. Unless you plan for sendmail to use your own customized rules in a complex configuration, you can leave the macro file and macro processor alone. For more information on changing sendmail's rules in the macro file, see the MailadminHOWTO on the CD-ROM.

An example of a macro in / is the OSTYPE macro that names the operating system. Remember that sendmail runs on many different operating systems — not just UNIX and Linux. On a Linux system, if you look at sendmail's macro file, you see the line:

```
OSTYPE(`linux')
```

which tells sendmail which operating system it's running on so that sendmail runs properly. On Linux, the OSTYPE macro comes predefined so that you don't need to worry about it.

If you really want complete, technical information about the macro file and how it works, read the /usr/lib/sendmail-cf/README file.

```
[ -f /usr/sbin/sendmail ] || exit 0

RETVAL=0

start() {
        # Start daemons.

    echo -n "Starting sendmail: "
    /usr/bin/newaliases > /dev/null 2>&1
    for i in virtusertable access domaintable mailertable ; do
            if [ -f /etc/mail/$i ] ; then
                makemap hash /etc/mail/$i < /etc/mail/$i
            fi
    done
daemon /usr/sbin/sendmail $([ "$DAEMON" = yes ] && echo -bd) \
                          $([ -n "$QUEUE" ] && echo -q$QUEUE)
```

Configuring POP3

The steps involved in setting up POP3 include:

1. Install the package that contains the POP3 daemon.

2. Edit the file, /etc/inetd.conf, to make POP3 services available.

3. Restart the inetd daemon to make the changes in step 2 take effect.

4. Check that the POP3 daemon is accepting connections.

Your Linux operating system installation procedure may have already set up POP3 for you. Before you start setting up POP3, therefore, you should use your favorite package manager to query whether POP3 is already installed. The command below, for example, uses rpm to display all installed packages on your system.

Tip

Some Linux distributions, such as Red Hat, bundle IMAP4 and POP3 software together. On Red Hat, for example, when you query the RPM database for POP3, you need to look for it under the IMAP name, as below:

```
root@flyingpenguin# rpm -q imap
```

Cross-Reference

Chapter 7, "Installing Software Packages" describes how to use various package managers to query and install packages.

Configuring IMAP4

To configure IMAP4, you follow the same basic steps as with POP3 in the previous section:

1. Install the package that contains the IMAP4 daemon.

2. Edit the file, /etc/inetd.conf, to make IMAP4 services available. This is usually taken care of when you install Linux.

3. Restart the inetd daemon to make the changes in step 2 take effect.

4. Check that the POP3 daemon is accepting connections. You can telnet to your own computer on port 143 as below to see whether IMAP4 is accepting connections:

```
Miss_scarlet@redbird# telnet localhost 143
Trying 127.0.0.1...
telnet:Connected to localhost.
Esc character is '^'.
* OK localhost IMAP4rev1 v11.240 server ready
```

Your Linux operating system installation procedure may have already set up POP3 for you. Before you start setting up POP3, therefore, you should use your favorite package manager to query whether POP3 is already installed.

Setting up aliases to make life easier

Mail aliases are useful for creating distribution lists and for making access to users more convenient. For example, if people have trouble spelling marshall_wilensky, you can create an alias, marshall_wilenski so that if someone misspells the name, the mail still reaches Marshall. You can also alias a nonexistent user to a real user. For example, you could set up an alias, author, which redirects all mail sent to "author" to user Candace. The aliases file is usually /etc/aliases. The example below contains entries for:

✦ System aliases for mailer-daemon and postmaster, which are required.

✦ Redirections for pseudo accounts such as lp, shutdown, and daemon. Most of these are all aliased to root by default, but you can change them.

✦ User aliases, such as wilenski

✦ Distribution lists, such as TCPAuthors.

```
# Basic system aliases -- these MUST be present.
mailer-daemon:  postmaster
postmaster:     root
# General redirections for pseudo accounts.
daemon:         root
lp:             root
sync:           root
shutdown:       root
usenet:         news
ftpadm:         ftp
ftpadmin:       ftp
ftp-adm:        ftp
ftp-admin:      ftp

# trap decode to catch security attacks
decode:         root

# Person who should get root's mail
root:           candace

#Users
miss_scarlet:       bad_girl
wilensky:                   marshall_wilenski, marshall

#Distribution lists
candace, marshall:                  TCPAuthors
emily, elly, emma@fakeremote.com   :   Kids
```

Tip   You can use either local or remote addresses. This feature can be handy when users move to another system. You can disable their accounts on your computer, but continue to forward their mail to their new address.

To create an entry in the aliases file, use your favorite editor. Each entry consists of the username, a colon, space(s) or tab(s), and the alias. After you save the file, you must run the newaliases command to make the changes take effect. This is because sendmail looks at the binary file /etc/mail/aliases.db to read alias information. The newaliases command reads your aliases text file and updates the binary file.

Other files and commands that work with sendmail

Glancing through your sendmail configuration file shows that sendmail uses several files. The following list describes some of these files. Your system may not use all of these files.

/usr/sbin/sendmail	Also /usr/lib/sendmail, depending on your distribution, the sendmail daemon executable image
mailq or sendmail -bp	Shows the contents of the mail queue as below:

```
root@redbird# mailq
/var/spool/mqueue is empty
root@redbird# sendmail -bp
/var/spool/mqueue is empty
```

/var/spool/mqueue	The file that holds the mail queue
depends on distro	The file that holds a user's mail (the mailbox file), as shown in the following example.

```
root@redbird# ls /var/spool/mail/*
-rw-rw----  1 candace  mail      0 Oct 21 23:53 /var/spool/mail/candace
-rw-rw----  1 marshall mail    554 Jan 25 20:48 /var/spool/mail/marshall
-rw-rw----  1 miss_pea mail      0 Jan 19  2000 /var/spool/mail/miss_peacock
-rw-------  1 miss_sca root    7396 Feb 21  2000 /var/spool/mail/miss_scarlet
-rw-------  1 root     root    6416 Jan 26 04:02 /var/spool/mail/root
-rw-rw----  1 sherlock mail    513 Oct 21 22:48 /var/spool/mail/sherloc
```

Tip For security, be sure that all mailbox files are readable and writable only by their owners.

/etc/mail/access	List of addresses not permitted to send mail to your system
/etc/mail/relay-domains	List of hosts that are permitted to relay e-mail through your system
/etc/mail/local-host-names	Other names for your system
/etc/mail/virtusertable	Maps e-mail addresses to usernames on the system

Configuring the E-mail Client Side

You need to configure an e-mail client (MUA) before you and your users can read and send e-mail. The MUA(s) you decide to configure depend on user preferences and which user interfaces are available on your computer. If your Linux system has no GUI, you must choose a text-based e-mail client. The sections below show you how to configure one GUI MUA (Netscape Messenger) and one text-based MUA (elm). Although the steps vary for other clients, the basic concepts are the same for configuring all MUAs.

Introducing Netscape Messenger

Most Linux users are familiar with Netscape Navigator, the browser that comes with Linux. Navigator is just one program in the Netscape Communicator suite. Another program in the Communicator suite is the Netscape Messenger e-mail client program. Since most major distributions include Netscape Communicator, you probably already have the package installed on your system. As usual with configuring software, you should use your favorite package manager query to be sure you have Messenger. The following example uses rpm (piped through grep to search for all packages that include "netscape" in their name) to query all installed packages to determine whether the Netscape package is installed.

```
root@flyingpenguin# rpm -qa | grep netscape
netscape-communicator-4.75-2
netscape-common-4.75-2
netscape-navigator-4.75-2
```

Cross-Reference Chapter 7," Installing Software Packages," describes how to install new software packages.

Tip There are many places on the Web to find Netscape Communicator and its tools. You can see a list of Communicator packages for various distributions at http://rpmfind.net/linux/rpm2html/search.php?query=netscape.

Netscape Messenger has several advantages:

✦ It's easy to configure.

✦ It's easy to use.

✦ It integrates well with Netscape Navigator.

The major disadvantage of Messenger is that it runs somewhat slowly.

Tip You can open the Messenger window from within the Navigator browser by pressing the keys, ALT-2.

Configuring Netscape Messenger

Setting up Netscape Messenger consists of three main parts:

1. Filling out forms.
    1. The Identity form tells Messenger who you are.
    2. The Mail Server form tells Messenger which e-mail server to retrieve your mail from.
3. Configuring the incoming Mail Server.
4. Configuring the outgoing Mail Server.

Filling out the Messenger form

To display the Identity and Mail Server forms, start Messenger and select Preferences from the Edit menu. Expand the "Mail and Newsgroups" item by clicking on its arrow as in Figure 24-1. Select Identity from the menu to display the Identity dialog box. Add your name and e-mail address in the dialog box as shown in Figure 24-2.

Note The figures show examples from Netscape Communicator, version 4.75-2. Some screens may differ from yours, depending on what version of Netscape Communicator you run.

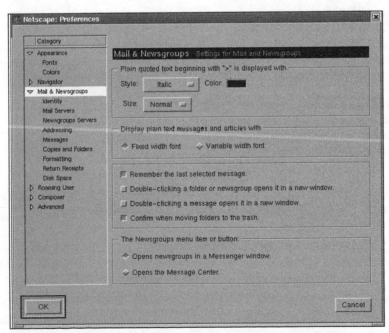

Figure 24-1: Expand Mail and Newsgroups to read the Identity and Mail Servers choices

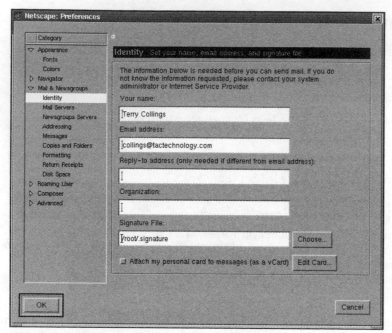

Figure 24-2: Add your username and e-mail address to create your e-mail identity

Filling out the Mail Server form

Next you need to let Messenger know which of your ISP's servers will deliver your e-mail. If you're a user, ask your system administrator for this information. If you're the system administrator, you will have already set this up when you selected an ISP.

Click on Mail Servers. A list of mail servers that Messenger can fetch mail from appears in the top part of the dialog box. Select a server to deliver your incoming mail and click the Edit button to fill in your username and local mail directory. When you're done filling in the form, click Add. In Figure 24-3, the Mail Servers box shows that both the POP3 server and the SMTP server reside at the ISP.

Caution Although the list may include multiple mail servers, you can only choose one mail server unless you use the IMAP4 protocol.

Configuring Messenger's Incoming Mail Server

When you click on the add button next to a server on the list, a form appears for you to fill in. You need to choose a server type from POP3 and IMAP4. You must specify your username and password and some protocol-related parameters.

Tip Be sure to type your username and password exactly the same as they are spelled on your ISP's server.

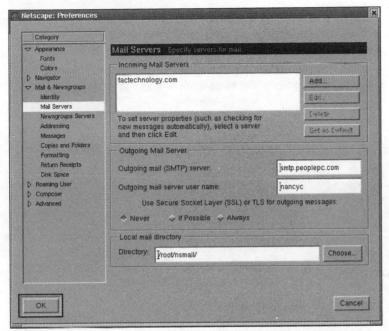

Figure 24-3: Set up your incoming and outgoing mail servers

If you are using an MTA such as sendmail (described earlier in this chapter) or smail with the fetchmail program (also described earlier), you need to select the `movemail` option. The mta and fetchmail cooperate to retrieve your mail messages and insert them into a mail folder, usually a subdirectory (named after your account) under /var/spool/mail. Be sure to tell Messenger the name of the subdirectory where movemail can find your e-mail.

Configuring Messenger's Outgoing Mail Server

The way you set up the Outgoing Mail Server depends on whether you run your own MTA and SMTP server or whether the SMTP server belongs to your ISP. If you have your own SMTP server and MTA, you choose the hostname of the computer where your SMTP server runs.

Tip If your SMTP server runs on the same computer as Messenger, you can select localhost.

If you want outgoing mail to go directly to your ISP, type the hostname of your ISP's SMTP server. Some ISP's require that you enter your account name again.

Using Netscape Messenger

Once Messenger is configured, you can run it separately or inside the Navigator window. The Messenger window contains three parts:

✦ A list of your folders

✦ A list of e-mail messages in the currently selected folder

✦ The e-mail message you are currently reading

Tip   You can resize the three parts of the Messenger window by dragging the separator lines.

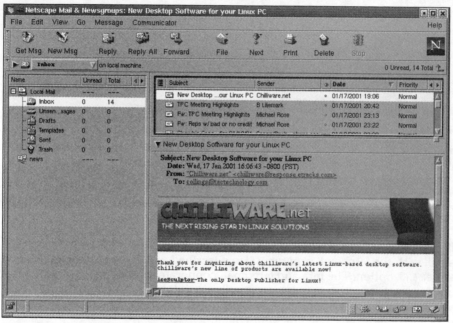

Figure 24-4: Looking inside the Messenger window

Within Messenger, you have three choices for retrieving your messages:

✦ From the File menu, select File/Get New Messages.

✦ Click on Get Msg on the toolbar.

✦ Press Alt+2.

Reading messages, storing them in folders, and deleting them is easy, but when in doubt, use the Help menu on the far right of the window.

Note   If your mail resides on a POP3 or IMAP4 server, Messenger asks for your password before retrieving your messages into your inbox folder.

You also have three choices for composing messages:

✦ From the Message menu, select Message/New Message.

✦ Click on New Msg on the toolbar.

✦ Press Alt+m.

Messenger displays a form where you enter the message and the e-mail addresses of the recipients. Figure 24-5 shows the Compose window with a message in progress. When you're finished composing your message you can either send it immediately or select Send Later from the File menu (the Alt+Shift+Enter key combination). If you want to send your message immediately, select Send Now from the File menu or press the Alt+Enter key combination.

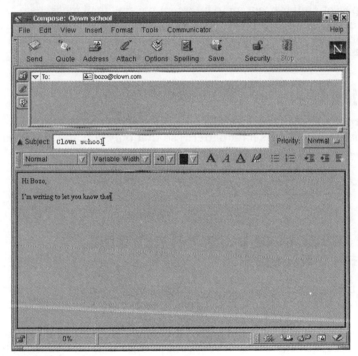

Figure 24-5: The Compose window

Caution

If you are using the SMTP server at your ISP, be sure that you are connected to the ISP before sending your message.

If you select Send Later, Messenger stores your mail message in the Unsent folder. The messages remain there until you connect to your ISP and select Send Unsent Messages from the File menu.

Tips for Securing your E-mail System

Do you think you have nothing to hide? Maybe you don't, but e-mail security is always a privacy issue even if you aren't mailing credit card numbers or corporate secrets. Using S/MIME for security is only a first step in protecting your users and you.

Protect against eavesdropping

Your mail message goes through more computers than just yours and your recipient's because of store and forward techniques. All a cracker has to do to snoop on your mail is use a packet sniffer program to intercept passing mail messages. A *packet sniffer* is intended to be a tool that a network administrator uses to record and analyze network traffic, but the bad guys use packet sniffers too. There are dozens of free packet sniffing programs available on the Internet.

Use encryption

Cryptography isn't just for secret agents. Many e-mail products allow your messages to be encrypted (coded in a secret pattern) so that only you and your recipient can read them. Lotus Notes provides e-mail encryption, for example.

Read Chapter 29, "Securing a Linux System," for more on encryption.

Protect your intranet or personal desktop computer with a firewall

If you receive mail from people outside your network, you should set up a firewall to protect your network. The *firewall* is a computer that prevents unauthorized data from reaching your network. For example, if you don't want anything from `snoopers.com` to penetrate your net, put your net behind a firewall. The firewall blocks out all `snoopers.com` messages. If you work on one computer dialed in to an ISP, you can still install a firewall. Several vendors provide personal firewalls, and some of them are free if you don't want a lot of bells and whistles.

Read Chapter 29, "Securing a Linux System," for more information on firewalling.

Don't get bombed, spammed, or spoofed

Bombing happens when someone continually sends the same message to an e-mail address either accidentally or maliciously. If you reside in the United States and you receive 200 or more copies of the same message from the same person, you can report the bomber to the U. S. Federal Bureau of Investigation. The FBI has a National Computer Crimes Squad in Washington, DC.

You can reach the National Computer Crimes Squad at the following telephone number: 202-325-9164.

Spamming is a variation of bombing. A spammer sends junk mail to many users (hundreds and even thousands) of users. It's easy to be an accidental spammer. If you choose your e-mail's "Reply All" function, and you send a reply to a worldwide distribution list, you are a spammer.

The person who goes on holiday and sets up an automatic mail responder program needs to be careful. A man who worked at a major U.S. corporation incorrectly set up his auto-responder message, "I'm out of the office on vacation for 10 days" to go to all mailing list messages he received. A thief used this information to rob the empty house.

Spoofing happens when someone sends you e-mail from a fake address. If spoofing doesn't seem like it could be major problem for you, consider this: you get e-mail from a system administrator telling you to use a specific password for security reasons. Many people will comply because the system administrator knows best. Imagine the consequences if a spoofer sends this e-mail faking the system administrator's e-mail address to all the users on a computer. All of a sudden, the spoofer knows everyone's passwords and has access to private and possibly sensitive or secret data.

Spoofing is possible because plain SMTP does not have authentication capabilities. Without authentication features, SMTP can't be sure that incoming mail is really from the address it says it is. Chapter 29 explains authentication in more detail. If your mail server allows connections to the SMTP port, anyone with a little knowledge of the internal workings of SMTP can connect to that port and send you e-mail that appears to be from a spoofed address. Besides connecting to the SMTP port of a site, a user can send spoofed e-mail by modifying his or her Web browser interfaces.

You can protect your data and configure your mail system to make mail fraud more difficult. If someone invades your mail system, you should report the intrusion to the Computer Emergency Response Team (CERT). You can find the reporting form on the Internet at `ftp://info.cert.org/pub/incident_ reporting_form`.

Be careful with SMTP

Use dedicated mail servers. First of all, keep the number of computers vulnerable to SMTP-based attacks to a minimum. Have only one or a few centralized e-mail central servers, depending on the size of your organization. (See the case study in the sidebar.)

Only allow SMTP connections that come from outside your firewall to go to those few central e-mail servers. This policy protects the other computers on your network. If your site gets spammed, you have to clean up the central e-mail servers, but the rest of your networked computers will be OK.

Case Study

The fictitious users (Miss Scarlet and her partners in crime) in this book use a central e-mail server that sits in a "DMZ" — demilitarized zone behind the computer that runs their company's firewall software and in front of the computers that serve up mail to the company's intranet. The central e-mail server runs an MTA and keeps a directory of users within the corporate intranet. The directory can be something as simple as a list of e-mail aliases, such as miss_scarlet@cardinalconsulting.com means miss_scarlet@redbird.cardinalconsulting.com. The directory means that when I send to mail to Miss Scarlet, I don't need to know exactly which computer is serving her mail.

Besides being a security technique, this is very convenient! When I send e-mail to Miss Scarlet, my message goes across the Internet to Miss Scarlet's firewall, which accepts or rejects my message based on my address. Once my message passes through the firewall, it continues to Miss Scarlet's intranet to the MTA on redbird, which serves up mail to Miss Scarlet and her coworkers. Finally, redbird forwards my message to Miss Scarlet's personal computer and notifies her that she has mail.

New Feature

If you use packet filtering, you only need to configure your e-mail servers. Packet filtering analyzes packets based on the source and destination addresses. The analysis decides whether to accept the packets and pass them through to your networks or to reject them as being unsafe. Firewalls often use packet-filtering techniques. The latest stable kernel, 2.4, has built-in packet filtering capabilities.

The News about News

News is a bit of a misnomer in the technology world. It really has nothing to do with journalism. *Newsgroups* are public electronic discussion groups called forums. A newsgroup may reside on a single computer with no network access or on any kind of network. Usenet is a TCP/IP service for the world's largest collection of newsgroups. Each newsgroup is an electronic conversation group about a particular topic. When computer users talk about "news," they usually mean Usenet news. At last count, there were over 30,000 newsgroups dedicated to pursuits as varied as culinary arts to skydiving.

To get news on any of these topics, you first need access to a news server. Usually, your ISP provides this access, but if you want to run your own news server, you need to set up your news transport software — the NNTP server.

Why would you want to run your own news server? If you manage a large intranet, it's more convenient and performs better to run your own news server on the intranet. Your news server must connect to the Internet if users want to participate in newsgroups outside of your intranet. Then users connect to your intranet's news server rather than each user having a separate connection to an ISP. Another benefit of running your own news server is that you can create private newsgroups as forums for business, organizational, and technical topics. These private news-groups are only available inside your intranet.

Activating the NNTP Server

NNTP, which stands for *Network News Transport Protocol,* is built into all current news handling software for Linux today. NNTP's success comes from the fact that it was one of the first news programs that used the TCP/IP style protocol in its con-nection between a news client and a news server.

The NNTP server can run as either a program managed by the all-important Internet daemon—inetd—that controls all Internet connections on a Linux box, or as a standalone server program that starts at boot time. If you decide to run NNTP at boot time, you need to edit the /etc/rc.inet2 file.

If you want to start it from the Internet daemon, complete the following steps.

1. Log in as the root administrative account.

2. Open the file /etc/inetd.conf.

3. Look for the following line in the file:

   ```
   #nntp  stream  tcp nowait  news /usr/etc/in.nntpd  nntpd
   ```

4. Delete the hash mark in front of the line, then save and quit. A hash mark in Linux tells the machine to ignore the line. Removing the mark is the equiva-lent to turning a switch to on, since Linux ignores it.

Tip

If you can't find the line to uncomment, type the line in yourself. Be sure to omit the hash mark.

5. Open the file /etc/services.

6. Look for the following line:

   ```
   #nntp 119/tcp readnews untp  # Network News Transfer Protocol
   ```

7. Again, uncomment this line or type it in.

8. Next, create a directory for your news to be stored (also known as *spooled*). It's best to create this in the /tmp directory so that it will be removed upon a reboot of the system. Do this by typing the following at the command prompt and pressing Enter.

   ```
   mkdir /var/spool/news/tmp
   ```

9. Finally, use the chown command to change the ownership of the file to the news system account:

   ```
   chown news.news /var/spool/news/tmp
   ```

Reading the Newsgroups in pine

The pine program allows you to read the Internet's newsgroups. While using pine as a newsreader has declined in recent years as Netscape has become more popular, this is still a good method, particularly if you're running an older, slower machine that could benefit from the relative quickness of a non-graphical newsreader.

To get your pine mail reader to handle newsgroups, you need to create the .newsrc file that pine reads to determine which newsgroups that you want to read. To do this, complete the following steps:

1. Using vi, create a file called .newsrc.

2. Type in the list of newsgroups you'd like to read about. For example, your list might include:

   ```
   misc.games
   alt.automobiles_used
   comp.linux.caldera
   ```

3. Save and quit the file.

4. Next, complete the process by configuring the pine mail program to handle NNTP-based news. Start pine at the command line by typing **pine**.

5. Type **S** for Setup

6. Type **C** to get to the configuration screen.

7. Use the down arrow key to move the cursor down to highlight nntp-server.

8. Press **C** to change the configuration.

9. Type in the name of your ISP's news server, then press Enter.

10. Type **Q** to exit pine.

11. When pine asks you if you want to save the changes, press **Y** for yes.

From now on, when you start up pine and look at your mail folders, you'll also have the option to look at your listed newsgroups.

Configuring Netscape for News

Today, the most popular option is to configure Netscape to handle your news as well as electronic mail for you. Netscape news is a lot more user friendly for many people because it looks like Outlook, Internet Explorer, or Eudora.

Note   You must be running a GUI to use Netscape.

To configure Netscape to handle news, perform the following steps:

1. Start Netscape Communicator.

2. Click the Edit pull-down menu at the top of the screen.

3. Select Preferences by clicking on it.

4. The Preferences screen appears. You'll see a list of Categories on the left-hand side of the Preference screen.

5. Mid-way down the list of choices is Mail & Newsgroups. Click on arrow immediately to the left of this setting. The arrow will flip down and you'll get a menu of different categories under the Mail & Newsgroups listing.

6. Click Newsgroups Servers. The screen to the right will list the settings, which will list only the default News, since you haven't set anything yet. (See Figure 24-6)

7. If you don't want to use the default or your ISP instructs you not to, click the Add button

8. A new screen appears where you can type in the server's name in the blank text field. (See Figure 24-7)

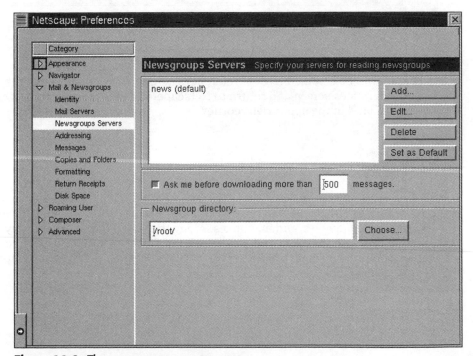

Figure 24-6: The newsgroup servers screen

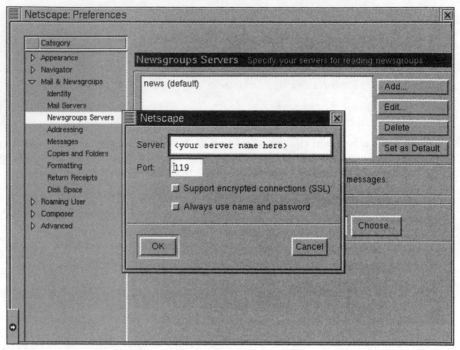

Figure 24-7: Adding a news server

9. Click OK when you're finished.

10. You will be returned to the Preferences screen. If you want to exit the Preferences screen and return to Netscape, click the close button, marked with an X in the upper right corner.

Summary

This chapter follows an e-mail message from sender to recipient as the message passes through MUAs, MTAs (sendmail), TCP/IP protocols, LDAs, mail notification programs, mail queues, and mailboxes. Along the way the chapter shows you how to configure both the client and server sides of an e-mail system. The chapter also shows you how to set up a news server so that users can read and participate in Usenet discussions and forums.

✦　　✦　　✦

Configuring an FTP Server

FTP is an acronym for *File Transfer Protocol,* which is a part of the TCP/IP suite of protocols. As the name indicates, this protocol is used to transfer files between two systems. The most widely used version of FTP was developed in the early 1990s at Washington University in St. Louis and is called wu-ftp.

Because FTP is part of TCP/IP, any system that uses TCP/IP can share files via FTP. Consequently, FTP is the most common way to share files of any type among systems, whether or not they are using the same operating system. A good example of this can be found on countless Internet sites that enable you to download files. In this example one of the systems acts as the server and the other is the client. For FTP to work, the server must be properly configured and accepting requests for FTP from the client system. In this chapter you will learn how to set up an FTP server and client and how to start an FTP session.

Obtaining and Installing the Software

Since FTP is the most common way to share files between systems, FTP is installed by default on all current distributions of Linux. Depending on your distribution — when it was installed and how often you update files — the version of wu-ftp on your system may not be the latest release. It is usually a good practice to upgrade to the latest version since new releases may fix any bugs that may be present.

The most recent version of wu-ftp can be obtained from the wu-ftp Web site at www.wu-ftp.org. The readme file at the wu-ftp site recommends obtaining the binary files, if possible, to save time and trouble. The file to obtain for a Linux system is wu-ftp-2.6.0-i386-linux.tar.gz; or get the rpm version of the file, wu-ftpd-inet-2.6.0-1.i386-Linux-6x.rpm. After obtaining the rpm version, I installed it on my system using kpackage, which is included with KDE.

Figure 25-1 shows the kpackage program that is used to install rpms.

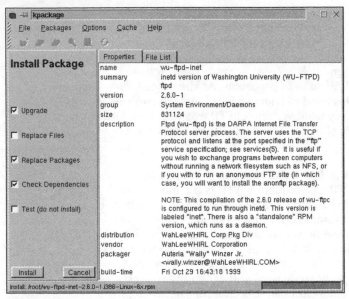

Figure 25-1: The kpackage program that is used to install rpms

Installing the package sets up everything required to make the FTP service available. The FTP service is controlled by the inetd daemon and is started when the system boots. The FTP daemon is called ftpd and you can verify if it will start at system startup by looking at the /etc/inetd.conf file and looking for the in.ftpd listing in the FTP line of the file. Figure 25-2 shows the inetd.conf file and the listing for the FTP server.

The inetd program listens for requests for services that have been configured in the /etc/inetd.conf file and also the /etc/services file. The /etc/services file defines which port the configured service will use. In the case of FTP, this is port 21. Figure 25-3 shows a typical /etc/services file.

When a request for FTP services is received by the inetd daemon, it starts the FTP daemon in.ftpd. To be sure that FTP is enabled, you just need to check the two previously mentioned files, find the lines referring to FTP, and remove the hash (#) from the beginning of the line if it is there.

After the server is configured, users gain access through user accounts. On a local network a user can just use his or her login id and password to authenticate to the FTP server, as shown in Figure 25-4.

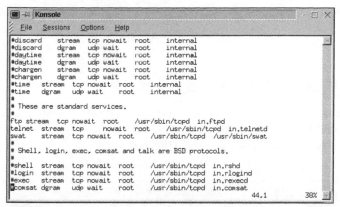

Figure 25-2: The line beginning with ftp shows that the FTP service is enabled by default

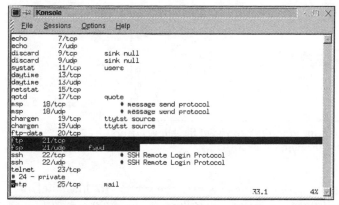

Figure 25-3: The /etc/services file shows that ftp is configured to use port 21

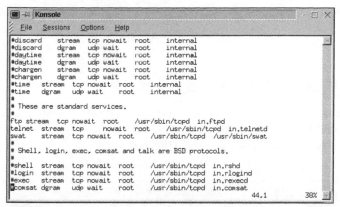

Figure 25-4: Local users can log in to an FTP session by using their login ids and passwords

This works fine for local users, but suppose you want to allow access to a remote user on the Internet. You need to allow that user to log in anonymously.

Understanding Anonymous FTP

Anonymous FTP is typically enabled by default when the FTP server software is installed. A user account login is also created for anonymous users in the /etc/passwd file. The account is called ftp and is shown in Figure 25-5.

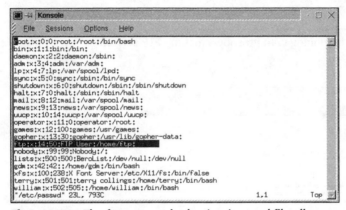

Figure 25-5: The ftp account in the /etc/passwd file allows users to log in using the name anonymous or ftp

Anonymous FTP enables anyone who can access the system to download, or upload if allowed, files from anywhere—regardless of his or her identity.

Understanding FTP Directory Locations

The FTP server installation program also creates an FTP directory structure, which is located at /home/ftp. The /home/ftp directory contains four sub-directories:

```
/home/ftp/bin
/home/ftp/lib
/home/ftp/etc
/home/ftp/pub
```

To grant access to files, you need only place them in the /home/ftp/pub directory. When a user logs in to FTP, he or she will have read-only access to any files, or directories, that you placed in the /home/ftp/pub directory. Users cannot access any files in the other three directories.

If you want to allow users to upload files, you can create a directory under /pub for this purpose. It is a good idea to create a separate partition for this directory to keep it from filling up and causing problems for the rest of your system. This directory should also be set to write only to enable you to check the content of any uploaded files before releasing them to the public.

Understanding Access Control

There are four ways to control who is allowed to access the FTP server. Three of these methods involve changing files and one is simply stopping the server. We'll look at changing files first.

The /etc/ftpaccess file, as its name indicates, is used to control who can access the server. This file is also used to configure messages that the user receives and the services he can perform while logged in. To disable access for user login, find the line beginning with class and remove the class of user. Figure 25-6 shows the /etc/ftpaccess file. More details about the /etc/ftpaccess file can be found in the ftpaccess man page.

The /etc/passwd file you looked at earlier (See Figure 25-5) contains an entry for the ftp user. By removing or commenting out the ftp user line, you are disabling all anonymous logins.

The /etc/ftpusers file contains a list of users who are not allowed to use the FTP server. To exclude additional users, just add them to the /etc/ftpusers file. Figure 25-7 shows the default /etc/ftpusers file.

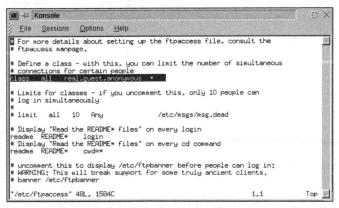

Figure 25-6: The class line shows the class of users allowed to access the FTP server

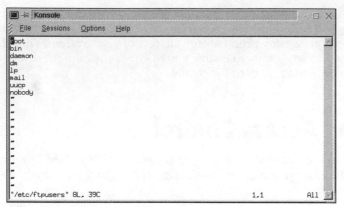

Figure 25-7: The /etc/ftpusers file shows the users who are not allowed to access the FTP server

The most drastic step you can use to control access to the FTP server is to shut it down. Simply issue the command `ftpshut` *time*, where *time* is the time for the server to shutdown. Whenever someone tries to login to the FTP server, the user will receive a message like that shown in Figure 25-8.

A file called shutmsg is created in the /etc directory that is read whenever someone tries to connect to the server. To enable the FTP server again, all you need to do is delete the /etc/shutmsg file.

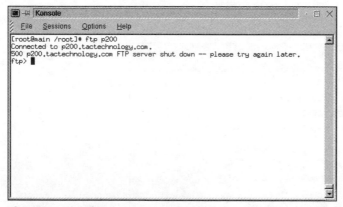

Figure 25-8: When a user tries to log in to an FTP server that has been shut down, a message appears

Understanding the FTP Client

All Linux distributions have a standard command-line FTP client. In addition, most distributions have a graphical client, such as the one included with the Netscape Web browser. The command-line FTP client is easy to use and many of the commands have the same function as other Linux commands. For example, the `ls` command that is used to show a directory listing at a Linux shell prompt also has the same function in FTP.

The first command you need to issue is the command to access the FTP server. The command is just `ftp` followed by the name of the FTP server. In Figure 25-9, I am logging into the server main on my local network. The server asks for a name and then a password. An anonymous user can enter either `ftp` or `anonymous` as the name, and whatever she likes as the password, but it is customary to provide an e-mail address as the password.

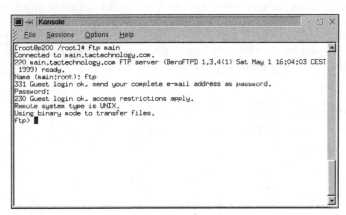

Figure 25-9: An anonymous user logs into our FTP server

When an anonymous user logs in to the FTP server, access is restricted to the /home/ftp/ directory that you looked at in the file directory location section. Anonymous users can see any files or directories located here, and can download files from the pub directory.

If a local user logs into the FTP server, that user will use his or her regular user name and password. The local user will be placed at his or her home directory. For example, the user Terry logs into the server and can then browse his home directory. (See Figure 25-10)

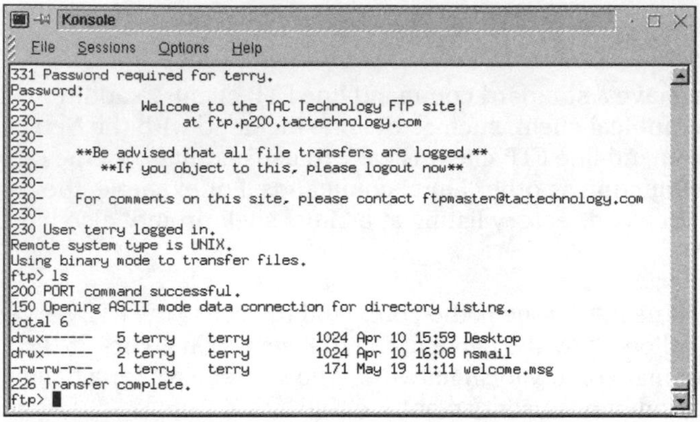

Figure 25-10: User Terry logs in and can browse his home directory

For both users logging in, the connection is made when the ftp> prompt appears. They can now choose from among many commands. For a listing of these commands type help or ? at the ftp> prompt. Further help can be obtained by typing help and then the item you want help with. Figure 25-11 shows the result of the help command and then requesting help on a specific item.

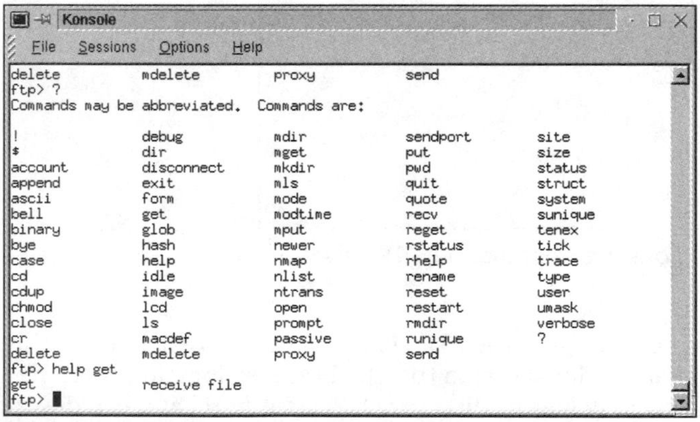

Figure 25-11: You can use the help command to get a list of commands and help on a specific command

Several of the commands switch between modes and parameters. To see a listing of the default modes or parameters, type status at the ftp> prompt. To change the mode from those listed as defaults by the status command, type the parameter you wish to change. For example, the default file-transfer mode is set to binary. To change it to ascii, just type the word ascii. Figure 25-12 shows the default status and Figure 25-13 shows the status after changing to ascii mode.

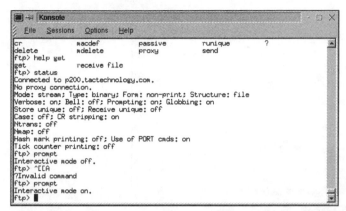

Figure 25-12: The status command shows the current ftp settings

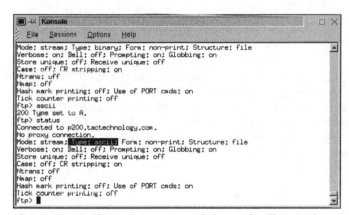

Figure 25-13: The status command shows the file-transfer mode changed from binary to ascii

Downloading files using the command-line ftp session is quite easy. You just need to locate the file or files you want to download by using the cd and ls commands to change to the appropriate directory and list the files. These two commands are exactly the same as the Linux cd and ls commands.

In Figure 25-14 I have changed to the /home/ftp/pub directory and then used the ls command to get a list of files. Then, using the mget command and answering y to the prompts, I download all the sawmill files.

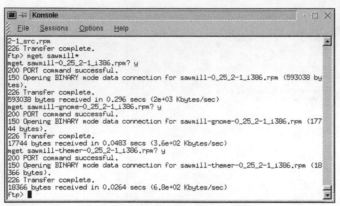

Figure 25-14: Downloading multiple files using the mget command
after using cd to change directories and ls to get a directory listing.

Summary

In this chapter you learned about File Transport Protocol (FTP). FTP is the most
commonly used protocol for transferring files across the Internet. FTP allows anyone to log in to an FTP server from any location without a password. Once logged
in, the client can access and download those files allowed by the FTP server. You
learned about obtaining the latest version of the FTP software and its installation
and configuration. You also learned how to access an FTP server as a client, browse
directories, and download files.

✦   ✦   ✦

Configuring a Web Server

In this chapter you'll learn about Web-server software — chiefly Apache Web Server, which is included with most current distributions of Linux.

The Apache Web Server

The most popular Web-server software in use today is the Apache Web server. According to the statistics from the Apache Web site more than 60 percent of all Web servers run the Apache software. All current Linux distributions include the Apache Web-server software and most of them install it by default.

In many cases the Web-server software is also started by default: it is probably already running on your system. You can easily see if this is the case by starting a Web browser under the X-server and typing `http://localhost` into the browser's location line. If you see a screen like the one in Figure 26-1, then your Apache Web server is running. Depending on your distribution, your page may appear slightly different from the one in the figure.

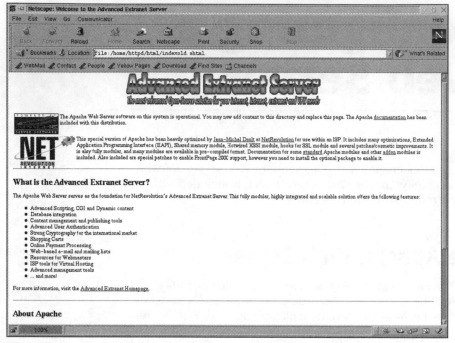

Figure 26-1: The default Apache Web-server main page for a Mandrake distribution

If the Web server is not running, it doesn't necessarily mean that it is not installed on your system. Check to see if the software is installed on your system by using the `locate`, `find`, or `whereis` command from a command prompt. If I use the `whereis` command on my system, I see the following:

```
/usr/sbin/httpd /etc/httpd /  /usr/man/man8/httpd.8.bz2
```

This indicates that the httpd daemon is in /usr/sbin, the httpd directory is in /etc, and the man page is in /usr/man.man8. If you see output like this, the software is installed on your system and just needs to be started. If you do not see the /etc/httpd directory, you will need to install Apache on your system. We will install Apache in the next section.

Obtaining and Installing the Software

The most recent release of Apache is version 1.3.14 and you can get it from the Apache Web site, www.apache.org. You can also get the source or binary files from the Apache site.

You can also download the package files for your distribution from the distribution's Web site or one of the mirror sites. I always try to find the packages specifically designed for the distribution that I am using. This saves a lot of time and trouble by eliminating the need to compile the source code and then install the software. The packages take care of both of these steps, and since they were built to work with the distribution, they rarely cause configuration problems.

Installing the Apache package for your distribution will create several directories and install documentation and configuration files. The configuration files are typically located in /etc/httpd/conf or /etc/httpd/apache/conf, depending on your distribution. The documentation files, which are provided by the Apache group to assist you in setting up the server and are quite extensive, are typically located in /home/httpd/html/manual.

Configuration files

If you look in the /etc/httpd/conf directory, you can see the main configuration file, httpd.conf. In earlier versions of Apache there were three configuration files: httpd.conf, srm.conf, and access.conf.

In version 1.3.14 there is just the httpd.conf file, so this is the only file with which you need to be concerned. The /etc/httpd/conf directory contains two more files: the magic file and the mime.types file.

Both of these files specify MIME types for different file extensions.

Finally, files ending with -dist are sample configuration files distributed by the Apache organization. You can use these files by removing the -dist extension.

Located in the /etc/httpd directory are the logs folder and the modules folder. Both of these are symbolic links containing logs pointing to /var/log/httpd and modules pointing to /usr/lib/apache, respectively. Remember that, depending on your distribution, these file locations may not be exactly the same on your system.

The directories that remote users can access are located at /home/httpd/html. This is the default directory that the server will search when someone accesses the system. Also located in /home/httpd are the cgi-bin and icon directories. These directories are available to remote users who can call them by going through the Web server.

Configuration directives

The /etc/httpd/conf/httpd.conf file, shown in Figure 26-2, contains many sections that provide instructions to the Web server about its operation. These sections contain configuration options, called *directives,* of which there are nearly 200. We look at some of the most common directives by dissecting the default httpd.conf file and looking at the default settings. For a complete listing of all directives and their uses, refer to the Apache manual located at /home/httpd/html/manual.

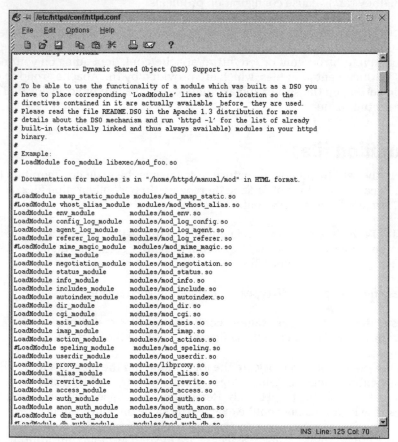

Figure 26-2: The httpd.conf file showing the Dynamic Shared Object section

The first section of httpd.conf is called Dynamic Shared Object (DSO) Support. In this section are the modules that will be loaded when the httpd daemon is started by the server. You must load the appropriate module to be able to use directives. The Apache manual contains a complete description of modules and how to use them.

Immediately following the DSO section of the httpd.conf file is the Name Space and Server Settings section. The directives in this section affect how the name space that users see will appear and also how requests will be handled and formatted for display.

The Name Space directives are shown in Table 26-1, each with a description and an example of its usage.

Table 26-1
Name Space Directives

Directive	Function	Example
DocumentRoot	The default directory location of files presented to users.	DocumentRoot /home/httpd/html
UserDir	The name of the directory appended onto a user's home directory when a user request is received.	UserDir public_html
DirectoryIndex	The files to use for HTML requests to the site.	files named index.htm, index.html
FancyIndexing	Indicates whether indexing should be fancy or standard toggle.	FancyIndexing on/off
AddIcons	Tells the server which icon to show for each file type.	AddIconByType (TXT,/icons/text.gif) text/*
DefaultIcon	Sets icon for files without an explicitly set icon.	DefaultIcon /icons/unknown.gif
ReadmeName	The default readme file.	ReadmeName readme
HeaderName	File name that should be prepended to directory indexes.	HeaderName header
IndexIgnore	File names that should be ignored by directory indexing.	IndexIgnore *filename1 filename2*
AccessFileName	A file in each directory that provides access control information.	AccessFileName .htaccess
TypesConfig	Specifies location of mime.types file.	TypesConfig /etc/httpd/conf/mime.types

Continued

Table 26-1 *(continued)*

Directive	Function	Example
DefaultType	Specifies default MIME type for documents with file types not listed.	DefaultType text/plain
AddEncoding	If supported by the browser, the browser can uncompress information as it is received.	AddEncoding x-gzip gz
AddLanguage	Specifies the default language of a document.	AddLanguage en .en
LanguagePriority	Sets the priority of the language displayed languages listed in decreasing priority.	LanguagePriority en el it
Redirect	Tells users where to find moved documents.	Redirect different url
Alias	Lists pointers to other items.	/icons /home/httpd/icons
ScriptAlias	Specifies directories containing server scripts.	ScriptAlias *fakename realname*
AddType	Allows you to change mime.types without editing the file.	AddType type/subtype ext1
AddHandler	Allows mapping of some file extensions to handlers.	AddHandler send-as-is asis
Action	Allows execution of scripts by defined media types when matching files are found. Eliminates need for repeated URL pathnames for frequently used cgi files.	Action media/type / cgi-script/location
MetaDir	Specifies directory where meta information files are located.	MetaDir .Web
MetaSuffix	Specifies the file-name suffix for the file containing the meta information.	MetaSuffix .meta
ErrorDocument	Allows specification of routines to handle errors. Returns a string as a value for the ErrorDocument, or the error can be redirected to a static page or cgi script. Examples are shown below.	
ErrorDocument 401	Redirects the user to a local URL for a subscription service.	

Directive	Function	Example
`ErrorDocument 403`	Displays the specified message.	
`ErrorDocument 404`	Redirects to either a local static page (ErrorDocument 404 */whatever*.html) or a cgi script (ErrorDocument 404 /cgi-bin/*whatever*.pl).	
`ErrorDocument 500`	An internal server error that does not display a message to the user.	
`MimeMagicFile`	Using the specified file, the server can get hints about file types.	**MimMagicFile** /etc/httpd/conf/magic
`BrowserMatch`	Disables keepalives and HTTP header flushes. Can also disable HTTP/1.1 responses to browsers that do not support the standard. Used for older browsers such as Netscape 2.x and Internet Explorer 4.0.	**BrowserMatch** "Mozilla/2" nokeepalive

BrowserMatch "MSIE4\.0b2;" nokeepalive downgrade-1.0 force-response-1.0

The next section of the httpd.conf file is called Global Access Configuration. This section specifies the directories the server can access and what services are enabled or disabled in the specified directories.

You can place one or more directives within <Directory> and </Directory> tags. The directives apply only to the named directory and subdirectories of the specified directory. You can use any directive that is allowed in a directory context. The directory is either the full path to a directory or a wild-card string. In a wild-card string, ? matches any single character and * matches any sequence of characters. You may also use character ranges as in the shell. For example:

```
<DIRECTORY /home>
Options Indexes Includes FollowSymLinks
AllowOverride none
</DIRECTORY>
```

Figure 26-3 shows the Global Access Configuration section of the httpd.conf file. As you can see, there are several directories shown in this file containing various directives. We look at the default settings of this section in Table 26-2.

```
#---------------------- Global Access Configuration -----------------------
# This section defines server settings which affect which types of services
# are allowed, and in what circumstances.
# This part of httpd.conf used to be split in access.conf

# Each directory to which Apache has access, can be configured with respect
# to which services and features are allowed and/or disabled in that
# directory (and its subdirectories).

# First, we configure the "default" set of permissions. Used to be
# restrictive, but tweaked by <jmdault@netrevolution.com> to enable
# FrontPage extensions and misc. performance patches.

<Directory />
Options Indexes Includes FollowSymLinks
AllowOverride None
</Directory>

# Note that from this point forward you must specifically allow
# particular features to be enabled - so if something's not working as
# you might expect, make sure that you have specifically enabled it
# below.

# This should be changed to whatever you set DocumentRoot to.

<Directory /home/httpd/html>

# This may also be "None", "All", or any combination of "Indexes",
# "Includes", "FollowSymLinks", "ExecCGI", or "MultiViews".

# Note that "MultiViews" must be named *explicitly* --- "Options All"
# doesn't give it to you.

Options Indexes Includes FollowSymLinks

# This controls which options the .htaccess files in directories can
# override. Can also be "All", or any combination of "Options", "FileInfo",
# "AuthConfig", and "Limit"

AllowOverride All

# Controls who can get stuff from this server.

order allow deny
```

Figure 26-3: The Global Access Configuration specifies the directories and services available to outside users

Table 26-2
Default Settings

Directive	Function
`Options`	Controls which features are available in the specified directory.
	`Indexes` — If a user requests a URL that maps to a directory, and there is no DirectoryIndex (for example,, index.html) in that directory, then the server will return a formatted listing of the directory.
	`Includes` — Server-side includes are enabled.
	`FollowSymLinks` — The server will follow symbolic links in this directory.

Directive	Function
	ExecCGI — Enables execution of CGI scripts.
AllowOverride	When the server finds a .htaccess file, this directive specifies options that the file is allowed to override. Usually set to all or none, but other options are available. See the Apache manual for more information.
order	Specifies the order in which deny and allow are interpreted.

Server configuration

The next section of httpd.conf is used for Server Configuration. When the httpd daemon starts, it reads this section to get IP information, the server name, and other server-related configuration information. Table 26-3 lists the directives in the server configuration section and their uses.

Table 26-3 Directives for Server Configuration	
Directive	**Function**
ServerType	Specifies how the server is run by the system. Options are inetd and standalone. The option recommended by Apache is standalone.
Port	Specifies to which port the standalone server listens. The default port is 80.
HostnameLookups	Specifies whether the names of clients are logged (if set to on) or IP numbers (if set to off).
User	Specifies the user who should run the server.
Group	Specifies the group that should run the server.
ServerAdmin	Specifies the server admin e-mail address (for example, ServerAdmin root@localhost).
ServerRoot	Specifies the location of the server's config, error, and log files (for example, ServerRoot /etc/httpd).
BindAddress	Supports virtual hosts. Specifies either *, an IP address, or a fully qualified domain name.
Listen	Specifies the port to which the server should listen for requests.

Continued

	Table 26-3 *(continued)*
Directive	**Function**
ErrorLog	Specifies the location of the error log file (for example, ErrorLog logs/error_log).
LogLevel	Specifies the number of messages written to the error_log (for example, LogLevel warn).
LogFormat	Specifies nicknames for CustomLog directives (for example, LogFormat "%h %l).
CustomLog	Specifies the location of the access logfile (for example, CustomLog logs/access_log common).
PidFile	Specifies the file to which the server logs the pid (for example, PidFile /var/run/httpd.pid).
ScoreBoardFile	Stores internal server process information (not used in Linux).
LockFile	Specifies path to lockfile.
ServerName	Specifies the host name returned to client for server.
UseCanonicalName	Specifies if the server should generate self-referencing URL from server name:port or from hostname: port.
CacheNegotiatedDocs	Enables caching of negotiated documents.
Timeout	Amount of time before sends and receives time out.
KeepAlive	Specifies whether or not to enable persistent connections (multiple connections).
MaxKeepAliveRequests	Specifies maximum number of keepalive requests allowed during persistent connections.
KeepAliveTimeout	Specifies the number of seconds to wait for the next request.
MinSpareServers	Specifies the minimum number of servers available to accept requests.
MaxSpareServers	Specifies the maximum number of servers available to accept requests.
StartServers	Specifies the number of servers to start.
MaxClients	Specifies the maximum number of clients that can connect at the same time.
MaxRequestsPerChild	Specifies the number of requests a child process can process before dying.
ProxyRequests	Enables proxy server.

Add-on modules and virtual hosts

The last section of the httpd.conf file is called Add-on Modules and Virtual Hosts. This section contains include statements for modules added after Apache is installed. Virtual host includes are also placed here to call the configuration file for the host. Each virtual host has its own configuration file. Figure 26-4 shows the Add-on Modules and Virtual Hosts section of the httpd.conf file for `tactechnology.com`, the sample domain I've been using for the examples in the networking section of this book.

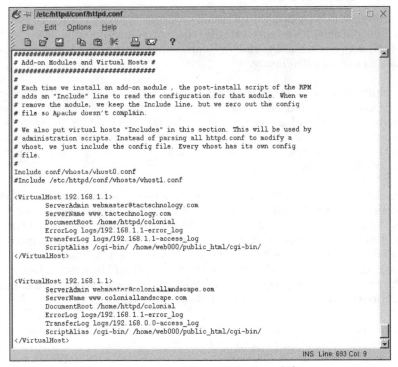

Figure 26-4: The virtual hosts section of httpd.conf shows two virtual hosts

Now that you have looked at the configuration file for the Web server, you are ready to actually configure the server. In the next section you look at several possible server configurations.

Web-Server Configuration

You can configure the Apache Web server to host one or many Web sites. Typically, the Web server runs on a single computer and is configured to serve more than one Web site. This is known as *virtual hosting* and this section shows you how to set it up.

Multiple instances of the Web server on the same computer

With this method, a different instance of the Web server runs for each Web site. This method draws heavily on the computer's resources and creates many processes for each instance of the Web server. It's not a very efficient way to deal with multiple Web sites.

Multiple IP addresses

With this method, each Web site has its own IP address. You can configure the server with multiple network interface cards (NIC), or you can configure one card with multiple IP addresses. Configuring one card with multiple IP addresses uses a feature in Linux known as *IP aliasing*.

Configuring multiple network interface cards in one computer is simply a matter of repeating the procedure you used to configure the first card. The second card will be eth1. You may need to add an append line to the /etc/lilo.conf file to let the kernel know about the i/o and interrupts of each card. You can use the ifconfig utility to assign the second IP address to the card. Refer to Chapter 20 for instructions on using the ifconfig utility.

To configure one card with multiple IP numbers requires that the kernel support IP aliasing. All current Linux distributions do, and setting it up is relatively easy. You can use the ifconfig utility to assign the IP address, but since there is only one NIC, you need to change the name of the NIC slightly so that it recognizes multiple addresses. The NIC with just one IP address was known as eth0. Now to recognize two (or more) addresses, the card is referred to as eth0:0 for the first address, eth0:1 for the second address, eth0:2 for the third address, and so on. The Linux kernel will support up to 256 IP aliases in its default configuration.

After you have set up the aliases for the NIC, you need to edit the /etc/httpd/ httpd.conf file so the Web server will listen to multiple addresses and respond to each one separately. You can do this with the <VirtualHost> directive. Place the information about each host in the /etc/httpd/conf/vhosts/vhost#.conf file, where the hash is the number of the vhost. Place an include statement in /etc/httpd/ conf/httpd.conf that calls the vhost#.conf file. The following example shows the <VirtualHost> entry for a domain using an IP address that's different from your main site address.

```
<VirtualHost 192.168.1.5>
    ServerAdmin Webmaster@coloniallandscape.com
    DocumentRoot /home/httpd/html
    ServerName www.coloniallandscape.com
    ErrorLog logs/192.168.0.2-error_log
    TransferLog logs/192.168.2.0-access_log
    ScriptAlias /cgi-bin/ /home/Web000/public_html/cgi-bin/
</VirtualHost>
```

Inside the <VirtualHost> section are directives related to the domain defined by the <VirtualHost>. The information is the name of the server (ServerName), the location of the document files (DocumentRoot), log file options (ErrorLog and TransferLog), and the way to handle script requests (ScriptAlias).

To add additional virtual hosts, repeat the preceding steps for each host. Directives and options for each host may be different depending on the results you want. The minimum requirement for each virtual host is an IP address and a DocumentRoot specification.

Multiple names for one IP address

Name-based virtual hosting assigns one IP address to multiple names. The Apache Web server software uses the same <VirtualHost> directive you saw in the previous section to enable you to assign the same IP address to multiple hosts.

Setting up name-based virtual hosting is not much different from setting up IP-based virtual hosting. You use the directive <NameVirtualHost>to specify the IP address used for name-based hosting. The <VirtualHost> sections contain the names to match for the host. You place the configuration information in the /etc/httpd/conf/vhosts/vhost#.conf file, which is called from the httpd.conf file. Figure 26-5 below shows the vhost1.conf file.

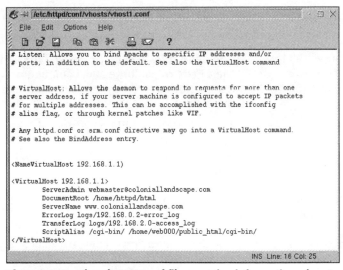

Figure 26-5: The vhost#.conf file contains information about the hosts served by the server

Server Security

You can use several directives to make the Web server. These directives can require that users have passwords to access the site, and restrict access based on IP addresses or hostnames. You can apply security restrictions to the entire Web site or to specific directories.

Host-based security

You can use the `allow` and `deny` directives to restrict access by host locations. For example:

`deny tellurium.net`	Deny access to anyone from the domain `tellurium.net`
`deny tony.tellurium.net`	Deny access to tony at `tellurium.net`
`deny all`	Deny access to everyone

To deny access to a specific IP address use the following:

`deny 192.168.1.3`	Deny access to the specified number
`deny 192.168.1.`	Deny access to the entire network specified

You can use the `order` directive to specify the order in which the `allow` and `deny` rules are interpreted. The basic principle is shown next:

`order`	`deny, allow`	The `deny` rules will be processed first, then the `allow` rules. If the rules conflict, or a host is not covered by a rule, then `allow` is the default.
`order`	`allow, deny`	The `allow` rules will be processed first, then the `deny` rules. If the rules conflict, or a host is not covered by a rule, then `deny` is the default.

Another directive you can use is `AllowOverride`. You place this directive inside of a <directory> section and it looks for a .htaccess file for instructions.

These types of restrictions are called *host-based restrictions*. They are easy to set up and are transparent to the user since they require no user input.

User-based security

Another type of restriction is known as *user-based* and does require input from the user. In order to enter a user-based site, a user must have a username and password.

While this type of site is more secure than a site with only host-based restrictions, it does require more work on the part of both the administrator and the user.

To help you set up each user's account, a program called htpasswd will automatically create a file called /etc/httpd/htusers to hold user information the first time it is used. Subsequent uses will add user accounts to the file. Figure 26-6 shows the htpasswd command being used to set up a user account.

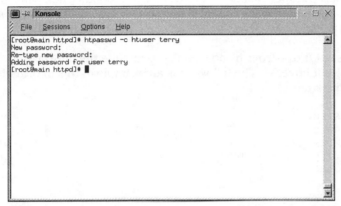

Figure 26-6: The htpasswd command creating the htuser file and adding the user terry

The -c option followed by htuser specifies that a file should be created with that name. The user terry is added to the file and the program prompts twice for the user's password. To add more users, just use the htpasswd command without the -c option. You can remove users by using a text editor to open the file and then just deleting them from the file.

You can also use a group file to make administration easier. Use any text editor to define a group as follows:

```
adduser:  terry
```

Be sure to use valid usernames that are shown in the htuser file. To enable the server to use these files you must modify the /etc/httpd/conf/httpd.conf file. You need to tell the server to use these two files by adding the following directives:

```
AuthUserFile   /path to file
AuthGroupFile /path to file
```

Next you need to configure the realm and type. Use the AuthName directive to enable the client's browser to identify the domain the client is logging into. This enables the user to enter his or her username and password. The AuthType directive defines the format of the information exchanged by the client and the server during the authorization process. There are two types of information, *basic* and *digest*. Basic is fully supported by all browsers while digest is not, so just use basic.

The last item you need to configure is access control for the users and group you created. You need to use the `require` directive to do this. There are three options:

✦ `require user` *username*

✦ `require group` *group name*

✦ `require valid user`

The first option enables the specified users to log in. The second option enables the users listed in the group file to log in. The third option enables any user listed in the htuser file to log in.

You must modify the /etc/httpd/conf/httpd.conf file to include the information about access control just covered. The following is an example of this information for a directory called testing.

```
<Directory /testing>
AllowOverride None
AuthUserFile /etc/httpd/htuser
AuthGroupFile /etc/httpd/htgroup
AuthName "testing"
AuthType Basic
require user terry
require group aduser
</Directory>
```

Secure Socket Layers (SSL)

Secure Socket Layers is a transmission protocol developed by Netscape to enable encrypted transmission between two machines using TCP/IP. Basically, one machine encrypts the data by using a key and transmits the data to the other machine, and the second machine uses a key to restore the information to its unencrypted form. If both machines use the same key to unencrypt the information, it is called a *private-key system* because the key is kept secret in order to protect the information. Transmitting data across the Internet poses something of a problem as the key, as well as the data, must be transmitted to the remote computer in order for the message to be unencrypted. Thus, a different kind of encryption system was developed, known as the *public-private key system*.

Using a public-private key system also enables you to use certificates that describe the Web server and its owner. Certificates are electronically signed by a trusted organization that verifies the content of the Web site and its owner and the authenticity of the certificate. The certificate provides some assurance that the client is actually communicating with the intended server.

Secure Web servers use a different protocol for communicating with the clients. This protocol is called HTTPS, which means *secure HTTP*. To access a secure server you must type the following:

```
https://www.server_name.com
```

Note The default TCP port for secure servers is 443, so you need to specify the correct protocol type in order for the server to accept secure requests from browsers.

The Apache software does not include support for SSL because of U.S. government export restrictions on encryption software. In order to add SSL capabilities to the Apache Web server, you must find third-party software and then compile and install it.

You can get this software from many places. The most common package is called mod_ssl, and you can get the source from `http://www.modssl.org`. In addition, you'll need two other sources, one called ssleay and the other called rsaref. Links to both of the sites containing the source are available from the mod_ssl site. You'll also find complete instructions for compiling and installing the software at the mod_ssl site.

Caution Be sure to pay very close attention to the warnings contained in the mod_ssl documentation about using this third-party software. The U.S. government takes exporting encryption software very seriously, and there are serious penalties for violating the laws.

Summary

In this chapter you learned about the Apache Web server software, which is usually included with most current distributions of Linux. The Apache Web server software is used on more than 60 percent of all Web servers. You learned about the configuration files and the directives that you can use in those files to configure the Web server to your requirements.

You also learned about server security and access control. Finally, you learned a little about the Secure Socket Layer protocol and where to get the additional software you need to add this feature to Apache.

✦   ✦   ✦

Advanced System Administration and Network Administration

Automating Tasks

Keeping a computer or network running smoothly means that you must regularly perform tedious maintenance tasks, such as collecting usage statistics, backing up filesystems, and running system-cleanup tasks. Linux provides a set of scheduling commands — batch, at, and cron — so that you can schedule tasks to run automatically. One benefit of these scheduling commands is that you can schedule tasks to run when the system is least busy, even if you are home sleeping.

Using at or batch to Schedule Infrequent Tasks

Use the at and batch commands to run a command or script once or very infrequently.

The batch command runs your script or command once whenever Linux determines that the system's workload is light.

Tip Help balance your system's workload. Use batch to run commands that use system resources (such as CPU or memory) heavily.

The at command queues your script or command to run once at (or near) the time you specify. Figure 27-1 shows how to use at. You provide at with two arguments:

◆ The date and 24-hour time (or just the time) to execute your command or script

◆ The command or script to run

CPU Load Limiting and at

Some systems use a *system load average*, a measure of how busy the system is, of 1.5 as the default. You can tell `atd` to run jobs only when your computer's CPU has extra capacity. By default, most Linux distributions consider the limiting load on your CPU to be 80% (.8). In other words, if you use the `-1` option when you start `atd`, the value .8 says, "Do not run a job until the CPU is less than 80% busy." If you have a single CPU computer, the default value is usually fine. However, symmetric multiprocessing systems (SMPs) — computers with more than one CPU inside — have more than 100% CPU capacity. Each CPU inside the computer counts as 100%, so if you have a dual-CPU machine, you have 200% processing power. In `atd -1` terms, this is 2. If you have three CPUs, that's 300% — that is 3 — and so on. With SMP computers, a common rule of thumb for setting CPU load limits for `at` is to use the number of processors minus 1. The value you use on the command, `atd -1`, also determines when `batch` jobs run. If you use the default (.8), `batch` jobs run immediately unless the CPU is more than 80% busy.

batch factoids

Linux controls the time that a batched command runs. You can use the `batch` command to run any Linux command or shell script, as follows:

```
batch
at> #type any command or script name here
at> #type more commands or script names here
at> #press <CTRL-D> when done
```

`batch` actually runs a form of `at`. That's why the `batch` command in the preceding example generates an at> prompt. With some Linux distributions, including Red Hat, you can type `at -b` instead of the `batch` command. A user may batch a long recursive listing and check the status with the `atq` command.

at factoids

Note the following characteristics of `at`:

✦ `at` takes a time option to submit a command or script to run unattended at a later time. Table 27-1 shows valid time formats for the `at` command.

✦ A variation of the `at` command, `atq`, displays a list of jobs scheduled to run.

✦ A variation of the `at` command, `atrm`, removes a queued `at` job.

✦ You do not need to be logged in for your `at` job to run. The shell script, `atd` (or, on older UNIX systems, `atrun`), runs the jobs you queue with `at`.

Caution Your at job is not guaranteed to run at exactly the time you specify. cron schedules the script, atd, which processes your queued at jobs. For example, if you tell your at command to run at 11:55, but cron schedules atd to run only on the hour and half-hour, atd won't examine the queue until 12:00. Your job will run at 12:00.

Figure 27-1: Use at to schedule infrequent commands

Table 27-1
Valid Time Formats for the at Command

Format	*Examples*
at *hh:mm*	at 23:58 (use the 24-hour clock)
at *hh:mm month day year*	at 23:58 jan 25 2000, at 12:40am Jan 1
at *now+count units*	at now+5 min (units can be minutes, hours, days, weeks)
at 4pm+3 days	

How at.allow and at.deny Work

The existence (or absence), and the contents, of the allow and deny files determine who may use `at` or `batch`.

✦ If the deny file exists, the usernames listed in it are not allowed to use `at` or `batch`, as shown in the following listing of /etc/at.deny:

```
# cat /etc/at.deny
nobody
bin
daemon
sys
lp
sync
mail
news
uucp
games
man
guest
ftp
```

By default, most system accounts are listed in at.deny.

✦ If the allow file doesn't exist, the system checks the deny file. No user listed in the deny file can use `at` or `batch`. Every user *not* mentioned in the deny file can use `at` or `batch`.

✦ If the deny file exists but is empty, every user can use `at` or `batch`.

✦ If neither file exists, only the superuser (root) can use `at` or `batch`.

Administering at and batch

The following sections deal with administering `at` and `batch`.

Granting (allowing) or denying access to users

If you want users to be able to control who can use the `at` and `batch` commands, you need to work with the two files — the allow and the deny files — that grant or deny permission:

✦ /etc/at.allow

✦ /etc/at.deny

Both of these files are text that you edit to allow or deny access to both at and batch. To grant access, edit the file /etc/at.allow and add the usernames of those who can use the cron system.

Tip   Don't forget to include the root username in cron.allow.

Starting and stopping the at daemon

The at daemon, `atd`, controls both `at` and `batch` processing. When Linux boots, it starts the at daemon automatically. The script /etc/rc.d/init.d/atd starts the daemon. You do not need to start the at daemon manually unless a system or user error causes the daemon to die.

Note   The script to start the at daemon runs automatically when the system starts run levels 2–6. The script to stop the at daemon runs automatically at run levels 0 and 1.

Using the cron System to Schedule Routine Tasks

If you need to run a command or a script at regular times — whether every minute of every day or once a week or once a year — you should use the cron system. System administrators use cron to automate routine maintenance scripts such as:

✦ Monitoring the state of your system, e.g. tracking available disk space, finding "disk hogs," generating capacity planning reports.

✦ Searching for core dumps (files created by operating system problems) and hardware errors.

✦ Backup.

✦ Cleaning up /tmp before the next reboot.

cron factoids

A few things to note about cron:

✦ The cron system consists of the cron daemon, a system crontab file, user's personal crontab files, and the `crontab` command.

✦ There are two types of crontab files — personal files for user tasks and a system file for system administration and maintenance tasks.

✦ You create your personal crontab file with the `crontab` command.

✦ You must know the root password or have UID 0 to create or edit system cron jobs.

✦ The `crontab` command submits your crontab file to the cron daemon, as shown in Figure 27-2.

✦ The system administrator can deny access to the cron system although this is unusual.

✦ cron on Linux includes more features than the basic UNIX cron, such as configuration options and added security.

Creating and submitting personal crontab entries

Follow these steps to submit non-privileged user tasks for periodic cron execution:

1. Create a personal crontab file.

2. Use the `crontab` command to submit your cron entries to the cron system.

Creating a personal crontab file

You can use your favorite editor or the `cat` command to create entries in your personal crontab file.

Tip

You can name your file anything you want. The cron daemon eventually renames its copy of your file according to cron naming standards.

The purpose of a crontab file is to tell cron, "Run these jobs at these times." Your crontab file consists of:

✦ Optional comments that begin with a hash (#).

✦ Scheduling entries, one per line, that represent tasks that you want to submit for scheduling.

Each entry begins with of a set of five time fields that describe how often you want the task to run. The remainder of the entry is the command you want to execute. Figure 27-2 shows a non-privileged user's crontab file, $HOME/emily/batch_tasks. Table 27-2 lists the five time fields that you can use in a crontab entry. You should separate fields with white space (a space or tab). An asterisk (*) in a field means to run the job at every possible value for that field.

Table 27-2		
crontab Time Fields		
Time Field	*Description*	*Legal Values*
minutes	Minutes past the hour	0–59
hours	Hours of the day	0 (midnight)–23

Time Field	Description	Legal Values
day of the month	Day of the month	1–31
month	Month of the year	1–12 or first three characters of the name, such as Jan
weekday	Day of the week	0–7 or first three characters of the name, such as Mon

Note

Each field in a crontab entry may consist of subfields. For example, if you want to run a job automatically every 10 minutes, the minutes field should look like this: 10,20,30,40,50,00. If you want to run a job on the first and fifteenth of the month, the month field should look like this: 1,15.

Figure 27-2: A personal crontab file consists of entries to run periodically

Using the crontab command to submit your job to the cron system

There is also a system crontab file for system administration and maintenance tasks. You can read about the system crontab file later in this chapter.

How the cron system works

The cron daemon starts automatically as part of the Linux startup procedure. It performs the following steps:

1. Checks the system crontab file, /etc/crontab to see what system tasks need to be done.

2. Searches /var/spool/cron for new or updated personal crontab files every minute. When a user runs the `crontab` command, the cron daemon generates file names that include that user's username.

3. Loads crontab files, if there are any, into memory for cron processing.

4. Checks for modified crontab files every minute in the directories /var/spool/cron and /the file etc/crontab.

5. Reloads any changed crontab files into memory. When you use the `crontab` command to create cron jobs, the `crontab` command modifies the date on the spool directory. Therefore, you do not need to restart the cron daemon each time anyone adds new cron entries.

6. Checks file entries. Each minute, the cron daemon checks the entries in both the user and system crontabs to see if it should execute any entries.

7. Executes the entry and notifies the owner. When the daemon executes an entry, it e-mails the output to the owner of the crontab file or to the user named in the `MAILTO` environment variable.

Administering the cron system

If you are the Linux system administrator, you set up protections on the cron system that allow or deny cron access to users.

Granting (allowing) or denying access to users

If you want users to be able to create personal crontab files in /var/spool/cron, you need to work with two files — the allow and the deny files — that grant or deny permission to use the cron system:

✦ /etc/at.allow or /etc/cron.allow

✦ /etc/at.deny or /etc/cron.deny

Both of these files are text that you edit to allow or deny access to cron. To grant access, edit the file /etc/cron.allow and add the usernames of those users who can use the cron system.

How cron.allow and cron.deny Work

The existence (or absence) of the allow and deny files, and their contents, determine who may use cron.

✦ If the allow file exists, the users whose usernames are listed in the allow file can use cron.

✦ If the allow file doesn't exist, the system checks the deny file. No user listed in the deny file can use cron. Every user *not* mentioned in the deny file can use cron.

✦ If the deny file exists but is empty, every user can use cron.

✦ If neither file exists, only the superuser (root) can use cron.

Starting and stopping the cron daemon

When Linux boots, it starts the cron daemon automatically. The script /etc/rc.d/init.d/crond starts the daemon. You do not need to start the daemon manually unless a system or user error causes the daemon to die.

Note The script to start the cron daemon runs automatically when the system starts run levels 2–6. The script to stop the cron daemon runs automatically at run levels 0 and 1.

Summary

Use batch and at to automate tasks that you run only once or infrequently. Use the cron system to automate regular unattended processing. Users must have permission to use personal crontab files. The system administrator maintains the system crontab file.

✦   ✦   ✦

Rebuilding the Kernel

The kernel is the heart of Linux. If you removed all of the applications and utilities, X Window from your system, what would remain is the kernel — the core of the operating system. It is the kernel that makes the keyboard, mouse, disk drives, and other hardware work. Every single program on any Linux system relies on the services the kernel provides. This chapter shows you how to rebuild the kernel, that is, to customize it to your system. Although you do not have to rebuild the kernel, there are three reasons why you might want to do so:

+ To add support for a new device by modifying and rebuilding your existing kernel.

Tip Each new release of the Linux kernel supports more devices than the previous release. If you acquire a new device that your kernel does not support, browse the official kernel source code Web site www.kernel.org to see if there is a new release of the kernel that supports your device.

+ To change the kernel's configuration, especially if you are tuning the operating system's performance.

+ To remove support for devices that you don't use and do not plan to use in the future.

Removing unneeded device support reduces the size of the kernel. The smaller the kernel, the more efficient it is. In this age of fast processors, giga-memory, and extra fast disks, some people don't worry about the kernel's efficiency. They let the hardware compensate for any unnecessary kernel overhead. However, not all Linux computers are state-of-the-art. In fact, that's one of the benefits of Linux as opposed to other popular operating systems. Linux can run on some really old computers that are underpowered for other operating systems. If that's the case at your site, give the kernel all the help you can by removing extraneous device support and rebuilding the kernel. Before you start changing the kernel you should decide whether you're going to add features to your existing kernel or upgrade to a new version.

Kernel Building Overview

You get the kernel in human-readable source-code files. That means you can print the files, display them on your screen, and edit them. Rebuilding the kernel involves compiling the source code to create an executable image that replaces the old kernel. The following steps, explained in detail in the rest of the chapter, outline general procedure for creating a new kernel,

1. Know what version of the kernel your computer is currently running.

2. Decide what version(s) of the kernel you want to build or upgrade to.

3. Get the source code.

4. Check your Linux symbolic (soft) link.

5. Decompress the source code.

6. Choose the appropriate kernel configuration tool for your user interface:

   * `make menuconfig`

   * `make xconfig`

   * `make config`

   * `make oldconfig`

7. Coordinate source-code dependencies.

8. Compile the kernel.

9. Install the kernel so that it takes effect the next time you boot.

10. Edit the LILO configuration file to recognize the new kernel.

11. Reboot immediately if you want to use your new kernel as soon as it is built.

Understanding terminology

There are a few terms that appear repeatedly in this chapter:

✦ *Dynamically loadable module* (*loadable module* or *module* for short) — device driver code that you can add and remove from the running kernel at any time. You do not need to rebuild the kernel and reboot to add or remove a module.

✦ *Build*—Building the kernel means compiling it and linking it into an executable image. The `make` utility does this.

✦ *Install*—Installing the kernel means making sure it's in the right directory (the `make` utility usually does this) and that LILO, the Linux Loader, knows about it.

✦ `make`—A utility that automates managing software builds. `make` gets its instructions from a text file called Makefile. When you run `make`, you specify an option that points into the Makefile at what you want to do. The Makefile comes with the kernel sources. All you need to do is run the `make` utility with the appropriate option. This chapter describes what the `make` options do and when to use them.

Before you start

If you've decided to rebuild the kernel, the first thing you need to do is get the kernel source-code files from your CD or download them from the Internet.

Deciding whether to modify the existing kernel or upgrade to a new version

Before you get the source code, you should know what version of the kernel is currently running and what version of the kernel source code you need. If you plan to upgrade to support new devices or kernel features, you need a newer release of the kernel source. If you want to add some additional options into your current kernel, you need the source code that matches your existing kernel version. There are different ways to find out the release number (version) of your currently running kernel. The easiest way is to use the `uname -a` command, as illustrated in the following short listing:

```
$ uname -a
Linux localhost.localdomain 2.2.14 #5 Mon Jan 22 07:55:25 MST
2001 i686
$
```

The output from the preceding `uname` command gives you information not only about your kernel, but also about your computer. The first field tells you that you're running Linux. You probably already knew that, but if this were a UNIX computer, `uname` would say something else. The second field lists the fully qualified domain name (FQDN) of your computer—in this case, because the system is not connected to a network of any sort, the name is localhost.localdomain. The third field tells you the kernel version number. The system is running kernel version 2.2.14. The fourth field tells you the number of times this version of kernel has been compiled so far (five), and the fifth field shows date (January 22) and time this kernel was compiled. The sixth field tells you that the kernel is running on an i686, which can be a Pentium II or Pentium III computer.

Understanding the Version Number

The Linux kernel source code for a specific version is called the *source tree* because the files — all 5,000+ of them — are arranged into a tree of directories and files. The kernel version numbers consist of three parts:

✦ The major version number

✦ The minor version number

✦ The patch level

The major version doesn't often change. Linux has had only two major versions in its history. The minor version represents the current level within the major version. Traditionally, even-numbered minor versions are stable releases. Version 2.0.30 is a stable kernel at patch level 30, for example. Odd-numbered minor versions, also called *development versions*, contain new features. Development versions are typically unstable, so they should only be used on systems that are not vital. Version 2.1.30 is a development kernel at patch level 30, for example. Odd-numbered minor versions aren't as stable as even-numbered versions. If you want to be on the cutting edge of kernel technology, upgrade your kernel as soon as a new release with an odd-numbered minor version becomes available. If you need the most stable and reliable kernel for running production systems, go with the most recent available even-numbered minor version. At some point, the odd-numbered version will have its bugs fixed and will be graduated to an even number. The patch level is the number of the patch file applied to the kernel. A patch is a binary file that fixes a feature that does not work as expected in the compiled kernel. Changes to the kernel sources are patch files. You use the `patch` utility to apply changes to the kernel source files. If, for example, you had the 2.0.29 kernel source tree and you wanted to move to the 2.0.30 source tree, you would obtain the 2.0.30 patch file and apply the patches, as in the following example.

```
$ cd /usr/src/linux
$ patch -p1 < patch-2.0.30
```

Finding kernel sources

If you have a Linux distribution on CD-ROM, and you need to modify your existing kernel, look on the distribution CD-ROM for the source code instead of going to the Internet.

You can download the kernel source code from many Web sites and FTP archives around the world. Table 28-1 lists many of the mirrors for Linux kernel source code.

Note   A *mirror* is an FTP archive or a group of files on a Web site that has been copied from one computer to another to reduce network traffic and make downloading Web files and FTP archives quicker and easier. The mirror is an exact copy of the original and is kept synchronized with the original.

The origin for all kernel mirrors is the kernel that Linus Torvalds maintains. This "official" kernel source keeps version numbers and patch levels consistent even though anyone can modify and release a kernel according to the GPL (GNU Public License). If you fix a bug in the kernel or add a new feature to it, you send it to Linus Torvalds, whose team tests it to be sure that it works without breaking anything else. If your fix or feature checks out, Linus sees that it becomes part of the next kernel release or patch level.

Table 28-1
Kernel Mirror Sites around the World

Country Code	Country	FTP Archive or Web Site
AD	Andorra	ftp or www.ad.kernel.org
AO	Angola	ftp or www.ao.kernel.org
AR	Argentina	ftp or www.ar.kernel.org
AT	Austria	ftp or www.at.kernel.org
AU	Australia	ftp or www.au.kernel.org
AV	Åland	ftp or www.av.kernel.org
AZ	Azerbaijan	ftp or www.az.kernel.org
BE	Belgium	ftp or www.be.kernel.org
BG	Bulgaria	ftp or www.bg.kernel.org
BO	Bolivia	ftp or www.bo.kernel.org
BR	Brazil	ftp or www.br.kernel.org
BW	Botswana	ftp or www.bw.kernel.org
BY	Belarus	ftp or www.by.kernel.org
CA	Canada	ftp or www.ca.kernel.org
CH	Switzerland	ftp or www.ch.kernel.org
CL	Chile	ftp or www.cl.kernel.org
CR	Costa Rica	ftp or www.cr.kernel.org
CX	Christmas Island	ftp or www.cx.kernel.org
CZ	Czech Republic	ftp or www.cz.kernel.org
DE	Germany	ftp or www.de.kernel.org
DK	Denmark	ftp or www.dk.kernel.org
EE	Estonia	ftp or www.ee.kernel.org

Continued

Table 28-1 *(continued)*

Country Code	Country	FTP Archive or Web Site
ES	Spain	ftp or `www.es.kernel.org`
FI	Finland	ftp or `www.fi.kernel.org`
FO	Faroe Islands	ftp or `www.fo.kernel.org`
FR	France	ftp or `www.fr.kernel.org`
GI	Gibraltar	ftp or `www.gi.kernel.org`
GL	Greenland	ftp or `www.gl.kernel.org`
GR	Greece	ftp or `www.gr.kernel.org`
GT	Guatemala	ftp or `www.gt.kernel.org`
HN	Honduras	ftp or `www.hn.kernel.org`
HR	Croatia	ftp or `www.hr.kernel.org`
HU	Hungary	ftp or `www.hu.kernel.org`
IE	Ireland	ftp or `www.ie.kernel.org`
IL	Israel	ftp or `www.il.kernel.org`
IS	Iceland	ftp or `www.is.kernel.org`
IT	Italy	ftp or `www.it.kernel.org`
JP	Japan	ftp or `www.jp.kernel.org`
KG	Kyrgyzstan	ftp or `www.kg.kernel.org`
KR	Korea, South	ftp or `www.kr.kernel.org`
KZ	Kazakhstan	ftp or `www.kz.kernel.org`
LI	Liechtenstein	ftp or `www.li.kernel.org`
LS	Lesotho	ftp or `www.ls.kernel.org`
LT	Lithuania	ftp or `www.lt.kernel.org`
LU	Luxembourg	ftp or `www.lu.kernel.org`
LV	Latvia	ftp or `www.lv.kernel.org`
MC	Monaco	ftp or `www.mc.kernel.org`
MD	Moldova	ftp or `www.md.kernel.org`
MG	Madagascar	ftp or `www.mg.kernel.org`
MU	Mauritius	ftp or `www.mu.kernel.org`
MW	Malawi	ftp or `www.mw.kernel.org`
MX	Mexico	ftp or `www.mx.kernel.org`

Country Code	Country	FTP Archive or Web Site
MZ	Mozambique	ftp or www.mz.kernel.org
NA	Namibia	ftp or www.na.kernel.org
NI	Nicaragua	ftp or www.ni.kernel.org
NL	Netherlands	ftp or www.nl.kernel.org
NO	Norway	ftp or www.no.kernel.org
NZ	New Zealand	ftp or www.nz.kernel.org
PA	Panama	ftp or www.pa.kernel.org
PL	Poland	ftp or www.pl.kernel.org
PS	Palestinian Territory	ftp or www.ps.kernel.org
PT	Portugal	ftp or www.pt.kernel.org
PY	Paraguay	ftp or www.py.kernel.org
RE	Reunion	ftp or www.re.kernel.org
RO	Romania	ftp or www.ro.kernel.org
RU	Russian Federation	ftp or www.ru.kernel.org
SC	Seychelles	ftp or www.sc.kernel.org
SE	Sweden	ftp or www.se.kernel.org
SG	Singapore	ftp or www.sg.kernel.org
SI	Slovenia	ftp or www.si.kernel.org
SJ	Svalbard and Jan Mayen Islands	ftp or www.sj.kernel.org
SK	Slovakia	ftp or www.sk.kernel.org
ST	Sao Tome and Principe	ftp or www.st.kernel.org
SV	El Salvador	ftp or www.sv.kernel.org
SZ	Swaziland	ftp or www.sz.kernel.org
TM	Turkmenistan	ftp or www.tm.kernel.org
TW	Taiwan	ftp or www.tw.kernel.org
UA	Ukraine	ftp or www.ua.kernel.org
UK	United Kingdom	ftp or www.uk.kernel.org
UM	United States Minor Outlying Islands	ftp or www.um.kernel.org
US	United States	ftp or www.us.kernel.org

Continued

Table 28-1 *(continued)*		
Country Code	**Country**	**FTP Archive or Web Site**
UY	Uruguay	ftp or `www.uy.kernel.org`
VA	Vatican	ftp or `www.va.kernel.org`
VE	Venezuela	ftp or `www.ve.kernel.org`
ZA	South Africa	ftp or `www.za.kernel.org`
ZM	Zambia	ftp or `www.zm.kernel.org`
ZW	Zimbabwe	ftp or `www.zw.kernel.org`

Choosing a source file format

On the Web, the kernel files, source code plus patches, come in three flavors of compressed files. The files that end in .tar.gz are `tar` archives, compressed by the `gzip` utility. The files that end in tar.bz2 are `tar` archives compressed by the `bzip2` utility. `bzip2` is similar to `gzip`, but compresses the files even further.

Tip   All Linux systems come loaded with the `gunzip` utility to unzip .gz files. If you also have the `bunzip2` utility, you can save some downloading time by getting the .bz2 files.

The file names that end in sign are PGP (Pretty Good Privacy) signature files. If you are downloading from a mirror site and want to make sure that the files are exactly the same as those in the official `www.kernel.org` site, you need to download the sign file. If you download the sign file, you need a public key to verify the files. You can get the public key at `www.kernel.org/signature.html`.

Cross-Reference   Read Chapter 29, "Securing a Linux System," to see how to use PGP signature files.

The `tar` archive named for the kernel version contains the sources for the kernel. For example, to build kernel Version 2.3 patch level 51, you need to surf to `http://www.kernel.org/pub/linux/kernel/v2.3/` or one of the mirror sites listed in Table 28-1. You need to download the file linux-2.3.51.tar.gz or linux-2.3.51.tar.gz and all the patch files up to and including patch-2.3.51.gz. Figure 28-1 shows part of the directory listing for version 2.3 files.

In the following section, the examples show how to download and unzip the source and patch files before configuring and building a kernel.

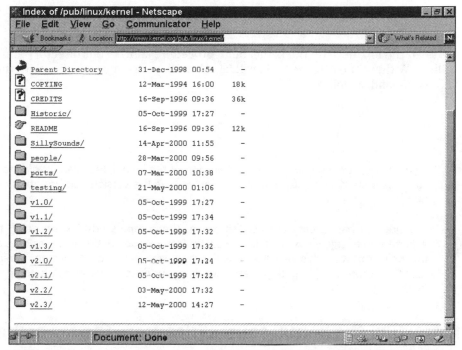

Figure 28-1: The kernel Web site contains a directory for the files in each kernel version

Unzipping (decompressing) the kernel source files

After downloading the compressed source code, you need to uncompress the files in the /usr/src directory. Change to the /usr/src directory for your starting point. Next, create a subdirectory for the unzipped files. Name your subdirectory after the version of the kernel you downloaded. Assuming you downloaded the file to /usr/src, the following commands create a directory for the kernel version 2.3.9 and use gunzip to decompress the tar archive for the kernel source code.

```
tweety$ cd /usr/src
tweety$ mkdir linux-2.3.9
tweety$ cd linux-2.3.9
tweety$ gunzip ../linux-2.3.9.tar.gz
```

In the previous example, note that the directory for the kernel previously built contains a symbolic link called linux. You need to change that link to point to the directory you just created. Use the rm command to remove the link and the ln -s command to recreate the link to point to your new directory. Type the name of the link followed by the subdirectory that points to the link. The following commands show you how.

```
tweety$ rm linux
tweety$ ln -s linux-2.3.9 linux
```

You need the link because the kernel build procedure knows your directory simply as linux. Without the link, the build will fail. You can verify your new link with the file command, as follows:

```
tweety$ file *
linux:        symbolic link to linux-2.3.9
linux-2.3.9   directory
```

Caution   If you have previously built a different version of the kernel, the /usr/src directory contains a subdirectory for that version as well as the version you are about to build.

Tip   Be sure you have plenty of free disk space. The compressed files are going to expand into a large file named linux-2.3.9.tar. You can delete the .gz or .bz2 file at this point to save disk space. If you have extra space, you should consider retaining the compressed file until you are sure that your decompressed file is going to work.

Extracting the kernel source files from the tar archive

Use the tar command to extract all the source files from the archive and store them in the source tree. You should be in the /usr/src directory to run tar as follows:

```
tweety$ cd /usr/src
tweety$ tar -xvf linux-2.3.9
```

tar automatically creates branches (subdirectories) in the source tree to hold the files.

Some of the messages that tar displays as it extracts and stores each file are shown in the following code listing. At the end of the listing you can see the du (disk usage) command, which shows you how much disk space the decompressed files use.

```
# Directories created and files extracted from the tar archive
linux/
linux/Makefile
linux/fs/
linux/fs/msdos/
linux/fs/proc/
linux/fs/minix/
linux/fs/isofs/
linux/fs/nfs/
linux/fs/ext2/
linux/fs/umsdos/
linux/fs/hpfs/
```

```
linux/fs/sysv/
linux/fs/smbfs/
linux/fs/fat/
linux/fs/vfat/
linux/fs/ncpfs/
linux/fs/ufs/
linux/fs/affs/
linux/fs/romfs/
linux/fs/ntfs/
linux/kernel/
linux/lib/
linux/mm/
linux/include/
linux/include/video/fbcon-vga-planes.h
linux/net/
linux/net/socket.c
linux/ipc/
linux/ipc/msg.c
linux/drivers/
linux/drivers/net/
linux/drivers/net/hamradio/
linux/arch/i386/
#other directories edited out to save space
60586    linux
[root@flyingpenguin]# # 60586 MB = the grand total
```

Note The options on the `tar` command in the preceding code mean extract files (x), file (f), and verbosely list the files being extracted (v).

Examining the source tree

After you extract the source code, you can see the tree of directories under /usr/src/linux. The following list briefly describes the contents of the /usr/src/linux directory's subdirectories.

/usr/src/linux/kernel	Main kernel code. It contains subdirectories for each hardware architecture, in arch/*/kernel, where * is the hardware architecture.
/usr/src/linux/arch	Hardware-specific kernel code, such as system-clock routines, interrupt-handling routines, and low-level I/O routines. It contains one subdirectory for each hardware architecture, such as i386, ppc (PowerPC), and alpha (Compaq Alpha).
/usr/src/linux/include	Header files for building the kernel. It contains sub-directories for each architecture. The subdirectory include/asm* is a symbolic link to the include directory for a specific hardware. For example, include/asm-i386 points to /usr/src/linux/arch/i386.

/usr/src/linux/init	Kernel initialization code (code that runs at boot time).
/usr/src/linux/mm	Memory-management code, such as memory-mapped file handling and swap-file management. It contains subdirectories for each hardware architecture in the form arch/*/mm/, where * is the specific hardware architecture, e.g. alpha.
/usr/src/linux/drivers	Device-driver code. It contains subdirectories for classes of device drivers such as block.
/usr/src/linux/modules	Holds any loadable modules.
/usr/src/linux/ipc	Kernel inter-process communications code, such as shared memory routines and semaphores (methods for synchronizing activities between processes).
/usr/src/linux/fs	Filesystem routines. It contains subdirectories for each filesystem, such as /usr/src/linux/fs/ext2 and /usr/src/linux/fs/vfat.
/usr/src/linux/net	Kernel-networking routines, such as code for TCP/IP, IPX, AppleTalk, and Ethernet.
/usr/src/linux/lib	Kernel libraries (shared routines). It contains architecture specific subdirectories in the form arch/*/lib/, where * is the hardware architecture.
/usr/src/linux/scripts	Scripts to build the kernel.

Configuring and Building a New Kernel

Once you have downloaded, uncompressed, and extracted the kernel source code, you are ready to begin building a new kernel. This section explains how to configure the kernel so that it matches your hardware and how to compile it.

Tip   To configure and build the kernel, you must be the superuser (root).

Caution   The kernel build routines use the C compiler to compile the code. The C compiler is named gcc, for GNU C Compiler. If you are running an old version of Linux, you should get a new version of gcc. Go to the GNU site, www.gnu.org/software/gcc, to download a new copy of the source code for gcc and to get instructions for building a new gcc. Trying to build a new kernel version with an old gcc is almost certain to cause errors.

You configure the kernel before you build it. Configuring the kernel means selecting the options and settings you want to build into the kernel. You have a choice of either three or four utilities for configuring the kernel, depending on whether you have an X interface or not. The following list of kernel configuration utilities is in order from most to least user-friendly.

`/usr/src/linux/make xconfig`	Requires X, menu driven
`/usr/src/linux/make menuconfig`	Menu driven
`/usr/src/linux/make config`	Question-and-answer
`/usr/src/linux/.config/make oldconfig`	Requires an input file

Note Did you notice that all the utilities above start with the `make` command? `make` is a utility that comes with Linux and automates building programs and large software systems. `make` automatically finds and builds all the individual files that are part of the software system according to a pre-defined order of dependencies. All of the kernel-configuring interfaces use `make` in the same way. The only difference is in the user interface of the various utilities.

Understanding kernel configuration options

You can configure a variety of options and services into your kernel. As new versions of the Linux kernel become available, there will be even more options and settings for you to consider. This section describes some of the configuration options you can set when running the preceding `make config` utilities. Your kernel probably supports many of the options and settings described in this section. However, if you want to make your kernel as lean as possible for best efficiency, you may want to consider configuring your kernel to remove extraneous device support.

When you remove an extraneous setting, be sure that it's not something you might want to use in the future. You can save yourself some work by keeping support for kernel options and settings that might be useful as your system and network grow. For example, the network used for the examples in this book is strictly a TCP/IP network, but all the kernels on all the computers include support for AppleTalk because it's conceivable that we might add an iMac or an iBook to the network in the near future.

Note If you remove support for an item from your kernel configuration and later need the kernel to support that item, don't panic. You simply need to reconfigure and rebuild the kernel to restore support for the deleted device or service.

Configuring general kernel options

Most configurable kernel options fall into categories such as processor, filesystems, devices, and so forth. There are also a few miscellaneous options that don't fall into any specific category, and these are called the *general kernel options*. General options include configuring PCI or Microchannel bus support and various miscellaneous binary files.

Configuring processor options

Processor options set the CPU specification for your kernel. You can set the kernel to run on a selection of hardware architectures, including Intel and Intel-like CPUs such as AMD, Alpha, Motorola 68000 (for PowerPC and Amiga), and Sparc and Sparc64 (for Sun Microsystems computers). The kernels that come with most Linux distributions are configured for the 386 CPU type, the lowest common denominator. If your CPU does not have a floating-point emulator, you can also configure the kernel to perform math emulation. If you have an SMP (Symmetric Multiprocessing) computer — a computer with more than one CPU — you should configure the kernel to support the multi-processing option.

Configuring device options

You can configure the types of devices you want the kernel to support. Block devices, such as disk drives, are devices that transfer data in blocks (chunks). When you configure block-device options, you specify the hard drives and CD-ROMs you want the kernel to support. The kernel supports all the popular hard drives and many of the less common ones. When you configure block-device support, you are usually trimming the kernel down for greater efficiency by removing support for devices you plan never to use. You can also configure whether or not the kernel supports floppy disks and whether or not it supports SCSI disks. You can even configure the kernel to pretend that your IDE disks are SCSI.

Character devices transfer data one character at a time. They are usually slower than block devices. When you configure character-device options, you are configuring support for virtual terminals, terminals connected to the serial ports, pseudoterminals for network access, speech cards, joysticks, and certain tape drives.

The several examples that follow use different interfaces to configure support for experimental device drivers, UNIX style (BSD) process accounting, the AppleTalk network protocol, and SCSI tapes.

Configuring filesystems

You can configure your kernel to support various filesystems. Most kernels come already configured for the ext2 filesystem, the native Linux filesystem, and others such as ISO9660 for CD-ROMs, MS-DOS, and VFAT. Other filesystems the kernel can support include the Macintosh filesystem, the OS/2 HPFS, Microsoft's NTFS, and the ancient Minix. You can also configure the kernel with preset limits on disk use for users.

Configuring network adapters

The kernel includes settings for a wide variety of network adapter cards, also called network interface cards or NICs. You may want to make your kernel smaller by removing support for all NICs that you plan never to use.

Configuring networking software

The networking options category includes just about everything you could possibly need to support an intranet, an extranet, or the Internet. The kernel supports the TCP/IP, IPX, and AppleTalk networking protocols, as well as some ancient but still operative protocols, such as the proprietary DECnet from Compaq Computer Corporation. You can also configure IP tunneling to support Virtual Private Networks (VPNs), and filtering so that you can allow (or disallow) certain types of network packets into your network. If your computer is going to be a router on your network, you can configure the kernel to optimize routing functions.

Configuring loadable modules

You can configure the kernel to support (or not) loadable modules (dynamically loadable device drivers). Using loadable modules is a way to keep the kernel smaller, because the modules are not built-in to the kernel. The kernel loads the modules at runtime when they are needed. If you plan to use loadable modules, you must tell the kernel which device drivers to use as loadable modules.

Note   You need to compile the loadable modules you select. You can read about how to compile loadable modules later in this chapter.

Configuring other kernel options and settings

There are some kernel options and settings that don't fall into any of the preceding categories. Those options include ISDN (Integrated Services Digital Network) support, support for a few very old sound cards, and even support for Ham radio via TCP/IP.

Tip   If you have an ancient sound card, don't bother trying to get your kernel to support it. Buy a new sound card.

Using the command line to configure the kernel

There are easier interfaces than `make config`, but I show it first because you can count on the non-graphical interface to be on any Linux system. To configure your kernel in a terminal window or a virtual console or on a non-graphical terminal, use the following command:

```
make config
```

This form of the make utility asks you questions, such as what kind of CPU you have, and you answer them. The answers are either yes/no or multiple-choice. There is always a default answer, although it might not be the right answer for you. The default answer is in upper case. For example, the first question asks if you want to configure experimental device drivers and shows [Y/n] as the possible answers. The uppercase Y (for yes) is the default. If you see the letter m as part of the answer, make config is asking if you want to support the option as a separate loadable module. If you're not sure what to answer, type ? for detailed help. The following example is long, and yet, it only shows some of the kernel options make config prompts you about. Each prompt lists the possible answers in brackets ([ ]). In the following example, the system administrator adds accounting features and SCSI tape and AppleTalk support to the kernel and presses Enter to accept most of the default settings for the rest of the options. The make config utility labels with an asterisk (*) the categories described in the section "Configuring Kernel Options."

I've edited out a lot of the make config dialog to save space.

```
[root@flyingpenguin]make config
#
# Information deleted to save space
#
# Using defaults found in arch/i386/defconfig
*
* Code maturity level options
*
Prompt for development and/or incomplete code/drivers
(CONFIG_EXPERIMENTAL) [N/y/?] y
*
* Processor type and features
*
Processor family (386, 486/Cx486, 586/K5/5x86/6x86,
Pentium/K6/TSC, PPro/6x86MX) [PPro/6x86MX]
  defined CONFIG_M686
Symmetric multi-processing support (CONFIG_SMP) [Y/n/?]
*
* Loadable module support
*
Enable loadable module support (CONFIG_MODULES) [Y/n/?]
*
* General setup
*
Networking support (CONFIG_NET) [Y/n/?]
PCI support (CONFIG_PCI) [Y/n/?]
BSD Process Accounting (CONFIG_BSD_PROCESS_ACCT) [N/y/?] y
* Block devices
*
Normal PC floppy disk support (CONFIG_BLK_DEV_FD) [Y/m/n/?]
Enhanced IDE/MFM/RLL disk/cdrom/tape/floppy support
(CONFIG_BLK_DEV_IDE) [Y/m/n/?]
* Additional Block Devices
*
```

```
RAM disk support (CONFIG_BLK_DEV_RAM) [N/y/m/?]
XT hard disk support (CONFIG_BLK_DEV_XD) [N/y/m/?]
Parallel port IDE device support (CONFIG_PARIDE) [N/y/m/?]
*
* Networking options
*
TCP/IP networking (CONFIG_INET) [Y/n/?]
The IPv6 protocol (EXPERIMENTAL)(CONFIG_IPV6) [N/y/m/?] (NEW)y
IPv6:enable EUI-64 token format(CONFIG_IPV6_EUI64)[N/y/?](NEW)y
IPv6:disable provider based
    addresses(CONFIG_IPV6_NO_PB)[N/y/?](NEW)
*
The IPX protocol (CONFIG_IPX) [N/y/m/?]
Appletalk DDP (CONFIG_ATALK) [N/y/m/?] y
DECnet Support (EXPERIMENTAL) (CONFIG_DECNET) [N/y/m/?] (NEW)
* SCSI support
*
SCSI support (CONFIG_SCSI) [Y/m/n/?]y
*
* SCSI support type (disk, tape, CD-ROM)
*
SCSI disk support (CONFIG_BLK_DEV_SD) [Y/m/n/?]
SCSI tape support (CONFIG_CHR_DEV_ST) [N/y/m/?] y
*
* Network device support
*
Network device support (CONFIG_NETDEVICES) [Y/n/?]
Ethernet (10 or 100Mbit) (CONFIG_NET_ETHERNET) [Y/n/?]
Mylex EISA LNE390A/B support (EXPERIMENTAL) (CONFIG_LNE390)
[N/y/m/?] (NEW)
Novell/Eagle/Microdyne NE3210 EISA support (EXPERIMENTAL)
(CONFIG_NE3210) [N/y/m/?] (NEW)
Racal-Interlan EISA ES3210 support(EXPERIMENTAL)
(CONFIG_ES3210)[N/y/m/?](NEW)
SMC EtherPower II (EXPERIMENTAL) (CONFIG_EPIC100)[N/y/m/?](NEW)
Zenith Z-Note support (EXPERIMENTAL) (CONFIG_ZNET) [N/y/?](NEW)
Pocket and portable adaptors (CONFIG_NET_POCKET) [N/y/?]
FDDI driver support (CONFIG_FDDI) [N/y/?]
*
*
#Support for Amateur Radio, IrDA, Old CD-ROM drivers edited out
*
* Character devices
*
Virtual terminal (CONFIG_VT) [Y/n/?]
Support for console on virtual terminal(CONFIG_VT_CONSOLE)
[Y/n/?]
Standard/generic (dumb) serial support (CONFIG_SERIAL)
[Y/m/n/?]
Support for console on serial port (CONFIG_SERIAL_CONSOLE)
[N/y/?]
```

```
Extended dumb serial driver options (CONFIG_SERIAL_EXTENDED)
[N/y/?]
Non-standard serial port support (CONFIG_SERIAL_NONSTANDARD)
[N/y/?]
Unix98 PTY support (CONFIG_UNIX98_PTYS) [Y/n/?]
Maximum number of Unix98 PTYs in use(0-2048)
(CONFIG_UNIX98_PTY_COUNT) [256]
Mouse Support (not serial mice) (CONFIG_MOUSE) [Y/n/?]
*
* # Mice,Joystick, Video, speech cards edited out
*
* USB drivers - not for the faint of heart
*
Support for USB (EXPERIMENTAL!) (CONFIG_USB) [N/y/m/?]
* Sound
*
Sound card support (CONFIG_SOUND) [N/y/m/?] *
*** End of Linux kernel configuration.
*** Check the top-level Makefile for additional configuration.
*** Next, you must run 'make dep'
```

Did you notice this line at the end of the make config example?

```
*** Next, you must run 'make dep'
```

After you select kernel configuration options, you need to tell Linux how to compile the source code and link it into the kernel image. Luckily, this is a simple process. Just execute the following command:

```
make dep
```

The output from the make dep command is quite extensive. Don't worry if you don't know exactly what's happening. The make dep command reviews the source files that will eventually become the kernel and finds all the interrelationships and inter-dependencies among the source files so that the compile and linking process happens.

```
[root@redbird]$ make clean
make[1]: Entering directory `/usr/src/linux/arch/i386/boot'
rm -f tools/build
rm -f setup bootsect zImage compressed/vmlinux.out
rm -f bsetup bbootsect bzImage compressed/bvmlinux.out
make[2]: Entering directory `/usr/src/linux/arch/i386/boot/compressed'
rm -f vmlinux bvmlinux _tmp_*
make[2]: Leaving directory `/usr/src/linux/arch/i386/boot/compressed'
make[1]: Leaving directory `/usr/src/linux/arch/i386/boot'
rm -f kernel/ksyms.lst include/linux/compile.h
rm -f core `find . -name '*.[oas]' ! -regex '.*lxdialog/.*' \
       ! -regex '.*ksymoops/.*' -print`
```

Where Did the .config File Come from?

The kernel configuration process creates a file, .config, that stores the kernel options you select when you run make config. The following example lists the file and displays the first few lines of options. You can see some of the new configuration options that the make config example set, such as support for experimental device drivers and UNIX-style (BSD) process accounting.

```
[root@flyingpenguin]ls -l .config
total 1
-rw-r--r--   1 root      root          8734 May 22 08:59 .config
[root@flyingpenguin]more .config
#
# Automatically generated make config: don't edit
# Code maturity level options
#
CONFIG_EXPERIMENTAL=y
# Processor type and features
# CONFIG_M386 is not set
# CONFIG_M486 is not set
# CONFIG_M586 is not set
# CONFIG_M586TSC is not set
CONFIG_M686=y
CONFIG_SMP=y
CONFIG_BSD_PROCESS_ACCT=y
#
# Loadable module support
#
CONFIG_MODULES=y
Handling Dependencies
```

More ways to configure the kernel

If you prefer to use a menu-driven kernel configuration utility you can use make menuconfig or make xconfig (if you have an X-based interface).

Using a character-based menu

You can use the menu-driven kernel configuration utility, make menuconfig, from either a text-based interface or in an X terminal window such as a GNOME or KDE terminal. The advantage of using a menu-driven interface is that you don't have to scroll through lots of questions when you plan to accept the defaults. In the preceding make config example, the system administrator has to answer over 50 questions to make only four changes to flyingpenguin's kernel. With the menu-driven interface, you use the arrow keys to go directly to the categories and options you want to change. Anything you don't touch remains unchanged. To run the text-based menu configuration utility, go to your Linux directory and type the following command in either a text-based terminal or a terminal window. After you type the command, you see the main menu. Figure 28-2 shows the menu with SCSI support selected. Figure 28-3 shows the prompt to save your configuration changes.

```
tweety# cd /usr/src/linux
tweety# make menuconfig
```

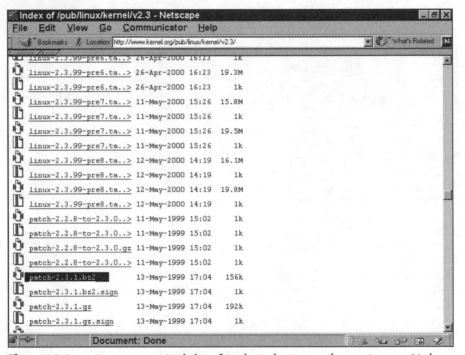

Figure 28-2: make menuconfig's interface is easier to use than make config's

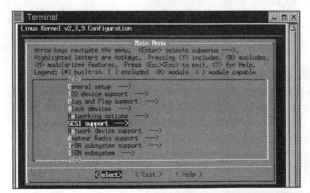

Figure 28-3: Be sure to save your kernel configuration changes

On the main menu, you arrow down to your selection or type the highlighted letter. On the main menu shown in Figure 28-2, I have selected SCSI support. This is the category that holds the SCSI tape-configuration option. Selecting a category on the main menu displays another menu with the specific options for the category. Each option has a Help button to the right. To build SCSI tape support into the kernel, arrow down to the SCSI tape-support option and type *. If you prefer SCSI tape support to be a loadable module rather than built into the kernel, type m. The legend shows you which options can become loadable modules. Hit Enter after you make your selection(s). When you are done selecting categories and options, hit Enter for the last time. Now you are ready to compile the kernel.

Using a graphical menu (X Window)

Running make xconfig is like running make menuconfig. Selecting a category on the main menu displays another menu with the specific options for the category. Each option has a Help button to the right. Pressing the Help button gives you detailed information about the option. The difference between make xconfig and make menuconfig is that you can use the mouse or any pointing device to move among categories and selections. Be sure to read the Help for the options you select. The Help boxes often point you to a HOWTO or a README file in the kernel sources. The Help box also lets you know whether you can configure an option as a loadable module.

Using the batch configuration method

If you want to configure the kernel without having to answer dozens of questions, execute make oldconfig. make oldconfig uses the existing .config file and only requires input for new options, that is, for kernel configuration options that are not present in .config.

Compiling the kernel

Regardless of how you configure your kernel, you need to build (compile) it. You've configured the kernel to support the devices and services you need by setting kernel options with the make config utility. To make those options part of the kernel, you must build the kernel, which means compiling the source code and installing the new kernel executable image that results. You use the make utility again to compile and install the kernel executable image. Usually you compile the kernel by typing make zImage.

Caution   Be careful to preserve the mixed case in the make zImage command.

If you have chosen so many options and device drivers that the kernel is too large to fit in the boot sector of the disk, you need to compile the kernel using the make bzImage command.

Both forms of the `make *zImage` command compile and link the kernel automatically, displaying lengthy messages as the build proceeds.

Causing the new kernel to take effect

At boot time, Linux expects the kernel to have the name vmlinuz. Linux also expects the kernel to reside in the /boot directory. Therefore, after you compile the kernel, you need to replace the existing kernel with the new one so that the new kernel takes effect.

Tip   If, after you reboot, the new kernel options don't seem to be working, check to see if you forgot to move the new kernel to the correct location.

Making a kernel on a boot floppy

To boot from a floppy disk, you need to compile the kernel and move it to a formatted floppy. There are two forms of the `make zdisk` command that compile the kernel, link it into an executable image, and copy the kernel image to the floppy disk.

To compile the kernel and make a bootable floppy, you usually use the `make zdisk` command, or, if the kernel is too big to fit into the floppy's boot sector, the `make bzdisk` command.

After compiling the kernel, both `make *zdisk` commands copy the resulting image file to a formatted floppy disk. To format the floppy disk, type the following command:

```
fdformat /dev/fd0
```

To make a backup copy of the new bootable floppy disk, change directory to /usr/src/linux and copy the kernel using the following command, substituting your computer's architecture for *xxx*.

```
cp arch/xxx/boot/zImage /dev/fd0
```

Automatically installing the new kernel

If you want to compile the kernel and automatically install it so that LILO (Linux Loader) can load it, you need to satisfy the following requirements:

✦ The LILO must be named /sbin/lilo.

✦ The LILO configuration file must be named /etc/lilo.conf.

When you are sure the LILO prerequisites are complete, you can compile and automatically install the new kernel (named vmlinuz) in the root directory with the `make zlilo` command—or, if the kernel is large, `make bzlilo`.

Note You can have more than one bootable kernel image on the same computer. For example, you might normally boot from your customized kernel and keep a more generic kernel available in case you need to troubleshoot your system. Keeping multiple kernel images can be especially helpful when you are running a development kernel (an odd-numbered kernel such as 2.3).

When LILO runs, it generates a map file from the configuration file. The map, /boot/map, holds the name and location of the bootable kernels. The map does the following:

✦ Tells Linux where (on what partition) to find the master boot record.

✦ Sets the `prompt` option so that the boot process can accept user input (for example, if you have a dual-boot system, you can respond to the prompt by selecting the operating system you wish to boot).

✦ If this is a dual-boot system, sets the timeout to wait for the user to enter the image of the operating system to boot.

✦ Sets the default image to boot. The default image is the first image line in the file. If you have built additional kernels, they should appear as additional image lines following the default image.

Tip If, when you boot your computer, you forget the name of the other images to boot, press Tab for a list of possible bootable images.

The LILO configuration file lists the bootable kernel. The following example is the LILO configuration file /etc/lilo.conf on the computer tweety, which is running Caldera OpenLinux. The line beginning with `image` lists the bootable kernel.

```
# /etc/lilo.conf - generated by Lizard
# target

boot = /dev/hda
install = /boot/boot.b

# options

prompt
delay = 50
timeout = 50
message = /boot/message

default = linux

other = /dev/hda1
        label = win
```

```
image = /boot/vmlinuz-pc97-2.2.14-modular
        label   = linux
        root    = /dev/hda2
        vga     = 274
        read-only
        append  = "debug=2 noapic nosmp"
```

Compiling and installing loadable modules

If, during the kernel configuration process, you selected any drivers to be dynamically loaded modules, you need to compile them and install them separately from the kernel build procedure. To compile all the selected modules, type `make modules`.

After the modules compile successfully, install them with yet another form of make: `make modules install`.

Tip   If you are using any new, experimental device drivers, consider building them as loadable modules. If you have any problems with the drivers, you can unload them at any time without having to build a new kernel.

Summary

The kernel consists of the low-level system settings and device drivers that make up the heart of Linux. For a full Linux operating system, you need both a kernel and the GNU tools and applications that surround the kernel with user functionality.

After you have the kernel source code, you use the `make` utility with different options to configure, build, and install the kernel. After installing the kernel, you build and install any loadable modules.

✦   ✦   ✦

Securing a Linux System

◆ ◆ ◆ ◆

◆ ◆ ◆ ◆

Security concerns and precautions are constantly changing. Since anything that one person can build, another person can take apart, you can't even guarantee security on a static system. As a system administrator, you need to be up to date on new viruses, worms, Trojan horses, and other exploits that malicious crackers may inflict on your systems and networks.

Understanding Security Terminology — What's the Worst that Can Happen?

The computer industry describes security hazards using many terms, some of them familiar, in specific ways. Before you read on, you need to understand how this chapter uses the following terms:

- ◆ Hacking and cracking
- ◆ Theft
- ◆ Spoofing
- ◆ Hacking versus cracking
- ◆ Password cracking
- ◆ Virus infection
- ◆ Worm infection
- ◆ Trojan horse loading
- ◆ Denial of service

Hackers or crackers? Hacking or cracking?

A fundamental distinction needs to made between the terms hackers and crackers and hacking and cracking. Unfortunately, popular media, particularly the movie *War Games* and the many news stories about computer viruses (*virii?*), have created and perpetuated a terrible misunderstanding. To make the distinction short and sweet, hackers are the good guys and hacking is a good thing; crackers are the bad guys and cracking is a bad thing

Hackers are benign, and hacking is a benign activity. *Hackers* refers to people who enjoy doing interesting, unusual things with computers, and especially with the source code to computer programs. Hackers might delight in playing with code, whether kernel source code or a small, unimportant shell script, not in obtaining unauthorized access to someone else's system. It is a group of self-described hackers that wrote the Linux kernel and that created many of the programs used on Linux and UNIX systems today.

Crackers are those malicious individuals, sometimes working in teams, who break into computer systems, deface Web pages, steal credit card numbers, and perform any other sort of unauthorized activity on a computer system to which they do not have legitimate, approved access. This type of activity, and the practice of breaking into computer systems in general, is called *cracking*. Make no mistake about it — cracking is illegal! All of the Linux users I know will knowingly have nothing to do with such people.

Besides stealing computers, the data store on computers is also at risk. Thieves break onto networks or into hosts to steal computing resources and/or data. A thief can be someone who, without authorization, telnets into a computer to use its CPU resources, or a cracker who steals proprietary business secrets. Combine physical security with filesystem, password, and network security to prevent theft.

Password cracking

Crackers often break into authorized users' accounts using a technique called *password-cracking*, systematically guessing their passwords, either through brute force, using special password- cracking programs, or both. One way to protect your computer and network from password cracking is based on the "it takes a thief to catch a thief" maxim. Obtain a password-cracking program and run it on all the computers in your network to see whose passwords are most vulnerable. Then educate those users as to how to choose more secure passwords.

Now to elaborate.

What is spoofing?

Crackers who pretend to be other people are *spoofers*. A cracker spoofs in order to use someone else's access rights, or to make hosts on a network assume the identities of other hosts — either to disguise the cracker's network identity or to send users to the wrong machines.

What is a virus?

A *virus* is a program or part of a program that makes copies of itself on your computer without your knowledge or permission. Viruses can do all sorts of damage to a computer and network. For example, viruses can grab all the physical and/or virtual memory and hang or crash your computer. A more damaging virus can corrupt data and system files. Some viruses can wipe out your entire operating system. Other viruses learn the system password and send it around the Internet, making it easy for all kinds of crackers to break into your system. Another kind of virus can infect the boot sector and make the computer impossible to boot.

Although we've had viruses on our Windows systems, and our VAX was hit by the 1988 worm, the Cardinal network used in the examples for this book has never been infected by a Linux virus. Why? By its very design and built-in security features, particularly file permissions, Linux is quite resistant to viruses because they cannot replicate themselves into key areas of the system. As long as you protect the root password, only log in as root when you need to, and are careful about using programs downloaded from the Internet, Linux is very well protected against viruses. You will learn more about the root password later in this chapter.

What is a worm?

A worm is a kind of virus that replicates itself across a network. The main difference between viruses and worms is in the way they spread. A virus infects files or the boot sector on a computer and spreads via file transfers between computers. The computers don't need to be networked for a virus to spread. A common non-networked way for viruses to spread is by shared floppy disks. A worm spreads via network connections. The Internet worm of 1988 copied itself across the Internet, infecting computers with so many copies of itself that the infected systems eventually became unusable. Many corporate networks had to disconnect from the Internet to recover from the worm and get vaccinated so that they would be immune to a re-infection.

What is a Trojan horse?

In terms of computer security, a Trojan horse is a malicious program disguised as something good. When a Trojan horse program executes, it usually loads a virus onto your system. For example, the program pkz300b.exe disguised itself as an archiving and compression utility, but it actually removed the contents of a hard-disk drive.

An Example of a Linux Trojan Horse

The util-linux package contains a group of system utilities for Linux, including the `fdisk` configuration tool and the login program. You can get the package from many different FTP servers around the world. In January of 1999, some delinquent placed a Trojan horse file named util-linux-2.9g.tar.gz on at least one FTP server, which may then have distributed the Trojan horse copy to mirror FTP sites. The infected util-linux package modified the program /bin/login to send the host name and UID of users who logged in to a system using the infected /bin/login to an address on the Internet. To make checking difficult, the Trojan horse file had the same date-time stamp as the legitimate version.

If you have a recent version of a Linux distribution or if you keep up to date with patches, you have the legitimate version of util-linux. If you're not sure whether you have the real thing or the Trojan horse, use the following command to check your package:

```
root@yourpc# strings /bin/login | grep "HELO"
```

If your util-linux package is okay, this command will return no output. If you have the Trojan horse version of util-linux, the strings command will return the following:

```
HELO 127.0.0.1
```

If you need to replace the Trojan horse version of util-linux-2.9, you can FTP a copy from `ftp://ftp.win.tue.nl/pub/linux/utils/util-linux/util-linux-2.9h.tar.gz`

One way of ensuring that you do not copy or receive Trojan horses is to accept only digitally signed data. A digital signature proves that data and messages are actually being sent by the person who claims to be sending them.

See the section in this chapter about PGP (Pretty Good Privacy) to read about public and private (secret) keys and how they work with digital signatures.

You create a digital signature with a private key and the data. The recipient verifies the data with your public key. Verifying the data validates the sender and also checks the contents of the data or message so that you know they have not been changed by a cracker during the transport.

When you are loading packages onto your computer, ensure that you are not loading a Trojan horse by checking that both source and binary packages are signed. You can use your package management software to do this. The following example shows how to use RPM to check for a valid digital signature. The command syntax is as follows:

```
rpm -checksig Package-file
```

The following example checks that the new `seahorse` binary package I just downloaded has a valid signature. The `seahorse` package is in my local directory. When you run `rpm`, be sure to `cd` to your package directory or use the full path of the package.

```
# rpm -checksig /seahorse-0.4.9-1.i386.rpm
/local/newpkg/seahorse-0.4.9-1.i386.rpm
```

The `OK` in the preceding output means that the package has a digital signature.

Tip   CERT[i] is the Computer Emergency Response Team. To learn more about Trojan horses, read the CERT[i] Advisory CA-1999-02 Trojan Horses, at `http://www.cert.org/advisories/CA-1999-02.html`.

What is a denial of service attack (DoS)?

A denial of service (DoS) attack occurs when malicious users send so much traffic to computers that authorized users can't perform normal activities because the computers and/or networks are too busy. The most common DoS attacks send multiple network packets to an Internet server, such as an e-mail, Web, or FTP server, and gobble up the server's resources, making the system unusable.

Tip   Using quotas on user filesystems (such as /home) helps protect against Denial of Service attacks because non-privileged users cannot fill the entire filesystem. Chapter 10, "Managing Filesystems and Swap Space," tells you how to establish filesystem quotas.

Devising a Security Strategy

Everyone involved in setting up security must consider a variety of questions. What are you protecting and from whom? Are the regular users on your network a greater threat than outsiders trying to break in? How much are you willing to pay, and for how much protection? How much inconvenience will legitimate users tolerate? Your security strategy for both individual computers and whole networks involves:

✦ Organization policies and procedures

✦ Physical security

✦ Password security

✦ Filesystem security

✦ Network security

Security policies and procedures

Your security strategy must cover three issues when users send and receive data both locally and across a network. These issues apply to your business's LAN (local area network) as well as to WANS (wide-area networks) such as the Internet. These issues are:

✦ Security

✦ Authenticity

✦ Integrity

Data security means that no one but the intended recipient can read your data. Encryption and public/private keys guarantee that only your intended audience can read any data you transmit. Authenticity means that the originator of the data (for example, the person who sent you an e-mail message) is really the person he or she claims to be, and that the host that originated the data is really the host it claims to be. Digital signatures guarantee authenticity. Integrity means that no one has modified the data during their trip across the network, so that the data you receive are exactly the data that were sent. Digital signatures guarantee that data in transit is not hacked.

Being connected to a network, and especially the Internet, comes with security risks. Are the risks and extra work worth it? For most people and organizations, the answer is yes, as long as there are policies and procedures to protect individual hosts as well as the entire network. Building these policies and procedures often involves office politics, which, if you're like most system and network administrators, you prefer not to be involved in. However, you need to work with management to set up training and education for users about keeping their accounts and data safe and about rules and regulations, including the consequences of breaking the rules.

Physical security

Physical security is the simplest and yet most underused area of security in the computer world. There are two aspects of physical security. First, you need to protect your computer from being stolen or worked on when you're not around. The idea is to restrict physical access to your machine to prevent vandalism or theft of your equipment by physical means, such as locked doors, as well as password-locking mechanisms. Next, you need to keep illegal devices off your network. For example, even if all your computers are well protected, if someone can physically tap into your network cable and add an unauthorized computer you may find your network in chaos.

Password security

Properly chosen password systems keep all but the most sophisticated crackers out of your system, while improperly chosen passwords are practically an invitation to unauthorized users.

Filesystem security

Permissions are important in preventing accidental damage to your files should you or someone else access or edit something that is better left alone.

Network security

Network security includes physical security, password security, and filesystem security for each individual client and server on the network, as well as methods to secure network connections, such as setting up firewalls, encrypting passwords and data that go across the network media, using network applications with built-in security, and tracking intruders who try to break into your system from a remote location.

Immediately after installing your Linux distribution, go to the distribution's Web site and see if there are any security patches for the release you just installed. There probably will be. For example, if you have just installed Red Hat 7, go to `www.redhat.com/support/errata/rh7-errata-security.html` to see a list of Red Hat 7 Security Advisories. The updates include patches for potential security problems with `ping`, `gnorpm`, possible local denial-of-service exploitation, and more. Whatever version and distribution you install, before allowing users on the system or enabling networking, download and install the security patches.

Linux developers on all distributions are constantly working to enhance default system-security features. However, the default security features of most Linux distributions are weak and the security features used vary from distribution to distribution. Be sure to find out what default security mechanisms your distribution provides.

For example, Caldera OpenLinux eServer, used on tweety, provides some of the most stringent default security features. Phat Linux provides fewer default security features. This does not mean that you can't have a secure Phat installation. It simply means that you may need to download additional security packages and modify the kernel to support them.

Securing your Physical Environment

Physical locks can be anything from a padlock to a door lock. If you work at a company with a lot of foot traffic through your computer areas or where there has been a theft problem in the past, consider a combination of any of the following:

✦ Door locks on the computer room with key access for administrative personnel only.

✦ A keycard system that logs entries into and exits from the computer room.

✦ A security camera system.

✦ A case-lock system for each computer console.

Most computer vendors, when selling machines to a lab-like setup, include a kind of case-lock system. Depending on the design, case locks can prevent your computer from being stolen. Case locks don't have to be 100% foolproof, but should function as a deterrent, much like noisy car alarms. Different case locks perform different functions. A case lock may prevent intruders from using the following attacks:

✦ Opening the case and using or stealing your hardware, unless the case is broken.

✦ Rebooting your computer from the intruder's personal boot floppy disk.

✦ Connecting new keyboards or mice.

The idea is to create enough of a disincentive that a thief may not bother to tamper with a computer.

Caution

Some computers, such as Sun SPARCs and Apple Macs, have a dongle on the back through which you can thread a cable. To break into these machines, attackers have to cut the cable or destroy the case. If you lock your computer to another object, such as a workbench or drafting table, make sure that the object can't be sawed through. Also remember that it's easy to pick simple discount-store-type locks.

Protecting the BIOS (Basic Input Output System)

All computers have machine-level code that determines how your computer boots and how the operating system communicates with the hardware. This low-level code is called by different names on different hardware architectures. For example, Macs call it firmware, while some Suns and older VAXes call it the boot PROM, and PCs and some Alphas call it the BIOS. The BIOS resides on a chip on the motherboard. The BIOS enables you to boot the computer. When you turn a computer on, one of the first messages you see is about the BIOS. The BIOS is the code that provides basic hardware functionality, such as managing the disk drives, serial ports, keyboard, and display.

Cross-Reference

You'll find the Linux BIOS home page at `http://www.acl.lanl.gov/linuxbios`.

The BIOS may be another vulnerable spot that you need to protect. By manipulating the BIOS, attackers can boot your computer, gaining unauthorized access to the operating system.

Many PC BIOSes let you set a boot password. A boot password can be a deterrent, but don't be lulled into a false sense of security. A BIOS password is a limited form of security. An expert cracker can reset the BIOS and even remove the chip if the computer case can be opened.

Some BIOSes enable you to specify additional security settings. Since each vendor's BIOS is different, check your BIOS documentation or go to the manufacturer's Web site to see what you can do. For example, you may be able to disable booting from floppy disks.

Securing Linux at the boot-loader level

Most Linux boot loaders enable you to set a boot password. LILO enable you to set password and restricted settings. The password setting requires a password at each boot. The restricted setting requires a boot password only if you specify options (such as `single`) at the LILO prompt. Be sure to check the lilo.conf man page. The following example shows an excerpt from the file /etc/lilo.conf that implements a LILO password following the image section. If you plan to use the `restricted` setting, add it to the lilo.conf file immediately following the password line, as in the following example.

```
root@flyingpenguin# cat /etc/lilo.conf
boot=/dev/hda
map=/boot/map
install=/boot/boot.b
prompt
timeout=50
default=linux
message=/boot/message
linear

image=/boot/vmlinuz-2.2.16-22
        label=linux
        read-only
        root=/dev/hda1
password="IheartLinux99"
restricted
```

Run the `lilo` command to make your changes take effect without rebooting. Be sure to set permissions for /etc/lilo.conf so that only root can read the file.

```
root@flyingpenguin# ls -l /etc/lilo.conf
-rw-r--r--    1 root    root  181 Oct 15 17:48 /etc/lilo.conf
root@flyingpenguin# chmod 600 /etc/lilo.conf
root@flyingpenguin# ls -l /etc/lilo.conf
-rw-------    1 root    root  181 Oct 15 17:48 /etc/lilo.conf
```

Caution

You always need to balance security methods with practicality. When you set a BIOS and/or LILO password, the computer cannot boot unattended because it waits for you to enter the BIOS password. Keep in mind when you consider whether to set BIOS and LILO passwords that someone would have to come in and supply the password in the event of a power failure at 2 AM on a national holiday. This is an especially important consideration for server computers.

Cross-Reference

Chapter 2, "Getting Ready to Install Linux," has more information about LILO.

Passwords Everywhere

Remember that setting passwords on various computer components means that you must remember those passwords. Using the same password for root, the BIOS, and LILO may be convenient, but if a cracker guesses one password, he or she has access to all components you think you have password-protected. If you decide to write all the passwords down, be sure to hide the paper. Don't forget where you hide it, and realize that if a cracker is serious, he or she will look in all the obvious and not-so-obvious places for a paper with passwords on it. Don't even think about attaching the paper to the computer.

Cross-Reference For tips on selecting secure passwords, see the section "Implementing Password Security."

Using display locks

Display locks are the beginning of security for any operating system with a GUI (Graphic User Interface). This includes any version of Linux that is running a desktop program like GNOME or KDE. When a machine with a display lock is left alone for a period of time, the screen saver appears, blocks out the view of the desktop, and won't let anyone return to the desktop without entering the correct password. Display locks are very helpful in preventing system and file vandalism by those who shouldn't be looking at unattended screens.

Note Since display locks aren't an integrated or networked function, you must go to each monitor on your network and enter the appropriate settings, as determined by the operating system in question.

You can implement the display-locking feature in Linux from your graphical desktop. The procedures for GNOME and KDE are similar. To configure your screen saver from the GNOME interface, follow these steps:

1. Click the Main Menu button on the GNOME panel.
2. Choose Settings ➪ Desktop ➪ Screensaver.
3. Select the Require Password checkbox by clicking it.
4. Click OK to exit.

The problem with display locks

Display locks do not necessarily prevent someone from switching out of the X Window System to a virtual-console login prompt, or to the virtual console that X11 was started from, and suspending it and your privileges — a reason not to be root unless you really need to be.

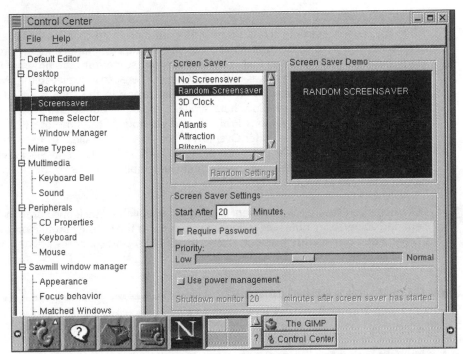

Figure 29-1: Selecting the Require Password checkbox

Tip   Don't log into a graphical system as root. Log in as an unprivileged user and create a terminal window where you can su to be root. If you leave your computer, even for a few minutes, close the root's terminal window.

Another security hole exists in some old versions of xlock, a commonly used display-locking program. xlock comes in most Linux distributions that support X, along with a man page that describes the options. You can run xlock from any xterm on your console and it will lock the display and require a valid password to unlock it. However, some old versions of xlock copy the encrypted root password, and if xlock crashes or a cracker deliberately crashes it, the encrypted root password will be available to run through one of the many publicly available password decrypters. Whoever decrypts it will then have unlimited access to your system. The CERT Advisory CA-1997-13, "Vulnerability in xlock," describes the problem in more detail.

If you have an old version of xlock (vintage 1997), be sure to download and install a patch to close the security hole. Another solution is to use a display locker that you know does not have this vulnerability, such as xlockmore.

Caution

While the xlock example refers to an old security problem that most readers don't have, you need to be aware that problems like this can surface in any program that runs with SUID and that enables a user to escape from the program to the shell. The xlock problem was particularly severe because it displayed the root password. The type of security hole that lets you escape to the shell is called a *buffer overflow*. A buffer overflow hole similar to xlock's surfaced in 1999 on servers running the FTP daemons ProFTPD and wu-ftpd. At the time of CERT(r)'s Advisory, CA-1999-03, "FTP Buffer Overflows," wu-ftp was installed and enabled by default on many popular Linux distributions, such as Red Hat and Slackware Linux. A more recent buffer-overflow security vulnerability in vixie-cron was reported to CERT in 2000.

On the CD-ROM

CERT helps you keep up with current security vulnerabilities. You'll find some incident and vulnerability notes regarding Linux security in the security bundle on the CD-ROM that comes with this book. Access the CERT Web site, www.cert.org, to stay up to date.

How do you lock a virtual console?

You can't use a graphical display lock, such as a screen-saver lock, if you don't use a GUI. If you are text-based, use a virtual console locker program such as vlock. vlock enables you to lock any or all of the virtual consoles on your Linux computer. It works with many Linux distributions, including Red Hat, Mandrake, TurboLinux, and OpenLinux.

Tip

If you don't have a virtual console locker, go to http://rpmfind.net/linux/ RPM/vlock.html to download an RPM-format package of vlock for your Linux distribution.

Nothing's perfect, especially in the security world. Locking your console prevents people from tampering with your current login, but it doesn't keep them from rebooting your computer and trying to break in via single-user mode. To keep someone from rebooting your computer to gain access, password-protect your BIOS and boot loader. However, it is trivially easy to reset a BIOS password on most IBM-compatible PCs by simply removing the CMOS battery and waiting a few minutes. To circumvent a boot loader password, all someone needs is a boot disk and the ability to set the BIOS to boot from a floppy disk.

Implementing Password Security

The most basic form of computer and network protection starts at the choice of passwords. Linux (and UNIX) automatically encrypt the password for every account.

Caution Just because Linux uses encrypted passwords, don't think that all passwords are safe. Password-cracking programs are publicly available on the Web.

Since passwords are the key to gaining access to Linux, they are the first line of defense against anyone who wants to log in, locally or remotely, with the intention of doing damage to files anywhere on your network. Therefore, it's in users' best interests to try to choose passwords that are difficult to crack. Passwords should never have a direct, obvious connection to a user. Don't use first names, last names, birthdates, usernames, or any combination of the above. In fact, it's best if you avoid using your nickname, your dog's name, or even a favorite quote as a password to the system.

The following is a list of suggestions for creating a password:

✦ Use a word or phrase that has no meaning to anyone but yourself. Such a word should not be a *compound word*. A compound word is two or more words stuck together to form a single word, such as theend or linuxuser. Do not use words that are found in the dictionary or encyclopedia, either, because password-cracking programs look for both compound words and dictionary words.

✦ Use the first letters of each word of a personal phrase, such as EITQOAT ("Emily is the queen of all things").

✦ Since Linux is case-sensitive, throw in a capital letter or two anywhere but at the first position in the password.

✦ Add numeric characters for added difficulty.

Caution Although some people think reversing words or names (turning johnny into ynnhoj) is clever, it's actually not a good idea. Many cracking programs do the same thing.

Assigning and changing user passwords

All of your password additions, subtractions, and alterations take place in the /etc/passwd or /etc/shadow file. You use the `passwd` command to create and change passwords.

Cross-Reference Chapter 14, "Logging in and Starting to Use Linux," shows how to use the `passwd` command to change a password. Each user can change his or her password, but only root can change someone else's password.

Encrypting Passwords — DES vs. PAM

The default algorithm, or mathematical cipher, that Linux uses to encrypt passwords is called DES (Data Encryption Standard). During a login attempt, the password entered from the Password: prompt is re-encrypted and compared with the encryption pattern stored in your /etc/passwd or etc/shadow file. Linux grants access if the encryption patterns match.

If you want to make decryption more difficult for crackers, consider using a different encryption scheme. You can use different encryption algorithms if you use PAM — Pluggable Authentication Modules. Sun Microsystems originally designed PAM, and most of the major Linux distributions, including Caldera, Debian, and Red Hat, support Linux-PAM.

Note   Configuring PAM is beyond the scope of a single chapter. See the PAM home page, `www.kernel.org/pub/linux/libs/pam`, for more complete information, including the PAM manual and the manual for configuring PAM in pam.conf.

PAM is a flexible mechanism for authenticating users. Using PAM allows programs to be independent of a specific authentication strategy and encryption algorithm, such as DES. To enable the programs' independence, the system administrator must configure *authentication modules*, which perform a certain kind of authentication selected by the administrator, to be attached to programs, including the login program, at runtime. PAM enables you to do more than replace DES encryption for passwords. By using PAM, you can also:

✦ Set resource limits, such as the maximum number of processes and maximum amount of memory a user can allocate, so that individual users will find it difficult to clog your system or perform denial-of-service attacks.

✦ Disable the use of .rhosts files and the `rexec` and `rlogin` programs.

✦ Add extra security rules, such as allowing specific users to log in only at specific times and/or from specific locations.

Using password and group shadow files

To add an extra layer to password and group security, you can use a technique called *shadowing*. Both password and group mechanisms move certain information from the world-readable standard files (passwd and/or group) into the root-only readable shadow files:

✦ /etc/shadow, which stores encrypted passwords and maintains additional password information, including:

- `PASS_MIN_DAYS`
- `PASS_MAX_DAYS`
- `PASS_WARN_AGE`

✦ /etc/gshadow, which stores encrypted group passwords, if any exist. Group passwords are not usually used.

Shadowing and unshadowing passwords

An alternative to storing encrypted passwords in the world-readable /etc/passwd file is moving the encrypted passwords from the world-readable passwd file to the shadow file /etc/shadow. Using a shadow file is one of the most important things you can do to protect your system and network because only the root account can read shadow password file. This mechanism helps protect users' encrypted passwords from password crackers.

When you install Linux, most distributions ask whether you want to use a shadow passwd file. Respond yes, and the installation procedure automatically creates /etc/shadow. If you're not sure whether your Linux system shadows passwords, look inside the /etc/passwd file. If you see an *x* in the password field for any account, your passwords are shadowed in /etc/passwd. The following are a couple of different ways to determine whether you have shadowed passwords:

```
root@flyingpenguin# tail -1 /etc/passwd
testing:x:751:751::/root/1xt:/bin/sh
root@flyingpenguin# head -1 /etc/passwd
root:x:0:0:root:/root:/bin/bash
```

When you see an *x* in the second field (the encrypted password field), the passwords have been moved to the shadow file. If the passwords are not shadowed, you see the encrypted password in the second field. Run the pwconv command as root to move the passwords to the shadow file, as in the following example:

```
root@flyingpenguin# pwconv
```

By default, most Linux systems use shadow passwords. You can make the change to using the shadow file for your passwords with the pwconv (password conversion) command. The fields in the /etc/passwd file are copied into the shadow file and hidden from all users except root.

The pwconv command creates /etc/shadow from /etc/passwd and moves the encrypted password to the shadow file. Here is an excerpt from a passwd file before conversion to shadowing:

```
root@flyingpenguin# more /etc/passwd
root:Glen$j8I5GzXipV:0:0:root:/root:/bin/bash
bin:*:1:1:bin:/bin:
   | (edited for brevity)
admin:cnO//1$fMCOfGL.:1000:500:Notes
Admin:/home/admin:/bin/bash
notes:ekuFzE$2aTRRl/:1001:501:Domino Server
account:/home/notes:/bin/bash
miss_scarlet:RBmUi$ET:500:506:emily lauren
scarlet:/home/miss_scarlet:/bin/csh
candace:V7ah9ak$F5fvZg:501:100:candace
leiden:/home/candace:/bin/bash
```

```
marshall:1Ox.UdKbBS8xcL4w0:502:100:marshall
wilensky:/home/marshall:/bin/bash
professor_plum:$xGmDQP8sv.:503:100:professor
plum:/home/prof_plum:/bin/bash
  | (edited for brevity)
```

After you run `pwconv` to shadow the passwords, the password file no longer contains any encrypted passwords. The *xes* are placeholders for the encrypted passwords. The following example enables password shadowing and displays the passwd file after shadowing.

```
root@flyingpenguin# /usr/sbin/pwconv
```

Tip

If the `pwconv` command is successful it returns to your shell prompt with no message.

```
root@flyingpenguin# more /etc/passwd
root:x:0:0:root:/root:/bin/bash
bin:x:1:1:bin:/bin:
    | (edited for brevity)
admin:x:1000:500:Notes Admin:/home/admin:/bin/bash
notes:x:1001:501:Domino Server account:/home/notes:/bin/bash
miss_scarlet:x:500:506:emily lauren
scarlet:/home/miss_scarlet:/bin/csh
candace:x:501:100:candace leiden:/home/candace:/bin/bash
marshall:x:502:100:marshall wilensky:/home/marshall:/bin/bash
professor_plum:x:503:100:professor
plum:/home/prof_plum:/bin/bash
        | (edited for brevity)
```

Password aging—it happens to everyone

If you've set values for PASS_MIN_DAYS, PASS_MAX_DAYS, and PASS_WARN_AGE in the file /etc/login.defs, `pwconv` includes that information in the shadow file. Each time you log in, these password-aging controls keep track of your password use and remind you when your password will expire.

```
root@flyingpenguin# more /etc/login.defs
# *REQUIRED*
#   Directory where mailboxes reside, _or_ name of file,
#       relative to the home directory.
#
   If you _do_ define both, MAIL_DIR takes precedence.

MAIL_DIR        /var/spool/mail

# Password aging controls:
#
```

```
#          PASS_MAX_DAYS   Maximum number of days you can use a
#                 password before it expires. 99999 never expires.
#          PASS_MIN_DAYS   Minimum number of days allowed between
#                 password changes.
#          PASS_MIN_LEN    Minimum acceptable password length.
#          PASS_WARN_AGE   Number of days warning given before a
#                 password expires.
#
PASS_MAX_DAYS    90
PASS_MIN_DAYS    5
PASS_MIN_LEN     9
PASS_WARN_AGE    7
#
# Min/max values for automatic uid selection in useradd
#
UID_MIN                    500
UID_MAX                    60000


#
# Min/max values for automatic gid selection in groupadd
#
GID_MIN                    500
GID_MAX                    60000


#
# If defined, this command is run when removing a user.
# It should remove any at/cron/print jobs etc. owned by
# the user to be removed (passed as the first argument).
#
#USERDEL_CMD      /usr/sbin/userdel_local


#
# If useradd should create home directories for users by
default
# On RH systems, we do. This option is ORed with the -m flag on
# useradd command line.
#
CREATE_HOME      yes
```

If you need to undo shadowing, use the /user/sbin/pwunconv to rebuild the encrypted passwords back into /etc/ and remove the shadow file.

Tip   If you prefer to manage password aging graphically, you can use either COAS or linuxconf, depending on what you have installed on your system. You may, in fact, have both installed: they run on other distributions in addition to Caldera and Red Hat.

Note   If you want to use linuxconf, invoke it from the main menu. You can do this from the KDE or GNOME main menu, as shown in Figures 29-2, 29-3, and 29-4.

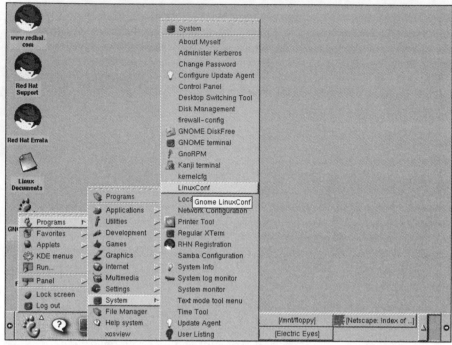

Figure 29-2: Invoking `linuxconf` from GNOME

Shadowing groups

If you use group passwords, which is not usual practice, you can use the `grpconv` and `grpunconv` commands to convert the standard /etc/group file to its shadowed counterpart, /etc/gshadow, and back again. The following example converts /etc/group to /etc/gshadow.

```
root@flyingpenguin# /usr/sbin/grpconv
root@flyingpenguin#
```

Tip   Errors in the password or group files, such as invalid or duplicate entries, may cause these shadow programs to generate unexpected results or fail completely. To prepare to run the shadow programs, run `pwck` and `grpck` commands to correct any possible errors before running `pwconv` or `grpconv`. Here is an example with warnings, but no errors that need correcting:

```
root@flyingpenguin# /usr/sbin/pwck
user adm: directory /var/adm does not exist
user uucp: directory /var/spool/uucp does not exist
user gopher: directory /usr/lib/gopher-data does not
exist
user gdm: directory /home/gdm does not exist
pwck: no changes
```

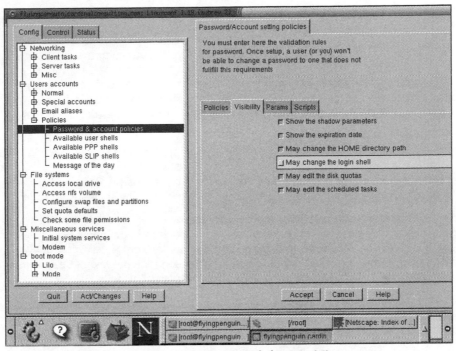

Figure 29-3: Using `linuxconf` to set password characteristics

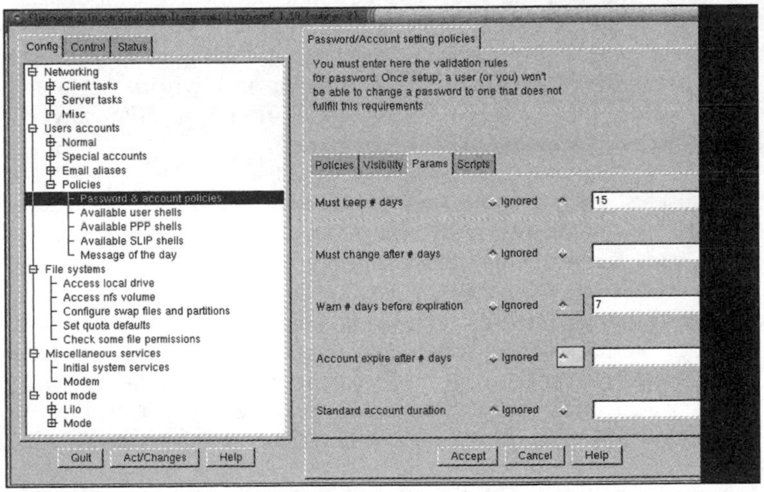

Figure 29-4: Setting more password characteristics with `linuxconf`

I Forgot the Root Password

If everyone forgets the root password, it's easy to boot your Linux computer into single-user mode at the LILO prompt by typing `linux single`. This logs you in as root without a password. Now that you're root, you can change the root password. Before you change the password, you need to `umount` and `mount` the root filesystem in read-write (`rw`) mode. On most Linux systems, booting into single-user mode mounts the root filesystem as `ro` (read-only).

Therefore, anyone who has physical access to your computer can sneak in, boot to single-user mode, change the root password, initialize full timesharing, and do all sorts of damage. Remember that no computer is secure if other people have physical access to the console, but adding a LILO password prevents users from breaking in using single-user mode.

If you forget both the root password and the LILO password, you may still be able to get in if you have a boot floppy. Boot your computer from your Linux boot floppy. Next, mount the root (/) filesystem in read-write (`rw`) mode and change the root password. Booting from the floppy automatically makes you root without any need for a password. Be sure to keep your boot floppy locked up so no one can invade your system with it.

If you forget both the root password and the LILO password, and you don't have a boot floppy, you need to reinstall Linux.

Checking passwords

To be completely sure that you and your users choose passwords that are hard to guess or crack, run a password-cracking program similar to the ones that the people who try to infiltrate your computer use. Password-cracking programs work by trying every word in the dictionary, and then variations and hybrids of those words, encrypting each one and checking it against your encrypted password. If they get a match, they've cracked your password.

Note   An attacker must first get into your system or network by means of some security weakness besides /etc/passwd in order to read your /etc/passwd file. Unfortunately, such security holes are too common.

Three favorite cracking programs are crackerjack, Crack (`http://www.ja.net/CERT/CERT-CC/tools/crack/`), and John the Ripper (`http://www.openwall.com/john`). If you run one of these programs, you can determine whether an attacker can get in using them. Notify users with crackable passwords, and run the program again after you've given them time to change to stronger passwords.

Tip   Cracking programs use lots of CPU time. To avoid affecting users, test your passwords when there are few other users logged in.

Tip

On a network, security is only as strong as the most unprotected host. If you have a mixed network, you may want to investigate cracking programs for your other operating systems, such as L0phtCrack, a Crack implementation for Windows 98 and NT. It's available from http://www.10pht.com for a free 15-day trial.

Cross-Reference

You can also password-protect things other than users, including the BIOS of your computer and LILO, the boot loader. See the earlier sections "Protecting the BIOS" and "Securing Linux at the boot-loader level."

su-ing to the root Account

When you need to be root, use the su command. Log into your regular non-privileged account and type su (switch user, substitute user). See the sidebar "Rules for root" for reasons why you should not log in as root directly. By default, su redefines the environment variables HOME and SHELL to the context of the user to which you are switching. However, su does not by default change the current directory. The following code is an example of using the su command to become root, where the user must cd to get to root's home directory.

```
login: miss_scarlet
Password:xxxxxxxxx
Last login: Sun Oct 8 14:53:21 from 192.168.0.5

HOWDY DOODY, Linux folks
        Have a nice day
----------------------------------------
You have mail.
miss_scarlet@flyingpenguin$ su
Password:xxxxxxxxxxxxx
root@flyingpenguin# whoami
root
root@flyingpenguin# pwd
/home/miss_scarlet
root@flyingpenguin# cd
root@flyingpenguin# /root# pwd
/root
```

In the example above, miss scarlet types the su command. She types the root password at the Password: prompt. Although she retains her login directory, the whoami command shows that miss_scarlet is now root. Her prompt still identifies her as miss_scarlet. Running the cd command relocates miss_scarlet to root's home directory. The fact that her bash prompt changes to reflect root's home directory is a function of how root's .bash_profile defines the PS1 variable.

Rules for root

✦ Don't log in as root. Be sure to have a "regular," non-privileged account for yourself. Log in as you, and su to root when you need to perform privileged tasks, such as adding a user or configuring a service. There are a few good reasons to take this precaution:

- When you run programs as root, you have effectively disabled all the protections that make Linux secure, including those protections that make Linux less vulnerable to virus infections.

- As root, a single typographical error can damage not only your own files and directories, but other users' as well.

- If any applications have security holes, logging in as a regular user limits the damage those programs can cause.

✦ Keep the value for root's PATH environment variable as short as possible. *Never* include . (the current directory) or writable directories in root's PATH. If you do, an attacker who gets in as root can modify existing binary files or add new binaries in a PATH directory, allowing those new bogus programs to run as root.

✦ Don't use the Berkeley r utilities (rlogin/rsh/rexec) at all because they send passwords in clear text, which is easily intercepted by network sniffer programs. The r utilities are especially dangerous when executed by the root user.

✦ Never create a .rhosts file for root. This makes it easy for someone to break into the root account without a password.

✦ Be discriminating when you set up the file /etc/securetty because it lists the terminals that can accept a root login. Suppose the lobby in your office building has a public terminal where guests can log in to check their e-mail. You don't want to allow users to try to guess the root password while they're waiting to meet you in the lobby. The following listing shows a typical /etc/securetty file:

```
root@flyingpenguin# cat /etc/securetty
tty1
tty2
tty3
tty4
tty5
tty6
tty7
tty8
```

✦ Check the default setup of /etc/securetty. The Red Hat installation, for example, creates this file to enable root logins only from local virtual consoles (vtys).

✦ If you need to log in remotely, always use your regular account and su if you need to (hopefully sending your password across the network encrypted via ssh or some other encryption mechanism).

✦ Think twice, type once.

Tip If you are running with a GUI such as the GNOME or KDE desktops, log in as your non-privileged account, create a terminal window, and type the `su` command as in the following example. Your graphical environment remains non-privileged while you work as root in the terminal window.

When you are finished with root chores, type exit or Ctrl-D to close the root job and return to being your "regular," non-privileged self, as follows:

```
root@flyingpenguin# exit
logout
miss_scarlet@flyingpenguin$ whoami
miss_scarlet
miss_scarlet@flyingpenguin$ pwd
/home/miss_scarlet
```

If you try to `su`, as miss_scarlet does in the example below, and don't know the correct password, `su` returns the message `incorrect password` and leaves you in your non-privileged account.

```
miss_scarlet@flyingpenguin$ su
Password: xxxxxxxxxxx
su: incorrect password
miss_scarlet@flyingpenguin$ whoami
miss_scarlet
```

Note You can also `su` (with the `-l` option) to another user's identity if you know the password. In the example below, miss_scarlet uses the `su` command to become professor plum.

```
miss_scarlet@flyingpenguin$ whoami
miss_scarlet
miss_scarlet@flyingpenguin$ su -l professor_plum
Password: xxxxxxxxxxx
professor_plum@flyingpenguin$ whoami
professor_plum
professor_plum@flyingpenguin$ exit
logout
miss_scarlet@flyingpenguin$
```

Logging su

Linux keeps track of all `su` attempts, both successful and failed, in a file called the sulog. The sulog resides in different directories in different Linux distributions. For example, Red Hat stores the sulog in the file, /var/log/messages. Wherever your distribution stores the sulog, you should use this log to see who has been using root's privileges as well as to see who may have been trying to break into the root account (or another user's). The sulog messages below show the following activities:

✦ miss_scarlet's attempt to su to root.

✦ miss_scarlet's authentication failure to login to root.

✦ miss_scarlet's successful su to root.

✦ miss_scarlet's normal exit (logout) from her successful root session.

```
Oct 13 14:17:42 flyingpenguin PAM_pwdb[19181]: authentication
failure;(uid=0)-> miss_scarlet for login service
Oct 13 14:17:43 flyingpenguin login[19181]: FAILED LOGIN 1 FROM
192.168.0.5 FOR miss_scarlet, Authentication failure
Oct 13 14:19:05 flyingpenguin PAM_pwdb[19195]: (su) session
opened for user root by miss_scarlet(uid=500)
Oct 13 14:29:18 flyingpenguin PAM_pwdb[19195]: (su) session
closed for user root
```

Note   The sulog matches up messages by an identifier that the su command assigns for each session.

Note   If you are root, you can su to any other user's account without knowing the password.

The rest of the story

Remember I told you there are reasons why you should not log in as root directly? Well here they are!

Checking Filesystem Security

Filesystem security is about restricting file and directory permissions, using SUID and SGID permissions sparingly, checking for and removing suspicious files, and setting a system-wide default permission scheme.

Cross-Reference   Chapter 19, "Securing a Linux System," explores setting file and directory access permissions for system security in detail.

Checking file permissions

Depending on the permissions you grant to a file or directory in Linux, it can be available to everyone, to members of a specific group, or to only one person. You set permissions based on what kind of access users can perform (read, write, execute) and the rights granted to the users (owner, group, other users).

Finding suspicious files

You should look for files that do not belong on your system, are security holes, or are not well protected. You can use the find command to locate these suspicious files. Write a script with the find commands in the tips below, and submit the script to cron to run automatically every night.

The following find command lists all world-writable files (except symbolic links, -type l) in a report file, worldwrite.rpt:

```
root# find / -perm -2 ! -type l -ls > worldwrite.rpt
root# more worldwrite.rpt
   6414      0 srw-rw-rw-   1 root     root            0
Oct  8 04:02 /dev/log
   4099      0 crw-rw-rw-   1 root     root       1,   3
May  5 1998 /dev/null
   4105      0 crw-rw-rw-   1 root     root      68,   0
Sep 24 1999 /dev/capi20
   4106      0 crw-rw-rw-   1 root     root      68,   1
Sep 24 1999 /dev/capi20.0
0
   4107      0 crw-rw-rw-   1 root     root      68,   2
Sep 24 1999 /dev/capi20.0
1
---------------- output edited --------------
 153605      1 -rw-rw-rw-   1 games    games           4
May 18 1999 /var/lib/games/xhextris-scores
```

The files in /dev must be world-writable. Be sure you know why other files are world-writable. For example, it's normal for shared game scores to be world-writable, but the executables should not be.

Check your system regularly for unowned files. They may be orphans or they may be back doors deliberately created by attackers. The following command starts at the top of the directory tree (/) and searches for all files that have no owner or group:

```
root@flyingpenguin# find / -nouser -o -nogroup -print
```

Look for .rhosts files in all users' directories. These files let other people access your system from remote computers with the identity and privileges of any user who has an .rhost file in the home directory. If you find .rhosts files, remove them and notify the user(s) who owned the file(s). The following command assumes that all users' directories reside below /home.

```
root@flyingpenguin# find /home -name .rhosts -print
```

Checking SUID and SGID settings

You may notice the Set SUID and Set SGID options under the special settings. These two settings should be used with care—preferably not at all, unless you are making a special Linux utility available to all users. This is because the SUID and SGID settings have the following characteristics.

SUID   This describes set-user-id permissions on the file. When the set user ID access mode is set in the owner permissions, and the file is executable, processes that run it are granted access to system resources based on the user who owns the file, as opposed to the user who created the process. This is dangerous because crackers exploit SUID-root programs to grab root permissions and leave a back door to get in again.

SGID   If set in the group permissions, this bit controls the set group id status of a file. SGID behaves like SUID, except that the group is affected instead of a single user.

Tip   Use the following command to find all SUID/SGID programs on your system:

```
root# find / -type f \( -perm -04000 -o -perm -02000 \)
------------------ output edited --------------------
/usr/bin/mahjongg
------------------ output edited --------------------
```

Most of the output from this find command showed system programs that need SUID to work. I did find a game running with SUID. Do I really want a game running as SUID? I didn't, so I removed it. You can also use the chmod command to disable SUID access if you find code that you are not familiar with running SUID.

The Debian Linux distribution automatically runs a nightly job to determine what SUID programs are on your system. It then compares these results to the previous night's run. You can look in /var/log/setuid* for this log.

Setting system-wide default permissions with umask

Adding a umask command to the system configuration file, /etc/profile, sets a default protection scheme for all user files on the system. You can't be sure that users protect their files carefully, but setting a default protection scheme system-wide provides at least some basic file protection. Every newly created file and directory takes its access permission from the umask in /etc/profile. Users can override the default by writing a umask command in their .login files. Remember that the umask is the octal complement of the permission setting. For example, in /etc/profile, the command umask 077 sets strict default protections for all files and directories. If a user wants to share a file, he or she must explicitly change the permissions on the file to be shared.

Guarding Privacy

Some of the terminology used for computer security and privacy comes straight out of the world of secret agents. Here are definitions of some of these concepts.

Cryptography	This is the process of scrambling (encrypting) and deciphering (decrypting) messages in secret code. We have seen some authors use the term *cryptology*, but as far as we know, that's the study of crypts.
Encryption	*Encryption* is the process of scrambling a message into code to conceal its meaning. A common method of encryption is to use a pair of keys — a public key and a private key — to encode data so that only the intended recipient can read it. If Colonel Mustard sends a message to Professor Plum, he encodes the message with Professor Plum's public key. The professor decodes the message with his private key. Only the professor's private key can decode the message. Miss Scarlet can't peek at what Colonel Mustard and Professor Plum are saying.
Encryption key	The *encryption key* is the essential piece of information — a word or number or combination — used in encrypting and decrypting the message.

Note

At the networking level, the new (but not commonly used) IPv6 protocol allows applications to encrypt an entire packet (maximum security) or just the data portion (minimum security) using various mathematical methods.

Public key/private key cryptography	In the public key/private key coding process, one encryption key (the public key) encrypts the message and another key (the private key) decrypts the message. These two keys are related to each mathematically: they are long prime numbers numerically related (factors of another, larger number). You need both keys to translate the message because anything encrypted with one can only be decrypted with the other. Your private key is protected by a passphrase. Never give out the passphrase, as that would virtually destroy the key's effectiveness in protecting your information.
Keys	Each user gets a unique pair of keys — one key is made public and the other is kept private. Public keys are stored in common areas, mailed among users, and may even be printed in newspapers. For Pretty Good Privacy, or PGP (the subject of the next section), to work you must store your private keys in a safe place and protect them. Anyone can have your public key, but only you should have your private key. It works something like this: "You talkin' to me? I won't listen unless you encrypt the message using my public key so that I know no one else is eavesdropping. Only my private key, which no one else has, can decrypt the message, so I know no one else can read it. I don't care that lots of other people have my public key because it can't be used to decrypt the message."

| Digital certificate | A digital certificate stores the public key together with the UID (user ID) of the owner and the creation date of the key. |
| Key ring | A file that stores keys. |

PGP (Pretty Good Privacy)

Would you want to receive all your postal mail by postcard? Of course not. Anyone can read the message on a postcard, which may be fine if the message is "Hi. Having a wonderful time," but which is not fine if the message contains personal information, such as a job offer or a medical report. Most of us want our personal messages and data to be mailed inside an envelope. This desire for privacy extends to e-mail and other forms of electronic communication.

To ensure privacy, there must be some way to guarantee that the person sending you messages and information really is the person he or she claims to be. If you receive a letter from your banker, you want to be sure that it is on official letterhead paper and properly signed. The same is true with e-mail and other computer information. If you get a message from cleiden@office.com, you may want a guarantee that this e-mail is really from Candace and not from someone claiming to be her.

Note   Authentication (usually in the form of a digital signature) ensures that the information you receive was sent by the source that claims to have sent it.

PGP, which stands for Pretty Good Privacy, is based on the cryptographic system called *public key/private key*, which I mentioned in the previous section. PGP guarantees the privacy and authenticity of messages and data sent through insecure channels, such as networks (including the Internet). PGP technology provides the technical underpinnings for secure applications and data. PGP is an exportable, public-domain (free) software package for public key/private key cryptography.

Note   Many versions of PGP, some commercial and some in the public domain, are available. This book uses the GNU Privacy Guard (another free program from the GNU Project), GnuPG, for its examples.

Introducing GnuPG (GNU Privacy Guard)

The GNU Privacy Guard is a free replacement for PGP. GnuPG contains all the functionality and features of PGP (plus a few extras), but does not use the patented algorithm that PGP uses. Since GnuPG is patent-free, you can use it under the GPL with no restrictions. GnuPG works with Linux on the following hardware architectures:

✦ x86 (Intel)

✦ alpha (Compaq)

✦ mips

Key Size versus Import and Export Regulations

For many years, the U.S. government refused to allow cryptographic products to be exported unless the key size was strictly limited. The U.S. defined exportable cryptographic products as "weak" — having a key size of no more than 56 bits.

The more bits there are, the harder it is to break the code. (By the way, 56-bit encryption products are about 64,000 times harder to break than 40-bit products and 128-bit products are way, way, way harder.) The reason for not sharing some of the best U.S.-designed encryption products was that the U.S. traditionally labeled encryption products that use keys with more than 40 bits as "weapons."

In January 2000, the U.S. restrictions on exporting cryptographic products were loosened to allow 128-bit software to be exported. The regulations were relaxed, enabling most United States citizens and business entities to export any cryptographic product without a license. If the end-user of the exported product is a foreign government, they *will* need a license. The U.S. government doesn't allow cryptographic products to be exported to embargoed locations. To see a list of embargoed locations, go to www.bxa.doc.gov.

Other countries have their own initiatives and import or export controls. China has some of the strongest restrictions on cryptographic products. Other countries that strictly control export and import of cryptographic products are Russia and Israel. France used to have strong restrictions on import and domestic use of encryption products, but the French government ended most of the restrictions in 1999. For information on national export controls, check out www.wassenaar.org site. (The Wassenaar arrangement is an international agreement that contributes to regional and international security and stability.)

✦ sparc64 (sun)

✦ m68000 (Apple Mac)

✦ powerpc (Apple)

Tip
GnuPG also runs on many versions of UNIX, on Windows 95/98, and on Windows *x*86 platforms for Windows NT/2000. To see if you have GnuPG installed on your system, use the following rpm command line. If the package is installed, rpm returns the package name, major and minor versions, and patch level.

```
root@flyingpenguin# rpm --query gnupg
gnupg-1.0.2-4
```

Tip
If you currently use PGP, and you would like to convert to GnuPG, you can use a special wrapper program called pgpgpg to translate PGP command syntax into GnuPG syntax. Go to the pgpgpg homepage, http://www.nessie.de/mroth/pgpgpg/, to download the program.

Getting GnuPG

On the Web, the GnuPG download page, `http://www.gnupg.org/download.html`, contains links to GnuPG's primary FTP server, `ftp.gnupg.org`, and to mirror sites in 20 different countries. GnuPG is available for download in three formats:

✦ Debian package

✦ RPM package

✦ Source code

If you download one of the package formats, you get the binary files and the tools you need to run GnuPG on your supported Linux platform. If you need GnuPG for a Linux distribution that does not support either package manager, you can download and build the source code.

Note Installing Red Hat Linux 6.2 automatically installs GnuPG by default.

New Feature Red Hat Linux 7.0 includes a graphical interface (SeaHorse) for configuring GnuPG.

Configuring GnuPG

If you download GnuPG in package format, you install it with your favorite package manager, for example, rpm, `dpkg`, `kpackage` on Caldera, or the COAS front end to RPM.

Cross-Reference See Chapter 7, "Installing Software Packages," for examples of using package managers.

If you download the source code, follow these steps to build and install GnuPG:

1. Unpack the `tar` archive, for example, to unpack the current release as of this writing:

   `tar xvzf gnupg-1.0.3.tar.gz`

2. `cd` to the directory where you put the source code.

3. Use the `make` command to build GnuPG.

4. Install GnuPG (copy the executable and man pages into the installation directory) with the `make install` command.

On the CD-ROM The GnuPG Mini HOWTO contains detailed instructions for building and installing GnuPG from the source code. There is a link to this HOWTO on the CD-ROM.

Tip GnomePGP is a GUI interface to GnuPG. It is available in French, German, Italian, Japanese, and English versions at `http://www.geocities.com/SiliconValley/Chip/3708/gpgp/gpgp.html`.

Working with keys

After you install GnuPG, the next step is to use the `gpg` command to create and manage keys, including:

Creating private and public keys	gpg –gen-key *command*
Exporting public keys	gpg –export *command*
Importing public keys	gpg –import *command*
Revoking private keys	gpg –revoke *command*
Deleting public keys	gpg –delete-key *UID command*

Creating keys

When you run `gpg --gen-key`, `gpg` creates a public/private key pair. You need to input the encryption algorithm and the size of the encryption key you want to use. The example at the end of this section creates a key pair using the default encryption algorithm (DSA and ElGamal) with the largest key size possible (2048 bits).

Tip To learn the technical specifics of various encryption algorithms, go to the PGP DH vs. RSA FAQ at `http://www.scramdisk.clara.net/pgpfaq.html`. DSA is a widely used, non-patented algorithm.

When choosing the key size, you need to decide which is more important to you: higher security or time to calculate the key. A large key decreases the risk for cracking the encryption, but also increases calculation time (and also CPU resources to compute the key). If you have an older processor, such as an early Pentium, computing time may be an issue. However, powerful new processors speed up arithmetic performance. The minimum key length for GnuPG is 768 bits. When security is a top priority, you should choose the largest key size available. After you choose the key size, the `gpg` command prompts for information such as your name, your e-mail address, and comments. Finally, you need to enter a password for the key so that you can revoke the key later if you need to. Follow the guidelines for choosing good passwords (with the `gpg` command, you can use spaces).

Tip Whenever you create a key pair, be sure to create a revoke license. If you ever need to revoke a stolen key, you must have a revoke license before you start. Be sure to keep the revoke license (on disk or paper) safely hidden so that no one else can revoke the key.

The following example creates a key pair that expires four months from the creation date. The passphrase protects the key and enables you to revoke it if necessary. At the end of a successful creation process, the key is created and signed.

```
root@flyingpenguin# gpg --gen-key
gpg (GnuPG) 1.0.4; Copyright (C) 2000 Free Software Foundation,
Inc.
This program comes with ABSOLUTELY NO WARRANTY.
This is free software, and you are welcome to redistribute it
under certain conditions. See the file COPYING for details.

Please select what kind of key you want:
   (1) DSA and ElGamal (default)
   (2) DSA (sign only)
   (4) ElGamal (sign and encrypt)
Your selection? 1
DSA keypair will have 1024 bits.
About to generate a new ELG-E keypair.
              minimum keysize is  768 bits
              default keysize is 1024 bits
    highest suggested keysize is 2048 bits
What keysize do you want? (1024) 2048
Do you really need such a large keysize? yes
Requested keysize is 2048 bits
Please specify how long the key should be valid.
         0 = key does not expire
      <n>  = key expires in n days
      <n>w = key expires in n weeks
      <n>m = key expires in n months
      <n>y = key expires in n years
Key is valid for? (0) 4m
Key expires at Thu 15 Feb 2001 11:17:46 AM EST
Is this correct (y/n)? y
You need a User-ID to identify your key; the software
constructs the user id from Real Name, Comment and Email
Address in this form:
    "Heinrich Heine (Der Dichter) <heinrichh@duesseldorf.de>"

Real name: candace leiden
Email address: cleiden@office.com
Comment: just to illustrate concept for Linux Bible. Will not
be used for actual production purposes.
You selected this USER-ID:
"candace leiden (just to illustrate concept for Linux Bible.
Will not be used for actual production purposes.)
<cleiden@office.com>"

Change (N)ame, (C)omment, (E)mail or (O)kay/(Q)uit? o
You need a Passphrase to protect your secret key.
```

What is a Digital Signature?

When you create a key pair, you get a message that the keys are created and "signed." The major security "gotcha" with public keys is authenticity keys. How do you know that the public key is really valid and not a fake created as an attempt to break your encryption? You add a digital signature to the key to guarantee its veracity. The signature guarantees that the UID of the key really owns that key. Encrypting is only guaranteed safe with the assurance that a digital signature provides. GnuPG guarantees the authenticity of keys based on the signatures and on the level of "ownertrust." Ownertrust represents a level of faith that the owner of a key has for a signature. The ownertrust information is stored in a separate file from the key file. The levels of ownertrust are:

1. Don't know

2. Do NOT trust

3. Trust marginally

4. Trust fully

Use the `gpg --edit-key` UID command to sign a key. The following example shows that the `gpg --edit-key` displays a command prompt where you type commands such as `sign`, `list-sigs`, `revoke-sigs`, and `help`. To add a digital signature, type the `sign` command as in the following example.

```
Enter passphrase: xxxxxxxxxxxx
Repeat passphrase: xxxxxxxxxxxx
We need to generate a lot of random bytes. It is a good idea to
perform some other action (type on the keyboard, move the
mouse, utilize the disks) during the prime generation; this
gives the random number
generator a better chance to gain enough entropy.
+++++.++++++++++++++++++++++++++++++++..++++++++++.+

public and secret key created and signed.
```

After you successfully create a key pair, gpg puts each key on a key ring. The file ~/.gnupg/pubring.gpg is your public key ring. The file ~/.gnupg/secring.gpg is your private (secret) key ring.

Note The key pair created in the following example was created strictly as an example for this book. It is not and has never been used on the Internet. It no longer exists.

Exporting keys

When you want other people to contact you securely, you must distribute your public key(s). You do this by exporting them. You can list the exported keys on your home page or on a public key server. (See Figure 29-5.) The procedure for exporting a key varies with the key server. For example, some key servers require you to paste the ASCII text into a window on the key server's Web page. Another way to submit a key is to e-mail a file containing your key. http://math-www.uni-paderborn.de/pgp/ accepts keys via e-mail. You mail the key to pgp-public-keys@uni-paderborn.de, making the word ADD the subject and the ASCII key the body of the e-mail.

```
root@flyingpenguin# gpg --export -o pgpkeyfile
root@flyingpenguin# ls -l pgpkeyfile
-rw-r--r--    1 root     root      1254 Oct 18 16:32 pgpkeyfile

root@flyingpenguin# file pgpkeyfile
pgpkeyfile: data
```

To export the keys into an ASCII file, use the -a option, your ID (in the case below, cleiden), and redirect the results into a file.

```
root@flyingpenguin# gpg -a --export cleiden ASCIIpublickeyfile
root@flyingpenguin# ls -l ASCIIpublickeyfile
-rw-r--r--  1 root   root   1855 Oct 21 16:07 ASCIIpublickeyfile

root@flyingpenguin# file ASCIIpublickeyfile
ASCIIpublickeyfile: PGP armored data public key block
```

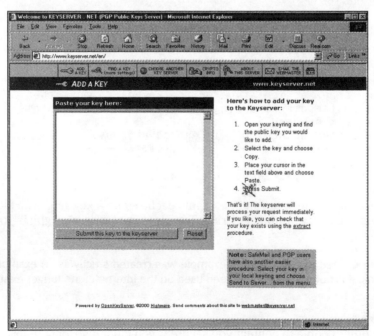

Figure 29-5: A Public key server

What is a Key server?

A public key server, like the one shown in Figure 29-5, is a host on the Web that serves as a repository of public keys. Anyone can submit public keys and certificates and query the database of keys free of charge. A key server stores keys; it does not guarantee that a key is valid. You must check the key's certificates for validation. A key server helps you to exchange keys with other people in order to communicate securely. Most key servers manage thousands and even hundreds of thousands of public keys. The following is a list of some of the many key servers around the world where you can export your key, as well as find someone else's public key.

```
http://belgium.key server.net
http://finland.key server.net
http://germany.key server.net
http://seattle.key server.net
http://thailand.key server.net
http://pgp.ai.mit.edu/
http://akpublic.research.att.com/~reiter/PathServer/
http://goliat.upc.es/~alvar/pks/pks-toplev.html
http://www.cl.cam.ac.uk/PGP/#pks
http://www.service.uit.no/pgp/servruit.eng.html
http://www.nic.surfnet.nl/pgp/pks-toplev.html
http://math-www.uni-paderborn.de/pgp/
http://pgp.tnjc.edu.tw/pgp/pks-toplev.html
http://pgp.uni-mainz.de/key server
```

Importing keys

If you receive someone's public key so that you can read an encrypted message, you must get the key and add it to your key ring before you can use it. You usually import a key from a file. The following is the import syntax:

```
gpg --import filename
```

If you want to type in the key from the keyboard, omit the file name and the gpg command will take the input from stdin.

Tip   You usually get other people's public keys from key servers, home pages, by fingering the other person's account, or from an e-mail message.

Remember that public keys are distributed freely. You don't need to encrypt them or hide them as you would your private key.

Revoking private keys

You may need to revoke a key if it is stolen. You will also need to revoke a key if you want to change the UID or key length. Use the gpg --gen-revoke command to create a revocation certificate.

Remember that you must have the revocation license you made when you originally created the key.

Deleting public keys

When you try to delete a public key, GnuPG checks to see if any private (secret) keys depend on this public key. You must delete private keys before deleting public keys. The following example shows the message GnuPG gives you when you try to delete a public key that still has a private-key dependency:

```
root@flyingpenguin# gpg -delete-key miss_scarlet
gpg (GnuPG) 1.0.4; Copyright (c) 2000 Free Software Foundation,
Inc.
This program comes with ABSOLUTELY NO WARRANTY.
This is free software, and you are welcome to redistribute it
under certain conditions. See the file COPYING for details.

gpg: there is a secret key for this public key!
gpg: use option "-delete-secret-key" to delete it first.
```

Setting permission on key files

GnuPG stores your keys and key rings in files. Therefore, you need to secure file access to both the directory, .gnupg, and the files inside it. After setting up the keys and signatures, check the default permissions. First, check the permissions on the .gnupg directory itself.

Don't forget the dot (.).

```
root@flyingpenguin# ls -la
        #---- output truncated -------
  drw-------   2 root     root    1024 Oct 18 17:59 .gnupg
        #---- output truncated -------
```

Use the chmod command in its octal form to make the .gnupg directory executable.

```
chmod 700 ~/.gnupg
drwx------   2 root      root         1024 Oct 18 17:59 .gnupg
```

Then check the default permissions on the files in the .gnupg directory.

```
root@flyingpenguin# ls -l .gnupg
total 20
-rw-r--r--    1 root      root     2823 Oct 15 08:32 options
-rw-r--r--    1 root      root     4003 Oct 18 17:59 pubring.gpg
-rw-r--r--    1 root      root     3147 Oct 18 14:29 pubring.gpg~
-rw-------    1 root      root      600 Oct 18 17:59 random_seed
-rw-------    1 root      root     4826 Oct 18 17:59 secring.gpg
-rw-r--r--    1 root      root     3000 Oct 18 14:29 trustdb.gpg
```

The system administrator (the root account) should be the owner of these files and the only person who has read permission. Change the permission so that only the owner has read and write permissions. The example below recursively (-R) uses the octal form of the chmod command to set permissions for root.

```
root@flyingpenguin# chmod -R 600 .gnupg

root@flyingpenhmod -ls -l .gnupg
total 20
-rw-------    1 root      root     2823 Oct 15 08:32 options
-rw-------    1 root      root     4003 Oct 18 17:59 pubring.gpg
-rw-------    1 root      root     3147 Oct 18 14:29 pubring.gpg~
-rw-------    1 root      root      600 Oct 18 17:59 random_seed
-rw-------    1 root      root     4826 Oct 18 17:59 secring.gpg
-rw-------    1 root      root     3000 Oct 18 14:29 trustdb.gpg
```

Getting information about keys

To get information about keys on your system, you can use the following commands:

gpg --list-keys	List all keys.
gpg --list sigs	List all keys and their signatures.
gpg --list-secret-keys	List all private (secret) keys.

The following terminal session shows examples of getting information about keys.

```
root@flyingpenguin# gpg list-keys
/root/.gnupg/pubring.gpg
------------------------
pub  1024D/80668234 2000-10-18 candace leiden (just  to
illustrate concept for Linux Bible. Will not be used for actual
production purposes.) <cleiden@office.com>
sub  2048g/AD887CB3 2000-10-18 [expires: 2001-02-15]
```

```
root@flyingpenguin# gpg --list-sigs
/root/.gnupg/pubring.gpg
------------------------
pub  1024D/80668234 2000-10-18 candace leiden (just  to
illustrate concept for Linux Bible. Will not be used for actual
production purposes.) <cleiden@office.com>

sig        80668234 2000-10-18  candace leiden (just  to
illustrate concept for Linux Bible. Will not be used for actual
production purposes.) <cleiden@office.com>

sub  2048g/AD887CB3 2000-10-18 [expires: 2001-02-15]

sig        80668234 2000-10-18  candace leiden (just  to
illustrate concept for Linux Bible. Will not be used for actual
production purposes.) <cleiden@office.com>

root@flyingpenguin# gpg --list-secret-keys
/root/.gnupg/secring.gpg
------------------------
sec  1024D/80668234 2000-10-18 candace leiden (just  to
illustrate concept for Linux Bible. Will not be used for actual
production purposes.) <cleiden@office.com>

ssb  2048g/AD887CB3 2000-10-18
```

A *fingerprint* is a 16-byte data structure that uniquely identifies a key. You use fingerprints to be sure that you have someone's legitimate key. Of course you can verify the complete key, but a fingerprint enables you to check the key by testing only 16 bytes rather than all the bytes in a key. Using a digital fingerprint to test identity instead of verifying a complete key is like a police laboratory using a human fingerprint to identify someone instead of performing a complete DNA test.

```
root@flyingpenguin# gpg --fingerprint
/root/.gnupg/pubring.gpg
----------------------
pub  1024D/80668234 2000-10-18 candace leiden (just  to
illustrate concept for Linux Bible. Will not be used for actual
production purposes.) <cleiden@office.com>

Key fingerprint = CE31 4D96 88DC 992E 8325  C4F5 3201 5181 8066
8234

sub  2048g/AD887CB3 2000-10-18 [expires: 2001-02-15]
```

If you prefer to use a GUI, you can run seahorse to list key information. Figure 29-6 shows a graphical query.

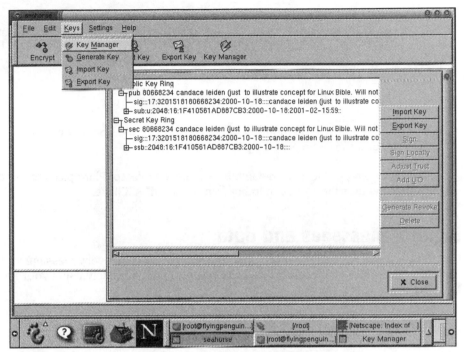

Figure 29-6: seahorse displays key information graphically

Using keys to encrypt data and messages

Once you have GnuPG installed and all your keys created, you can begin to encrypt messages and data. The GnuPG syntax for encrypting keys is:

```
gpg -e recipients <filename>
```

The GnuPG syntax for decrypting keys is:

```
gpg -d <filename>
```

Note Instead of the -e and -d command options, you can use the double-dashed options: --encrypt and --decrypt.

Suppose that Professor Plum wants to send a list of his favorite hideaways to Miss Scarlet and Colonel Mustard. The Professor does not want anyone else to see the data. Before e-mailing the hideaway file, Professor Plum encrypts it:

```
prof_plum@flying_penguin$ gpg -ea miss_scarlet colonel_mustard hideaway.txt
```

By encrypting the hideaway file, Professor Plum has created an additional file named hideaway.pgp. The hideaway.pgp file contains the text file encoded in a way that only Miss Scarlet's and Colonel Mustard's private keys can decrypt. When the Miss Scarlet and Colonel Mustard receive the Professor's e-mail, they detach the file and decrypt the information by typing:

```
miss_scarlet@flying_penguin$ gpg -d hideaway.pgp
```

The decrypted data goes to stdout by default. However, Miss Scarlet could use the -o option to send the decrypted output to another file.

Note The hideaway.pgp file is, by default, binary. Since Professor Plum plans to e-mail this file, he uses the -a option to build an "armored" ASCII file.

Signing messages and data

In addition to encrypting data, you should also digitally sign every message and file that you encrypt so that other users can be sure no one is falsely using your identity. The syntax for signing information is:

```
gpg -s <data>

prof_plum@flying_penguin$ gpg -s hideaway.txt
```

The -s option also compresses the data. If you want to sign the information without compressing it, use the -clearsign option. If you want to write your signature in a file that's separate from the data, use this syntax:

```
gpg -b <data>
```

Note You can also use double-dashed options to sign data:--sign (instead of -s)-- detach-sign (instead of -b)

To encrypt and sign the hideaway file, Professor Plum types:

```
prof_plum@flying_penguin$ gpg -se miss_scarlet hideaway.txt
```

If you need to verify a digital signature, you can use the

```
gpg -verify data
```

command, as in the following example:

```
miss_scarlet@flyingpenguin$ gpg -verify hideaway.txt
```

Note   GnuPGCheck the GNU home page, http://www.gnu.org/, for updates to GnuPG. It contains an overview of GnuPG, news flashes such as the release of new versions of GnuPG, a list of supported operating systems, links to other PGP-related sites, and links to French, Italian, German, and Spanish versions of the home page.

Securing root Access from Terminals

The file /etc/securetty file controls which terminals root can log in from. You create an entry for each terminal that allows root login in the securetty file. The entry consists of the terminal's identifier in the /dev directory. When a user tries to log in as root, the login program checks /etc/securetty to see whether root is allowed on that terminal.

The following listing shows that only the virtual consoles (vc) and hardwired terminals (tty) are permitted to log in as root.

```
root@flyingpenguin# cat /etc/securetty
vc/1
vc/2
vc/3
vc/4
vc/5
vc/6
vc/7
vc/8
vc/9
vc/10
vc/11
tty1
tty2
tty3
tty4
tty5
tty6
tty7
tty8
tty9
tty10
tty11
```

Securing Root Access across a Network

When a user has multiple accounts on different computers on a network, the file $HOME/.rhosts simplifies remote logins for that user. For example, if you have a .rhosts file in your home directory on a remote computer, when you login to your remote account via telnet or rlogin you don't need to type your password.

That's because the .rhosts file contains a list of hosts wherein you have accounts that you can log into without typing your password. The hosts in your .rhosts file are called *equivalent hosts*. In the following .rhosts file, miss_scarlet trusts herself on flyingpenguin and bigbird. She also trusts professor_plum to enter her account from two remote computers: turbopenguin and burgessmeredith.

```
miss_scarlet@tweety$ cat .rhosts
# $HOME/.rhosts - User miss_scarlet
# Equivalent hosts where I do not need to type my password
#        when I telnet, rlogin, rcp, etc. in to this system
flyingpenguin
bigbird
# Equivalent hosts from which I will allow professor_plum
# remote acces to tweety as me.
# Computer          User I trust - a lot!
turbopenguin        professor_plum
burgessmeredith professor_plum
```

According to the preceding .rhosts file, the owner of the file miss_scarlet can remotely access her accounts on flyingpenguin and bigbird from tweety without being prompted for a password. If professor_plum logs in as miss_scarlet on turbopenguin or burgessmeredith, he gets into miss_scarlet's account without being challenged for a password. To access tweety in the same convenient way from the other computers on the network, miss_scarlet must create a similar .rhosts file on each computer and add an entry for tweety.

Caution   If someone breaks into miss_scarlet's account on tweety, that cracker will also be able to access flyingpenguin and bigbird as miss_scarlet. If someone cracks into professor_plum's account on turbopenguin or burgessmeredith, he or she will have free access to miss_scarlet's account on tweety. Never give root a .rhosts file. The security risk is too great. If you need to telnet to a computer and behave as root, telnet in as a non-privileged user and su to root.

Securing Remote Access Utilities

First, use ssh. If you don't use ssh, follow the other tips and guidelines in this section of the chapter. You should disable all remote-access daemons that your users don't need. For example, if your system is a Web server, you don't need other daemons running other TCP/IP services on the computer.

Why use ssh (secure shell)?

Most TCP/IP applications send your password in clear (unencrypted) text across the network. Anyone with a sniffer or network analyzer connected to your network can steal the clear-text data.

Note A *sniffer* is a program that monitors data transmitted across a network, any network, ranging from a small corporate intranet to the Internet. Network and system administrators use sniffers for legitimate network monitoring. Crackers use sniffers for stealing clear (unencrypted) text from a network. Sniffer programs are easy to get. There are several public sites on the Internet for downloading sniffers.

Note A network analyzer is either hardware or software or a combination of the two that captures information about network traffic, including source and destination IP addresses, port addresses, timestamps, number of packets and bytes, and types of network service. A network analyzer is an extremely useful tool for network and system administrators to analyze, and especially to use to troubleshoot networking. It is also a favorite tool for crackers looking to get into your network.

`ssh` is a suite of programs that provide the same remote access functionality as `telnet`, `rlogin`, `rsh`, `ftp`, and other popular remote access services and applications, with better security. `ssh` (secure shell) provides encrypted communication between untrusted clients and servers. The `ssh` applications are a more secure alternative to `telnet`, `ftp`, `rlogin`, `rsh`, and `rcp` because `ssh` encrypts the username and password in a remote login session. You can turn off `inetd` and replace it with `ssh` without losing any remote-access functionality. `ssh` protects you from the following types of intrusions:

✦ *IP spoofing*, wherein a remote host sends out packets that seem to come from a trusted host.

✦ *IP source routing*, wherein a host tricks you into thinking that an IP packet comes from a trusted host.

✦ *DNS spoofing*, wherein an attacker forges nameserver records.

✦ Intercepting unencrypted passwords and other data.

✦ Modifying data in transit on an intermediate host.

✦ Listening to X authentication traffic and spoofing X11 server connections.

Caution `ssh` encrypts passwords and data so that snoopers can't grab and read TCP/IP packets that contain your password. However, it doesn't encrypt everything in the TCP/IP packet. The packet header, for example, remains in clear text.

On the CD-ROM There is a tutorial for `ssh` in the NHF (Newbie-ized Help Files), which you can link to from the CD-ROM that comes with this book. The tutorial walks you through:

Getting `ssh` if it is not included with your Linux distribution.

Creating an entry for `ssh` in the /etc/hosts file.

Generating `ssh` keys with the `ssh-keygen1` command.

Configuring your identity.

Setting file permissions.

Connecting to a remote computer with ssh.

New Feature Red Hat Linux 7 (on the operating system CDs) includes the following ssh packages: Openssh-clients, Openssh Secure Shell protocol server (sshd), Openssh free Secure Shell (ssh) implementation.

Tip A network is no more secure than its most crackable system. If your network includes non-Linux clients, such as various flavors of Microsoft Windows, you should use ssh from those clients that access your Linux servers. There are several freely available Windows-client implementations, including the ones at www.depot.berkeley.edu/software/SSH/ssh.html and www.zip.com. au/~roca/ttssh.html

Finding running network services and open sockets

To find out which remote access daemons are running on your system, use the following netstat command. Anything netstat displays in the LISTEN state and that uses tcp is a service (implemented by a daemon) that is listening for a connection from the network.

```
root@flyingpenguin# netstat -a | grep LISTEN
tcp        0      0 *:X                   *:*         LISTEN
tcp        0      0 *:netbios-ssn         *:*         LISTEN
tcp        0      0 *:www                 *:*         LISTEN
tcp        0      0 *:printer             *:*         LISTEN
tcp        0      0 *:ssh                 *:*         LISTEN
tcp        0      0 *:linuxconf           *:*         LISTEN
tcp        0      0 *:finger              *:*         LISTEN
tcp        0      0 *:login               *:*         LISTEN
tcp        0      0 *:shell               *:*         LISTEN
tcp        0      0 *:telnet              *:*         LISTEN
tcp        0      0 *:ftp                 *:*         LISTEN
tcp        0      0 *:auth                *:*         LISTEN
tcp        0      0 *:1024                *:*         LISTEN
```

Since the system shown in the preceding example runs ssh, a good security measure would be to disable telnet, ftp, and finger. The example in the following section, "Disabling unnecessary network services," shows how to disable the finger daemon.

Note Depending on the command options you use, the netstat utility may display network connections, routing tables, interface statistics, masquerade connections, and multi_cast memberships.

Securing telnet and FTP without SSH

Other secure remote access utilities use SSLeay, a free implementation of Netscape's SSL (Secure Socket Layer)—the software encryption protocol behind the Netscape Secure Server and the Netscape Navigator Browser. (You pronounce SSLeay by saying each individual letter.) The SSLeay protocol protects the clear-text passwords and data in applications like telnet and FTP. While not as flexible as ssh, SSLeay-based telnet and FTP provide similar protection against password crackers and data thieves. You can find Secure telnet and Secure FTP by starting with the SSLeay and SSLapps FAQ, available at http://maga.di.unito.it/security/resources/mirrors/SSLeay/SSLeayFAQ.html.

Anything using udp (an alternative to tcp) and displaying *.* is a socket waiting for a remote connection. When you run netstat, search (grep) for udp.

```
root@flyingpenguin# netstat -a | grep udp
udp        0        0 flyingpengu:netbios-dgm *:*
udp        0        0 flyingpengui:netbios-ns *:*
udp        0        0 *:netbios-dgm           *:*
udp        0        0 *:netbios-ns            *:*
udp        0        0 *:ntalk                 *:*
udp        0        0 *:talk                  *:*
udp        0        0 *:1025                  *:*
udp        0        0 *:965                   *:*
udp        0        0 *:1024                  *:*
udp        0        0 *:sunrpc                *:*
```

Disabling unnecessary network services

When you decide which remote daemons to disable, you must take into account the needs and wants of your users and weigh those needs and wants against possible security threats. finger is an example of a utility where the wants of the users may conflict with the security needs of your system and network. Your users may find such utilities quite convenient, but actually the convenience they provide is completely offset by the security hole they open. Here's an example of finger output:

```
root@flyingpenguin# finger root@localhost
Login: root                              Name: root
Directory: /root                         Shell: /bin/bash
On since Sun Oct 15 20:54 (EDT) on :0 (messages off)
On since Sun Oct 15 20:55 (EDT) on pts/0 from :0
    1 day 23 hours idle
On since Wed Oct 18 12:12 (EDT) on pts/2 from :0
    2 days 22 hours idle
New mail received Sat Oct 21 04:02 2000 (EDT)
    Unread since Sun Mar 12 23:42 2000 (EST)
No Plan.
```

This is far too much public information about root. The example below fingers miss_scarlet across a LAN (local area network).

```
root@redbird# finger miss_scarlet@flyingpenguin
Login: miss_scarlet                        Name: emily lauren
scarlet
Directory: /home/miss_scarlet         Shell: /bin/csh
On since Sat Oct 21 15:40 (EDT) on pts/4 from 192.168.0.5
Mail last read Sun Sep 24 19:41 2000 (EDT)
Plan:
Get a life starting 12-Dec, on holiday in Bahamas.
Contact Professor Plum in case of emergency.
Back in the office 12-Jan-2001.
```

Did you notice that Miss Scarlet has a plan? You implement a plan for fingering by creating the text file ~/.plan. It's informative that Miss Scarlet is going on vacation — informative enough that crackers will know that December 12 is a good time to try to break into her account. If you do not disable finger, at least encourage your users not to create .plan files.

Caution   If gentle persuasion does not work, as system administrator you can find all .plan files on your system, examine them, and delete them.

Caution   I know of one person whose house was robbed in part because of a holiday plan.

Here's another finger example. Notice that you cannot get finger information about the miss_scarlet account on the computer tweety. tweety does not accept finger connections because the finger daemon on tweety is disabled in /etc/inetd.conf.

```
root@flyingpenguin# finger miss_scarlet@tweety
Connection refused.
```

finger works via the finger daemon, in.fingerd. To disable finger, you need to disable its daemon. Since your inetd daemon controls most of the other daemons on your system, the easiest way to disable finger is to comment out its entry in the configuration file /etc/inetd.conf. The following code excerpt is from inetd.conf. This file looks the same on all Linux distributions.

```
$ more /etc/inetd.conf
#
# inetd.conf
#This file describes the services that will be available
#      through the INETD TCP/IP super server. To reconfigure
#      the running INETD process, edit this file, then send the
```

```
#                   INETD process a SIGHUP signal.
#
# Version:          @(#)/etc/inetd.conf    3.10     05/27/93
#
# Authors:          Original taken from BSD UNIX 4.3/TAHOE.
#                   Fred N. van Kempen,
<waltje@uwalt.nl.mugnet.org>
#
# Modified for Debian Linux by Ian A. Murdock
<imurdock@shell.portal.com>
#
# Modified for RHS Linux by Marc Ewing <marc@redhat.com>
#
# <service_name> <sock_type> <proto> <flags> <user>
#<server_path> <args>
#
# Echo,discard,daytime,and chargen are used primarily for
testing.
#
# To re-read this file after changes,type 'killall -HUP inetd'
#
#echo    stream  tcp     nowait  root     internal
#echo    dgram   udp     wait    root     internal
#discard         stream  tcp     nowait   root    internal
#discard         dgram   udp     wait     root    internal
#daytime         stream  tcp     nowait   root    internal
#daytime         dgram   udp     wait     root    internal
#chargen         stream  tcp     nowait   root    internal
#chargen         dgram   udp     wait     root    internal
#time    stream  tcp     nowait  root     internal
#time    dgram   udp     wait    root     internal
#
# These are standard services.
#
ftp     stream  tcp nowait  root  /usr/sbin/tcpd  in.ftpd -l -a
telnet  stream  tcp nowait  root     /usr/sbin/tcpd  in.telnetd
#
# Shell, login, exec, comsat and talk are BSD protocols.
#
shell   stream  tcp nowait  root     /usr/sbin/tcpd  in.rshd
login   stream  tcp nowait  root     /usr/sbin/tcpd  in.rlogind
     ----------- output edited -------------
# Finger, systat and netstat give out user information which  #
may be valuable to potential "system crackers."  Many sites
# disable some or all of these services to improve security.
#
finger stream  tcp nowait root /usr/sbin/tcpd in.fingerd
#cfinger stream tcp nowait root    /usr/sbin/tcpd  in.cfingerd
#systat stream  tcp nowait guest  /usr/sbin/tcpd  /bin/ps -
auwwx
#netstat stream  tcp nowait  guest /usr/sbin/tcpd /bin/netstat
```

When a client requests a `finger` connection, inetd passes the connection to the `finger` daemon, which is waiting for connection requests. When the `finger` daemon receives a connection request, it either delivers the `finger` information to the requestor or refuses the connection. To disable `finger`, comment out (with the hash character) the `finger` line in the inetd.conf file. When you disable your computer's `finger` daemon, users on that computer can still finger other users across the network on computers where the `finger` daemon is permitted to run. After you edit the inetd.conf file, you can make the edits take effect immediately without rebooting if you send a HUP (hangup) signal to `init` (job 1), as in the command that follows. Remember that `kill` is really a command that sends a signal. It doesn't kill everything it touches unless the signal you send is `KILL`.

```
root@tweety# killall -HUP inetd_pid
```

Tip   Use `ps -aux` to find out the pid of the inetd.

Caution Your Linux system can be fingered by any operating system that has the `finger` TCP/IP application installed and the daemon running, including most flavors of Microsoft Windows.

Tip   You can use firewall software (which I describe later in this chapter) to refuse `finger` requests from outside your network. That means that even if computers on your LAN run `finger` daemons, no `finger` requests from the Internet can pass through the firewall to the local computers.

Using tcp wrappers

TCP wrappers, created by Wietse Venema, are a set of binary file wrappers that execute Internet services such as `telnet` and `ftp`, more securely. The wrappers log each attempt to use inetd (or xinetd, in Red Hat 7.x) service connections and compares each attempt against the allow and deny (/etc/hosts.allow and /etc/hosts.deny) files. If the file entry permits the connection, the wrappers send the connection to the appropriate daemon, such as telnet. If the connection is not valid according to the allow and deny files, the wrapper drops the connection. Configuring TCP wrappers in Linux is simply a matter of creating or editing the /etc/hosts.allow and /etc/hosts.deny files to list IP address and/or networks from which your system will accept (or deny) connections. For connections you want to allow, add entries to /etc/hosts.allow. In the hosts.deny file, deny `ALL`. After checking the deny file, Linux checks the allow file for specific addresses. The addresses in the allow file override the `ALL` entry in the deny file.

Caution Linux allows connections from everywhere by default.

The following excerpt is from an allow file.

```
root@flyingpenguin# cat /etc/hosts.allow
#
# hosts.allow   This file describes the names of the hosts
# which are allowed to use the local INET services, as decided
#               by the '/usr/sbin/tcpd' server.
# Format of each entry is:
# Service:   IP address or network:       ALLOW or DENY
in.telnetd: 192.168.0.241 : ALLOW
in.ftpd: 192.168.0.2 :ALLOW
```

The following example illustrates denying all access to all sources in /etc/hosts. deny.

```
root@flyingpenguin# cat /etc/hosts.deny
#
# hosts.deny    This file describes the names of the hosts
# which are *not* allowed to use the local INET services, as
# decided by the '/usr/sbin/tcpd' server.
#
# The portmap line is redundant, but it is left to remind you
# the new secure portmap uses hosts.deny
ALL: ALL DENY
```

Using Security Programs and Tools to Protect your System and Network

Since security is such a rapidly evolving field, there are more software packages on the market than ever that do port- or service-based scanning. What's more, you can perform this scanning either on a single machine or on an entire network. For a comprehensive list of effective security tools, read CERT's Security Tools document, `http://www.cert.org/tech_tips/security_tools.html`.

You can also read the security tools document on the CD-ROM that accompanies this book. The article is in the Tech Tips included in the CERT bundle.

PortSentry

PortSentry is part of the Abacus Project suite of security tools. It is a program designed to detect and respond to port scans against a target host in real time. PortSentry is part of the Abacus Project suite of security tools.

The CD-ROM included with this book contains a tutorial on setting up PortSentry. The tutorial, entitled "Setting Up PortSentry," is in the NHF collection. The tutorial guides you through the following steps:

Downloading the program.

Unpacking the compressed file.

Editing the configuration file, portsentry.conf, to tell PortSentry which ports to listen on and how to respond if your system is scanned.

SATAN

Despite its evil-sounding acronym, which stands for (Security Administrator's Tool for Analyzing Networks), SATAN is an effective port scanner with a Web interface. SATAN is a wonderful tool in that it is preventative in nature; it runs light, medium, or strong scans on a machine or a network of machines, and then volunteers to fix network-security loopholes that it finds. The SATAN site, `http://www.connix.com/~psantoro/satan.html`, contains a tutorial by Peter Santoro on building SATAN, including a quick and easy Linux-ready way. You can download SATAN from `http://www.ibiblio.org/pub/packages/security/Satan-for-Linux`.

SAINT

SAINT (Security Administrator's Integrated Network Tool) is a newer and more comprehensive tool than SATAN. It's also more time-consuming and harder to build and configure. SAINT gathers information about your networking environment and reports on both potential and actual security holes. You can also use SAINT to report on your network configuration, including which services are running and the hardware and software used on your network. SAINT, which is licensed under the GPL, is freely available for download from `www.wwdsi.com/demo/saint`. To run SAINT, you need Perl (v5.0 or higher) and a C compiler to build the components. After you build SAINT, you configure it in the file saint.cf.

Before downloading and configuring SAINT, read the overview at `/saint_overview.html`. Pay strict attention to the sections "System requirements" and "Dangers of SAINT."

SAINT can report by:

✦ Levels of danger, including:

   • Critical

   • Area of concern

- Potential

- Services that do not appear to be vulnerable to attack

- Other

✦ Kinds of vulnerabilities

✦ Hosts, including:

- Names and system types

- Class of service

- Trusted and/or trusting

- Hosts in a specific Internet domain

- Hosts in a specific subnet

Tip Many tools are available for analyzing Linux security on a single host or on a network. Check out /www.linuxsecurity.com/resources/host_security-1. html and host_security2.html for downloads of security programs, including SAINT, GnuPG, Psionic Port Sentry, and TIGER. TIGER is a collection of scripts that scan your Linux system looking for security problems. CNET's Linux Central site, http://linux.cnet.com/linux/, is another good place to find downloads of free software, shareware, and demos of commercial security products for Linux.

Protecting your Intranet behind a Firewall

Traditionally, a firewall was defined as a fireproof door or wall set into an otherwise inflammable area to stop the flames from progressing beyond a certain point. Today's firewalls are aptly named, as their purpose is much the same as that of a steel wall in a wooden building; to prevent damage beyond a certain point.

How a firewall works

The firewall examines each packet and decides whether it is allowed to pass, either in or out. If the firewall refuses to let it pass, the packet is thrown away. The sending system gets the idea when there's no response. Most applications take the lack of response as bad news, and they may respond either by trying again or giving up. Either way, the firewall software logs the event.

There are two types of firewalls that you can set up on a system, one at the network level, and one on the hardware level. The first is the *filter* type of firewall, which is a sort of network "choke point" that blocks unauthorized packets from getting onto your network. The other is the *proxy* type of firewall, which monitors or blocks entire network connections from taking place.

The filtering firewall

Packet filtering is the type of firewall built into the Linux kernel. You build your packet-filtering firewall by establishing filters. A *filter* is a rule that you establish on the router to train the router to drop certain packets on purpose. Nothing less intelligent than a router can do this because of the software required.

The three fields that can trigger the filters are the source address, the destination address, and the port number:

✦ The *source address* answers the question, "Where did this packet come from?" The root account can alter a computer's IP address to anything, including a false address. Depending on how a computer is attached to the network and how its packets reach your computer, you may or may not be able to trust the validity of that source address. Your filter can essentially say, "I don't trust this computer at all and will not talk to it."

✦ The *destination address* answers the question, "Where is this packet going?" When the destination is one of your computers, you can decide whether any packet is allowed to go there at all. Your filter can say, "This computer doesn't receive packets directly from outside the intranet." Sometimes you may choose to redirect the packet to a special server. In this case, your filter can say, "The packet is okay, but send it over there instead." E-mail is a good example of a service that you may want to redirect. You can disallow receipt of e-mail directly from outside, arranging instead for all e-mail to be routed through a single point of contact. The DNS mail-exchange records, known as *MX records,* are designed specifically for this.

✦ The *port number* answers the question, "For what service is this packet destined?" If you're not running a particular server, why should you accept any packets of that protocol? For example, if you're not running a World Wide Web server, you can freely and safely configure your filter to ignore any HTTP packets.

Typically, if you purchase network routers from Cisco or other major routing-hardware manufacturers, the ability to perform a filter firewall service comes bundled with the hardware. The Linux kernel provides support for packet-filtering firewalls.

Adaptive firewall technology

Adaptive firewall technology goes a step beyond the static packet-filtering firewall described above. Where packet-filtering firewalls only read brief information about your packet in a structure called a *wrapper*, adaptive firewalls inspect the entire packet.

Note   The more information a firewall inspects, the more effective it is at protecting your intranet from unwanted packets. On the other hand, the more information a firewall inspects, the more likely it is to use large amounts of CPU resources.

While the static packet-filtering firewall runs from rules you give it, the adaptive firewall starts with your static rules and triggers new rules dynamically based on network traffic.

The proxy server model

A proxy server is a computer whose purpose is to control or monitor outbound traffic. The two main types of proxy servers are application proxies and SOCKS proxies.

In its base form, an application proxy server simply automates the creation of a telnet session to the proxy server, and from telnets to the outside world. The proxy server handles the process of connecting to the server you want on the Internet. A further security advantage of this method is that the server can log all the actions a user takes while online. This includes the URLs of Web sites visited and the files transferred to and from the system via FTP proxies. This allows you to monitor the sites visited and scan for downloaded viruses.

SOCKS servers, which work by cross-wiring your connection through the system to another outside server, work only with TCP/IP type point-to-point connections. As with the filter type of firewall, you won't be able to provide user authentication, though SOCKS servers can provide logging services much like an application proxy can, such as noting which machines a user connected to while online.

If you want to set up a proxy server, the overall best package to get started is Trusted Information System's FWTK, or Firewall Toolkit, which can be found at http://www.tis.com/research/software/.

 Note   If you're using a dial-up service such as an ISDN line and you're setting up a machine to use as a firewall, consider using an additional network card specifically for filtering packets. This increases the level of control and further isolates incoming packets by keeping them off your regular network.

Network-management considerations for setting up a firewall

A simplistic firewall is a single router that links the internal and external networks, examines every packet, and decides whether or not to let each one pass. A single router offers some protection, but is it enough? In this most basic approach, there may also be a question of ownership and control: Who owns the router, you or your Internet service provider? Where is the router installed, on your premises or the service provider's?

Some organizations choose to add another router and another network segment. The Internet Service Provider owns one router and you own the other. Fortunately, routers are invisible to the network users. Under this arrangement, you must decide carefully how the network's computers are arranged — the computers must be placed on the correct network segment, based on their function within the network.

This intermediate approach has one major advantage: If you decide to disconnect from the Internet by turning off your own router, your organization still appears to be on the network, because some of your computers are still active, even though no traffic is coming in. E-mail can be queued for later delivery inside; external users can still get to the anonymous FTP server; and users can still browse the World Wide Web. On the other hand, if the service provider must turn off its router, your organization is off the network!

Some computers, such as your anonymous FTP server and your World Wide Web server, must be accessible from outside your organization (that is, from the Internet side of the firewall). But do they have to be directly accessible from inside your organization (that is, from your side of the firewall) as well? You can always move files onto the servers by floppy or other external media, but that would be pretty inconvenient. Is the trouble worth the benefit of the extra level of security?

Some computers and services must be accessible from both inside and outside your organization in order to be useful. E-mail and `telnet` are prime examples.

Configuring a firewall

To create a packet filtering firewall, you don't need any additional software outside of your distribution. The kernel supports packet filtering. You need to follow these general steps to configure a firewall on Linux:

1. Compile firewall support into your kernel (if it is not already there). You need support for the following:

    a. Loadable modules

    b. Network firewalls

    c. IP firewalls

Tip   Using `make menuconfig` to rebuild the kernel resolves any kernel dependencies that might occur.

2. Configure two network cards.

3. Configure the IP addresses.

4. Use the `ifconfig` and route `commands` to test both incoming and outgoing connections to your network ().

5. Secure the firewall by disabling certain remote-access daemons.

6. Set up filtering rules with the `ipchains` command and create /etc/rc.d/rc.firewall (if it is not already there).

On the CD-ROM   The Firewall and Proxy Server HOWTO explains the preceding steps in detail, including examples and sample scripts from which you can copy or cut and paste. There is a link to this HOWTO on the CD-ROM for this book.

Diagnosing Break-in Attempts

You should establish a regular routine of performing general tasks to scan your system for possible break-ins and break-in attempts. These tasks should include looking for suspicious files and file permissions and analyzing the system log files for unauthorized access and failed access attempts.

Checking files and permissions for risky or suspicious properties

Regularly check the SETUID and SETGID permissions on files. There should be no setuid and/or setgid that you don't know about. The following command starts at the top of your directory hierarchy (/) and searches through every filesystem for setuid permissions. Depending on the size of your directory, this command may take a long time to run. You may want to run it in the background and redirect the results to a file (using the > operator).

```
root@flyingpenguin# find / -perm +4000 -print | xargs ls -l
find: /proc/6/fd: Permission denied
find: /proc/19885/fd/4: No such file or directory
-rwsr-xr-x 1 root    root       55356 Aug 5 11:08 /bin/mount
-rwsr-xr-x 1 root    root       20604 Aug 8 06:51 /bin/ping
-rwsr-xr-x 1 root    root       14184 Jul 12 20:47 /bin/su
-rwsr-xr-x 1 root    root       25404 Aug 5 11:08 /bin/umount
-r-sr-xr-x 1 root    daemon     18567 Jul 23 1999 /opt/linuxworld-demo
-r-sr-xr-x 1 root    daemon     18402 Oct 4 1999 /opt/lotus/notes/5020/linux/bindsock
-r-sr-xr-x 1 root    root       14732 Aug 22 21:19 /sbin/pwdb_chkpwd
-r-sr-xr-x 1 root    root       15340 Aug 22 21:19 /sbin/unix_chkpwd
-rwsr-xr-x 1 root    root       21248 Aug 24 18:30 /usr/bin/test
```

In the preceding example, two entries are suspect. Since Linuxworld has come and gone, it is probably not necessary to maintain the linuxworld-demo program. In any event, running a demo at a trade show under setuid is risky. The other suspicious entry is the last line, which shows a program named `test` running under setuid. Be sure you know exactly what that program does and that it does not enable users to escape from the program into the shell with all the privileges of the program. If you did not configure that test program, someone probably cracked the root password and has installed the test program as setuid to provide entry to your entire system.

Look at the file-creation times in root's home directory. One way to do this is to use the command ls -lc. If you see files that don't seem familiar and that have strange creation dates, remove them. If you see files that you recognize but that have creation dates that don't seem right, replace them. They may be Trojan horses. For example, you know that you wrote gawkscript.1b, but you originally created it in July. The creation date in the listing shows that someone may have replaced the script more recently. Examine the script and restore your July version to be safe. The file testprog is unprotected. Also check the creation dates on all gpg or PGP key files to be sure that no one has cracked the root account and created unauthorized keys.

```
root@flyingpenguin# ls -lc |more
total 1005489
-rw-r--r-- 1 root    root          0 Jan 20  2000 1
-rw-r--r-- 1 root    root          0 Jan 26  2000 1000
-rw-r--r-- 1 root    root          0 Jan 26  2000 1001
-rw-r--r-- 1 root    root       1855 Oct 21 16:07 ASCIIpublickeyfile
-rw-r--r-- 1 root    root       5580 Oct 21 16:06 asciipgpfile
-rw-r--r-- 1 root    root        282 Dec 24 07:59 gawkscript.1b
-rw-r--r-- 1 root    root          0 Oct 21 16:04 rootpublickeyfile
-rw-rwxrwx 1 root    root         87 Sep 24 22:20 testprog
```

Check the creation dates and permissions on the network-configuration files. Users and applications need read access to these files, but only the root should have write permissions.

```
root@tweety# ls -l /etc/hosts* /etc/ftp* /etc/services /etc/protocols
-rw-------  1 root        root          484 Aug  9 05:55 /etc/ftpaccess
-rw-------  1 root        root          456 Aug  9 05:55 /etc/ftpconversions
-rw-------  1 root        root           39 Aug  9 05:55 /etc/ftpgroups
-rw-------  1 root        root          104 Aug  9 05:55 /etc/ftphosts
-rw-------  1 root        root           74 Jan 27  2000 /etc/ftpusers
-rw-r--r--  1 root        root          278 Mar 23  2000 /etc/hosts
-rw-r--r--  1 root        root          161 Jan 12  2000 /etc/hosts.allow
-rw-r--r--  1 root        root          347 Jan 12  2000 /etc/hosts.deny
-rw-r--r--  1 root        root         1567 Jan 12  2000 /etc/protocols
-rw-r--r--  1 root        root        11958 Oct 15 17:01 /etc/services
```

Consider finding and removing all .rhosts files.

Check the /etc/aliases file. Be sure mail goes to the right people. Be very careful to check the root entry. root's mail should go only to the system administrator.

Note

There is some disagreement among system administrators at our site as to whether there should be an e-mail alias for root. Those who prefer to have an alias, use it to avoid logging in as root. With an alias, you can log in as your normal non-privileged self and read root's e-mail without needing to su.

```
#  This file lists the default mail aliases for Caldera
OpenLinux.
#
#  Aliases in this file will NOT be expanded in the header from
#  Mail, but WILL be visible over networks or from /bin/mail.
#
#                    IMPORTANT NOTE:
#
#  After you make any changes to this file, you have to run
#
#    /usr/sbin/mta-switch newconfig
#
#  or the program `newaliases' (works for smail and sendmail).
#  Otherwise the changes won't be visible to your MTA.
#

# Basic system aliases -- these MUST be present.
MAILER-DAEMON:        postmaster
postmaster:   root

# General redirections for pseudo accounts.
bin:          root
daemon:       root
adm:          root
games:        root
ingres:       root
system:       root
toor:         root
news:         root
uucp:         root
operator:     root
ftp:          root
nobody:       root

# Well-known aliases.
manager:      root
dumper:       root
newsadm:      news
newsadmin:    news
usenet:       news
netnews:      news
gnats:        root
ftpadm:       ftp
ftpadmin:     ftp
ftp-adm:      ftp
ftp-admin:    ftp


# trap decode to catch security attacks
decode:       root

# Person who should get root's mail
#root:         col
```

If you use NFS to export filesystems to other computers on the network, check the creation and modification dates for the file /etc/exports. Be sure that the exported filesystems are read-only. You can use the `showmount` utility to check. Also be sure to exclude a localhosts entry and to use fully qualified domain names for other hosts.

Cross-Reference   Read Chapter 22, "Configuring the Network Filesystem (NFS)," for more complete information on NFS.

Analyzing log files for security-related events

Log files record what is happening on your system, including successful events and failed attempts. You need to check your logs carefully to see if anyone is trying to perform any unauthorized operations. Most logs reside in the directory /var/log. Your directory listing may differ slightly from the following listing, depending on your Linux distribution and the software you are running. The files in bold type are the log files that contain security and possible break-in information. Files that end in a number, such as messages.2 and messages.3, are sorted in order. The largest number indicates the oldest file.

Tip   The file /var/log/messages is your main system-error or message log.

```
root@flyingpenguin# ls /var/log
XFree86.0.log  dmesg          messages.2     savacct        usracct
XFree86.9.log  fax            messages.3     secure         vbox
boot.log       htmlaccess.log messages.4     secure.1       wtmp
boot.log.1     httpd          netconf.log    secure.2       wtmp.1
boot.log.2     lastlog        netconf.log.1  secure.3       xferlog
boot.log.3     lastlog.1      netconf.log.2  secure.4       xferlog.1
boot.log.4     maillog        netconf.log.3  spooler        xferlog.2
btmp           maillog.1      netconf.log.4  spooler.1      xferlog.3
cron           maillog.2      news           spooler.2      xferlog.4
cron.1         maillog.3      pacct          spooler.3
cron.2         maillog.4      postgresql     spooler.4
cron.3         messages       sa             squid
cron.4         messages.1     samba          statistics
```

Before you check individual log files, look for some general clues that someone may have tampered with your logs. Intruders may try to cover their tracks by editing their entries out of your log files or deleting a log file completely. Check log files for:

✦ File size (short or incomplete logs)

✦ Missing logs

✦ Unusual timestamps

✦ Incorrect file permissions and/or ownership

Analyzing /var/log/wtmp

This accounting file is not a text file. You need to use the last command to read the contents of the wtmp accounting file. For each login, last shows who, when, and where from. The following example shows some serious security lapses.

```
root@flyingpenguin# last
miss_sca  pts/4        192.168.0.5      Sun Oct 22 12:04    still logged in
marshall  pts/5        192.168.0.2      Sat Oct 21 17:38 - 17:39  (00:01)
professo  pts/4        192.168.0.5      Sat Oct 21 15:40 - 20:11  (04:30)
root      pts/2        :0               Wed Oct 18 12:12    still logged in
root      pts/2        :0               Sun Oct 15 21:25 - 21:25  (00:00)
root      ftpd1056     192.168.0.5      Sun Oct 15 21:04 - 21:05  (00:01)
root      pts/1        :0               Sun Oct 15 20:55 - 12:13  (2+15:18)
root      pts/0        :0               Sun Oct 15 20:55    still logged in
root      :0                            Sun Oct 15 20:54    still logged in
reboot    system boot  2.2.16-22        Sun Oct 15 20:53          (6+15:11)
root      tty1                          Sun Oct 15 20:44 - 20:45  (00:01)
candace   pts/2        192.168.0.5      Sun Oct 15 18:23 - 20:38  (02:14)
root      pts/1        :0               Sun Oct 15 17:58 - 20:44  (02:45)
root      pts/0        :0               Sun Oct 15 17:58 - 20:44  (02:45)
root      :0                            Sun Oct 15 17:55 - down   (02:56)
reboot    system boot  2.2.16-22        Sun Oct 15 17:52          (02:59)
root      pts/1        :0               Sun Oct 15 16:10 - down   (00:10)
root      pts/0        :0               Sun Oct 15 16:10 - down   (00:10)
reboot    system boot  2.2.12 20        Sun Oct 15 16:09          (00:11)
reboot    system boot  2.2.12 20        Sun Oct 15 16:07          (00:00)
reboot    system boot  2.2.12-20        Sun Oct 15 15:52          (00:01)
root      pts/0                         Sun Oct 15 11:44 - 11:45  (00:00)
kendunca  pts/0        192.168.0.5      Sun Oct 15 08:14 - 10:47  (02:33)
emilyd    pts/8        192.168.0.5      Sat Oct 14 16:16 - 18:53  (02:37)
katherin  pts/0        192.168.0.5      Fri Oct 13 14:47 - still logged in
miss_sca  pts/0        192.168.0.5      Sun Oct  8 14:53 - 00:22  (09:28)

wtmp begins Sun Oct  8 14:53:21 2000
```

Notice the entries that are still logged in. root and katherin stay logged in for days. Educate your users to log out when they are finished. As root, you should know better than to leave your sessions logged in when you are not there. Even if you use a screen saver with a password to lock your display, you are leaving your system open to attack.

Also check the times that last shows system reboots. If these are unexpected, an intruder may be shutting down and rebooting the system in order to break in. You may also have power problems. Check the unexpected reboot times to see whether there is a pattern — for example, someone unknown rebooting the system every Sunday at 22:30.

Analyzing /var/log/boot

This file contains the boot messages. Check it for any unauthorized system reboots. Also check within the boot message file for any new daemons that start. If you see a `finger` daemon starting when you know that it should be disabled, a cracker may have broken into your system and changed the startup procedure to run the daemon.

Analyzing /var/log/messages

The messages file lists various types of system messages. To see security messages, search for strings that include `su`, `authentication`, and `PAM`, such as the following:

```
Sep 24 11:18:56 flyingpenguin PAM_pwdb[7454]: authentication
failure; miss_scarlet(uid=500) -> root for su service
Sep 24 11:19:02 flyingpenguin PAM_pwdb[7455]: (su) session
opened for user root by miss_scarlet(uid=500)
```

In the following excerpt from the messages file, user candace tried to `telnet` into flyingpenguin as root.

```
Sep 24 20:14:50 flyingpenguin pam_rhosts_auth[8074]: denied to
miss_scarlet@flyingpenguin.cardinalconsulting.com as candace:
access not allowed
```

The messages file also lists device initializations. Look for the network-controller messages to be sure that no one has installed an additional network card. In the following excerpt, `eth0` refers to the Ethernet controller.

```
Oct  6 14:02:36 flyingpenguin cardmgr[392]: executing: './network start eth0'
```

If you see an additional network controller that you did not install, a cracker may be planning to configure it to enable IP forwarding. *IP forwarding*, redirecting packets destined for one IP address to another IP address, enables crackers to have your computer's data automatically forwarded to them without manual intervention (e.g. without having repeatedly to break to e-mail stolen data). IP forwarding also enables crackers to use your ISP connection. By configuring IP forwarding on their "secret" network controllers, crackers could also launch attacks on other computers in your network.

Analyzing /var/log/secure

This file records connect and login messages. It also stores the sulog.

 See the section "su-ing to the root Account" for more information about the sulog, a virtual log within the secure file.

If a user logs in across the network, such as via `telnet` or `rlogin`, as shown in the following excerpt, /var/log/secure shows the daemon that logged the connection and the user's original IP address.

```
Sep 24 11:18:51 flyingpenguin login: LOGIN ON 0 BY miss_scarlet
FROM 192.168.0.5
Sep 24 20:14:50 flyingpenguin in.rlogind[8074]: connect from
192.168.0.241
Sep 24 20:14:52 flyingpenguin login: LOGIN ON 3 BY candace FROM
flyingpenguin
```

When you analyze the log for possible security intrusions, look for unrecognized IP addresses and hostnames connecting to your machine, strange connection times, or a succession of connections very close together.

Tip
Don't make it easy for a non-privileged user to erase wrongdoing in a log file. Be sure to set file permissions so that only root (or members of root's group, wheel) have access to the log files.

/var/log/maillog

This file contains messages from sendmail transactions.

Cross-Reference
Chapter 24 describes the sendmail Mail Transfer Agent.

Analyzing log files

Reading your daily logs can be quite a chore. The simple bash script below extracts one day's worth of messages from the log files — messages, secure, and maillog — and e-mails them to a "responsible" person who reads them daily. The following example shows the bash code as well as a sample run and mail message.

```
root@flying_penguin# cat logreport
# 31-Oct-2000  logreport
# Script to extract yesterday's logged messages from their log
files into a report and e-mailed to candace.
#! /bin/bash
/bin/cat /var/log/messages  > /tmp/tmp_logs
/bin/cat /var/log/secure    >> /tmp/tmp_logs
/bin/cat /var/log/maillog   >> /tmp/tmp_logs

/bin/cat /tmp/tmp_logs  | grep "$(date +"%b %d" | sed 's/ 0/
/g')" | sort -o /tmp/yesterday_log +2
/bin/cat /tmp/yesterday_log | mail -s "Yesterday's Logged
Events" candace@flyingpenguin
# You could remove the files, tmp_logs and yesterday_log, here.
root@flying_penguin# bash logreport

candace@flyingpenguin$ mail
Mail version 8.1 6/6/93. Type ? for help.
"/var/spool/mail/candace": 1 message 1 new
>N  1 root@flyingpenguin.c  Sat Oct 21 23:37 311/26225 "Daily
Log Reports"
&1
```

```
Oct 21 04:02:00 flyingpenguin CROND[11790]: (root) CMD (run-
parts /etc/cron.daily)
Oct 21 04:02:00 flyingpenguin anacron[11794]: Updated timestamp
for job `cron.daily' to 2000-10-21
Oct 21 04:02:26 flyingpenguin PAM_unix[11954]: (system-auth)
session opened for user news by (uid=0)
Oct 21 04:02:29 flyingpenguin PAM_unix[11954]: (system-auth)
session closed for user news
Oct 21 04:02:48 flyingpenguin sendmail[12018]: e9L82mE12018:
from=root, size=440, class=0, nrcpts=1,
msgid=<200010210802.e9L82mE12018@flyingpenguin.cardinalconsulti
ng.com>, relay=root@localhost
Oct 21 04:02:48 flyingpenguin sendmail[12018]: e9L82mE12018:
to=root, ctladdr=root (0/0), delay=00:00:00, xdelay=00:00:00,
mailer=local, pri=30440, dsn=2.0.0, stat=Sent
Oct 21 04:06:38 flyingpenguin rhnsd[12020]: running program
/usr/sbin/rhn_check
Oct 21 04:06:42 flyingpenguin rhnsd[900]: command returned:
ERROR: unable to read system id.
Oct 21 15:40:39 flyingpenguin PAM_unix[12295]: (system-auth)
session opened for user miss_scarlet by (uid=0)
Oct 21 15:40:42 flyingpenguin PAM_unix[12308]: (system-auth)
session opened for user root by miss_scarlet(uid=500)
Oct 21 20:24:44 flyingpenguin PAM_unix[12754]: authentication
failure; miss_scarlet(uid=500) -> root for system-auth service
Oct 21 22:49:04 flyingpenguin sendmail[12898]: e9M2n4E12898:
to=emilyd, delay=00:00:00, mailer=local, pri=0, dsn=5.1.1,
stat=User unknown
Oct 21 22:49:04 flyingpenguin sendmail[12898]: e9M2n4E12898:
to=princesspaws2000, delay=00:00:00, mailer=local, pri=0,
dsn=5.1.1, stat=User unknown
```

If you want something more sophisticated than the preceding logreport script, you can download free utilities that analyze log files. logcheck, a free program available from the Psionic Web site, http://www.psionic.com/abacus/logcheck/, reports on abnormalities, security threats, and security violations it finds in your log files and e-mails the report to you. logsurfer is a similar free log analyzer that you can get at the Logsurfer Web site, http://www.cert.dfn.de/eng/logsurf. The following output is from the logcheck program.

Note   The following output has been edited to remove specific IP addresses and user-account names.

```
From: candace
To: root
Subject: burgessmeredith debian system

Security Violations
Dec 16 16:30:23 burgessmeredith su: 'su' failed for
miss_scarlet
```

```
Dec 16 16:30:35 burgessmeredith login: LOGIN FAILURE ON
/dev/ttyp5 FROM localhost
Dec 16 16:36:44 burgessmeredith deny
host=tweety.cardinalconsulting.com/service=ipop3d

Unusual System Events =-=-=-=-=-=-=-=-=-=-=
Dec 16 16:32:40 burgessmeredith sshd[21624]: log: Connection
from
Dec 16 16:32:44 burgessmeredith sshd[21624]: log: Password
authentication for candace accepted.
Dec 16 16:32:48 burgessmeredith sshd[21624]: log: Closing
connection to
```

Controlling and Repairing Damage after a Break-in

Once you detect a compromised system or network, there are several measures that you need to take immediately.

Close the breach

Disconnect compromised system(s) from the network completely. If you leave the compromised system on the network, the intruder may still be there, undoing all the actions you perform to repair the damage.

Look for evidence of a sniffer program. Crackers often break in to install a sniffer to steal user-account and password information.

To determine whether a sniffer is installed on your system, look for a network interface running in promiscuous mode. Normally, your *network interface card* (NIC) is only interested in looking for packets addressed to it — it ignores all the rest. Some network monitoring and management software, however, is able to place the network interface card in promiscuous mode, making it keep and display every packet. These kinds of tools are useful for debugging network problems, but they should be available to and used by authorized network administrators only. If any interface is in promiscuous mode, a sniffer could be installed on your system. Note that you will not be able to detect promiscuous interfaces if you have rebooted your machine or are running the system in single-user mode since your discovery of this intrusion.

Use the ifstatus program to check all network interfaces on the system and report all that are in debug or promiscuous mode. The sidebar, "Getting the ifstatus Program," shows how to set up ifstatus, beginning with downloading the program if you don't already have it.

Getting the ifstatus Program

This example uses a terminal window interface to download the ifstatus program using FTP.

```
root@flyingpenguin# ftp ftp.cerias.purdue.edu
Connected to ftp.cerias.purdue.edu.
220-ftp.cerias.purdue.edu NcFTPd Server (free educational
license) ready.
220-          Welcome to the CERIAS Security FTP Archive
220-
220-Users must provide their e-mail addresses as passwords. All
activity
220-is logged and may be monitored. If you object to this, do not
log into
220-this service. Before downloading any tools, tips, tricks or
other bits
220-of information from this site, please read and understand all
of the
220-implications of the information provided located in the root
directory.
220-
220-         Limitation of Liability - README.liability
220-            Export Restrictions - README.export
220-            Copyright Notice - README.copyright
220-
KERBEROS_V4 rejected as an authentication type
Name (ftp.cerias.purdue.edu:miss_scarlet): anonymous
331 Guest login ok, send your complete e-mail address as
password.
Password:
230-
230-                    Purdue University
230-
230-            CERIAS - Security Archive
230-          ---------------------------------------
230-          Center for Education and Research in
230-             Information Assurance and Security
230-----------------------------------------------------------------
-----------
230-        Local time is Mon Oct 23 09:40:21 2000. User 15 of
100.
230-
230- All transfers are logged with your host name and email
address. If you
230-              don't like this policy, disconnect now!
230-    For more information on CERIAS go to
http://www.cerias.purdue.edu
```

```
230-
230 Logged in anonymously.
Remote system type is UNIX.
Using binary mode to transfer files.
ftp> cd pub/tools/unix
250-"/pub/tools/unix" is new cwd.
250-
250-------------------------------------------------------------------
-----------
250-                           Purdue University
250-
250-                       CERIAS Security Archive
250-                   -----------------------------------------
250-                   Center for Education and Research in
250-                     Information Assurance And Security
250-
250-           Send comments to security-archive@cerias.purdue.edu
250-------------------------------------------------------------------
-----------
250-
250-crypto     - Cryptographic software
250-daemons    - Daemons
250-firewalls  - Firewalls and firewall configuration utilities
250-ids        - Intrusion Detection Systems
250-libs       - Security-aware libraries
250-logutils   - Logging and log management utilities
250-netutils   - Network utilities
250-pwdutils   - Password utilities
250-scanners   - Network and host scanners
250-sysutils   - System utilities
250-
250-------------------------------------------------------------------
-----------
250
ftp> cd sysutils
250 "/pub/tools/unix/sysutils" is new cwd.
ftp> cd ifstatus
250 "/pub/tools/unix/sysutils/ifstatus" is new cwd.
ftp> ls
227 Entering Passive Mode (128,10,252,10,211,196)
150 Data connection accepted from 24.218.228.45:1084; transfer
starting.
-rw-rw-r--   1 ftpuser   ftpusers        730 Jun 14 17:40
README.local
-rw-rw-r--   1 ftpuser   ftpusers      12295 Jun 14 17:40
ifstatus2.2.tar.gz
```

Continued

Continued

```
226 Listing completed.
 ftp> mget *
mget README.local? y
227 Entering Passive Mode (128,10,252,10,211,210)
150 Data connection accepted from 24.218.228.45:1092; transfer
starting for READ
ME.local (730 bytes).
226 Transfer completed.
730 bytes received in 0.00024 seconds (2.9e+03 Kbytes/s)
mget ifstatus2.2.tar.gz? y
227 Entering Passive Mode (128,10,252,10,211,212)
150 Data connection accepted from 24.218.228.45:1093; transfer
starting for ifst
atus2.2.tar.gz (12295 bytes).
226 Transfer completed.
12295 bytes received in 0.24 seconds (51 Kbytes/s)
ftp> close
221 Goodbye.
ftp> bye
root@flyingpenguin# ls *z
ifstatus2.2.tar.gz
root@flyingpenguin# gunzip *z
root@flyingpenguin# ls if*
ifstatus2.2.tar

root@flyingpenguin# tar -xvf ifstatus*.tar
ifstatus/
ifstatus/Makefile
ifstatus/ifstatus.c
ifstatus/ifstatus.man
ifstatus/if-generic.c
ifstatus/if-solaris.c
ifstatus/install.sh
ifstatus/if-solaris26.h
ifstatus/RCS/
ifstatus/RCS/if-solaris.c,v
ifstatus/RCS/if-solaris25.h,v
ifstatus/RCS/Makefile,v
ifstatus/RCS/if-solaris26.h,v
ifstatus/if-solaris25.h

root@flyingpenguin# cd ifstatus
root@flyingpenguin# ls
Makefile  if-generic.c  if-solaris25.h  ifstatus.c   install.sh
RCS       if-solaris.c  if-solaris26.h  ifstatus.man
```

```
root@flyingpenguin#

-- TCP/IP LOG -- TM: Tue Nov 15 15:12:29 --
     PATH: not_at_risk.domain.com(1567) =>
at_risk.domain.com(telnet)
```

Back up the compromised system(s)

While this step may seem strange, you should make a backup of your system if at all possible before repairing the damage. You may need to restore the state of the compromised machine to analyze it further. Also, in the case of legal action, you may need the compromised system for evidence.

Analyze the intrusion

Check file permissions and modifications as I described earlier in the section "Diagnosing break-in Attempts." Check any strange IP addresses you find in the log files in the appropriate whois database. For a .com, .edu, .net, or .org top-level domain, you can query the InterNIC's whois database, http://rs.internic.net/tools/whois.html.

If you are running an integrity-checking program like Tripwire, use it to perform an integrity check. It should help to tell you what has been compromised.

Reporting the intrusion to CERT

CERT, the Computer Emergency Response Team, is an independent agency that helps organizations defend themselves against attacks. CERT's mission is to assist members of the Internet community to deal with computer-security incidents and to research ways to improve computer-system security. CERT also maintains information on the security weaknesses of operating systems and applications and how to repair them. CERT doesn't publicize security vulnerabilities without telling you how to work around the problem or how to get a patch to fix it. You can send e-mail to cert@cert.org or go to CERT's Web site, www.cert.org, to fill out an electronic incident report.

 Note   There are regional CERTs around the world.

What is whois?

whois is a TCP/IP protocol, service, and application that enables you to look up information about networks, networking organizations, domains, and the people who manage them. The information is stored in a database on the Internet.

The following whois sites are maintained by various Internet registrars (the organizations that give out IP addresses):

✦ whois.ripe.net—The RIPE NCC (Reseaux IP Europeans Network Coordination Centre), the regional Internet registrar for Europe. (The RIPE database does not contain information on all European domain names. Searching for IP numbers will get you better results than searching for domain names.)

✦ whois.apnic.net—The Asia Pacific Network Information Center.

✦ whois.nic.mil— The U.S. military's Internet registrar; only maintains registration information for domains ending in .mil.

✦ whois.nic.gov— The U.S. Government; for finding domains ending in .gov and .fed.us. Here's where you can find information about the U.S. White House, home office of the President. If you search for whitehouse.com, whois tells you "Sorry, no match for whitehouse.com."

Recovering from the intrusion

The safest way to recover from an intrusion is to reinstall the operating system to guarantee that all operating-system components, including the kernel, binaries, datafiles, processes, and memory, are clean. Other steps you should take to recover include:

✦ Disabling unnecessary services.

✦ Installing all the security patches for your distribution. You get these at the vendor's Web site.

New Feature

The Red Hat Network is a new service that, for a small fee, automatically notifies you of new patches. The service currently supports Red Hat 7 only, but will eventually support version 5.2 as well. Visit www.redhat.com for more information.

✦ Change passwords for everyone.

✦ Consult CERT and AusCERT advisories and security bulletins. You can get AusCERT advisories from http://www.auscert.org.au/Information/ Advisories/aus_advisories.html. You can get AusCERT External Security Bulletins from http://www.auscert.org.au/Information/Advisories/ esb_advisories.html.

✦ Reconnect to the Internet.

✦ Review your security policies and procedures, updating them if necessary.

Caution   Since legitimate network monitors and protocol analyzers set a network-interface card to promiscuous mode, finding an interface in promiscuous mode does not necessarily mean that a cracker's sniffer is running on your computer.

Keeping up to Date on Viruses, Vaccines, and Security Alerts and Fixes

Your best bet for keeping your system updated in the ongoing evolution of security breaches and fixes is to check CERT at `www.cert.org`. In addition to incident response activities, CERT researches and writes reports on security vulnerabilities, prevention of vulnerabilities, system-security improvement, and the ability of large-scale networks to survive security-related attack or compromise.

Pay special attention to CERT advisories — documents that describe a serious security problem and its impact, along with instructions on how to obtain a patch or construct a workaround.

Consider adding your name to the CERT mailing list. To subscribe to the CERT advisory mailing list, send e-mail to `majordomo@cert.org`. In the body of the message, type

```
subscribe cert-advisory
```

Additionally, regularly consult the security pages on your Linux vendor's Web site. The major Linux vendors, such as Caldera, Red Hat, Slackware, regularly publish security advisories for the products and release patches for programs discovered to be vulnerable to security exploits. They also have full time security experts or quality assurance departments specifically charged with detecting and fixing bugs and breaches.

Some vendor specific sites are:

✦ Caldera's page of security fixes: `http://www.caldera.com/tech-ref/security/`

✦ Debian's security page: `http://www.debian.org/security/`

✦ Red Hat's own Security Page for its latest release, Red Hat 7: `http://www.redhat.com/support/errata/rh7-errata-security.html`

✦ SuSE Security Page: `http://www.suse.de/security/`

Additional sites you may want to check out include:

✦ Rootshell.com, a great site for seeing what exploits crackers are currently using: `http://www.rootshell.com/`

✦ Finally, Infilsec runs a vulnerability engine that can tell you what vulnerabilities affect a specific platform: `http://www.infilsec.com/vulnerabilities/`

Summary

Security involves everything and everyone on a computer and network. This chapter helps you set up security policies to protect against attacks and actively check for possible break-ins. If the worst should happen, this chapter also helps you repair damage from intrusions on your systems and networks. This chapter also points you to numerous sources of tools to monitor security-related activities and documents.

✦   ✦   ✦

Shell Scripting for System Administrators

This chapter provides a miscellaneous collection of scripting hints, tips, and examples for system administrators. The scripts in this chapter build on the basic scripting techniques described in Chapter 18.

Cross-Reference To understand the examples and concepts in this chapter, you must understand the information in Chapter 18.

The First System Admin Script

As a system administrator, even if you never write a script, you still need to be able to work with the initialization scripts in the subdirectories below /etc/rc.d and the /etc/rc.local script.

Note In Linux files and directories, rc stands for *run command*.

When you start your system, Linux executes all the init scripts for the run level you are booting.

Note A run level is a Linux configuration that specifies which system processes and daemons should run. You must be root or have a UID of 0 to change run levels.

These init scripts reside in the directories /etc/rc.d/rc*.d (where * is 0, 1, 2, 3, 4, 5, or 6). The init scripts' file names begin with either K (for *kill a process*) or S (for *start a process*). For example, if you are going to run level 0 (single user mode),

Linux kills all the processes since you are halting the system. Therefore, all the scripts in /etc/rc.d/rc0.d begin with K. The following directory listing shows the files in the directory /etc/rc.d/rc0.d on Caldera's OpenLinux eServer:

```
total 0
lrwxrwxrwx  1 root    root   15 Feb 27  2000 K09samba -> ../init.d/samba
lrwxrwxrwx  1 root    root   15 Feb 27  2000 K12squid -> ../init.d/squid
lrwxrwxrwx  1 root    root   13 Feb 27  2000 K25gpm -> ../init.d/gpm
lrwxrwxrwx  1 root    root   15 Feb 27  2000 K25httpd -> ../init.d/httpd
lrwxrwxrwx  1 root    root   17 Feb 27  2000 K30logoutd -> ../init.d/logoutd
lrwxrwxrwx  1 root    root   15 Feb 27  2000 K44dhcpd -> ../init.d/dhcpd
lrwxrwxrwx  1 root    root   13 Feb 27  2000 K50mta -> ../init.d/mta
lrwxrwxrwx  1 root    root   14 Feb 27  2000 K55ldap -> ../init.d/ldap
lrwxrwxrwx  1 root    root   15 Feb 27  2000 K55snmpd -> ../init.d/snmpd
lrwxrwxrwx  1 root    root   13 Feb 27  2000 K59atd -> ../init.d/atd
lrwxrwxrwx  1 root    root   14 Feb 27  2000 K60cron -> ../init.d/cron
lrwxrwxrwx  1 root    root   13 Feb 27  2000 K60nfs -> ../init.d/nfs
lrwxrwxrwx  1 root    root   13 Feb 27  2000 K65lpd -> ../init.d/lpd
lrwxrwxrwx  1 root    root   15 Feb 27  2000 K65mysql -> ../init.d/mysql
lrwxrwxrwx  1 root    root   13 Feb 27  2000 K70amd -> ../init.d/amd
lrwxrwxrwx  1 root    root   13 Feb 27  2000 K70ntp -> ../init.d/ntp
lrwxrwxrwx  1 root    root   13 Feb 27  2000 K74ipx -> ../init.d/ipx
lrwxrwxrwx  1 root    root   20 Feb 27  2000 K79nis-client -> ../init.d/nis-client
lrwxrwxrwx  1 root    root   18 Feb 27  2000 K80netmount -> ../init.d/netmount
lrwxrwxrwx  1 root    root   20 Feb 27  2000 K80nis-server -> ../init.d/nis-server
lrwxrwxrwx  1 root    root   15 Feb 27  2000 K82quota -> ../init.d/quota
lrwxrwxrwx  1 root    root   14 Feb 27  2000 K85inet -> ../init.d/inet
lrwxrwxrwx  1 root    root   15 Feb 27  2000 K90named -> ../init.d/named
lrwxrwxrwx  1 root    root   16 Feb 27  2000 K94pcmcia -> ../init.d/pcmcia
lrwxrwxrwx  1 root    root   16 Feb 27  2000 K95syslog -> ../init.d/syslog
lrwxrwxrwx  1 root    root   17 Feb 27  2000 K95urandom -> ../init.d/urandom
lrwxrwxrwx  1 root    root   17 Feb 27  2000 K99network -> ../init.d/network
lrwxrwxrwx  1 root    root   13 Feb 27  2000 K99zap -> ../init.d/zap
lrwxrwxrwx  1 root    root   14 Feb 27  2000 S99halt -> ../init.d/halt
```

Note   The init scripts in the rc directories are actually links to the master copies in the /etc/rc.d/init.d directory.

When you boot to run level 5, all the scripts in /etc/rc.d/rc5.d begin with S. The init scripts for run levels 1, 2, and 3 contain a mixture of K and S scripts.

Looking at a simple rc.local initialization file

If you plan only one or two small system-specific initialization tasks, it's easiest to edit them into rc.local. If you plan to run some complex customized initialization routines, you should create K or S scripts and add them to the appropriate run-level directories. This approach keeps rc.local small and simple, and keeps your complex initialization scripts organized with similar Linux initialization procedures.

From init to rc.local

init (job 1) is the parent of all processes. When you boot your system, Linux reads the file /etc/inittab to see how to set up processes for each run level. On most Linux distributions, init levels range from 0 to 6:

0 - Halt

1 (or S or s) - Single-user mode

2 - Multiuser (timesharing) mode without networking

3 - Multiuser (timesharing) mode with networking

4 - Usually unused

5 - Multiuser mode with networking and the X Window System

6 - Reboot

After Linux executes all the init scripts needed for a run level, it executes the file /etc/rc.local. On Berkeley-style UNIX, system administrators put all their own system specific initialization material in rc.local. You can do this in Linux as well. However, since Linux provides specific run-level directories, most Linux system administrators prefer to add their own initialization scripts into the rc1 through rc5 directories.

When you perform an upgrade installation to move to a new Linux release, Linux may add new or edited init scripts to the rc*.d directories. The upgrade installation preserves the site-specific scripts that you add to these directories. However, a good system administrator is a paranoid system administrator, so I recommend that you back up your customized init files just in case something unexpected happens during the upgrade.

The following section examines two different versions of the rc.local file - one from a Sony VAIO notebook, tweety, which runs Caldera's OpenLinux eServer, and the other from a Dell laptop, flyingpenguin, which runs Red Hat Linux.

In this book, tweety and flyingpenguin are the two computers used most often, though not exclusively, to generate examples. Other examples come from PHAT Linux, TurboLinux, Debian, and SuSE Linux.

The following file is the rc.local script without any system-administrator customizations from tweety, a notebook computer that runs Caldera's OpenLinux eServer. The installation procedure creates the basic rc.local file.

On most Linux distributions, the init scripts, including rc.local, are Bourne shell (sh) scripts. However, bash is compatible with sh, so you can use most of the syntax you see in a Bourne shell script in a bash script.

```
#!/bin/sh

# This script will be executed *after* all the other init scripts.
# You can put your own initialization stuff in here if you don't
# want to do the full Sys V-style init stuff.

if [ -r /etc/.issue ]; then
    cat /etc/.issue > /etc/issue
else
    cat << EOI > /etc/issue

Caldera OpenLinux(TM)
Copyright (C) 1996-1998 Caldera, Inc.

EOI
fi

cp -f /etc/issue /etc/issue.net
echo >> /etc/issue
```

> **Note** This rc.local script creates a simple informational message, including the name, version, and copyright of the Linux distribution, shown each time someone logs in to the system. The next text file, /etc/issue, stores the message. Notice that the version number is hardcoded into the file.

This is the resulting /etc/issue file that rc.local creates.

```
Caldera OpenLinux eServer
Version 2.3
Copyright 1996-1999 Caldera Systems, Inc.
```

Adding complexity to rc.local

The next example of rc.local comes from flyingpenguin, which is running Red Hat Linux. The Red Hat rc.local does basically the same thing as Caldera's rc.local file: it displays the informational message stored in /etc/issue. The difference between the files is that the Red Hat version does more checking on the system architecture than does the Caldera version. For example, the rc.local file below determines how many processors are in your computer and, if the architecture is SMP (Symmetric Multiprocessing, that is, more than a single CPU), rc.local outputs the number of processors as part of the system information message. Another difference between the two rc.local files is that the Red Hat version does not hardcode the release number into the /etc/issue file. It checks for the existence of an extra file, /etc/redhat-release, which holds the release number.

```
$ cat /etc/rc.d/rc.local
#!/bin/sh
#
```

```
# This script will be executed *after* all the other init scripts.
# You can put your own initialization stuff in here if you don't
# want to do the full Sys V-style init stuff.

if [ -f /etc/redhat-release ]; then
    R=$(cat /etc/redhat-release)

    arch=$(uname -m)
    a="a"
    case "_$arch" in
            _a*) a="an";;
            _i*) a="an";;
    esac

    NUMPROC=`grep -cl "^cpu[0-9]+" /proc/stat`
    if [ "$NUMPROC" -gt "1" ]; then
        SMP="$NUMPROC-processor "
        if [ "$NUMPROC" = "8" -o "$NUMPROC" = "11" ]; then
            a="an"
        else
            a="a"
fi
    fi

# This will overwrite /etc/issue at every boot. So make any changes you
# want to make to /etc/issue here or you will lose them when you reboot.
echo "" > /etc/issue
echo "$R" >> /etc/issue
echo "Kernel $(uname -r) on $a $SMP$(uname -m)" >> /etc/issue

cp -f /etc/issue /etc/issue.net
echo >> /etc/issue
fi
#
#       Site-specific customizations go here.
#
# Start sshd (secure shell daemon).
#
/usr/local/sbin/sshd
# Start any PCMCIA devices
if [ -x /etc/rc.d/rc.pcmcia ] ;
then
. /etc/rc.d/rc.pcmcia start
fi
# Check the rc.modules file to see if dynamic modules need to be
# loaded. If so, go ahead and load them.
if [ -x /etc/rc.d/rc.modules ];
then
. /etc/rc.d/rc.modules
fi
```

Note   The last part of the file above starts sshd, the secure shell daemon. This line is a site-specific customization inserted by the system administrator.

Scripting Tips and Techniques from rc.local

Although shell scripting is an easily acquired skill, there are some subtle points that typically trip up a beginner. This section presents a few tips you can use when creating new scripts or modifying existing ones that will help you avoid common pitfalls.

Tip 1. Always check that files exist before you access them.

The first if test in the Red Hat version of rc.local checks for the existence of a file, /etc/redhat-release.

```
if [ -f /etc/redhat-release ]; then
    R=$(cat /etc/redhat-release)
```

If the redhat-release file is a regular file that exists, rc.local continues processing with the statement(s) that follow the then clause. If the file redhat-release does not exist, processing skips over the then clause and continues processing with the next statement in the script.

Cross-Reference   See Chapter 18 for more information on if-clause syntax and options.

When you write scripts that access other scripts or files, always check first that the files exist. If the files you reference don't exist, your script will generate an error like the following and exit immediately:

```
cat: redhat release: No such file or directory
```

A common system-administration task is to generate reports from the passwd file. You can do this in a variety of ways in Linux: using a shell script, an awk program, a Perl program, or even a standard 3GL (third-generation language) such as C or FORTRAN. The excerpt below shows how to test that the passwd file exists and how to generate your own error message and set an exit status if Linux can't find the file:

```
#/bin/bash
# bash script, checkfile.bsh
# Check for the passwd file.
```

```
#         Candace Leiden
#         Cardinal Software Group
#      12-Dec-2000
# Verify that the passwd file exists.
if [ -f "/etc/passwd" ];
then
    echo "Password file exists."
    # Set a successful exit status of 0.
    exit 0
else
    # Display an error message and set a failed exit status
    echo "No such file. Please notify system admin immediately."
    exit 1
fi
```

Note   Although the checkfile.bsh script above is a bash script, it uses the same `if` syntax as Red Hat's rc.local Bourne shell script.

Cross-Reference   See Chapter 18 for information about setting the exit status.

Tip 2. Store the results of a command in a variable for later use.

The first `if` test in rc.local takes the results of the `cat` command and stores those results in a variable named R:

```
if [ -f /etc/redhat-release ]; then
    R=$(cat /etc/redhat-release)
```

The rc.local script later uses the value in R to display the contents of the release file.

If the file /etc/redhat-release does not exist, processing continues, and when rc.local displays the system information message, you don't see the release number. You can either create the /etc/redhat-release file or modify rc.local to code a release number into the script by adding an `else` clause that stores a hardcoded value in the variable, R:

```
if [ -f /etc/redhat-release ];
    then
        R=$(cat /etc/redhat-release)
    else
        R="release 6.1 (Cartman)"
```

Tip   Rather than modifying rc.local, in this case a better idea is to create the file /etc/redhat-release. When you upgrade to a new release, it will be easier and safer to modify the redhat-release file rather than rc.local.

Tip 3. In a multi-architecture environment, write a single script that works for all architectures.

The rc.local script performs a simple action based on the hardware architecture of the computer that is booting. The architecture check in the code below is setting up correct English grammar for the /etc/issue file. If the architecture begins with a (for alpha) or i (for Intel), rc.local plans to deliver a message that says "an alpha" or "an intel." If it's any other architecture, rc.local delivers a message referring to "a mips," "a ppc," and so forth.

```
arch=$(uname -m)
    a="a"
    case "_$arch" in
            _a*) a="an";;
            _i*) a="an";;
    esac
```

First, rc.local runs the uname -m command to determine the architecture of the machine. Putting the command in parentheses following a $ takes the result of the command and stores it in the variable on the left side of the =. The first line in the preceding excerpt stores the architecture in the variable arch.

Caution   In the previous example, arch is a variable. On Linux, there is also an arch command, which is the same as uname -m. Be careful to distinguish between the variable and the command.

Note   The case statement compares a string to a set of values. In the previous example there are two values: anything starting with a, and anything starting with i. At the first match, Linux executes the corresponding statement(s). After executing the statement(s), Linux exits the case statement and proceeds to the statement following esac. If there is no match, Linux resumes processing after esac. See Chapter 18 for more about the case statement.

Cross-Reference   See Chapter 18 for more information on case-statement syntax.

While the architecture checking in rc.local is simply grammatical, you can use architecture checking to make your bash scripts run on any hardware architecture. For example, the script below decides which welcome message to display based on hardware architecture.

Note   The following script replaces uname -m with the arch command. Linux supports the arch command as well as uname -m. If you are writing scripts that need to run on both Linux and UNIX, keep in mind that some UNIX versions only support uname -m.

```
candace@redbird$ cat archi_script
#/bin/bash
# bash script, archi_script.bsh
# Check for the hardware architecture.
#       Candace Leiden
#       Cardinal Software Group
#       15-Dec-2000
# Display the hardware architecture before proceeding.
# First get the node name; then get the architecture.
Node=$(uname -n)
Hardware=$(arch)
case "$Hardware" in
"mips") echo "Welcome to the MIPS system, $Node";;
#
#       You could insert more mips-specific processing here.
#
"i686") echo "Welcome to an Intel system, $Node";;
#
#       You could insert more mips-specific processing here.
#
"sparc") echo "Welcome to a Sun system, $Node";;
#
#       You could insert more mips-specific processing here.
#
"i386") echo "Welcome to the dark ages. It still works;;"
esac
#       Add further generic processing here.

OffenderFile bash archi_script.bsh
Welcome to a Sun system, redbird.cardinalconsulting.com
```

Note Possible return values for the arch command include:

i386	alpha	m68k
i486	sparc	mips
i586	arm	ppc
i686		

Tip If you have a multi-architecture environment, you may have multiple scripts that perform basically the same function with a few modifications for architectural differences. Having multiple scripts instead of a single script is a maintenance burden. You need to keep track of all the scripts, back them all up, decide which one(s) to restore if a file is lost or corrupted, and edit all of them to add the same functionality. Instead of maintaining separate scripts based on architecture, try building a case statement that does processing for varied architectures in a single script.

Further hardware checking

If you work in a Symmetric Multiprocessing (SMP) environment, your script may need to know the number of processors. In the example below from rc.local, the script gets the number of processors to add to the informational message in /etc/issue. The first step in the following excerpt is to retrieve the number of processors from the file /proc/stat in the /proc filesystem. The grep command searches for the number of CPUs and stores that number in the variable NUMPROC. If NUMPROC is greater than 1, the script defines a variable, SMP, as the string NUMPROC-processor. For example, if redbird has four processors, the value of the SMP variable is 4-processor. Next the code does some English-language manipulation. As in the preceding architecture example, this rc.local decides whether to say "a" or "an" in the /etc/issue message. If the computer has eight processors, for example, the message reads "an 8-processor."

 Cross-Reference   You can read more about finding system information in the /proc filesystem in Chapter 32, "Monitoring and Optimizing Linux Performance."

```
NUMPROC=`grep -cl "^cpu[0-9]+" /proc/stat`
    if [ "$NUMPROC" -gt "1" ]; then
        SMP="$NUMPROC-processor "
        if [ "$NUMPROC" = "8" -o "$NUMPROC" = "11" ]; then
            a="an"
        else
            a="a"
fi
```

The file /etc/issue shows a message from an SMP computer with four CPUs.

```
Red Hat Linux release 6.1 (Cartman)
Kernel 2.2.12-20 on a 4-processor sparc
```

The rest of the rc.local script uses the echo command to write the system message to the file /etc/issue. Then rc.local copies /etc/issue to /etc/issue.net so that telnet sees the same system message.

```
# This will overwrite /etc/issue at every boot. So make any changes you
# want to make to /etc/issue here or you will lose them when you reboot.
echo "" > /etc/issue
echo "$R" >> /etc/issue
echo "Kernel $(uname -r) on a $a $SMP$(uname -m)" >> /etc/issue

cp -f /etc/issue /etc/issue.net
echo >> /etc/issue
fi
```

Tip 4. Add pre-login security measures to rc.local.

On the network used to generate most of the examples in this book, one of the customizations to the various rc.local files is to comment out all lines that write messages to /etc/issue. Most security conscious organizations don't want to provide any information to unauthorized users. Therefore, we write no system information to /etc/issue and /etc/issue.net. Instead we create /etc/issue with the line, "Authorized Access Only." The "real life" rc.local file from a Red Hat system, flying-penguin, is below.

```
$ cat /etc/rc.d/rc.local
#!/bin/sh
#
# This script will be executed *after* all the other init scripts.
# You can put your own initialization stuff in here if you don't
# want to do the full Sys V-style init stuff.

#if [ -f /etc/redhat-release ]; then
#    R=$(cat /etc/redhat-release)

#    arch=$(uname -m)
#    a="a"
#    case "_$arch" in
#            _a*) a="an";;
#            _i*) a="an";;
#    esac

#    NUMPROC=`grep -cl "^cpu[0-9]+" /proc/stat`
#    if [ "$NUMPROC" -gt "1" ]; then
#       SMP="$NUMPROC-processor "
#       if [ "$NUMPROC" = "8" -o "$NUMPROC" = "11" ]; then
#            a="an"
#       else
#            a="a"
#       fi
#    fi

# This will overwrite /etc/issue at every boot. So make any changes you
# want to make to /etc/issue here or you will lose them when you reboot.
#echo "" > /etc/issue
#echo "$R" >> /etc/issue
#echo "Kernel $(uname -r) on $a $SMP$(uname -m)" >> /etc/issue
#
#    cp -f /etc/issue /etc/issue.net
#    echo >> /etc/issue
#    fi
#
#    **** Site-specific customizations go here. ***
# Don't give away any info. Add security message.
echo "" > /etc/issue
echo "     Authorized Access Only" >> /etc/issue
echo "     --------------------" >> /etc/issue
cp -f /etc/issue /etc/issue.net
# Start sshd (secure shell daemon).
#
/usr/local/sbin/sshd
# Start any PCMCIA devices
```

```
if [ -x /etc/rc.d/rc.pcmcia ] ;
then . /etc/rc.d/rc.pcmcia start
fi

$ cat /etc/issue

Authorized Access Only
----------------------
```

Tip

If you prefer to keep the pre-login message as it comes in your distribution, consider adding a line to the /etc/issue file to the effect that unauthorized access is not permitted.

Debugging Your Scripts

If a script fails, bash usually sends you a message giving you the reason why the script failed and a line number near where the error occurred. For example,

```
OffenderFile bash test_debug.bsh
test_debug.bsh: test_debug.bsh: line 29: syntax error:
unexpected end of file
```

Tip

The meaning of an error message may not always be obvious. For example, the syntax error in the test_debug script above is a missing fi to complete an if block. Use cat -n to display your script file with line numbers, as below:

```
$ cat -n test_debug.bsh
     1  if [ -f /etc/redhat-release ]; then
     2      R=$(cat /etc/redhat-release)
     3
     4      arch=$(uname -m)
     5      a="a"
     6      case "_$arch" in
     7              _a*) a="an";;
     8              _i*) a="an";;
     9      esac
    10
    11      NUMPROC=`grep -cl "^cpu[0-9]+" /proc/stat`
    12      if [ "$NUMPROC" -gt "1" ]; then
    13          SMP="$NUMPROC-processor "
    14          if [ "$NUMPROC" = "8" -o "$NUMPROC" = 11" ]; then
    15              a="an"
    16          else
    17              a="a"
    18  fi
    19          fi
    20
    21  # This will overwrite /etc/issue at every boot. So make any changes you
    22  # want to make to /etc/issue here or you will lose them when you reboot.
    23  echo "" > /etc/issue
```

```
24  echo "$R" >> /etc/issue
25  echo "Kernel $(uname -r) on $a $SMP$(uname -m)" >> /etc/issue
26
27  cp -f /etc/issue /etc/issue.net
28  echo >> /etc/issue
$
```

Note Notice that there is no line 29 in the script to correspond to the error message. bash is looking for something that should be on line 29. Remember that line numbers in bash error messages are only approximate.

To do some simple logic debugging, invoke your script with the following syntax:

```
bash -x script-name
```

The -x option displays all the steps the script follows. Unexecuted code and comments do not appear in the output of bash -x. *script-name* is the name of the script. The example below runs the script from Tip 3. You can see each step displayed in the order in which it is executed. If you have logic errors, especially in loops, debugging your script with bash -x can show you where your logic and flow goes wrong.

```
OffenderFile bash -x archi_script.bsh
++ uname -n
+ Node=flyingpenguin.cardinalconsulting.com
++ arch
+ Hardware=i686
+ echo Welcome to an Intel system,
flyingpenguin.cardinalconsulting.com
Welcome to an Intel system,
flyingpenguin.cardinalconsulting.com
OffenderFile
```

Caution A script can't execute until it is free of syntax errors. Using the -x option to debug script execution does not help debug syntax errors. Here is the output of bash -x on a script that is missing a fi from an if block:

```
OffenderFile bash -x test_debug.bsh
test_debug.bsh: test_debug.bsh: line 29: syntax error:
unexpected end of file
```

Keeping Users Informed

The echo command is a simple command that you should use to display informational messages from a script, especially when users won't see output for a few seconds. You can either echo a character string or redirect the echo results to a file, as you saw rc.local direct information to /etc/issue earlier in this chapter.

The command:

```
echo "Working. . ."
```

can help users understand that something is happening even if they don't know what.

Another way to use the echo command is as an alternative to bash -x to trace the execution of a shell script. Using echo at key points in the logic of the code tells you how far the script has gotten and what's happening. Here is the output from a simple script:

```
miss_scarlet@tweety$ info
Sun Sep 24 20:09:23 EDT 2000
./knife
./lead_pipe
./rope
./candlestick
./.kde/share/config/ksnapshotrc
./mail
./friends/colonel_mustard
./friends/emily
./friends/marshall
./friends/miss_scarlet
./x
./gobbige
./databases
./Emmy_Horse_File
./ch15_newpics
miss_scarlet  pts/0     Sep 24 18:10
Login         Name           Tty    Idle   Login Time
candace       candace leiden  /3            Sep 24 20:14 (flyingpenguin)
candace       candace leiden  /5            Sep 24 20:15 (192.168.0.5)
miss_scarlet  emily lauren scar /0  1:27    Sep 24 18:10 (192.168.0.5)
miss_scarlet  emily lauren scar /4          Sep 24 19:27 (:0)
root          root            /1     2d     Sep 10 22:12 (:0)
root          root            /2     2d     Sep 10 22:12 (:0)
```

There are two problems with the output above that using echo can resolve:

1. The user may not be aware that the script is working if it is slow to display output.

2. The user may not understand the output.

Adding echo commands solves both of these problems. The code for the script follows, with echo commands added. You can see the improved output following the source code.

```
echo "Retrieving today's date . . ."
echo ". . . . . . . . . . . . . ."
date
echo ""
echo "Looking for empty files. Please delete. . ."
echo ". . . . . . . . . . . . . ."
find -empty
echo ""
echo "Finding local logged in users . . ."
echo ". . . . . . . . . . . . . ."
who
echo ""
echo "Fingering logged in users . . ."
finger
echo "End of processing. Have a nice day. . ."
echo "========================================="

miss_scarlet@tweety$ bash info
Retrieving today's date . . .
. . . . . . . . . . . . . .
Sun Sep 24 20:09:23 EDT 2000

Looking for empty files. Please delete . . .
. . . . . . . . . . . . . .
./knife
./lead_pipe
./rope
./candlestick
./.kde/share/config/ksnapshotrc
./mail
./friends/colonel_mustard
./friends/emily
./friends/marshall
./friends/miss_scarlet
./x
./gobbige
./databases
./Emmy_Horse_File
./ch15_newpics

Fingering logged in users . . .
Login          Name            Tty   Idle  Login Time   Office     Office Phone
candace        candace leiden  /5          Sep 24 20:15 (192.168.0.5)
miss_scarlet   emily lauren scar /0   1:32  Sep 24 18:10 (192.168.0.5)
miss_scarlet   emily lauren scar /4         Sep 24 19:27 (192.168.0.5)
root           root            /1    2d    Sep 10 22:12 (:0)
root           root            /2    2d    Sep 10 22:12 (:0)
End of processing. Have a nice day. . .
=========================================
```

Implementing a Simple Menu

Earlier in this chapter you saw a case statement used in rc.local to set a value depending on the computer's architecture. Another common use for a case statement is for evaluating and acting on users' menu choices. If you want users to access commands and applications only through a menu, you can write a script like the one following and invoke it from the user's .bash_profile file. Executing the script from .bash_profile causes the menu to display automatically when the user logs in and uses bash.

```
#! /bin/bash
#   /home/miss_scarlet/bash_profile_menu
#
# Display the menu
echo "Please select an option from the menu "
echo "Option          Description"
echo "------          -----------"
echo " L              List files in your current directory"
echo " D              Display a file"
echo " P              Print a file"
echo " R              Remove a file"
echo " E              Exit"
# Get the user's menu selection.
read menu_choice
# Use a case statement to relate a menu choice to an action.
# Accept either upper or lower case.
case $menu_choice in
L|l) ls -l;;
D|d) echo "File(s) to display?"
read file_list
more $file_list;;
P|p) echo "File(s) to print?"
read file_list
lp $file_list;;
R|r) echo "Name of file(s) to remove?"
read file_list
rm -i $file_list;;
*) echo "Exiting";;
esac

miss_scarlet@tweety$ bash bash_profile_menu
Please select an option from the menu
Option          Description
------          -----------
    L              List files in your current directory
    D              Display a file
    P              Print a file
    R              Remove a file
    E              Exit
```

```
r
Name of file(s) to remove?
xxxxxxxxx.tst
rm: remove write-protected file `xxxxxxxxx.tst '? n
```

Tip Because you used rm with the -i option, the command automatically confirms that the user really wants to remove the file.

The menu example above is quite simple. If you build a menu for your users, you may want to add a prompt to ask a user if he or she wants another menu selection and loop back to the case statement. For example, you could set up a while loop that continuously reads the user's menu choice as long as the user does not select Exit. Chapter 18 shows several ways to control the logic flow with loops and if tests.

Using Functions

You can further extend your scripts' functionality by using functions. To write a function, use the following syntax.

```
function_name()
{
Statements
}
```

To call a function from a script, simply type its name and pass it any necessary parameters. The function uses optional parameters the same way a script uses positional parameters. For example, to call a function, type its name followed by a list of parameters, if any.

Function Factoids

✦ When you invoke (call) a function from a script, bash does not *fork* (spawn) a new process to interpret the function.

✦ Functions accept positional parameters.

✦ Usually the calling script and the function share variable values.

✦ You can define variables that are local to the function. That is, only the function and its children, if any, can see the local variable. Use the built-in command local name=value.

✦ Functions can invoke other functions.

✦ The function definition can appear either before or after the main program.

```
function_name param1 . . . param-n
```

Note   A function consists of shell commands, like a shell script. The difference is that you use functions to perform repetitive actions without having to duplicate the code.

Writing a simple function to check disk-space usage

Unless your users are careful about using disk space, you need to run regularly a script that reports on the disk hogs. Even if you can't control disk usage with quotas (sometimes an organization's procedures make disk quotas impractical), you should know who is using the most space. Monitoring disk usage also helps with the capacity-planning and forecasting processes. The following script assigns variables and constants and uses the cut and grep commands to generate a report file that contains disk-usage information for a user's home directory. The script consists of three parts:

1. An initialization section that sets up variables and constants.

2. A function named space_used. A function is a section of code that returns a value to the calling program. The function may also accept input parameters from the calling program.

3. The main program. A main program contains the basic program logic and may call functions to do some of the processing work.

Note   The cut command outputs selected pieces of lines in a file. The syntax is cut [option] [file].

The default output device is stdout. The script below uses the -d and -f options. The -d option specifies a delimiter between fields, in this case a colon. The default for -d is the Tab character. The -f option specifies a field or fields. In this case, -f6 means the sixth field in the password file, which is the home directory.

Cross-Reference   See Chapters 17 and 18 for details on defining and using variables, constants, and regular expressions.

```
#!/bin/bash
# /root/disk_report.bsh
#          ******* INITIALIZATION SECTION ********
# Define variables and constants

# Dh_File holds the report,\.
Dh_File="/root/disk_hog.rpt"
DiskHogFile="/root/disk.hog"
# OffenderFile is where to write information about hogs
#
OffenderFile="offender"
#
#          ******* FUNCTION ********
space_used()
  # Accepts a user name as an input parameter.
  # Returns the disk space for the user's home directory.
```

```
    # The home directory is the sixth field in /etc/passwd.

{
    Home_Dir=`grep ^$1: /etc/passwd | cut -d: -f6`
  # du separates fields with tabs, and we only need the first field
    used=`du -s $Home_Dir | cut -f1`
}

#           ******* MAIN PROGRAM ********
# Main Program
#
while read username
do
    space_used $username
    echo "$username has used $used"
done < $DiskHogFile
```

Using a function to test user input

If you test for user error within your scripts, you can make your scripts easier to use. One of the most common usage errors users make is to forget to pass in the correct number of command-line arguments your script requires. You can create a simple function that checks for the command-line arguments and displays a syntax hint if the user has entered an incorrect number of arguments.

```
#! /bin/bash
# usage_check.bsh
# Checks for positional parameters on the command line
# Includes a usage function to display a syntax hint.

usage ()
{
    echo "Error"
    echo      "Correct usage: disk_report.bsh username"
    echo      "Reports on disk use by user"
}

# test whether 1 positional parameter is on the command line.
# If the number of positional parameters is not 1, invoke the
#  usage function and exit.
if [ $# != 1 ]
then
    usage
    exit
fi
# Continue report processing.

root@flyingpenguin# chmod a+x $HOME/check_usage.bsh
root@flyingpenguin# $HOME/check_usage.bsh
Error
```

```
Correct usage: disk_report.bsh username
Reports on disk use by user
root@flyingpenguin# $HOME/check_usage.bsh emily miss_scarlet
Error
Correct usage: disk_report.bsh username
Reports on disk use by user
root@flyingpenguin# $HOME/check_usage.bsh emily
# usage is correct, report processing continues here.
```

Summary

This chapter used rc.local as an example to show some of the bash scripting techniques you can use as a system administrator, such as:

✦ Checking for a file's existence.

✦ Storing the result of a command in a variable.

✦ Determining the hardware architecture of the computer on which a script is executing.

✦ Executing the actions in a case statement based on hardware type.

This chapter also showed you how to debug your scripts, create menus, and write simple functions to use within your scripts. This chapter is not intended to deliver complete bash programming information. bash scripting is a whole book of its own. However, this chapter combined with Chapter 18 gives you enough information to get started reading scripts that exist on your system and writing simple useful scripts of your own.

✦   ✦   ✦

Introduction to Perl Programming for System Administrators

This chapter introduces Perl and gives you enough basics to build some simple system-administration scripts in Perl.

What is Perl?

Perl is a language for working with text, files, and processes. It's non-proprietary, runs on most operating systems, and is free. Perl is often called "the duct tape of the Web" because it's the most popular Web-programming language. Linux interprets Perl at runtime, so it's dynamic, as opposed to the C language, which you must compile into static object code.

Why use Perl?

You know that Linux offers you many different ways to do the same thing. You can do the examples in this chapter in something besides Perl, such as a C program or a bash script. You may choose to use Perl, however, for a few reasons:

   ✦ Perl syntax is easier than C.

   ✦ Perl syntax is more flexible and concise than shell scripting.

✦ Perl includes a superset of sed and awk.

✦ You don't need a compiler.

✦ A dynamic interpreter offers runtime flexibility.

✦ Perl is free, and included with most Linux distributions.

The most recent stable version of Perl is available on the Web at `http://www.perl.com/pub/language/info/software.html`. This site includes both source code and binary versions of the most recent stable release, older releases, and the latest developer's experimental release.

Note   You can get translator software to convert sed and awk scripts into Perl.

Your First Perl Program

Regardless of the language, most programming books and courses start you off with a Hello World program. Here it is in Perl:

```
print "Hello World\n";
```

Perl versus perl

You may notice that you see both Perl and perl in this book. There is a difference. You spell *Perl* the language with an uppercase *P*. The program that interprets your Perl program and tells the computer what to do with your Perl statements is *perl* the interpreter, spelled with a lowercase *p*. You write Perl statements. perl interprets the Perl statements and runs the program.

Compiled versus Interpreted

When you compile a program written in a traditional programming language, such as C, FORTRAN, or COBOL, the compiler converts the program into a binary format easily understood by the CPU. Perl, unlike C, FORTRAN, or COBOL, is an interpreted language.

Interpreted languages do not get compiled, which means that the instructions are not compiled into a binary format, but are decoded on the fly. The perl interpreter sends instructions to the operating system based on the instructions in a Perl program.

The perl interpreter scans your Perl program and builds it into a memory data structure and processes it very quickly. The interpreter optimizes your Perl code in many of the same ways that compilers optimize traditional programming languages.

You can find all the Perl programs in this chapter on the CD-ROM included with this book.

Understanding the primary Perl syntax rules

The Hello World program illustrates some basic Perl syntax rules:

✦ The verb `print` is a Perl statement that displays a value on stdout.

✦ You must enclose the string to print in double quotes (").

✦ The `\n` is a Perl expression that means "include a linefeed (new line) after the printed value."

✦ Perl statements end with semicolons (;).

Forgetting the semicolon (;) is the most common mistake Perl programmers make. When your program generates error messages that you don't understand, first check that all your semicolons are in place.

✦ The hash (#) character is the comment character.

✦ Perl ignores blank lines, so you can use as many as you want to improve the readability of your program.

Running your first program

To run the program, pass it to the Perl interpreter. In accordance with the Linux philosophy that there's more than one way to do things, here are three ways to run a Perl program:

1. Invoke Perl at the shell prompt with the `-e` option to execute a Perl statement, and enclose the whole program with single quotes ('). The examples below are in order of ease of use:

```
$ perl -e 'print "Hello World\n";'
Hello World

$
```

2. Use an editor to put your program into a file. Invoke Perl and pass it the file name for your program. See Listing 31-1.

Listing 31-1: **Your first perl program**

```
# hello.pl - First Perl program
print "Hello World\n";
```

Note All the file names that contain Perl programs in this chapter, end in the extension .pl. The .pl extension is not required, but is a common Perl file-naming convention.

Tip No matter how simple your Perl program is, get in the habit of adding comments with the # character.

```
$ perl hello.pl
Hello World
$
```

3. Simply use the pathname of the program as a command at the shell prompt. To run the Perl program as a command, you need to follow the same steps you followed in Chapter 17, "Shell Scripts." This method is shown in Listing 31-2.

   a. Use the hash bang (#!) in the file to direct the shell to use the Perl interpreter to run the program.

   b. Change the permissions on the file so that people can execute the program.

Listing 31-2: Using hash bang in a script

```
#!/usr/bin/perl
# hello.pl - First Perl program
$ chmod a+x hello.pl
$ ls -l program1.pl
-rwxr-xr-x  1 miss_sca bad-guys 91 Aug 9 14:17 hello.pl
$ ./hello.pl
Hello World
```

Playing with the print Statement

Listing 31-1 used one of the most basic and common statements in Perl — print. You use the print statement to send output, usually to the screen.

Listing 31-3 presents another short Perl program.

Listing 31-3: The print statement

```
#!/usr/bin/perl
# add.pl - Using the print statement
print "1 + 2 = 3";
```

When you run the program,

```
miss_scarlet@tweety./add
1 + 2 = 3miss scarlet@tweety$
```

you see the output, followed immediately by the bash prompt. This is confusing at best, ugly at worst. To make the output more readable, you need to put a linefeed between the output and the next bash prompt. You use Perl's \n (linefeed or new line) to tell perl to add a linefeed after the output and before the next line. Change the print statement so that it resembles the following

```
print "1 + 2 = 3\n";
```

Now, when you run the program,

```
miss_scarlet@tweety$ ./add.pl
```

you see two lines on the display. The first line below is the output from the program. The second line is the bash prompt waiting for another command.

```
1 + 2 = 3
miss_scarlet@tweety$
```

Using Scalar Variables to Hold Values

A variable is a symbol that represents a value. Variables enable you to make your programs flexible. Rather than hardcoding data directly into your program, you can use variables to represent the data. When a user runs your program, perl (or any other compiler or interpreter) replaces the variables with real data. Perl supports the following kinds of variables:

✦ Scalar

✦ Filehandle or directory handle

✦ Arrays (indexed by number and indexed by character string)

✦ Subroutine name

✦ Wild card

A *scalar* variable is a variable that holds a single distinct value. It can be either a character string or a number. Scalar variables are the most commonly used variables in Perl. Each scalar starts with a dollar sign ($). This interchangeability of numeric and string types is a special Perl feature. Contrast this with most other programming languages, where you need a separate numeric type and a separate character type. For example, the line

```
$name_var = <STDIN>;
```

initializes the value of the variable, $name_var, to whatever the user enters. If you don't initialize a variable, it automatically takes either ' ' (null) or 0 as its starting value. Depending on how you use the variable, Perl automatically sets a datatype for your variable. You can even assign a command to a scalar variable.

Caution   This warning is for C and C++ programmers only. Unlike C, Perl does not end a character string with a null. If you are converting C or C++ code to Perl, remember to strip off the nulls. This warning probably doesn't mean anything to you if you do not work with C or C++. That's OK.

The following examples show some scalar variable assignments:

```
$dir = 'pwd';                               #command
$preteen = 'Emily';                         #character string
$preteen = "Emily";                         #character string
$preteen = `Emily`;                         #character string

$meaning_of_life = 42;                      #number (integer)
$price = 2.49;                              #number (decimal)
$big_price = 2.49e15;                  ·     #number (real)
$beware = 'Police line. Do not cross. \n';  #character string
escaped by \n
```

Note   Did you notice that there are three character strings above, only differing in the use of quotes? You can use double quotes ("), single quotes ('), or backticks (`) to surround a string variable. Perl doesn't care.

Escaping Special Characters

If you want to use a special character, such as double quotes, within a character string, you must use a backslash (\) to escape the meaning of the special character. The value of the variable below includes a set of \" characters surrounding the young philosopher's saying.

```
$Philosophy = "Emmy says  \"Don't lose your inner child. \""
```

The following table lists a few of Perl's other useful escape characters.

Escape Character	Meaning
\\	Backslash
\f	Form feed
\t	Tab
\%	Percent sign
\@	Ampersand
\c	Control character (followed by the control character)

Scalar Factoids

You can perform calculations with scalar variables, e.g. $total = 3 +6;

Perl automatically converts datatypes when necessary. The following line assigns a character string, 8, to the variable crime_counter. The single quotes change the number 8 to the character 8.

```
$crime_counter = '8';
```

When you try to add the number 1 to the character 8, perl realizes that you can't add numbers and letters, so it converts 8 to 8 before doing the addition, and prints the numeric sum.

```
print $crime_counter +1;
9
```

The combination $_ is a special scalar variable that usually stores the current line.

If you want to undefine a variable within a program, use the undef function, as in the following example, where I define preteen and teen and print them both and then undefine preteen and print both variables again.

```
miss_scarlet@flyingpenguin$ perl -e '
> $preteen="Emily"; $teen="Sarah"; print "1. $preteen  $teen
\n";
> undef $preteen;  print "2. $preteen  $teen \n";
> '
1. @SB code:Emily Sarah
2. @SB code:Sarah
```

Tip   Perl is case-sensitive. $A is different from $a.

Backticks (`) also enable you to use a command as a scalar variable or as a literal in a print statement. The following example shows how to use the ls command to list a Linux directory from Perl.

```
miss_scarlet@flyingpenguin$ perl -e 'print `ls *.perl`;print "\n";'
array.perl              open_directory.perl  program1.perl  program2c.perl
file_search_tool.perl  passwd_report.perl   program2.perl  temp.perl
```

The example above uses three kinds of quotes, each for a different purpose. The single quotes (') surround the entire Perl program since it is executing as part of the perl -e command line. The backticks surround the Linux command ls *.perl. The double quotes (") are needed to set the \n (newline) character apart from the ls command.

Note gawk (and awk) use the field $0 as the value of the current line.

Listing 31-4 assigns values to two variables, adds the values, and assigns the result to a third variable.

Listing 31-4: **Scalar calculations**

```
#!/usr/bin/perl
# adding.pl - Doing addition
$var1 = 1;
$var2 = 2;
$var3 = $var1 + $var2;
print "$var1 + $var2 = $var3\n";
```

The calculation actually happens when you assign the sum of the scalar variables, $var1 and $var2 to $var3, also a scalar variable. When you run the program, the print statement displays the result:

```
miss_scarlet@tweety$ adding.pl
1 + 2 = 3
```

Listing 31-4 uses two arithmetic operators, + and =.

Table 31-1 lists some commonly used Perl operators with examples.

Note Most Perl operators are the same as the C programming language operators.

Table 31-1 Commonly Used Perl Operators			
Operator	**Meaning**	**Type**	**Example**
<	Less than	Numeric comparison	2 < 4
>	Greater than	Numeric comparison	4 > 2
<=	Less than or equal to	Numeric comparison	2 <= 4
>=	Greater than or equal to	Numeric comparison	4 >= 2
=	Equal to	Numeric comparison	2 =2
lt	Less than	String comparison	$two lt $four
gt	Greater than	String comparison	$four gt $two

Operator	Meaning	Type	Example
le	Less than or equal to	String comparison	`$two le $four`
ge	Greater than or equal to	String comparison	`$four ge $two`
cmp	Compare	String comparison*	`$four cmp $two`
+	Plus	Arithmetic	`$count + 1`
–	Minus	Arithmetic	`$count -1`
*	Multiply	Arithmetic	`$count * 10`
/	Divide	Arithmetic	`$count / 5`
**	Exponent	Arithmetic	`$count **2`
.	Concatenate	String	`"Hello" . "World"`
x=	Repetition	String	`blank = " "; blank = x= 80`
..	Range	Array	`@legal_values = (0..100);`

* Compares two strings. Based on the value of the first string, returns -1 for less, 0 for equal, 1 for greater

Listing 31-4 isn't very useful because it only works if you want to add the hard-coded digits, 1 and 2. You can make this program much more flexible, and hence, more useful, by letting the user specify which numbers to add. The next section shows you how to prompt a user for input.

Prompting for Input

Instead of saying Hello to the World, you can modify your first Perl program to greet each user who runs the program. To make this happen, you need to prompt the user for a name, accept the user's input, and display the user's name as part of the greeting. Here are the individual steps to follow to create a Hello *<your name here>* program:

1. Use the hash-bang to make the program runnable as a command. This is optional, but good programming practice for all but single-line programs.

2. Use comments to document your program.

   ```
   # myprog.pl - Does something useful
   ```

3. Use the `print` command to display the prompt. Don't forget to end each line with a semicolon (;).

   ```
   print "What is your Name? ";
   ```

4. Declare a variable to hold the user's response from stdin (whatever the user types on the keyboard). It doesn't matter what you name the variable. It's a placeholder to hold the user's response. Perl requires that you precede the variable with a $. The $ tells Perl that the variable can be either a character string or a number. By assigning STDIN to the variable, you accept whatever the user types into name_var. Surrounding STDIN with angle brackets (<>) tells perl to prompt the user to type a value at the keyboard.

```
$name_var = <STDIN>;
```

Note Perl calls <STDIN> a predefined filehandle. The filehandle <STDIN> represents the keyboard.

5. Display the greeting:

```
print "Hello $name_var,"\n";
```

Tip Perl provides several predefined filehandles for you to use. In Listing 31-5, you see <STDIN> used to hold whatever a user types. Other handy Perl predefined filehandles are:

STDOUT, the standard output (stdout), device, usually the screen.

STDERR, the standard error (stderr), device, usually the screen.

ARGV, a list of file names to use with the program.

You can also define your own filehandles to use in Perl programs.

Performing calculations on user input variables

You know that the way to take user input from the keyboard is to assign a variable with angle brackets, as below:

```
$var1 = <>;
```

When your program executes that line, perl waits for the user to type input and press the Enter key. Pressing Enter generates a carriage return. The carriage return tells perl that the user is done typing. Perl assigns the user input to the variable — in the Listing 31-5, the scalar variable, $var1, and later, $var2.

Note In the example below, be sure to notice how perl automatically handles the decimal number as well as the integers. In most other programming languages you have to tell the language the datatype of both kinds of numbers.

Tip Don't forget to make your Perl program executable if you want to run it as a command.

Listing 31-5: **A Perl based adding machine**

```perl
#!/usr/bin/perl
# calc.pl - An adding machine

print "What is your name? ";
$name_var = <STDIN>;
print "Hello $name_var\n";

print "Please enter a number: ";
$var1 = <>;
chop($var1);
print "Please enter another number: ";
$var2 = <>;
chop($var2);
$var3 = $var2 + $var1;
print "$var1 + $var2 = $var3\n";
```

Here is how this program might look if you execute it:

```
miss_scarlet@tweety$ ./calc.pl

What is your name? Emily
Hello Emily

Please enter a number: 1
Please enter another number: 2
1 + 2 = 3
miss_scarlet@tweety$ ./calc.pl

What is your name? Emily
Hello Emily

Please enter a number: 99876
Please enter another number: 3452.3
99876 + 3452.3 = 103328.3
```

Note the use of the chop statement. Perl adds the linefeed generated when you press Enter; therefore, in order to eliminate the extra linefeeds, the program uses Perl's special formatting command, chop, which chops off the last character from a variable. Chopping $var1 and $var2, turns them back into simple 1 and 2, which perl can add easily. You see lots of chopping in Perl programs.

Tip   Surround the object of the chop command with parentheses.

Handy Command-Line Options for perl

So far, the examples in this chapter have run the perl interpreter with either no options or the -e option (to enter a line of Perl between two single quotes). Perl has almost 20 options you can use on the command line. Some of the most useful include:

-c   Check for syntax errors, but do not execute the program. This option is quite useful when you are working with large, complex programs. You can do Perl syntax checking without spending the time to run the program and possibly write incorrect data. For example:

```
miss_scarlet@flyingpenguin$ perl -c passwd_report.perl
passwd_report.perl syntax OK
```

Here's an example that lets you know you have syntax errors:

```
miss_scarlet@flyingpenguin$ perl -c file_search_tool.perl
syntax error at /home/miss_scarlet/file_search_tool.perl line 4,
near ""$path_variable") "
syntax error at /home/miss_scarlet/file_search_tool.perl line 11,
near "}"
/home/miss_scarlet/file_search_tool.perl had compilation errors.
```

-w   Same as -c.

-S   Look for the Perl program on the PATH variable.

-v   Display the version and patch level of your perl interpreter, as in the following example. Your output may look different, depending on the version of perl you are using.

```
miss_scarlet@flyingpenguin$ perl -v

This is perl, version 5.005_03 built for i386-linux

Copyright 1987-1999, Larry Wall

Perl may be copied only under the terms of either the Artistic
License or the GNU General Public License, which may be found in
the Perl 5.0 source kit.

Complete documentation for Perl, including FAQ lists, should be
found on this system using `man perl' or `perldoc perl'. If you
have access to the Internet, point your browser at
http://www.perl.com/, the Perl Home Page.
```

Using array variables

An *array variable* is a list of scalar variables prefixed with the @ character instead of the $ character. The following assignment statements create arrays and initialize them with values:

```
@weapon  = ("knife","lead pipe", "rope", "candlestick", "gun");
@room = ("conservatory", "hall", "kitchen");
@birthdates = (1921,1947,1949,1954,2000,1957,1981,1989,2001)
```

Each value separated by commas inside the parentheses is an element of the array. @weapon is a an array of five character elements. @room is an array of three character elements, and @birthdates is an array of nine numeric elements. Each individual element in an array variable is a scalar variable. To access a specific element of the array, you use an index—the number of the element in the list, starting from 0. Therefore, the fourth element, the candlestick, is array element 3. To indicate the candlestick, type the name of the array followed by a set of square brackets enclosing the number of the candlestick, as below:

```
$weapon[3]
```

Tip   Since each individual array element is one scalar variable, use a $ to precede it. Only use the @ when you refer to the entire array.

Referring to a numeric element is no different from referring to a character-string element. For example, to refer to the fourth element of the birthdates array (1954), you would type:

```
$birthdates[3]
```

Tip   Notice that the @ changes to a $ because a single element is a scalar variable. Remember that Perl numbers elements beginning with 0.

Listing 31-6 shows how using an array in different contexts affects how Perl displays the array.

> ## Listing 31-6: **Using an array in different contexts**

```
miss_scarlet@tweety$ cat array.pl
   # Set up the array
@weapon = ("knife","lead pipe","rope","candlestick","gun");
   # Use the /n to add a new line after each line of output.
   # Display the basic array. The output is not easily
readable.
print @weapon.""."\n";
   #Display the array again. Notice how the "" generate spaces
   #     between each element.
```

Continued

Listing 31-6: *(continued)*

```
print @weapon, "\n";
    #Display the number of elements in the array. Note the ".".
print "@weapon","\n";
    # Display the index of the last element.
    # Remember the first element is numbered 0.
print $#weapon,"/n";

# Run the program.
miss_scarlet@tweety$ perl array.pl
knifelead piperopecandlestickgun
knife lead pipe rope candlestick gun
5
4
```

Working with Files

An important part of a system administrator's job is to review data in log files to monitor performance, review usage patterns in accounting files, and look for possible system problems. These files contain meaningful system data mixed with not-so-important data. Perl makes it possible to parse these large, primitively formatted files and generate readable reports that contain the information you need to manage a system efficiently. Before you can generate these nice reports, you need to understand some elementary Perl file-handling techniques. The basic steps for dealing with a file in Perl are:

1. Open the file.

2. Assign a filehandle.

3. Tell perl the path of the file you want to open.

4. Operate on the file (for example, read, write, or extract).

5. Close the file.

The open statement opens a file for read, write, or append access. You need to pass a filehandle and the path of the file name. The example below opens the Linux passwd file ands assigns a filehandle called PASSWDFILE.

Tip   By convention, Perl filehandles are uppercase to make them easy to identify when you read through program code. You can choose to use any case you want.

```
open (PASSWDFILE, "/etc/passwd"); # Open the file for reading.
```

The filehandle acts like a nickname that you create and use to access the file for the rest of the program.

Although you can pass the entire pathname, it's better programming style to use the scalar variable that defines the file. The second parameter is an expression denoting the file name.

```
open (PASSWDFILE, "$passwd_path"); # Open the file for read.
```

Tip   If you type the pathname in quotes, as in the definition of PASSWDFILE above, perl treats it as a literal value and does not do any expansion. Therefore, if you use a symbol, such as the tilde (~), perl does not interpret it successfully. For example, if you use the expression, `~/professor_plum/datafile` as the shortcut to Professor Plum's home directory, you need to do something to tell perl to expand the tilde properly. To cause the tilde to expand, surround the path with angle brackets (e.g. `<~/professor_plum/datafile>`) instead of quotes.

If you need to open the file for some sort of write access, including delete, tell perl the access mode by using the > (write or delete) or >> (append) characters. Table 31-2 shows the file access mode characters you can use with the `open` function. The following lines show how to open the passwd file for write and append access.

```
open (PASSWDFILE, ">$passwd_path");  # Open the file to create
a new version and write.
```

Caution   Curses! The example above overwrote my existing PASSWDFILE. Use the example below to add a user account to an existing file.

```
open (PASSWDFILE, ">>$passwd_path"); #Open the file for
append.
```

Tip   An alternate syntax for opening to read is:

```
open (PASSWDFILE, "<$passwd_path"); # Open the file for
read.
```

Table 31-2
File Open Access Characters

Prefixed Character	Access Mode	Example
none	Read	open (PASSWDFILE, "$passwd_path");
<	Read	open (PASSWDFILE, "<$passwd_path");
+<	Read and write	open (PASSWDFILE, "+<$passwd_path");
>	Create and write	open (PASSWDFILE, ">$passwd_path");

Continued

Prefixed Character	Access Mode	Example
+>	Write and read	`open (PASSWDFILE, "+>$passwd_path");`
>>	Append	`open (PASSWDFILE, ">>$passwd_path");`
-	Read from stdin	`open (PASSWDFILE, '-');`
>-	Read from stdout	`open (PASSWDFILE, '>-');`

Table 31-2 *(continued)* is shown above.

Caution In contrast to shell return status, Perl returns a non-zero value if the open function is successful.

Reading and Writing Files

Reading and writing files in Perl is easy. In both cases you must use a filehandle to open the file first.

Reading files

Once a file is open, you can read it one line at a time by assigning the filehandle to a variable, as in the following example where the variable is $account_data and the filehandle is <PASSWDFILE>.

```
$account_data=<PASSWDFILE>
```

The preceding code reads the first line of the file and assigns it to the $account_data variable. The filehandle in angle brackets (<>) is like the data that Listing 31-5 accepted from <STDIN>. The only difference in Listing 31-7 is that it accepts data from the file.

Listing 31-7: **Reading data from a file**

```perl
#!/usr/bin/perl
# readpasswd.pl - File I/O

# Assign a scalar variable to hold passwd records
open(PASSWDFILE, "/etc/passwd");
$account_data=<PASSWDFILE>;
# Display the data on the screen
```

```
print "$account_data\n";
# Get the second record into the variable
$account_data=<PASSWDFILE>;
# Display the next line of the file
print "$account_data\n";
close (PASSWDFILE);

root@tweety# /root/readpasswd.pl
root:x:0:0:root:/root:/bin/bash

bin:x:1:1:bin:/bin:

root@tweety#
```

The preceding program only reads the first two lines of the passwd file. This is because each line needs to have its own variable assignment and `print` statement. Since `$account_data` is assigned to the `<PASSWDFILE>` handle and printed twice, you only see two lines of output. To read the whole passwd file, you could assign the variable and print as many times as there are lines in the passwd file. Using this technique creates a much larger Perl program than is really necessary.

 Tip   Large programs usually use more memory and don't perform as well as smaller programs.

Instead of writing a long Perl program to assign a variable and print multiple times, you can create a loop that repeats until the entire file has been read. The following program is a variation on the Read_Passwd program above. This program uses a loop to read and display the contents of the passwd file. The `while` statement in the program below is a loop that says, "While there are records in the passwd file, continue to read them and print them."

 Cross-Reference   There is more information on how to use loops in Perl programs later in this chapter.

Listing 31-8: **Using a while loop**

```
#!/usr/bin/perl
# readallpasswd.pl - Read and print all passwords

open(PASSWDFILE,"/etc/passwd") || die "Can't open the file.\n";
while(<PASSWDFILE>)
    {  print; }
```

The syntax for the `while` loop takes a condition in parentheses — in this example

```
(<PASSWDFILE>)
```

This means that while there are data in the PASSWDFILE and an action or set of actions within curly braces, in this example,

```
{  print; }
```

means print each line of data.

Note   The statement(s) within the curly braces constitute a block of code. The braces can be on the same line as the statements in the block, as above or on separate lines, as in the following example:

```
{
        print;
{
```

Whether you indent the statements or not is up to you and your sense of programming style and readability.

After perl completes the loop, it goes ahead to the next statement in the program. In the readallpasswd.pl example above, there is no statement following the loop, so perl exits.

After setting the file to be executable (`chmod a+x`), you can run the program, and the output should resemble the following:

```
root@tweety# /root/readallpasswd.pl
root:x:0:0:root:/root:/bin/bash
bin:x:1:1:bin:/bin:
daemon:x:2:2:daemon:/sbin:
adm:x:3:4:adm:/var/adm:
lp:x:4:7:lp:/var/spool/lpd:
sync:x:5:0:sync:/sbin:/bin/sync
shutdown:x:6:0:shutdown:/sbin:/sbin/shutdown
halt:x:7:0:halt:/sbin:/sbin/halt
mail:x:8:12:mail:/var/spool/mail:
news:x:9:13:news:/var/spool/news:
uucp:x:10:14:uucp:/var/spool/uucp:
operator:x:11:0:operator:/root:
games:x:12:100:games:/usr/games:
gopher:x:13:30:gopher:/usr/lib/gopher-data:
ftp:x:14:50:FTP User:/home/ftp:
nobody:x:99:99:Nobody:/:
xfs:x:100:233:X Font Server:/etc/X11/fs:/bin/false
admin:x:1000:500:Notes Admin:/home/admin:/bin/bash
notes:x:1001:501:Domino Server account:/home/notes:/bin/bash
```

```
miss_scarlet:x:500:506:emily lauren
scarlet:/home/miss_scarlet:/bin/csh
candace:x:501:100:candace leiden:/home/candace:/bin/bash
marshall:x:502:100:marshall wilensky:/home/marshall:/bin/bash
professor_plum:x:503:100:professor
plum:/home/prof_plum:/bin/bash
gdm:x:42:42::/home/gdm:/bin/bash
-------- output edited  ----------
```

This program didn't name a variable to store each line from the <PASSWDFILE>. Nor was the program specific about what to print. A handy Perl feature is the default variable, $_. Perl automatically uses $_ if you don't name a variable. In the example above, perl reads the lines of the passwd file into $_ and prints the value of $_ to the screen.

Writing to files

You use the print statement to write to a file in the same way that you display a line on the screen. First you must open the file for write access. Listing 31-9 writes a line of user account data to the /etc/passwd file.

Tip   Use the close (*filehandle*) statement to tell Perl you're done using the file.

From now on in your program, refer to the file by its filehandle. Use the print statement to write a line into the file.

Listing 31-9: **Writing to a filehandle**

```
#!/usr/bin/perl
# writepasswd.pl - Appends an entry to the password file
open(PASSWDFILE,">>/etc/passwd");
print PASSWDFILE "mallory:x:1001:100:Kathy Mallory:/home/mallory:/bin/bash\n";
close (PASSWDFILE);
```

After executing the program, you can verify that it added the new user to the passwd file using the grep command:

```
root@flyingpenguin# grep mallory /etc/passwd
mallory:x:1001:100:Kathy Mallory:/home/mallory/bin/bash
```

Note   Be sure to delete the added line from the password file!

Handling a file open error

If the open statement fails for some reason, the rest of the preceding program will not work. It's good programming practice to check for an error on the open and exit the program if the open fails. Use the die command to handle the error, display a message to the user, and exit the program. Listing 31-10 contains a typographical error: there is no /etcc directory on the computer, so perl cannot find the passwd file.

Listing 31-10: **Using the die command**

```
#!/usr/bin/perl
# writepasswd.pl - Appends an entry to the password file

open(PASSWDFILE,">>/etcc/passwd") || die "Can't open file";
print PASSWDFILE "mallory:x:1001:100:Kathy
Mallory:/home/mallory:/bin/bash\n";
close (PASSWDFILE);
```

Note   The die command handles the error and exits the program, but it will only be invoked if the open command fails. The or operator, ||, says, "execute the open command or, if that fails, execute the die command."

To make the error message more meaningful, you could include the file name so that the user knows exactly which file can't be opened.

Writing Loops and Conditionals

Perl includes several looping and conditional statements so that you can repeat an action or test a variable or constant and perform an action based on the value. These flow-control statements include:

   ✦ while
   ✦ until
   ✦ foreach
   ✦ if
   ✦ unless

Writing a while loop

The while loop performs the actions inside the body of the loop as long as a condition is true. For example, earlier in this chapter, you saw the statement

```
while(<PASSWDFILE>)
    {   print; }
```

The condition in the `while` loop above is (`<PASSWDFILE>`), meaning "as long as the PASSWDFILE has data, perform each of the statements enclosed in braces." As long as there are data in the PASSWDFILE, the condition enclosed in parentheses is true. The loop keeps going, performing the same statements in the loop body on each line of the PASSWDFILE. When there are no more lines in the PASSWDFILE, the condition becomes false, so program control moves to the statement following the loop.

Note   The actions in the loop are enclosed in curly braces (`{ }`).

The example above prints passwd records until there are no more. Another way to write a condition is to use a counter. You can count up to a certain point, but more common programming practice is to count down to 0. To set up a counter, follow these steps:

1. Assign a variable for the counter that contains the number of times to perform the loop.

2. Use a `while` loop to perform the same actions repeatedly.

3. Use the counter as the condition of the `while` loop. Perl will keep going through the loop as long as the counter is not 0. (Remember, you're counting down.) Use the `!=` operator to mean *not equal*.

4. Subtract 1 from the counter each time you do the loop action.

5. When the counter reaches 0, Perl automatically exits the loop and executes the first statement outside the loop.

Listing 31-11 illustrates using a loop counter.

Listing 31-11: **Using a loop counter**

```perl
#!/usr/bin/perl
# read5passwdlines.pl - Decrementing a loop counter.
open(PASSWDFILE,"/etc/passwd") || die "Can't open file\n";
$counter = 5;
while($counter != 0)                # While the counter is not 0
    {                               # Begin the loop body
        $account_data=<PASSWDFILE>; # These commands are in the loop body
        print $account_data;
        $counter=$counter - 1;
    }                               # This is the end of the loop
print "**** The end \n";            # This executes when counter is 0
```

What is True?

Perl regards a value as true when the value is neither a null string nor the number 0 nor the string 0. When an operator returns a value, Perl decides on whether it is true. For example, in the Listing 31-11, the != operator returns 1 when the value of the counter is not 0. When the value of the counter is finally 0, Perl realizes that the not-equal condition has become false.

The output of a sample run of this program should resemble the following:

```
$ ./read5passwdlines.pl
root:x:0:0:root:/root:/bin/bash
bin:x:1:1:bin:/bin:
daemon:x:2:2:daemon:/sbin:
adm:x:3:4:adm:/var/adm:
lp:x:4:7:lp:/var/spool/lpd:
**** The end
$
```

Later in this chapter, you can see how to count down using a for loop.

Writing a for loop

Like most programming languages, Perl includes syntax to perform a for loop. A for loop executes a statement or block of statements for the number of times you specify. The basic syntax is as follows:

```
for (initialization_expression; conditional_expression; looping_expression)
     { statement(s) }
```

The example in this section uses a for loop to count down from a counter variable and print the first five lines of the passwd file, just like the example in the previous section, "Using a while loop."

To set up the for loop, follow these steps:

1. Assign a variable in the initialization expression of the for loop. This variable is the number of times to go through the loop.

2. Set up a condition for the variable in the conditional expression of the for loop. Perl checks that this condition is true before each iteration of the loop. If the conditional expression is not true, Perl exits the loop.

3. Set up the loop expression in the for loop that tells Perl what to do before beginning each iteration of the loop. In the example below, we want to decrement (subtract one from) the counter each time we go through the loop. The example uses Perl's auto-decrement function (--) to increment the counter.

Note   Besides an autodecrement function, Perl also has an autoincrement function, ++, to use when you are counting up.

Listing 31-12 rewrites Listing 31-11 using a for loop.

Listing 31-12: **Using a for loop**

```
#!/usr/bin/perl
# read5for.pl - Using a for loop
open(PASSWDFILE,"/etc/passwd") || die "Can't open file\n";
$counter = 5;
for($counter = 5; $counter > 0; $counter--)
    {
        $account_data=<PASSWDFILE>;
          print $account_data;
    }
print "**** The end \n";
```

Writing a foreach loop

The foreach statement is useful for writing a loop that goes through an array of variables.

 Cross-Reference   Remember from the section "Using array variables" that an array is a list of scalar variables prefixed with the @ character.

The foreach syntax looks like this:

```
foreach variable (list)
{   statement or block of statements }
```

For example, to add the numbers 1 through 5:

```
foreach $counter (1..5)
    {
        print $total += $counter, "\n";
    }
```

Each time Perl goes through the loop, it assigns the next value in the 1 .. 5 list to the counter variable. This automatic list handling is a special feature of Perl. The example below uses a foreach statement to display the entire passwd file. Each line of the passwd file is an element in the array @passwd_array. The variable

`$element` represents a single line. For each element in the array, the loop prints the line. When there are no more elements in the array — that is, when there are no more passwd records — control passes out of the loop. Listing 31-13 illustrates using the `foreach` statement.

Listing 31-13: Using the `foreach` **statement**

```
#!/usr/bin/perl
# read5foreach.pl - Using a foreach loop
open(PASSWDFILE,"/etc/passwd") || die "Can't open file\n";

@passwd_array=<PASSWDFILE>;
foreach $element (@passwd_array)
    {
        print $element;
    }
```

The output from a sample run of this program should resemble the following:

```
$ ./read5foreach.pl
root:x:0:0:root:/root:/bin/bash
bin:x:1:1:bin:/bin:
daemon:x:2:2:daemon:/sbin:
adm:x:3:4:adm:/var/adm:
lp:x:4:7:lp:/var/spool/lpd:
sync:x:5:0:sync:/sbin:/bin/sync
shutdown:x:6:11:shutdown:/sbin:/sbin/shutdown
```

Writing if tests

Based on a condition, the `if` statement sends you along a certain path of action (logic). The basic `if` syntax is as follows:

```
if (CONDITION)
    { actions to perform if condition is true }
else
    { # actions to perform if condition is false }
```

Some possible conditions might be:

✦ If the user has a UID of 0 (superuser), there might be a special path of action to follow:

```
if ( $userid eq 0 ) {. . . action . . . }
```

✦ Based on the value of a counter, you might continue reading a file or stop reading a file:

```
if ( $counter > 10 ) { . . . action . . . }
```

✦ Based on a user's account name, you might allow or disallow access to a program:

```
if ($username eq "root") { . . . action . . . }
```

✦ Based on the value of a character string, such as a user name, you might perform an action, such as print her passwd record, as in the example in the following section.

Using an if test on a glob of files

This section shows you how to grab a *glob* (group) of files, search for a particular string within those files, and display records that include that search string. The following example illustrates a common system-administration task: Searching through log files for records that pertain to a certain user. Some of the information you can find in the various log files in the /var/log directory include

✦ When the user switched identity to root.

✦ When the user logged in remotely from a different computer on the network.

✦ When the user had any bad login attempts.

✦ When the user last read Usenet news.

✦ When the user last accessed Web pages.

✦ When the user last submitted a cron job.

Now that you know how to open a file and read from and write to it, you can expand those techniques to a group of files. *File globbing* is the technique of accessing a group of files at once.

Note   While it may sound cute or strange, depending on your point of view, *file globbing* is a real technical term. Some programming languages even have a glob command.

To glob a group of files, set up a while loop based on a pathname (it can have wild cards) assigned to a variable, like this:

```
while($filegroup = </root/*>) { . . . . . . }
```

The variable in the statement above is named filegroup and is assigned to all (*) the files in the /root directory. Perl can read all the file names in any directory if you use the syntax above. If you only want to read some of the files — for example, files that end in .dat — change the wild-carding on the path to this:

```
while($filegroup = </root/*.dat>) { . . . . . . }
```

The Perl program in Listing 31-14, fsrch.pl, searches for a text string, perl, in files that end with .pl in the current directory, and prints the path of the file ($_) and the string if it finds the search string.

Listing 31-14: **File globbing in Perl**

```perl
#!/usr/bin/perl
# fsrch.pl - Using the if statement
while($path_variable = <*.pl>)
    {
        open(FILE,"$path_variable") || die "Can't open $path_variable\n";
        while(<FILE>)
            {
                if(/perl/)
                    { print "$path_variable: $_\n"; }
            }
    }
```

The output of this program might resemble the following:

```
$ ./fsrch.pl
add.pl: #!/usr/bin/perl
adding.pl: #!/usr/bin/perl
calc.pl: #!/usr/bin/perl
fsrch.pl: #!/usr/bin/perl
fsrch.pl:                    if(/perl/)
read5for.pl: #!/usr/bin/perl
read5foreach.pl: #!/usr/bin/perl
read5passwdlines.pl: #!/usr/bin/perl
readallpasswd.pl: #!/usr/bin/perl
readpasswd.pl: #!/usr/bin/perl
writepasswd.pl: #!/usr/bin/perl
```

Understanding the fsrch.pl program

The preceding program uses the following familiar concepts:

✦ Defining a variable ($path_variable).

✦ Using a while loop.

✦ Using a filehandle (FILE).

✦ Using the die command to exit the program if a file is not found.

✦ Using the print command.

✦ Using the default variable, $_.

An Exhortation about Error Handling

If your program causes an error, Perl doesn't crash the program. It tries to continue as best it can. For example, if you try to open a file, but the file doesn't exist, the program continues executing statements. Of course the file statements won't work, but some others might. You might get unexpected or even wrong results from the program. Here's another example: The program calls a subroutine and expects the subroutine to return variables to the main program. The subroutine returns no variables. Does Perl crash your program? No. It pads out the variables it was expecting with spaces or zeroes and continues to process. If the program is doing calculations, the results will definitely be wrong, but Perl doesn't care. Therefore, it's up to you to add error handling to your programs. For example, when you tell Perl to open a file, ensure that Perl actually does open the file. If Perl can't open the file, it's up to you to relay the bad news to the user. Take error-handling responsibility. In some cases, that means adding error handling to every Perl statement in your program, telling Perl what to do if something fails.

The program also introduces some new concepts:

✦ Using the `if` conditional statement.

✦ Nesting loops within loops.

Nesting loops

You can include loops within loops, called a *nested loop*. Listing 31-14 contains two `while` loops. The second loop is inside the first loop. The basic structure looks like this:

```
while ( some condition is true )
    {
    perform action(s) in this outer block
    while ( some other condition is true )
        {
            perform action(s) in this inner block
        }
    }
```

Notice the use of optional white space for readability in the syntax above. I use white space to set each loop apart. You can nest loops deeply. Just be sure that each opening curly brace at the beginning of a block has a matching end brace at the end of the block.

Expanding if statements

So far in this chapter, the `if` test has been used as an either/or option: either you process the actions or you fall through to the statement that follows the `if`'s ending brace (}). However, you can use the `elseif` and `else` statements to set up alternate conditions. For example, the `if` condition might be `if you are root`. The `elseif` condition might be `if you are miss_scarlet`, another `elsif` condition might be `if you are holmes`, and an `else` condition might be `if you are anyone besides root, miss_scarlet, or holmes`. The syntax is below:

Note   Be sure to spell elsif correctly. Perl drops the second "e."

```
if (condition)
{
    Perform actions if condition is true.
}
elsif (alternate condition)
{
    Perform actions if alternate condition is true
}
elsif (other alternate condition)
{
    Perform other actions if other alternate condition is true
}
    as many other elsifs as you need
else
{
    Perform actions if none of the above conditions are true
}
```

Tip   Notice how the actions for each condition have their own set of matching curly braces ({ }). The indentations make it easier to see each block separately.

Here is a fragment of a program that sends different greetings based on who is running the program:

```
if($username eq "root")
{
    print "Hello, root.\n"
}
elsif( $username eq "miss_scarlet")
{
    print "Hello, Miss Scarlet. Did you leave a clue?\n"
}
elsif($username eq "holmes")
{
    print "Hello, Holmes. Do you have a clue?\n"
}
elsif($username eq "Sarah")
{
    print "Hello, Sarah. Did Emily do it?\n"
}
else
{
    print "This program is not for you\n"
}
```

Writing unless tests

Both the if and unless statements take a condition. Where the if statement takes a condition and executes actions if that condition is true, the unless statement takes a condition but only executes actions if that condition is false. For example, suppose you are root. The if example below executes the print action:

```
if ($username eq "root")
{
    print "Hello, root, you are all-powerful in Linux."
}
print "   The End/n";
```

In the next example, you are still root, but the print action does not happen for you. The print action happens for everyone else. All you see is The End.

```
unless ($username eq "root")
{
    print "Hello, you have no power in Linux."
}
print "   The End/n";
```

Introducing Perl Functions

Most programming languages, whether compiled or interpreted, have some notion of subroutines, often called functions. A *function* is a routine that you can call from a program. The function must return a value to the calling (main) program. The calling program may optionally pass input values to the function. Perl includes a rich set of built-in functions and also enables you to write your own functions and subroutines. For a system administrator, some of the most useful Perl functions are those that grant access to the passwd file. Table 31-3 lists some of the Perl passwd file functions.

Table 31-3
Perl Functions for Accessing the Password and Group Files

Function	Input Value	Return Value
getpwent	None	User name, UID, GID, quota, comment, home directory, login shell.
getpwnam	User name	User name, UID, GID, quota, comment, home directory, login shell.
getpwuid	UID	User name, UID, GID, quota, comment, home directory, login shell.

Continued

Table 31-3 (continued)		
Function	**Input Value**	**Return Value**
getgrent	None	Group name, GID, group members.
getgrgid	GID	Group name, GID, group members.
getgrnam	Group name	Group name, GID, group members.
getgrp	PID	Current group for the input PID.

Since Perl functions return a value, the way to invoke them is to assign the name of a variable to the function. In the example below, the getpwent function returns a password record into an array variable named @user_array.

Tip   The @ sign reminds you that the user_array variable is an array.

Listing 31-15 uses the getpwent function to retrieve each user's passwd record and display the user name and login shell. If a user name has no shell listed, the program displays Bourne, for the default shell. Listing 31-15 shows how to use two of the Perl functions shown in Table 31-3.

Listing 31-15: **Showing the username and login shell**

```
#!/usr/bin/perl
# getlogin.pl - Displays the username and the login shell.

print "Name\tShell\n";
while (@user_array=getpwent)
{
    ($name,$passwd,$uid,$gid,$quota,$comment,$gcos,$dir,$shell)
= @user_array;
    if ($shell  ne "")
    {
        print "$name\t$shell\n";
    }
}
```

Tip   When you use the built-in functions for accessing the passwd and group files, you don't need to open the files explicitly.

The output from a sample run of this program should resemble the following:

```
Name    Shell
root    /bin/bash
bin     defaults to Bourne
daemon  defaults to Bourne
adm     defaults to Bourne
lp      defaults to Bourne
sync    /bin/sync
shutdown        /sbin/shutdown
...
```

Formatting Reports

The output from this program is clear, but not attractive, and could be much easier to read. Fortunately, Perl's format function lets you "pretty" your output by adding headers and writing simple picture clauses that show how the data should look on the screen or on the page. The following output shows how the output would appear if you used Perl's formatting statements to set up a header and format the output lines.

```
            Login Shells Report

    User Name               Login Shell
----------------------------------------------
    root                    /bin/bash
    bin                     defaults to Bourne
    daemon                  defaults to Bourne
    adm                     defaults to Bourne
    lp                      defaults to Bourne
    sync                    /bin/sync
    shutdown                /sbin/shutdown
    halt                    /sbin/halt
    mail                    defaults to Bourne
    news                    defaults to Bourne
    uucp                    defaults to Bourne
    operator                defaults to Bourne
    games                   defaults to Bourne
    gopher                  defaults to Bourne
    ftp                     defaults to Bourne
    man                     defaults to Bourne
    majordom                /bin/false
    postgres                /bin/bash
    mysql                   /bin/false
    nobody                  /bin/false
    emilyd                  /bin/bash
    holmes                  /bin/bash
    kendunca                /bin/bash
```

```
        candace              /bin/bash
        mustard              /bin/bash
        peacock              /bin/bash
        plum                 /bin/bash
        scarlet              /bin/bash
        white                /bin/bash
        wilensky             /bin/bash
        ****** End of the Shells Report ******
```

The program shown in Listing 31-16 illustrates how to use Perl's format statement.

Listing 31-16: **Perl's report formatting capabilities**

```perl
#!/usr/bin/perl
# getlogin.pl - Displays the username and the login shell

format top =
        Login Shells Report

User Name          Login Shell
--------------------------------------
.
format STDOUT =
@<<<<<<<<<<<<<<      @<<<<<<<<<<<<<<<<<<
$name              $shell
.

while (@user_array=getpwent)
{
    ($name,$passwd,$uid,$gid,$quota,$comment,$gcos,$dir,$shell) = @user_array;
    if ($shell  ne "")
    {
        write;
    }
    else
    {
        $shell = "defaults to Bourne";
    {
    write;
}
```

The write function writes a record formatted with picture clauses to a filehandle or to standard output (using STDOUT). To use the write statement, first declare a picture format using the format statement and give it a name. This picture format describes the output. The line following the picture format lists the data, usually variables, to write, in the same order as the picture clauses.

Formatting Factoids

Perl writes formatted lines exactly as they appear in the picture clauses.

A picture clause contains certain fields that represent values to insert into the display line.

While you can create a page header with the `top` keyword, there is no corresponding `bottom` or `footer` function available in the format clause.

A picture field that begins with the @ character is the most commonly used picture field. It contains padding and justification characters.

Do not confuse the format clause's use of @ with the array variable symbol, also @.

A < symbol following the @represents the number of spaces for a left-justified field, e.g.

```
@<<<<<<<<<<<<<<<<
```

A > following the @ character represents the number of spaces for a right-justified field.

A | following the @ character represents the number of spaces for a centered field.

If the width of the formatting clause is less than the width of the data, the `write` command truncates the data. For example:

```
@<<<<<
$name
```

yields the following output for the user, miss_scarlet:

```
miss_
```

The `write` statement is not the opposite of the `read` statement. They're totally unrelated.

```
format STDOUT =
@<<<<<<<<<<<<<<<<<<@<<<<<<<<<<<<<<<<<<<<
$name              $shell
.
```

Tip To write the report to a file, use a filehandle instead of `STDOUT`.

Summary

This chapter got you started using Perl by showing you the syntax you need to write some basic programs and create simple reports. The examples were geared toward system administration use, and you can follow the basic concepts to create any sort of Perl program. Perl is the scripting language choice of many system administrators because of its forgiving and flexible syntax and rich functionality. You don't need to be a programmer to write basic Perl programs. For example, you don't need to be well versed in datatype concepts to use variables and constants in Perl programs, yet Perl provides most of the same features as a language such as C or FORTRAN. This chapter covered reasons to use Perl, how to run Perl programs, and the syntax for writing Perl programs.

✦   ✦   ✦

Monitoring and Optimizing Linux Performance

To *tune* is to improve performance without adding hardware. This chapter explains how to decide whether you can tune a Linux system without purchasing hardware or whether additional hardware will make the system perform better. This chapter also shows you how to monitor system performance so that you can determine whether tuning is even required and, if it is, how to make changes and measure the resulting performance improvements.

Using a Performance Methodology

Before you start to monitor your system, consider using a methodology to help you collect information about your system and to help you analyze and solve performance problems.

What is a methodology?

A methodology is simply a consistent method of monitoring performance, analyzing the results of the monitoring, and improving specific areas of performance. Although you can buy "off-the-shelf" methodologies that include documentation, record-keeping tools, and analysis tools, this chapter shows you how to use what's already included with Linux for your methodology. It's not really important what methodology you use. What's important is that you plan ahead and consistently use the same methodology.

Why use a methodology?

When you tune system performance, you should be able to demonstrate your results to your boss or your teammates as well as to yourself. A methodology guides you so that you manage your system's or network's performance systematically and measure and document the end results.

Understanding the Terminology

The following list explains the terms used in this chapter and their definitions:

Response time	Elapsed time between when a user ends a query or command and when the system displays the first character of the response on the screen.
Throughput	Amount of a certain type of work, such as disk reads and writes or the number of network packets processed, that a computer can do in a certain time period.
Bandwidth	Rate at which an I/O component, such as a disk controller or subsystem, can transfer bytes of data; sometimes called the *transfer rate*. Bandwidth is especially important for applications that perform large sequential data transfers, such as large downloads.
System resources	Computer components and subsystems, such as the CPU, the I/O subsystem, the memory subsystem (including physical RAM and available swap space), network cards, and so forth.
CPU	Central Processing Unit, the chip that controls the logic circuitry and performs machine instructions that make the operating system and applications run. The fastest system resource.
Memory subsystem	Electronic location for program instructions and data, which resides on hardware (RAM, DRAM chips), plus the swap daemon and swap space(s) on disk for managing virtual memory. The second fastest resource.
I/O subsystem	Hardware devices (hard disks, floppy disks, writable CD-ROMs, RAID arrays, tape drives) that provide both data input and output, plus their controllers. The slowest resource of the big three—CPU, memory, and I/O.
Saturation	When a resource has no available capacity and cannot service requests.

Bottleneck	Literally, a bottleneck is the narrow part of a bottle near the cork or cap. *The American Heritage® Dictionary of the English Language, Third Edition* (Houghton Mifflin 1996) defines a bottleneck as: "1. a. A narrow or obstructed section, as of a highway or a pipeline. b. A point or an area of traffic congestion. 2. A hindrance to progress or production." A performance bottleneck is usually a saturated resource that requests must wait their turn for, and that consequently slows down system performance.
Baseline	Performance statistics for your current system before you start to tune and/or optimize system-resource use. After tuning, monitor your system and compare the results to the baseline.

Collecting System Information

Before you start to improve system performance, be sure you understand the factors that affect performance. There are three basic tasks you need to carry out before you can effectively improve the performance of any computer resource:

✦ Identify the hardware components that make up your system.

✦ Identify the software applications that run on your system. For example, an e-mail server performs very differently from a database server.

✦ Monitor current system performance so that you have a baseline against which to compare any tuning and optimization results.

Identifying your hardware

If you selected the hardware you work with, you may already know exactly what your system's hardware capabilities and limits are. However, if you are the system administrator (SA) of a large network, you may need to remind yourself of the system configuration for the machine(s) you need to tune. You have a wide choice of tools for inventorying your hardware. This chapter shows examples of identifying hardware capabilities using the following utilities and tools:

✦ The /proc filesystem

✦ Harddrake

✦ COAS (Caldera Open Administration System, developed by Caldera)

✦ linuxconf (developed by Red Hat)

✦ Control panel

Examining /proc to inventory your hardware

The /proc filesystem consists of directories and files associated with the running kernel. The files store information about the system's resource use (the amount of memory, swap space, and CPU currently being used), and information about each running process

One of the performance-collecting tools shown later in this chapter is top, which gets most of its system resource usage numbers from the /proc filesystem. top is a useful administration tool as it displays a "live" readout of the CPU and memory resources being used by each process on the system. You don't need to use top to investigate the /proc filesystem; you can display, edit, or print the files in the /proc filesystem to see how your computer's resources are being used. The following examples use simple display commands such as cat, more, head, and tail to show /proc information.

See Chapter 10, "Managing Filesystems and Swap Space," for more information about the /proc filesystem.

The /proc/cpuinfo file holds information about the processor (CPU):

```
$ cat /proc/cpuinfo
processor       : 0
vendor_id       : GenuineIntel
cpu family      : 6
model           : 5
model name      : Pentium II (Deschutes)
stepping        : 2
cpu MHz         : 267.278241
cache size      : 512 KB
    — output truncated —-
```

The CPU in cpu family is an Intel 686.

Display the /proc/meminfo file to find out how much memory the system has and how much is free. You can also check swap-space use here. In the following example (from flyingpenguin), you can see that very little swap space is being used. If this is the case under normal and peak processing times, the system administrator might consider reducing the swap-space size to free up some space for a user partition. flyingpenguin is a document-production and application-testing machine that is often low on disk space. Apparently it has plenty of memory and doesn't need to swap much.

An assumption about system performance based on a single snapshot of memory use is an ill-founded assumption. You must monitor the system regularly over time to determine whether you are looking at regular usage or an anomaly. In fact, flyingpenguin frequently uses about 30 per cent of its swap space when database testers are testing commercial relational-database products.

```
$ cat /proc/meminfo
total:     used:        free:  shared: buffers:  cached:
Mem: 131022848 126824448 4198400 56238080 11476992     456256
Swap: 608628736  6848512 601780224
MemTotal:     127952 KB
MemFree:        4100 KB
MemShared:     54920 KB
Buffers:       11208 KB
Cached:        46344 KB
SwapTotal:    594364 KB
SwapFree:     587676 KB
```

To see individual swap spaces, display the /proc/swaps file.

```
$ cat /proc/swaps
Filename        Type         Size    Used   Priority
/dev/hda6       partition    594364  6688   0
```

Note The type of swap space is "partition." You can also choose to implement swap space in a file. It's easier to manage that way, but that method is not as efficient for performance and is consequently less common.

Get a list of all the partitions on all devices by displaying /proc/partitions, as below. You can also use fdisk to see the same information. The flyingpenguin computer has one hard drive, hda, and one mounted CD-ROM, hdc.

```
$ cat /proc/partitions
major minor  #blocks   name

   3      0   6342840  hda
   3      1   4200966  hda1
   3      2         1  hda2
   3      5   1542208  hda5
   3      6    594373  hda6
  22      0    626254  hdc
```

Examine the file /proc/net/dev to find out what active network devices exist on your system.

```
$ cat /proc/net/dev
Inter-|   Receive                          |  Transmit
 face |packets errs drop fifo frame|packets errs drop fifo
colls carrier
    lo:    91    0    0    0    0     91    0    0    0    0    0
  eth0:     0    0    0    0    0     60    0    0    0    0   60
```

The preceding excerpt shows that flyingpenguin has two active network devices. The loopback device for testing is lo. The Ethernet interface (NIC) is eth0. If your system has multiple Ethernet interfaces, the display will also show eth1, eth2, and so forth.

Tip   The preceding display is useful for troubleshooting network interfaces. If flying-penguin has two NICs, for example, this display shows that one of those devices is not working.

Cross-Reference   Chapter 33, "Monitoring and Optimizing Network Performance," explains how to interpret the rest of the output in the preceding example.

Using Harddrake to inventory your hardware

Linux-Mandrake's utility, Harddrake, is a GUI tool that gives you comprehensive information about your hardware. Besides examining the hardware (see Figure 32-1), Harddrake can also set IO, IRQ, and X86 characteristics, as shown in Figure 32-2. You can use Harddrake with the Mandrake and Red Hat distributions and you can build it for other distributions as well.

Tip   You can download the Harddrake packages from `http://www.linux-mandrake.com/lothar/download.html`.

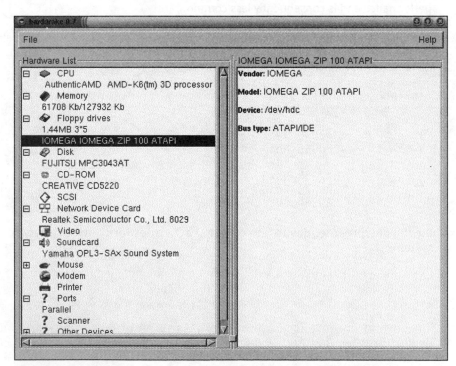

Figure 32-1: Harddrake is a GUI-based tool for inventorying hardware

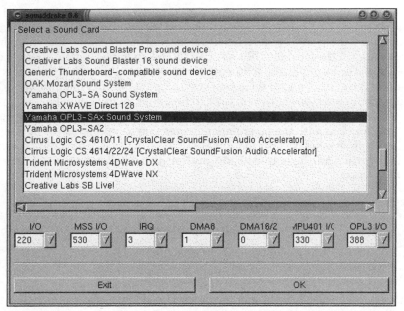

Figure 32-2: Harddrake provides information about IO, IRQ, and X settings

Identifying software and understanding what users are doing

You can use RPM or another package manager such as Caldera's COAS or Debian's dpkg (Debian Package Management System) to see what software packages are installed on your system. However, just because a package is installed, doesn't mean that people are using it. What you really want to know about software, after all, is what software people are really using and what resources they are consuming when they run the applications. You have a choice of tools to see what software is running and who is using it. Further sections in this chapter describe:

✦ The `ps -elf` (or `ps -aux`) command, which shows what each process is running, including processes that are not attached to terminals (detached processes), such as daemons.

✦ The `top` command, which also shows the commands that users are running.

✦ The accounting utilities, which can provide a thorough look at what users are doing, how often they log in, and how often they run various commands and programs.

When you list the application software that runs on your computer, you should also identify the daemons that run on your system. You have a choice of tools with which to do this. If you run ps regularly, you can see what daemons run on your system by looking at the far right column (CMD.) The daemons' names usually end with the letter *d*. For example, the following ps excerpt shows several daemons running, including the system logger daemon (syslogd), the Internet daemon (inetd), and the line printer daemon (lpd). Don't try to decipher all the columns in the ps display yet. You can see a full explanation of the ps columns later in this chapter. Using the -elf options with the ps command gives you a complete look at your system. The e option displays information about all processes. The l option displays the long format for the output. The f option gives a full listing.

```
$ ps -elf
F   S UID  PID   PPID C  PRI  NI ADDR SZ  WCHAN  STIME TTY     TIME     CMD
100 S root 1     0    0  60   0   -   276 do_sel May05 ?      00:00:04 init [5]
140 S root 314   1    0  60   0   -   289 do_sel May05 ?      00:00:01 syslogd
140 S root 404   1    0  60   0   -   281 do_sel May05 ?      00:00:00 inetd
140 S root 448   1    0  60   0   -   294 do_sel May05 ?      00:00:00 lpd
140 S root 534   1    0  60   0   -   288 do_sel May05 ?      00:00:01 rwhod
```

Tip   Removing (and not starting) daemons you don't need frees up system resources. Removing remote access daemons that you don't need improves performance. For example, the rwho and ruptime commands require the rwhod daemon. Since rwho (find people who are logged in across the network) and ruptime (get uptime summaries for machines on the network) are very resource-intensive commands, removing the daemon effectively disables the rwho and ruptime commands.

The top command shows information on processes, sorted by CPU usage, including the commands users are running. In the following top example, look at the far right to see the commands the users are running. Table 32-1 describes fields commonly displayed in the output of various performance-monitoring tools, including top.

```
$ top
─────── output edited ─────────────────
  PID USER     PRI NI  SIZE  RSS SHARE STAT  LIB %CPU %MEM  TIME COMMAND
26568 miss_sca 11  0  1032 1032   820 R      0   3.8  0.8  0:00 top
26543 miss_sca  4  0   992  992   772 S      0   0.0  0.7  0:00 bash
26542 root      0  0  1100 1100   856 S      0   0.0  0.8  0:00 login
26541 root      0  0   880  880   684 S      0   0.0  0.6  0:00 in.telnetd
26516 candace   0  0   768  768   628 S      0   0.0  0.6  0:00 vi
26503 candace   0  0   948  948   768 S      0   0.0  0.7  0:00 bash
26502 root      0  0  1100 1100   856 S      0   0.0  0.8  0:00 login
26501 root      0  0   880  880   684 S      0   0.0  0.6  0:00 in.telnetd
26500 candace   0  0  1064 1064   788 S      0   0.0  0.8  0:00 in.ftpd
24993 nobody    0  0  1356 1348  1244 S      0   0.0  1.0  0:00 httpd
24994 nobody    0  0  1356 1348  1244 S      0   0.0  1.0  0:00 httpd
```

Note By default, `top` displays the top 15 processes sorted in CPU order. The preceding display appeared when the user pressed `a` to sort the processes in descending order by age.

<table>
<tr><td colspan="2" align="center">Table 32-1
Commonly Displayed Performance Fields</td></tr>
</table>

Field	Meaning
PID	The process id. After a process terminates, a new process may reuse the pid.
USER	Username.
PRI	Current process priority, set and dynamically adjusted by the kernel, depending on what the process is doing.
NI	"Nice" setting, ranging from -20 (the highest) to +19 (the lowest). The default is 0. Users can use the `nice` command to reduce their priority to keep CPU intensive jobs from bottlenecking other interactive processes. Root can "nice" a process it doesn't own. Only root can make a nice setting higher.[1]
SIZE	Amount of *virtual* memory currently allocated to a process.[2]
RSS	Size of physical memory currently allocated to a process.[3]
SHARE	Amount of shared memory currently being used by a process.
STAT	The process state.
%CPU	Percentage of CPU capacity currently being used by a process.
%MEM	Percentage of physical memory currently being used by a process.
TIME	Total CPU time used by the process since it started. In cumulative mode (`S`), this totals the CPU time of all the process' dead children.
COMMAND	The process' command name (may be truncated). Parentheses indicate that the process is outswapped.

1. Experience says: Don't depend on users to be "nice." If priorities of CPU hogs need to be lowered, the system administrator must do it.

2. The SIZE column *does not* include the amount of physical memory that the process is using.

3. A process can have a large virtual memory SIZE but use only a small RSS.

Tip %CPU is a percentage of the total available CPU capacity, which is more than 100% on a SMP (Symmetric Multiprocessing) computer because each processor represents 100%. Therefore, a computer with four processors has a total of 400% CPU capacity. If a process is using 25% of the CPU in a four-processor environment, it is using the equivalent of all of one processor. If you add together all the %CPU statistics for all users, the total is not exactly 100%.

Collecting system information

The original purpose of the accounting utilities was to be able to charge users for their usage of system resources — from CPU down to each piece of paper they printed on. Using accounting this way is rare on Linux and UNIX systems. However, accounting is still useful. By setting up login and process accounting, you can learn about how people are using the computer and get an idea of what kinds of activities constitute normal processing.

Login accounting

Each time someone logs in or out, the job with PID 1, init, writes the following information to the login accounting file, /var/log/wtmp:

✦ XE "/var/log/wtmp *username*
✦ Login time
✦ Terminal port logged into
✦ Logout time

You use the last command, as shown in the code that follows this list, to display the following information stored in the login accounting (wtmp) file:

✦ Who has logged in and out. Especially notice how often root has logged in. This is important security information. If you are root, and you see root logins occurring when you are not working, someone is breaking in.

✦ Who is currently logged in across the network and from where.

✦ The total connect time for each login.

```
root@flyingpenguin# last
professo pts/3       192.168.0.5     Sun Jul 30 20:29   still logged in
miss_sca pts/2       192.168.0.241   Sun Jul 30 20:25   still logged in
root     pts/1       :0              Sun Jul 30 14:54   still logged in
root     pts/0       :0              Sun Jul 30 14:54   still logged in
reboot   system boot 2.2.12-20       Sun Jul 30 14:53       (05:37)
miss_sca pts/1       192.168.241     Sat Jul 29 17:44 - 21:33  (03:48)
miss_sca pts/1       192.168.0.241   Sat Jul 29 17:11 - 17:12  (00:00)
miss_sca pts/2       192.168.241     Sat Jul 29 07:09 - 15:12  (08:02)
              --- output truncated ---
```

Tip

Using the last command on a regular basis gives you a foundation for capacity planning. Watch the trends. If you see the number of logins or the length of sessions increasing, you may need to start planning for more hardware to service the increasing system load. If you see the number of network logins steadily increasing, you may need to add a server or increase network capacity to satisfy the growing number of requests.

The lastb command displays the same information as the last command. The difference is that lastb queries the /var/log/btmp file, which lists bad logins. In the following example, the last three entries show that someone tried to log in locally (from localhost) as root. The IP addresses in the third column show that all other failed logins originated on the same computer across the network.

```
root@flyingpenguin# lastb
root      pts/2     192.168.0.2       Wed May 31 16:26 - 16:26  (00:00)
miss_sca  pts/2     192.168.0.241     Wed May 31 16:26 - 16:26  (00:00)
candace   pts/2     192.168.0.2       Wed May 31 16:26 - 16:26  (00:00)
candace   pts/2     192.168.0.2       Wed May 31 16:26 - 16:26  (00:00)
          pts/2     192.168.0.2       Wed May 31 16:25 - 16:25  (00:00)
root      pts/2     192.168.0.2       Wed May 31 16:25 - 16:25  (00:00)
root      pts/2     192.168.0.2       Wed May 31 16:25 - 16:25  (00:00)
          pts/3     localhost         Wed May 31 16:14 - 16:14  (00:00)
root      pts/3     localhost         Wed May 31 16:14 - 16:14  (00:00)
root      pts/3     localhost         Wed May 31 16:14 - 16:14  (00:00)
```

Caution   The accounting utilities only log information in the wtmp and btmp files if those files exist. To enable login accounting, use the touch command to create the empty files. For example, create the wtmp file with the following command:

```
touch /var/log/wtmp
```

Using ac to total connect times

The ac command also shows some basic login information. The ac command, /usr/bin/ac, displays connect times. Like last, ac displays a report based on /var/log/wtmp, the login accounting file. The ac command is part of the psacct package.

Note   If you don't have the ac command installed, use your distribution's package manager, such as RPM, to install the psacct package.

Using the ac command with no options simply displays a grand total of connect times for all users connected to the system.

```
root@tweety# ac
        total      116.39
```

Using ac without arguments is not usually useful. Choose one of the following options to see daily or user totals.

To get more information from ac, you can use the -d option to display totals for each day, as in the following example:

```
root@flyingpenguin# ac -d
May  1  total       0.06
May  7  total       0.01
May 13  total      23.14
May 14  total      26.18
```

```
May 15   total           19.16
May 16   total            1.55
May 17   total            4.66
May 21   total           11.48
May 22   total           15.67
May 23   total            7.66
May 24   total            0.91
May 25   total            0.29
Today    total            5.63
```

To see individual totals for each user, use the -p option, as in the following example:

```
root@flyingpenguin# ac -p
        miss_scarlet                    80.12
        marshall                        35.78
        root                             0.50
        total          116.40
```

Combine the -p and -d options to see daily totals for each user, as in the following excerpt, which gives you a general idea of who uses the system the most.

```
root@flyingpenguin# ac -pd
        miss_scarlet                     0.03
        marshall                         0.03
        candace                          0.03
   May  1  total      0.09
        root                             0.01
   May  7  total      0.01
        root                             5.98
        marshall                        17.15
   May 13  total     23.14
        miss_scarlet                    10.18
        marshall                        16.00
   May 14  total     26.18
        miss_scarlet                    20.06
        professor_plum                   6.12
   May 15  total      4.66
        miss_scarlet                     8.86
        marshall                         2.60
        root                             0.02
```

Note   ac shows connect times. This may give you an idea of who is working the most on the computer, but just because a user is logged in does not necessarily mean that that user is working. The user may log in and go to a meeting followed by lunch. This user is accumulating connect time, but is not using any significant amount of system resources.

Using sa to summarize process activity and resource use

The command /sbin/accton toggles process accounting on and off. The sa command summarizes process accounting data about previously executed commands, as recorded in the acct file /var/log/pacct. You can also use sa to save these data into the file /var/log/savacct. /var/log/savacct lists the number of times the sa command was called and the system resources it used. You can also summarize the data per user. Table 32-2 shows the many options you can use with sa.

The output from sa includes:

cpu   Total (in seconds) of system and user time.

re   "Real time" in CPU seconds.

k   CPU-time averaged core usage, in 1k units.

avio   Average number of I/O operations per execution.

tio   Total number of I/O operations.

k*sec   CPU storage integral (kilo-core seconds).

u   User CPU time in CPU seconds.

s   system time in CPU seconds.

If you see an asterisk (*) in the output, it means that a process forked another process without calling the usual exec system service. By default, sa sorts the output by CPU use (user plus system time).

Tip   Notice the many different GNOME components that are active. GUIs, whether GNOME, KDE, or X, have many parts, all of which use system resources. If your computer is resource-poor, consider eliminating the GUI.

```
[root@flyingpenguin]#/usr/sbin/sa -a |more
   7611 1444514.04re      620.65cp        0avio       317k
    147       0.54re        0.32cp        0avio       364k    gawk
      1   69905.07re        0.26cp        0avio      1027k    enlightenment
     55       2.64re        0.19cp        0avio       293k    ls
      1   69905.07re        0.16cp        0avio      2156k    panel
      1   69905.07re        0.14cp        0avio      1489k    gnomepager_appl
     12       1.09re        0.08cp        0avio       231k    rpm
    274       0.15re        0.06cp        0avio       418k    inn-cron-nntpse
      1   45962.58re        0.06cp        0avio      2132k    kfm
     21    1757.84re        0.06cp        0avio       417k    in.telnetd
      2  115692.89re        0.05cp        0avio      1424k    gnome-terminal
    298       0.06re        0.05cp        0avio       266k    runlevel
     27  118508.38re        0.04cp        0avio       437k    bash
      1   69905.07re        0.02cp        0avio      1343k    gnome-smproxy
      1   69905.07re        0.02cp        0avio      1398k    gnome-session
     23    1066.36re        0.02cp        0avio       389k    su
      5       0.33re        0.01cp        0avio       282k    vmstat
     19       0.34re        0.00cp        0avio       279k    sa
      1   47098.54re        0.00cp        0avio      4188k    netscape-commun

—More—
```

Table 32-2 Some Options for the sa Command	
Option	**Description**
-h	Display the usage syntax.
-a	List all.
-c	Display percentages of time for user and system values.
-d	Sort by average number of disk I/Os.
-D	Sort by total number of disk I/Os.
-l	Don't add system and user time for CPU. Show both values.
-r	Sort in reverse order.
-u	Display the uid and command for each line.

Monitoring Performance and Creating a Baseline

Before you make any changes to your system, monitor performance over time to get an idea of how your system is currently performing. Monitor both average loads and peak loads so that you can decide what changes will improve day-to-day performance and what you might need to do to optimize performance at unusually heavy times. For example, your system's performance may be perfectly fine most of the time, but at the end of the month, when one department is running month-end financial reports, people in other departments may have a hard time getting work done because the system is so slow and non-responsive. In that case, you need to figure out what you can do to improve month-end processing without harming normal daily processing.

Caution   Whenever you modify your system to address a performance problem, it's possible that your change may slow down some other aspect of performance. That's why it's so important to make only a few changes at a time and monitor them until you're satisfied that they actually help.

It's important to monitor performance regularly. If you monitor performance for just a few days, you may not get a representative sample of what's happening on your system. For example, suppose you monitor performance for the three days that the heaviest users are out of town at a conference. The performance figures you collect are not representative of a typical load, and any changes you make based on those non-representative numbers won't be the right changes. After you monitor performance for an adequate length of time (and that depends on your environment), you need to analyze the data you collected to figure out:

✦ Do you even have a performance problem?

✦ If so, what system resources are stressed?

✦ Do you have a performance bottleneck?

✦ Do you need to improve response time, throughput, or both?

✦ Can you tune the system without buying any additional hardware?

✦ Are there any low-risk, low-effort changes that will improve performance?

✦ What major changes are required?

Getting baseline data

If you are the system administrator, you should understand the current level of resource use and what level of performance is normal for your computers (or network). Before you start tuning and optimizing, you need to create a baseline set of data about your current system resource use so that you can measure the results of your tuning and optimizing. Collect performance data pertaining to your current configuration, including CPU use, memory use, I/O throughput, and network activity. Keep a record of both average performance and peak demands. This baseline set of data will help you select the optimal tuning strategies to implement. After you optimize an area of system performance, monitor the system again and compare the results with the baseline.

Caution

Don't assume that tuning an element will improve overall system performance. For example, suppose you get a faster CPU for your system. Be sure to monitor performance and compare it to the baseline. If you see no improvement, it's possible that your I/O subsystem can't keep up with the new CPU, and consequently that processes are waiting in line to read or write to disk or to access the disk controller before they can take advantage of the CPU. The processes waiting for disk resources constitute a *disk queue*. On the other hand, if CPU performance is fine, and you add I/O resources, the CPU may slow down. An improved I/O rate may mean that more requests get to the CPU faster than before. Everything is interrelated.

Finding bottlenecks

After you have collected some basic performance data over time, you should analyze those data and look for bottlenecks. One possible indicator of performance problems is users or processes hogging a particular system resource. This is only a possible indicator because it's possible that the "resource hog" is the only process requesting that resource, and that Linux is offering the entire amount until someone else needs to share it. Of course, if other processes are waiting to use the resource, the "hog" is causing a bottleneck.

What are people doing?

You need to understand the normal kind of work people do on your computer for both security and performance reasons. If you identify one user consistently using a large percentage of CPU resources, often called a *CPU hog*, you need to know what that person is doing. If he or she is a programmer, compiling and building complex programs, that person is doing a job. If that person plays lots of CPU-intensive games, then he or she is a CPU hog, and you may need to terminate his or her process.

 Cross-Reference

You also need to know how people use the system in order to identify potential security breaches. If your site has no programmers and you see someone using the C compiler regularly, you need to know why. Perhaps the user is doing homework for a programming course. On the other hand, the user could be trying to write break-in programs. Chapter 29, "Securing a Linux System," has more information about identifying security breaches.

If you know what level of resource use is normal, you can recognize extraordinary events, such as a filesystem filling up or a system-wide e-mail failure. If you recognize these events quickly, you can notify users of the problem before they all call you at once, and begin the repair process quickly.

Monitor services in addition to the system resources. Besides collecting statistics about memory, CPU, network and disk use, you need to be able to recognize when a daemon has crashed or when a network cable is not connected.

Is anyone waiting?

The way to find out if users are stuck waiting for a resource is to monitor process states. The command ps auxWw displays comprehensive output, including the following process states:

D   Waiting for disk I/O; indicates a queue of processes that are waiting for disk access.

R   Runnable; indicates a queue of processes that are on the CPU queue (run queue).

S   Sleeping.

T   Stopped.

Z   Defunct (a "zombie").

If users are queued for a resource such as I/O or CPU, the next step is to find out whether a resource hog is blocking access or whether usage is normal and you need to add system resources. If a hog is the reason for a CPU or I/O queue, you can solve the problem by:

✦ Killing the process that is hogging the resource (kill -9 pid).

✦ Changing the process' priority (nice).

✦ Buying and installing more of the resource.

Using Monitoring Tools

Have you ever heard or said, "My system is running slow. How do I find and fix the problem?" Your first step should be to look at the number and type of running processes. Then you can narrow it down to the process or processes causing the slowdown and determine whether a resource is the bottleneck or whether the application is inefficient and needs to be rewritten. Many tools for monitoring Linux performance are available. This part of the chapter introduces you to a few of them. You have already seen ps, top, and GNU accounting examples in this chapter. The following sections introduce you to using vmstat, top, and Bonnie to monitor system performance and resource use.

Caution

While tools provide a lot of numbers to look at, none of them interprets the numbers to tell you where problems exist, or tell you how to solve those problems.

Using vmstat to see an overview of your computer's performance

Your first step in monitoring system performance is to collect data that give you a general overview of system resource use. Using the vmstat tool gives you information about CPU, memory, and I/O use.

Although the name vmstat implies a tool for monitoring virtual memory, vmstat provides comprehensive information about your running system. The vmstat output below shows column headings for process information (procs), memory use, swapping activity (swap), disk I/O (io), and CPU use (CPU).

```
root@flyingpenguin} vmstat
   procs                      memory    swap        io     system      cpu
 r  b  w   swpd  free   buff  cache  si  so    bi   bo    in   cs  us  sy  id
 0  0  0   6688  19628  17240  26312  0   0     0    0    1    12   0   1   7
```

Running vmstat with no options generates a report like the preceding example that displays system averages since the last reboot. The subfields for each category are as follows:

✦ procs

  • r—Number of processes ready to run. Since only one process can run at a time on a single CPU, this column measures the CPU run queue.

- • b—Number of processes sleeping.
- • w—Number of processes that are runnable, but swapped out.

✦ memory (in KB)

- • swpd—Amount of virtual memory in use.
- • free—Amount of available memory.
- • buff—Amount of memory used for system buffers.

✦ swap (in KB)

- • si—Amount of memory swapped in from disk.
- • so—Amount of memory swapped out to disk.

✦ io (in 1-KB blocks, except for 2-KB CD-ROM blocks)

- • bi—Blocks sent to block devices, such as a disk.
- • bo— Blocks received from block devices.

✦ system

- • in—Interrupts per second. An interrupt is a signal from a device or a program that tells Linux to stop what it's doing and decide what to do next. Each interrupt request (IRQ) sends a number to the kernel indicating which device is requesting service.
- • cs—Context switches per second. Context switching occurs when a process' time slice is up and the CPU schedules the next runnable process. If the original process is not finished, the CPU saves that context— that is, the instructions and data that the program is using—before servicing the next process in the queue. Saving the contents and pointers for one process in order to service another process allows the CPU to resume processing where it left off when it is the original process's turn. Context switching is an expensive (in performance terms) CPU activity.

✦ cpu (percentages of the total time)

- • us—User time (time spent servicing user code).
- • sy—System time (time spent servicing privileged kernel code).

✦ id—Idle time (time the CPU is not busy).

Using top to see an overview of system resource utilization

The top command displays basic information about the system load and all the running processes. The top display in Figure 32-3 begins with a header that describes the general state of the system. After the header, top displays a list of all running processes and the system resources they are consuming.

The top summary display

The top header lists how long the computer has been up and running, and how many users are logged in. The header also summarizes the load averages, process states, CPU states, memory use, and swap-space use for your computer. The following is a list of the information you'll find in the top header:

✦ The load average represents the length of the system run queue averaged over the last one minute, five minutes, and fifteen minutes.

✦ The process state gives the total number of processes and summarizes how many are in each state: sleeping, running, zombie, stopped, and on CPU.

✦ The memory-use line displays the total amount of physical and virtual memory available, the total amount in use, and the total amount that is free.

The top process display

See Table 32-1 for an explanation of fields in the top process display. Figure 32-3 and Figure 32-4 show two aspects of resource use.

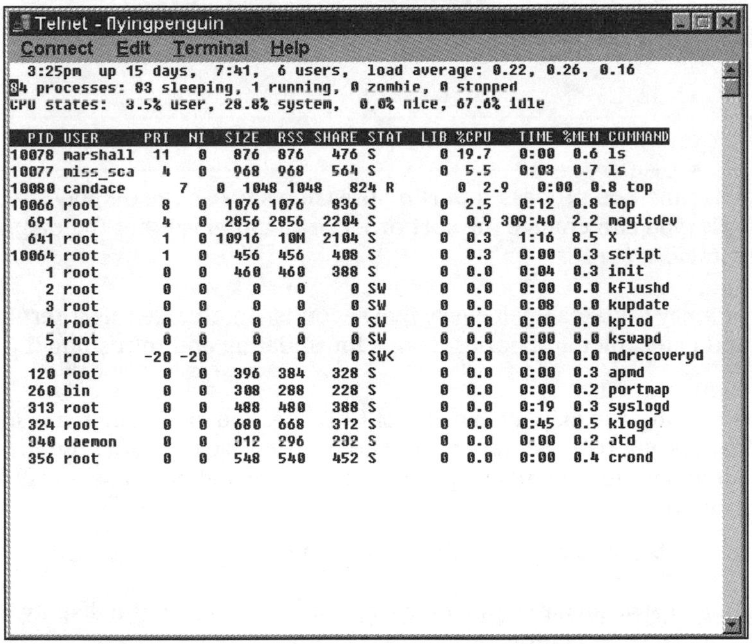

Figure 32-3: The top summary displays overall system-resource use

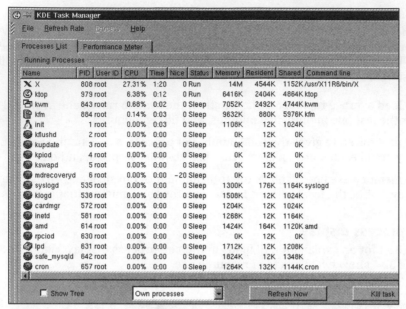

Figure 32-4: The top process display shows per-process resource use

top tips

You can customize the top process report by pressing keys as the display is running. For example, you can change the sort order or the interval that the display uses to update itself.

- ✦ The top display updates itself every five seconds. To change this interval, press s and enter the number of seconds for updating and refreshing the display.

- ✦ top sorts the process display in order of CPU use. You can change the sort default by pressing the first letter of the column you want to sort by. For example, if you prefer to sort the process display by memory use, press M (upper case M).

- ✦ Press q to quit top and return to the command line.

To use interactive top commands, just type the command during the display. Interactive top commands include:

Space	Update display.
^L	Redraw the screen.
fname	Add and remove field *names*.
ofields	Sort in the order of the listed *fields*.

h or ?	Display the list of interactive commands.
S	Toggle between interactive and cumulative mode.
i	Toggle display of idle processes.
c	Toggle display of command name/line.
l	Toggle display of load average.
m	Toggle display of memory information.
t	Toggle display of summary information.
k	Kill a task (with any signal).
r	Renice a task.
N	Sort by pid.
A	Sort by age.
P	Sort by CPU usage.
M	Sort by resident memory usage.
T	Sort by time/cumulative time.
u	Show only a specific user.
n or #	Set the number of process to show.
s	Set the delay in seconds between updates.
W	Write configuration file ~/.toprc.
q	Quit.

Using a graphical top

If you are using the KDE interface, you can run KTOP to see general system information. KTOP has two types of displays. You can see either a list of processes and
their resource use (see Figure 32-3), or the performance meter showing the system
load and memory use (like the top summary). Figure 32-5 shows a performance
meter.

The free command is another memory-monitoring tool. It displays (in KB) the total
amount of free and used physical memory and swap space on your computer, and
the shared memory and buffers used by the kernel. Command options include:

-b	Display memory in bytes.
-k	Display in kilobytes (default).
-m	Display in megabytes.
-t	Display the totals.

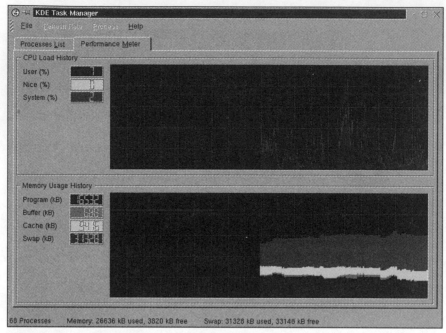

Figure 32-5: KTOP displays a performance meter

Improving Disk I/O Performance

An old saying holds that a computer's fastest performance is determined by its slowest component. In most systems, the slowest components are typically the hard disks. This section discusses improving the performance of your system's hard disk(s).

The I/O subsystem, which consists of disks and disk controllers, operates very slowly compared to CPU and memory speeds. A fast CPU can easily saturate an underpowered I/O subsystem, especially on a server that uses IDE disks. To see if your I/O subsystem can keep up with your CPU, use the vmstat command to identify processes waiting for disk I/O (blocked processes -b) or the ps command to identify processes in D state. The I/O subsystem is a bottleneck if the number of blocked processes (b) regularly exceeds the number of processes waiting to run (r).

Tip   Use vmstat as preventive medicine. If the number of I/O blocked processes (b) is usually the same as or close to the number of runnable processes (r), then the I/O subsystem is not yet a bottleneck but is about to become one. Tune I/O to avert a problem before it happens.

Disk I/O Terminology

Before you tune the I/O system, you should be familiar with the terminology and concepts pertaining to disk and controller performance.

✦ *Seek time* — The amount of time a disk head takes to position itself at a specific track.

✦ *Rotational latency* — The amount of time a disk takes to rotate to a specific sector.

✦ *Access time* — A common measure of disk performance that combines seek time and rotational latency.

✦ *Sequential access* — A setup wherein data are read from or written to contiguous (adjacent) logical disk blocks.

✦ *Random access* — A setup wherein data are read from or written to blocks in non-contiguous locations on a disk.

✦ *Filesystem I/O* — The I/O to a disk partition that contains a filesystem.

✦ *Raw I/O* — The I/O to a disk partition that does not contain a filesystem. Raw I/O does not use filesystem buffers and caches. Relational databases such as Informix and Oracle typically use raw, that is, unformatted, disk. The operating system and database-application software often use I/O. Relational database systems usually give you the option of using raw I/O for database operations since it might provide better performance than filesystem I/O.

Monitoring performance with shareware (Bonnie)

The Bonnie program performs a series of tests on a file of known size. The default file size is 100 MB. On most servers, you should set the file size to be at least twice the size of the available RAM.

✦ If your computer has 64-bit architecture (for example, if you have an Alpha), Bonnie works with 64-bit pointers.

✦ For each test, Bonnie reports the bytes processed per elapsed second, bytes processed per CPU second, and the percentage of CPU usage (user and system).

Go to http://www.textuality.com/bonnie to download the source code. After downloading the Bonnie source code, run the make command to build the code. Bonnie uses the following syntax:

```
Bonnie [-d scratch-dir] [-s size-in-Mb] [-m machine-label] [-html]
root@flyingpenguin# Bonnie -s750 -malpha1
——-Sequential Output——— --Sequential Input- —Random—
            -Per Char- —Block—- -Rewrite- -Per Char- —Block—- —Seeks--
Machine   MB K/sec %CPU K/sec %CPU K/sec %CPU K/sec %CPU K/sec %CPU  /sec %CPU
alpha1   750   534 65.7  1236 22.5   419 17.5   564 74.3  1534 32.8  35.0  8.3
```

Bonnie's output fields mean:

alpha1	This test was run with the option -m alpha1. alpha1 is the label for this test.
750	This test used the file-size option -s 750.
1941	File output was 534 KB per second.
65.7	Writing the file consumed 65.7% of the CPU. This Alpha is old and has a slow CPU.
1236	File output to a 750-MB file was 1,236 KB per second.
22.5	Writing the file using efficient block writes used 22.5% of one CPU's time.
419	Creating, changing, and rewriting each block of a file was measured at 418 KB per second.
17.5	Creating, changing, and rewriting each block consumed 17.5% of one CPU's time.
564	Reading the file using 750 million getc() macro invocations used an input rate of 564 KB per second.
74.3	Reading the file consumed 74.3% of one CPU's time. This is quite high.
1534	File reads occurred at an input rate of 1,534 KB per second.
32.8	Reading the file with block reads consumed 32.8% of one CPU's time.
35.0	Bonnie created four child processes and had them execute 4000 seeks to random locations in the file. On 10% of these seeks, the processes changed the blocks that they had read and re-wrote them. The disk's effective seek rate was 32.8 seeks per second.
8.3	The seeking process consumed 8.3% of one CPU's time.

Is IDE performance sufficient?

Let's start with some terminology.

Ultra-ATA drives	The latest generation of drives. These drives are backwards-compatible with IDE drives, but they have a maximum throughput that is twice that of older IDE drives.
SCSI	Small Computer System Interface

The best Ultra-ATA drives usually have as much cache as most SCSI drives (512 KB) and spin at the same speed as many SCSI drives (7200 RPM). However, IDE drives lack certain features, particularly the ability to use their I/O processing chips to handle disk I/O. As a result, IDE drives dramatically affect overall system performance because they rely on the system's main CPU to handle I/O requests, unlike SCSI disks and controllers, which handle I/O without relying on the main CPU. SCSI controllers can write to multiple devices at once; IDE controllers can't. A general guideline is that if the computer is a single-user workstation, IDE disks are adequate and will save you money. If the computer is a server with a large disk farm used by many concurrent processes, choose SCSI. SCSI is also the best choice for either a workstation or server if the computer has more than two hard drives.

If performance is the only consideration, choose SCSI. If cost is the only consideration, choose IDE (EIDE).

Using hardware RAID to improve disk I/O

Hard disks configurations can include hardware RAID (Redundant Array of Independent Disks) subsystems, which expand the number of disks that can be connected to a single bus and provide both performance and availability features, but the performance depends on the RAID level selected. There are four main RAID levels and one hybrid level:

RAID 0 (disk striping)	Divides data into disk chunks called stripes and distributes the stripes across an array of multiple disks. Distributing the disk I/O load across disks almost always improves throughput because it allows parallel data access increased bandwidth.
RAID 1 (mirroring)	Stores identical copies of data on different disks in an array. Duplicating data on different disks improves both data availability and disk-read performance. You can mirror striped disks by combining RAID 1 and RAID 0. RAID 1 is a more expensive performance solution than RAID 0 because you need to double the amount of storage you would normally use. If you don't need the high availability of RAID 1, use RAID 0.
RAID 3 (a rarely used parity RAID)	Stripes the data across an array of disks, as in RAID 0, and also stores redundant parity information on a separate disk. If a disk in the data array fails, the parity regenerates the lost data. However, the parity disk is a single point of failure. An inexpensive, but less reliable, availability solution.
RAID 5 (a type of parity RAID for high availability)	Stripes data and redundant parity across disks. Striping the parity information removes parity as the single point of failure. On disk writes, updating the parity information may slow down I/O performance. If multiple disks fail, data can still be available although performance will slow down.

| Adaptive RAID 3/5 (the hybrid, dynamic parity RAID) | Supported by some high-performance RAID controllers to combine RAID 3 and RAID 5 to improve I/O performance. The amount of I/O workload controls how Adaptive RAID 3/5 dynamically adjusts between data transfer intensive operations and I/O operations. If multiple disks fail, data can still be available although performance will slow down. |

Tip   Using hardware RAID also improves CPU performance by offloading some of the behind-the-scenes CPU operations involved in overseeing I/O processing.

Fight fragmentation

Ideally, a disk file is a set of contiguous disk blocks. However, on full disks, when a file is written, Linux can't always find a set of contiguous blocks. A file that is not contiguous is fragmented. It takes longer to read a fragmented file, since the disk's read-write head has to jump around to the various fragments of the file.

The ext2 filesystem attempts to keep fragmentation at a minimum by keeping all blocks in a file close together, even if they can't be stored in consecutive sectors. Ext2 always allocates the free block that is nearest to other blocks in a file. With ext2, it is therefore seldom necessary to worry about fragmentation unless your disk is over 90% full. However, you should check other filesystem types for fragmentation.

Improve memory performance

Since swapping involves disk I/O, improving swap performance indirectly improves disk-I/O performance.

Improving CPU Performance

Before digging into the details of improving CPU performance, it is important to understand how a given CPU's design affects its performance. In particular, you need to understand the different types of processor cache, which is a small amount of memory set aside solely for high-speed access by the CPU.

CPUs come in different processor speeds and onboard-cache sizes. For example tweety, one of the computers used to generate the examples in this book, is a Mobile Pentium MMX processor that runs at a speed of 200 MHz, with 256 KB of secondary cache. Tweety is not a very powerful computer for Windows 98 or 2000, but it has resources to spare for the Linux environment in which it runs. When both operating system and application programs run, the operating system moves data and instructions through caches (on the processor itself and on the motherboard), physical memory, and disk swap space. The speed at which a CPU can access data and instructions, depends on the location of its cache.

Note A CPU chip accesses several caches that are either built into the chip or that are located very close to it. The size of these caches depends on the make and model of your computer. If you are using an Intel Pentium P60 processor, don't expect much in the way of cache size. If you are using an Alpha computer from Compaq, you will be blessed with large on-chip caches up to a maximum of 64 KB, depending on the Alpha processor. These caches help the CPU(s) run as fast as possible. The secondary data cache is not on the CPU, but is usually on the motherboard. After the CPU cache, secondary cache is the fastest access component in your computer. The size of the secondary cache ranges from 128 KB to 8 MB, depending on the make and model of your processor and computer. Some powerful computers, such as certain Alphas, contain a tertiary cache that functions as an additional secondary cache.

A computer does not necessarily have only one CPU. You can use Symmetrical Multiprocessing (SMP) computers, where multiple CPUs in the same cabinet share physical memory and the same version of the operating system, and execute program instructions simultaneously. CPU-intensive environments, such as large scientific systems, often use multiprocessing systems to handle the workload.

Finding a CPU bottleneck

A CPU bottleneck occurs when the CPU is saturated, and processes that are ready must queue up and wait to run. Look at the r (run queue) column of the vmstat output to identify bottlenecks. Sometimes a single process can grab most of the CPU resources. When this happens, this process is called a *runaway process*. You can find a runaway process by using ps or top to check for one process consuming abnormal amounts of CPU time.

CPU bottleneck solutions

To free up a CPU bottleneck, you have a few choices:

✦ Redesign and optimize applications that use the CPU heavily. This is a high-risk solution since it involves recoding and recompiling, which often introduces new bugs into the applications. Additionally, redesigning for performance doesn't guarantee improved performance. In fact, sometimes the redesign reduces performance.

✦ Schedule CPU-intensive applications to run at non-peak hours using cron or at.

✦ Move some applications to other computers that have CPU idle time.

✦ Buy a more powerful CPU.

✦ Use a SMP (Symmetric Multiprocessing) computer, a computer that contains multiple CPUs.

✦ Use hardware RAID to offload some of the processing load to the RAID controllers. This also improves I/O performance because the CPU assists in managing certain aspects of I/O requests behind the scenes.

✦ Optimize memory performance. Behind the scenes, the CPU assists in memory operations such as swapping.

Before selecting one or the other of the optimization strategies described in the preceding list, you must baseline the system's performance, then test each strategy and measure its impact on both the problem you are trying to solve and on overall system performance and responsiveness.

Improving Memory Performance

The total amount of physical memory comes from the capacity of the memory boards installed inside your computer. The virtual-memory subsystem tracks and manages this memory and supplements it with swap space. Because memory operations are much faster than disk I/O operations, buffer caching keeps recently used data read from disk in physical memory. When applications use cached data, performance improves because an in-memory access retrieves data, preventing slow disk access.

Tip   A quick way to detect physical memory (RAM) shortages is to watch `vmstat`'s `sr` (scan rate) column. A traditional performance guideline is that the `sr` that is consistently over 200 indicates a memory bottleneck.

Determining memory requirements

The primary consideration when determining your system's memory requirement is to learn as much as you can about the applications and data on your system so that you can size memory adequately. Sufficient memory (both physical and virtual) is necessary for adequate system performance. In Linux, sizing memory is a cross between a science and an art. If you don't know much about the applications and data on your system, sizing memory is at best a shrewdly educated guess and, at worst, a hopelessly doomed endeavor. When deciding how much memory you need, add up the following:

✦ The amount of memory needed to load the operating system into memory, which includes its normal data tables, the metadata and filesystem buffer caches, and dynamically allocated data structures.

✦ Total memory that processes need to hold data and data structures such as heap storage and stack space.

✦ Total memory required for filesystem data cache.

✦ For each network connection, the computer requires a small amount of memory to support internal structures and buffers such as the following:

- Kernel socket structure.

- Internet protocol control-block (inpcb) structure.

- TCP control-block structure.

- The socket buffer space needed as packets arrive and the kernel processes them.

See Chapter 10, "Managing Filesystems and Swap Space," for more information about sizing physical and virtual memory.

No matter how fast your hard disk is, its access speed is nowhere near that of memory. That's why RAM disks are so fast. They're chunks of memory dedicated to functioning like hard disks.

Reduce swapping

Try to avoid swapping on busy servers. By adding memory, you can keep more programs and data in memory and relieve Linux of the need to swap them out to make room for other programs and data.

Spread swap-file activity across hard disks

On busy servers, you may not be able to add enough memory to eliminate paging and swapping. Creating multiple swap partitions of equal sizes on different physical hard disks improves paging and swapping performance and disk I/O by balancing swap load.

If you spread swap partitions across multiple logical disks (partitions) on the same physical disk, performance degrades because the disk's read/write head must move across many areas of the same disk. When swap partitions are spread across multiple disks, the read/write heads on one disk have a chance to reposition themselves before a read/write operation on another disk finishes.

Sort the ps output by process memory use using the following command:

```
ps -aux | sort -r +
```

More swapping tips

For multiple swap partitions on different disks, use the same priority in fstab so that swap activity can be balanced evenly between the disks — it works like striping the swap space. This works even better with SCSI disks on dual SCSI channels. Keep swap space on disks that are not already heavily accessed.

Always use at least a little swap space even if your computer is rich in physical memory. If you have swap space, Linux swaps inactive processes to use their memory for disk cache and buffers. You are restricting the Linux virtual-memory management system if you don't give it some swap space to play with.

Size swap space big enough to hold a core dump without running out of space. Core dumps are helpful in determining why your system crashed, but since the core file is as large as physical memory, sizing swap space to hold it may not always be practical.

Using hardware to improve memory speed

Improve memory-intensive workloads by choosing computers with large onboard CPU and secondary (and possibly tertiary) caches.

Other Performance Tips

This section offers tips and hints for improving your system's performance that do not fall neatly into the categories discussed earlier in the chapter.

Optimize the X Window System and hardware

The traditional minimum setup for running XFree86 is a 486 processor with at least 16 MB of physical memory. For optimal performance, be sure to have an accelerated video card, such as one that uses, for example, a Matrox or GeForce graphics chip set card that Linux supports.

Tip

Read the Usenet newsgroups `comp.windows.x.i386` and `comp.os.linux.misc.` to see postings about benchmarks for video cards that run under XFree86.

Read all the documentation:

✦ The XFree86 documentation in /usr/X11R6/lib/X11/, especially the XFree86 configuration tutorial file, README.Config.

✦ The README files in /usr/X11R6/lib/X11 for your video chip, such as README.Cirrus and README.S3. Look for a file that applies to your video card. Not all video cards have README files.

✦ The XFree86 man page.

✦ The XF86Config man page.

✦ The man page for your XFree86 server program, such as XF86_SVGA.

Know where to go for help

Subscribe to the Linux-perf mailing list by e-mailing `majordomo@www.klinik.uni-mainz.de` with subscribe linux-perf as the subject.

Browse `linux.com/tuneup/database.phtml/Administration` for hundreds of tips.

Summary

You should monitor system performance regularly. The best way to do this is to use a consistent methodology and set of tools. Linux provides a variety of tools, both command-oriented and GUI, for monitoring disk I/O performance, memory throughput, and CPU use. After collecting enough performance information to form a representative sample of your system's average and peak workloads, identify any bottlenecks. Make system changes only one or two at a time so that you can accurately determine their effectiveness. You may need to add to or replace existing hardware to achieve a satisfactory level of performance.

The following chapter describes how to monitor and optimize network performance. Optimizing network performance can affect disk I/O performance, memory throughput, and CPU use disk I/O performance, memory throughput, and CPU use.

✦　　✦　　✦

Monitoring and Optimizing Network Performance

Network performance involves much more than the packets that flow across a cable or other connection medium. Before you start optimizing your network, be sure that you understand what's involved:

✦ What networking topology (wiring scheme) will you use—Ethernet or token ring?

✦ What kind of network interface cards (NICs) do you use?

✦ What type of connections do you have to the Internet (such as, T1 link or dial-up)?

✦ What computers and other networks are you connected to?

✦ Are your computers clients, servers, or both?

✦ If your computer is a server, what kind of services does it provide?

✦ What applications do you use that require networking?

Note This chapter is about the TCP/IP internetworking protocol suite. Linux supports other networking protocols, such as IPX/SPX and DECnet (in the 2.3 experimental kernel), and while much of the information in this chapter applies to general networking concepts and performance, this chapter does not specifically discuss other protocols.

Is your Local Host a Server? What Kind of Server?

Servers and clients must be configured for networking in different ways and will make different performance demands on the network configuration. For example, a laptop client that browses the Web and performs occasional FTP downloads places a much different load on the network from an enterprise-wide file or Web server. This chapter is primarily about network servers. The next few sections describe the most common types of network servers.

What's a file server?

Although the term *server* traditionally refers to software that services client requests, this chapter expands that definition to include software that works on a dedicated computer. Therefore, in this chapter, the term *file server* refers to software and hardware that work together to provide file-handling and storage functions for multiple users on a LAN or WAN.

Cross-Reference   Chapter 22, "Configuring the Network File System (NFS)," describes the most popular file-sharing software in the networking environment.

What's a mail server?

Although the term *server* traditionally refers to software that services client requests, this chapter expands that definition to include software that works on a dedicated computer. Therefore, in this chapter, the term *mail server* refers to the software and hardware that provide email services.

Cross-Reference   Chapter 24, "Configuring E-mail and Other Communications Services," describes MTAs (Mail Transfer Agents).

What's a Web server?

Although the term *server* traditionally refers to software that services client requests, this chapter expands that definition to include software that works on a dedicated computer. Therefore, in this chapter, the term *Web server* refers to software and hardware that work together to store Web pages and provide services so that your browser can connect to the Web server, and request and receive Web pages. Most Web-server software includes features such as URL redirection, HTTP and SSL (Secure Socket Layer) support, server management, monitors, log files, CGI scripting, and access control for multiple users on a LAN or WAN.

Cross-Reference   Chapter 26, "Configuring a Web Server," describes Apache, the most widely implemented Web-server software on the Internet.

What's a compute server?

Although the term *server* traditionally refers to software that services client requests, this chapter expands that definition to include software that works on a dedicated computer. Therefore, in this chapter, the term *compute server* refers to software and hardware that work together to accept client requests in the form of tasks, provide CPU cycles to perform the tasks (computations), and return the results to the clients on a LAN or WAN. The server computes the results and manages the system resources needed to do the job.

The SETI@home project is an example of a special-purpose compute server. The SETI compute server is a group of networked PCs around the world running the SETI@home screen saver. The screen saver is the glue that attaches the PCs to form a single special-purpose compute that searches for messages from space. When SETI@home sees idle cycles on any PC running its screen saver, the SETI server uses those extra CPU cycles to search for artificial signals of extraterrestrial origin within radio-telescope data.

Your compute server may not perform tasks as exotic as SETI. Your server may simply be an IBM AS400 running Linux to provide shared expense-reporting services to clients on your intranet. Nonetheless, it is as much a compute server as the SETI server is.

Using Tools to Find the Bottleneck

To optimize network performance, you need to monitor both the network and the hosts on the network. The performance of one affects the performance of the other. When host performance is slow, the actual problem may be a saturated network. Conversely, when it takes too long to send and receive data across the network, you may find that the network has plenty of unused capacity because host-performance problems prevent the efficient use of the available network bandwidth. On the other hand, if you solve certain host-performance problems, a network that had been functioning efficiently may suddenly become saturated. Solving host problems may enable the host to send more data more quickly across the network.

Linux has network-monitoring tools built into the operating system. Those tools include the following programs:

- ✦ ping
- ✦ netstat
- ✦ nfstat

Beyond using the tools listed above, you should also examine your system and application logs for network events. A network analyzer is another indispensable tool for monitoring and troubleshooting networks.

Using ping

When you can't reach a machine on your network, your first check should be to use ping. It sends a message across the network to the remote system requesting a response. When ping responds, as in the following example, it confirms that the remote host is responding to requests, and that there is a valid, functional route from your computer to the remote computer. If the system doesn't respond, you've got a problem. Possibly networking services are malfunctioning or the remote host is down, or there is a network hardware problem. ping doesn't tell you a lot about what's wrong. However, if you cannot reach a remote host through an application, such as FTP, but you can ping that host, you can eliminate the network as the problem.

```
root@flyingpenguin# ping bigbird
PING bigbird.cardinalconsulting.com (192.168.0.1) from
192.168.0.241 : 56(84) by
tes of data.
64 bytes from 192.168.0.1: icmp_seq=0 ttl=128 time=1.1 ms
64 bytes from 192.168.0.1: icmp_seq=1 ttl=128 time=0.7 ms
64 bytes from 192.168.0.1: icmp_seq=2 ttl=128 time=0.6 ms

--- bigbird.cardinalconsulting.com ping statistics ---
3 packets transmitted, 3 packets received, 0% packet loss
round-trip min/avg/max = 0.6/0.8/1.1 ms

root@flyingpenguin# ping tweety
ping: unknown host tweety
#-- It turns out, Tweety's PC Card Network Interface is broken
```

Using ifconfig to display and modify network-card settings

Use ifconfig to see both the TCP/IP and hardware settings of your network-interface card. Two important configuration values for you to troubleshoot are the interrupt and base address. These values correspond to the IRQ and I/O Port addresses for the network card. If Linux can't see your network card, these values may be incorrect or conflicting with some other device.

```
marshall@flyingpenguin$ /sbin/ifconfig eth0
eth0      Link encap:Ethernet  HWaddr 00:60:08:F5:27:09
          inet addr:192.168.0.241  Bcast:192.168.0.255  Mask:255.255.255.0
          UP BROADCAST RUNNING MULTICAST  MTU:1500  Metric:1
          RX packets:5879 errors:0 dropped:0 overruns:0 frame:0
          TX packets:2111 errors:0 dropped:0 overruns:0 carrier:0
          collisions:1225 txqueuelen:100
          Interrupt:3 Base address:0x300
```

ifconfig lists collisions for the Ethernet interface. Examining the collisions statistic helps you determine whether packets are reaching their destinations as quickly as possible without needing to be retransmitted. All of the hosts attached to your Ethernet segment share the cable (or other transmission medium). When multiple systems try to send packets at the same time, a collision occurs as a packet from one host bumps into a packet from a different host. Only one packet can go on the wire at the same time. Collisions are a fact of life on most Ethernets. If the number of collisions increases steadily (compared to the total network traffic), network performance degrades. In the preceding example, the number of collisions is high compared to the total number of received (RX) and transmitted (TX) packets.

Other important information in the ifconfig display includes:

Hardware address	Also known as the MAC address, the address built into the network card. The MAC address is bound to the card, not the computer. Since the network for this book connects to the Internet via cable modem, when I bought a new network card for the server I had to notify the cable company of the new hardware address on the new card. If you have multiple network cards installed, each one has its own unique hardware address.
MTU	The Maximum Transmission Unit, the largest block of data the connection can carry. Ethernet limits the MTU size to 1500 bytes.
inet (IP) address	This is the host's IP address, followed by the broadcast address and the subnet mask.

 Tip Ethernet works well for a workload of up to about 75% capacity. As use increases over 75%, collisions begin to degrade performance. The network in the preceding code example was very slow at the time the example was captured.

Besides reporting on the network interface(s), ifconfig enables you to update the configuration of the interface if you believe it to be inaccurate.

Looking for problems and events in system log files

Check system log files regularly for network problems. The following example lists the files in the path /var/log. You can tell from the names which of these log files are network-related, such as the directory /var/log/httpd.

```
root@flyingpenguin # pwd
/var/log
root@flyingenguin# ls -R
.:
```

```
boot.log      cron.4           maillog.4        netconf.log.4   spooler     xferlog
boot.log.1    dmesg            messages         news            spooler.1   xferlog.1
boot.log.2    htmlaccess.log   messages.1       pacct           spooler.2   xferlog.2
boot.log.3    httpd            messages.2       savacct         spooler.3   xferlog.3
boot.log.4    lastlog          messages.3       secure          spooler.4   xferlog.4
btmp          lastlog.1        messages.4       secure.1        squid
cron          maillog          netconf.log      secure.2        usracct
cron.1        maillog.1        netconf.log.1    secure.3        vbox
cron.2        maillog.2        netconf.log.2    secure.4        wtmp
cron.3        maillog.3        netconf.log.3    sendmail.st     wtmp.1

httpd:
access_log    access_log.2    access_log.4   error_log.1   error_log.3
access_log.1  access_log.3    error_log      error_log.2   error_log.4

news:
OLD  news.crit  news.err  news.notice
```

The following example displays the contents of the file secure.1. The secure.# files show network access. The computer at IP address 192.168.0.5 is opus, an IBM ThinkPad running Microsoft Windows 95.

```
root@flyingpenguin# more secure.1
Jul 23 18:13:43 flyingpenguin in.telnetd[3300]: connect from 192.168.0.5
Jul 23 18:13:54 flyingpenguin login: LOGIN ON 2 BY miss_scarlet FROM 192.168.0.5
------------- output edited ----------------
```

Using the /proc filesystem to find network-device information

The directory /proc/net contains current information about your network interfaces. The following example displays the file /proc/net/dev.

```
root@flyingpenguin# more /proc/net/dev
Inter-|   Receive                                                |  Transmit
 face |bytes      packets errs drop fifo frame compressed multicast|bytes      packe
ts errs drop fifo colls carrier compressed
    lo:   12342     216    0    0    0    0           0         0    12342       2
16   0    0    0    0        0         0

  eth0: 1831259   10532    0    0    0    0           0         0  1843188      48
28   0    0    0   42        0         0
```

The information in the preceding code example is basically a list of counters for each network interface on the computer. The line for eth0 is for the Ethernet card. The Receive and Transmit byte and packet counters show data moving across the network. On your hosts, check the errs, drop, and carrier columns for both

Transmit and Receive. These columns indicate errors and problems on the network. For example, the carrier column counts attempts to move data across the network that were interrupted by a problem with the connection. It's not unusual to see occasional errors popping up: that's to be expected. If your network is slowing down over time, the values in these columns have most likely been steadily increasing. If you need to watch these values closely, you can write a bash script that prints out the values regularly.

Cross-Reference Chapter 30, "Shell Scripting for System Administrators," includes a simple script that automatically monitors /proc/net/dev every three seconds.

Using netstat to monitor network connections

You can use the netstat command on your local host to monitor network connections (sockets), send queues, routing tables and interface performance. To monitor the local host's network status, use the netstat command followed (if you wish) by the command options. If you use the netstat command with no options, the default display shows the open sockets. The following example shows the default netstat output.

```
marshall@flyingpenguin# netstat
Active Internet connections (w/o servers)
Proto Recv-Q Send-Q Local Address          Foreign Address         State
tcp      1      0 flyingpenguin.card:1057 vwww-mv1.netscape.c:www CLOSE_WAIT
tcp      1      0 flyingpenguin.card:1056 vwww-mv1.netscape.c:www CLOSE_WAIT
tcp      1      0 flyingpenguin.card:1055 vwww-mv1.netscape.c:www CLOSE_WAIT
tcp      0      0 flyingpenguin.card:1054 ads.web.aol.com:www     TIME_WAIT
tcp      0      0 flyingpenguin.card:1053 h-207-200-83-93.net:www TIME_WAIT
tcp      0      0 flyingpenguin.card:1052 myvipa.netscape.co:www  TIME_WAIT
tcp      0      0 flyingpenguin.card:1051 ads.web.aol.com:www     TIME_WAIT
tcp      0      0 flyingpenguin.ca:telnet 192.168.0.5:1196        ESTABLISHED
            --- very long local socket output edited ---
```

The preceding example shows all the active Internet sockets. The first column, Proto, lists the protocol. When this example was captured, only tcp appeared in the Proto column. You may also see udp in this column. The next two fields are very important fields to monitor. They are Send-Q and Recv-Q, which display the length of the network send queue and receive queue. The send and receive queues show the number of bytes of data ready and waiting to be sent or received, respectively. If the send queue for most connections across the network segment is steadily growing, that network may be saturated with traffic. If you see a single high send-queue value, monitor the local host to see if it has a performance problem. The Local Address column is the host you're monitoring. The Foreign Address column is where you're connected. (In this example, people were using the Netscape Navigator browser to surf to netscape.com and aol.com.) The State column displays the current connections to the Internet.

The most useful options for netstat are:

✦ -i, which displays the current interface status. (Pay attention to sent and received packets, collisions, and errors.)

✦ -r, which displays the current routing table and flags for the current status of each route.

✦ -a, which displays the information for a specific connection

✦ -s, which lists the statistics for connections, packets transmitted and received, errors, and forwarding. The information varies with the Linux distribution.

Using netstat with the -i option shows information similar to that shown by ifconfig (see Table 33-1). The following example shows that operations on the Ethernet interface (eth0) are error free, and that no packets are being dropped. About twice as many packets are being received (RX-OK) as transmitted (TX-OK). No packets have been dropped (DRP), or have errors (ERR) or overruns (OVR).

```
marshall@flyingpenguin# netstat -i
Kernel Interface table
Iface  MTU Met    RX-OK RX-ERR RX-DRP RX-OVR    TX-OK TX-ERR TX-DRP TX-OVR Flg
eth0   1500   0    6284      0      0      0     2334      0      0      0 BRU
lo     3924   0       9      0      0      0        9      0      0      0 LRU
```

Table 33-1
Meaning of netstat -i Output Fields

Field	Meaning
Iface	Name of the interface.
MTU	Maximum transmission unit. The size of data transferred (except for interface specific headers).
RX-OK	Number of error-free packets received.
RX-ERR	Number of packets received with bugs.
RX-DRP	Number of dropped received packets.
RX-OVR	Number of packets not able to be received.
TX-OK	Number of error free packets transmitted.
TX-ERR	Number of packets transmitted with bugs.
TX-DRP	Number of dropped transmitted packets.
TX-OVR	Number of packets that could not be transmitted.

Field	Meaning
Flags	Attributes of the interface.
A	Able to receive all multicast addresses.
B	Able to receive broadcasts.
D	Debugging is on.
M	Promiscuous mode. This mode looks at all packets on the LAN, regardless of destination.
N	No trailers.
O	No Address Resolution Protocol (ARP).
P	Point-to-Point connection.
R	Interface is running.
U	Interface is up.

Tip

Using `netstat -s` shows yet another view of your network. The most important statistic in the following example is the retransmission count under TCP. Compare it to the data-transmission count. A retransmission percentage of 20%–25% (or more) suggests a bottleneck.

```
[miss_scarlet@redbird$ netstat -s
Ip:
    10972 total packets received
    0 forwarded
    0 incoming packets discarded
    5872 incoming packets delivered
    5049 requests sent out
Icmp:
    34 ICMP messages received
    0 input ICMP message failed.
    ICMP input histogram:
        destination unreachable: 27
        echo requests: 4
        echo replies: 3
    65 ICMP messages sent
    0 ICMP messages failed
    ICMP output histogram:
        destination unreachable: 61
        echo replies: 4
Tcp:
    24 active connections openings
    0 passive connection openings
```

A Brief Overview of Sockets

A *socket* is a method used to enable communication between a client and a server. The socket can be implemented across a network or locally on a single host. A typical set of client/server activities that sockets implement is shown in the following table.

On the Server	On the Client
Wait for a sendto request from some client.	Sendto requests Web page.
Process the sendto request.	Send the HTML page.
Perform the sendto, reply to the client request.	Recvfrom receives the Web page.

```
      0 failed connection attempts
      0 connection resets received
      1 connections established
      5066 segments received
      4232 segments send out
      5 segments retransmited
      0 bad segments received.
      0 resets sent
Udp:
      2595 packets received
      34 packets to unknown port received.
      0 packet receive errors
      767 packets sent
TcpExt:
      27 ICMP packets dropped because they were out-of-
window
```

See Chapter 20, "Configuring the Network," for an explanation of the protocols listed above (TCP, IP, UDP, and ICMP).

Table 33-2 lists some `netstat` command options.

See the man pages on the CD included with this book for a complete list of `netstat` options.

Table 33-2
Some netstat Command Options

Option	Description
-A	Display the address of associated protocol-control blocks.

Option	Description
-a	Show information for all sockets.
-faddress_family	Show statistics or address-control block reports for the specified address_ family.
-Iinterface	Display information about interface.
-i	Display status for autoconfigured interfaces.
-m	Display memory-use data.
-n	List numeric network addresses
-r	List the routing tables.
-s	Display statistics per protocol.

Using nfsstat to find NFS performance problems

nfsstat displays help you find network-performance problems that are caused by NFS (the Network File System). For example, you can use nfsstat to determine whether your network is having connection problems.

✦ The badcalls statistics show the number of defective RPC messages processed by the system. badcalls could mean that you have authentication problems (these occur when a user is in too many groups) or that people have been trying to access exported filesystems as root.

✦ The nullrecv and badlen statistics show the number of empty or incomplete messages. A nullrecv greater than 0 means empty messages. NFS requests are not arriving fast enough to keep all of the nfsd daemons busy. Reduce the number of NFS server daemons until nullrecv is 0. This saves CPU and returns memory to your host's operating system. It also removes the useless network overhead of moving empty messages.

✦ The xdrcall statistics show the number of errors in understanding messages.

Tip

Because NFS uses RPC (Remote Procedure Calls) for client/server communication, nfsstat also displays RPC statistics by default. Use the -n option to see only NFS statistics.

The following example uses the -s option to show only server statistics.

```
# nfsstat -s
Server RPC:
calls        badcalls     nullrecv     badlen       xdrcall      duphits      dupage
50852        0            0            0            0            0            0.00
```

```
Server NFS:
calls        badcalls
50852        0
null         getattr       setattr       root          lookup        readlink
1  0%        233  0%       0  0%         0  0%         1041  2%      0  0%
read         wrcache       write         create        remove        rename
49498 97%    0  0%         0  0%         0  0%         0  0%         0  0%
link         symlink       mkdir         rmdir         readdir       fsstat
0  0%        0  0%         0  0%         0  0%         75  0%        4  0%
```

Finding and Fixing Network and Server Bottlenecks

The next sections briefly discuss how disk I/O, memory, and CPU performance affect network performance. Read the basics about monitoring and optimizing those areas of performance in Chapter 32. What seems to be a network bottleneck may actually be a performance problem on a host. What seems to be slow performance on a host may actually be the result of a network bottleneck.

Collision advice

In addition to collisions caused by simultaneous transmissions on the same network segment, various other extenuating conditions might cause errors in transmission or reception of data. Hardware problems, such as defective hubs and switches or malfunctioning network cards, might be responsible for high collision statistics. High collision rates can also result from rare and strange events. In one case that I know of, network performance in a harborside building degraded from collisions every time a naval vessel entered or left port. The electromagnetic field from devices on the ship, not even in the same building as the network, interfered with network functioning. The solution was to move the offices and their network segment away from the outside wall above the harbor to an inner office suite. The bottom line is that as the number of collisions and other errors on your network increases — regardless of why it increases — the performance of the network suffers.

One way to reduce collisions and improve network performance is to upgrade the network hardware. Fast Ethernet, running at 100 Mbps (Megabits per second) is 10 times faster than Ethernet. Fast Ethernet's capacity reduces collisions, thereby improving performance under heavy workloads. Gigabit Ethernet, running at 1 Gigabit per second, 10 times faster than Fast Ethernet, radically improves performance if collisions are the cause of a network bottleneck. For token-ring fans, FDDI, at 100 Mbps, is an alternative to Ethernet. A Web server connected with Ethernet that had a 23 percent collision rate measurably benefited by connecting the router to the Internet via Fast Ethernet. Both Fast and Gigabit Ethernet have a tradeoff — cost for speed. You need to purchase network cards, switches, and hubs that support the faster Ethernet flavors.

Where's the bottleneck on file servers?

On a file server, the area of performance most likely to cause problems is disk I/O. Whether the computer services Samba or NFS clients, those clients are requesting disk files to be sent across the network. Saturated network bandwidth is the second-most common bottleneck. Be sure that your network hardware has enough bandwidth to deliver those files. The performance of the network card(s) should be a primary concern. At the least, you should use SCSI hard drives, but consider Ultra-SCSI. If you use IDE disks, you should also be concerned about the associated CPU overhead on the server.

Where's the bottleneck on mail servers?

Mail servers run into the same bottlenecks as file servers. SMTP mail servers have considerations and requirements that are similar to those of file servers. The main responsibility of a mail server is to move e-mail onto or off the network. Disk I/O is a key area to monitor and optimize. Be sure to use a high-performance network card(s).

There are performance implications for the various client/server mail protocols: POP3 versus IMAP4 versus HTTP (Web mail such as HotMail, Office.com, Yahoo Mail, and others). Of course, in all cases the number of simultaneous users is the biggest performance factor.

POP3 (Post Office Protocol 3) is a fairly simple protocol designed to help end users download mail from the server to their local computers. This means that a POP3 mail server basically acts like an ordinary file server. The file server must be able to support the I/O for delivering e-mail files to the client. Other than that, POP3 has a low performance penalty, because it provides very simple functionality.

IMAP4 (Internet Message Access Protocol 4) is a richer environment than POP3 and provides the end user with more features and functionality. Your IMAP4 server receives and stores your e-mail. If you wish, you can review just the header and sender of the message before deciding whether to download your mail. You can also create and manage folders and messages across the network on the server. IMAP4 requires access to the server while you work with your e-mail. Since the mail server that uses IMAP4 has to work harder than a POP3 server to support those features, IMAP4 has higher performance penalty on a server.

When a Web server (HTTP — Hypertext Transfer Protocol) provides mail services, it is doing more than just providing static HTML Web pages. The server has to process users' requests to create, read, forward, and delete messages, to store them in folders, upload and download attachments, manage contacts — all the things you expect a mail system to be able to do.

Caution If you decide to improve functionality or server performance by switching your users to a different protocol, you have to (re)train them on the new client software and features/functionality.

Where's the bottleneck on Web servers?

On a LAN (Local Area Network) where the organization's data sharing is Web-based, your intranet Web servers are heavily loaded and require top-of-the-line hardware to satisfy network requests without making users wait. For both Ethernet and token ring, use a 100 Mbs link. Be sure you know whether your Web servers dish up mostly static content (HTML pages) or dynamic content (Dynamic HTML and/or CGI pages and/or Java Server Pages).

Tip   The advantage of running a server suite such as Lotus Domino is that instead of running separate server tasks (SMTP, LDAP, POP3, IMAP4, HTTP) written by a committee of committees, you run an integrated suite of services that include security and are designed to work together.

Disks and the network are the places to look for bottlenecks when your Web server serves mostly static (HTML) pages. CPU power is usually not an issue. You can even use an old Pentium system to function as a Web server. The main function of the CPU in this environment is to dish out pages from disk to the network. Because processing is limited to taking static HTML pages off the disk(s) and throwing them onto the wire, you don't need a powerful CPU. There's no real computing going on. The bottleneck is either disk I/O or a network configuration that is too slow to handle the load.

Where's the bottleneck for dynamic content?

With dynamic content, the bottleneck potential shifts to the host's CPU and the network bandwidth.

Is the CPU a bottleneck?

The CPU has much more work to do to support delivering dynamic content, which is delivered on demand. For example, CGI is interpreted as it runs. With DHTML, the whole point is that the server can't store static pages. It must create them on demand for the users. CPU replaces disk I/O as the potential bottleneck on the server. If your server only has one network card installed, all the traffic goes through that single network card. The http daemon (httpd) is probably active and busy all the time. The CPU has to be powerful enough to support the requirements of the httpd server and to generate the Web pages on demand. Upgrading to a SMP (symmetric multiprocessing) host can relieve the CPU bottleneck.

Is it a network bottleneck?

One limiting factor on network bandwidth is the bus to which the network card is connected. (The *bus* is the connection between the computer and its device interfaces — in this case, the network card.)

Multithreading

Think about dining in a restaurant. Multiple servers (waiters) serve a wide variety of multi-course meals to a large group of diners who are in a wide variety of stages of their meals. Each waiter is a single multithreaded executable capable of remembering the context and status for each table's meal. If you're at a table with a good waiter, you have no idea that you're sharing your waiter with other tables (timesharing). The bottleneck is the door in and out of the kitchen. The waiters are efficient, but they sometimes queue up at the door waiting to get through. Sometimes a waiter going into the kitchen collides in the doorway with a waiter going out. How can the restaurant owner maximize the performance of his very efficient servers? The owner can upgrade the entrance to the kitchen by installing a separate door for each waiter. That way a waiter never needs to wait to go through the door.

Multiple NIC cards equals multiple doors to/from the kitchen (the network).

ISA is a common bus on older PCs that only allows 16 bits at a time to flow between the motherboard circuitry and the network card. So if you have an ISA bus architecture, the bus bandwidth is very likely to limit the amount of data getting to the network card and, therefore, is very likely to be the bottleneck. To relieve a bus bottleneck, upgrade to a computer with a PCI bus. One of the reasons PCI is so much faster than ISA is that PCI allows either 32 or 64 bits at a time (depending on the number of pins in the connector) to flow between the motherboard circuitry and the network card. It's especially important to use PCI if the server handles many users or uses 100 Mbit Ethernet.

Another potential network bottleneck is the network-interface card. Be sure that the host's network card can use the full capacity of the network. This means choosing a network card that supports the best transmission methods and speeds of the network. For example, if the network supports Full Duplex mode, make sure you are running in full duplex, with network-card configuration software, switches, and so forth all set to full duplex mode.

Note   The term *full duplex* refers to data-transmission methods on a bidirectional cable or network medium. Full duplex means that clients can transmit network data in both directions (send/receive) at the same time. 10 Mbps Ethernet is usually half-duplex, meaning that traffic can flow in only one direction at a time. 100 Mbps is full duplex.

Additionally, if the network card is a multiple interface card that automatically detects 10 Mbit or 100 Mbit Ethernet, do a sanity check and verify that it has really switched to 100 Mbits where the network supports it.

If the bottleneck lies in getting to the network, you can add more network capacity by adding more network cards to the host. Using multiple network cards multithreads access to the network.

Summary

For most sites, it's a fact of life that the more network bandwidth you offer to users, the more they use and the more they need. Network and system administrators monitor and optimize their networks more often now than they ever have before. While Linux provides built-in tools to monitor a network, understanding the output requires that you understand both the hardware and software that make up your network. You must also tune each server host on the network so that a computer-performance problem does not masquerade as a network-performance problem. Improving a network's performance usually requires major time and money.

This chapter showed you some of the tools Linux provides to monitor network performance. Additionally, this chapter described some common performance problems that beset various kinds of network servers, and solutions and recommendations to those problems.

This chapter dealt with basic networking issues for the TCP/IP protocol suite and Linux hosts. The next chapter moves further into networking by telling you how to form a network by combining Linux hosts with hosts running other operating systems.

✦   ✦   ✦

Integrating Linux into Heterogeneous Networks

In this chapter you will learn how to connect a computer running Linux to a computer running Microsoft Windows 95 or greater. You will also learn how to print from your Linux computer to a printer connected to a Windows computer.

Sharing Linux Filesystems with MS Windows 95, 98, 2000, and NT

Computers running Windows 95 or greater use a protocol called *Server Message Block* (SMB) to communicate with each other and to share services like file and print sharing. Using a program called Samba, you can emulate the SMB protocol and connect a PC running Linux to a Windows network to share files and printers. The Linux PC will appear in the Windows Network Neighborhood window and the files on the Linux PC can be browsed using the Windows Explorer.

Installing Samba

Before you can use Samba to connect to the Windows computers, it must first be installed on the Linux PC. All current distributions of Linux include Samba, but it may not have been installed during the system installation. Even if it is has been installed, it is always a good idea to check for the latest version, to find out if any problems have been fixed by the latest release. To check if Samba is installed on your system, type the following command:

```
rpm -q samba
```

If Samba is not installed, the command returns the output shown in Figure 34-1.

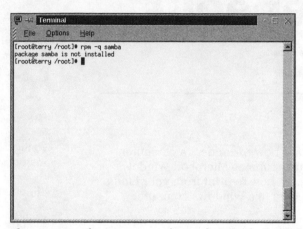

Figure 34-1: The rpm query shows that Samba is not installed on this system

If Samba is installed, the rpm query returns the version number as shown in Figure 34-2.

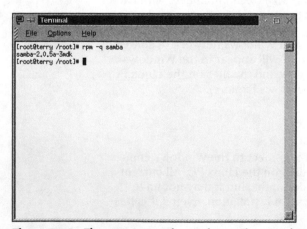

Figure 34-2: The rpm query shows the version number of Samba that is installed on this system

Note You can get the latest version of Samba at the Samba Web site: `http://www.`
`samba.org`. The current version as of this writing is 2.0.7. Follow the instructions
at the site for downloading the rpm file for your distribution.

After downloading the Samba rpm file, install it as follows:

```
rpm -i samba(number of version downloaded)
```

If you are unable to download the rpm version, or you want to compile the program
yourself, then download the file samba-latest.tar.gz. Extract the file using the following command:

```
tar -xfvz samba-latest.tar.gz
```

Change to the directory containing the extracted files (usually /usr/src) and then
type `./configure`. Press Enter and wait for the command prompt to return. From
the command prompt type `make` and then press Enter and wait for the command
prompt to return. Finally, type `install` from the command prompt. If all goes well,
when the command prompt returns, Samba is installed. Now you will need to configure it.

In order for Samba to provide its services, you must configure both the Linux PC
and the Windows PC. We'll start with the Linux PC and then move on to the
Windows PC. In this chapter I will refer to the Linux PC as the *Samba server* and the
Windows PC as the *Samba client*.

Configuring the Samba server

Beginning with version 2.0, Samba includes a utility called SWAT, the Samba Web
Administration Tool. This tool makes setting up Samba very easy. The main Samba
configuration file is /etc/smb.conf. SWAT enables you to use a Web browser as the
interface to /etc/smb.conf and will make the necessary modifications to this file.
While you are using SWAT to make the configuration changes, you will learn more
about the smb.conf file. A sample smb.conf file was created during the installation,
and you can use it for reference. It would be a good idea to rename this file because
you will be creating a new smb.conf using SWAT and it will overwrite the original file.

The smb.conf file

The smb.conf file is divided into several sections, which are shown with the title of
the section in brackets. Listing 34-1 shows the smb.conf file from one of the computers on my home network. Following the listing is a complete description of the
items in the smb.conf file.

Listing 34-1: **smb.conf file**

```
# Samba config file created using SWAT
# from localhost (127.0.0.1)
# Date: 2000/05/25 10:29:40
# Global parameters
[global]
    workgroup = ONE
    netbios name = TERRY
    server string = Samba Server
    security = SHARE
    log file = /var/log/samba/log
    max log size = 50
    socket options = TCP_NODELAY SO_RCVBUF=8192 SO_SNDBUF=8192
    dns proxy = No
    wins support = Yes
    hosts allow = 192.168.1.
    hosts deny = All
[homes]
    comment = Home Directories
    read only = No
[printers]
    comment = All Printers
    path = /var/spool/samba
    guest ok = Yes
    print ok = Yes
    browseable = Yes
[nancy]
    path = /oldwin
    valid users = nancy
    read only = No
    guest ok = No
    browseable = yes
```

Each section contains a list of options and values in the following format:

```
option = value
```

There are hundreds of options and values and you will look at the most common ones here, as shown in Listing 34-1. For a complete listing of options, refer to the smb.conf man page.

The [global] section

The first section of the smb.conf file is the [global] section.

workgroup   ONE is the name of the workgroup shown in the
                         Identification tab of the Network Properties box on the
                         Windows computer.

netbios name	TERRY is the name by which the Samba server is known to the Windows computers on my network.
Server string	Samba server is the name of the Samba server.
security	SHARE is the level of security applied to server access. Possible options are user, which is the default setting, domain and server. Using SHARE makes it easier to create anonymous shares that do not require authentication, and it is useful when the netbios names of the Windows computers are different from other names on the Linux computer.
log file	/var/log/samba/log is the location of the log file.
max log size	50 is the maximum size in kilobytes that the file can grow to.
socket options	TCP_NODELAY SO_RCVBUF=8192 SO_SNDBUF=8192 allows the server to be tuned for better performance. TCP_NODELAY is a default value. The BUF values set send and receive buffers.
dns proxy	No indicates that the netbios name will not be treated like a DNS name and that there is no DNS lookup.
wins support	Yes tells the Samba server to act as a WINS server.
hosts allow	192.168.1. means that requests from this network will be accepted.
hosts deny	All hosts' requests will be denied.

The [homes] section

The next section of the smb.conf file is [homes]. This section allows the server to give users quick access to their home directories. Refer to the smb.conf man page for a more complete description of how the [homes] section works.

comment	Home Directories is a comment line.
read only	No specifies that users can write to their directories.

The [printers] section

This section sets the options for printing.

path	/var/spool/samba is the location of the printer spool directory.
guest ok	Yes allows guest access to the printer.
print ok	Yes enables clients to send print jobs to the specified directory. This must be set or printing will not work.
browseable	Yes means that the printer will appear in the browse list.

The [nancy] section

The last section of this smb.conf file is called [nancy]. This is the computer that my wife uses so I named this share for her.

path	/oldwin is the path to the directory accessible by nancy.
valid users	nancy specifies the users that can use the shares.
read only	No allows write access to the directory.
guest ok	No prevents guest acess.
browseable	Yes means that the share will be visible in browse lists.

The smb.conf file you just analyzed was created using the SWAT program (as indicated by the comment lines at the beginning of the file). It is also possible to create this file from scratch by entering values for the options shown above, or by modifying the smb.conf file that is installed along with the program. Remember that you looked at a simple file for a small network. Always refer to the smb.conf man page for complete details about options and values.

Now you will use SWAT to configure smb.conf.

Using SWAT

Before you can use SWAT, you need to change two files to enable it. The first file is /etc/services. This file is a list of Internet services and their port numbers and protocols. You need to add the following line to /etc/services:

```
swat        901/tcp
```

Next you need to add a line to /etc/inetd.conf. The inetd daemon runs at system startup and listens for connections at specific ports. The inetd.conf file lists the programs that should be run when the inetd daemon detects a request at one of the ports. You need to add the following line:

```
swat        stream  tcp     nowait.400      root /usr/sbin/swat
```

If you're interested in more details about the line you added, look at the inetd man page.

Finally, you need to restart the inetd daemon so it will read the changes you made to inetd.conf. To do this, type the following at the command prompt:

```
killall -HUP inetd
```

Now you can start a Web browser and get ready to run SWAT. (Since most distributions include Netscape, I'll use this browser to start SWAT.) In the location box enter the address for localhost and the port number for SWAT as `http://localhost:901`. This will open a box asking for a user ID and password as shown in Figure 34-3.

Figure 34-3: After you enter the address for localhost and the port number used by SWAT, you are prompted for a user ID and password

You have to be root in order to configure Samba, so enter root as the user ID and the password for root. The main SWAT screen, as shown in Figure 34-4, will appear after entering the user ID and password.

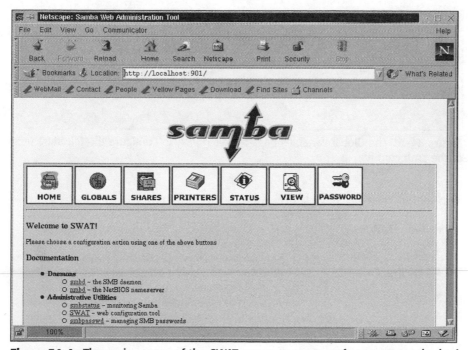

Figure 34-4: The main screen of the SWAT program appears after you enter the login information

You will begin configuring the [globals] section by clicking on the Globals icon. The Global Variables page appears as shown in Figure 34-5. The values shown are being read from the smb.conf file that already exists on the system. As I mentioned earlier, all systems include a default smb.conf that will be used by SWAT. The values shown in your file will be different from those shown in the figures since I have already made configuration changes.

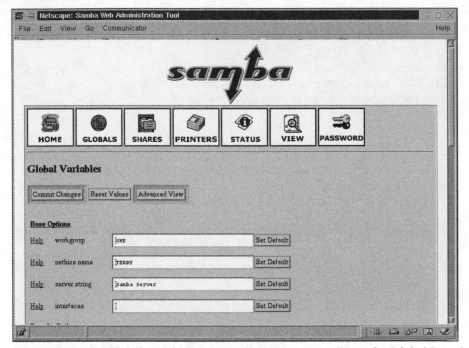

Figure 34-5: The Global Variables page makes it easy to configure the [globals] section of the smb.conf file

The Global Variables page is divided into six sections:

✦ Base Options

✦ Security Options

✦ Logging Options

✦ Tuning Options

✦ Browse Options

✦ WINS Options

Figure 34-6 shows the Base and Security Options sections.

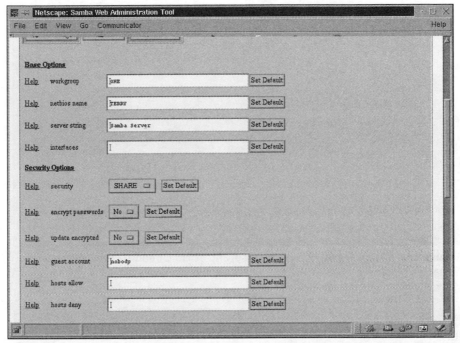

Figure 34-6: The Base and Security Options sections of the Global Variables page of SWAT

As you can see, the options shown here are the same options you looked at in the smb.conf file. The values shown are the values you previously saw for my system. To configure Samba for your system, use your own values for the options in these sections. Figure 34-7 shows the remaining four sections of the Global Variables page.

After you have entered the appropriate values for your system, click the Commit Changes button to save them to the file. Next you will create shares by clicking on the Shares icon. This will open the Share Parameters page as shown in Figure 34-8.

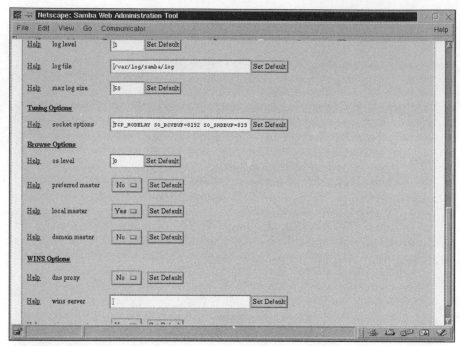

Figure 34-7: The Logging, Tuning, Browse, and WINS Option sections of the Global Variables page

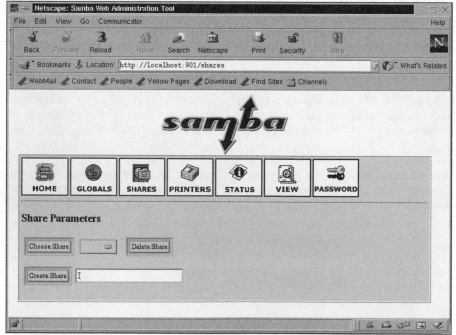

Figure 34-8: The Share Parameters page enables you to create and modify shares

To create a new share, fill in a name for the share and click the Create Share button. An expanded Share Parameters page, as shown in Figure 34-9, will appear.

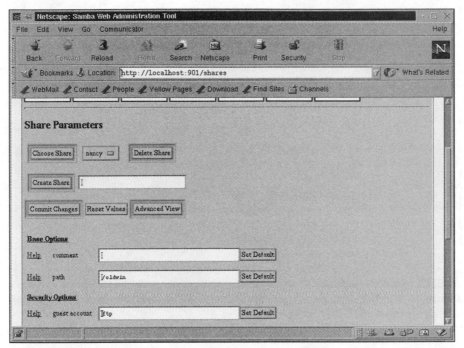

Figure 34-9: The expanded Share Parameters page enables you to enter the configuration information for Windows computers that can access the Samba server

As you can see in Figure 34-9, I have entered the appropriate information for the share [nancy], which is my wife's computer running Windows 95. (The information here is the same information we discussed earlier when looking at the smb.conf file.) Enter the appropriate information for your computer and then click Commit Changes to save them to the smb.conf file.

Next you will set up a printer that the Windows computer can use for printing. Clicking the Printers icon will open the Printer Parameters page where you can create and modify printer information. This page is similar to the Share Parameters page except that you need to create or select a printer rather than a share. To create a new printer, type in the name of the printer and click Create Printer. If you already have a printer configured, it will be marked with an asterisk and you can select it from the dropdown list. An expanded Printer Parameters page, as shown in Figure 34-10, will open.

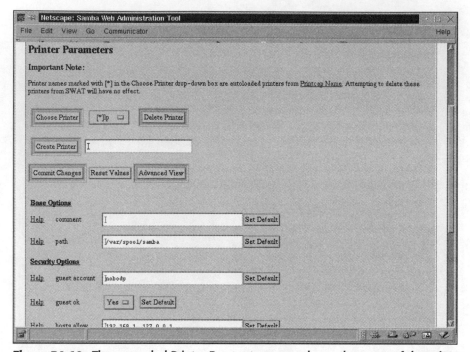

Figure 34-10: The expanded Printer Parameters page shows the name of the printer share you selected

As you can see, I have entered the appropriate information for the [printer] share. The information here is the same information we discussed earlier when looking at the [printer] section of the smb.conf file. Pay attention to the Important Note at the top of the Printer Parameters page. If you already have a printer configured in Linux, Samba will use it as the default printer and you will not be able to delete it from the list. Be sure to click Commit Changes to save the information to the smb.conf file.

After the smb.conf is created you can run a utility called `testparm` that checks the file for errors. At a command prompt, type `testparm`: if all is well, you should see output like that shown in Figure 34-11.

After making changes to the smb.conf file you must start (or restart) Samba services. Do this by choosing the Status icon. The Server Status page, as shown in Figure 34-12, tells you if the Samba daemons are running or not. The two daemons are smbd and nmbd; you can start or restart them by clicking on the appropriate buttons.

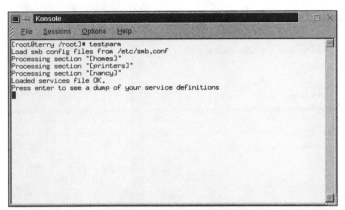

Figure 34-11: The testparm utility checks the smb.conf file for errors

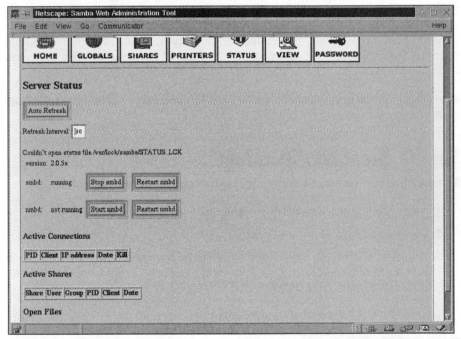

Figure 34-12: The Server Status page shows the current status of the Samba daemons

You can also start Samba from a command prompt. The command to start Samba is /usr/sbin/samba start or /etc/rc.d/init.d/samba start, depending on your distribution. After starting Samba, you can run smbclient on your localhost to get some configuration information. Issue the command smbclient -L localhost and press Enter at the password request. You should see output similar to what is shown in Figure 34-13.

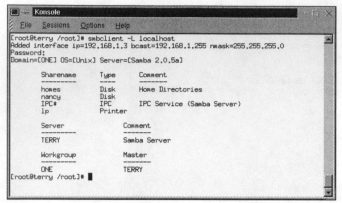

Figure 34-13: Checking the smbclient on your local host gives you Samba configuration information about the server

The last thing you need to do on the server is create the user that will use the share you created. On my home network, which I used in this example, I called the share [nancy]; I need to create a user called nancy. I'll type useradd nancy at a command prompt. Then I'll assign a password for this account by using the passwd command to assign a password.

Everything is now configured on the server, but you can't connect to any Windows computers yet because you haven't set them up.

Samba client configuration

To configure the Samba client, follow these steps:

1. From the Windows desktop, click Start.

2. Choose Settings and then Control Panel to open the Control Panel window.

3. Double-click the Network icon. In the Network dialog box, check for File and Printer Sharing and Client for Microsoft Networks in the Configuration window. See Figure 34-14 below.

If these two items are not installed, you will need to install them. To install the Client for Microsoft Networks, follow these steps:

1. Click the Add button to open the Select Network Component Type dialog box.

2. Click Client and then Add in the Select Network Component Type box.

3. Next, click Microsoft and then click Client for Microsoft Networks in the Select Network Client box that appears.

4. Click OK.

Figure 34-15 shows the entire process.

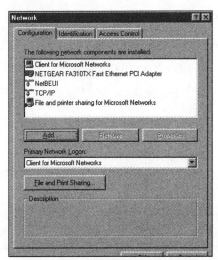

Figure 34-14: The Configuration tab window lists installed components and enables you to install others

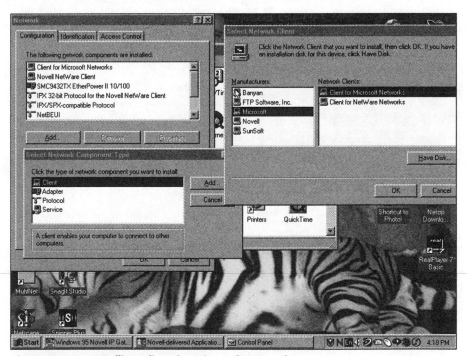

Figure 34-15: Installing Client for Microsoft Networks

Next you need to install File and Print Sharing for Microsoft Networks.

1. Click the Add button to open the Select Network Component Type dialog box.

2. Click Service, and then click Add in the Select Network Component Type box.

3. Click Microsoft, and then click File and printer sharing for Microsoft Networks in the Select Network Service box.

4. Finally, click OK and restart the computer.

After the computer restarts, you will see a network login window asking for a user name and password. Click Cancel for now, as there are a few more items you need to set up.

Note   Some users (like myself) do not like having a password or any prompt when the machine reboots. Setting the default logon as "Windows" instead of "Client for MS-Networks" and deleting the .PWL file will still keep the computer active on the network, and will not ask for a password.

There should now be a Network Neighborhood icon on the desktop. Right-click this icon and choose Properties from the dropdown list. In the Network Properties window click the Identification tab. In this window you will enter a computer and workgroup name, as shown in Figure 34-16. These names appear when you're browsing the network. The computer description does not appear in the Network Browse list.

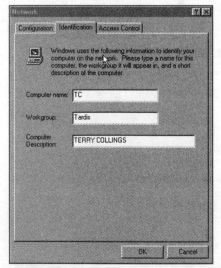

Figure 34-16: The Identification window is where you enter a name for your computer and its workgroup

Click the Access Control tab and the Share Level Access Control button (as shown in Figure 34-17), then click OK.

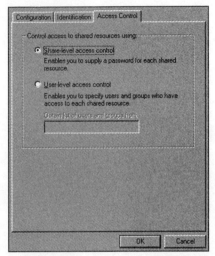

Figure 34-17: Choose Share Level Access Control in the Access Control window

Click the Configuration tab and then click the File and Print Sharing button. In the File and Print Sharing window check both options (as shown in Figure 34-18), then click OK.

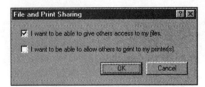

Figure 34-18: Choose both options in the File and Print Sharing window

Click the TCP/IP listing for the network card and then click the Properties button. In the TCP/IP properties windows click IP Address (if it is not already selected). Click the Specify an IP address button and then fill in the IP address and subnet mask for this computer, as shown in Figure 34-19.

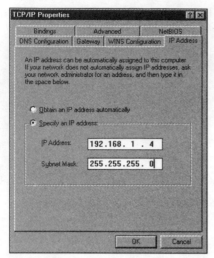

Figure 34-19: Enter an IP address and subnet mask for the Windows computer

 Note   Assigning an IP address manually works well for a network with a small number of computers. For a network with a large number of computers, it would be best to automatically assign IP addresses using the Dynamic Host Configuration Protocol (DHCP).

Next, click the WINS Configuration tab and then select Enable WINS Resolution. Enter the IP address of the Samba server (Linux computer) as the Primary WINS Server, as shown in Figure 34-20. Click OK when finished.

Figure 34-20: Enter the IP address of the Linux computer for the primary WINS server

Now click the Bindings tab and make sure that Client for Microsoft Networks and File and printer sharing for Microsoft Networks are there and checked as shown in Figure 34-21. Click OK to close the window.

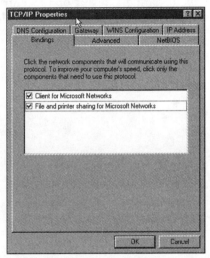

Figure 34-21: Checking the Bindings tab to be sure the components are there

Highlight File and printer sharing for Microsoft Networks in the list from the Configuration tab window. Click the Properties button and ensure that Browse Master is set to Disable and LM Announce is set to No, as shown in Figure 34-22. Click OK when finished.

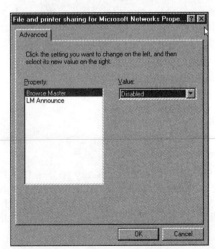

Figure 34-22: Setting the Browse Master and LM Announce properties

Close the Network Properties window by clicking OK. You will be asked to reboot the computer again so Windows can write all the changes you made to the registry.

When the computer has rebooted, open My Computer and right-click a drive icon. The popup menu will now contain an entry called Sharing. Clicking on this entry opens a window where you can enter the name and access type of the shared drive. See Figure 34-23.

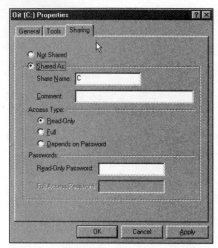

Figure 34-23: Entering the name and access type for the shared drive

If you have a printer connected to your Windows computer and you would like to use it from the Linux computer, double-click the Printers icon in My Computer and enable sharing for the printer as I described earlier for the disk share. You will need to reboot the Windows computer again and add some configuration information about the Windows printer to the Linux box. You can do this while the Windows computer is rebooting.

Using a Windows Printer from the Linux Computer

Since all distributions include a printer configuration tool, it is easy to use this tool to help configure the printer. Red Hat Linux includes `printtool`, and this is what I use to configure the printer. Type `printtool` at a command prompt and after the program starts, click Add. Then choose SMB/Windows95.NT printer and click OK, as shown in Figure 34-24.

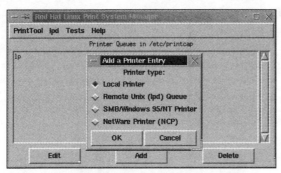

Figure 34-24: Using the Red Hat printtool to configure a Samba printer

A dialog box will appear, warning you about passwords and Samba. After reading this warning, click OK to go to the printer entry box. Configuring the printer connected to the Windows computer is a lot like configuring a printer connected to a Linux computer — with a few exceptions. The hostname of the print server is the name of the Windows computer. Enter the IP address of the Windows computer in the IP number of Server box, and then enter the name of the printer. You can leave the other boxes blank and click OK when finished. See Figure 34-25.

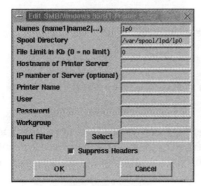

Figure 34-25: Entering the configuration information about the Windows printer

From the Printer Manager page of `printtool`, highlight the entry for the printer you just created. Click Tests and print the first two test pages, as shown in Figure 34-26.

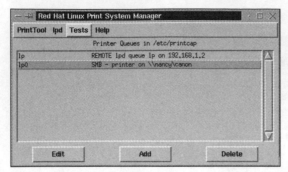

Figure 34-26: Testing the printer configuration of the Windows printer

Now you are ready to test everything you have done so far. On the Windows computer, double-click Network Neighborhood. In the Network Neighborhood window you should now see a listing for the Windows computer and the shares you made available. You should also see the Linux computer and, if you open it, the directories you made available from it.

If you double-click the directory from the Linux computer, you will be prompted for a user name and password to enter the directories. In our example you created one directory called oldwin, so this is the directory you should see from the Browse list.

On the Linux computer you can use the smbclient utility to access the directories on the Windows computer. Enter the following command:

```
Smbclient //nancy/directory name
```

This utility is a lot like the FTP utility. You can get a list of commands by typing help at the smbclient command prompt.

That's all there is to it. Now you can share files between your Linux computers and your Windows computers. In this example you set up Samba for just two computers, but you can follow the same steps to set up any number of computers on the network.

Why use Samba Instead of NFS?

In Chapter 22 you set up the Network File System to enable file sharing across your network. Why didn't you just use NFS to share the Windows files? Well, you could have, but it makes more sense to use Samba to communicate with Windows computers. Windows computers use the Server Message Block (SMB) to communicate with each other. It is the Windows native protocol for sharing files and printers. By using the same protocol, you are ensuring that file and printer sharing will operate with a minimum of difficulty.

Summary

In this chapter you learned how to configure a Linux computer to be a server for computers running Microsoft Windows. First you installed a program called Samba on the Linux server. Samba is an implementation of the Server Message Block protocol used by Microsoft Windows to communicate with other Windows computers. Next you learned about the smb.conf file that contains the configuration information required by Samba. You modified the smb.conf file by using a program called SWAT, which can be run from a standard Web browser.

After finishing the server configuration, you set up the Samba client to communicate with the Samba server. You installed the client for Microsoft Networks and file and print sharing on the computer running Windows. Finally, you configured your Linux system to print to a printer connected to a computer running Microsoft Windows.

✦   ✦   ✦

Appendixes

About the CD-ROM

The *Linux Bible* CD-ROMs contain reference information and software that you may find useful. Here's what you'll find on the CDs:

System Requirements

Make sure that your computer meets the minimum system requirements listed in this section. If it doesn't, you may have problems using the contents of the CD.

What You'll Find

Here's a summary of the software on this CD, arranged by category.

Red Hat Linux 7.1 Publisher's Edition

Red Hat Linux 7.1 Publisher's Edition is a complete and feature-rich Linux distribution. In addition to the wide variety of popular Linux software, including the KDE and GNOME window managers, and the Netscape Communicator suite, Red Hat Linux includes a graphical installer named Anaconda that makes installing Linux a breeze, even for a complete Linux newcomer.

Links to Linux HOWTOs and NHFs

The Linux HOWTOs and mini-HOWTOs are detailed instructional documents about specific subjects. The HOWTO index lists all HOWTOs and mini-HOWTOs along with short descriptions. These documents tell you how to do just about anything on Linux, no matter how simple or complex.

Newbie-ized Help Files (NHFs) are a new form of documentation aimed at users with little or no UNIX experience and need extra help as they make the transition to Linux. NHFs differ from traditional HOWTO files because they include tips and tricks the authors have gathered from their own personal experience with Linux.

Note   You can link to the most current (as of this writing) Linux HOWTOs and NHFs from this book's CD-ROM.

Sample code from the programming chapters

The CD-ROM includes all the shell scripts and Perl programs used as examples in the book.

Security tools and information

The CD-ROM contains selected information and tools from the CERT (Computer Emergency Response Team) Coordination Center. CERT is part of the Networked Systems Survivability Program, a branch of Carnegie Mellon University's Software Engineering Institute. The tools and information include:

✦ Incident Notes and Vulnerability Notes containing security information useful to the Internet community.

✦ CERT Security Improvement Module Deploying Firewalls, a document that describes both the security issues behind the need for firewalls and recommended practices for setting up firewalls.

✦ Falcon Firewall Project is an Internet community project whose goal is to build a "Free Application-Level CONnection" gateway.

Tools and utilities

Adobe Acrobat Reader enables you to view and print files stored in Adobe PDF format.

Kratsu's Downloader for X is a graphical program for downloading files. If the server supports the ability to resume interrupted file transfers (most servers do), you can use Downloader to restart interrupted downloads.

Netscape Navigator is a popular Web browser.

VisualPulse is a program that runs on a Web server to monitor network status and performance. You can view its output with a Java applet running in your Web browser. You can install VisualPulse with VisualRoute Server.

VisualRoute is a graphical version of `traceroute` that displays its results on a map of the world.

VisualRoute Server eliminates the need for the dedicated VisualRoute client software by providing a Java applet to your Web browser.

WINE is a free implementation of the Windows APIs on top of Linux and the X Window System. With WINE, you can run Windows programs under Linux.

✦   ✦   ✦

The Linux Directory Structure

This appendix describes a typical Linux directory tree by following the branches of the main filesystems. These are the root, /usr, /var, and /home. The Linux directory tree is structured to work efficiently on a standalone computer or in a network of Linux machines that may share files using NFS (the Network Filesystem).

The Root Filesystem (/)

The root filesystem contains the files you need to boot the system. It is the only filesystem automatically mounted in single-user mode. The root directory generally consists only of subdirectories and the kernel executable image file. Other files reside in the following subdirectories of the root filesystem:

✦ /bin — Commands, mostly for users.

✦ /sbin — Commands, mostly for system administrators.

✦ /etc — System configuration files.

  • /etc/rc?.d — Scripts and subdirectories of scripts that run whenever the run level changes, include when the computer boots.

  • /etc/passwd — The user account file, which may not include encrypted passwords if a shadow file is used.

  • /etc/fdprm — The floppy-disk parameter table.

  • /etc/fstab — Lists the filesystems mounted automatically at startup.

- /etc/group — The group file listing groups other than users's default groups.

- /etc/inittab — Contains entries for run levels.

- /etc/magic — Contains the descriptions of various file formats. Used by the file command.

- /etc/motd — The message-of-the-day file, displayed after a user logs in.

- /etc/mtab — Lists the currently mounted filesystems.

- /etc/shadow — Shadow password file, which contains encrypted passwords for all user accounts.

- /etc/printcap — Printer-configuration file.

- /etc/profile — System-wide profile file for users of bash and the Bourne shell.

- /etc/csh.login, /etc/csh.cshrc — System-wide environment files for C-shell users.

- /etc/securettys — Lists secure terminals that enable root login.

- /etc/shells — Lists all trusted shells.

- /etc/termcap — The terminal configuration file.

✦ /root — The home directory for the user account, root.

✦ /lib — Shared libraries used by the programs stored in the root filesystem.

✦ /lib/modules — Dynamically loadable kernel modules.

✦ /dev — Device special files and, in some distributions, the MAKEDEV script.

✦ /tmp — Temporary files, usually automatically created by applications transparently to the user.

✦ /boot — Files needed by LILO or another boot loader. Also, some kernel images may be stored in /boot.

✦ /mnt — Mount point for temporary mounts for testing filesystems. If you need to test multiple filesystems at once, you can create subdirectories under /mnt.

✦ /proc, /usr, /var, /home — Mount points for other filesystems described in more detail in the next few sections of this appendix.

The /usr Filesystem

The /usr filesystem contains system files for commands, libraries, and manual pages. Files in /usr, such as manual pages, are good candidates for sharing across a network via NFS because most of these files are static and rarely change. Indeed, many system administrators mount the /usr filesystem read-only to enhance system security. In older UNIX systems, /usr/users was the traditional location for users' home directories. Today, the /home filesystem typically contains users' home directories.

✦ /usr/X11R6 — X Window System files.

✦ /usr/X386 — Similar to /usr/X11R6, but for X11 Release 5.

✦ /usr/bin — User commands. Other user commands are in the root filesystem in /bin.

✦ /usr/sbin — System administration commands that are not needed to boot the system.

✦ /usr/include — Header files for the C and C++ programming languages.

✦ /usr/lib — Data files used by system programs. The name *lib* is derived from *library*.

✦ /usr/local — Locally installed software.

The /var Filesystem

The /var filesystem contains various files of varying size and purpose, such as spool directories (for mail, news, printers, etc), log files, and pre-formatted manual pages. Sharing /var across the network is rare because the /var files and directories are computer-specific. Files in /var include:

✦ /var/catman — Stores man pages that are formatted on demand from source files in /usr/man/man *.

✦ /var/lib — Volatile files that change as the system is running.

✦ /var/local — When the system administrator installs new programs in /usr/local, any data files associated with those programs are installed in /var/local.

✦ /var/lock — Lock files, such as the lock file for vipw.

✦ /var/log — Log files, including login accounting files, the kernel log, if enabled, and system-message files.

✦ /var/run — Files that contain information about the system that is valid only until the next system boot. For example, /var/run/utmp contains information about the users currently logged in.

✦ /var/spool — Directories for spooled data, including mail, news, and printer queues. Each spooler has its own subdirectory. For example, the users' mailboxes are in /var/spool/mail.

✦ /var/tmp — Temporary files in addition to those in /tmp (usually with special requirements, such as larger size or longer life than that allowed for /tmp).

The /home Filesystem

The /home filesystem contains users' home directories. The system administrator can assign users' home directories to any directory or filesystem. However, keeping users' files in a single directory (/home is the standard convention), makes it easier to back up user data. If /home is very large, it's good practice to spread it across multiple filesystems, such as /home/europe, /home/pacific, and /home/asia.

The /proc Filesystem

The volatile /proc filesystem exists only in memory. Unless you copy it to disk, the files and directories in /proc do not use any disk space. /proc stores system and process information and is useful for debugging mysterious process failures. Subdirectories and files in /proc include:

✦ /proc/* — Subdirectories with information about processes. Each process has a directory below /proc named after the pid. For example, the subdirectory with information about the `init` process is /proc/1.

✦ /proc/cpuinfo — Information about the CPU, such as its type, manufacturer, and model.

✦ /proc/devices — A list of device drivers configured into the running kernel.

✦ /proc/filesystems — A list of filesystems configured into the kernel.

✦ /proc/interrupts — A list of how many of each type of interrupt have occurred.

✦ /proc/kcore — An image of physical memory.

✦ /proc/kmsg — Kernel messages.

✦ /proc/meminfo — Information about physical- and virtual-memory swap use.

✦ /proc/modules — A list of kernel modules currently loaded.

✦ /proc/stat — Performance statistics about the system, such as the number of page faults since the system was booted.

✦ /proc/uptime — The amount of time the system has been running.

✦ /proc/version — The kernel version.

✦   ✦   ✦

Internet Resources for Linux

I f, as some industry analysts claim, Linux is the operating system for over fifty percent of the servers on the World Wide Web, it seems appropriate that the Web and FTP archives on the Internet can help you to learn almost anything about Linux. You can browse and download complete books and manuals, white papers about technical topics, tutorials on a wide variety of Linux methods, and a large set of documents called the Linux HOWTOs.

On the CD-ROM There is a link on the CD-ROM to all of the HOWTOs available as of this writing. Therefore, this appendix does not cover the HOWTOs.

Who Hosts the Web Sites

Different groups and organizations, as well as interested individuals, maintain Web sites about Linux. This appendix lists a few of the Web sites maintained by:

✦ Linux software vendors.

✦ Hardware vendors who ship hardware that works with Linux.

✦ Organizations dedicated to promoting the use of Linux.

✦ Individuals interested in Linux who contribute technical Linux information.

Getting Linux Information from Operating-System Vendors

The following list includes only a few of the many vendors who have produced Linux distributions. They appear on this list because they offer valuable information about Linux in addition to distributions that you can download or buy.

www.calderasystems.com	Caldera has a great installation program and the retail version includes a special version of PartitionMagic to help you partition your disks for Linux without risking damage to existing data.
www.debian.org	Debian Linux is another Linux distribution. Debian offers lots of additional Linux software, especially for developers.
www.mandrake.org	Mandrake Linux is based on Red Hat, with enhancements.
www.redhat.com	Red Hat was the first Linux vendor to offer shares publicly. Red Hat developed the RPM (Red Hat Package Manager) that other Linux distributions also use. Recent versions of Red Hat Linux have improved the installation program's autodetection of hardware.
www.slackware.com	Slackware is one of the oldest distributions and it keeps incorporating new features into new releases. Slackware is probably the version of Linux that's most like traditional UNIX.
www.suse.com	Pronounced like *Sousa*, as in John Philip Sousa, the composer, SuSE is a Linux distribution that's growing fast, especially in Europe. SuSE distributes both a German and English version of Linux. It also includes a huge amount of applications and tools with its distribution.
www.turbolinux.com	Turbolinux comes in three languages: Japanese, Chinese, and English. The TurboLinux installation program is based on Red Hat's installation, and TurboLinux comes in both server and workstation versions.

Getting Linux Information from the ".orgs"

You can find distributions for add-on software, such as the latest versions of GUIs, as well as the "official" word on features planned for future releases, at these sites. Many of these sites are also looking for volunteers if you're interested in becoming an active member of the Linux community.

www.gnome.org	Many distributions include the GNOME graphical interface. If you don't have GNOME, go to this site to download a copy. You'll also find technical information and documentation about using GNOME.
www.kde.org	Most distributions include the KDE graphical interface. However, KDE developers work constantly at improving and extending the interface, and the version of KDE that you receive with your Linux distribution may not be the most recent. To see if you have the latest and greatest version of KDE, visit this Web site. You can download KDE if there is a version that is newer than the one you already have. You can also find KDE tips and documentation at this site.
www.linuxdoc.org	Do you need Linux documentation? Maintained by the Linux Documentation Project, this is the place to find man pages, FAQs (Frequently Asked Questions), and all the newest HOWTOS, books and guides. You can even read the online magazine, *The Linux Gazette*. If you need Linux information in a language other than English, this site includes links to documentation in Chinese, Croatian, Czech, Danish, Dutch, Estonian, Finnish, French, German, Hellenic, Hungarian, Indonesian, Italian, Japanese, Korean, Malaysian, Norwegian, Polish, Portuguese, Romanian, Russian, Singapore, Slovenian, Spanish, Swedish, Thai, Turkish, and Walloon.
www.linux.org	This site is a huge clearinghouse for diverse Linux information, including the "Rampantly Unofficial Linus Torvalds FAQ," the HOWTO collection, listings of upcoming Linux-oriented events, links to Linux-user groups worldwide, and a selection of recent news articles.

`www.xfree86.org`	If you are having problems with the X Window System, this is the site to go to first. You can find XFree86 documentation in Japanese and English here, as well as lists of supported video cards. You can also download the most recent release of XFree86, and read about X-related security issues and plans for future releases.
`www.gnu.org`	This is the GNU project site. You can find information in several languages, including Catalan, Chinese, Dutch, English, French, German, Hungarian, Italian, Japanese, Korean, Portuguese, Spanish, and Turkish. If you are looking for software, browse GNU's software catalog for applications, games, security packages, tools and utilities, and libraries.
`www.kernel.org`	This is the main site for the Linux kernel source code, but you can find more than just kernels here. If you want to download kernel sources using `ftp`, this site points to the `ftp` archive `ftp://ftp.kernel.org/pub`.
`www.linuxnewbie.org`	This site is useful even if you're past being a Linux newbie. If you think the usual Linux HOWTOs are too detailed, look at the NHFs (Newbie-ized HOWTO Files). If you're moving to Linux from Windows, there's bound to be something you need at this site. You can find help with almost any problem you might have with Linux, and get a T-shirt too!
`www.lpi.org`	Start here, at the Linux Professional Institute, if you're interested in becoming certified Linux administrator.

Getting Linux Information from the ".coms"

There are way more commercial sites with Linux information and software on the Internet than we can even begin to include in this appendix. Here are a few of our favorites.

`www.internet.com/ sections/linux.html`	If you go to only one site, make this the one. You'll find links to many of the individual sites we list in this appendix. The internet.com Corp. links to 117 Web sites, 171 online newsletters, and 117 discussion forums, many of them about Linux. Look there for tutorials, Linux news, product reviews, downloads, and expert advice.

www.linuxhq.com	This site contains a series of guides, such as the Network Administrator's Guide and the Linux User's Guide, kernel documentation and patches, a HOWTO collection, and a large set of links to other useful Linux sites.
www.zdnet.com	This site, run by the Ziff-Davis media company, contains articles about Linux (and more) and a large archive of downloads. You can also watch technology broadcasts at this site if your computer supports multimedia.
www.cnet.com	CNET is a media company that provides online technology news, product reviews, comparison shopping, and a large download archive. You can find a lot of Linux information here.
www.4front-tech.com	If you need a sound driver for your computer, 4Front Technologies offers a large choice of sound drivers for a modest fee. 4Front is trying to build a comprehensive sound architecture for Linux with its Open Sound System (OSS).
www.tomshardware.com	Tom's hardware guide is filled with tidbits about hardware, especially Intel, that you might not be able to find elsewhere.
www-4.ibm.com/software/is/mp/linux/	I know. You think of IBM as a mainframe company. Well, it is, but now you can run Linux on mainframes. You can find downloads of new IBM products for Linux, including ViaVoice, DB2, and Lotus Domino (trial versions). This site also includes an online magazine, *Hot Topics in Linux*, in English, Portuguese, French, French-Canadian, German, Italian, and Spanish. This somewhat surprising fountain of Linux information also lists upcoming international Linux events and webcasts pertaining to Linux technology.

✦   ✦   ✦

Advanced Commands Glossary

Options, syntax, and examples for the commands are listed alphabetically in this appendix.

Getting help

apropos
: Search the `whatis` database for commands that contain a text string.

apropos *keyword*

```
$ apropos less
jpegtran (1)          - lossless transformation
of JPEG files
less (1)              - opposite of more
lesskey (1)           - specify key bindings
for less
raid0run (8)          - starts up old
(superblock-less) RAID0/LINEAR arrays
UNIVERSAL (3)         - base class for ALL
classes (blessed references)
```

info
: Display online help (in `emacs`) for various commands.

info

help
: `bash` help for commands that are defined internally to bash.

help, help *command_name*

```
# help builtin
builtin: builtin [shell-builtin [arg ...]]
Run a shell builtin.  This is useful when you
wish to rename a
```

shell builtin to be a function, but need the functionality of the builtin within the function itself.

man   **Read the online manual pages;** man -k **is the same as** apropos.

man [*options*] [*section*] *command*

```
# man whatis
whatis(1)
NAME
    whatis - search the whatis database for complete words.
SYNOPSIS
    whatis keyword ...
DESCRIPTION
    whatis  searches  a set of database files containing short
    descriptions of system commands for keywords and  displays
    the result  on  the  standard output.  Only complete word
    matches are displayed.
    The  whatis  database  is  created  using  the  command
    /usr/sbin/makewhatis.
SEE ALSO
        apropos(1), man(1).
```

whatis   **Similar to** man -k**, but searches only for complete key-words.**

whatis *keyword*

```
$ whatis less
less (3) perl pragma to request less of something from compile
```

Working in the user Environment

alias/unalias   **Assign/deassign a shortcut for a command.**

alias **(lists all aliases)**

alias [*name*] **(lists the alias for** *name*)

alias [*name*[=*command*] **(defines an alias for** *command*)

```
$ alias
alias cp='cp -i'
alias ll='/bin/ls -lA'
alias lsl='ls -la'
alias mv='mv -i'
alias rm='rm -i'
# alias j='jobs -l'
# alias j
alias j='jobs -l'
# unalias j
```

```
# alias j
alias: `j' not found
```

    chsh   **Change to another shell.**

```
        chsh [ -s shell ] [ -l ] [ -u ] [ -v ] [ username ]
```

```
$ chsh
Changing shell for miss_scarlet.
Password:
Warning: your password will expire in 38 days
New shell [/bin/bash]: /bin/csh
Shell changed.
```

    cal   **Show the calendar for a month or year.**

```
cal [-mjy] [month [year]]
```

    groups   **List the groups that a user belongs to.**

```
groups [option]... [username]...
# groups root
root : root bin daemon sys adm disk wheel
# groups
bad-guys emmys-friends
```

    id   **Display user information.**

```
        id [options] [username]
```

```
scarlet@flyingpenguin$ id
uid=500(miss_scarlet) gid=506(bad-guys) groups=506(bad-guys),503(emmys-friends)
scarlet@flyingpenguin# id candace
uid=501(candace) gid=100(users) groups=100(users),503(emmys-friends),504(databas
e)
```

    passwd   **Change password.**

```
passwd [-k] [-l] [-u [-f]] [-d] [-S] [username]
```

    printenv **List the current environment variables.**

```
printenv [option]... [variable]...S] [username]
```

    tty   **Display the device name of the terminal.**

```
tty [-s] [--silent]
# tty
/dev/pts/2
```

    type   **Show a command's full path**

```
type [-all] [-type | -path] [name ...]
# type set
set is a shell builtin
```

Managing Files/Directories

cd   **Change working directory.**

cd [*path*]

```
$ cd
$ pwd
/home/miss_scarlet
$ cd ~candace
$ pwd
/home/candace
```

chmod   **Set file/directory permissions.**

```
chmod [option]... mode[,mode]... file...
$ ls -l dead.letter
-rw-------   1 miss_sca bad-guys      1357 Feb 21 18:03
dead.letter
$ chmod a+rx dead.letter
$ ls -l dead.letter
-rwxr-xr-x   1 miss_sca bad-guys      1357 Feb 21 18:03
dead.letter
```

chown   **Change file ownership.**

```
chown [OPTION]... OWNER[.[GROUP]] FILE...
# chown candace dead.letter
# ls -l dead.letter
-rwxr-xr-x  1candace bad-guys 1357 Feb 21 18:03 dead.letter
```

file   **Display information about a file's structure.**

file [-bcnsvzL] [-f *filename*] *filename*

```
$ file -s /dev/hda1
```

/dev/hda1: Linux/i386 ext2 filesystem

find   **Find a file.**

```
find [path] [expression]
$ find -empty
./Desktop/Autostart
./Desktop/Trash
./knife
```

head   Display the first few lines of a file.

```
head [OPTION]... [FILE]...
```

less   Display a file so that you can page backward and forward.

```
less [options] filename
```

ln   Create hard or symbolic (ls -s) links to files and directories.

```
ln [OPTION]... TARGET [LINK_NAME]
ln [OPTION]... TARGET... DIRECTORY
```

locate   Find files listed in a system database.

```
locate [-q][-d <path>][--database=<path>] <searchstring>
slocate (security enhanced version of locate)

$ locate dead*
/home/miss_scarlet/dead.letter
```

ls   Display a directory listing.

```
ls [OPTION]... [FILE]...
$ ls -l /etc/group
-rw-r--r--  1 root    root    787 May 13 13:12 /etc/group
```

mkdir   Make a directory.

```
mkdir [OPTION] DIRECTORY...
$ mkdir --verbose database_files
mkdir: created directory `database_files'
```

more   Display a file so that you can page forward through it.

```
more [-dlfpcsu] [-num] [+/ pattern] [+ linenum] [file ...]
$ more -3 clues
emily   duncan  lead pipe       rope    revolver
helen   duncan  chair           cat     fingerprint
prof    plum    pipe            shoe    tobacco
--More--(47%)
```

mv   Rename or move files.

```
mv [OPTION]... SOURCE DEST
```

```
     mv [OPTION]... SOURCE... DIRECTORY

$ mv -b --verbose home.txt newhome.txt
home.txt -> newhome.txt
```

rm   **Remove files.**

```
 rm [OPTION]... FILE...
$ rm -i --verbose junk
rm: remove `junk'? y
removing junk
```

rmdir   **Remove directories.**

```
rmdir [OPTION]... DIRECTORY...
$ rmdir -p --verbose francais/amis
rmdir: removing directory, francais/amis
rmdir: removing directory, francais
```

pwd   **Print (display) the current working directory.**

```
pwd -[--help] [--version]
$ pwd
/home/miss_scarlet
```

sort   **Sort text.**

```
sort [OPTION]... [FILE]...
$ cat detectives
     Maigret
        Morse
Poirot
Arkady

$ sort detectives
        Morse
     Maigret
Arkady
Poirot

$ sort -b detectives
Arkady
     Maigret
        Morse
Poirot
```

tail   **Display the last few lines of a file.**

```
tail [OPTION]... [FILE]...
```

```
$ tail -3 --verbose detectives
==> detectives <==
      Morse
Poirot
Arkady
$ tail --bytes 3 --verbose detectives
==> detectives <==
dy
```

touch   **Create a file.**

```
touch [OPTION]... FILE...
$ touch Emmy_Horse_File
$ ls -l Emmy*
-rw-r--r--   1 root      root             0 Jul 23 20:29
Emmy_Horse_File
```

whereis   **Find files in directories of executable images.**

```
whereis [ -bmsu ] [ -BMS directory...  -f ] filename ...

$ whereis -m *
GnomeScott:
Mail: /usr/man/man1/Mail.1
MakeTeXPK: /usr/man/man1/MakeTeXPK.1
```

which   **Find files along your** PATH **variable.**

```
which [options] [--] programname [...]
$ which *bin*
which: no *bin* in
(.//home/miss_scarlet:/usr/bin:/sbin:/usr/sbin:/bin)
```

Working with files

cat   **Concatenate a file to a device.**

```
cat [OPTION] [FILE]...
$ cat -n terminfo.txt
     1  /usr/share/terminfo/v/vt100
     2  /usr/share/terminfo/v/vt100-am
     3  /usr/share/terminfo/v/vt100-bm
     4  /usr/share/terminfo/v/vt100-bm-o
     5  /usr/share/terminfo/v/vt100-bot-s
     6  /usr/share/terminfo/v/vt100-nam
```

cp   Copy file(s).

```
cp [OPTION]... SOURCE DEST
cp [OPTION]... SOURCE... DIRECTORY
$ cp --verbose newbeaniebabies.dat retired_beanies.dat
newbeaniebabies.dat -> retired_beanies.dat
```

dd   Copy and convert the format according to the command options.

```
dd [options]
```

```
$ dd if=ps of=short_ps_file obs=1
13+1 records in
6712+0 records out
```

grep,   Search for regular expressions in a file.
egrep,
fgrep

```
egrep [options] [pattern] file(s)
```

```
$ egrep -i -n SCARLET *
grep: Desktop: Is a directory
grep: databases: Is a directory
grep: friends: Is a directory
allfiles.txt:7725:/home/Miss_Scarlet:
mbox:9:To: miss_scarlet@flyingpenguin.cardinalconsulting.com
rlogin.txt:4:login: miss_scarlet
```

zcat   Decompress and display a file.

zless   Decompress and display a file for backward and forward paging.

zmore   Decompress and display a file for forward paging.

Text processing

cut   Cut strings of text from each line in a file.

diff   Compare two text files.

expand   Convert tabs to spaces

fold   Wrap text to fit a specified width.

nl   Display (on stdout) all lines in a text file that are not blank.

paste   Concatenate specified lines from multiple filesystems.

patch   Using the diff results, update a text file.

tr   Substitute characters throughout a file.

uniq	Remove duplicate lines of text.
wc	Display the number of lines, words, characters.

Printing

lpr	Spool to a printer.
lpq	Check the status of the print queue.

Archiving

compress	Compress files (not as powerful as the GNU algorithms).
cpio	Copy files to an archive.
dd	Convert and copy.
dump	Backup a filesystem.
gunzip	GNU unzip (uncompress) compressed files.
gzip	GNU zip (compress) files.
restore	Restore from a dump archive.
tar	Work with a tar archive (good personal backup utility).
uncompress	Decompress files compressed with the compress command.

Controlling processes

bg	Move to the background.
fg	Move to the foreground.
nice	Lower the base priority of a process.

Managing filesystems and swap

cfdisk/fdisk	Partition a hard disk.
efs2ck/fsck	Check/repair a filesystem.
fdformat	Format a floppy disk.
MAKEDEV	Make a device special file.
mkfs/mke2fs	Make a filesystem/make ext2 filesystem.

mkswap	Make a swap partition (or file)
mount	Mount a filesystem into the directory tree.
swapon	Enable swap partitions.
swapoff	Disable a swap partition.
sync	Write data from buffers to filesystem.
umount	Dismount a filesystem.

Monitoring the System

df	Show space available for all mounted filesystems.
du	Show disk-use statistics.
free	Show the amounts of physical memory. and swap space free and in use.
ps	Show process status.
pstree	Like ps with parent-child process relationships.
top	Display the processes using the most CPU and memory.
uname	Display kernel and system information.

Handle with Care

date	Show/set date and time.
halt	Shut down Linux and halt the computer. You may still need to turn of the power switch.
kill	Send a signal, such as terminate or hangup.
reboot	Shut down and restart.
su	Switch to another user environment.

✦   ✦   ✦

Glossary

$HOME Environment variable that points to your login directory.

$PATH Environment variable that lists the directories Linux should look in to find commands.

/ Root directory.

/dev Device special file directory.

/dev/null Device special file for the null device. Also known as the *bit bucket*.

/etc/group The group file, containing information about groups and the users they contain.

/etc/inittab Lists the active terminal ports passed to getty for login prompts and daemons to start at system boot.

/etc/motd file Optional file containing the message-of-the-day.

/etc/passwd Contains user account information and, possibly, the account passwords. The password might actually be in another file, /etc/shadow, to protect it from attacks.

/etc/profile System-file that sets shell characteristics for all users of the bash, Bourne, and Korn shells.

{ } Braces.

[ ] Brackets.

| See *pipe*.

ar Archive utility.

awk Text-manipulation language. gawk is GNU awk. See also *gawk*.

background process Process with input disconnected from the interactive session. A user should redirect input and output and errors to a file.

bash GNU Bourne Again SHell, based on sh (Bourne shell), the original command interpreter.

block-special device file Used to communicate with block-oriented I/O devices, such as disks and most tape drives.

boot To initialize (start) the operating system.

C shell Another shell. It features C-like syntax.

cat Concatenate files usually to the display or the printer. Can also be used to create a new file.

character special device file Used to communicate with character-oriented I/O devices such as terminals, printers, and network-communications lines. They perform I/O byte by byte as opposed to block by block.

child process See *subprocess*.

child shell See *subshell*.

command-line editing The act of recalling a previously entered command, modifying it, and then executing the new version.

command-line history The commands you've executed previously and that are available for recall.

command-line parameters Parameters passed to a program or script. Also known as *command-line arguments*.

command prompt Characters that the shell displays indicating that the user should enter a command.

CPU Central Processing Unit. The chip that is the "brain" of the computer, such as Intel 486, Alpha, and the like.

daemon A background process that provides system services.

device special file A file under the /dev directory that represents a physical device.

directory A special kind of file that holds other files and directories (subdirectories). The root (/) directory is the top level of the Linux directory tree and every other directory is contained in it (directly or indirectly).

DNS Domain Name Service. Translates human-readable host names, for example, www.cardinalconsulting.com, to machine-readable numbers (IP addresses)

DoS Denial of Service. A class of computer attacks that cripple the target system to the degree that users are prevented from using it normally, that is, denied the system's services.

DOS Disk Operating System, such Microsoft's MS-DOS or IBM's PC-DOS.

ed Line-oriented text editor.

elm Interactive mail program.

emacs An editor, written by Richard M. Stallman, that can also function as an environment; part of the GNU software distribution. emacs is available for many platforms.

environment variables See *variables, environmental.*

Ethernet The standard networking technology that runs the Internet.

expression A combination of variables, constants, literals, and operators.

file name The name at the end of a path that identifies a specific file. You don't need to type the full path if the file is in your current working directory.

filesystem A piece of the directory tree that is connected (mounted) to the entire tree at a mount point (directory). Filesystems live in partitions.

firewall Software (and optionally hardware) that sits between your local network and the outside world (the Internet). Enables users behind it to access the Internet but keeps users on the Internet at large from accessing your internal network.

foreground Interactive processes connected to your session.

FTP File Transfer Protocol. An application for transferring files between computer systems.

GID Group ID number.

GNOME A *graphical user interface*, similar to but newer than KDE. The default GUI on Red Hat Linux. You can run KDE applications from GNOME.

GNU A recursive acronym standing for GNU's Not UNIX. Also the name of a large group of programmers that create, maintain, and distribute much of the free software that makes up a Linux system.

GPL GNU General Public License that allows to you copy, edit, and distribute open-source software.

grep A tool used to search a file for a pattern. egrep enables you to search for extended regular expressions; fgrep searches for text fast.

GUI Graphical user interface, such as GNOME or KDE.

inode The pointer to a file.

ISO International Standards Organization. ISO also refers to the file format used to create CD-ROMs.

KDE A graphical user interface, similar to but more mature than GNOME. The default GUI on most Linux distributions. You can run GNOME applications from KDE.

kernel The core of the operating system that handles communication among applications, the operating system and the hardware, memory management, interrupt servicing, input and output, and process management.

keys, control These are keys or key combinations that do not display a character but instead cause some function to occur. For example, the end-of-file key, usually Ctrl+D, tells Linux that there is no more input.

link, hard A directory entry that provides an alias to another file within the same file system. Every file has one hard link to itself. Created by the ln command.

link, soft See *link, symbolic*.

link, symbolic A directory entry that provides an alias to another file or entire directory in the same or a different file system. Created by the ln -s command.

login The process that grants a user access to Linux system.

lp Line printer.

lpc Line-printer control program.

lpd Line-printer daemon.

man page Online reference page (for *manual*).

manual page See *man page*.

memory, physical The amount of RAM (random-access memory) installed in the system, also known as RAM.

memory, virtual Portions of disk drives used as RAM.

metacharacter A character with special meaning to the shell. For example, the wild-card asterisk (*).

NFS Network File System. A TCP/IP service and protocol that enables you to access to remote file systems as if they were local.

NIS Network Information Service. A TCP/IP service and protocol that enables computers on a network to share system files such as the passwd file.

NNTP Network News Transport Protocol. Transmits Usenet news over TCP/IP.

operator A symbol, such as >, <, or | that performs a function on values or variables.

options Indicators added to the command line to modify the behavior of a command.

parameters Data, also called *arguments*, passed to a program, usually on the command line.

parent process A process that controls another process.

parent process identifier The process identifier of the parent process. See also *PPID*.

partition Part of a disk drive allocated for a specific purpose and logically distinct from other areas on the disk drive.

pathname An *absolute pathname* is the full file specification, from the root directory to the file. A *relative pathname* is a partial file specification, from the current working directory to the file.

Perl An interpreted (rather than compiled, like C) programming language (Practical Extraction and Report Language) developed by Larry Wall. It incorporates the best features of shells, awk, sed, and C. Perl is the name of the language; perl is the name of the interpreter.

permissions Access controls on a file or directory. Assigned for owner, group, and other. The permissions are r for read, w for write, and x for execute

PGP Phil Zimmerman's Pretty Good Privacy encryption scheme, which is based on public key/private key cryptography.

PID Process Identifier.

pine An interactive mail program.

pipe (|) A method, known as *redirecting*, of making the output of one program the input of another.

POSIX Portable Operating System Interface. The POSIX Shell and Utilities standard, developed by IEEE Working Group 1003.2 (POSIX.2), concentrates on the command-interpreter interface and utility programs.

PPID The parent process identifier. See also *Parent Process Identifier.*

PPP Point-to-Point Protocol, typically used to enable the TCP/IP protocol to function over dial-up lines.

pppd The Point-to-Point-Protocol daemon.

printcap The printer capability database.

process A running program.

process identifier The unique number assigned to each process.

quota A limit on the amount of system resources — such as disk space, memory usage, CPU time, number of open files — a user can use.

quoting The use of single and double quotes to influence how the shell understands characters.

redirection The process of directing data to something other than stdin, stdout, stderr. See also *stdin*, *stdout*, *stderr*.

regular expression A way of specifying and matching strings.

rlogin The Berkeley remote login program, similar to `telnet`.

root The username of the superuser with all privileges. Also the top of the directory tree.

router A computer with routing software that moves network traffic from one network to another, deciding which path to take when there is more than one possible connection path.

RPC The Remote Procedure Call service. Gives you the ability to call functions or subroutines that run on a remote computer.

RPM The Red Hat Package Manager, for managing and loading software packages.

script A file of Linux commands that can have program-like logic. Not compiled. See also *shell scripts*.

SCSI The Small Computer System Interface (pronounced "skuzzy") for disks and other peripherals.

sed A stream-text editor for manipulating large amounts of text.

shell The Linux command handler. See also *bash*.

shell script A file containing shell-specific commands that can be run like a program. Shell scripts can also contain typical programming constructs, such as conditional statements(if-then) and loops (while). Shell scripts are not compiled.

signal A special flag or interrupt that sends special events to programs by the operating-system and user processes. The kill command, for example, sends signals to processes.

SLIP The Serial Line Internet Protocol. Dialup protocol for a serial line (modem). Usually replaced by PPP.

stderr The standard destination for error messages: the default is the screen. Can be redirected to a file or to another command.

stdin The standard input source; the default is the keyboard. Input can also be read from a file or from another command's output.

stdout The standard output destination; the default is the screen. Can be redirected to a file or to another command.

subdirectory See *directory*.

subnet A portion of a network.

subshell A shell running under the control of a parent shell. See also *shell*.

SUID Set user ID.

superuser Anyone with a UID of 0 (usually the root user). See also *UID*.

system administrator The person who takes care of the operating system and user administrative issues on Linux systems. Also called a *system manager*. May perform network-administrator functions as well.

system manager See *system administrator*.

tar Tape archiving utility for personal backups and other small archiving functions.

TCP Transmission Control Protocol.

TCP/IP Transmission Control Protocol/Internet Protocol. The pair of protocols and the suite of protocols, services, and applications that the Internet uses.

telnet TCP protocol, service, and application for terminal access to remote computers. Similar to `rlogin`, but older.

terminal A hardware device that normally consists of a screen and a keyboard. Can be a "dumb" terminal with a character-cell (text) interface or an X Window graphical terminal.

top A system-monitoring tool.

UID User-ID number. Anyone with a UID of 0 is the *superuser*.

URL Uniform Resource Locator. The name and location of a resource, such as a file, on the Internet.

Usenet News Discussion groups on the Internet.

UUCP UNIX-to-UNIX copy program. Allows primitive dialup networking between two systems for e-mail and news-reading.

variables, environment A name (nickname) for values that the shell or overall process environment can use. Whenever you use the name of the variable, the shell substitutes its value.

variable substitution The act of dereferencing a variable name to obtain its value.

WAN Wide Area Network.

Web See *World Wide Web*.

white space Blanks, spaces, and tabs.

wild card A special character in file name(s) that represents one or more missing characters.

World Wide Web Internetworked servers and services on the Internet that communicate via HTTP (Hypertext Transfer Protocol).

WWW See *World Wide Web*.

X See *X Window System*.

X Window System A IEEE standard windowing and graphics system. GNOME and KDE are layered on top of the X Window System. Also called X or X11.

X11 See *X Window System*.

Index

Continued

Continued

U

red**hat**®

www.redhat.com

GNU General Public License

Version 2, June 1991

Copyright © 1989, 1991 Free Software Foundation, Inc.

59 Temple Place, Suite 330, Boston, MA 02111-1307, USA

Preamble

The licenses for most software are designed to take away your freedom to share and change it. By contrast, the GNU General Public License is intended to guarantee your freedom to share and change free software — to make sure the software is free for all its users. This General Public License applies to most of the Free Software Foundation's software and to any other program whose authors commit to using it. (Some other Free Software Foundation software is covered by the GNU Library General Public License instead.) You can apply it to your programs, too.

When we speak of free software, we are referring to freedom, not price. Our General Public Licenses are designed to make sure that you have the freedom to distribute copies of free software (and charge for this service if you wish), that you receive source code or can get it if you want it, that you can change the software or use pieces of it in new free programs; and that you know you can do these things.

To protect your rights, we need to make restrictions that forbid anyone to deny you these rights or to ask you to surrender the rights. These restrictions translate to certain responsibilities for you if you distribute copies of the software, or if you modify it.

For example, if you distribute copies of such a program, whether gratis or for a fee, you must give the recipients all the rights that you have. You must make sure that they, too, receive or can get the source code. And you must show them these terms so they know their rights.

We protect your rights with two steps: (1) copyright the software, and (2) offer you this license which gives you legal permission to copy, distribute and/or modify the software.

Also, for each author's protection and ours, we want to make certain that everyone understands that there is no warranty for this free software. If the software is modified by someone else and passed on, we want its recipients to know that what they have is not the original, so that any problems introduced by others will not reflect on the original authors' reputations.

Finally, any free program is threatened constantly by software patents. We wish to avoid the danger that redistributors of a free program will individually obtain patent licenses, in effect making the program proprietary. To prevent this, we have made it clear that any patent must be licensed for everyone's free use or not licensed at all.

The precise terms and conditions for copying, distribution and modification follow.

Terms and Conditions for Copying, Distribution, and Modification

0. This License applies to any program or other work which contains a notice placed by the copyright holder saying it may be distributed under the terms of this General Public License. The "Program", below, refers to any such program or work, and a "work based on the Program" means either the Program or any derivative work under copyright law: that is to say, a work containing the Program or a portion of it, either verbatim or with modifications and/or translated into another language. (Hereinafter, translation is included without limitation in the term "modification".) Each licensee is addressed as "you".

Activities other than copying, distribution and modification are not covered by this License; they are outside its scope. The act of running the Program is not restricted, and the output from the Program is covered only if its contents constitute a work based on the Program (independent of having been made by running the Program). Whether that is true depends on what the Program does.

1. You may copy and distribute verbatim copies of the Program's source code as you receive it, in any medium, provided that you conspicuously and appropriately publish on each copy an appropriate copyright notice and disclaimer of warranty; keep intact all the notices that refer to this License and to the absence of any warranty; and give any other recipients of the Program a copy of this License along with the Program.

You may charge a fee for the physical act of transferring a copy, and you may at your option offer warranty protection in exchange for a fee.

2. You may modify your copy or copies of the Program or any portion of it, thus forming a work based on the Program, and copy and distribute such modifications or work under the terms of Section 1 above, provided that you also meet all of these conditions:

a) You must cause the modified files to carry prominent notices stating that you changed the files and the date of any change.

b) You must cause any work that you distribute or publish, that in whole or in part contains or is derived from the Program or any part thereof, to be licensed as a whole at no charge to all third parties under the terms of this License.

c) If the modified program normally reads commands interactively when run, you must cause it, when started running for such interactive use in the most ordinary way, to print or display an announcement including an appropriate copyright notice and a notice that there is no warranty (or else, saying that you provide a warranty) and that users may redistribute the program under these conditions, and telling the user how to view a copy of this License. (Exception: if the Program itself is interactive but does not normally print such an announcement, your work based on the Program is not required to print an announcement.)

These requirements apply to the modified work as a whole. If identifiable sections of that work are not derived from the Program, and can be reasonably considered independent and separate works in themselves, then this License, and its terms, do not apply to those sections when you distribute them as separate works. But when you distribute the same sections as part of a whole which is a work based on the Program, the distribution of the whole must be on the terms of this License, whose permissions for other licensees extend to the entire whole, and thus to each and every part regardless of who wrote it.

Thus, it is not the intent of this section to claim rights or contest your rights to work written entirely by you; rather, the intent is to exercise the right to control the distribution of derivative or collective works based on the Program.

In addition, mere aggregation of another work not based on the Program with the Program (or with a work based on the Program) on a volume of a storage or distribution medium does not bring the other work under the scope of this License.

3. You may copy and distribute the Program (or a work based on it, under Section 2) in object code or executable form under the terms of Sections 1 and 2 above provided that you also do one of the following:

a) Accompany it with the complete corresponding machine-readable source code, which must be distributed under the terms of Sections 1 and 2 above on a medium customarily used for software interchange; or,

b) Accompany it with a written offer, valid for at least three years, to give any third party, for a charge no more than your cost of physically performing source distribution, a complete machine-readable copy of the corresponding source code, to be distributed under the terms of Sections 1 and 2 above on a medium customarily used for software interchange; or,

c) Accompany it with the information you received as to the offer to distribute corresponding source code. (This alternative is allowed only for noncommercial distribution and only if you received the program in object code or executable form with such an offer, in accord with Subsection b above.)

The source code for a work means the preferred form of the work for making modifications to it. For an executable work, complete source code means all the source code for all modules it contains, plus any associated interface definition files, plus the scripts used to control compilation and installation of the executable. However, as a special exception, the source code distributed need not include anything that is normally distributed (in either source or binary form) with the major components (compiler, kernel, and so on) of the operating system on which the executable runs, unless that component itself accompanies the executable.

If distribution of executable or object code is made by offering access to copy from a designated place, then offering equivalent access to copy the source code from the same place counts as distribution of the source code, even though third parties are not compelled to copy the source along with the object code.

4. You may not copy, modify, sublicense, or distribute the Program except as expressly provided under this License. Any attempt otherwise to copy, modify, sublicense or distribute the Program is void, and will automatically terminate your rights under this License. However, parties who have received copies, or rights, from you under this License will not have their licenses terminated so long as such parties remain in full compliance.

5. You are not required to accept this License, since you have not signed it. However, nothing else grants you permission to modify or distribute the Program or its derivative works. These actions are prohibited by law if you do not accept this License. Therefore, by modifying or distributing the Program (or any work based on the Program), you indicate your acceptance of this License to do so, and all its terms and conditions for copying, distributing or modifying the Program or works based on it.

6. Each time you redistribute the Program (or any work based on the Program), the recipient automatically receives a license from the original licensor to copy, distribute or modify the Program subject to these terms and conditions. You may not impose any further restrictions on the recipients' exercise of the rights granted herein. You are not responsible for enforcing compliance by third parties to this License.

7. If, as a consequence of a court judgment or allegation of patent infringement or for any other reason (not limited to patent issues), conditions are imposed on you (whether by court order, agreement or otherwise) that contradict the conditions of this License, they do not excuse you from the conditions of this License. If you cannot distribute so as to satisfy simultaneously your obligations under this License and any other pertinent obligations, then as a consequence you may not distribute the Program at all. For example, if a patent license would not permit royalty-free redistribution of the Program by all those who receive copies directly or indirectly through you, then the only way you could satisfy both it and this License would be to refrain entirely from distribution of the Program.

If any portion of this section is held invalid or unenforceable under any particular circumstance, the balance of the section is intended to apply and the section as a whole is intended to apply in other circumstances.

It is not the purpose of this section to induce you to infringe any patents or other property right claims or to contest validity of any such claims; this section has the sole purpose of protecting the integrity of the free software distribution system, which is implemented by public license practices. Many people have made generous contributions to the wide range of software distributed through that system in reliance on consistent application of that system; it is up to the author/donor to decide if he or she is willing to distribute software through any other system and a licensee cannot impose that choice.

This section is intended to make thoroughly clear what is believed to be a consequence of the rest of this License.

8. If the distribution and/or use of the Program is restricted in certain countries either by patents or by copyrighted interfaces, the original copyright holder who places the Program under this License may add an explicit geographical distribution limitation excluding those countries, so that distribution is permitted only in or among countries not thus excluded. In such case, this License incorporates the limitation as if written in the body of this License.

9. The Free Software Foundation may publish revised and/or new versions of the General Public License from time to time. Such new versions will be similar in spirit to the present version, but may differ in detail to address new problems or concerns.

Each version is given a distinguishing version number. If the Program specifies a version number of this License which applies to it and "any later version", you have the option of following the terms and conditions either of that version or of any later version published by the Free Software Foundation. If the Program does not specify a version number of this License, you may choose any version ever published by the Free Software Foundation.

10. If you wish to incorporate parts of the Program into other free programs whose distribution conditions are different, write to the author to ask for permission. For software which is copyrighted by the Free Software Foundation, write to the Free Software Foundation; we sometimes make exceptions for this. Our decision will be guided by the two goals of preserving the free status of all derivatives of our free software and of promoting the sharing and reuse of software generally.

No Warranty

11. BECAUSE THE PROGRAM IS LICENSED FREE OF CHARGE, THERE IS NO WAR-RANTY FOR THE PROGRAM, TO THE EXTENT PERMITTED BY APPLICABLE LAW. EXCEPT WHEN OTHERWISE STATED IN WRITING THE COPYRIGHT HOLDERS AND/OR OTHER PARTIES PROVIDE THE PROGRAM "AS IS" WITH-OUT WARRANTY OF ANY KIND, EITHER EXPRESSED OR IMPLIED, INCLUDING, BUT NOT LIMITED TO, THE IMPLIED WARRANTIES OF MERCHANTABILITY AND FITNESS FOR A PARTICULAR PURPOSE. THE ENTIRE RISK AS TO THE QUALITY AND PERFORMANCE OF THE PROGRAM IS WITH YOU. SHOULD THE PROGRAM PROVE DEFECTIVE, YOU ASSUME THE COST OF ALL NECESSARY SERVICING, REPAIR OR CORRECTION.

12. IN NO EVENT UNLESS REQUIRED BY APPLICABLE LAW OR AGREED TO IN WRITING WILL ANY COPYRIGHT HOLDER, OR ANY OTHER PARTY WHO MAY MODIFY AND/OR REDISTRIBUTE THE PROGRAM AS PERMITTED ABOVE, BE LIABLE TO YOU FOR DAMAGES, INCLUDING ANY GENERAL, SPECIAL, INCI-DENTAL OR CONSEQUENTIAL DAMAGES ARISING OUT OF THE USE OR INABILITY TO USE THE PROGRAM (INCLUDING BUT NOT LIMITED TO LOSS OF DATA OR DATA BEING RENDERED INACCURATE OR LOSSES SUSTAINED BY YOU OR THIRD PARTIES OR A FAILURE OF THE PROGRAM TO OPERATE WITH ANY OTHER PROGRAMS), EVEN IF SUCH HOLDER OR OTHER PARTY HAS BEEN ADVISED OF THE POSSIBILITY OF SUCH DAMAGES.

End Of Terms And Conditions

Hungry Minds, Inc.
End-User License Agreement

license agreements recorded on the Software Media. These limitations may include a requirement that after using the program for a specified period of time, the user must pay a registration fee or discontinue use. By opening the Software packet(s), you will be agreeing to abide by the licenses and restrictions for these individual programs that are detailed in Appendix A and on the Software Media. None of the material on this Software Media or listed in this Book may ever be redistributed, in original or modified form, for commercial purposes.

5. Limited Warranty.

(a) HMI warrants that the Software and Software Media are free from defects in materials and workmanship under normal use for a period of sixty (60) days from the date of purchase of this Book. If HMI receives notification within the warranty period of defects in materials or workmanship, HMI will replace the defective Software Media.

(b) HMI AND THE AUTHOR OF THE BOOK DISCLAIM ALL OTHER WARRANTIES, EXPRESS OR IMPLIED, INCLUDING WITHOUT LIMITATION IMPLIED WARRANTIES OF MERCHANTABILITY AND FITNESS FOR A PARTICULAR PURPOSE, WITH RESPECT TO THE SOFTWARE, THE PROGRAMS, THE SOURCE CODE CONTAINED THEREIN, AND/OR THE TECHNIQUES DESCRIBED IN THIS BOOK. HMI DOES NOT WARRANT THAT THE FUNCTIONS CONTAINED IN THE SOFTWARE WILL MEET YOUR REQUIREMENTS OR THAT THE OPERATION OF THE SOFTWARE WILL BE ERROR FREE.

(c) This limited warranty gives you specific legal rights, and you may have other rights that vary from jurisdiction to jurisdiction.

6. Remedies.

(a) HMI's entire liability and your exclusive remedy for defects in materials and workmanship shall be limited to replacement of the Software Media, which may be returned to HMI with a copy of your receipt at the following address: Software Media Fulfillment Department, Attn.: *Linux Bible*, Hungry Minds, Inc., 10475 Crosspoint Blvd., Indianapolis, IN 46256, or call 1-800-762-2974. Please allow four to six weeks for delivery. This Limited Warranty is void if failure of the Software Media has resulted from accident, abuse, or misapplication. Any replacement Software Media will be warranted for the remainder of the original warranty period or thirty (30) days, whichever is longer.

(b) In no event shall HMI or the author be liable for any damages whatsoever (including without limitation damages for loss of business profits, business interruption, loss of business information, or any other pecuniary loss) arising from the use of or inability to use the Book or the Software, even if HMI has been advised of the possibility of such damages.

(c) Because some jurisdictions do not allow the exclusion or limitation of liability for consequential or incidental damages, the above limitation or exclusion may not apply to you.

7. **U.S. Government Restricted Rights.** Use, duplication, or disclosure of the Software for or on behalf of the United States of America, its agencies and/or instrumentalities (the "U.S. Government") is subject to restrictions as stated in paragraph (c)(1)(ii) of the Rights in Technical Data and Computer Software clause of DFARS 252.227-7013, or subparagraphs (c) (1) and (2) of the Commercial Computer Software - Restricted Rights clause at FAR 52.227-19, and in similar clauses in the NASA FAR supplement, as applicable.

8. **General.** This Agreement constitutes the entire understanding of the parties and revokes and supersedes all prior agreements, oral or written, between them and may not be modified or amended except in a writing signed by both parties hereto that specifically refers to this Agreement. This Agreement shall take precedence over any other documents that may be in conflict herewith. If any one or more provisions contained in this Agreement are held by any court or tribunal to be invalid, illegal, or otherwise unenforceable, each and every other provision shall remain in full force and effect.

CD-ROM Installation Instructions

Additional software and utilities, as well as code examples from the book, are also included on the accompanying CD-ROMs. To install the software, follow the instructions provided with each program. To use the code examples, copy to your hard drive.

Limited Warranty

HMI warrants that the Software and Software Media are free from defects in materials and workmanship under normal use for a period of sixty (60) days from the date of purchase of this Book. If HMI receives notification within the warranty period of defects in materials or workmanship, HMI will replace the defective Software Media.

Hungry Minds, Inc. (HMI) AND THE AUTHOR OF THE BOOK DISCLAIM ALL OTHER WARRANTIES, EXPRESS OR IMPLIED, INCLUDING WITHOUT LIMITATION IMPLIED WARRANTIES OF MERCHANTABILITY AND FITNESS FOR A PARTICULAR PURPOSE, WITH RESPECT TO THE SOFTWARE, THE PROGRAMS, THE SOURCE CODE CONTAINED THEREIN, AND/OR THE TECHNIQUES DESCRIBED IN THIS BOOK. HMI DOES NOT WARRANT THAT THE FUNCTIONS CONTAINED IN THE SOFTWARE WILL MEET YOUR REQUIREMENTS OR THAT THE OPERATION OF THE SOFTWARE WILL BE ERROR FREE.

This limited warranty gives you specific legal rights, and you may have other rights that vary from jurisdiction to jurisdiction.

The book includes a copy of the Publisher's Edition of Red Hat Linux from Red Hat, Inc., which you may use in accordance with the license agreements accompanying the software. The Official Red Hat Linux, which you may purchase from Red Hat, includes the complete Official Red Hat Linux distribution, Red Hat's documentation, and may include technical support for Official Red Hat Linux. You also may purchase technical support from Red Hat. You may purchase Official Red Hat Linux and technical support from Red Hat through the company's web site (www.redhat.com) or its toll-free number 1.888.REDHAT1.